Cambridge Handbook of Project Behavior

Despite careful planning, projects often deviate from their assigned paths. Delays, cost overruns, benefit underruns, stakeholder disappointments, and sustainability shortfalls are common challenges during project initiation and execution. The *Cambridge Handbook of Project Behavior* addresses the underlying causes of project behavior and misbehavior, while offering evidence-based strategies for remediation. Featuring guidance for anticipating project outcomes and practical advice for dealing with projects when they branch off assigned paths and veer off track, this *Handbook* is a valuable resource for practitioners, policymakers, and project professionals responsible for delivering high-profile and complex projects. It includes contributions from leading experts in the field of project management, providing a unique international perspective. As mega-projects become increasingly prevalent on the global stage, understanding the dynamics of project behavior and misbehavior has never been more critical. The *Cambridge Handbook of Project Behavior* offers essential insights and solutions for successfully navigating the challenges of project management.

LAVAGNON A. IKA is Professor of Project Management in the Telfer School of Management at the University of Ottawa, Canada. Professor Ika is at the forefront of the project behavior discussion as protagonist of the Planning Fallacy versus Hiding Hand debate and proponent of Fifth Hand theory. He is the author of the PMI award-winning book *Managing Fuzzy Projects* (2023) and his work on project behavior has won two International Project Management Association (IPMA) research awards.

JEFFREY K. PINTO is Andrew Morrow and Elizabeth Lee Black Chair in Management Technology in the Black School of Business at Penn State–Erie, The Behrend College. Professor Pinto has been considered one of the top scholars in his field for nearly three decades. He has written and edited 27 books and several hundred scientific papers, and has received numerous awards for his research in project management.

Cambridge Handbook of Project Behavior

Edited by

LAVAGNON A. IKA
University of Ottawa
JEFFREY K. PINTO
Pennsylvania State University

CAMBRIDGE
UNIVERSITY PRESS

CAMBRIDGE
UNIVERSITY PRESS

Shaftesbury Road, Cambridge CB2 8EA, United Kingdom

One Liberty Plaza, 20th Floor, New York, NY 10006, USA

477 Williamstown Road, Port Melbourne, VIC 3207, Australia

314–321, 3rd Floor, Plot 3, Splendor Forum, Jasola District Centre, New Delhi – 110025, India

103 Penang Road, #05-06/07, Visioncrest Commercial, Singapore 238467

Cambridge University Press is part of Cambridge University Press & Assessment, a department of the University of Cambridge.

We share the University's mission to contribute to society through the pursuit of education, learning and research at the highest international levels of excellence.

www.cambridge.org
Information on this title:www.cambridge.org/9781009322768

DOI:10.1017/9781009322737

When citing this work, please include a reference to the DOI 10.1017/9781009322737

First published 2025

Cover image: ImageZoo / Alamy Stock Photo

A catalogue record for this publication is available from the British Library

A Cataloging-in-Publication data record for this book is available from the Library of Congress

ISBN 978-1-009-32276-8 Hardback

Contents

Figures

Tables

Contributors

Fran Ackermann Curtin University, Business School

Maude Brunet HEC Montreal, Department of Management

Stewart Clegg University of Sydney, School of Project Management

Andrew Davies University of Sussex Business School, Science Policy Research Unit

Kate Davis Cranfield University, School of Management

Therese F. Dille University of South Eastern-Norway

Francesco Di Maddaloni University College London, The Bartlett School of Sustainable Construction

Katharina Eåmeyer University of Konstanz

Joana Geraldi Copenhagen Business School, Department of Organization, Centre for Organization and Time

Alicia Gilchrist Australian National University, College of Business and Economics

Joseph W. Harrison University of Bath, Information, Decisions and Operations (IDO) Division, School of Management

Lavagnon A. Ika University of Ottawa, Telfer School of Management

Dicle Kortantamer University of Leeds, School of Civil Engineering

Ann Langley HEC Montreal and University of Warwick

Michael A. Lewis University of Bath, Information, Decisions and Operations (IDO) Division, School of Management

Peter E. D. Love Curtin University, School of Civil and Mechanical Engineering

Liz Machtynger Cranfield University, School of Management

Ashwin Mahalingam IIT-Madras, Department of Civil Engineering

Miia Martinsuo University of Turku

Gerry McGivern King's College London, King's Business School

Jack Meredith Wake Forest University

Ralf Müller BI Norwegian Business School

Kim van Oorschot BI Norwegian Business School

Jeffrey K. Pinto Penn State University, Black School of Business

Jens K. Roehrich University of Bath, Information, Decisions and Operations (IDO) Division, School of Management

Graham Room University of Bath, Department of Social & Policy Sciences

Maximilian Schriewersmann Technische Hochschule Ostwestfalen-Lippe, Stands for Service Kommunikation IT and Media

Wolfgang Seibel University of Konstanz

Regis Signor Brazilian Federal Police

Jonas Söderlund Linköping University, Sweden

Verena Stingl Aalborg Universitet, Department of Materials and Production

Siiri Tuominen Tampere University, Faculty of Management and Business, Industrial Engineering and Management

Greg Usher University of Southern Queensland, School of Business

Rebecca Vine University of Sussex Business School, Science Policy Research Unit

Gro Holst Volden Norwegian University of Science and Technology

Morten Welde Norwegian University of Science and Technology

Ofer Zwikael ANU College of Business and Economics, Department of Civil and Environmental Engineering

Introduction

LAVAGNON A. IKA and JEFFREY K. PINTO

Project-based work has always been fraught with challenges and setbacks (Hirschman, 1967; Ika & Saint-Macary, 2023). No project is a long and quiet river, the adage says. As the French writer Molière wrote in *Tartuffe*, or *The Impostor* in 1664, "There's a long way from the project to the thing." We know from years of collective experience and research that projects tend to have a complicated life (or "behavior") of their own with plenty of detours, out-turns, inflection points (Williams, 2005), peripeties (Engwall & Westling, 2004), drift or dead ends (Kreiner, 2020), branching off assigned paths, going off track, zigzagging, and ending perhaps as tragedies (Bröchner, 2022) or, if one is fortunate, happily (Hirschman, 1967). Targets set may be realized anywhere but on target, from near misses to outright failures (Ika et al., 2022), as projects routinely experience "the potential for breakdown and repair" (Strauss, 1988, p. 172). As Ika et al. (2022, p. 3319) note, "projects harbor tensions between projections and plans, decisions and actions, outputs and outcomes, success criteria and success, and project *management* success and project success, the ignorance of which may be the reason why projects fail more than they succeed."

At the core of "how projects work" (Love et al., 2019a, 2019b) is a schism between the projected and the realized future (Kreiner, 2014, 2020), which may explain why projects systematically deviate from assigned plans and paths and result in far too common project management paradoxes (Ika et al., 2022). For instance, on the one hand, the development of major projects, those time-bound initiatives that are of a large-scale, inter-organizational, or complex nature, is significantly increasing, aimed at delivering economic, social, and institutional infrastructure and/or tackling grand challenges. The world's most pressing issues such as climate change, global pandemics, and unsustainable development all fall into this latter category. Between China's various "Belt and Road" initiatives, infrastructure redevelopment under "Build Back Better" funding in the US and Europe, and the huge increase in developing world projects, multi-trillion ($USD) investments are widely anticipated. On the other hand, these major projects often make headlines for the wrong reasons, due to their chronic underperformance. Typically, they suffer from a fivefold intersection of considerable delays at their completion, staggering cost overruns, dismal benefit shortfalls, painful stakeholder disappointments, and harmful sustainability outcomes (Flyvbjerg & Gardner, 2023; Ika & Saint-Macary, 2023).

The consequences of major projects failing on these criteria are well-reported; however, we hear far less about why these failures occur and what are the contingencies, especially the unanticipated events or opportunities and threats, that arise (Schutz, 1973; Strauss, 1988; Browning & Ramasesh, 2015; Ika & Saint-Macary, 2023). Evidence suggests that the development life cycle of major projects rarely follows a logical path that sophisticated planning and risk management might chart at their outset (Hirschman, 1967; Ika et al., 2022). As is often the case, many projects fail during ideation, whether through technical shortcomings, funding failures, or changes in strategic direction. Many others initially appear to show promise in their front-end phase but quickly become bogged down. The California High-Speed Rail project provides a fitting illustration. The target cost of the project, approved in 2008 and scheduled to be complete by 2020, ballooned to some $100 billion over its initial budget and it has yet to connect Los Angeles to San

We are indebted to Prof. Stewart Clegg for extensive comments on an earlier draft which have undoubtedly improved the substance and form of the chapter.

Francisco, its original objective (Shalby, 2024), as politicians struggle to salvage a fraction of value from the venture.

Still other major projects commence only to be abandoned completely or partially. Among recent examples of completely canceled projects is the decade-long and $ 10-billion Apple car project. Dubbed "Project Titan," it suffered what some of Apple's employees call "Titanic disaster," as it became clear that "Apple would never be able to sell vehicles at its expected margins, especially with the declining EV market and competitors racing to the bottom" (Hilliard, 2024). The HS2 project in the UK, a high-speed railroad that was planned to connect London and the North of England, is a further case of a partial cancellation. It was initially proposed in 2009 with an estimated cost of £37.5 billion. Since then, the project costs have spiraled out of control and the current cost estimate for the full business case is over £100 billion. In October 2023, the UK government announced that the Birmingham to Manchester leg, part of Phase 2, had been canceled, and instead, some of the money would be spent on upgrading existing infrastructure and improving connectivity between northern cities (Tetlow & Pattison, 2023).

A recurring theme in the lives of many projects is that they are delivered only after significant hiccups along the path to completion. Consider, for example, the Crossrail megaproject, in London, UK. While the project concept goes back to 1974, it has taken different out-turns and exhibited many instances of systematic deviations from plans over its lifetime. Indeed, not only was the £2.5 billion (1991 prices) project shelved in 1996, but it had to evolve in scope subsequently from a cross-London to a commuter railway, directed by a single actor to becoming a temporary alliance with the Greater London Authority, before later including, in addition to suppliers, groups of local stakeholders outside project governance boundaries. Continuing in fits and starts, the anticipated budget had reached £16 billion by 2007 (including a contingency of £5 billion) and £18 billion by 2009. Taking advantage of the concurrent recession and pressure to reduce the budget, the completion date was delayed before the project finally moved into its construction phase. After several additional adjustments, Crossrail was budgeted at £15 billion. By 2019, when, due to the coronavirus pandemic, the project had to be stopped to put in place new safety measures, the supplier costs increased by 53 percent over the 2008 forecast. Such a complicated behavior in the face of changing scope and end date, governance alterations, and shifting economic environment, explains much of its cost overruns (Gil & Fu, 2022).

It is in the context of the projects we have discussed and their persistent failure to perform or succeed as expected that the objective of this book was forged. It is to examine a fascinating, elusive, and complex phenomenon that occurs in the lifetime of major projects: the observance of project behavior in which there are systematic deviations between project initiation and execution (Ika et al., 2022). Following Schutz (1967, 1973), we consider *projecting* and *comporting* to be interrelated phenomena. Projecting, in the Schutzian sense, is a throwing forward to some *imagined* end while comporting, a term that Heidegger (1985, p. 41) made his own, is an *act* that is a directing-itself-toward some end. We take this to suggest that project delivery and project behavior are two sides of the same coin since complexity and uncertainty intervene between imagination and action, a gap that characterizes major project work (Daniel & Daniel, 2018; Love et al., 2024a, 2024b).

In this introductory chapter, we begin by explaining what project behavior is and why it matters for project management scholars and practitioners alike. Next, we review the key principles of project behavior and how they each connect to project complexity, risk, uncertainty, and performance, from both a scholarly and practical standpoint. We then provide a historical context for the different theories of project behavior before offering our typology. Finally, we will provide a summary of the chapters in the handbook and how they advance our thinking in terms of project behavior theory and practice.

What Is Project Behavior and Why It Matters

The notion of project behavior dates back at least to the seventeenth century. In what is perhaps the antetype of the project management discipline (Cleland & Ireland, 2007; Winch et al., 2023), the English novelist Daniel Defoe offered an essay on projects and the "projecting age" in reference to his times in the UK in particular and Europe in general. He depicts a "project-oriented behavior," where the notion of the major project is "a vast undertaking, too big to be managed, and therefore likely enough to come to nothing" (Defoe, 1697, p. 20), and is seen, above all, as an instrument in the hands of "projectors," that is, promotors of schemes, to deliver social, cultural, political, literary, and scientific change, not always for personal gains (Maldonado, 2002; Novak, 2008).

More than three centuries later, the notion of project behavior abounds in the project management literature (Wynn et al., 2021; Ika et al., 2022). To get a sense of the interest of scholars in the notion of project behavior, we undertook a search in June 2024 using the keyword "project behavior" and generated some 4,680 results in Google Scholar. The same search in the two leading journals in the project management field yielded respectively 1,665 results for *International Journal of Project Management* and 1,060 results for *Project Management Journal*, with half of these results appearing in the last 10 years alone. This is a testament to the worldwide use of the term by scholars and practitioners.

Notably, research that seeks to understand the overall behavior of the project as a system of systems (Daniel & Daniel, 2018) or to model events, such as project completion or resource allocation behaviors, is common (Colon & Garland, 1993). Likewise, it is not rare to come across research that investigates the effects of the project manager's leadership, team management behavior (Bendoly & Swink, 2007), or other stakeholders' behaviors (Beringer et al., 2013), including project sponsors (Kloppenborg et al., 2014) on project performance, such as the escalation of commitment (Keil et al., 2000). We read often about the human behavioral aspects of those working in project settings (Slevin & Pinto, 2007; Pinto, 2022) such as normalization of deviance (Pinto, 2014), collaborative and opportunistic behaviors of contractors (Galvin et al., 2021), and optimistic and pessimistic project status reporting behavior (Kaufmann & Kock, 2023). We also come across multiple studies on behavioral decision-making in projects (Stingl & Geraldi, 2017) including the role of cognitive biases such as overconfidence (Shore, 2008), strategic misbehaviors such as lies (Flyvbjerg et al., 2002), smart heuristics (Love et al., 2024a, 2024b), and the "cognitive gear switching" of project managers between their gut-feelings and rational choice tools (Nowińska & Pedersen, 2024) in project delivery. In short, the field of project management has long plumbed the depths of work on system and human behavior when exposed to the unique challenges of the project setting, but in a larger context, what does the notion of project behavior entail and why does it matter?

A Working Definition of Project Behavior

Project behavior remains an elusive idea that is often referenced yet very rarely delineated. For example, Söderlund (2004) suggests theories of the project should "explain and predict" project behavior without providing a clear definition of the concept. More recently, Gil and Fu (2022) trace the systematic escalation of capital costs over time to governance adaptations during the lifetime of large-scale projects, calling for a "grand model of megaproject behavior" and yet falling short of defining what this term implies. In short, we see the need to understand project challenges within the context of behavior, yet fail to follow the trail to its defining principles. Adopting a complex systems perspective and assuming that projects can take many different and complex out-turns, project behavior can be understood as a nonlinear and counterintuitive phenomenon (Williams et al., 1995; Forrester, 1997), stemming from "systemic interrelated sets of causal factors rather than tracing effects to single causes" (Williams, 2005, p. 499), making it "difficult for the human brain to predict and understand intuitively" (Daniel & Daniel, 2018, p. 193). As Cicmil et al. (2006, p. 683) write:

> The systemic models show behaviour arising from the complex interactions of the various parts of the project; they demonstrate how behaviour arises that would not be predicted from an analysis of the individual parts of the project and thus show

> how the traditional decomposition models in some circumstances can be inadequate. The project behaviour shown in this body of work is complex and non-intuitive. It shows causal feed-back, leading to non-linear behaviour, and produces effects which can sometimes manifest themselves after significant time-delays.

In this book, following the work of Ika et al. (2022), we recognize project behavior as the study of how projects work, or develop, and along the way, take different and complex out-turns over their lifetime. To borrow the words from an early systems thinker and project behavior scholar, Albert Hirschman, the author of *Development Projects Observed*, project behavior "should go far in explaining and anticipating successes and failures, systematic veerings from pre-assigned paths, propensities toward specific difficulties, as well as opportunities for special payoffs" (Hirschman, 1967, p. 4). It is important to note, however, that this book is articulated around the behavior of project systems and their production and management subsystems as well as their interactions (Daniel & Daniel, 2018), *not* that of individuals or work groups/teams, which is often the focus of organizational behavior–orientated studies in project management (Chiocchio et al., 2015; Ika et al., 2022). Put differently, our focus is on the study of the behavior *of* projects in true system behavior and system dynamics tradition, not the behavior *in* projects in true organizational behavior tradition (Unterhitzenberger, 2021).

Project behavior research includes behavioral decision-making and action-taking. Most notably, in the face of complexity and uncertainty, we see this phenomenon as capturing, inter alia, (1) project investment decisions and critical junctures (or "forks in the road"); (2) project governance choices; (3) project execution actions from sponsors, managers, and other stakeholders; and (4) risks, complexities, and uncertainties. We also experience these behaviors as evidence of project performance, along with systematic deviations of projects from initial plans and paths, including project failures, successes, serendipities, and the shades of gray between success and failure (Ika et al., 2022). Put differently, we are more concerned with what Geraldi and Söderlund (2018) term the meso level of project studies, as we seek to understand project behavior at the level of the overall project system. The meso level forms that critical link between the individual/team (micro) level where people's skills, careers, and psychology matter and the supra organizational and societal (macro) level where the impacts of the project on strategy, policy, and society count the most. As Hirschman (1967) teaches us, project behavior is rooted in the nexus between the project's structural complexity and the sociopolitical complexity of the surrounding environment, including society at large (Ika & Söderlund, 2016).

Project Behavior: The Role of Projecting and Future Perfect Thinking

Where there is a project, there is projecting, as an actor or an extension/collection of actors (for example, a group of stakeholders or an organization or even a society), "project" a future and uncertain situation and, in so doing, give meaning to the project to be accomplished. Put differently, there is no project without the intent or motive of a project actor or Defoe's projector (Schutz, 1967; Boutinet, 2005). When project actors seek to "make the uncertainty attached to the future something that can be dealt with in advance of it occurring," the projected future is imagined as if it were already a reality that they may look back on and imagine the steps that will have taken them there, using what has been termed a "future perfect strategy" (Pitsis et al., 2003, p. 574). As Schutz (1967, p. 61) advances, the future perfect is the cognitive process by which

> an actor projects his actions as if it were already over and done with and lying in the past .... Strangely enough, therefore, because it is pictured as completed, the planned act bears the temporal character of pastness .... The fact that it is thus pictured as if it were simultaneously past and future can be taken care of by saying that it is thought of in the future perfect tense.

Thus, future perfect thinking carries an "in-order-to" motive for action inherent with the projected future or what Schutz (1967) terms *protention* (that is, the forward-looking projection of the future).

Protention is experienced by the project actor as a feeling or a sense of what comes next, as opposed to a "because" motive for behavior inherent with what Schutz (1967) calls *retention*, which is a perception of the past. The realized future will be fundamentally different from the projected future. Indeed, the projected future forms what the philosopher Ryle (2000) calls a course of action, which, out of many alternatives available to the project actor, provides meaning and significance to the particular action that the project actor will take in a particular situation that is fraught with uncertainty (Kreiner, 2014, 2020). Uncertainty implies that project-based work remains a process of filling in empty horizons (Schutz, 1973), as abstract protention only shows the direction of travel, not the journey whose steps need to be taken (Winch & Sergeeva, 2022), based on experiences of how a course of action will typically develop. As Schutz (1973, p. 69) notes: "Projecting like any other anticipation carries along its empty horizons which will be filled in merely by the materialization of the anticipated event. This constitutes the intrinsic uncertainty of all forms of projecting."

Project Behavior versus Project Actor Behavior and Action

According to Schutz (1967), the project is a quintessential unit of action. However, in contrast to Heidegger (1962, p. 185) who argues that "projecting has nothing to do with comporting oneself towards a plan that has been thought out," Schutz (1967) believes that projecting and comporting are different yet interrelated phenomena. That is, there is a recursive relation between the action and the behavior of a project actor (Winch & Sergeeva, 2022). According to Schutz (1967) and in contrast to Weber (1978) who suggests action is meaningful behavior, what distinguishes action from behavior is the presence of a project "more or less implicitly preconceived" (p. 59) or that "action is the execution of a projected act" (p. 61). As Schutz (1967, p. 60) adds: "What is projected is an act, which is the goal of an action and which is brought into being by an action." For example, a project actor (e.g., Steve Jobs) can take the action of launching a project (e.g., the original iPhone project) through a formal kick-start meeting. Such a forward-looking human activity (Winch & Sergeeva, 2022) is thus ordered under a corresponding projected act (e.g., to conquer the world's smartphone market), which provides it with meaning. Therefore, a difference exists between the action, considered as something in progress, and the completed act, considered as something already achieved (Schutz, 1967).

In contrast, the behavior of the project actor is oriented toward the present and the past (Winch & Sergeeva, 2022); it may, for example, be unintentionally optimistic about the prospect of the project but intentionally aggressive about the project schedule and its time-to-market choice. Put differently, the behavior of the project actor may be both deliberate and unintentional. A projected act, for its part, involves a chain of coordinated actions, which collectively shed light on the lived experience of leading the project or what Cicmil et al. (2006) call the actuality of the project, whether it is completed or imagined as already over. Both actions and acts are thus mediated by the project actor in a particular situation (Schutz, 1967).

For example, Steve Jobs' request to change the screen of the iPhone from plastic to glass to avoid it getting scratched was a projected act. This was not possible without a chain of coordinated actions, including testing all the glass options on the market; convincing Wendell Weeks, CEO of Corning Inc., a NewYork–based manufacturer of special glass to have that company produce the scratch-resistant glass within six months and finally delivering it just a few days before the iPhone went on sale (Amil, 2022). As the iPhone screen example and Steve Jobs' leadership suggest, the project actor's action tends to be social "insofar as its subjective meaning takes account of the behavior of others and is thereby oriented in its course" (see Weber 1978, p. 4). Likewise, project behavior is always social. Observed project behavior may be deliberately intended, as in the project actor intentionally manipulating project forecasts to gain project approval, or unintentional as in a project being late and over budget because of the unforeseen COVID-19 contingency that has impeded its execution, a socially constructed category, the legitimacy of which all can apprehend.

At this juncture, however, we hasten to note that project behavior collectively concerns the past, present, and future. Past strategic decisions and actions led to commitment to the project; present day mundane managerial decisions inform the project as to what information to share in a meeting as well as actions in sharing that information in a certain manner during the project's course, and the future will depend on the decisions and actions to be taken that lead to project completion and termination. At all stages in this unfolding, much attention to events will occur. Events might mean the departure of the project manager or a change in the competitive environment, or what is subsequently seen as managerial inaction and indecisiveness. One might argue that while the project actor may take action, the project as whole, strictly speaking, cannot because it lacks human agency (Emirbayer & Mische, 1998; Winch & Sergeeva, 2022). We, however, argue that both the project actor and the project as a whole may behave. Put differently, while the project may be anthropomorphized, project behavior is predicated on both the behavior of the project as a thing and the behavior of the project as actors. Indeed, the project is more than a thing since the actors are what makes the project (Ika & Saint-Macary, 2023). As the French philosopher and anthropologist Bruno Latour's actor-network theory teaches us, the project may even act as a nonhuman actor, with significant consequences such as delays in that a tunnel boring machine may get stuck in a hole and it may take months if not years to release it through creative problem-solving, as was the case in the Hoosac Tunnel project in the US.

Deviations from the Planned Behavior over Time

In the context of major projects, project organizing remains a deliberate, social activity in which projects are consciously, professionally, and skillfully designed, planned, executed, and evaluated and the projection of the future is rationally operationalized in terms of project goals and performance targets (Kreiner, 2014; Ika & Saint-Macary, 2023). In this instance, there is no project without a project actor – say a client or some other funder – deciding to commit to the project, which is seen as a reasoned and purposive human action. The premises under which this decision is made will generally inform how the project should be delivered, at least from a rational standpoint, and the project planning process predetermines and anticipates the future situations the project will face (e.g., think about a risk register) (Kreiner, 2014, 2020).

As Ika and Saint-Macary (2023, p. 210) write about major project delivery in a professional setting, "The way the project is structured, as well as the decisions and actions, must be based on reason and logic, not on personal experience or emotion." Thus, the project plan, which helps rationally reduce complexity and serves as a road map (Ika & Saint-Macary, 2023), offers a purposive action meaning and specifies such action in time and space, making specifications, deliverables, schedules, and budgets, etc. inherent aspects of the project planning process. However, since major projects are systems of designed and planned action, these decisions and the project delivery conditions they entail do *not* determine the subsequent project management process. Tasks, conducted under uncertainty, do not just adhere to the plan, as rational project management perspectives would have it (Kreiner, 2014, 2020). "Plans may be poor descriptions of actions that are actually carried out, but they are nevertheless important as providing 'space' for action. Plans thus carry a symbolic meaning" (Lundin & Söderholm, 1995, p. 448).

As Ika and Saint-Macary (2023) note, the project delivery does not happen *in vitro*, that is, within the closed environment of a laboratory, but instead *in vivo* and *in situ*. In other words, delivery is heavily dependent on context, with many actors involved inside and outside the project structure. Further, taking inspiration from Schutz (1967), we know that purposive action implies that both means and ends are always temporally in flux, marked by high degrees of indeterminacy. Thus, over time, things happen in a project and contingencies or events are bound to occur that defy the oft-flawed plan (Ika et al., 2024). There is a schism between meaning (as a multidirectional compass) and plan (as a road map); consequently, the emergent behavior may not be the planned behavior of the project, as complexity theory teaches us (Kreiner, 2020; Ika & Saint-Macary, 2023). As the Canadian strategic management author Henry Mintzberg argues, it's even all about the emergent behavior. As a result, when aspiration collides with political realities, as in the case of the original hopes for the UK's HS2 rail line versus its final adjudication, evidence of this schism is most profoundly observed.

When, over time, these deviations from plan and targets happen or when discrepancies exist between outcomes and anticipations – that is, emergent project behavior deviates from planned project behavior – then actors are quick to suggest there was poor planning and/or poor implementation of the plan or there were underperformances or failures in terms of the project management process or in terms of the project's long-term goals (Kreiner, 2014). Indeed, the disconnect between project *management* success and project *success* where the project may be delivered on time and/or within budget and yet fails to deliver expected outcomes (Ika & Pinto, 2022) can be explained by contingencies or environmental events that occur during a project's life cycle and are often beyond the project team (Pinto & Slevin, 1988). These events may be external – including the market and technology – and internal – including personnel changes such as team turnover or replacing the project manager – (Kunisch et al., 2017; Ika et al., 2024). As Kreiner (2014) argues, when these events occur and the plan is not on par with reality, project actors experience the drama that represents "the gap between living forward with flawed foresight and understanding backward with equally flawed but mischievously seductive hindsight" (Weick 1999, p. 134).

Indeed, time is at the core of project organizing, behavior, and performance (Lindkvist et al., 1998; Ika et al., 2024). Additionally, there exists a clear expectation of "institutionalized termination" for projects (Lundin & Söderholm, 1995) and thus a preset deadline (Lindkvist et al., 1998) in any project. However, time is woven into project performance factors such as events and processes that may affect the delivery of short-term project outputs and long-term project benefits (Ika & Saint-Macary, 2023). In response to such events, project actors may apply changes to the project over time and, in so doing, recognize windows of opportunities or favorable periods of time for the adaptation of the project to its environment (Kunisch et al., 2017; Ika et al., 2024). They may thus select the appropriate timing, pace, or speed to deliver success in the project (Shenhar & Dvir, 2007). Again, in practical terms, a key project sponsor may conduct an environmental scan that shows a lessening of stakeholder support for a pet project, necessitating the decision to delay the project until additional support can be garnered.

Project actors interact differently with the past, present, and future and may have different time horizons. For example, some may bring to the project experiences from previous interactions and expectations of potential collaborations, as they derive lessons from the performance of past projects to deal with the challenges of the present project and seek to trigger funding for the next project (Vaagaasar et al., 2020). While some project actors (such as project managers) may have a short-term concern for the delivery of the project within budget, others (such as project funders) may have a longer-term concern for the delivery of project benefits (Meredith & Zwikael, 2019). Hence, there may be tensions between different actors' temporal orientations and horizons, prompting a need to change or balance the prevailing temporal structures, such as schedules, event-based targets, or cultural norms pertaining to the extent to which a project may, for example, exceed a budget target (Vaagaasar et al., 2020). As well, there are tensions between short-term and long-term project performance, illustrating the paradox of intertemporal choice (Slawinski & Bansal, 2015), where what is best in the short term (e.g., to deliver a project within budget) may not be ideal in the long term (e.g., to deliver socioecological value) (Ika et al., 2024). This is notably the case of grand challenges, with their fuzzy goals, long-term value focus, and the pressing need for project behavior theory and practice to make the world a better place where no one is left behind (Ika & Munro, 2022).

Tapping into their agency and thus reacting to the fuzziness inherent with major projects (Ika & Saint-Macary, 2023), actors would strive to alter, through action, the project's strategy (Shenhar & Dvir, 2007), governance (Ika et al., 2024), plan (Dvir & Lechler, 2004), and scope (Love et al., 2019a). They are compelled to strategically respond to changing threats and opportunities (Kunisch et al., 2017), as well as luck, good or bad (Ika, 2018), and in doing so, they shape the emergent project behavior. Due to the important role that contingencies (including chance, happenstance, and unintended consequences) play in shaping the project, success and failure are intertwined in meaning and action and project behavior does not have a linear relationship with project performance (Hirschman, 1967; Ika et al., 2022).

Project success and failure thus become social constructions and as such involve, throughout the project life cycle, individual and collective symbolic and rhetorical evaluations and attributions of project performance by project actors, which may not have much to do with the delivery of the project within constraints of time, cost, and quality (Kreiner, 2014; Ika & Pinto, 2022). Yet, as practice would have it:

> In project management, our assessment of success is mainly based on criteria set in the beginning (ex ante) to measure results at the end (ex post). This approach is a slippery slope since it can result in what psychosocial theorists call a *fundamental attribution error*. It leads us to assess success using subjective assessments of what we observe while ignoring external and contextual factors that occur or fall outside our purview. (Ika & Saint-Macary, 2023, p. 151)

In so doing, we blame any deviations from plans and targets on the project team actors and underestimate the role of complexity and uncertainty in projects (Kreiner, 2014). As we learn from attribution theory (Ross, 1977), there is a pervasive tendency to underestimate the influence of context on behavior. Project behavior theories may fall foul to such attribution error and thus they "may at best represent attribution errors about project performance." (Ika et al., 2022, p. 3323) Table I.1 provides a synopsis of some of the key concepts of project behavior.

A Family of Five Principles of Project Behavior

Recent years have witnessed a conversation about two competing principles of project behavior: Daniel Kahneman's *Planning Fallacy* and Albert Hirschman's *Hiding Hand* (Hirschman, 1967; Kahneman, 2011; Flyvbjerg, 2016; Ika, 2018) (see Table I.2 for examples and read Chapters 1 and 2 of this book for ample discussion).

The Planning Fallacy, supporting belief in the tendency for projects to over-promise and under-deliver, suggests that forecasts of project schedules, costs, and benefits are by and large unrealistically close to best-case-scenarios (Kahneman, 2011). According to Planning Fallacy proponents (Flyvbjerg & Gardner, 2023), systematic biases, such as optimism bias, and misbehaviors, such as strategic misrepresentation, creep into how projects are selected, managed, and reported on. Optimism bias is the belief that decision-makers are less likely to face risks than statistical judgment warrants. Strategic misrepresentation stands for the deliberate manipulation of cost and benefit estimates, typically intended to paint a rosier picture than true estimates might warrant, in the belief that it is better to get a project started and later "beg for forgiveness" than submit real expected cost numbers that could kill the project at the outset. Psychology and power thus combine to explain the dreadful underperformance of entire classes of projects, including mega dams, rail and infrastructure, Information Technology, and Olympic Games. So resonant are the warnings of Planning Fallacy champions that public sector decision-making has been significantly affected; for example, the requirement in some UK government departments that all new project proposals be subjected to a "reference class multiplier" for cost estimation or the 2016 decision by Virginia Raggi, mayor of Rome, to withdraw her city's bid to host the 2024 Olympics, citing historical evidence of huge cost overruns. In these and other ways, it is clear that Planning Fallacy supporters have created a hugely influential perspective that is guiding both decision-makers and project management researchers.

A competing perspective known as the Hiding Hand, however, suggests that this propensity for

Table I.1 Project behavior: Definitional concepts

Key concepts	Definitions
Projecting	The looking-forward process, where an actor or an extent of actor, say a group of stakeholders or an organization or even a society, gives meaning to the project to be accomplished and, in so doing, "projects" themselves into a future situation where uncertainty almost always looms large (Defoe, 1697; Boutinet, 2005).
Projected future	The imagined desirable situation or anticipated state of affairs that is lying in store through purposive action (Schutz, 1967).
Future perfect	The cognitive process by which "an actor projects his actions as if it were already over and done with and lying in the past" (Schutz, 1967, p. 61).
Protention	The forward-looking projection of the future or the "cognitive process of looking towards the future" (Winch & Sergeeva, 2022, p. 49).
Retention	The backward-looking visualization of the past or "cognitive process of drawing on past experience" (Winch & Sergeeva, 2022, p. 49).
Decision	A conscious judgment or choice for a course of action out of many alternatives (e.g., Brunsson, 1982).
Action (of an actor)	A forward-looking human activity or "the execution of a projected act" (Schutz 1967, p. 61). It is "orientated towards the future by protention" (Winch & Sergeeva, p. 49).
Act (of an actor)	That "which is the goal of an action and which is brought into being by an action" Schutz (1967, p. 60).
Behavior (of an actor)	Consists in "human activity orientated towards the present and past by retention" (Winch & Sergeeva, 2022, p. 49).
Filling in	"The delivery process of working towards the desired future state as the lived experience of projecting" (Winch & Sergeeva, 2022, p. 49).
Project behavior	The study of how projects work, or develop, and along the way, take different and complex outturns over their lifetime (Ika et al., 2022). It "should go far in explaining and anticipating successes and failures, systematic veerings from pre-assigned paths, propensities toward specific difficulties, as well as opportunities for special payoffs" (Hirschman, 1967, p. 4).
Human agency	It is "the temporally constructed engagement by actors of different structural environments – the temporal-relational contexts of action – which, through the interplay of habit, imagination, and judgment, both reproduces and transforms those structures in interactive response to the problems posed by changing historical situations" (Emirbayer & Mische, 1998, p. 970).
The fundamental attribution error	"The tendency for attributors to underestimate the impact of situational factors and to overestimate the role of dispositional factors in controlling behavior" (Ross, 1977, p. 183).
Complexity	A property of a project that consists of many varied parts with a multitude of existing and emerging interrelations, which make it difficult to understand, foresee, and control its overall behavior, even when there is enough information (Vidal et al., 2011).
Risk	A situation where the exhaustive and mutually exclusive set of future states of the world (that is, *all* relevant alternatives) and all their consequences and probabilities are known for sure (Knight, 1921; Gigerenzer, 2020).
Uncertainty	A situation where *some* of the alternatives, consequences and probabilities are unknown (Knight, 1921; Gigerenzer, 2020).

promoters to overestimate the benefits and underestimate the costs and difficulties of their assigned projects is not always bad, as creativity may come to the rescue in unforeseen circumstances (Hirschman, 1967). In other words, Hiding Hand proponents (Ika & Saint-Macary, 2023) suggest that data arguing that most projects are "dead on arrival" due to systemic errors in initial estimation coupled with willful misrepresentation, as argued in the Planning Fallacy, grossly over-represents this position, arguing that such premeditated culpability is simply one potential source of project

Table I.2 Three prevailing principles of project behavior: Illustrations

Key principles of project behavior	Illustrations
Hiding Hand	The Rideau Canal: A near miss In 1826 in Canada, the Rideau Canal was envisioned as a navigable waterway from the Ottawa River to Kingston, with the goal to provide a safe supply and communication route. The project, however, took six years to complete, had a final cost of £822,000 (some 115 million in today's pounds) as opposed to an initial budget of £576,757 (about 72 million in today's pounds), and experienced significant setbacks. Faced with the stringent challenge to build not only locks but water control dams, the project team still dug deep into their creativity and found unplanned ways to deliver the canal (Ika & Söderlund, 2016). Looking back, if Colonel By and other promoters had known about the difficulties they would encounter, they would have most likely never done the project. But had it not been built, it would not have been an engineering marvel or the successful recreational waterway that it has become over decades. As Ika (2018, p. 371) suggests: "This is an example of how ignorance and poor planning can make decision-makers low-ball the real costs and challenges of a project, and heavily understate their own creativity to overcome project-related problems." This kind of happy ending is what Hirschman (1967) describes in what he calls the Principle of the Hiding Hand.
Planning Fallacy	The A 380: A flop In 2000, the A380 superjumbo jet project was proposed by Airbus to compete with the Boeing 747 at a budget of about $10 billion. However, the double-decker passenger aircraft of 600–800 seats turned out to be an implementation nightmare, as it struggled with massive electrical wiring problems, paid over $6 billion of penalties due to delivery delays, and had CEOs leaving a company forced to restructure. After a few postponed releases, it was delivered to its launch customer in 2007, with billions of cost overruns. Despite the $25 billion plane project being the largest passenger plane ever built, Airbus was forced to announce the end of production in 2021, as it hoped to sell as many as 750 but actually reached about a third of that target (Prisco, 2020). Looking back, the A380 project was plagued by optimism bias on the part of its promoters, leading them to underestimate its times, costs, risks, and benefits. With the benefit of hindsight, the project should never have been started, at least according to some close observers, since it was too big for a market that was already turning from a "hub and spoke" model to embrace "point to point" travel. As Flyvbjerg (2016, p. 176) notes, "the average project is in fact undermined by a double whammy of substantial cost hikes compounded by substantial benefits shortfalls." This sort of fiasco illustrates what Kahneman (2011) coins the Planning Fallacy.
The Fifth Hand	The Aurora VA Hospital: Shades of gray between success and failure In 2011, the Aurora VA Hospital project in the US was pegged at a budget of $678 million to deliver a state-of-the-art facility to treat up to 400,000 veterans suffering from various disabilities. Despite scope changes to cut costs and a change in contractor to put it back on track, the project ballooned to $2 billion at its formal ribbon-cutting ceremony in 2018, years behind schedule. Additional millions had to be spent three years after "completion" to fix a litany of quality issues, making the hospital one of the most expensive health facilities in the world. The project was also the site of a legal battle between the Department of Veterans Affairs and its primary construction contractor. While the Congressional Budget Office argued that unbridled optimism coupled with willful concealment of costs explain the project's underperformance, contractors suggested the snowballing of errors including a deficient collaboration among key stakeholders were the real culprits. In hindsight, the project drift was due to a perfect storm of optimism bias and a litany of errors. As Ika et al. (2023, pp. 68 and 70) write, "The checkered and controversial history of the development of the VA Aurora hospital (Colorado) illustrates the critical nature of creating a means for satisfying the bias versus error debate . . . we can see elements of both bias and error at play." This kind of joint bias *and* error project behavior is typical of what Ika et al. (2022) call the Fifth Hand principle, which combines elements of the Planning Fallacy and the Hiding Hand to explain project underperformance under uncertainty.

failure but does not consider how initial miscues may actually unexpectedly spur creativity and make projects turn into success. This is the case of many UNESCO world heritage sites or other great engineering feats of the modern world such as the Hoosac Tunnel in the US and the Sydney Opera House in Australia. Clearly, these projects would not have been undertaken if their promoters had known the real costs and difficulties that they would confront. In other words, cost-benefit analysis, as recommended by Planning Fallacy proponents, could have ended up costing the world a great deal indeed.

A debate has thus emerged in the project management literature over whether the Planning Fallacy outweighs the Hiding Hand or whether bias (e.g., optimism bias) trumps error (e.g., scope changes, complexity, and uncertainty) as the most likely explanations of project underperformance (Flyvbjerg et al., 2002; Flyvbjerg, 2016; Ika, 2018; Love et al., 2019a, 2019b). As competing theories of cost overruns and benefit shortfalls, these views shape much of the debate on project planning; to wit, are decision-makers deliberately (or even subconsciously) prone to misbehaviors and biases at the outset (leading to poor project outcomes) or do simple planning and execution errors account for most project underperformance? Readers can quickly understand how this debate about project behavior is important when it comes to best curbing project underperformance, either through applying "bias uplifts" or "best practices." Because the presumed cause of underperformance is quite different, adherents to each school of thought promote very different (and potentially expensive or unhelpful) solutions to project delivery and governance. Yet, while some headway has been made in the debate, we still do not know in what circumstances the principles of behavior such as the Hiding Hand and the Planning Fallacy work and how project actors can deal with complex outturns during the lifetime of their assigned projects (Love et al., 2019a, 2019b). As it has been shown that the protagonists of the debate (e.g., Flyvbjerg *versus* Ika/Love and Kahneman *versus* Hirschman) hold antagonistic worldviews about projects and project management (Kreiner, 2020; Ika et al., 2022), one of the goals of this handbook is to examine this debate through the perspectives of different scholars and different schools of thought and address these outstanding questions from both a theoretical and practical perspective.

Two additional project behavior principles, lesser known in the project management literature, have been added for a total of four, including: (1) the Hiding Hand or Benevolent Hand, (2) the Planning Fallacy or Malevolent Hand, (3) the Passive Hand (which leads decision-makers to stifle creativity and avoid risks), and (4) the Protecting Hand or precautionary principle (which tackles ignorance through risk management and scenario-planning). Put differently, the twin principles of the Hiding Hand and the Malevolent Hand are part of a family of *Four Hands* (Anheier, 2017).

Each of these four principles of behavior is associated with the forward-looking appreciation of the complexity (e.g., underestimation or overestimation) and uncertainty (e.g., ignorance or awareness) of the project, which are common features of major projects (Browning & Ramasesh, 2015; Ika & Saint-Macary, 2023). As we learn from Anheier (2017), the Hiding Hand, the equivalent of the Apollo mission's "Houston, we have a problem here," emerges as a result of the combination of ignorance and underestimation of complexity, whereas the Malevolent Hand is the product of the combination of an awareness of full knowledge and willful underestimation of project complexity. The Protecting Hand appears to be at work when there is concomitantly an awareness of a lack of full knowledge and an overestimation of complexity. The Passive Hand is about overestimation of project complexity when the state of knowledge is such that few unknowns should come as a surprise.

While these four principles of project behavior offer superior explanation for project underperformance, they fail to account for the shades of gray between success and failure or between optimism and pessimism. Therefore, Ika et al. (2022) propose the Fifth Hand principle of project behavior, which offers a pluralistic approach to understanding major project cost overruns and benefit shortfalls by combining elements and assumptions embedded both in the Planning Fallacy and the Hiding Hand and recognizing that effective diagnosis of underperformance requires a willingness to accept the existence of multiple causes, both bias and error (see Table I.2 for illustration) (Pinto, 2023). The Barcelona 1992 Olympics also offers a mix of both the Hiding Hand and the Planning Fallacy as strategic misrepresentation about the capacity of the Olympic stadium occurred (strategic overoptimism) and yet optimism bias (sincere overoptimism) also triggered enough creativity to turn the project into a success in the end. As Casellas and Lehtonen (2024, p. 7) write: "For the megaproject literature, the Barcelona case demonstrates that sincere and strategic overoptimism operated in tandem, and that the distinction between the 'Hands' is not necessarily the most important aspect."

Theories of Project Behavior: A Brief Historical Context and Underlying Assumptions

As we have seen, project behavior captures complex out-turns during the course of the project along with initial decisions and actions, events and emerging decisions and actions, and inaction and indecisiveness (March, 1994; Stingl & Geraldi, 2021). While there may be "decisions without actions and actions without decisions" (Brunsson, 1982, p. 32) as in the case of the iPhone project where the action of producing the scratch-resistant screen was taken by Corning CEO Wendell Weeks before a decision was made (Amil, 2022), the project behavior literature has primarily focused on decisions.

As projects require a wide variety of decisions (Stingl & Geraldi, 2017, 2021), historically, project management techniques, as taught in universities and training programs, have focused on the use of myriad decision-making tools. These tools include: (1) direct evaluation techniques such as checklists; (2) deterministic criteria-based evaluation techniques such as weighted scoring models, Analytic Hierarchy Process (AHP), Choosing By Advantages (CBA), and financial models such as cost-benefit analysis, net present value (NPV), and internal rate of return (IRR); (3) stochastic criteria-based evaluation techniques such as decision trees and risk-based profitability analysis; (4) deterministic planning techniques such as decision gates, Work Breakdown Structure (WBS), and CPM; and (5) stochastic planning techniques such as expected monetary value, risk sensitivity analysis, and PERT. Most of these techniques, we note, have been devised in the nineteenth and twentieth centuries to tame the projected future (Rolstadås et al., 2015). In short, our longtime focus was on developing and promoting the use of these toolkits as a means for aiding managers in their organizational and decision-making challenges when running projects.

As decision-making under conditions of perfect or near-perfect certainty is nearly impossible to come by (Kahneman, 2011), the project behavior literature has increasingly focused on decision-making under risk; that is, a context where, according to Knight (1921), an individual making a choice knows the potential outcomes of each available option and their probabilities of occurrence (see Table I.1). As such, project behavior under risk is dominated by probability logic. For example, Reference Class Forecasting (RCF), which is a widely used method to curb cost overruns, is a technique of predicting the future or the likely outcome of a purposive action, based on the forecast error of similar past actions; that is, the discrepancy between their projected costs and their actual costs. In constructing confidence intervals for future project costs based on historical performance of projects within the similar reference class, the technique is based on the probability distribution of expected, "true" costs (Lovallo & Kahneman, 2003; Flyvbjerg, 2006).

The above-mentioned original stream of project behavior research is grounded in the economics literature, which sought to understand individuals' preferences in games of chance (Kahneman, 2011). Bernoulli (1738) proposed expected utility theory where he demonstrated how individuals do not choose the available option with the highest expected value of an outcome but instead the expected utility of an action or the sum of the products of the utilities and probabilities for each of the outcomes that could result from the decision. The key question remains: How should individuals choose an action from a set of possible actions?

von Neumann and Morgenstern (1944) then derived a number of decision-making axioms that posit that rational individuals should choose the available option with the highest expected utility theory, which represents the rational choice.

As the theory goes, to maximize their expected utility, the decision-maker needs to know the exhaustive and mutually exclusive set of actions and their future outcomes and probabilities. As is often the case, this theory evolved over time. As Gigerenzer (2020, p. 1370) remarks: "This basic theory has been modified in many ways, such as in prospect theory, and the learning of probabilities has been modified by Bayes' rule." Despite its widespread appeal, the expected utility theory came under attack in economics for its ill-suited computations, its underlying assumption of perfect knowledge about the exhaustive sets of actions and future outcomes, and lack of evidence for the existence of its stable utility functions (Gigerenzer, 2020). Over time, however, expected utility theory and its variants such as prospect theory, provided the rational prescriptions on which much of the descriptive literature on decision-making under risk in the management field is based (Holmes et al., 2011).

Expected utility theory remains a powerful explanation of project behavior. We can point to two examples to make this point in the project management field. First, as Michele Alacevich, a historian of the World Bank, writes, cost-benefit analysis, a premier project appraisal tool, offers an interesting illustration of these rational prescriptions:

> Cost-benefit analysis had been taking shape in the 1920s as a technique in water-resources development, cultivated mostly by engineers, which subjected public investment decisions to economic analysis and evaluated alternative projects in terms of the maximization of public "utility." It received a further stimulus during the 1930s expansion of public investment activity in the United States, especially thanks to the Flood Control Act of 1936, which dictated that only projects whose benefits were projected to exceed their costs could receive federal funds. (Alacevich, 2014, p. 160)

Second, Piney (2003) provides an application of expected utility theory to project risk management. The author discusses the shortcomings of applying expected monetary value as a tool for assessing and mitigating risks and presents an alternative based on the subjective view of stakeholders (the "utility function") to explain project behavior.

It is against the rational prescriptions of decision-making under risk and in particular tools such as cost-benefit analysis that the principle of the Hiding Hand (Hirschman, 1967), "a theory" of behavior at the project level, was developed. As Alacevich (2014, p. 160) notes:

> Hirschman had already shown doubts about the accuracy of cost-benefit analysis in his preliminary work for the Bank. In that specific case, however, Hirschman seemed more concerned about the possible inhibitory role of cost-benefit analysis than about its role as ex post justification: "were costs underestimated as is frequently the case? If so, was this error matched by an underestimate of benefits (also frequent) so that the Bank's judgment of the actually experienced cost-benefit ratio would have been poorer if just its cost estimate had been more nearly correct?"

Ironically, the Hiding Hand had long been unrecognized and uncredited in the project management literature, with only a few exceptions (e.g., Ika & Söderlund, 2016). Scholars in the meantime had turned to two alternative theories to expected utility theory to explain risk-related behaviors while departing from many of the theory's rational prescriptions: the theory of temporary organizations (Lundin & Söderholm, 1995) and the Planning Fallacy principle (for management, see Kahneman & Tversky, 1977 and Lovallo & Kahneman, 2003 and for project management, see Flyvbjerg, 2006, 2016). Both the theory of temporary organizations and the Planning Fallacy principle form part of the behavioral decision theory literature in project management that directly challenges the precepts of expected utility theory (Holmes et al., 2011; Stingl & Geraldi, 2017).

Lundin and Söderholm's (1995) theory of temporary organizations also helps us understand project behavior – how and why things happen – and its wider implications on creativity, learning, and innovation throughout the project life cycle (Geraldi & Söderlund, 2018). The theory of temporary organizations is inspired by the behavioral theory of the firm (March & Simon, 1958; Cyert & March, 1963) but it differs as it is an action-based, not decision-based, theory, or as the authors put it: "There may not be any logical connection between decisions and actions" (Lundin & Söderholm, 1995, p. 438). The behavioral theory of the firm, which operates at the organizational level, not at the individual level as does expected utility theory, posits that bounded rationality prevails because humans are limited in accessing, processing, and using information (Simon, 1955, 1957); this theory provides a detailed account of decision-making processes in organizations, which may compare their performance to aspiration levels, thereby shaping their risk-taking preferences (Holmes et al., 2011).

For its part, the Planning Fallacy principle, which sheds light on the behavior of projects where underestimation of costs and overestimation of benefits prevail, is based on prospect theory (see Kahneman & Tversky, 1979 and Tversky & Kahneman, 1992 for management and Ika et al., 2022 and Chapter 1 in this book for project management). As Ika et al. (2022, p. 3310) write: "Under the banner of prospect theory, the Planning Fallacy emerges as a phenomenon whereby planners and managers display optimism bias during the framing and valuation phases of projects. The upshot is the tendency for forecasts of project times, costs, and benefits to be close to best-case scenarios." Prospect theory is not a normative theory like expected utility. Rather, it relaxes the assumption of logical rationality of people in favor of their bounded rationality and emphasizes the role that the latter plays in their decision-making. Prospect theory, which offers a unified theory of individual risk taking, was developed in the context of controlled experiments where individual choices between alternatives are assessed, each of which involves potential outcomes and their respective probabilities of occurrence. As such, though the Planning Fallacy is assumed to be working at the project level, its underlying prospect theory operates at the individual level of decision-making and explains if not predicts decisions under risk (Holmes et al., 2011).

The Fifth Hand, which we earlier discussed, also operates at the project level (Ika et al., 2022). Like the Hiding Hand, it assumes that the risk context of decision-making differs from the uncertainty context of decision-making (Knight, 1921; Gigerenzer, 2020) where probability logic falls short as "we need to consider how we should make decisions when some of the alternatives, consequences, and probabilities are unknown (i.e., this requires heuristics and intuition)" (Love et al., 2024a, p. 205). The Fifth Hand principle is based on the theory of ecological rationality (Todd & Gigerenzer, 2012). This theory of decision-making under uncertainty, not risk, which puts forth an "adaptive toolbox" of heuristics – a set of evolved and learned rules that project actors deliberately and intuitively use to help deliver projects – stipulates that a heuristic is good when it matches the structure of the context where it is applied (Gigerenzer, 2020). The Fifth Hand and its underlying ecological rationality may thus help understand the circumstances under which projects successfully or unsuccessfully work (Ika et al., 2022; Love et al., 2024a, 2024b). Table I.3 compares the key theories of project behavior and their underlying assumptions.

A Rough Typology of Theories of Project Behavior

The question of how to explain project behavior has preoccupied researchers and practitioners alike for decades. As we have mentioned, many project behavior theories have sought to explain, and even predict, project behavior. Following the work of the German psychologist, Gerd Gigerenzer, longtime director at the Max Planck Institute for Human Development, we may distinguish between "tools-to-theories," "as-if-theories," and "adaptive toolbox theories."

Tools-to-Theories of Project Behavior

According to Gigerenzer (2020, p. 1367), tools-to-theories prevail in the case where "new theories can be inspired directly by new tools rather than by new data." In project management, these tools-to-theories correspond to optimization or computation tools such as cost-benefit analysis, CPM, and

Table I.3 A comparison of key theories of project behavior and their underlying assumptions

Project behavior theories (Underlying decision-making theories)	Expected utility theory (Expected utility theory)	Hiding Hand	Planning Fallacy (Prospect theory)	Theory of temporary organizations (Behavioral theory of the firm)	The Fifth Hand principle (Ecological rationality)
Level of analysis	Individual	Projects	Individual/projects	Projects as temporary organizations	Projects
Type of rationality	Logical rationality	Bounded rationality	Bounded rationality	Bounded rationality	Bounded rationality
Decision or action rationality?	Decision	Action	Decision	Action	Action
Decision-making context	Risk	Uncertainty	Risk	Risk	Uncertainty
Key authors	Piney (2003); Bernoulli (1738); von Neumann and Morgenstern (1944)	Hirschman (1967); Ika (2018)	Flyvbjerg (2006, 2016); Kahneman and Tversky (1979); Tversky and Kahneman (1992)	Lundin and Söderholm (1995); Cyert and March (1963); March and Simon (1958)	Ika et al. (2022); Todd and Gigerenzer (2012); Gigerenzer (2020)

PERT where planned project schedules and costs determine project behavior and allow tight monitoring and control of the project to get the project back on track in case of deviations from the plan (Kreiner, 2014; Rolstadås et al., 2015). These tools preceded the so-called best-practice theories of project behavior, where project planning is the best practice par excellence, and they are concerned with what project behavior should be rather than what it really is. As Ika and Saint-Macary (2023, p. 180) write: "In short, the project defines the mandate, and the mandate defines the project. To succeed in one is to succeed in the other." As an example, a tool-to-theory such as critical chain project scheduling reminds us that the interest of the project does not coincide with the interests of all project actors; for example, project team members and managers may engage in self-preservation behavior and endeavor to protect themselves by padding project estimates (Goldratt, 1997). Nevertheless, critical chain still remains a statistical tool to optimize project duration and resources.

By and large, tools-to-theories project the formal structure of statistical tools inspired by Neyman and Pearson's statistical decision theory onto project behavior theories and thus cultivate the illusion that the real world of major projects is about risk rather than uncertainty and thus only optimization, not satisficing, can deliver success (Gigerenzer, 2020; Love et al., 2024a, 2024b). Notably, these tools-to-theories of project behavior focus on project management processes (Rolstadås et al., 2015) but they emphasize a sort of *in vitro* project behavior that can be controlled by the decision-maker; the project, which is "reified," is assumed to be "a well-oiled process designed to deliver a product or service that meets a specific need" (Ika & Saint-Macary, 2023, p. 177).

Tools-to-theories can also inspire new theories with other computational features: "new tools for data processing are introduced into a scientific community, from which new theories emerge that in turn require new kinds of data" (Gigerenzer, 2020, p. 1369). It might be argued that a most recent example of a tool-to-theory is the RCF technique, which, as we have noted previously, seeks to debias project cost estimates based on data on past similar projects, and thus has led to the development of what some might call "bias uplift theory" or "RCF theory" (Baerenfold, 2023) to apply *post hoc* corrections to cost estimates made by a project team (Flyvbjerg, 2006). This remains a case of tools-to-theories, considering the fact that

RCF has been used in practice (Flyvbjerg & Cowi, 2004) before its underlying theory has been unraveled in project management (Flyvbjerg, 2006).

As-If Theories of Project Behavior

The economist Milton Friedman (1953) in one of the memorable defenses of expected utility theory suggests that the realism of a theory does not count. What counts is only the accuracy of the theory in predicting behavior. As Gigerenzer (2020, p. 1370) recounts, "an explanation is only *as-if*. People behave *as if* they maximized expected utility... Friedman's as-if argument is still the standard interpretation of expected utility models in economics today."

In the area of project behavior, the classic example of an as-if theoretical principle is the Planning Fallacy. Project leaders behave *as if* they have perfect foresight of the future outcomes of their actions and updated probabilities consistent with Bayes' rule. Notably, Planning Fallacy proponents construe a project as "a consciously designed and planned *leap into a designed and desired future*" and, while the road to success may be bumpy, the destination appears to be known, as "it is given by human choice and purpose"; project management processes are by essence inconsequential for project success, as it was envisioned at the outset; and the project plan "allows us to see if subsequent events fit and, if not, to take corrective action." (Kreiner, 2020, p. 404). Further, the Planning Fallacy searches for correlations between project misbehavior and project underperformance, rather than underlying causes. The rationale is seductive but misleading: If there are cost overruns, then there is concomitantly (naïve or strategic) cost underestimation, which, in turn, without any empirical evidence, *should* explain cost overruns (Flyvbjerg et al., 2002; Flyvbjerg, 2016). Thus, we are left with the question: Where are the causal links between cost underestimation and cost overruns (Love et al., 2022; Pinto, 2023)?

To suggest project management processes are not critical according to the Planning Fallacy explanations of project behavior is, however, not surprising. It is a typical feature of as-if-theories of behavior. We note that prospect theory, the underlying explanation of Planning Fallacy, predicts behavior, yet it is "relatively silent on the cognitive processes underlying such behavior" (Holmes et al., 2011, p. 1078) After all, an as-if-theory tends to be "immune to critique of the reality of its assumptions" about project management processes "and can only be tested by predictions about behavior" (Gigerenzer, 2020, p. 1372) Thus, any practical application of the Planning Fallacy principle may represent a complex as-if normative benchmark to combat cost overruns and benefit shortfalls, which may, at best, work under risk (Ika et al., 2022). As Gigerenzer (2020, p. 1377) suggests, "As-if theories assuming expected utility maximization and Bayesian updating apply instead to situations of risk, where they can provide a normative benchmark but without insight into the cognitive processes."

Adaptive Toolbox Theories of Project Behavior

As-if theories of project behavior such as the Planning Fallacy are unfit for decision-making under uncertainty, where the probability calculus *cannot* deliver the optimal solution (Ika et al., 2022). As Savage (1954, p. 16), who is the author of modern Bayesian decision theory, notes, it would be "utterly ridiculous" to apply it to non-"small world" situations such as "planning a picnic" where probability calculus falls short. Thus, the question, how does project decision-making occur under uncertainty remains to be addressed. Taking inspiration from the great American political scientist and organizational decision-making scholar Herbert Simon, a fierce critic of the universal use of as-if-theories of behavior (Simon, 1955, 1957), Gigerenzer sought to understand how experts make decisions under uncertainty, not risk, and devised formal models of heuristics to guide behavior "quickly and accurately" in true ecological rationality tradition, where these smart rules should match with the structure of their environment (Todd & Gigerenzer, 2012). He coined the term *adaptive toolbox* (Gigerenzer et al., 1999), which, again, he defines as the repertoire of heuristics an individual or an organization has learned over time, including the cognitive capacities that are needed to use these heuristics. Here, "behavior is a function of heuristics, which need to be adapted to the problem at hand" (Gigerenzer, 2020, p. 1373).

As we earlier discussed, the Fifth Hand conceptualization offers such an adaptive toolbox theory of project behavior, as it seeks to understand under what circumstances statistical tools – including probability calculus – work and in what circumstances heuristics and gut-feelings work (Ika et al., 2022). The Fifth Hand does not take project management processes for granted or construe them as inconsequential in the manner of as-if theories of project behavior such as the Planning Fallacy. But the key difference between the Fifth Hand, on the one hand, and tools-to-theories such as cost-benefit analysis and PERT, on the other hand, is that it operates under uncertainty, not risk. The ideas of the Fifth Hand have been applied to the determination of the cost contingency of major projects (Love et al., 2024a, 2024b). And although we are slowly but steadily peeling the layers back in our understanding of project behavior, additional work is necessary if we are to understand how project actors make decisions and take actions under uncertainty. This is even more crucial as their agency, creativity, learning, and innovation are crucial when it comes to delivering these major undertakings, and the stakes are high when we consider them in light of grand challenge projects (Ika & Munro, 2022).

The topic of project behavior, far from offering an esoteric or peripheral vision of projects in modern times, operates directly at the heart of our understanding of the organizational, social, political, human behavioral, computational/tool-based, and structural workings of projects aimed at addressing and alleviating a host of challenges quite literally worldwide. As our chapter has suggested, these challenges are at once definitional ("What do we mean?") and action-oriented ("What can we do?") imperatives that require modern scholars and practitioners alike to rethink the project puzzle, elevating and broadening their perspective, in order to face the "brave new world" of projects in a rapidly evolving, technology-driven, and "megathreats"-ridden era. It is with these goals in mind that we can turn our attention to the organization of this book and the contributions of our authors.

The Structure of the Book

This handbook on project behavior (and misbehavior) is organized in three parts and contains chapters by a well-regarded and engaged set of international project management scholars to reflect on a broad spectrum of perspectives. Part I discusses the principles of project behavior and why they matter for project management theory and practice. Chapter 1, by Lavagnon Ika, entitled "The Rise and Fall of the Planning Fallacy: From the Impulsion to the Compulsion to Theorize," offers a historical and critical evaluation of the nature of Planning Fallacy explanations for project behavior, especially as they relate to project underperformance. His chapter presents a fuller picture of both the utility and shortcomings arising from this conceptualization. Graham Room (Chapter 2) follows with a chapter that lays out the key features of the Flyvbjerg/Hirschman controversy in the project literature, addressing the elements of both the Planning Fallacy and Hiding Hand while exploring some of the popular mythology and misunderstandings that continue to color our evaluation of these models. Along the way, he offers a defense of the Hiding Hand, suggesting that much of the resistance to Hirschman's views comes from a fundamental misunderstanding of his theory, his experimental setting, and the conclusions he drew. In this chapter, Room makes an important contribution to our recognition of project behavior as evidenced by two of its most well-known alternative theories.

Chapter 3 in Part I, on voyages of discovery, by Rebecca Vine, Dicle Kortantamer, and Andrew Davies, borrows its title from the well-known description of project behavior by Hirschman. In their chapter, these authors probe a critical theme in projects, recognizing that an open system characterized as one seeking discovery will fundamentally clash with closed-system imperatives, such as control or too-rigid governance. How a project can balance this critical junction of leadership, control, and capabilities is a resonant thesis that the authors address. In "Temporal Structuring and Project Behavior" (Chapter 4), Ann Langley and Gerry McGivern offer a fascinating appraisal of temporal structures and the lengths to which key project participants go to retain an open system, with frequent input from partners and the positive midcourse corrections to the plan that these interventions spawn. They demonstrate that time and temporality matter for project behavior, referring to the ways in which participants engage with projects and varying according to whether the project operates in a context where deadlines are immutable or not. Finally, Part I concludes with Fran Ackermann's contribution (Chapter 5) on the challenges of managing complexity and uncertainty in projects – two critical and interacting features that shape project behavior – through engaged stakeholder participation and continuous reappraisal. As stakeholder coalitions wax and wane through the project's life, it is necessary to frequently monitor and make midcourse adjustments based on their composition and evolving perceptions of project requirements. They conclude that attempts by project managers to respond to uncertainty may well result in added complexity that they need to confront in turn, making project behavior a dynamic and challenging phenomenon in practice.

Part II of the book is organized around the thorny problems found in project complexity and uncertainty. Van Oorschot, Dille, and Söderlund (Chapter 6) address the challenges of "averaging behavior," where complex projects composed of several sub-projects are susceptible to a form of balancing, in which divergent opinions of the status of the various sub-projects can lead to a desire to find a middle ground that actually results in overestimation of actual project performance. In presenting a longitudinal process study of an information systems project, they found that its hierarchy of sub-projects promoted unfavorable project behavior. Ralf Müller's (Chapter 7) exposure of the vagaries of intra- and inter-organizational project governance sheds important light on forms of subsequent project behavior. Notably, he takes the analogy of project personality to describe different types of project behavior, which may depend, for example, on whether projects take an inward or outward perspective, or they focus on the consequences of actions or instead their correctness. Miia Martinsuo and Siiri Tuominen (Chapter 8) elaborate on a critical feature of macro-project phenomena, discussing project portfolio management and behaviors that are sparked through strategic portfolio alignment, dealing with uncertainties, and pressures toward portfolio realignment. Using examples from five projects, they show that project behavior is both a source of uncertainty and a potential mechanism for activating and promoting strategic realignment.

Kate Davis, Liz Machtynger, and Francesco Di Maddaloni (Chapter 9) offer a deeper dive into the challenges and mechanisms by which project-based firms can identify and formulate strategies for stakeholder management. Further, they address project behavior challenges when including different stakeholder perceptions for project performance. Their chapter demonstrates that it is essential to control the project's outcome parameters through stakeholder expectations to minimize the chances of failure and maximize performance. Maude Brunet (Chapter 10) continues the focus on project governance with an intriguing chapter that identifies the dynamic nature of governance, as it can operate on three different models – hierarchical, heterarchical, and network – and to understand that shifts in project governance – proactive, reactive, radical, or evolutionary – provide turning points that shed light on project behavior, with far-reaching impacts on performance. Wolfgang Seibel and Katharina Eåmeyer (Chapter 11) provide a unique chapter that examines, through an extended case example, the issue of corruption in a project environment, specifically focusing on money laundering. They show how the tensions between the rationality of politicians and the rationality of administrative experts can challenge the delivery of the project and complicate its behavior over time. Continuing the theme of project behavior as pathology, the final chapter in Part II by Regis Signor and Peter Love (Chapter 12) focuses on the nature of mega-project corruption in the Brazil construction industry, reviewing a variety of causes and consequences of this ongoing challenge. Taking corruption as a willful, deceitful, and criminal project misbehavior enacted for monetary gain, they offer a chronological analysis of relevant facts and successive decisions taken by politicians and managers in specific mega-project cases and thus provide a context to understand how strategic misbehaviors occur in project settings.

Part III offers some chapters that address practical guidelines and applicable measures for dealing with project behavior, and more specifically, with varieties of misbehaviors. Ofer Zwikael, Alicia Gilchrist, and Jack Meredith (Chapter 13) kick off this part of the book with a discussion of the need for and methods to employ in setting realistic project goals, arguing that misbehaviors often occur in the margins; that is, where goals remain nebulous or open to multiple interpretations, there is a tendency for self-serving behaviors to exert themselves amongst the various stakeholders. Their contribution focuses on the analysis of seven major projects and offers ten practical recommendations to help managers set more realistic project goals. Their chapter is followed by Joana Geraldi, Verena Stingl, and Maximilian Schriewersmann's treatment (Chapter 14) of the use of decision heuristics to improve project screening, arguing that better initial selection through smart heuristics can militate against potentially ruinous investments that were undertaken for unclear reasons and help smooth front-end project behavior. Their chapter consists in an empirical study on heuristics used by senior managers to screen and select which of the tendering opportunities of major infrastructure projects to pursue. Joseph Harrisson, Jens Roehrich, and Mike Lewis (Chapter 15) continue the focus on project front-end in their chapter with clear suggestions on how to apply project governance methods – contractual and relational governance mechanisms – to manage and minimize misbehaviors – at the individual, team, and project levels – that can snowball once the project is fully under way. They show how the two functions of control and coordination of the contractual and governance mechanisms can help tackle project misbehaviors such as strategic misrepresentation at the project level, normalization of deviance at the team level, and narcissistic traits of leaders at the individual level.

Ashwin Mahalingam's contribution (Chapter 16) on twists and turns in project delivery provides a unique and highly readable account of his recent role in managing his own project – a residential construction – and discovering firsthand the manner in which misbehaviors and various out-turns occurred. Combining theory and real experience, his chapter is a refreshing look at the real way project vagaries assert themselves. Jeffrey Pinto and Greg Usher's chapter on project disruptions (Chapter 17) introduces the theme of calculated responses. It is common to talk of robustness, resilience, and antifragility as types of responses to project disruptions. This chapter examines each of these responses to disruption in turn, arguing that circumstances and proactive decision-making can result in disrupted projects that actually recover as stronger and more value-creating than originally envisioned. The final chapter in Part III, by Morten Welde and Gro Holst Volden (Chapter 18) presents some important guidance on addressing two of the thorniest behavior problems in new project delivery – exploring the means for minimizing benefit shortfalls while curbing cost increases. Their work with the Concept Research Program in Norway for many years has resulted in a chapter of practical and cutting-edge expertise.

The book concludes with an Afterword by Stewart Clegg. Modeled on a similar approach taken by the late Professor Peter Morris for *Making Projects Critical* by Hodgson and Cicmil (2006), we asked Professor Clegg to offer his unique perspective on the nature of project behavior, his critical assessment on the chapters herein contained, and thoughts on research and theory gaps that can form a roadmap for future studies. His chapter, looking at the contributions in this handbook, forms a wonderful concluding word on the subject and a call for future effort in continuing to examine the nature of project behavior.

This handbook has been the result of years of reflection and active scholarship on the nature of project behavior, the ways it can be understood to impact project development and delivery, and the pathologies so often found both causing and resulting from the myriad vagaries and out-turns that projects take. In noting that where projects are concerned, "there is many a slip 'twixt the cup and the lip," this handbook is the logical outworking of a stream of research that has been internationally recognized and ongoing for some years now. We would be remiss to not offer our greatest and most sincere thanks to Professor Peter Love, who has been a major source of inspiration, guidance, motivating light, and supportive colleague as we conclude this handbook. It is fair and appropriate to state that the book itself, as well as the theoretical understanding of project behavior, would not have seen the light of day were it not for his personal contributions and support. Likewise, we extend our many thanks to Valerie Appleby, Tobias Ginsberg, and Caroline Parkinson from Cambridge University Press who have helped us successfully navigate the complicated steps in this handbook project. Our gratitude also goes to the reviewers who have worked tirelessly to help authors improve their chapters.

To conclude, we noted at the outset that the current debate on large-scale projects overruns and overspends has been front and center in the project management literature for the past several years, with debates and positions being exchanged in the pages of a number of academic journals as well as the popular press. Given the likely unabating interest in the topic and the divergence of opinions being offered (particularly in this age of rapid development of mega-projects around the globe), we strongly believe that the time is ripe for a scholarly handbook on the current state of this challenge, perspectives on project behavior and misbehavior, and its implications for practitioners and project professionals responsible for delivering these high-profile and highly complex projects. Collecting the reasoned perspectives of a broad array of widely respected scholars has given us the opportunity to create a book that has both academic validity and practical power.

References

Alacevich, M. (2014). Visualizing uncertainties, or how Albert Hirschman and the World Bank disagreed on project appraisal and what this says about the end of "high development theory." *Journal of the History of Economic Thought, 36*(2), 137–168.

Amil, I. F. (2022). "You can do it" – The day Steve Jobs changed the world. North America Vision Magazine. *Vision Magazine* (visionmagazineus.com).

Anheier, H. K. (2017). Infrastructure and the principle of the Hiding Hand (pp. 1–20). In K.Wegrich, G. Kostka, and G.Hammerschmid, G. (eds.). *The governance of infrastructure*. Oxford University Scholarship Online.

Baerenbold, R. (2023). Reducing risks in megaprojects: The potential of reference class forecasting. *Project Leadership and Society*, 100103.

Bendoly, E., and Swink, M. (2007). Moderating effects of information access on project management behavior, performance and perceptions. *Journal of Operations Management, 25*(3), 604–622.

Beringer, C., Jonas, D., and Kock, A. (2013). Behavior of internal stakeholders in project portfolio management and its impact on success. *International Journal of Project Management, 31*(6), 830–846.

Bernoulli, D. (1738). Specimen theoriae novae de mensura sortis, in Commentarii Aca-demiae Scientiarum Imperialis Petropolitannae; translated from Latin into English by L. Sommer, "Exposition of a new theory on the measurement of risk." *Econometrica, 22*, 23–36.

Boutinet, J.-P. (2005). *Anthropologie du projet*. Quadrige.

Bröchner, J. (2022). Project tragedies. *International Journal of Project Management, 40*(5), 467–470.

Browning, T. R., and Ramasesh, R. V. (2015). Reducing unwelcome surprises in project management. *MIT Sloan Management Review* 56(3), 53–62.

Brunsson, N. (1982). The irrationality of action and action rationality: Decisions, ideologies, and organizational actions. *Journal of Management Studies*, 29–44.

Casellas, A., and Lehtonen, M. (2024). The Hiding Hand controversy as an analytical approach in the study of urban megaevents. *Cities, 147*, 104773.

Chiocchio, F., Kelloway, E., and Hobbs, B. (eds.). (2015). *The psychology and management of project teams*. Oxford University Press.

Cicmil, S., Williams, T., Thomas, J., and Hodgson, D. (2006). Rethinking project management: Researching the actuality of projects. *International Journal of Project Management, 24*(8), 675–686.

Cleland, D. I., and Ireland, L. R. (2007). *Project management: Strategic design and implementation*. McGraw-Hill.

Conlon, D. E., and Garland, H. (1993). The role of project completion information in resource allocation decisions. *Academy of Management Journal*, *36*(2), 402–413.

Cyert, R. M., and March, J. G. (1963). *A behavioral theory of the firm*. Blackwell.

Daniel, P. A., and Daniel, C. (2018). Complexity, uncertainty and mental models: From a paradigm of regulation to a paradigm of emergence in project management. *International Journal of Project Management*, *36*(1), 184–197.

Defoe, D. (1697). *An essay upon projects*. Cockerill.

Dvir, D., and Lechler, T. (2004). Plans are nothing, changing plans is everything: the impact of changes on project success. *Research Policy*, *33*(1), 1–15.

Emirbayer, M., and Mische, A. (1998). What is agency? *American Journal of Sociology*, *103* (4), 962–1023.

Engwall, M., and Westling, G. (2004). Peripety in an R&D drama: Capturing a turnaround in project dynamics. *Organization Studies*, *25*(9), 1557–1578.

Flyvbjerg, B. (2006). From Nobel Prize to project management: Getting risks right. *Project Management Journal*, *37*(3), 5–15.

Flyvbjerg, B. (2016). The fallacy of beneficial ignorance: A test of Hirschman's hiding hand. *World Development*, *84*, 176–189.

Flyvbjerg, B., and Cowi (2004). Procedures for dealing with optimism bias. In Transport Planning Guidance Document. Department for Transport: London, UK.

Flyvbjerg, B., and Gardner, D. (2023). *How big things get done: The surprising factors that determine the fate of every project, from home renovations to space exploration and everything in between*. Signal.

Flyvbjerg, B., Holm, M. K. S., and Buhl, S. L. (2002). Underestimating costs in public works projects: Error or lie. *Journal of the American Planning Association*, *68*(3), 279–295.

Forrester, J. W. (1997). Industrial dynamics. *Journal of the Operational Research Society*, *48*(10), 1037–1041.

Friedman, M. (1953). *Essays in positive economics*. University of Chicago Press.

Galvin, P., Tywoniak, S., and Sutherland, J. (2021). Collaboration and opportunism in megaproject alliance contracts: The interplay between governance, trust and culture. *International Journal of Project Management*, *39*(4), 394–405.

Geraldi, J., and Söderlund, J. (2018). Project studies: What it is, where it is going. *International Journal of Project Management*, *36*(1), 55–70.

Gigerenzer, G. (2014). *Risk savvy: How to make good decisions*. Penguin Group.

Gigerenzer, G. (2020). How to explain behavior? *Topics in Cognitive Science*, *12*(4), 1363–1381.

Gigerenzer, G., Todd, P. M., and ABC Research Group (1999). *Simple heuristics that make us smart*. Oxford University Press.

Gil, N., and Fu, Y. (2022). Megaproject performance, value creation and value distribution: An organizational governance perspective. *Academy of Management Discoveries*, *8*(2), 224–251.

Goldratt, E. (1997). *Critical chain*. The North River Press.

Heidegger, M. (1962). *Being and time*. Harper.

Heidegger, M. (1985) *History of the Concept of Time: Prolegomena*, translated by T. Kiesel. Indiana University Press

Hilliard, W. (2024). Abandoned $10 billion Apple Car project referred to as 'Titanic disaster' by employees. Appleinsider.com. https://appleinsider.com/articles/24/02/29/abandoned-10-billion-apple-car-project-referred-to-as-titanic-disaster-by-employees.

Hirschman, A. O. (1967). *Development projects observed*. The Brookings Institution.

Hodgson, D., and Cicmil, S. (2006). *Making projects critical*. Bloomsbury.

Holmes R. M., Jr., Bromiley, P., Devers, C. E., Holcomb, T. R., and McGuire, J. B. (2011). Management theory applications of prospect theory: Accomplishments, challenges, and opportunities. *Journal of Management*, *37*(4), 1069–1107.

Ika, L. A. (2018). Beneficial or detrimental ignorance: The straw man Fallacy of Flyvbjerg's test of Hirschman's Hiding Hand. *World Development*, *103*, 369–382.

Ika, L. A., Love, P. E. D., and Pinto, J. K. (2022). Moving beyond the Planning Fallacy: The emergence of a new principle of project behavior. *IEEE Transactions on Engineering Management*, *69*(6), 3310–3325.

Ika, L. A., Meredith, J., and Zwikael, O. (2024). Project governance: The impact of environmental changes on governance adaptations in large-scale projects. *International Journal of*

Managing Projects in Business, *17*(4/5), 829–854.

Ika, L. A., and Munro, L. T. (2022). Tackling grand challenges with projects: Five insights and a research agenda for project management theory and practice. *International Journal of Project Management*, *40*(6), 601–607.

Ika, L. A., and Pinto, J. K. (2022). The "re-meaning" of project success: Updating and recalibrating for a modern project management. *International Journal of Project Management*, *40*(7), 835–848.

Ika, L. A., Pinto, J. K., Love, P. E., and Pache, G. (2023). Bias versus error: Why projects fall short. *Journal of Business Strategy*, *44*(2), 67–75.

Ika, L. A., and Saint-Macary, J. (2023). *Managing fuzzy projects in 3D: A proven, multi-faceted blueprint for overseeing complex projects*. McGraw-Hill Education.

Ika, L. A., and Söderlund, J. (2016). Rethinking revisited: Insights from an early rethinker. *International Journal of Managing Projects in Business*, *9*(4), 931–954.

Kahneman, D. (2011). *Thinking fast and slow*. Doubleday Canada.

Kahneman, D., and Tversky, A. (1977). *Intuitive prediction: Biases and corrective procedures* Defense Advanced Research Projects Agency. https://apps.dtic.mil/sti/tr/pdf/ADA047747.pdf.

Kahneman, D., and Tversky, A. (1979). Prospect theory: An analysis of decision under risk. *Econometrica*, *47*(2), 263–292.

Kaufmann, C., and Kock, A. (2023). The performance effects of optimistic and pessimistic project status reporting behavior. *International Journal of Project Management*, *41*(7), 102514.

Keil, M., Mann, J., and Rai, A. (2000). Why software projects escalate: An empirical analysis and test of four theoretical models. *Mis Quarterly*, 631–664.

Kloppenborg, T. J., Tesch, D., and Manolis, C. (2014). Project success and executive sponsor behaviors: Empirical life cycle stage investigations. *Project Management Journal*, *45*(1), 9–20.

Knight, F. H. (1921). *Risk, uncertainty and profit*. Houghton Mifflin.

Kreiner, K. (2014). Restoring project success as phenomenon (pp. 21–40). In R. A.Lundin and M. Hällgreen (eds.). *Advancing research on projects and temporary organizations*. Copenhagen Business School Press & Liber.

Kreiner, K. (2020). Conflicting notions of a project: The battle between Albert O. Hirschman and Bent Flyvbjerg. *Project Management Journal*, *51*(1), 400–410.

Kunisch, S., Huy, N. Q., and Bartunek, J. M. (2017). Time in strategic change research. *The Academy of Management Annals*, *11*(2), 1005–1064.

Lindkvist, L., Soderlund, J., and Tell, F. (1998). Managing product development projects: On the significance of fountains and deadlines. *Organization Studies*, *19(6)*, 931–951.

Lovallo, D., and Kahneman, D. (2003). Delusions of success: How optimism undermines executives' decisions. *Harvard Business Review*, July, 56–63.

Love, P. E. D., Sing, M. C. P., Ika, L. A., and Newton, S. (2019a). The cost performance of transportation projects: The fallacy of the Planning Fallacy account. *Transportation Research Part A: Policy and Practice*, *122*(1), 1–20.

Love, P. E. D., Ika, L. A., and Ahiaga-Dagbui, D. (2019b). On de-bunking 'fake news' in a post-truth area: Why does the Planning Fallacy explanation for cost overruns fall short? *Transportation Research A: Policy and Practice*, *126*, 397–408.

Love, P. E. D, Ika, L. A., and Sing, M. C. (2022). Does the planning fallacy prevail in social infrastructure projects? Empirical evidence and competing explanations. *IEEE Transactions on Engineering Management*, *69*(6), 2588–2602.

Love, P. E. D., Ika, L. A., Matthews, J., and Fang, W. (2024a). Risk and uncertainty in the cost contingency of transport projects: Accommodating bias or heuristics, or both? *IEEE Transactions on Engineering Management*, *71*(1), 205–218.

Love, P. E. D., Ika, L. A., and Pinto, J. K. (2024b). Homo heuristicus: From risk management to managing uncertainty in large-scale infrastructure projects. *IEEE Transactions on Engineering Management*, *71*(1), 1940–1949.

Lundin, R. A., and Söderholm, A. (1995). A theory of the temporary organization. *Scandinavian Journal of Management*, *11*(4), 437–455.

Maldonado, T. (2002). Defoe and the "Projecting Age." *Design Issues*, *18*(1), 78–85.

March, J. G. (1994). *Primer on decision making: How decisions happen*. Simon and Schuster.

March, J. G., and Simon, H. A. (1958). *Organizations*. John Wiley.

Meredith, J., and Zwikael, O. (2019). When is a project successful? *IEEE Engineering Management Review*, *47*(3), 127–134.

Novak, M. E. (ed.). (2008). *The Age of projects* (vol. 9). University of Toronto Press.
Nowińska, A., and Pedersen, T. (2024). Project managers and decision making: Conditional cognitive switching and rationally stepping up. *Long Range Planning*, *57*(1), 102414.
Piney, C. (2003). Applying utility theory to risk management. *Project Management Journal*, *34*(3), 26–31.
Pinto, J. K. (2014). Project management, governance, and the normalization of deviance. *International Journal of Project Management*, *32*(3), 376–387.
Pinto, J. K. (2022). No project should ever finish late (and why yours probably will, anyway). *IEEE Engineering Management Review*, *50*(3), 181–192.
Pinto, J. K. (2023). Is this how big things get done? *International Journal of Project Management*, *41*(1),102484.
Pinto, J. K., and Slevin, D. P. (1988). Critical success factors across the project life cycle. *Project Management Journal*, *19*(3), 67–75.
Pitsis, T. S., Clegg, S. R., Marosszeky, M., and Rura-Polley, T. (2003). Constructing the Olympic dream: A future perfect strategy of project management. *Organization Science*, *14*(5), 574–590.
Prisco, J. (2020). Airbus A380: The wondrous giant that never quite took off. CNN. www.cnn.com/travel/article/airbus-a380-birth-and-death/index.html.
Rolstadås, A., Pinto, J. K., Falster, P., and Venkataraman, R. (2015). Project decision chain. *Project Management Journal*, *46*(4), 6–19.
Ryle, G. (2000). Courses of action or the uncatchableness of mental acts. *Philosophy*, *75*(3), 331–344.
Ross, L. (1977). The intuitive psychologist and his shortcomings: Distortions in the attribution process. In L.Berkowitz (ed.). *Advances in experimental social psychology* (vol. 10). Academic Press.
Savage, L. J. (1972). *The foundations of statistics*. Wiley.
Schalby, C. (2024). Despite some progress, state's high-speed rail is $100 billion short and many years from reality. *Los Angeles Times*. www.latimes.com/california/story/2024-03-21/high-speed-rail.
Schutz, A. (1967). *The phenomenology of the social world*. Northwestern University Press.
Schutz, A. (1973). *Collected papers I: The problem of social reality*. Martinus Nijhoff.
Shenhar, A. J., and Dvir, D. (2007). *Reinventing project management: The diamond approach to successful growth and innovations*. Harvard Business School Press.
Shore, B. (2008). Systematic biases and culture in project failures. *Project Management Journal*, *39*(4), 5–16.
Simon, H. A. (1955). A behavioral model of rational choice. The Quarterly Journal of Economics, 99–118.
Simon, H. A. (1957). *Models of man*. John Wiley.
Slawinski, N., and Bansal, P. (2015). Short on time: Intertemporal tensions in business sustainability. *Organization Science*, *26*, 531–549.
Slevin, D. P., and Pinto, J. K. (2007). An overview of behavioral issues in project management (pp. 1–19). In *Wiley guide to project organization & project management competencies*. Wiley.
Söderlund, J. (2004). Building theories of project management: Past research, questions for the future. *International Journal of Project Management*, *22*(3), 183–191.
Stingl, V., and Geraldi, J. (2017). Errors, lies and misunderstandings: Systematic review on behavioural decision making in projects. *International Journal of Project Management*, *35*(2), 121–135.
Stingl, V., and Geraldi, J. (2021). A research agenda for studying project decision-behaviour through the lenses of simple heuristics. *Technological Forecasting and Social Change*, *162*, 120367.
Strauss, A. (1988). The articulation of project work: An organizational process. *Sociological Quarterly*, *29*(2), 163–178.
Tetlow, G., and Pattison, J. (2023). HS2: costs and controversies. How much has the HS2 project cost since its inception? Institute for Government. www.instituteforgovernment.org.uk/explainer/hs2-costs
Todd, P. M., and Gigerenzer, G. (2012). *Ecological rationality: Intelligence in the world*. Oxford University Press.
Tversky, A., and Kahneman, D. (1992). Advances in prospect theory: Cumulative representation of uncertainty. *Journal of Risk and uncertainty*, *5*, 297–323.
Vaagaasar, A. L., Hernes, T., and Dille, T. (2020). The challenges of implementing temporal shifts in temporary organizations: Implications of a situated temporal view. *Project Management Journal*, *51*(4), 420–428.
Vidal, L. A., Marle, F., and Bocquet, J. C. (2011). Measuring project complexity using the Analytic

Hierarchy Process. *International Journal of Project Management*, *29*(6), 718–727.

Von Neumann, J., and Morgenstern, O. (1944). *Theory of games and economic behavior*. Princeton University Press.

Weber, M. (1978). *Economy and society*, 2 vols. Edited by R.Guenther and C.Wittich. University of California Press.

Weick, K. E. (1999). That's moving theories that matter. *Journal of Management Inquiry*, *8*(2), 134–142.

Williams, T. (2005). Assessing and moving on from the dominant project management discourse in the light of project overruns. *IEEE Transactions on engineering management*, *52*(4), 497–508.

Williams, T., Eden, C., Ackermann, F., and Tait, A. (1995). The effects of design changes and delays on project costs. *Journal of the Operational Research Society*, *46*, 809–818.

Winch, G. M., and Sergeeva, N. (2022). Temporal structuring in project organizing: A narrative perspective. *International Journal of Project Management*, *40*(1), 40–51.

Winch, G. M., Brunet, M., and Cao, D (2023). Introduction to research handbook on complex project organising (pp. 1–10). In G. M.Winch, M.Brunet, and D.Cao (eds.). *Research handbook on complex project organising*. Edward Elgar.

Wynn, C., Smith, L., and Killen, C. (2021). How power influences behavior in projects: A theory of planned behavior perspective. *Project Management Journal*, *52*(6), 607–621.

PART I

Guiding Principles

What Is Project Behavior and Why It Matters

CHAPTER 1

The Rise and Fall of the Planning Fallacy

From the Impulsion to the Compulsion to Theorize

LAVAGNON A. IKA

Introduction

> The ideas of economists and political philosophers, both when they are right and when they are wrong, are more powerful than is commonly understood .... Indeed, the world is run by little else. Practical men, who believe themselves to be quite exempt from any intellectual influence are usually the slaves of some defunct economist .... It is ideas, not vested interests, which are dangerous for good or evil. (Keynes, 1953, p. 306)

For centuries, project leaders have grappled with the uphill challenge of getting their major projects right. While failure and underperformance statistics should be taken with a grain of salt (Chapman, 2024), some authors suggest that 50 percent of projects of different types fail to deliver their expected benefits (Ika & Saint-Macary, 2023) and 91.5 percent of them fail to come in either on time or within budget (Flyvbjerg & Gardner, 2023). Indeed, the history of projects is rife with optimistic plans, which may cause dismal failures if not costly disasters (Hall, 1980; Pinto, 2023). These benefit shortfalls in the long term may be compounded with time and cost overruns in the short term, leading perhaps to a bleak recurrent cycle of projects that are delivered "over time, over budget, under benefits, over and over again," a phenomenon that former Oxford professor Bent Flyvbjerg terms the "Iron Law of Megaprojects" (Flyvbjerg, 2017).

The search for explanations for such a pattern of project behavior – that is, how projects take different and complex out-turns between initiation and execution or experience over their lifetime systematic deviations from plans (Ika et al., 2022) – is a long-standing quest, which Love et al. (2022a) equate to "hundreds of years of pain, with minimum gain." For example, Albert Hirschman, a rather unsung pioneer of project management research and one of the most influential economists and social scientists of the twentieth century, posits the Hiding Hand principle, which stipulates that it is not always bad for leaders to overestimate the benefits and underestimate the costs, the difficulties and risks of proposed projects, because they may also underestimate their own creativity ex ante. Hence, once things begin to go wrong, they rise to the challenge and "stumble into success" (Hirschman, 1967). Indeed, a playful variant of Adam Smith's Invisible Hand, Hirschman's Hiding Hand "beneficially hides difficulties from us" and suggests ignorance can be good for projects (Hirschman, 1967, p. 13). But, for half a century, except for the work of Ika and Söderlund (2016), "Hirschman's seemingly unimpactful ideas about projects were left to rest in peace" and "never caught on in the rest of the field of project management" (Kreiner, 2020, p. 401).

However, this was not the fate of another theoretical explanation of project behavior, which did not go unnoticed, although it had emerged in the fields of psychology and economics: Nobel Prize–winner Daniel Kahneman's Planning Fallacy principle, that is, the tendency for forecasts of project schedules, costs, and benefits to be unrealistically close to best-case scenarios, *even if it contradicts past plans and performances* (Lovallo & Kahneman, 2003; Kahneman, 2011). While the Planning Fallacy, whereby project leaders tend to overpromise and under-deliver, initially focused on project completion time (Kahneman & Tversky, 1977; Buehler et al., 1994), it is in this encompassing sense that, with the seminal work of Flyvbjerg, it came of age in the project management field (Flyvbjerg, 2006), as a novel but competing explanation to the Hiding Hand (Ika & Söderlund, 2016). Notably, as Harvard professor and influential behaviorist Cass Sunstein notes, the *Benevolent* Hiding Hand, which is of course Hirschman's principle, has its "evil twin," the *Malevolent* Hiding Hand, "which also hides obstacles and difficulties, but in situations in which creativity does not emerge, or emerges too late, or cannot possibly save the day." (Sunstein, 2015, p. xii) However, it is still not clear whether the Malevolent Hiding Hand argument trumps the Benevolent Hiding Hand argument in both theory and practice.

Flyvbjerg (2016, p. 176) is all for the Malevolent Hiding Hand as he is not impressed with the Benevolent Hiding Hand argument, which he considers "the oldest and most common justification of why low-balled cost estimates and optimistic business cases are considered acceptable in large projects." Put differently, Flyvbjerg (2016, p. 176) rejects Hirschman's Hiding Hand, champions instead Kahneman's Planning Fallacy, and suggests ignorance is *always* bad as it leads to ''starting projects that should not have been started." Soon, the Planning Fallacy was heralded as the "best theory" for "how projects work," thereby making behavioral bias the most robust explanation for cost overruns and benefit shortfalls (Flyvbjerg et al., 2018). Some two decades after the coming of age of the Planning Fallacy principle, while it has enjoyed considerable support in project management theory and practice, it is in danger of falling from its exalted pedestal. Indeed, the fact that the Planning Fallacy is still regarded as the prominent explanation of project behavior with little causal testing and empirical validation to show for it (Love et al., 2022a, 2022b) begs for an inquiry on what explains the appeal of the so-called theory and, more importantly, whether it will reach a dead end and why.

As Shenkar and Ellis (2022, p. 783) write, this complex inquiry calls for arguments in the realms of both the philosophy (Malisoff, 1934) and the sociology (Ben David & Sullivan, 1975) of science:

> The dominance of a theory in a particular domain is determined not only by its internal logic and validity, but also by the characteristics of the scholarly environment in which it operates and evolves.

Accordingly, this chapter focuses on the timely rise and looming fall of the Planning Fallacy and asks: Is the Planning Fallacy principle a theory anyway and, if yes, is the theory complete? Is the theory too narrow in scope or does it cater to complexity and uncertainty? Will it lose support from the scientific community? I hasten to note that my intent is not to provide complete answers to these questions but offer mid-range conclusions.

I argue that the reasons for the timely rise and looming fall of the Planning Fallacy are still hardly understood. I posit that the fall of the Planning Fallacy may not rest with the sociology of science but will rather lie in the philosophy of science. I suggest that while the rise can be attributed to an *impulsion* to theorize at a time when a theory of cost overruns was not forthcoming, the fall may be due to a companion *compulsion* to theorize since it seeks to explain almost everything after the fact (see Table 1.1 for definitions of these theory-related terms).

In our quest for project behavior knowledge, we are witnessing a Planning Fallacy of the theory, as the principle falls foul to overestimating its own theoretical power. I hence note that the cure to the Planning Fallacy is not on par with expectations and that the evil of the Iron Law it purports to thwart is not receding much according to its proponents. Indeed, we continue to see the same planning setbacks, over and over again, since error and bias keep creeping into project plans. I thus suggest that similar costly theoretical and practical misadventures are up for grabs in years to come if project management scholars continue to borrow "hand-me-down" theories from other fields without sufficient evaluation.

In the rest of the chapter, I begin with a historical section on the rise of the Planning Fallacy and discuss the impulsion to theorize that propels its appeal. Then, I focus on the fall of the Planning Fallacy and examine the compulsion to theorize that will eventually fuel its disavowal. I conclude the chapter with a dilemma for scholars.

Table 1.1 Theory terminology

Key theory concepts	Definitions
Theory	"A theory is an organized, heuristic, coherent, and systematic set of statements related to significant questions that are communicated in a meaningful whole" (McDonald et al., 2004, p. 28).
Theorizing	A trial-and-error process that draws on empirical data to produce "informed knowledge claims" (Cornelissen et al., 2021) or "a short-hand for a better understanding of how a theory is put together; how it is handled in empirical research – and how it can be taught in an effective manner" (Swedberg, 2016, p. 6).
Impulsion to theorize	The urge to "see" and problematize things under study thereby identifying patterns and regularities to make sense of the world and thus offer "possible" accounts to tackle a societal puzzle (Blum, 1970).
Compulsion to theorize	The tendency to "compulsively" and "mindlessly" seek sweeping law-like explanations for a phenomenon under study, which would fit a prevailing theory or "line of causation" (Hirschman, 1970).
Concepts	Abstract theory terms "that specify the features, attributes, or characteristics of the phenomenon in the real or phenomenological world that they are meant to represent and that distinguish them from other related phenomena" (Podsakoff et al., 2016, p. 3).
Hypothesis	A preliminary answer to a research question or "a conjectural statement about the relation between two or more variables" (Pedhazur & Schmelkin, 2013, p. 194).

The Rise of the Planning Fallacy: The Impulsion to Theorize

In this section, I take a chronological view and describe the rise of the Planning Fallacy principle, its key concepts, streams of research, and practical applications in project management. I then highlight the concomitant impulsion to theorize in project management research, which offers a window of opportunity for the principle to shine.

Genesis of the Planning Fallacy

The Planning Fallacy was first introduced to the psychology literature by two fathers of behavioral economics, the late Daniel Kahneman and Amos Tversky, whose work has had a profound impact in many fields from psychology to economics to finance to project management. For example, the recent passing of the Nobel Prize–winner Kahneman at the time of the writing of this chapter, that is 28 years after the death of his coauthor and friend Tversky, has led to a flurry of obituaries in prestigious outlets such as the *Guardian*, the *New York Times*, *The Economist*, *Le Monde*, *China Daily*, and *Times of India*, a testament of the genius of the man and the high esteem in which his ideas have been held.

Kahneman and Tversky posit that individuals mainly rely on intuitive but inaccurate judgments when making *project* forecasts based on singular information related to the project under consideration and thus commit errors that "are often systematic rather than random, manifesting bias rather than confusion" (Kahneman & Tversky, 1977, pp. 1–1). Hence, the Planning Fallacy, "a consequence of the tendency to neglect distributional data" (Kahneman & Tversky, 1977, pp. 2–2) from past projects. As they observe:

> Scientists and writers, for example, are notoriously prone to underestimate the time required to complete a project, even when they have considerable experience of past failures to live up to planned schedules. (Kahneman & Tversky, 1977, pp. 2–2)

As it will soon turn out, the Planning Fallacy is powered by prospect theory, proposed by Kahneman and Tversky (1979) as an alternative to expected utility theory for predicting individual decision-making under risk. Prospect theory suggests that decision-making processes involve two phases. In the framing phase, people make a preliminary evaluation and develop a simplified representation of the prospects. In the evaluation phase, people assign each potential outcome of a prospect a decision weight and select the prospect whose outcomes have the highest total of weighted values (Bromiley & Rau, 2022). As Kahneman and Tversky (1979, p. 283) argue:

> Because people are limited in their ability to comprehend and evaluate extreme probabilities, highly unlikely events are either neglected or overweighted, and the difference between high probability and certainty is either neglected or exaggerated.

This behavior occurs in many projects where bias may loom large and, leaders, tricked by the Planning Fallacy, settle for unrealistic estimates during project framing and evaluation (Ika et al., 2022). Interestingly, while they coined the term Planning Fallacy, Kahneman and Tversky (1977) were *not* the first to write about project "underestimation bias" (e.g., Epton, 1972). So, where does the idea of the Planning Fallacy come from?

The Planning Fallacy can be described as an accidental discovery of a theoretical principle in an area – project management – that has been described as "the accidental profession" since the 1970s. In his 2011 best seller *Thinking, Fast and Slow*, Daniel Kahneman recounted the story of his Eureka moment during a textbook project in 1976. While, after one year of hard work, the team estimated the project would be complete in two years, the curriculum expert surprisingly realized, based on experience, that it took seven years for teams better than theirs to finish a similar project with a 40 percent chance of failure. Yet, despite such a dire warning and many unanticipated challenges, the team continued the work and eventually delivered the project eight years later, only to discover that the textbook would never be used (Kahneman, 2011).

Kahneman (2011, p. 247) took away two key lessons: (1) The Planning Fallacy occurs in projects with estimates unrealistically close to best-case scenarios; (2) two distinct approaches to forecasting exist: the "inside view," which focuses on the project at hand and contemplates intuitive guesses about its costs and benefits, and the "outside view," which statistically focuses on past similar projects that are part of a reference class to temper planners' rose-colored expectations (cf. Lovallo & Kahneman, 2003). As we learn from Kahneman's (2011) dual process analogy, while the inside view relies on System 1, the brain's intuitive mode of thinking, the outside view builds on System 2, the brain's deliberate mode of thinking.

Though anecdotal, Kahneman's single case reminds us of an all-too-common observation where we are confident that our assigned project will go as planned even though most projects from a relevant comparison set do not meet their planned targets (Buehler et al., 1994). Kahneman and Tversky (1982) defined the original Planning Fallacy as the tendency for individuals to underestimate the time it takes to complete a project, even when they have significant experience of past failures to live up to planned schedules.

Thus, the Planning Fallacy cannot be equated with general "optimism bias" (Buehler et al., 1994), the belief that people are less likely at risk than statistical reality warrants when experiencing a negative consequence (Kahneman, 2011; Sunstein, 2015). As Kahneman (2011) notes, the Planning Fallacy is a special case of a widespread optimism bias. The Planning Fallacy calls us to revisit George Bernard Shaw's view that "We learn from history that we learn nothing from history" (Shaw, 1903, p. 485). Optimism bias instead prompts us to dig into the deep psychology of Lionel Tiger's claim that "Thinking rosy futures is as biological as sexual fantasy" (Tiger, 1979, p. 35). Table 1.2 provides a lexicon of the fundamental concepts of the Planning Fallacy.

Bemoaning the overoptimistic forecasts of projects even in the face of a rather pessimistic history of similar projects, Lovallo and Kahneman (2003) expanded the scope of the Planning Fallacy to include costs and benefits. This all-encompassing Planning Fallacy transpires in much of the project management literature today (Flyvbjerg, 2021; Ika et al., 2022).

The Emergence of the Planning Fallacy in Project Management: Old Wine in New Bottles?

While Kahneman and Tversky (1977) specifically referred to "projects," not too many took note in project management. However, when they postulated the Planning Fallacy, much like time underestimation bias (e.g., Epton, 1972), cost

Table 1.2 The Planning Fallacy lexicon

Key Planning Fallacy Concepts	Definitions
The Planning Fallacy	The tendency for forecasts of project schedules, costs, benefits, and odds of success to be unrealistically close to best-case scenarios, *even if this contradicts past plans and performances* (Kahneman & Tversky, 1977; Lovallo & Kahneman, 2003).
Optimism bias	The belief that people are less likely at risk than statistical reality warrants when experiencing a negative consequence. This cognitive bias may lead to a naïve underestimation of costs and overestimation of benefits of projects (Kahneman, 2011; Sunstein, 2015). Hence, *delusion* or *the honest Planning Fallacy* (Flyvbjerg et al., 2009; Ika et al., 2022).
Strategic misrepresentation	The deliberate and systematic ploy to distort or misstate facts, that is, to make numbers lie and thus secure project approval and funding (Wachs, 1989; Jones & Euske, 1991). Hence, *deception* or *the intentional Planning Fallacy* (Flyvbjerg et al., 2009; Ika et al., 2022).
Inside view	An approach to forecasting, which looks forward, focuses on the project at hand and contemplates intuitive guesses about its costs and benefits. Thus, a focus on *System 1* (Lovallo & Kahneman, 2003; Kahneman, 2011).
Outside view	An approach to forecasting, which looks backward, statistically focuses on past similar projects that are part of a reference class. Thus, a focus on *System 2* (Lovallo & Kahneman, 2003; Kahneman, 2011).
System 1	The brain's faster, automatic, intuitive, and emotional mode of thinking (Kahneman, 2011).
System 2	The brain's slower, more effortful, and deliberate mode of thinking (Kahneman, 2011).
Reference Class Forecasting (RCF)	A debiasing technique that relies on the outside view to produce distributional data on past similar projects and thus correct the errors that creep into the intuitive guesses of the inside view (Lovallo & Kahneman, 2003; Flyvbjerg, 2006).
Optimism bias uplifts	Post hoc correction of estimated costs and benefits to account for potential bias (Flyvbjerg, 2006).

underestimation bias (e.g., Merrow et al., 1979) was not new. Meanwhile, for decades, cost overrun research has relied on single case studies if not anecdotal evidence (Love et al., 2022a).

Against this backdrop, Flyvbjerg et al.'s (2002) statistical analysis of a sample of 258 transportation infrastructure projects delivered worldwide was groundbreaking. They reveal nine out of ten projects experience cost overruns and suggest cost underestimation is systematic. They proffer that the best explanation is not "forecasting errors" but strategic misrepresentation, which is "the planned, systematic distortion, or misstatement of fact – lying – in response to incentives in the budget process" (Jones & Euske, 1991, p. 437) or, simply put, the deliberate deception of "making numbers lie" (Wachs, 1989).

Flyvbjerg et al. (2002) hence opt for economic explanations such as incentives to keep costs low in the interest of the public (e.g., Merewitz, 1973) and political explanations such as strategic misrepresentation (e.g., Wachs, 1989). They, however, discount technical explanations such as honest mistakes (e.g., Morris & Hough, 1987) and psychological explanations such as appraisal optimism on the part of planners (e.g., World Bank, 1992). Surprisingly, while Flyvbjerg et al. (2002) focus on cost underestimation bias, neither the terms "optimism bias" and "Planning Fallacy" nor the names Kahneman and Tversky appear in their work. As Flyvbjerg (2021, p. 532) recounts in a spirited debate spurred by the *Harvard Business Review* (*HBR*) editor who asked, "So which of the two theories is right?":

> As a psychologist, Kahneman explained outcomes in terms of cognitive bias, especially optimism bias and the planning fallacy. As an economic geographer, I explained the same phenomena in terms of political economic bias, specifically strategic misrepresentation.

This absence of optimism bias in Flyvbjerg's theorizing would soon change and the Planning Fallacy would rapidly rise to theoretical stardom.

The Planning Fallacy's Streams of Research: Optimism Bias and Strategic Misrepresentation

In project management, Flyvbjerg (2006) was the first to put the Planning Fallacy front and center in his writings. Learning from the *HBR* debate and connecting the dots between what he later calls "cognitive bias" and "political bias" (Flyvbjerg, 2021), Flyvbjerg (2006) bases his work on the behavioral insights of Kahneman and Tversky (1977) and Lovallo and Kahneman (2003). For example, arguing that the problem is bias and not inaccuracy, Flyvbjerg (2016, p. 7) describes the Planning Fallacy in these terms: "Thus, people will underestimate the costs, completion times, and risks of planned actions, whereas they will overestimate the benefits of the same actions."

Moreover, Flyvbjerg (2006), again, rules out technical explanations. However, in contrast to his ideas four years earlier (cf. Flyvbjerg et al., 2002), he retains both political and psychological explanations as the most significant causes of the Planning Fallacy. Further, except for a cursory mention of so-called political-economic explanations, the economic explanations critical in Flyvbjerg et al.'s (2002) conclusions are conspicuously discarded from the Planning Fallacy argument. Flyvbjerg's (2006, p. 6) remarks are clear-cut:

> Psychological explanations account for inaccuracy in terms of optimism bias; that is, a cognitive predisposition found with most people to judge future events in a more positive light than is warranted by actual experience. Political explanations, on the other hand, explain inaccuracy in terms of strategic misrepresentation. Note that while optimism bias is unintentional (that is, deception of self), strategic misrepresentation is intentional (deception of others).

While optimism bias and strategic misrepresentation constitute two streams of the Planning Fallacy research, much of the research focuses on the former (Ika & Feeny, 2022; Chen et al., 2023), as evidence on the latter is hard to come by since those who game the system or manipulate project estimates need to admit to their intentional deception (Flyvbjerg et al., 2002). The High Speed 2 railway project in the UK provides a fitting example, as an inquiry found that HS2 Ltd. and the Department for Transport deliberately lied and withheld information about the project and its underperformance (Love et al., 2022a).

Reference Class Forecasting: The Putative Cure of the Planning Fallacy

Flyvbjerg (2006) also builds on Kahneman and Tversky's (1977, pp. 2–3) suggestion that the forecaster should move from the biased inside view to the unbiased outside view where they ask how long (much) such projects usually last (cost). Applying the outside view, Flyvbjerg (2006) simplifies the five-step approach developed by Lovallo and Kahneman (2003, p. 62) to build a reference class for a project under consideration using historical evidence from past similar projects. Flyvbjerg (2006) thus devises a three-step approach, a tool that he coins reference class forecasting (RCF) and presents as the cure for optimism bias. Hence, a subset of the optimism bias stream of the Planning Fallacy research now focuses on RCF (Baerenbold, 2023).

RCF consists of a procedure for debiasing confidence intervals and correcting non-regressive project forecasts (Kahneman & Tversky, 1977; Lovallo & Kahneman, 2003). Put differently, RCF regresses the intuitive guess toward the most likely case of the reference class. That is, if planners want a X percent likelihood of hitting their cost forecast, they should inflate their intuitive guess by some corresponding Y percent based on the established probability distribution of the reference class. Thus, RCF, a debiasing "technique that attempts to retain what is most valid in the intuitive process while correcting errors" (Lovallo et al., 2023, p. 141), provides "bias uplifts," which are adjustments to overly optimistic project forecasts (Flyvbjerg, 2006).

The first instance of RCF application was when the UK Department of Transport, appointed Flyvbjerg and COWI in 2004 to develop a procedure for dealing with optimism bias and that, the same year, an outside view was taken to debias the Edinburgh Tram Line 2 cost forecast with the just established bias uplifts, based on the entire business case of capital projects at the time of the decision to build (Flyvbjerg, 2006). Hence, the arrival of the Planning Fallacy on the scene of project management practice in 2004 and project management theory in 2006!

The Impulsion to Theorize

Human beings have a natural tendency to seek understanding for their lives or the world to the point that the sociologist Jack Douglas suggests that each of them is their "own sociologist" (Douglas, 1970, p. vii). Since Aristotle, it has become clear they may contemplatively engage in theorizing, that is, turning one's mind in "a certain direction" or, observing the world, driven by "a certain interest," for example, to go forward in life (Blum, 1970, p. 303). This urge, which I call impulsion to theorize in this chapter (see Table 1.1), is even more salient in scholarship (e.g., Blum [1970] speaks of "the impulse to theorize," p. 309 and the "possibility-for-seeing," p. 314 that it allows researchers to gain), not just in social sciences (Swedberg, 2016) but also in management, where theory "forms the 'currency' in which we trade insights with one another and through which we claim to have developed a sufficiently novel and distinct contribution" (Cornelissen et al., 2021, p. 2). In project management, while theorizing may not be the be-all and end-all of scholarship, it is becoming more and more important (Svejvig, 2021).

In particular, the coming of age of the Planning Fallacy seemingly responded to the emerging impulsion to theorize in project management research, where the top two specialist journals – *International Journal of Project Management* and *Project Management Journal* – now stress theoretical contribution as a linchpin of publication in their pages. Notably, the Planning Fallacy's double hypothesis of overoptimism (delusion) and strategic misrepresentation (deception) had reached an inflection point when Flyvbjerg (2014) suggested the Hiding Hand is not valid and, therefore, implied that, in practice, project forecasts based on the underlying behaviors of the Planning Fallacy lead to the overarching rule of project selection being often survival of the unfittest. This phenomenon would be best explained by the Planning Fallacy, which Flyvbjerg et al. (2018) herald as the "best" underlying theory to explain project drift and which even critics admit is a "paradigm-breaker" in cost overrun research (Love et al., 2022b).

According to Pinto (2023, p. 1), the timing of the Planning Fallacy argument "was superb." Notably, apart from the longtime unrecognized Hiding Hand principle, "there was an absence of a theory to guide and give meaning to the cost overrun problem" (Love et al., 2022b, p. 57).

The Planning Fallacy thus fits with the drive to explain cost overruns and benefit shortfalls through "a conceptual leap" from the topic to the resource of behavioral science. It thus provides "a preliminary step" to formulate propositions, thereby offering a form of theorizing that Cornelissen et al. (2021) term "propositional." As Flyvbjerg (2016) writes, his focus appears to be "on theory as explanation" (p. 179), which he construes as "an idea, or a system of ideas, used to account for or explain a situation" (p. 186). Consequently, at a time when some lament the rigor-relevance gap in project management research (Meredith, 2022), the Planning Fallacy principle is an outstanding contribution to the project management field as it considers theory as conceptualization and provides key concepts that both scholars and practitioners can use (cf. Table 1.2).

The Looming Fall of the Planning Fallacy? The Compulsion to Theorize

In this section, I first take stock of empirical evidence, present the clash between the Planning Fallacy and competing principles of project behavior, and explore its theoretical and methodological pitfalls as well as practical relevance. Next, I shed light on the compulsion to theorize that the Planning Fallacy succumbs to and explore three outstanding issues in the realms of the philosophy and sociology of science that may lead to its decline as the overarching principle of project behavior. These issues are articulated around the incompleteness of the Planning Fallacy as a theory, the narrowness of its theoretical scope under complexity and uncertainty, and the chances that the support it garners from the scientific community will wane over time.

Where Is the Empirical Evidence on the Planning Fallacy?

To bolster his case for the Planning Fallacy principle, which so far rests on anecdotes or case studies (Flyvbjerg et al., 2009), Flyvbjerg (2016) undertakes a statistical test of the Hiding Hand with a large dataset of 2,062 projects of different types, of which 327 have data for both cost and benefit performance. In true propositional theorizing tradition (Cornelissen et al., 2021), he adopts an economic cost-benefit lens and conjectures that, if the Hiding Hand were at work, then, on average, benefit shortfalls would exceed cost overruns. Such a test of the Planning Fallacy with a focus on the more general optimism bias lacks data on comparable projects at the time of their initiation. Notwithstanding, Flyvbjerg (2016) reveals the Planning Fallacy outweighs the Hiding Hand and accounts for 80 percent of the projects. Accordingly, the average project experiences a "double whammy" of significant cost overruns and benefit shortfalls. Flyvbjerg (2016, p. 186) therefore describes the Hiding Hand as a "fallacy of beneficial ignorance" and considers Hirschman "a victim, not a student, of bias" and "a case of how damaging optimism can be."

To further advance the case for the Planning Fallacy, now with the public at large, Bent Flyvbjerg and the Canadian journalist Dan Gardner recently authored a bestseller titled *How Big Things Get Done*. Flyvbjerg and Gardner (2023) reveal that 99.5 percent of projects in their sample of 16,000 projects do not come in either on time or within budget or deliver benefits as planned and that the Planning Fallacy explains their underperformance. And if you ask: "So what are the universal drivers that make the difference between success and failure?," Flyvbjerg's response is straightforward: psychology and power (Flyvbjerg & Gardner, 2023, p. 6) in that people and organizations are tricked into misjudgements and inappropriate decision-making by optimism bias while they compete for resources and jockey for position (Pinto, 2023). And, if you add: How does Hirschman's Hiding Hand fare against the Planning Fallacy, he writes: "If he's right, I'm wrong and vice versa" (Flyvbjerg & Gardner, 2023, p. 6).

Flyvbjerg and associates' work has provoked a twofold debate where (1) Daniel Kahneman's Planning Fallacy is pitted against Albert Hirschman's Hiding Hand as the best theoretical explanation for project underperformance and (2) Bias competes with error as the root cause of cost overruns and benefit shortfalls. Hence the birth of what I (with coauthors) call the "Planning Fallacy debate" (Love et al., 2019a). I hasten to note that, in the context of the Planning Fallacy debate, bias means "a systematic deviation between the (average) judgment of a person or a group and a true value or norm, or in most cases in the Planning Fallacy debate, a deviation from a statistical principle" whereas error consists in "the use of imperfect techniques, making honest forecasting and execution mistakes, lacking experience, and having inadequate data" (Ika et al., 2022, p. 3311).

The bias *versus* error debate, which connects to the Planning fallacy *versus* Hiding Hand debate as I demonstrate next, notably confronts two schools of thought on cost-and-benefit performance research with eponymous names (Ika et al., 2023). The bias school seeks to tackle psychological and political pitfalls and ensure decision-makers are accountable. In short, it proffers that cost overruns and benefit shortfalls are caused by the Planning Fallacy (Flyvbjerg, 2016). Instead, the error school aims to counteract economic and technical pitfalls by applying project management best practices. It attributes project underperformance to scope changes during the project lifecycle and happenstances associated with complexity and uncertainty. In short, this argument suggests that projects fall short because we continue to make mistakes (Love et al., 2022b).

While the bias school relies on Kahneman's (2011) Planning Fallacy principle, the error school may draw on Hirschman's (1967) Hiding Hand Principle as exemplar theory (Ika et al., 2023). Notably, the Hiding Hand celebrates the crucial role of error as leaders may underestimate project costs and their resourcefulness in the face of unexpected challenges through what Hirschman (1967,

p. 35) terms "creative error" and "beneficial ignorance." After all, if the Planning Fallacy trumps the Hiding Hand, bias trumps error and thus scholars cannot afford to ignore these a priori convictions. Table 1.3 summarizes empirical insights from the Planning Fallacy debate.

Does Bias Outweigh Error?

In contrast to the bias school thesis, there is little empirical evidence to support the presence of causal influences that result in project underperformance (Love & Ahiaga-Dagbui, 2018). Adding to the paucity of empirical evidence, the

Table 1.3 Empirical evidence on the prevalence of the Planning Fallacy

Planning Fallacy concepts	Evidence	Key authors
Original Planning Fallacy (completion time)	Anecdotal	Kahneman and Tversky (1977)
Planning Fallacy (completion time) *Three hypotheses*: (1) People underestimate their own but not others' completion times; (2) when making their predictions, people focus on plan-based scenarios rather than on pertinent past experiences; (3) people's attributions diminish the relevance of past experiences	Empirical evidence from five experiments with 684 students corroborates all three hypotheses	Buehler et al. (1994)
All-encompassing Planning Fallacy (schedules, costs, benefits)	Anecdotal	Lovallo and Kahneman (2003)
Strategic misrepresentation	A sample of 258 projects, 86 percent of which experience cost overruns	Flyvbjerg et al. (2002)
Optimism bias	Anecdotal	Flyvbjerg (2006)
Optimism bias and strategic misrepresentation	Anecdotal	Flyvbjerg et al. (2009)
Optimism bias and strategic misrepresentation: The Planning Fallacy occurs when the average benefit overrun is less than the average cost overrun	A sample of 327 projects, 80 percent of which are prone to the Planning Fallacy; the Planning Fallacy trumps the Hiding Hand	Flyvbjerg (2016)
Planning Fallacy: The Planning Fallacy occurs within the category of project management and project failures	A sample of 161 projects, 3 percent of which are prone to the Planning Fallacy vs 13 percent for the Hiding Hand; Hiding Hand trumps Planning Fallacy	Ika (2018)
Optimism bias: The Planning Fallacy occurs when cost estimates are higher than actuals	A sample of 85 projects, 53 percent of which are prone to the Planning Fallacy	Love et al. (2019b)
Optimism bias: The Planning Fallacy occurs when cost estimates are more optimistic than actuals	A sample of 47 projects, 57 percent of which are prone to the Planning Fallacy	Love et al. (2022b)
Optimism bias: If project economic rates of return (ERRs) are econometrically lower at closure than approval, then the Planning Fallacy occurs	A sample of 2,800 projects, 60 percent of which are prone to optimism bias; Optimism bias reduces odds of project performance up to 20 percent	Ika and Feeny (2022)
Planning Fallacy: The Planning Fallacy occurs within the category of project management and project failures or when average benefit overrun is less than average cost overrun	A sample of 43 projects, 75% of which more successful than planned vs. 25% of failures; Hiding Hand trumps Planning Fallacy (33 percent v. 21 percent)	Olasehinde-Williams and Jenkins (2023)

datasets used by Flyvbjerg et al. (2002) and Flyvbjerg (2016) are heterogeneous and prone to selection bias. Therefore, I and my coauthors consider that the presence of the Planning Fallacy, and thus the role of bias, may have been misconstrued (Love et al., 2019a). For example, it is not clear whether the Planning Fallacy is due to optimism bias or a "rational" response of planners to prevailing organizational incentives (Ika & Feeny, 2022).

A few studies provide some further empirical insights. Love et al. (2019b) and Love et al. (2022b) in their study of infrastructure transport projects delivered in Hong Kong, both economic (N = 85) and social (N = 47), respectively find that 47 percent and 43 percent of them incurred a cost underrun. They suggest that the Planning Fallacy may explain 53 percent to 57 percent of projects. Therefore, the Planning Fallacy *and* competing explanations prevail in infrastructure projects.

If we compare apples with apples, this rate is estimated at 51.5 percent in the study of Flyvbjerg and Gardner (2023). In a research that examines 228 road projects and 96 rail projects in Sweden, Chapman (2024) demonstrates that, respectively, 58 percent and 46 percent of them were delivered over budget and that 7 percent and 30 percent of them did not achieve their intended benefits. In their study of 2,800 World Bank–funded projects, Ika and Feeny (2022) show optimism bias affects 60 percent of projects and reduces the odds of overall project performance up to 20 percent.

An offshoot of the bias *versus* error debate is whether RCF works. While the idea of debiasing project forecasts goes at least back to Kahneman and Tversky (1977), rarely has it been applied in practice. However, soon after its introduction in the UK in 2004, RCF prescriptions were officially endorsed by the American Planning Association (APA), which recommended that planners use it complementary to traditional forecasting techniques (Flyvbjerg, 2006). "Despite little research into the method and its applicability" (Baerenbold, 2023, p. 2), over the last 20 years, RCF has become a requirement for large-scale transportation and construction projects in the UK, Denmark, Germany, Norway, Sweden, Switzerland, the Netherlands, and the EU (Park, 2021).

However, the empirical evidence on RCF has been mixed at best. While some suggest RCF performs better than comparable approaches (Park, 2021), others maintain it does not provide more accuracy and that the construction of the reference class remains problematic (Themsen, 2019). Hence, the use of Similarity-Based Forecasting (SBF), an application of RCF but with a reference class where cases are not weighted equally but by similarity (Lovallo et al., 2023). Further, as RCF falls short of the requisite complexity that large-scale project delivery requires, the idea of developing "RCF 2.0" has emerged (Chen et al., 2023). Still others remain severely critical of RCF. Love et al. (2024, p. 1942), for example, are adamant that:

> In short, RCF fails to address the causes of such cost overruns and attempts to "smooth" estimates after their development: the equivalent, perhaps, to fixing the problem of a teenager's late arrivals at home by adjusting their watch an hour ahead each evening as they leave the house.

Put differently, while RCF purports to counter bias, it is itself prone to bias. With bias uplifts, things may become worse when knowing a piggy bank exists, many powerful stakeholders make requests asking the project to do more in terms of value distribution but hold no accountability for their claims (Gil & Fu, 2022). RCF remains fraught with unintended consequences from professional mediocrity to massaging cost-and-benefit numbers to deficiency in accountability. "Thus, RCF remains a Band-Aid over a recurring, self-inflicted wound" (Pinto, 2023, p. 6). As Baerenbold's (2023, p. 4) literature review of 41 papers on RCF concludes, "there is not enough evidence to conclude whether RCF is more useful or better than other cost estimation approaches."

In sum, I suggest that, notwithstanding Flyvbjerg et al.'s (2018) claim, the bias *versus* error debate is far from being over. Indeed, leaders may spend a lot of time and resources on removing assumed optimism bias in cost estimates at the expense of optimizing best practices, not to mention the critical but little studied role of other cognitive biases such as confirmation bias and group compliance (Flyvbjerg, 2021; Ika & Saint-Macary, 2023).

Does the Planning Fallacy Outweigh the Hiding Hand?

Flyvbjerg's (2016) so-called refutation of Hirschman's (1967) Hiding Hand did not go unnoticed. As Hirschman's intellectual biographer Michele Alacevich from the University of Bologna in Italy writes: "Flyvbjerg's attack caused a little brouhaha, with replies from other scholars counter-criticizing Flyvbjerg's premises and conclusions" (Alacevich, 2022, p. 132). For example, Room (2018) advances that the statistical analysis fails to consider the interconnections between and within projects and their wider social, economic, and political impacts. However, only my rejoinder (Ika, 2018) and Olasehinde-Williams and Jenkins (2023)'s work sought to replicate Flyvbjerg's (2016) findings and understand whether the Hiding Hand is more malevolent than benevolent (Sunstein, 2015), that is, the Planning Fallacy is more common than the Hiding Hand (Flyvbjerg, 2016).

I detect three main flaws in Flyvbjerg's (2016) work:

- (1) a strawman – a common argumentation fallacy – in that a weaker version of the Hiding Hand argument devoid of key concepts such as "creativity" and "difficulties" was knocked down: higher-than-estimated project costs (cost overrun) are typically outweighed by even higher-than-estimated project benefits (benefit overrun);
- (2) an empirical deficiency in that the statistical demonstration focuses on the type of project – infrastructure – where the Hiding Hand is least likely to emerge because of the prevailing "plan-your-work-and-work-your-plan" philosophy, which promotes the idea that everything can be planned in advance, an idea that clashes with the Hiding Hand;
- and (3) a methodological shortcoming of considering only actual construction costs and first-year benefits or the failure to account for the full life cycle costs and benefits and unintended project effects so critical for a valid test of the Hiding Hand.

I postulate that the Hiding Hand explanation makes sense for projects that, although *successful* in terms of benefit delivery in the long run, would be considered project *management* failures by standard metrics of time and/or budget adherence in the short run (de Wit, 1988; Ika & Pinto, 2022). On the contrary, the Planning Fallacy explanation concerns the category of projects that experience not only time and/or cost overruns but also fail to deliver expected benefits. I then draw on a sample of 161 World Bank projects of different types and apply this hypothesis: "If Flyvbjerg is correct, then the Hiding Hand would typically be less empirically common than the Planning Fallacy" (p. 378). My findings are instructive: the Hiding Hand outweighs the Planning Fallacy in terms of frequency of occurrence (13 percent v. 3 percent). I conclude that Flyvbjerg's statistical analysis treats the project management function as a "black box" and hence fails to capture the messy and complex processes that surround project execution and characterize the Hiding Hand (Ika, 2018).

Building on the above two pioneering statistical tests of the Hiding Hand (Flyvbjerg, 2016; Ika, 2018) and drawing on a sample of 43 World Bank–funded hydro dam projects for which both ex-ante and ex-post evaluation data is available, Olasehinde-Williams and Jenkins (2023) demonstrate that the Hiding Hand outweighs the Planning Fallacy in terms of frequency of occurrence (33 percent v. 21 percent), and that, in the end, 75 percent of the projects were even more successful than planned – while 25 percent of the projects ended up failing, thereby supporting my claims.

The Fifth Hand Principle: The False Choice of Error or Bias and the Power of Error and Bias

Neither the Planning Fallacy nor the Hiding Hand account for the shades of gray between success and failure or even the differing expectations of stakeholders. Notably, the gloomy view that the Planning Fallacy bears (Ika et al., 2022) rests on a negative view of the human mind where people are deemed bad at decision-making (Gigerenzer, 2014). In contrast, the serendipitous view that the Hiding Hand proffers rests on a "bias for hope" (Adelman, 2013) and a disdain for "the propensity to see gloom and failure everywhere" (Hirschman, 1970, p. 337).

The Hiding Hand, where naïve overoptimism prevails and yet projects stumble into success, is at work in organizational contexts where risk-taking and problem-solving behavior prevail. Conversely, the Planning Fallacy, where strategic overoptimism reigns and projects underperform, is at play when promoters practice profiteering and corruption as they seek to profit from information asymmetries and other market and governance failures (Anheier, 2017). Further, the Planning Fallacy and the Hiding Hand rely on two conflicting notions of projects (Kreiner, 2020). The Planning Fallacy proffers that projects are "deliberate leaps into a planned future" and that managers already know what success is and how to measure it. In contrast, the Hiding Hand foregrounds a broader notion of projects as "processes of pursuit, experimentation, and discovery" where, under uncertainty, agency plays a key role in "successfulness" and managers cannot presume what success is going to be and how to measure it.

Because neither principle sufficiently captures the current state of project underperformance, I (with coauthors) propose the principle of the "Fifth Hand," a pluralistic theorizing where elements and assumptions embedded in both the Planning Fallacy and the Hiding Hand are combined and both bias and error are recognized as overarching causes of project underperformance (Ika et al., 2022). A good example of the Fifth Hand is the Philharmonic Hall of Paris where the project costs ballooned from 173 million euros at the time of the launch in 2006 to 386 million at its inauguration in 2015 due to not only scope changes and excessive ambition on the part of promoters (that is, error) but also a systematic underestimation of the budget (that is, bias) (Ika et al., 2023).

The Fifth Hand is based on the pioneering work of the German psychologist Gerd Gigerenzer, longtime director at the Max Planck Institute for Human Development and Daniel Kahneman's strongest critic over the years, and their debate over whether human decision-making is error-prone or success-prone. The Fifth Hand is powered by ecological rationality (Gigerenzer, 2014), as it seeks to provide an understanding of the circumstances in which heuristics and even projects work or not (Ika et al., 2022; Love et al., 2024). The Fifth Hand thus offers a pragmatist synthesis, which helps to move past *dualisms* like Planning Fallacy *versus* Hiding Hand (Flyvbjerg, 2016; Ika, 2018) or bias *versus* error (Flyvbjerg et al., 2018; Love & Ahiaga-Dagbui, 2018) to *dualities* of Planning Fallacy *and* Hiding Hand or bias *and* error, which altogether better reflect the lived experience of project delivery (Ika et al., 2022). While the Fifth Hand may help understand project performance in hindsight as it allows for complexity and uncertainty to take hold, it also distinguishes uncertainty from risk where all the relevant alternatives, consequences, and probabilities can be known. The Fifth Hand can empower project leaders to understand when to use statistical analysis – which works under risk – or heuristics – which work under uncertainty – (Ika et al., 2022). In this sense, the Fifth Hand may well be called the "Savvy Hand," as it summons project leaders to be project context "savvy" (see Gigerenzer's 2014 book *Risk Savvy*).

In sum, the Planning Fallacy debate has yet to provide a conclusive outlook. The empirical evidence for the Planning Fallacy for completion time (Kahneman & Tversky, 1977) is compelling, especially at the individual decision-maker level (Buehler et al., 1994). Regrettably, the empirical evidence of the all-encompassing Planning Fallacy remains anecdotal for strategic misrepresentation and, at best, mixed for optimism bias. Further, methodological shortcomings including the cherry-picking of the data weaken such empirical evidence, if any (Love et al., 2019a; Pinto, 2023). Measuring accurately the Planning Fallacy (Love et al., 2022b), finding similar past projects (Lovallo et al., 2023), and rigorously applying RCF (Baerenfold, 2023) remain challenging.

The Compulsion to Theorize

Theorizing, pushed to the extreme, may become a hindrance to understanding. This excess deserves a name and an elaboration. Hirschman (1970, p. 329) suggests the term "compulsion to theorize" (cf. Table 1.1), that is, "the tendency toward compulsive and mindless theorizing," and laments how scholars may succumb to this "prevalent and debilitating disease" in social sciences where "the prestige of the theorist is towering." Such compulsion to theorize extends to the management field where there prevails what Hambrick (2007, p. 1346) calls a "theory fetish," that is, "an articulation of theory in everything we write," which may in fact retard our ability to comprehend a phenomenon under study, especially when no theory is available and, paradoxically, revealing facts are "banned" from reporting. While not everybody is so far busy theorizing, the field of project management is not shielded from theorizing disease (Meredith, 2022) or what Hirschman (1970), borrowing from the French writer, Gustave Flaubert, coins "la rage de vouloir conclure," the academic temptation to try to bring everything to conclusion (Adelman, 2013, p. 355).

As a case in point, the *impulsion* to theorize that propels the Planning Fallacy to glory has come over the years with an evil twin, the *compulsion* to theorize (Love et al., 2019a). I (with coauthors) speculate that confirmation bias is at work in the compulsion to theorize the Planning Fallacy, because of Flyvbjerg's (2017) Iron Law and the search for explanations that aim to support his Planning Fallacy "theory," rather than an open-minded quest to understand why projects underperform (Love et al., 2019a). As my coauthors and I suggest, the compulsion to theorize of the bias school is unfortunately akin to what Hirschman (1970) terms "cognitive style," that is, "the kind of paradigms we search out, the way we put them together, and the ambitions we nurture for their powers" (p. 338). However, these insights fail to demonstrate the conjecture of a compulsion to theorize.

As I show below, much like Kahneman's (2011) System 1 *versus* System 2 (Fox, 2014; see also Table 1.2), the Planning Fallacy principle does not predict anything. Still, it explains almost everything after the fact (Ika et al., 2022). This is cause for concern and will precipitate its fall. While empirical refutation may be hard to achieve, the Planning Fallacy is in danger of losing ground as the premier theoretical principle of project behavior. I turn to that demonstration in what follows and suggest that the reasons for the fall of the Planning Fallacy may lie much in the realm of the philosophy of science – the internal logic and validity of the principle including theoretical and methodological deficiencies as well as practical relevance challenges (Malisoff, 1934) – and little in the realm of the sociology of science – the surrounding scholarly environment of the principle including the role of the scientific community and the competition between schools of thought (Ben David & Sullivan, 1975).

Three Issues That Will Cause the Fall of the Planning Fallacy

The well-documented methodological deficiencies of the Planning Fallacy did not seem to have threatened its theoretical appeal (Love et al., 2019a) or its practical relevance (Lovallo et al., 2023). I argue that they might not be a significant cause of its decline. For example, prospect theory, which underlies the Planning Fallacy, remains popular despite methodological concerns over "whether the hypotheses scholars have attributed to prospect theory really fit the theory and context" (Bromiley & Rau, 2022, p. 137).

For lack of space, I will not belabor these validity issues (Malisoff, 1934). Instead, following the approach of Shenkar and Ellis (2022), I focus on these remaining questions, which I justify below: Is the Planning Fallacy principle a theory anyway and, if yes, is the theory complete? Is the theory too narrow in scope or does it cater to complexity and uncertainty? Will it lose support from the scientific community?

- Is the Planning Fallacy a theory and, if yes, is it a complete theory?

As noted earlier, Flyvbjerg suggests the Planning Fallacy is a theory (Flyvbjerg, 2016) and I consider its theorizing to be propositional (Cornelissen et al., 2021). But is it a theory anyway? As readers are aware, a theory is not just a collection of ideas, but, among other things, it may be considered in the hypothetico-deductive tradition of theorizing (Blum, 1970) as a carefully crafted depiction of a phenomenon under study, including its underlying variables and concepts (the what), the relationships between variables (the how), and the explanations for these relationships (the why)

(Whetten, 1989). The Planning Fallacy appears to meet these criteria (cf. the double hypothesis of optimism bias and strategic misrepresentation to explain project underperformance).

The theory also appears, at first, to meet Bacharach's (1989) Popperian criterion of being falsifiable (refutable) and useful (able to explain and predict). To reiterate, a closer look, however, suggests such empirical validation is lacking. To make things worse, the theory may explain any project underperformance from time overruns to cost overruns to benefit shortfalls by underestimation or overestimation bias on the part of leaders, even when we have no idea of past similar projects and their performance! Moreover, its practical fix, the post-hoc correcting RCF, does not go to the source of the project underperformance problem (Pinto, 2023; Love et al., 2024). More importantly and at best, the Planning Fallacy appears to be an "incomplete" theory in that it does not provide the ability to explain the underlying prediction that necessarily comes with the predictive power of a theory (Bacharach, 1989). The Planning Fallacy does not yet offer a cogent formulation of what Whetten (1989) calls the "why" of a theory. Perhaps, the theory has sacrificed explanation at the altar of parsimony, two key features of a typical theory (Bacharach, 1989).

Notably, as the "goal post" of project success (the dependent variable) has been moving over the years to include benefits, both expected and unexpected (Ika & Pinto, 2022), the Planning Fallacy (the independent variable) remains fixated on a narrow cost-benefit lens where it does not consider the full lifecycle costs and benefits (Ika, 2018) or stakeholder expectations if not value distribution (Gil & Fu, 2022). The all-too-simple conceptualization and operationalization of project performance that underlies the Planning Fallacy argument has not caught up with the reimaginings of project success that have occurred over the last twenty years, especially regarding critical considerations such as stakeholder satisfaction, benefits realization, sustainability, and green success (Ika & Pinto, 2022).

Relatedly, while the Planning Fallacy offers some degree of face validity when it comes to effects (that is, project underperformance), its causal links (that is, the variables that cause this project underperformance) are yet to be empirically and longitudinally demonstrated, making these effects "statistically unmoored" causes (Pinto, 2023, p. 4). Strictly speaking, however, purists may consider the Planning Fallacy as a theoretical principle, not a theory, since its underlying theory is prospect theory, as noted earlier (Kahneman & Tversky, 1979; Bromiley & Rau, 2022).

- Is the theory too narrow in scope or does it cater to complexity and uncertainty?

As the philosophy of science suggests, a narrow or misplaced scope may doom a theory to failure "that is, the range of the phenomena it covers is too limited to sustain interest to scholars, and relevance to practitioners" (Shenkar & Ellis, 2022, p. 791). The cost is that a theory becomes unappealing and fails to connect with other theories or practices. As noted earlier, the Planning Fallacy argument does not consider what goes on between the upstream and downstream phases of projects, thereby downplaying the complexity and uncertainty surrounding their delivery (Ika, 2018). For example, Anheier (2017) observes that by emphasizing the Planning Fallacy at the expense of the Hiding Hand, Flyvbjerg's (2016) view is too *narrow* and unable to see the broader problem of incomplete information and uncertainty that resides in planning processes.

Therefore, the Planning Fallacy is a reductionist principle that fails to connect to critical theories in project delivery such as contingency, complexity, stakeholder, and time theories, not to mention best practices (Ika et al., 2022). As Bromiley and Rau (2022, p. 137) observe about its underlying theory: "Prospect theory does not apply to situations of uncertainty. It is a theory of decisions under risk" (Bromiley & Rau, 2022, p. 137). Thus, the Planning Fallacy may work under risk, not under uncertainty (Ika et al., 2022). Further, the underlying probability logic of the Planning Fallacy is akin to an "'illusion of certainty" (Gigerenzer, 2014; Love et al., 2024) and RCF as a solution to the complex problem of cost overruns remains an oversimplification (Ika et al., 2022). Therefore, the Planning Fallacy principle may not fit projects that are "processes of pursuit, experimentation, and discovery" due to their relatively high complexity and uncertainty (Kreiner, 2020).

- Will the Planning Fallacy lose support from the scientific community?

Theories do not exist in a vacuum, as science is a social activity (Ben David & Sullivan, 1975; Shenkar & Ellis, 2022). The Planning Fallacy is no exception. Arguably, the Planning Fallacy is the most impactful contribution to project management theory and practice over the last twenty years. For example, Flyvbjerg, a formidable proponent of the Planning Fallacy, has had much research productivity and career success. Fifty years ago, Merton (1973) theorized that such academic productivity and career success may be measured against universalistic norms of science, where it is all about the merits of the work, not who produces it, and particularistic norms of science, where the personal characteristics and the social networks of the scholar matter.

Accordingly, I consider first the merits of Flyvbjerg and colleagues' work. According to Google Scholar, Flyvbjerg is arguably the most cited author in the project management field, and he has shaped not only megaproject scholarship but public policy (Pinto, 2023). For example, Flyvbjerg et al.'s (2002) paper, which has garnered some 2,500 citations in the last 22 years, that is, on average more than 100 citations a year, is a landmark contribution to project management theory even according to the Planning Fallacy critics (Love et al., 2022b). His message that it is not error but lie that explains cost overruns did not leave any practitioner indifferent. As Lovallo et al. (2023, p. 142) observe, "RCF represents one of the few cases wherein an academic proposition has relatively quickly become a widely applied public governance technique."

Further, Flyvbjerg's message strongly resonates outside academia, as attests his bestseller *How Big Things Get Done*. I have always admired the clarity in which he communicates his theories. As Pinto (2023, p. 2) opines in his review of the book:

> One thing I have personally appreciated about Flyvbjerg's output is the fluency with which he presents his ideas. He has always communicated in a lucid, easy to grasp manner – whether in academic publications, conference speeches, and now this book.

At the time of the 2002 paper, Flyvbjerg, as a planning scholar with a PhD in economic geography from the University of Aarhus (Denmark) and a post-doc from UCLA (US), was already enjoying considerable renown in social sciences. Flyvbjerg's (2006) paper was astutely titled "From Nobel Prize Winner to Project Management." It certainly helps when your arguments are based on a Nobel Prize–winning theory. Notably, Flyvbjerg does not often miss an occasion to point out his connections to Kahneman. As he notes:

> Others have commented on Kahneman's generosity in academic interactions. He invited me to visit him at home, first in Paris and later in New York, to develop the thinking on political and cognitive bias and how they may be interrelated. (Flyvbjerg, 2021, p. 533)

This rhetorical appeal to authority, as the French philosopher and anthropologist Bruno Latour would call it, is not futile. As Shenkar and Ellis (2022, p. 798) write:

> Scholars must determine who are the leaders and who are the supporters of the various competing theories, or which of the leading schools are associated with these theories and scholars, and from whom they can get financial and academic support.

It certainly does not hurt when scholars are in a prestigious institution such as Oxford, which Flyvbjerg joined in 2009. They can, for example, enlist coauthors worldwide. For example, Flyvbjerg was not alone for his rejoinder in *Transportation Research Part A* to Love and Ahiaga-Dagbui's (2018) critique of his work. No fewer than fourteen coauthors accompanied him including Lovallo, a coauthor of Kahneman. These coauthors were from three countries where he held a professorship (the UK, Denmark, and the Netherlands) and Australia, as well as from business schools, technology schools, and mathematical schools. While this may not be problematic behavior, research suggests such coauthoring and research field heterogeneity contribute to a researcher's productivity and career success (Seibert et al., 2017). They may in some cases help "strengthen a research school and enhance community cohesion and resilience and ultimately the ability of the school to face external threats from rival schools or theories" (Shenkar & Ellis, 2022, p. 800), Cass Sunstein is, perhaps, a vivid example, as he was able to praise the Hiding Hand in the preface of Hirschman's book in 2015 but reject it squarely in an empirical paper coauthored with Flyvbjerg, an extraordinary feat, which Alavevich (2020, p. 132) calls a "virtuoso effect."

All in all, it is fair to conclude that considering the outstanding support the theory has garnered in the scientific community over the last 20 years, the fall of the Planning Fallacy would not be spurred by issues belonging to the sociology of science (Ben David & Sullivan, 1975).

Conclusion

The Planning Fallacy principle has had an immense influence on project management scholarship, stemming from an apparent belief that bias outweighs error. Hence, it has led to a lively debate. I show that while the rise of the Planning Fallacy can be attributed to an impulsion to theorize, its fall may be due to a companion compulsion to theorize. As the practical relevance and the methodological pitfalls of the Planning Fallacy principle are well-established in the literature, in true tradition of the philosophy and sociology of science, I focus my argument on three outstanding questions: Is the Planning Fallacy principle a theory anyway and, if yes, is the theory complete? Is the theory too narrow in scope or does it cater to complexity and uncertainty? Will it lose support from the scientific community?

I contend that the looming fall of the Planning Fallacy may be due to the incomplete nature of the "theory" (that is, its failure to establish clear-cut links between causes and effects) and its limited scope (that is, its inability to capture the complexity and uncertainty that surround project delivery), which together form its "Achille heel." Hence, the popular appeal of the Planning Fallacy principle has vastly overstepped its ultimate viability. The Planning Fallacy presents the field of project management with a paradox where, since the 1970s, at least, we have known that bias and error are fundamental planning setbacks, yet they keep creeping again and again into project plans and deliveries, only to cause cost overruns and benefit shortfalls (Epton, 1972; Love et al., 2022a). The Planning Fallacy principle is thus a Planning Fallacy from a theoretical point of view, as it falls foul to overestimating its own theoretical power. Prospect theory is among the "hand-me-down" theories that project management scholars borrow from other fields without sufficient evaluation (see Bromiley & Rau, 2022 for management research as a whole). As Ika et al. (2022, p. 3310) warn:

> Indeed, the shoehorning of these imported theories to project settings may create a false currency or prompt a debate based on misguided or misinterpreted assumptions. The upshot in this instance can be confusion, which can adversely impact decision-making and jeopardize the performance and practice of projects.

We are now left with two choices to deal with the theoretical conundrum of the Planning Fallacy principle: either we desperately try to refute it despite its popularity and the herculean task of measuring its variables or we move on and let other theoretical principles of project behavior such as the Fifth Hand (Ika et al., 2022) to "wallow in their blood," to start anew at the risk of perpetuating the problem (Shenkar and Ellis, 2022). Are we up to the task?

References

Adelman, J. (2014). *Worldly philosopher: The odyssey of Albert O. Hirschman*. Princeton University Press.

Alacevich, M. (2020). *Albert O. Hirschman: An intellectual biography*. Columbia University Press.

Anheier, H. K. (2017). Infrastructure and the principle of the Hiding Hand (pp. 1–20). In K. Wegrich, G. Kostka, and G. Hammerschmid (eds.). *The governance of infrastructure*. Oxford University Scholarship Online.

Bacharach, S. B. (1989). Organizational theories: Some criteria for evaluation. *Academy of Management Review*, *14*, 496–515.

Baerenbold, R. (2023). Reducing risks in megaprojects: The potential of reference class forecasting. *Project Leadership and Society*, 100103.

Ben-David, J., and Sullivan, T. A. (1975). Sociology of science. *Annual Review of Sociology*, *1*, 203–222.

Blum, A.F. (1970). Theorizing (pp. 301–319). In J. D., Douglas (ed.). *Everyday life: Reconstruction of social knowledge*. Routledge.

Bromiley, P., and Rau, D. (2022). Some problems in using prospect theory to explain strategic management issues. *Academy of Management Perspectives*, *36*(1), 125–141.

Buehler, R., Griffin, D., and Ross, M. (1994). Exploring the "planning fallacy": Why people underestimate their task completion times. *Journal of Personality and Social Psychology*, *67*(3), 366.

Chapman, P. (2024). Revisiting project delivery performance: Evidence from Swedish transport infrastructure. *Project Management Journal*, https://journals.sagepub.com/doi/full/10.1177/87569728241257391.

Chen, Y., Ahiaga-Dagbui, D. D., Thaheem, M. J., and Shrestha, A. (2023). Toward a deeper understanding of optimism bias and transport project cost overrun. *Project Management Journal*, *54*(5), 561–578.

Cornelissen, J., Höllerer, M. A., and Seidl, D. (2021). What theory is and can be: Forms of theorizing in organizational scholarship. *Organization Theory*, *2*(3), https://journals.sagepub.com/doi/full/10.1177/26317877211020328.

De Wit, A. (1988). Measurement of project success. *International Journal of Project Management*, *6*(3), 164–170.

Douglas, J. D. (1970). Preface (pp. vii–xii). In J. D., Douglas (ed.). *Everyday life: Reconstruction of social knowledge*. Routledge.

Epton, S. R. (1972). The underestimation of project duration: An explanation in terms of a time-horizon. *R&D Management*, *2*(3), 141–142.

Flyvbjerg, B. (2006). From Nobel Prize to project management: Getting risks right. *Project Management Journal*, *37*(3), 5–15.

Flyvbjerg, B. (2014). What you should know about megaprojects and why: An overview. *Project Management Journal*, *45*(2), 6–19.

Flyvbjerg, B. (2016). The fallacy of beneficial ignorance: A test of Hirschman's Hiding Hand. *World Development*, *84*, 176–189.

Flyvbjerg, B. (2017). *The Oxford handbook of megaproject management*. Oxford University Press.

Flyvbjerg, B. (2021). Top ten behavioral biases in project management: An overview. *Project Management Journal*, *52*(6), 531–546.

Flyvbjerg, B., and Gardner, D. (2023). *How big things get done: The surprising factors that determine the fate of every project, from home renovations to space exploration and everything in between*. Signal.

Flyvbjerg, B., Garbiou, M., and Lovallo, D. (2009). Delusion and deception in large infrastructure projects: Two models for explaining and preventing executive disaster. *California Management Review*, *51*(2), pp. 170–193.

Flyvbjerg, B., Holm, M. K. S., and Buhl, S. L. (2002). Underestimating costs in public works projects: Error or lie. *Journal of the American Planning Association*, *68*(3), pp.279–295.

Flyvbjerg, B., Ansar, A., Budzier, A., Buhl, S., Cantarelli, C., Garbuio, M., Lavallo, D., Lunn, D., Molin, E., Ronnest, A., Stewart, A., and van Wee, B. (2018). Five things you should know about cost overruns. *Transportation Research A: Policy and Practice*, *118*, 174–190.

Fox, J. (2014). Instinct can beat analytical thinking. *Harvard Business Review*. https://hbr.org/2014/06/ instinct-can-beat-analytical-thinking. Accessed on: April 17, 2024.

Gigerenzer, G. (2014). *Risk savvy: How to make good decisions*. Penguin Group.

Gil, N., and Fu, Y. (2022). Megaproject performance, value creation and value distribution: An organizational governance perspective. *Academy of Management Discoveries*, *8*(2), 224–251.

Hall, P. (1980). *Great planning disasters*. Penguin Books.

Hambrick, D. C. (2007). The field of management's devotion to theory: Too much of a good thing? *Academy of Management Journal*, *50*(6), 1346–1352.

Hirschman, A. O. (1967). *Development projects observed*. The Brookings Institution.

Hirschman, A. O. (1970). The search for paradigms as a hindrance to understanding. *World Politics*, *22*(3), 329–343.

Ika, L. A. (2018). Beneficial or detrimental ignorance: The straw man Fallacy of Flyvbjerg's test of Hirschman's Hiding Hand. *World Development*, *103*, 369–382.

Ika, L. A., and Feeny, S. (2022). Optimism bias and World Bank project performance. *The Journal of Development Studies*, *58*(12), 2604–2623.

Ika, L. A., Love, P. E. D., and Pinto, J. K. (2022). Moving beyond the Planning Fallacy: The emergence of a new principle of project behavior. *IEEE Transactions on Engineering Management*, *69*(6), 3310–3325.

Ika, L. A., and Pinto, J. K. (2022). The "re-meaning" of project success: Updating and recalibrating for a modern project management. *International Journal of Project Management*, *40*(7), 835–848.

Ika, L. A., Pinto, J. K., Love, P. E., and Pache, G. (2023). Bias versus error: Why projects fall short. *Journal of Business Strategy*, *44*(2), 67–75.

Ika, L. A., and Saint-Macary, J. (2023). *Managing fuzzy projects in 3D: A proven, multi-faceted blueprint for overseeing complex projects*. McGraw-Hill Education.

Ika, L. A., and Söderlund, J. (2016). Rethinking revisited: Insights from an early rethinker. *International Journal of Managing Projects in Business*, *9*(4), 931–954.

Jones, L. R., and Euske, K. J. (1991). Strategic misrepresentation in budgeting. *Journal of Public Administration Research and Theory*, *1*(4), 437–460.

Kahneman, D. (2011). *Thinking fast and slow*. Doubleday Canada.

Kahneman, D., and Tversky, A. (1977). *Intuitive prediction: Biases and corrective procedures* Defense Advanced Research Projects Agency. https://apps.dtic.mil/sti/tr/pdf/ADA047747.pdf.

Kahneman, D., and Tversky, A. (1979). Prospect theory: An analysis of decision under risk. *Econometrica*, *47*(2), 263–292.

Kahneman, D., and Tversky, A. (1982). Intuitive prediction: Biases and corrective procedures (pp. 414–421). In D. Kahneman, P. Slovic, and A. Tversky (eds.). *Judgment under uncertainty: Heuristics and biases*. Cambridge University Press.

Keynes, J. M. (1953). *The general theory of employment, interest and money*. Harcourt Brace Jovanovich.

Kreiner, K. (2020). Conflicting notions of a project: The battle between Albert O. Hirschman and Bent Flyvbjerg. *Project Management Journal*, *51*(1), 400–410.

Lovallo, D., Cristofaro, M., and Flyvbjerg, B. (2023). Governing large projects: A three-stage process to get it right. *Academy of Management Perspectives*, *37*(2), 138–156.

Lovallo, D., and Kahneman, D. (2003). Delusions of success: How optimism undermines executives' decisions. *Harvard Business Review*, July, pp. 56–63.

Love, P. E. D., and Ahiaga-Dagbui, D. D. (2018). Debunking "fake news" in a post-truth era: The plausible untruths of cost underestimation in transport infrastructure projects. *Transportation Research A: Policy and Practice*, *113*, 357–368.

Love, P. E. D., Ika, L. A., and Ahiaga-Dagbui, D. (2019a). On de-bunking "fake news" in a post-truth area: Why does the Planning Fallacy explanation for cost overruns fall short? *Transportation Research A: Policy and Practice*, *126*, 397–408.

Love, P. E. D., Sing, M. C. P., Ika, L. A., and Newton, S. (2019b). The cost performance of transportation projects: The fallacy of the Planning Fallacy account. *Transportation Research Part A: Policy and Practice*, *122*(1), 1–20.

Love, P. E. D., Pinto, J. K., and Ika, L. A. (2022a). Hundreds of years of pain, with minimal gain: Capital project cost overruns, the past, present, and optimistic future. *IEEE Engineering Management Review*, *50*(4), 56–70.

Love, P. E. D., Ika, L. A., and Sing, M. C. (2022b). Does the planning fallacy prevail in social infrastructure projects? Empirical evidence and competing explanations. *IEEE Transactions on Engineering Management*, *69*(6), 2588–2602.

Love, P. E. D., Ika, L. A., and Pinto, J. K. (2024). Homo heuristicus: From risk management to managing uncertainty in large-scale infrastructure projects. *IEEE Transactions on Engineering Management*, *71*(1), 1940–1949.

McDonald, K. M., Graham, I. D., and Grimshaw, J. (2004). Toward a theoretic basis for quality improvement interventions (pp. 27–37). In K. G. Shojania, K. M. McDonald, K. R. Wachter, and D. Owens (eds.). *Closing the quality gap: A critical analysis of quality improvement strategies*. Agency for Healthcare Research and Quality. p. 27–37.

Malisoff, W. M. (1934). Editorial: What is philosophy of science? *Philosophy of Science*, *1*, 3–4

Meredith, J. (2022). Holey moley, the poppycock syndrome, and academic drift. *International Journal of Project Management*, *40*(1), 15–18.

Merewitz, L. (1973). Cost overruns in public works (pp. 277–295). In W. Niskanen, A. Hansen, R. Havermann, R. Turvey, and R. Zeckhauser (eds.). *Benefit cost and policy analysis*. Aldine.

Merrow, E. W., Chapel, S. W., and Worthing, C. (1979). A review of cost estimation in new technologies: Implications for energy process plants. A report prepared for the U.S. Department of Energy, RAND Corp., R-2481- DOE, p. 132. Available: www.osti.gov/servlets/purl/6002293.

Merton, R. K. (1973). *The sociology of science: Theoretical and empirical investigations*. University of Chicago Press.

Morris, P. W., and Hough, G. H. (1987). *The anatomy of major projects: A study of the reality of project management*. John Wiley & Sons.

Olasehinde-Williams, G., and Jenkins, G. P. (2023). A test of Hirschman's hiding hand principle in World bank-financed hydropower projects. *Journal of Benefit-Cost Analysis*, *14*, 1–20.

Park, J. E. (2021). Curbing cost overruns in infrastructure investment. *European Journal of Transport and Infrastructure Research*, *21*(2), 120–136.

Pedhazur, E. J., and Schmelkin, L. P. (2013). *Measurement, design, and analysis: An integrated approach*. Psychology Press.

Pinto, J. (2023). Is this how big things get done? *International Journal of Project Management*, *41*(1), 102484.

Podsakoff, P. M., MacKenzie, S. B., and Podsakoff, N. P. (2016). Recommendations for creating better concept definitions in the organizational, behavioral, and social sciences. *Organizational Research Methods*, *19*, 159–203.

Seibert, S. E., Kacmar, K. M., Kraimer, M. L., Downes, P. E., and Noble, D. (2017). The role of research strategies and professional networks in management scholars' productivity. *Journal of Management*, *43*(4), 1103–1130.

Shaw, G. B. (1903). *Man and superman: A comedy and a philosophy*. Cambridge University Press.

Shenkar, O., and Ellis, S. (2022). The rise and fall of structural contingency theory: A theory's "autopsy." *Journal of Management Studies*, *59*(3), 782–818.

Sunstein, C. R. (2015). Albert Hirschman's hiding hand: Foreword. In A. O. Hirschman (ed.). *Development projects observed*. Brookings Institution.

Svejvig, P. (2021). A meta-theoretical framework for theory building in project management. *International Journal of Project Management*, *39*(8), 849–872.

Swedberg, R. (2016). Before theory comes theorizing or how to make social science more interesting. *British Journal of Sociology*, *67*(1), 5–22.

Themsen, T. N. (2019). The processes of public megaproject cost estimation: The inaccuracy of reference class forecasting. *Financial Accountability & Management*, *35*(4), 337–352.

Tiger, L. (1979). *Optimism: The biology of hope*. Simon and Schuster.

Wachs, M. (1989). When planners lie with numbers. *Journal of the American Planning Association*, *55*(4), 476–479.

Whetten, D. A. (1989). What constitutes a theoretical contribution? *Academy of Management Review*, *14*(4), 490–495.

World Bank. (1992). Effective implementation: Key to development impact (Report No. 11536). World Bank.

CHAPTER 2

Unveiling the Hiding Hand

GRAHAM ROOM*

"Hiding Hand" is a metaphor or principle that Albert Hirschman used to characterize the international development process (Hirschman, 1967b, ch. 1). It was based on the experience of the projects he studied across several decades and several continents.

It states that international development projects typically incur major cost overruns and other implementation problems, which put in question the decision to launch them in the first place. Indeed, had these difficulties been known in advance, the projects might never have been even tried. Nevertheless, human ingenuity often finds a way around these difficulties and can indeed discover unforeseen benefits, which may then justify the project after all. The "Hiding Hand" thus confers "providential" or "beneficial ignorance" (Alacevich, 2014, p. 157) and encourages even the risk-averse to be bold. In the process, it enables them to learn better project appraisal and management. The principle may not apply in every case, but Hirschman believed it to be generally true.

The Hiding Hand has in recent years come in for strong criticism, by writers such as Flyvbjerg, based on his own analysis of projects, their costs, and their effects. He argues that Hirschman's argument is conceptually confused, empirically untrue and rhetorically disingenuous. This however misunderstands Hirschman. Flyvbjerg has "tested" the Hiding Hand at only a very limited micro level of the individual project. In doing this, he misses Hirschman's account of the larger environment within which international development projects and the Hiding Hand operate. That, at least, is the argument of this chapter.

The Hiding Hand is a metaphor for the creative processes of learning-by-doing in which we all in some degree engage: striving to transform the world around us, making sense of the obstacles we encounter and discovering new vistas that then open up. It is only by actively trying to change the world that we make better sense of it, and only by wrestling mightily with the obstacles that we meet, that we take the next steps in our self-transformative journey.

The next section of this chapter is concerned with Flyvbjerg's critique of Hirschman – and with Flyvbjerg's failure to set the individual project within the larger political economy of its macro-context. The third section addresses that macro-context, as viewed by Hirschman; from there it then turns back to the individual project and its evaluation. The following section situates the Hiding Hand in relation to larger debates on economic and political development. The final section considers the responsibility of social scientists to hold international development actors and the political community to account.

Flyvberg and the Hiding Hand

The Critique

Flyvbjerg (2016) sets out to test the Hiding Hand empirically. He has over recent decades built a dataset incorporating over 2,000 projects of eight different types, primarily concerned with infrastructure such as roads and power plants. For each of these he has robust data on costs and benefits. He demonstrates that within each of the eight categories of project, there are typically significant

* I am grateful to Marlies Morsink for reading this chapter in a succession of drafts and making numerous suggestions for improvement. I am also grateful to James Copestake for his helpful suggestions.

cost overruns: evidence of just the sort of unforeseen difficulties that, had they been known in advance, might indeed have discouraged anyone from ever starting them. What then of the *benefit* overruns that Hirschman celebrated – evidence that human ingenuity and serendipity often find a way around these difficulties and even discover additional benefits? Across all eight types of projects, Flyvbjerg concludes that the benefits proved less, not more than expected – no evidence therefore of a happy ending to the story. The Hiding Hand may be valid in some individual cases, but across the dataset as a whole, it is resoundingly refuted.

Flyvbjerg also assesses the evidence for saying that the Hiding Hand enables the community of decision-makers to learn collectively over time how to judge acceptable and non-acceptable risks – with their general performance progressively improving. Across his 2,000 projects, his data reveal no such trend in the assessment of cost and benefit risks. These results also are statistically robust.

This is not all. Flyvbjerg charges Hirschman with having taken a very small sample – and with having selected projects in which the "Hiding Hand" was especially apparent. This, he argues, runs contrary to the most basic principles of theory testing, whatever we may think of Hirschman as a stimulating and creative thinker on international development practice.

Finally, Flyvbjerg argues, Hirschman tended to reject the views of his respondents that their projects had failed, instead seeking to instill a sense of hope and optimism. He then allowed this to shape his own judgment of the project. This "made it appear that the Hiding Hand was an attribute of the projects he studied, when it was . . . more an attribute of his biases and the 'story he spun'" (Flyvbjerg, 2016, p. 180).

Flyvbjerg's article has stimulated a range of critical responses. They are concerned, first, with Flyvbjerg's claim to have provided a more robust quantitative analysis of international development project performance and a more rigorous test of the Hiding Hand thesis. Ika, for example, questions Flyvbjerg's decision to limit his gaze to the first year of a project's development, in the belief that the first year of activity is a sufficient predictor of the project's progress over a longer period (Ika, 2018, section 7).

There is, secondly, the question of whether Hirschman was indeed guilty of sloppy research practice: most obviously, in confining his attention to a sub-group of the projects available. As Adelman points out, many of the projects available were disordered in their approaches and their data collection (Adelman, 2013, pp. 388–389). Hirschman as fieldworker was faced not with a neat dataset but with the messy and practical reality of project teams (Room, 2018, section 2). No wonder he stuck to a small number of projects, so that he could personally visit and observe each of them and make sense of their idiosyncratic experience. Flyvbjerg does not say how many of the 2,000 projects in his own database he himself visited, exposing himself similarly to their messy and practical reality.

Third, there is the status of the "Hiding Hand" itself, as a mechanism of project learning and action (Lepenies, 2018, section 4). Is it, as Flyvbjerg believes, just a provocative or teasing metaphor, of little or no analytical value? If so, he is doing Hirschman a service, in taking his thesis seriously enough to merit empirical testing. Or is the Hiding Hand, as we will argue, itself an (intellectual) project under development, which can open up a range of productive new vistas? In that case, we must find a way to extract from Hirschman's metaphor such insights as it may offer, even if we also critique his usage, where it obscures more than it reveals.

Flyvbjerg's focus is on the micro-economics of individual projects, their costs and effects, and the rationality or otherwise of individual action. This chapter, in contrast, sets those micro-behaviors within the larger political economy in which these projects sit, the strategic intent of national and international development agencies, and the complex dynamics that their international development programmes set in motion.[1]

[1] Since his 2016 article, and in response to the debate this stimulated, Flyvbjerg has produced a succession of writings to defend and elaborate his position. This includes his book (Flyvbjerg & Gardner, 2023) written not for academic peers so much as policymakers and the broader public. Pinto's review, while respectful, finds little here that adds to the scholarly debate (Pinto, 2023).

The Benevolent and Malevolent Twins

For Flyvbjerg, the "Hiding Hand" as portrayed by Hirschman is an empirical generalization. International development projects commonly incur major cost overruns and other implementation problems; but these, more often than not, are dwarfed by the unforeseen benefits that then arise, when those problems are addressed and overcome.

Flyvbjerg accepts that this may indeed sometimes be the case. We can then be grateful that the extra efforts that turn out to be required were not evident at the start – had they been, the project might well have been abandoned. The Hiding Hand was "benevolent." In other cases, however – and Flyvbjerg reckons that this is more usual – the extra efforts undertaken do not produce those extra benefits. Here a different Hiding Hand is at work, one that Flyvbjerg deems "malevolent," inasmuch as it exploits the unjustified optimism of the international development workers (Flyvbjerg & Sunstein, 2016).[2] Even so, Olasehinde-Williams and Jenkins (2023, p. 312) in their empirical study of World Bank–financed hydropower projects, using Flyvbjerg's approach, find that the benevolent Hiding Hand is much more common than its malevolent twin.

Hirschman is not without fault. His primary focus is on the learning and innovation processes in which practitioners are involved, as they encounter and wrestle with unforeseen obstacles. However, by couching his argument in terms of the "hand of providence," he has unnecessarily obscured the more fundamental insights that he wishes to espouse.

Any international development project embodies the state of knowledge that the international development agents have acquired, applied to a specific situation. It is especially when a project applies a proven method – and expects therefore that the application in the new locale will be routine – that possible difficulties and therefore costs will be underestimated. This may also of course assist in obtaining the funding required (Hirschman, 1967b, pp. 17, 21). Unforeseen problems then force a stock-taking; the urgency of finding a solution drives efforts to find a way around or through the obstacles, as we improvise new capabilities of understanding and action. Necessity is the mother of invention and may indeed produce innovations on a much wider scale (Ika, 2018, section 4).[3]

This process is of course one that many other writers have captured, albeit using other terms and varying in their emphasis. They include, for example, Schon's "reflective practitioner" (Schon, 1983). Nevertheless, Hirschman's account of the Hiding Hand emphasizes the *collective* as well as the individual nature of this journey. In then moving between the individual and the collective, we must not miss the rival economic and political interests that champion competing views of the journey.

From Behavioral Nudges to Political Economy

Hirschman sees international development project managers as enjoying the providential influences of the Hiding Hand. Whatever difficulties they encounter, ways around are also likely to appear. Flyvbjerg is understandably impatient with such vagueness; his efforts to operationalize this generalization empirically and rigorously are to be applauded.

But Flyvbjerg is not just impatient; he charges Hirschman with having imposed this optimistic view of the world on project managers, even when their own experience suggested otherwise (and aligned better indeed with what Flyvbjerg's own statistical work has now revealed). What Hirschman's Hiding Hand hides is Hirschman's own efforts to offer false hope. The "Hiding

[2] These tendencies on the part of international development project leaders have also been discussed in terms of the so-called Planning Fallacy – where projects are allegedly guilty of ill-founded optimism. See, for example, Loveal. (2022).

[3] Hirschman (1958, pp. 20–21) adds that especially for projects where we do not have a proven method, and where early problems are quite likely to appear (with the risk that the project is abandoned), it is wise to develop it initially as a pilot-experimental project on a small scale, gathering experience.

Hand" is no less and no more than Hirschman himself sprinkling bonhomie and confidence across the projects he visits. That at least is Flyvbjerg's view.

For Flyvbjerg, international development workers would be better off to be hard-headed about the difficulties they face. As rational actors, they should fend off Hirschman's optimistic nostrums and avoid wasting their energies on an uphill struggle. Nevertheless, it is evident that many of them remain unduly optimistic and that many others just keep going, whatever the contrary evidence.

To explain this, Flyvbjerg resorts to such writers as Kahneman (2011) and Thaler and Sunstein (2009). The latter encourage policy analysts to move away from models of the "rational actor" and instead to start from social actors as they actually are, as illuminated by empirical research in the behavioral sciences. This research suggests that in many ways social actors blunder through life with cognitive biases – some *persisting in the inertia of existing habits*, no matter what new opportunities arise, others inspired by *unrealistic optimism*, no matter what countervailing evidence is available. Just therefore as a parent nudges a child, clear-sighted policymakers, concerned to optimize social and economic well-being, will "nudge" these actors in a direction that will truly benefit them – and which they themselves, on reflection, will agree is for the best. This is "libertarian paternalism" (Thaler & Sunstein, 2009, pp 4–6). Flyvbjerg indeed unites with Sunstein to strengthen his critique of Hirschman (Flyvbjerg & Sunstein, 2016): they present behaviorist psychology as underpinning the patterns of individual action, which Flyvbjerg claims to have laid bare in his account of infrastructure projects and their typical trajectories.

Nudge is not without value, in the analysis of project performance management (Bukoyeet al., 2022). Nevertheless, it hardly suffices as a robust basis for Flyvbjerg's critique of Hirschman's project planners and managers. If some of these social actors are characterized by *inertia*, this may attest not to their cognitive biases but to the social, institutional and political obstacles they face and their uncertainty as to the consequences of any particular train of action (Room, 2016a, ch. 8; 2016b).[4] They can hardly be expected to make "unbiased" assessments of the risks that they confront, in a world that is being disrupted and re-worked by political and corporate big actors. Too much turbulence and uncertainty – and these small actors will "hunker down" and wait for times to get better. This inertia, rather than being evidence of a "cognitive bias," may thus be the logical response to that uncertainty. "Nudge" – whether as analytical framework or as policy prescription – fails to set such behaviors within an understanding of political economy and of the larger socio-political order.

Meanwhile sustained *optimism*, on the part of some of these project managers, may express their sense of being able, as creative and agile actors, to reshape the world around them, if only on a modest scale. Their optimism may moreover be "rational" to the extent that they are able to attach themselves to the bigger actors of their society, the first movers, and can follow in their wake.[5] It is by keeping close to those big actors that they may be best able to glimpse the future, limit the uncertainty that they face and carry through their own strategies of action. It is also via these big actors – and their connections – that they may be able to access and secure the additional resources that these strategies will require.

[4] Thaler and Sunstein (2009) may have moved away from economic orthodoxy's fixation on the rational actor; but they retain its very weak or "thin" notion of social institutions. There is reference (ch. 3) to "following the herd" but little to the cues and nudges that are mediated through the social institutions in which we are all involved and into whose rules we are socialized. Instead, the great majority of the examples that they cite involve physical cues associated with the built environment and electronic cues associated with machines and IT systems. In this they remain wedded to a rather abstract form of methodological individualism (Lukes, 1973).

[5] There is a well-developed literature on "first mover dynamics" (Pierson, 2004). Those who move first into a new market or a new technology may be able to establish a self-reinforcing position of advantage. Second movers may then be able to develop secondary niches of their own (see the literature on the so-called minority game, starting from Arthur [1994]).

This points beyond individual behavior to the economic, political, and indeed ideological dimensions of power and inequality in society. This is something that the behaviorist literature largely ignores. Flyvbjerg and Sunstein (2016) do admittedly engage fleetingly with questions of power; but this is mainly in the context of agents who deliberately and deviously seek "to make the project look good on paper" (pp. 984–985). They also recognize (p. 983) that in developing countries in particular, there are "lots of unknowns": as Hirschman himself points out, "confidence in creativity is lacking" (Hirschman, 1967b, p. 15). They do not however engage analytically with these social inequalities in the distribution of power.

In contrast, Hirschman himself sets the Hiding Hand within his political economy and his overall scheme of thought. We now therefore turn from the individual behavior with which Sunstein and Flyvbjerg are concerned, to Hirschman's strategy of economic development at the macro-level. We will then be better equipped to return to the discussion of international development projects at the micro-level with which we began.

Hirschman's Strategy of Economic Development

Strategy and Dynamics at a Macro-Level

A decade before the "Hiding Hand" essay, Hirschman published *The Strategy of Economic Development* (1958), concerned with national approaches to economic development. The mainstream literature saw the preconditions for economic development in terms of natural resources, capital, entrepreneurs, etc. However, as Hirschman points out, it often proves difficult to agree empirically on which of these is key; and indeed, once development gets going, somehow they all fairly readily appear.

Hirschman therefore offers an alternative view. Many of these resources may be latent rather than immediately available. What seems to matter more than any particular resource are the "interlocking vicious circles" that hold development back and, in contrast, the "upward spirals" that can bring forth all the resources that are needed (p. 5). These interlocking vicious circles are reminiscent of the language of "wicked problems" (Rittel & Webber, 1973). The upward spirals that can bring forth all the resources that are needed may offer corresponding "smart solutions," where, by careful attention to the interrelationships of those wicked problems, they can be more effectively addressed.

The focus should therefore be not on the resources themselves but on the "essential dynamic and strategic aspects of the development process" (p. 6). Development depends on mobilizing and combining these purposefully, in a spirit of experimentation – trying out different makeshift adaptations and finding which ones will work. It is this capacity – to mobilize and combine, to adapt and redeploy – that Hirschman therefore places at the centre of development strategy. It is inappropriate therefore to embrace a strategy of "balanced growth," hoping to make simultaneous progress across all sectors. Instead, "if the economy is to be kept moving ahead, the task of development policy is to maintain tensions, disproportions and disequilibria" – mobilizing in force, so as occupy strategically important positions (p. 66).

Hirschman sits within a larger literature concerned with strategy and strategic walks – military, business, political (Clausewitz, 1984; Freedman, 2013). This recognizes a range of possible futures. It recognizes multiple actors pursuing interdependent but potentially conflicting aims, each of whose plans of action must be taken into account. It acknowledges uncertainty in relation to the larger social, economic and physical environment, within which the strategy will unfold. It recognizes fateful choices – the paths not taken, the windows of opportunity ignored, the relationships of mutual benefit never explored.

Strategy is therefore not just about allocating and combining resources to specific ends or testing a well-defined approach. Instead, it speaks of the new dynamic capabilities that will be required (Teece, 2009) and the stages, the intermediate steps, by which we will reach our strategic goal: whether this is to cross Antarctica on foot, to put a man on the moon, to eliminate smallpox, to achieve "net zero" in emissions. There is an extensive literature on such capabilities – distinguishing project-specific and operational as against strategic and dynamic capabilities but also exploring the reciprocal relations between the two (see, for example, Davies and Brady [2016]).

To speak of strategy often carries the idea of an opponent or competitor. The task is to figure out where and when to concentrate effort so as to set new dynamics in motion and undermine the opponent's position, while simultaneously advancing your own. The terrain of struggle is after all not a smooth undifferentiated space, in terms of your deployment and that of the opponent, and you must use your strengths to exploit his vulnerability.

Strategy is not however directed just against an opponent. It includes the mobilization of allies, consolidating them into a coherent and effective coalition for change, and the neutralization of other stakeholders, who might oppose what you are doing. It also includes the building of morale – for example, among troops and between the army and the civilian population (Clausewitz, 1984, book III, chs. III–IV). This may help to explain why Hirschman went round the projects, seeking to instill a sense of hope and optimism (Adelman, 2013, pp. 390–393).

In all these instances, the strategic actor is faced not with a set of inert problems but with interlocking "vicious circles" – and perhaps also, in due course, some "upward spirals." But to see through the mist, to discern these opportunities and to mobilize actors around these positives, is far from straightforward. These are the "dilemmas of social reform" (Marris & Rein, 1974).

Flyvbjerg speaks of the resources that are allocated and that project leaders then combine, to achieve a particular goal. Decision-making can, for him, be boiled down to the rational calculation and comparison of alternative inputs and outputs and the associated costs and benefits. This ignores the intermediate positions to be occupied, the capabilities that must be built and the order in which this must be done, as we move across different points in a complex landscape. There are moments to wait, allowing time for the landscape to shift, and moments to act, where we can escape from wicked problems and find smart solutions. The interactions among multiple actors unfold over time, and they cannot be entirely predicted. "Timescapes" are complex (Room, 2022). The strategic policymaker must wait and watch – and intervene only when the moment is right. Such overall strategic development is the business of generals. It is not what we expect of the captains of individual battalions or projects. Nevertheless, the generals must try to ensure that their overall direction of strategic development enables those captains to make progress on their local landscapes. Hirschman therefore goes on to consider how action within local contexts can respond to the larger interplay of strategic intent at macro-level.

From Macro-Strategy to Micro-Action

There may be multiple strategic actors with diverse plans for the development of a country – the national government, the World Bank, international NGOs and corporations, which offer their organizational capabilities and resources. They may however envisage quite different – perhaps even mutually incompatible – futures for the society in question, entailing political choices and trade-offs at key turning points. An individual development project will have to take account of these various strategic actors – their exercise of social, economic, and political power and their diverse requirements as to what the projects they fund should be doing.

Hirschman's *Strategy of Economic Development* describes the practical situation that the development worker thus confronts. No local development project – and its local skirmishes – can be thought of as free-standing and in isolation; it is caught in a wider tangle of interlocking obstacles and possibilities. These are however incompletely visible: to this extent, the costs and effort required to take the project forward can only in part be estimated in advance. They are "unknown unknowns."

Hirschman expects each development project to be sufficiently agile and imaginative, to break out from the tangled constraints and path dependencies that it encounters – and then to mobilize these interactions in "upward spirals" – with benefits not only to its own progress but maybe also that of other projects. Indeed, the boundaries among these different projects may prove somewhat artificial: and it may prove necessary to think of the broader range of costs and benefits, as individual projects link up in a larger development process. Their micro-actions are thus no less strategic than that of the nationally and internationally based macro-actors – albeit driven by the linkages they seek to weave on a more local landscape.[6]

There is however no way of knowing in advance what these linkages will be – the interlocking obstacles and tangles that increase the effort that will be required, the interlocking spirals that may secure enhanced benefits. Development agents may learn to recognize and distinguish the signs of each: but every judgment is provisional and may have to be revised in the light of experience. (This is what Schon would term "reflective practice.") In all this, the capacity to mobilize and redeploy is key but so also are human ingenuity, agility, and, indeed, optimism.

This is the Hiding Hand in operation: a process of learning-by-doing, as practitioners encounter unforeseen obstacles to development but then in some degree surmount or bypass those obstacles and find new vistas that open up.

Flyvbjerg, in his empirical testing of Hirschman's Hiding Hand, makes little or no reference to these dynamic linkages. Nor does he consider the implications for the way he assesses his 2,000 projects. He treats these projects as free-standing and discrete: with their respective costs and benefits, estimated ex ante and recorded ex post, quite independent of any wider development calculus. And indeed, having argued that it is sufficient to look at just the first year of a project's progress, in order to evaluate the Hiding Hand, Flyvbjerg cannot capture these evolutions of projects over a longer period – the very processes of learning with which the Hiding Hand is centrally concerned.

This is not the only limitation of his approach. An international development project typically involves a contract, awarded by one or more of the aforementioned national or international actors to a locally based organization, which may have existed for some time and that brings various actors together in that local community. The data used by Flyvbjerg refer to the specific contract and the funds awarded, but they may say little or nothing about the local organization and its micro-strategy over many years, perhaps using a succession of funds from different sources in combination.

It may be by combining funds from different sources – and thus leveraging a range of meso- and macro-level sponsors – that the local organization is able to bring about change. This plurality may then give them resilience: when one source of funds runs out, they are able to call down other funds and connections and capabilities, so as to avoid a hiatus in funding. This may not show up in the accounts that a project provides to any one funder nor, therefore, in Flyvbjerg's database. It will however show up in the project's notebooks, such as those that they showed to Hirschman.

In short: the local project organization has a specific local context and history from which it draws much of its capability (Engwall, 2003). It will however have to be wily and inventive, if it is to survive and prosper. Those that are not will likely disappear. Development involves trying out different makeshift adaptations and finding which ones will work. This applies, not least, to the politics of the funding ecosystem within which projects find themselves and which – perhaps over many years – they have in some degree made their own.

Even so, nothing stays the same: the winds of change will shift, favouring some funding niches and bypassing others. The heads of projects will need to be alert to those changing circumstances so as to enhance the effectiveness of their efforts and to make their inventive best of the new obstacles and tangles that they then encounter.[7]

Evaluating Projects

In his empirical testing of Hirschman's Hiding Hand, Flyvbjerg assesses more than 2,000 projects.

[6] There are resonances here with the literature on project strategy: see, for example, Patanakul and Shenhar (2012). Kreiner's essay on Hirschman and Flyvbjerg also has strong resonances with the argument here – albeit with a focus more on project design, development and learning, rather than project strategy across contested spaces, central to my contribution here (Kreiner, 2020).

[7] This is what Clausewitz, one of the great authorities on strategy, refers to as "friction" (Clausewitz, 1984, book 1, ch. VII).

He records their respective costs and benefits, estimated ex ante and recorded ex post, for the first year of their development. He pays little or no regard to subsequent evolutions, nor to the dynamic linkages that Hirschman deems fundamental.

The danger is that funders then embrace the illusion that the trajectory of a given project is fully controllable, rather than a matter of "muddling through" (Lindblom, 1959). This in turn risks setting unrealistic terms for their funding, so that practitioners have little choice but to submit unrealistically optimistic proposals if they are to get any funding at all. This may then paradoxically provide more "evidence" for the likes of Flyvbjerg, that the project should not have been undertaken in the first place.

Given however the real world in which projects operate, what sorts of data *might* Flyvbjerg have included in his database relevant to these progressions? What would be relevant, on the one hand, to academic theories of international development – and, on the other, to development strategists and development project workers?

The evaluation of projects such as these has been a recurrent subject of methodological debate going back at least to the 1960s and the launch by SAGE of its *Evaluation Studies Review Annuals* from 1976 onward. Those debates included the critical juxtaposition of more "positivistic" approaches to evaluation, stressing inputs and outputs, costs and benefits, and more "humanistic" approaches, allowing for competing perspectives on project goals, processes of learning and negotiation, and the crystallization of lines of conflict (Room, 1986, ch. 2). In some ways, Flyvbjerg and Hirschman respectively epitomize those two approaches.

During 1985–89, I led the evaluation of a programme of 92 "pilot" projects launched by the European Commission to combat poverty at the local level. I briefly highlight a few elements of those evaluation studies that are relevant here (Room, 1993).

My colleagues and I visited all the projects on a number of occasions. We familiarized ourselves with their internal documentation, as well as collecting data through standardized monitoring. This included data on the costs and outcomes of the projects in quantitative terms, so as to identify different levels of "success" and the antecedent factors that seemed to be significant (ch. 5). We also, however, collected the projects' accounts of the processes of learning-by-doing that their work entailed and that their internal evaluation procedures enabled them to articulate (pp. 36ff). These focussed, in particular, on the obstacles encountered and the light this shone on institutional and other barriers to relieving poverty – at local, regional and national levels. In some cases, this learning-by-doing produced a substantial shift in the way the project was working, with a view to surmounting the barriers revealed.

One third of the projects pre-dated the European programme. All of them, in order to qualify for European funding, had first to secure matching funds from within their own countries. They were thus enmeshed in a variety of institutional niches within their national funding ecosystems; these shaped in significant ways the direction in which their work then developed and the way they interpreted the barriers they encountered in their work. These variations figured in our evaluation (chs. 3, 6).

The European funding – and the cross-national conferences and visits among projects that this funding permitted – then enabled individual projects to develop links with each other and to develop a collective voice with NGOs at European level. Whether intentionally or not, the European Commission provided projects with new capabilities, for operating on the European stage. Opportunistically making the most of this new terrain, the projects were better able to lever strategic success on their local terrain and to remove some of the barriers they had been encountering there (ch. 8).

All of these elements would surely have been relevant to an empirical test of the Hiding Hand. It included costs and effects but also the processes of contingent learning and action with which Hirschman was concerned – international development projects serendipitously leveraging new openings and possibilities. It laid bare some of the interlocking tangles and the upward spirals that such projects commonly encounter but with no assurance that the Helping Hand would necessarily prevail.

This evaluation was no less "rigorous" than Flyvberg's analysis of his project database – but it was addressed to perhaps more significant questions, including those which Hirschman poses.

The Hiding Hand as an Intellectual Project

It is time to take stock of the Hiding Hand – and to situate it in relation to larger debates on economic and political development.

Hirschman's treatment of the Hiding Hand is far from being a well-formed theory. It is an (intellectual) project under development. As Flyvberg demonstrates, it has come up against a range of objections. Nevertheless, if we study these carefully – and revise the perhaps inappropriate presuppositions with which the objectors came to the project – we find new and fruitful vistas opening up.

As we have seen, Hirschman asks the individual development project leader to take stock of the connections that can be made to other social and economic actors – mobilizing these linkages in "upward spirals." So also, for the intellectual project of the Hiding Hand, we can take stock of the wider theoretical landscape and the fruitful synergies and novel insights that those connections may afford.

Hirschman speaks of and to development project leaders, as they confront the challenges of social and economic development across the territory in question. The individual development project does not, however, work in a vacuum; multiple strategic actors are involved, both national and international. The project is thus caught in a wider tangle of the interlocking possibilities and obstacles that those big actors set in train. It may be able to mobilize these interactions in "upward spirals" or it may get caught in "interlocking vicious circles."

Hirschman is thus in many ways a forerunner of the writings on complex systems that have flourished in recent decades (Room, 2011; Ika & Söderlund, 2016; Room, 2016b, ch. 1). But whereas much of that writing leaves little place for strategic actors who re-work the systems in question, this is centre-stage for Hirschman. His development project leaders wait and watch, to see how their socio-economic world will unfold. They study the obstacles and vicious circles that form; they build new capabilities and connect them in new ways; they pivot in hope of catching new upward spirals. They build connections from their local efforts to regional and national partners and new coalitions for change. In short, each project seeks to reshape system parameters for their own positional advantage and in order, we might say, to "occupy the future" (Room, 2016b, ch. 5). Nevertheless, nothing is assured; rival developments are also underway; they may therefore get left behind or even find themselves on a "burning platform."

What goes for projects at the microlevel goes also for policies at the national level. Indeed, international development projects, if "carried out in the zones of dynamism and turmoil of the developing world," may spill out "beyond narrow goal achievement" and serve as tools of national economic and social transformation (Picciotto, 2020, p. 477). Hirschman thus offers a more appropriate and active way of thinking about steering a national economy – whether advanced or developing – as a complex system, in a dynamically interconnected world.

Conclusion: The Hiding Hand and the Public Good

Hirschman evidently relished announcing a principle in terms that resonate with Adam Smith's "invisible hand." His juxtaposition of the two hands signals that for him, the Hiding Hand is, *pace* Flyvbjerg, much more than just a statement about individual development projects and their perception of the costs and effects of their activities. It is also a statement about promotion of the public good, at the level of society as a whole.

Adam Smith had argued that the *Invisible Hand* of the market would align private interests with each other and with the public good. The *Hiding Hand* aligns present action with overall future net benefit and the public good. Both Adam Smith's pin manufacturer and Hirschman's development project manager could therefore act with some confidence that a wider good would result, even if this was not immediately obvious at the time.

Since Adam Smith, that simple notion of the Invisible Hand has however been regularly contested. It may be that the market can indeed align private interests with each other but only to the extent that inequalities in private interests (as expressed in market power) are taken as a given and only to the extent that government ensures the overall good functioning of market institutions. Those at least would seem to be the lessons emerging from both the 1930s depression and the 2008 financial crash (Keynes, 1936; Skidelsky, 2009).

Nor does the Invisible Hand seem sufficient to ensure the rapid adoption of new technologies and concomitant shifts in institutions and modes of governance (Hidalgo et al., 2007). Politicians who surrender economic policy to the Invisible Hand cannot therefore expect to deliver structural change and the development of new national capabilities – whether within poor or rich countries. To this extent, the Invisible Hand is an abnegation of government.

Can the Hiding Hand be relied on, any more than the Invisible Hand, to deliver the public good?

The Hiding Hand is concerned with the costs of an international development project and its effects. A whole range of local stakeholders and businesses may however have been positively or negatively affected: thus losers as well as winners. These go far beyond the costs and effects for the project itself, as recorded in its reports under the funding contract it has been awarded, by a development bank at national or international level.

Schumpeter, the champion of "creative destruction," did not foresee compensation for the losers. Nor does Hirschman. On the contrary, such compensation – if exacted from the development project – would itself be a barrier to innovation (Hirschman, 1958, p. 60; 1967a, pp. 15–16). The Hiding Hand, concealing as it does the full range of costs that the project will generate (not least, for other local actors) – reinforces the optimism of the project staff, that whatever the barriers they face, history – and the major development funders – will be on their side. Only when the full range of the project's costs and effects are revealed may some more complete reckoning be demanded.

Much of the development discourse (in Europe as well as in the Global South) is oriented to the poor. The poor however are often precisely those whose lives have been disrupted without compensation by the changemakers of the past. Theirs is the Losing Hand. To prevent those predations – or at least to compensate the victims – is arguably more important than funding further uncompensated destruction. But for a time at least, this is in part what the Hiding Hand hides (Ika, 2018, esp. section 4).

As well as the victims of development, both Hirschman and Flyvbjerg also recognize undeserved *gains*. A development agent may underestimate costs and over-estimate benefits in order to win a contract from development funders. This could be one reason why international development projects then appear to underperform. Others may overstate costs, if they are confident of getting the contract anyway, by virtue of their influence with funders. These are all examples of what we might call the "Grubby Hand."[8] This is not peculiar to aid in developing countries: see, for example, Galbraith's study of the US as *The Predator State* (Galbraith, 2009) and Klein's studies of "disaster capitalism" (Klein, 2007). See also more recent revelations on corrupt lobbying of Western governments[9] and illicit public procurement contracts.[10]

International development projects thrive in part by skilfully representing their work as playing to several different tunes. As victors in the funding game, they are then well-placed to write the history

[8] This is not the same as the "Malevolent Hand" (see above). That referred to the extra efforts that projects are commonly obliged to undertake to achieve overly optimistic goals – efforts that are often frustrated, according to Flyvbjerg. Here, in contrast, we refer to the distribution of the benefits of a given project – and the sometimes undeserved extraction of the lion's share of those benefits by predatory "insiders." This may then indeed be one reason why the public benefit of a project may appear meagre – and the Malevolent Hand may appear to have been at work.

[9] The *Guardian* view on the Uber files: A tech immorality tale, editorial.

[10] Fifth of UK Covid contracts "raised red flags for possible corruption," Coronavirus, *Guardian*.

of their own success; even if in time that history is contested, when and if the unmerited losers and winners of the development process are revealed. As Hirschman nicely comments, all this is reminiscent of Hegel's "Cunning of Reason" (*List der Vernunft*) – only at dusk does the Owl of Minerva spread its wings (Hirschman, 1958: p 59). Nevertheless, Hegel's metaphor, while alluring, is perhaps no more helpful than Hirschman's.

Abandoning metaphors, we might instead follow Max Weber, and speak of the responsibility of social scientists, to hold development actors and the political community to account, for the world they are creating and the stories they tell (Weber, 1948a, 1948b). The hidden history is thereby laid bare. It is with that responsibility that Hirschman's essay on the Hiding Hand, when seen in the context of his work as a whole, is ultimately concerned.

References

Adelman, J. (2013). *Worldly philosopher: The odyssey of Albert O. Hirschman*. Princeton University Press.

Alacevich, M. (2014). Visualising uncertaities, or how Albert Hirschman and the World Bank disagreed on project appraisal and what this says about the end of "High Development Theory." *Journal of the History of Economic Thought 36*, 137–168.

Arthur, W. B. (1994). Inductive reasoning and bounded rationality (the El Farol problem). *American Economic Review 84*, 406–411.

Bukoye, O. T., et al. (2022). Using nudges to realize project performance management *International Journal of Project Management 40*(8), 886–905.

Clausewitz, C. v. (1984). *On war*. Princeton University Press.

Davies, A., and Brady, T. (2016). Explicating the dynamics of project capabilities. *International Journal of Project Management 34*(2), 314–327.

Engwall, M. (2003). No project is an island: Linking projects to history and context. *Research Policy 32*(5), 789–808.

Flyvbjerg, B. (2016). The fallacy of beneficial ignorance: A test of Hirschman's Hiding Hand. *World Development 84*, 176–189.

Flyvbjerg, B., and Gardner, D. (2023). *How big things get done: The surprising factors behind every successful project, from home renovations to space exploration*. Macmillan.

Flyvbjerg, B., and Sunstein, C. R. (2016). The principle of the Malevolent Hiding Hand; or the Planning Fallacy writ large. *Social Research 83*(4): 979–1004.

Freedman, A. (2013). *Strategy – a history*. Oxford University Press.

Galbraith, J. K. (2009). *The predator state*. Free Press.

Hidalgo, C. A., et al. (2007). The product space conditions the development of nations." *Science*. www.sciencemag.org.

Hirschman, A. O. (1958). *The strategy of economic cevelopment*. Yale University Press.

Hirschman, A. O. (1967a). The principle of the Hiding Hand. *The Public Interest* (Winter), 10–23.

Hirschman, A. O. (1967b). *Development projects observed*. The Brookings Institution.

Ika, L. A. (2018). Beneficial or detrimental ignorance: The straw man fallacy or Flyvbjerg's test of Hirschman's Hiding Hand. *World Development 103*, 369–382.

Ika, L. A., and Söderlund, J. (2016). Rethinking revisited: Insights from an early rethinker. *International Journal of Managing Projects in Business 9*, 931–954.

Kahneman, D. (2011). *Thinking, fast and slow*. Allen Lane.

Keynes, J. M. (1936). *The general theory of employment, interest and money*. Macmillan.

Klein, N. (2007). *The shock doctrine*. Penguin.

Kreiner, K. (2020). Conflicting notions of a project: The battle between Albert O. Hirschman and Bent Flyvbjerg. *Project Management Journal 51*(4), 400–410.

Lepenies, P. H. (2018). Statistical tests as a hindrance to understanding: What the controversy around the "Hiding Hand" conceals about research in the social sciences and conceals about project management. *World Development 103*, 360–365.

Lindblom, C. E. (1959). The science of "muddling through." *Public Administration Review 19*(2), 79–88.

Love, P. E. D., Ika, L. A., and Sing, M. C. (2022). Does the Planning Fallacy prevail in social infrastructure projects? Empirical evidence and competing explanations." *IEEE Transactions on Engineering Management 69*(6), 2588–2602.

Lukes, S. M. (1973). *Individualism*. Basil Blackwell.

Marris, P., and Rein, M. (1974). *Dilemmas of social reform*. Penguin.

Olasehinde-Williams, G., and Jenkins, G. P. (2023). A test of Hirschman's Hiding Hand principle in

World Bank–financed hydropower projects. *Journal of Benefit-Cost Analysis 14*(2), 298–317.
Patanakul, P., and Shenhar, A. J. (2012). What project strategy really is: The fundamental building block in strategic project management. *Project Management Journal 43*(1), 4–20.
Picciotto, R. (2020). Towards a "new project management" movement? An international development perspective. *International Journal of Project Management 38*(8), 474–485.
Pierson, P. (2004). *Politics in time*. Princeton University Press.
Pinto, J. K. (2023). Is this how big things get done? *International Journal of Project Management 41*, 1–7.
Rittel, H. W. J., and Webber, M. M. (1973). Dilemmas in a general theory of planning. *Policy Sciences 4*(2): 155–169.
Room, G. (1986). *Cross-national innovation in social policy*. Macmillan.
Room, G. (1993). *Anti-poverty action-research in Europe*. SAUS.
Room, G. (2011). *Complexity, institutions and public policy: Agile decision-making in a turbulent world*. Edward Elgar.
Room, G. (2016a). Nudge or nuzzle? Improving decisions about active citizenship. *Policy Studies 37*(2), 113–128.
Room, G. (2016b). *Agile actors on complex terrains: Transformative realism and public policy*. Routledge.
Room, G. (2018). The Hiding Hand: A rejoinder to Flyvbjerg on Hirschman." *World Development 103*, 366–368.
Room, G. (2022). Strategic policymaking within complex timescapes. *Complexity, Governance and Networks 7*(1), 15–28.
Schon, D. A. (1983). *The reflective practitioner*. Basic Books.
Skidelsky, R. (2009). *Keynes: The return of the master*. Allen Lane.
Teece, D. J. (2009). *Dynamic capabilities and strategic management*. Oxford, Oxford University Press.
Thaler, R. H., and Sunstein, C. R. (2009). *Nudge: Improving decisions about health, wealth, and happiness*, rev. ed. Penguin.
Weber, M. (1948a). Politics as a vocation (pp. 77–128). In H. H. Gerth and C. W. Mills (eds.). *Max Weber: Essays in sociology*. Routledge and Kegan Paul.
Weber, M. (1948b). Science as a vocation (pp. 129–156). In H. H. Gerth and C. W. Mills (eds.). *Max Weber: Essays in sociology*. Routledge and Kegan Paul.

CHAPTER 3

Voyages of Discovery

Balancing Leadership, Control, and Capabilities in Megaproject Delivery

REBECCA VINE, DICLE KORTANTAMER, and ANDREW DAVIES

Introduction

Over the last decade, there have been significant advances in our understanding of innovation and how megaproject delivery models can be organized to productively respond to project misbehavior (Davies et al., 2017a, 2017b). Yet megaprojects often struggle to take advantage of unforeseen opportunities that emerge over the project life (Anheier, 2016; Ika, 2018; Kreiner, 2020). This chapter examines the social and institutional architectures that enable megaprojects to strategically adapt to opportunities for learning and innovation when they emerge during the execution of a project.

In this chapter, we return to Hirschman's description of project implementation as a "long voyage of discovery" (Hirschman, 1967, p. 32) from his classic study of the behavior of international development projects. Here he describes how unforeseen events can have a trojan horse quality, translating uncertainty into a blessing in disguise (Picciotto, 2015; Ika & Söderlund, 2016). This picture of success assumes that the downstream capacity to innovate during project execution cancels out problems overlooked by planners (Davies, 2017). Fundamentally, Hirschman asserts that despite initial flawed plans, projects can become successful if they mobilize creative resources. This chapter examines the Voyage of Discovery (VoD) principle in more depth.

We also challenge the traditional view that control and leadership practices seek to mitigate project misbehavior by constraining novelty and discovery. This perspective focuses on megaproject governance as a set of control mechanisms that manifest "planning one's work and then working one's plan" (Ika et al., 2022, p. 3312) to keep the program on its predetermined track. This reduces project leadership to a set of skills adopted by project managers or the senior executives of a megaproject to produce an optimum level of performance (Damayanti et al., 2021; Drouin et al., 2021; Wan et al., 2020). In this chapter, we reconcile these seemingly opposing concepts of discovery and robust governance by examining situated contexts where control and leadership practices respond to both complexity and incertitude by actively seeking out novel solutions. Furthermore, we examine the role of new delivery models in balancing capabilities alongside leadership and control practices in a complementary way to enable innovative action.

Finally, to contribute to the Fifth Hand principle of project behavior (Ika et al., 2022) we avoid making a priori assumptions about the optimistic or pessimistic roles of major actors or their preference for bias or error. Instead, this chapter focuses on the adaptive and flexible processes that balance tensions between routine and innovative responses to change. This is particularly important because megaproject behavior is notoriously unpredictable and structural interdependencies can create systemic complexity (Shenhar & Dvir, 2007) and small changes are amplified into intense pressures to deviate from predetermined plans. This means that during different phases of a project life cycle different types of adaptive response may be needed.

The remainder of the chapter is structured as follows. Hirschman's VoD principle is revisited to consider how it might be used to better understand responses to the "forks in the road" (Kreiner, 2020, p. 405) observed in megaprojects. This is followed by an examination of recent research on megaproject delivery models and how capabilities can be organized to encourage a sustained search for innovative solutions. We then consider project governance and the role of control and leadership practices as constraints or enablers of discovery. Finally, we return to the VoD principle and consider how capabilities, control, and leadership combine to create complementary drivers for learning and innovation.

Conceptualizing Megaproject Delivery as a Voyage of Discovery

The idea that megaprojects can be conceptualized as delivery models was explored at length in Davies et al. (2019), a special issue of the *Project Management Journal.* Here a megaproject is defined as a large-scale project with a capital cost *greater than $1 billion* and a delivery model refers to *how* the project is managed to create and capture value (Davies et al., 2019). The special issue articles examined new business model evolution across institutions (Hall & Scott, 2019), technologies (Whyte, 2019), and routines (Bygballe & Swärd, 2019) and delivery model governance choices (Eriksson et al., 2019; Solheim-Kile et al., 2019). However, what was missing from this work was consideration of delivery model behavior. In particular, the notion that some delivery models are designed with flexibility in mind, as a VoD facilitating innovative action in response to unforeseen uncertainties.

Hirschman's VoD principle conceptualizes the implementation of a project as a journey, "setting sail for a destination (perhaps an unattainable one) but arriving in the event at quite a different one (perhaps much more important than the imagined one)" (Singer, 1969, p. 23). Despite this, Hirschman argues that it is possible for projects to still be a success, when there is a creative "spirit of enterprise" (Hirschman, 1967, p. 25):

> The forks in the road that the beaten track lures us into ignoring and to exercise the necessary pragmatic judgement in choosing between alternative routes, hoping to escape the predestined ill fate of projects managed according to conventional project management wisdom. (Kreiner, 2020, p. 405)

This perspective reframes project execution as a "pursuit" rather than the accomplishment of a plan (Kreiner, 2020, p. 405). It challenges the notion of project implementation as overseeing a fatalistic course (Adelman, 2013) setup during the early planning and design stage. In fact, Hirschman warns against the "pseudo-imitation" (Hirschman, 1967, p. 20) technique, arising from adopting a flawed assumption that all projects are immutable one-size-fits-all organizational solutions responding to complexity and uncertainty in a similar way. Moreover, he argues that if international development projects are thought of as a "pseudo-comprehensive" program (p. 20), it creates an illusion that failure is caused by departing from regulated routines and the expert advice of bureaucrats and administrators. Instead, he observes that international development projects may be subject to a constellation of uncertainties, with serendipity inspiring learning effects, echoing the proverb "that which does not destroy me, makes me stronger" (Hirschman, 1967, p. 25).

Fundamentally, Hirschman emphasizes the "power of context" (Ika & Söderlund, 2016, p. 933) in guiding responses to deviations from plan. In some contexts, he recognizes that projects might run into trouble because of a turbulent social or political environment, technological supply-side uncertainties, or volatile demand. He also introduces the concept of "latitudes" (Hirschman, 1967; Ika & Söderlund, 2016) to describe how far a project is tightly controlled. At one end of the spectrum, there is *narrow latitude* when the project requires stringent leadership, control, and monitoring. On the other hand, a *broad latitude* project is where plans can be adapted as learning opportunities emerge. At the far end of the spectrum are projects that go beyond adaptation (Ika & Söderlund, 2016) to developing a project environment that fosters novelty. Hirschman labeled this as "trait-making" because there is a sufficiently *broad latitude* to experiment and challenge existing behavioral and institutional structures (Hirschman, 1967, p. 126).

The VoD principle and latitude concepts raise important points about managing projects during deep levels of uncertainty. In response to incertitude, Hirschman warns against judging success based purely on the efficiency of planned delivery. Instead, he recommends explicitly recognizing the value of acquiring new knowledge (Hirschman, 1963; Alacevich, 2014) and creating an environment to foster novel ideas and improvement rather than just doing things differently. This notion of proactive trait-making in broad latitude contexts echoes the sentiments of scholars who emphasize the importance of strategically developing flexible and adaptive capabilities to response to "unknowns" (Loch et al., 2006; Davies et al., 2017a, 2017b; Dougherty, 2017).

In many ways, megaprojects face similar challenges to the broad latitude projects that Hirschman observed. In particular, their scale, the challenge of multiple stakeholders, and long durations. Megaproject research observes that delivery models have an initial front-end planning stage to set its structure and objectives. This is followed by the execution stage organized into design, construct, integrate, and handover to operations (Davies & Brady, 2016a; Davies et al., 2017a). Project risks are viewed as foreseeable uncertainties to be addressed using risk management and contingency planning. However, efforts to identify risks at the start cannot possibly foresee all the changes in technologies, markets, users, and financial requirements that may occur while the project is underway. When projects encounter unforeseeable uncertainties – or "unknown unknowns" – that cannot be predicted at the outset (Loch et al., 2006; Ramasesh & Browning, 2014), traditional risk management techniques encourage efforts to go back to the baseline plan. However, unforeseeable uncertainties may require organizations to change direction (Edmondson, 2012) and engage in innovative learning and parallel trials (Loch et al., 2006). The structural and dynamic effect of exogenous change may combine to influence the transition across the project life cycle (Brady & Davies, 2014; Zerjav et al., 2018). Interwoven interdependencies between project phases may have systemic effects across the whole megaproject. In response to these challenges, new delivery models have been developed that organize specific "dynamic" capabilities enabling flexible and adaptive responses to change (Davies et al., 2017a & 2017b).

In summary, Hirschman was a major proponent of innovation and counseled against trivializing the skills needed when faced with complex and uncertain contexts. The concept of innovation is derived from the Latin verb *innovare*, meaning to introduce something new or to make it better. The VoD principle recognizes the huge potential for applying innovation during execution as well as in the early design stages (Davies, 2017). The concept of latitude recognizes the importance of control and leadership practice as major enablers of performance improvement. However, Hirschman does not elaborate on how the capacity to innovate might be mobilized or how latitudes (control and leadership) should be organized to become drivers of innovation. These points are examined in more depth in the following sections.

Megaproject Capabilities

Many of the classic studies of megaprojects recognize that those responsible for project delivery must strike a balance between routine and innovative action. In their study of North Sea oil and gas projects, Stinchcombe and Heimer (1985) show how they require planned routines when conditions are stable and predictable but rely on innovation when conditions change and new opportunities arise. In their study of NASA's space program, Sayles and Chandler (1971) found that there is a need for a compromise between frozen and flexible planning depending on the conditions encountered. In his study of the Polaris missile program, Sapolsky (1972) introduced the concept of "disciplined flexibility" to show that managers must have the discipline to meet predefined schedules and flexibility to explore innovative possibilities and solve unexpected problems when the project is underway. A more recent study by Lenfle and Loch (2010) finds that "targeted flexibility" provides a solution to the innovation-routine balancing act. Different elements of uncertainty can be broken down into routines for dealing with predictable conditions and innovative, adaptive processes for unforeseeable ones.

Based on research on the management of UK infrastructures conducted between 2005 and 2015, Davies et al. (2017b) distinguish between two contrasting types of delivery models based on the approach to innovation and uncertainty. The traditional delivery model, frequently used to manage UK megaprojects during the 1980s, 1990s, and early 2000s (e.g., Channel Tunnel, Heathrow Express, Swanwick Air Traffic Control, and Jubilee Line Extension), assumed that the uncertainties likely to impact on a project during delivery could be identified up front and addressed in a fixed-price contract. Organizations responsible for delivering the projects resisted introducing new ideas and innovative methods, preferring to rely on established procedures and proven technologies. Efforts were made to freeze the design as early as possible and execute the project as planned, using contingency funds to address risks and foreseen problems while the project was underway. However, when unforeseen events disrupted the projects, disputes over responsibility resulted in legal disputes, cost overruns, and delays.

New delivery models follow the approach adopted on the Heathrow Terminal 5 (T5) project completed in 2008. This used a combination of innovative and flexible processes to incentivize collaborative behaviors needed to respond rapidly to uncertain and changing conditions. Organizations responsible for these projects rely on risk-sharing or risk-bearing contracts with contractors through integrated project teams. By freezing the design progressively, clients are more able to deal with changing requirements and circumstances as they arise during execution. When unforeseeable events do occur, members of integrated project teams are expected to work collaboratively to resolve problems, explore alternatives, and find innovative solutions.

Drawing on the strategy literature (Teece et al., 1997; Eisenhardt & Martin, 2000; Eisenhardt & Sull, 2001), scholars suggest that organizations responsible for delivering large projects need specific "dynamic capabilities" to enable innovation (Brady et al., 2012; Davies et al., 2016a, 2016b; 2017a, 2017b; 2019). These capabilities include strategic processes and simple rules that are assembled and mobilized through the megaproject's delivery model. Longitudinal case-based research on new delivery models identifies five sets of capabilities for balancing routine and innovative action in response to varying degrees of uncertainty (Davies et al., 2017a, 2017b): (1) search capabilities are relied upon to address the uncertainty facing the project during the planning stage and select the best combination of novel ideas, practices, and technologies for dealing with it; (2) adaptive problem-solving capabilities are used to deal with uncertainties encountered during execution; (3) test and trial capabilities help to identify and resolve any risks associated with unproven technologies or new practices prior to their introduction on the project; (4) strategic innovation capabilities are used to exploit the innovative resources of the project supply chain and other parties; (5) balancing capabilities are developed to manage the trade-offs between performing routines in predictable parts of the project and promoting innovation for unpredictable elements.

In summary, megaproject research highlights that the capacity to innovate during the execution of a project is linked to adaptive delivery model architectures balancing trade-offs between routine and innovative action. Strategic capabilities enable search, test and trial, collective problem-solving, and strategic innovation with suppliers. This creates flexibility and adaptability to take advantage of unforeseen events. However, these points have implications for project governance and control. Lenfle and Loch (2017) contend that modern-day projects typically avoid uncertainty, preferring one-size-fits-all phased control practices (e.g., stage-gate reviews) that reward routine execution and budgetary control rather than innovation. Classic studies of project performance, such as Polaris (Sapolsky, 1972), reduce the role of project control frameworks, such as Program Evaluation and Review Technique (PERT), to political window dressing. This literature suggests that when faced with uncertainty and complexity, traditional project control approaches foster bureaucratic architectures that significantly constrain and hinder innovation. The next section examines these points in more depth.

Megaproject Control

Megaproject governance takes place through an architecture of control practices and technologies designed to steer conduct toward a "value system, responsibilities, processes and policies" (Müller 2012, p. 306). The current project management paradigm taught in certified project management programs can be traced back to 1950s America (Hodgson & Cicmil, 2007; Brady et al., 2012; Engwall, 2012). By the 1960s, the ex-industrialist Robert McNamara became the US Secretary of Defense, spearheading the diffusion of cost control techniques to control the performance of large-scale military projects. The McNamara Revolution (Blight & Lang 2005; Lenfle & Loch 2010) led to an overhaul of defense procurement and new contracts were expected to provide detailed budgets and schedules. Performance was controlled using standardized frameworks to monitor and evaluate performance, such as PERT and Critical Path Analysis (CPA). The management of projects emphasized the delivery of plans through sequential stages converging toward predetermined goals.

At the time, these practices were framed as innovations in management science, enabling more robust budgetary control. The creation of work breakdown structures provided a basis to assign accountability for work packages and hold distributed teams to account against cost, schedule, and scope targets (Peck & Scherer, 1962; Johnson et al., 1964). The Project Management Office (PMO) consolidated planning and budgeting information while routinely monitoring cost efficiency against baseline plans. It was claimed that the production of more management control data (costs, schedule estimates, and targets) would improve the quality of decisions, making them appear more rational and objective. These rationalistic approaches viewed project control as a routine activity where the project manager protected baseline plans, so that "outcomes remain safe, strategically aligned and beneficial to stakeholders, as agreed at the time of approval" (Cicmil & Braddon, 2012, p. 222).

Hirschman (1967) disagreed with the view that planning and control innovations, such as cost-benefit benchmarking, would guarantee better project performance. He warned that one-size-fits-all frameworks seeking to manage international development projects as routine endeavours were deeply misguided (Hirschman, 1967, p. 165). Hirschman was not alone. By the late 1950s, several classic studies challenged the assumption that the adoption of planning and control frameworks would automatically lead to better performance. For example, Ackoff (1967) pleaded for research to question the implicit assumption of a positive causal relationship between performance and accounting control systems. Weber (1958, 1969) questioned an oversimplistic view that accounts and economic calculations are always synonymous with more rational decisions. Sapolsky (1972) noted that standardized control frameworks such as PERT could not provide a silver bullet to guarantee project success. Pettigrew (1973, 1979) recognized that meaning and significance is bestowed on accounting systems through organizational processes.

For over fifty years, accounting researchers have studied the dynamics of the relationship between performance and control techniques (Walker, 2016). Much of this research examines how far calculations that claim to enable *better* decisions, actually translate into action. In particular, classic research by Burchell et al. (1980) examines the different roles that calculations can play under conditions of uncertainty and complexity.

The framework in Figure 3.1 describes four different roles of calculations in the giving and receiving of accounts. Starting in the upper left quadrant, it describes a situation where objectives are undisputed and the causation of action is known (low complexity), then decision-making can be supported by using quantified computations. Here probabilistic risk models, performance management metrics, and performance ratios (such as return on investment) act as "answer machines" providing computational responses. Moving clockwise, if causation remains predictable (low

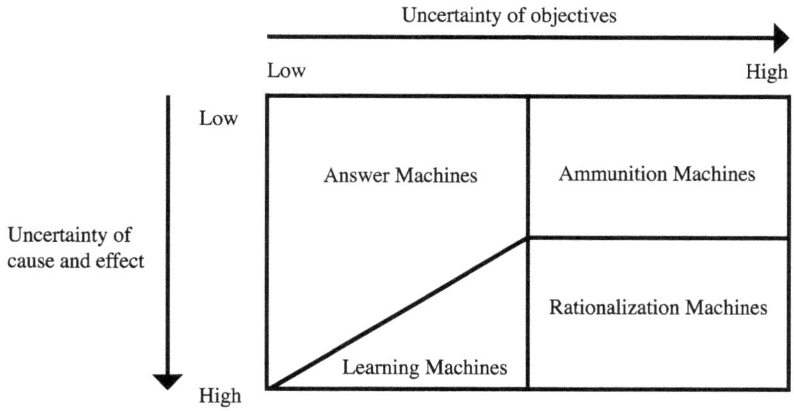

Figure 3.1 Uncertainty and complexity: Roles of calculations.
Source: Burchell et al., 1980, p. 14

complexity) but objectives are not agreed, then the criteria for resource allocation becomes unclear. Here calculative practices become deeply implicated in the bargaining for resources and used as "ammunition machines" to promote political positions (Pettigrew, 1973). If complexity increases and objectives are disputed, calculations become "rationalization machines" to legitimize and justify what has already been decided (ex-post). When objectives are more certain, but causal complexity is still high, calculative practices become sense-making "learning machines" for innovation and experimentation by using them in iterative routines (test, trial, and scenario planning).

This framework sheds light on skepticism about claims that computational practices always have a positive relationship with rational and objective judgment. In particular, Hirschman's disdain for ranking international development projects against uniform computational indices, such as cost-benefit indices, echoes this skepticism. This is because international development projects are inherently uncertain with a high possibility of misbehavior (Hirschman, 1963, 1967). This is explained by Burchell et al.'s (1980) framework, which illustrates that the assumption that computations are always "answer machines," and an objective mirror of reality to enable accurate predictions of performance, is fundamentally flawed. Although international development projects may have clear strategic objectives, such as the enhancement of economic and social progress, there is often causal indeterminacy of how this translates into outcomes. In this context, project execution becomes a VoD, using misbehavior to innovate, experiment, and better understand drivers of performance. This approach resonates with the "learning machines" approach, where calculations are used as tools for learning by testing the parameters of performance.

Megaprojects can also be adversarial settings fraught with competing objectives. Some projects remain turbulent and political, a competing "coalition of interests," (Cyert & March, 1963) where plans, targets, and standards are intentionally used to cynically advance vested interests. Here plans and metrics are used as "ammunition machines" to bargain for resources or "rationalization machines" to justify decisions after they have been taken. Returning to Polaris, Sapolsky (1972) argued that Polaris developed PERT for political purposes (Engwall, 2012) to deter external interference from government bureaucrats. This enabled the Special Projects Office (SPO) to focus on the development of a technological strategy and disciplined flexibility through high-performing autonomous teams. Within this setting, PERT helped to sustain the political support of the Pentagon (Nightingale & Brady, 2012), used as "rationalization machines" (Burchell et al., 1980) that legitimized decisions.

Burchell et al. (1980) argue that calculations govern performance by playing multiple roles. When governance processes engender common objectives, they may inspire learning and innovation. This can create an environment where the project becomes a vehicle for collective problem-solving and the use of common control routines "reduce uncertainty, define focus, and create a foundation for common organizational action" (Engwall, 2012, p. 611). Delivery models make this possible by fostering mutual adjustment, for example, by pledging to avoid legal claims between integrated team members and the full reimbursement of baseline costs (Levitt & Scott, 2017). Risk management literature describes this as a strong risk culture, one that acts upon and processes uncertainties by encouraging interaction and an appetite for new knowledge when unforeseen risks emerge (Power, 2020). This was observed on Heathrow T5 (Vine, 2018). Here a proactive risk management dialogue was encouraged, and team-based endeavours were rewarded. This shifted the focus away from opportunistic behavior and encouraged collaborative problem-solving (Davies et al., 2017a). Echoing Burchell et al. (1980), plans, standards, and metrics were used as learning machines to drive innovative action amongst teams.

The Heathrow T5 delivery model placed the client in a leadership role (Davies et al., 2009), governing progress by purposively rewarding collective inquiry. The client sustained disciplined flexibility (Sapolsky, 1972) by balancing the contradictory demands of capitalizing on existing knowledge with flexible responses to unexpected situations (Davies et al., 2016b). The Heathrow T5 example raises important questions about the role that leadership should play in other complex and uncertain megaproject settings, particularly when leading distributed teams in a way that continues to inspire innovation while mitigating risk averse behaviors and anxieties that may emerge when teams are faced with deep levels of incertitude. These points are more fully examined in the next section.

Leadership in Megaprojects

Traditionally, project leadership literature assumes that the project manager knows what is best for the project (Cleland, 1995; Lundy & Morin, 2013; Aga et al., 2016; Maqbool et al., 2017; Damayanti et al., 2021; Drouin et al., 2021) and they engage in heroic efforts to optimize project delivery by drawing on specific combinations of leadership skills and behaviors (Wan et al., 2020; Damayanti et al., 2021; Drouin et al., 2021). This idea of optimization can arguably be traced to the tendency of the project management literature to position the project manager as the "optimizer," a rational, goal-driven agent that systematically produces and executes a delivery plan (Brady et al., 2012). It is also consistent with the mainstream leadership literature that positions individuals in senior positions as agents with oversight responsibility who have access to the required level of information and expertise to determine the right course of action (Tourish, 2020). This is not to say that individuals in senior positions should not guide project teams toward solutions, but rather, when examining project leadership, it is important to recognize that megaprojects are notoriously unpredictable and leadership activities play a key role in actively shaping both situational demands and responses (Grint, 2005).

Hirschman (1967) makes a distinction between narrow and broad latitude projects, where the former inspires directive forms of leadership and the latter a shared spirit of enterprise. In a similar vein, leadership scholars also recognize that deeply uncertain contexts need collective inquiry, shifting the role of leadership from one that *provides* answers to one that *asks* questions (Grint, 2005, 2020). This may require moving beyond the idea of sharing leadership by temporarily transferring leadership to another team member (Müller et al., 2018a, 2018b, Scott-Young et al., 2019), toward one that facilitates collective inquiry (Grint, 2005). However, regardless of whether collective inquiry is orchestrated by an individual in a senior position or through informal leadership or self-organization (Bolden et al., 2009), it needs to be accompanied by the recognition that debates on uncertain problems can become problematic if timely closure cannot be achieved and there are delays in responding to urgent situations (Grint, 2005, 2020). Furthermore, inquiry into unexpected events across organizational boundaries may give rise to the emergence of competing vested interests (Anheier, 2016) resulting in distracting, destabilizing or destroying of valuable contributions (Clegg et al., 2021; Whyte et al., 2022). These observations echo Hirschman's observations about the power of a project's context and the need for flexible forms of leadership able to adapt to broad or narrow latitude settings. For example, transformational leadership is a popular approach that creates an illusion of control in order to reinforce the discourse sponsored by senior managers (Tourish & Vatcha, 2005). This can be combined with "constructive dissent" strategies to encourage enterprising individuals to contribute to shaping the way forward in a helpful way (Grint, 2010).

Although Hirschman (1963, 1967) recognized the important link between project context and governance responses, he did not elaborate on how the work of leadership might be accomplished. Here the theoretical traditions of ambidextrous leadership and paradoxical leadership offer useful insights into how to best balance the contradictory demands of maintaining predictable conditions and developing flexible responses. They suggest that an individual in a senior position should actively switch between directive and participative behavior (Denison et al., 1995; Rosing et al., 2011) that the exploration of innovative possibilities can be combined with the exploitation of past routines (Klonek et al., 2021; Lawrence et al., 2021), and that contradictory demands can be mitigated by distributed leadership work (Smith, 2014; Knight & Cuganesan, 2020). Notwithstanding their value, these theories remain surprisingly silent on how to cope with the vulnerabilities of collective inquiry across organizational, professional, or group boundaries when faced with deep levels of incertitude. Moreover, their translation into the project management literature tends to privilege the project manager's behavior (Buchanan & Boddy, 1992; Aubry & Lièvre, 2010) and interactions with team members (Havermans et al., 2015).

Complexity leadership theories go much further by suggesting that leadership should respond to the dual demands of enabling innovative responses and maintaining predictable conditions. Research describes how complexity leadership can play a central role in shaping tensions to trigger collective search for alternative solutions (Marion & Uhl-bien, 2001; Uhl-bien & Arena, 2017). It posits that multiple individuals may catalyze the emergence of innovative solutions and connect them to operational improvements through various mediators such as simple rules, standards, and targets. Unfortunately, not only is there a relative neglect of these ideas within traditional project management literature, but also their translation into project settings typically reproduces the tradition of identifying the skills and behaviors of the project manager in coping with uncertainty (Remington, 2011).

In summary, project management research has traditionally taken a reductionist approach to leadership, in terms of its tendency to focus on the attributes of the project manager as a rational goal-driven agent focused on delivering the optimal course of action. However, in megaprojects, scale combines with complexity to create volatile and uncertain project behavior. The VoD principle encourages scholars and practitioners to acknowledge the importance of responding to unpredictability with leadership approaches that foster a shared spirit of enterprise in response to unforeseen "forks in the road" (Kreiner, 2020, p. 405). In this setting, complexity and paradoxical and ambidextrous leadership research offers practical insights into how leadership can strike a balance between innovative and routine responses. However, far more research is required to understand how to best do this in a way that draws on the worldviews of a broad range of actors while maintaining timely closure.

Toward a Comprehensive Understanding of Megaproject Behavior

Traditional project management literature reduces project execution to a bureaucratic activity (Lenfle & Loch, 2010) that emphasizes the importance of regulation and associates project failure with the project manager not following the plan and ignoring the advice of project administrators (Kreiner, 2020). In contrast, the VoD principle recognizes the huge potential for applying innovation across the whole project life cycle, during execution as well as the early design stages. The concept of latitude (Hirschman, 1967) differentiates between regulated projects and projects that can accommodate more flexibility. From a project behavior perspective, these theoretical concepts underline the importance of understanding the specific context of a megaproject while treating project execution as a learning journey (Ika & Söderlund, 2016; Ika et al., 2022). In addition to coping with complexity, scale, long duration, and multiple stakeholders, uncertainty is also a major challenge. Hirschman (1967) conceptualizes uncertainty as the propensity for project misbehavior and latitude as the ability of project leadership to mold and direct a project (Ika & Söderlund, 2016). At the furthest end of the spectrum are the "trait-makers" (Hirschman, 1967, p. 121) responding to incertitude by challenging the status quo.

This chapter describes how megaproject delivery models adopt risk management techniques to manage known contingencies. This is augmented with dynamic capabilities that enable disciplined responses to unforeseen uncertainty. Project delivery models orchestrate this by carefully developing sophisticated search and learning routines. To accommodate unforeseen opportunities, balancing capabilities facilitate switching between routine and innovative responses. However, balancing does not happen automatically. It is only possible when control and leadership practices combine to encourage flexible responses. This requires control frameworks that position plans, standards, and metrics as learning machines (Burchell et al., 1980) and leadership practices to integrate supplier interests (Grint, 2005, 2020). Research describes how delivery models play a critical role in ensuring that capabilities, control, and leadership work together. For example, the Heathrow T5 delivery model placed the client in an oversight role acting as the systems integrator (Davies et al., 2009). This encouraged team interaction, common purpose, and mutual adjustment (Vine, 2020). Leadership and control architectures were modified to sustain an appetite for discovery among suppliers using governance mechanisms (incentives, team-based rewards) to carefully balance trade-offs between risks and opportunities (Davies et al., 2017a, 2017b; Vine, 2018).

This research reveals that some megaprojects can successfully navigate *both* complexity and uncertainty. It opens a debate about how far capabilities, control, and leadership can be organized to *drive* innovation rather than just *responding* to it. This is important because Hirschman's trait-makers *respond* to unforeseen opportunities with novel solutions that challenge existing behavioral and institutional structures. Furthermore, the VoD principle focuses on improvised creative *responses* that stimulate valuable payoffs. However, in this chapter, we extend these ideas further by examining how megaproject delivery models are deliberately designed to improve project performance by systematically switching between innovative and routine action (Davies, et al., 2017b). This may need a different type of balancing capability focused on sustaining common purpose. Striking this delicate balance can be difficult because structural and dynamic complexity (Brady & Davies, 2014) may mean that small changes result in amplified systemic effects that significantly destabilize progress. Moreover, fears of spiraling out of control can exacerbate commercial tensions (Davies, et al., 2016b).

Balancing the trade-offs between executing existing plans and innovation when faced with deep levels of incertitude requires delivery models that are sensitive to the destabilizing effects of rapid change. However, there is a substantive gap in studies of megaproject leadership and control that address these seemingly contradictory demands. The leadership approaches that have been neglected, such as complexity leadership, paradoxical leadership, and ambidextrous leadership offer important entry points to address this gap. More research is required in this area – research that explicitly considers the distinct features of temporary organizing (Bakker et al., 2016) to develop theories that are adequate for leading in a megaproject setting. Further megaproject control research is also needed to examine the multiples roles (Burchell, 1980; Power, 2020) that calculations might play to inspire discovery and reposition deviations from plan as opportunities for improvement rather than indicators of failure.

In summary, this chapter develops a more comprehensive picture of project behavior when faced with complexity and uncertainty. It fundamentally moves away from positioning project governance (control and leadership) in opposition to innovation as a dualism that cannot exist in the same setting. Instead, it echoes the sentiment of the Fifth Hand (Ika et al., 2022), which acknowledges that on a practical level, managing project performance may require a broad range of different responses to accommodate changes in scope, complexity, risk, and unexpected "surprises down the road" (Ika et al., 2022, p. 3320). Further research is now needed that breaks delivery models down into the distinct roles of a sponsor, client, suppliers, and/or delivery organizations. This should deepen our understanding of the situated context enabling delivery model innovation. Methodologically, we also recommend in-depth case study research that carefully observes the "actuality of projects" (Cicmil et al., 2006; Ika & Söderlund, 2016) by immersing the researcher in a delivery model context and studying the actual performance of roles.

Conclusion

In conclusion, this chapter uses Hirschman's Voyage of Discovery principle to examine how project misbehavior might provide an opportunity for improved performance. To do this, we examine new delivery model architectures in megaprojects that successfully take advantage of opportunities for innovation during the execution of a project. This research reveals the importance of balancing capabilities that switch between routine and innovative action as well as control and leadership practices that settle tensions, reward learning, and inspire discovery. These points reveal that control and leadership can be viewed as complementary drivers of innovation alongside capabilities rather than crowding innovation out. However, further project-based research is needed to examine ambidexterity and complexity leadership as well as the multiple roles that project control practices might inspire when engaging different parties through megaproject delivery models.

References

Ackoff, R. L. (1967). Management misinformation systems. *Management Science*, *14*(4), 147–156.

Adelman, J. (2013). *Worldly philosopher: The essential Hirschman*. Economics Books.

Aga, D. A., Noorderhaven, N., and Vallejo, B. (2016). Transformational leadership and project success: The mediating role of team-building. *International Journal of Project Management*, *34*(5), 806–818.

Alacevich, M. (2014). Visualizing uncertainties, or how Albert Hirschman and the world bank disagreed on project appraisal and what this says about the end of "high development theory." *Journal of the History of Economic Thought*, *36*(2), 137–168.

Anheier, H. K. (2016). Of hiding hands and other ways of coping with uncertainty: A commentary. *Social Research*, *83*(4), 1005–1010.

Aubry, M., and Lièvre, P. (2010). Ambidexterity as a competence of project leaders: A case study from two polar expeditions. *Project Management Journal*, *41*(3), 32–44.

Bakker, R. M., DeFillippi, R. J., Schwab, A., and Sydow, J. (2016). *Organization Studies*, *37*(12), 1703–1719.

Blight, J. G., and Lang, J. M. (2005). *The fog of war: Lessons from the life of Robert S. McNamara*. Rowman & Littlefield.

Bolden, R., Petrov, G., and Gosling, J. (2009). Distributed leadership in higher education: Rhetoric and reality. *Educational Management Administration & Leadership*, *37*(2), 257–277.

Brady, T., and Davies, A. (2010). Learning to deliver a mega-project: The case of Heathrow Terminal 5 (pp. 190–212). In N. Caldwell and M. Howard (eds.). *Procuring Complex Performance*. Routledge.

Brady, T., and Davies, A. (2014). Managing structural and dynamic complexity: A tale of two projects. *Project Management Journal*, *45*(4), 21–38.

Brady, T., Davies, A., Nightingale, P., Söderland, J., and Geraldi, J. (2012). Dealing with uncertainty in complex projects: Revisiting Klein and Meckling. *International Journal of Managing Projects in Business*, *5*(4), 718–736.

Buchanan, D., and Boddy, D. (1992). *The expertise of the change agent: Public performance and backstage activity*. Prentice Hall International.

Burchell, S., Clubb, C., Hopwood, A., Hughes, J., and Nahapiet, J. (1980). The roles of accounting in organizations and society. *Accounting, Organizations and Society*, *5*(1), 5–27.

Bygballe, L. E., and Swärd, A. (2019). Collaborative project delivery models and the role of routines in institutionalizing partnering. *Project Management Journal*, *50*(2), 161–176.

Cicmil, S., and Braddon, D. (2012). Fading glory? Decision-making around the project – how and why "glory" projects fail (pp. 221–255). In T. M. Williams and K. Samset (eds.). *Project Governance*. Palgrave Macmillan.

Cicmil, S., Williams, T., Thomas, J., and Hodgson, D. (2006). Rethinking project management: Researching the actuality of projects. *International Journal of Project Management*, *24*(8), 675–686.

Clegg, S. R., Skyttermoen, T., and Vaagassar, A. L. (2021). *Project management: A value creation approach*. Sage.

Cleland, D. I. (1995). Leadership and the project-management body of knowledge. *International Journal of Project Management*, *13*(2), 83–88.

Cyert, R. M., and March, J. G. (1963). *A Behavioral Theory of the Firm*. Prentice Hall.

Damayanti, R., Hartono, B., and Wijaya, A. (2021). Complexity, leadership, and mega project performance: A configuration analysis. *Journal of Industrial Engineering and Management*, *14*(3), 570–603.

Davies, A., (2017). *Projects: A very short introduction*. Oxford University Press.

Davies, A., Gann, D., and Douglas, T. (2009). Innovation in megaprojects: Systems integration at London Heathrow Terminal 5. *California Management Review*, *51*(2), 101–125.

Davies, A., and Brady, T. (2016a). Explicating the dynamics of project capabilities. *International Journal of Project Management*, *34*(2), 314–327.

Davies, A., Dodgson, M., and Gann, D. (2016b). Dynamic capabilities for a complex project: The case of London Heathrow Terminal 5. *Project Management Journal*, Special Issue: Innovation and Project Management: Bridging Contemporary Trends in Theory and Practice, *34*, 314–327.

Davies, A., Dodgson, M., Gann., D., and MacAulay, S. (2017). Five rules for managing large, complex projects. *MIT Sloan Management Review*, *59*(1), 73–78.

Davies, A., Dodgson, M., and Gann., D. (2017). Innovation and flexibility in megaprojects: A new delivery model (pp. 313–339). In B. Flyvbjerg (ed.). *The Oxford handbook of megaproject Management*. Oxford University Press.

Davies, A., MacAulay, S., and Brady, T. (2019). Delivery model innovation: Insights from infrastructure projects. Special Issue: Innovation in infrastructure delivery models, *Project Management Journal*, *50*(2), 1–9.

Denison, D. R., Hoojberg, R., and Quinn, R. E. (1995). Paradox and performance: Toward a theory of behavioral complexity in managerial leadership. *Organization Science*, 6(5), 524–540.

Dougherty, D. (2017). Taking advantage of emergence for complex innovation eco-systems. *Journal of Open Innovation: Technology, Market, and Complexity*, *3*(3), 14.

Drouin, N., Sankaran, S., van Marrewijk, A., and Müller, R. (2021). *Megaproject leaders: Reflections on personal life stories*. Edward Elgar.

Edmondson, A. (2012). *Teaming: How organizations learn, innovate, and compete in the knowledge economy*. Wiley.

Eisenhardt, K. M., and Martin, J. A. (2000). Dynamic capabilities: What are they? *Strategic Management Journal*, *21*, 1105–1121.

Eisenhardt, K. M., and Sull, D. N. (2001). Strategy as simple rules. *Harvard Business Review* January, 107–116.

Engwall, M. (2012). PERT, Polaris, and the realities of project execution. *International Journal of Managing Projects in Business*, *5*(4), 595–616.

Eriksson, K., Wikström, K., Hellström, M., and Levitt, R. E. (2019). Projects in the business ecosystem: The case of short sea shipping and logistics. *Project Management Journal*, *50*(2), 195–209.

Grint, K. (2005). Problems, problems, problems: The social construction of "leadership." *Human Relations*, *58*(11), 1467–1494.

Grint, K. (2010). Wicked problems and clumsy solutions: The role of leadership (pp. 169–186). In S. Brookes and K. Grint (eds.). *The new public leadership challenge*. Palgrave MacMillan.

Grint, K. (2020). Leadership, management and command in the time of the Coronavirus. *Leadership*, *16*(3), 314–319.

Hall, D. M., and Scott, W. R. (2019). Early stages in the institutionalization of integrated project delivery. *Project Management Journal*, *50*(2), 128–143.

Havermans, L. A., Den Hartog, D. N., Keegan, A., and Uhl-Bien, M. (2015). Exploring the role of leadership in enabling contextual ambidexterity.

Human Resource Management, 54(S1), 179–200.

Hirschman, A. O. (1963). *Journeys towards progress observed.* The 20th Century Fund.

Hirschman, A. O. (1967). *Development projects observed.* Reissued in 1995. The Brookings Institution.

Hodgson, D., and Cicmil, S. (2007). The politics of standards in modern management: Making "the project" a reality. *Journal of Management Studies, 44*(3), 431–450.

Ika, L. A. (2018). Beneficial or detrimental ignorance: The straw man fallacy of Flyvbjerg's test of Hirschman's hiding hand. *World Development, 103*, 369–382.

Ika, L. A., Love, P. E., and Pinto, J. K. (2022). Moving beyond the planning fallacy: The emergence of a new principle of project behavior. *IEEE Transactions on Engineering Management, 69*(6), 3310–3325.

Ika, L. A., and Söderlund, J. (2016). Rethinking revisited: Insights from an early rethinker. *International Journal of Managing Projects in Business, 9*(4), 931–954.

Johnson, R. A., Kast, F. E., and Rosenzweig, J. E. (1964). Systems theory and management. *Management Science, 10*(2), 367–384.

Klonek, F. E., Volery, T., and Parker, S. K. (2021). Managing the paradox: Individual ambidexterity, paradoxical leadership and multitasking in entrepreneurs across firm lifecycle stages. *International Small Business Journal: Researching Entrepreneurship, 39*(1), 40–63.

Knight, E., and Cuganesan, S. (2020). Enabling organisational ambidexterity: Valuation practices and the senior-leadership team. *Human Relations, 73*(2), 190–214.

Kreiner, K. (2020). Conflicting notions of a project: The battle between Albert O. Hirschman and Bent Flyvbjerg. *Project Management Journal, 51*(4), 400–410.

Lawrence, E. T., Tworoger, L., Ruppel, C. P., and Yurova, Y. (2021). TMT leadership ambidexterity: Balancing exploration and exploitation behaviors for innovation. *European Journal of Innovation Management, 25*(3), 703–719.

Lenfle, S., and Loch, C. (2010). Lost roots: How project management came to emphasize control over flexibility and novelty. *Californian Management Review, 53*(1), 32–55.

Lenfle, S., and Loch, C. (2017). Has megaproject management lost its way? Lessons from history (pp. 21–38). In B. Flyvbjerg (ed.). *Oxford handbook of megaproject management.* Oxford University Press.

Levitt, R. E., and Scott, R. S. (2017). Institutional challenges and solutions for global megaprojects (pp. 96–117). In B. Flyvbjerg (ed.). *Oxford handbook of megaproject management.* Oxford University Press.

Loch, C., De Meyer, A., and Pich, M. (2006). *Managing the unknown: A new approach to managing high uncertainty and risk in projects.* Wiley.

Lundy, V., and Morin, P. P. (2013). Project leadership influences resistance to change: The case of the Canadian public service. *Project Management Journal, 44*(4), 45–64.

Maqbool, R., Sudong, Y., Manzoor, N., and Rashid, Y. (2017). The impact of emotional intelligence, project managers' competencies, and transformational leadership on project success: An empirical perspective. *Project Management Journal, 48*(3), 58–75.

Marion, R., and Uhl-bien, M. (2001). Leadership in complex organizations. *The Leadership Quarterly, 12*(4), 389–418.

Müller, R. (2012). Project governance (pp. 297–320). In P. Morris, J. Pinto, and J. Söderlund (eds.). *The Oxford handbook of project management.* Oxford University Press.

Müller, R., Zhu, F., Sun, X., Wang, L., and Yu, M. (2018a). The identification of temporary horizontal leaders in projects: The case of China. *International Journal of Project Management, 36*(1), 95–107.

Müller, R., Sankaran, S., Drouin, N., Vaagaasar, A.-L., Bekker, M. C., and Jain, K. (2018b). A theory framework for balancing vertical and horizontal leadership in projects. *International Journal of Project Management, 36*(1), 83–94.

Nightingale, P., and Brady T. (2012). Projects, paradigms and predictability (pp. 83–112). In G. Cattani, S. Ferriani, L. Frederiksen, and F. Täube (eds.). *Project-based organizing and strategic management – advances in strategic management.* Emerald Group.

Peck, M. J., and Scherer, F. M. (1962). The weapons acquisition process: An economic analysis. *IEEE Transactions on Engineering Management,* 1, 51–52.

Pettigrew, A. M. (1973). *The politics of organizational decision-making.* Tavistock.

Pettigrew, A. M. (1979). On studying organizational cultures. *Administrative Science Quarterly*, 24(4), 570–581.

Picciotto, R. (2015), Hirschman's ideas as evaluation tools. *Journal of Multidisciplinary Evaluation*, 11(24), 1–11.

Power, M. (2020) Risk culture and information culture: Why an "appetite for knowledge' matter (pp. 42–72). In M. Tuveson, D. Ralph, K. Alexander (eds.). *Beyond bad apples: Risk culture in business*. Cambridge University Press.

Ramasesh, R. V., and Browning, T. (2014). A conceptual framework for tackling knowable unknown unknowns in project management. *Journal of Operations Management*, *32*, 190–204.

Remington, K. (2011). *Leading complex projects*. Gower.

Rosing, K., Frese, M., and Bausch, A. (2011). Explaining the heterogeneity of the leadership-innovation relationship: Ambidextrous leadership. *The Leadership Quarterly*, *22*(5), 956–974.

Sapolsky, H. M. (1972). *The Polaris system development: Bureaucratic and programmatic success in government*. Harvard University Press.

Sayles, L., and Chandler, M. K. (1971). *Managing large systems*. The Free Press.

Scott, W. R., and Meyer, J. W. (1994). *Institutional environments and organizations: Structural complexity and individualism*. Sage.

Scott-Young, C. M., Georgy, M., and Grisinger, A. (2019) Shared leadership in project teams: An integrative multi-level conceptual model and research agenda. *International Journal of Project Management*, *37*(4), 565–581.

Shenhar, A. J., and Dvir, D. (2007). Reinventing project management: The diamond approach to successful growth and innovation. Harvard Business Review Press.

Singer, H. W. (1969), Albert O. Hirschman: Development projects observed. *Institute of Development Studies Bulletin*, *1*(3), 22–25.

Smith, W. K. (2014). Dynamic decision making: A model of senior leaders managing strategic paradoxes. *The Academy of Management Journal*, *57*(6), 1592–1623.

Solheim-Kile, E., Lædre, O., and Lohne, J. (2019). Public-Private Partnerships: Agency Costs in the Privatization of Social Infrastructure Financing. *Project Management Journal*, *50*(2), 144–160.

Stinchcombe, A. L., and Heimer, C. A. (1985). *Organization theory and project management: Administering uncertainty in Norwegian offshore oil*. Norwegian University Press.

Teece, D. J., Pisano, G., and Shuen, A. (1997). Dynamic capabilities and strategic management. *Strategic Management Journal*, *18*(7), 509–533.

Tourish, D. (2020). Introduction to the special issue: Why the coronavirus crisis is also a crisis of leadership. *Leadership*, *16*(3), 261–272.

Tourish, D., and Vatcha, N. (2005). Charismatic leadership and corporate cultism at Enron: The elimination of dissent, the promotion of conformity and organisational collapse. *Leadership*, *1*(4), 455–480.

Uhl-bien, M., and Arena, M. (2017). Complexity leadership: Enabling people and organizations for adaptability. *Organizational Dynamics*, *46*(1), 9–20.

Vine, R. (2018). The intelligent client: Learning to govern through numbers at Heathrow Airport. Thesis, University of Sussex.

Vine, R. (2020). Riskwork in the construction of Heathrow Terminal 2. SPRU Working Paper Series 2020-20, 1–38.

Walker, S. P. (2016). Revisiting the roles of accounting in society. *Accounting, Organizations and Society*, 49, 41–50.

Wan, J., Le, Y., Wang, G., Xia, N., and Liu, X. (2020). Carrot or stick? The impact of paternalistic leadership on the behavioral integration of top management teams in megaprojects. *International Journal of Managing Projects in Business*, *13*(5), 937–960.

Weber, M. (1958). *The Protestant ethic and the spirit of capitalism*. Charles Scribner's Sons.

Weber, M. (1969). *Economy and society*, 3 vols. Bedminster Press.

Whyte, J. (2019). How digital information transforms project delivery models. *Project Management Journal*, *50*(2), 177–194.

Whyte, J., Naderpajouh, N., Clegg, S., Matous, P., Pollack, J., and Crawford, L. (2022). Project leadership: A research agenda for a changing world. *Project Leadership and Society*, *3*.

Zerjav, V., Edkins, A., and Davies, A. (2018). Project capabilities for operational outcomes in inter-organisational settings: The case of London Heathrow Terminal 2. *International Journal of Project Management*, *36*(3), 444–459.

CHAPTER 4

Temporal Structuring and Project Behavior

ANN LANGLEY and GERRY MCGIVERN

Over 25 years ago, Lundin and Söderholm (1995) outlined the elements of a theory of temporary organization that has become particularly influential in the project management literature. They argued that four concepts – time, task, team, and transition – and their interrelationships were key to theorizing about temporary forms of organizing. They placed "time" at the heart of their framework because of the centrality of temporal boundaries (beginnings, middles, and ends) in distinguishing temporary forms of organization from ongoing concerns (see also Bakker, 2010; Burke & Morley, 2016; Whyte & Nussbaum, 2020) and because of the way in which the three remaining elements in their framework are shaped by these temporal boundaries. Thus, "task" refers to the activities to be accomplished within those boundaries and constitutes the raison-d'être of the project. "Team" refers to the people involved in project tasks. The notion of "transition" refers to qualitative differences (between before and after) produced by the temporary organization (Lundin & Söderholm, 1995, p. 439).

Lundin and Söderholm (1995) further elaborated on the time dimension of temporary organizations by considering sequential activities that accompany progression from the beginning to the middle and the end of a project. According to the authors, these involve entrepreneurialism to get projects started (beginning); decoupling, task partitioning, planning, and guarding to manage their execution (middle); and finally, recoupling, institutionalization, and bridging to complete the transition to more permanent structures (end).

The centrality of time to project organizing is also clearly evident in the prescriptive literature on project management, represented by the classic planning tools such as critical path methods, Gantt charting and stage-gate processes, as well as in more contemporary practices such as Agile and Scrum, and variations thereof (Gemino et al., 2021; Project Management Institute, 2017). While traditional project management tools adopt a predictive approach characterized by schedules and deadlines, more recent formal methodologies allow increased flexibility in adjusting tasks to unforeseen developments but nevertheless prescribe rhythmic work patterns involving repetitive cycles of coordinated effort and feedback.

In other words, project management necessarily embeds some form of "temporal work" defined, following Bansal et al. (2022), as any individual, collective, or organizational effort to influence, reinforce, or redirect the temporal assumptions or structures that shape action. In practical terms, formal temporal structures may include schedules, event-based targets, time horizons, and prescribed rhythms. Less explicit temporal assumptions that may nevertheless orient organizational action could include, for example, taken-for-granted norms and practices embedded in particular organizational and cultural settings (e.g., norms concerning the degree of tardiness expected and allowed) (Orlikowski & Yates, 2002; Vaagaasar et al., 2020).

Yet, despite the recognized importance of time and temporality in project work, Burke and Morley (2016) suggest that there is a need for greater attention to temporal structuring and its role in orienting behavior in temporary organizations. Recent work in both the specialized project management literature (e.g., Vaagaasar et al., 2020; Whyte & Nussbaum, 2020; Kalff, 2022; Nachbagauer, 2022) and in the wider organization studies and management literature (e.g., Bakker et al., 2013; McGivern et al., 2018; Blagoev &

Schreyogg, 2019; Kremser & Blagoev, 2021; Lifshitz-Assaf et al., 2021) has begun to move in this direction. However, we have not seen concerted attempts to synthesize the cumulative learning from these studies. The purpose of the current chapter is therefore to address these shortcomings in the existing literature on time and temporality in projects. Specifically, we ask: *How do the temporal structures and assumptions associated with project tasks influence project behaviors?* By project behaviors, we refer here to the ways in which participants engage with projects, and how they then play out to produce outcomes, a definition that is close to, though not identical with, that suggested by Ika et al. (2022).

Indeed, we know that a wide variety of options for temporal structuring may exist depending on the nature of the project and the temporal work of participants and stakeholders. For example, while some projects (e.g., putting on the Olympic games) may have apparently immutable deadlines that everyone will work to respect (Pitsis et al., 2003), other projects (e.g., eradicating an infectious disease, developing radical innovation), though influenced by time pressure, may lack fixed clock-time targets or repeatedly violate them because of inherent uncertainties. Their endpoints are desired states that are temporally open-ended and that can only be fully apprehended as they are approached. Gustavsson and Hallin (2015) label such projects as "goal-seeking" rather than "goal-oriented." In addition, some projects may have short and well-defined time horizons (the writing of this chapter), while others – notably megaprojects – may have extended lifecycles that extend well beyond many so-called permanent organizations (Brookes et al., 2017).

As we see from these examples, issues of temporality are clearly dependent on and intertwined with the nature of the project task. Moreover, there can also be many uncertainties associated with both dimensions. The nature of the task may be influenced by the temporal structures that frame it, and the temporal structures developed may be influenced by the nature of the task. In addition, it is important to consider the "team" (or "who") dimension as well: consensus, conflict, and politics may also influence the temporal and task dimensions and their consequences for project behavior, enhancing ambiguities.

We organize our review in this chapter around three main headings. First, we review studies that examine project behaviors in contexts of "temporal closure" where overarching temporal structures are tightly constraining and immutable. Second, we examine project behaviors in situations of "temporal ambiguity," where the task defines the desired endpoint, or where other factors such as environmental uncertainty or political influence loosen the link between task and time and potentially enact tensions and accommodation between the two. The working hypothesis driving the organization of the chapter is that the degree of temporal closure or temporal ambiguity can make a difference to project behaviors. In the third section of the chapter, we draw on the findings in the prior sections to suggest an agenda for future research.

Temporal Closure: Fitting Task to Time

Project management from a traditional perspective involves the creation of artifacts in the form of time lines that indicate which tasks will be carried out by whom and when. As Yakura (2002) shows, building on Hassard (1991), time lines as "boundary objects" generally serve three functions inherent to project management: scheduling (i.e., indicating when the overall task or subtasks will be completed), synchronizing (i.e., coordinating the work of interdependent people), and allocating (i.e., managing resources – notably human resources – allocated to tasks). A time line is a future oriented "narrative" that, by projecting who will do what when orients action – in other words, it is performative, channeling actors into certain roles and activities and creating accountabilities that influence behavior in ways that help to enact the timeline (Deuten & Rip, 2000; Yakura, 2002).

As Yakura (2002) also shows, and as Kalff (2022) points out, project managers are both custodians of time lines, sustaining their role in disciplining project activities, but also nevertheless engage in revising them continually and on the fly to deal with inevitable and unexpected task contingencies. According to Kalff (2022), this is the essence of project management. It explains, in part, how and why projects appear to be "organized" and do not for the most part descend into complete chaos, while almost never playing out as planned, and often violating projected deadlines. We will revisit situations of temporal ambiguity in more detail later.

However, in some cases, temporal structures are less malleable, and deadlines appear to be fixed and immutable – a situation we refer to as "temporal closure" (e.g., see the examples given above). How then do people deal with these situations, notably when task uncertainties persist? A first interesting and basic contribution to this question comes from Gersick's (1988) study of eight naturally occurring task groups, subsequently replicated in a laboratory experiment (Gersick, 1989). It is important to note that the naturally occurring groups Gersick (1988) studied were clearly engaged in "projects" oriented around designing something new, but they were not officially guided by formal project management techniques and their time lines were quite short (from seven days to six months). The groups did however have clear deadlines that in most cases were not flexible.

Moreover, it is evident from Gersick's (1988, 1989) findings that these deadlines were very important in orienting the task behaviors of participants. Specifically, the author found that the groups started their lives by committing to a particular approach to the task, but precisely in the middle of their allocated time span, they engaged in a "mid-point transition," taking stock of where they had been and reorienting their task approach (often quite radically) in order to successfully meet their deadline. Subsequent studies (Okhuysen & Waller, 2002; Waller et al., 2002) have confirmed the presence of midpoint transitions in many, though not all, cases of groupwork, suggesting that their presence may be contingent on certain other conditions surrounding the group (e.g., familiarity among members).

Nevertheless, all these studies tend to support the intuition that deadlines tend to concentrate the mind and that time markers such as a midpoint may make them more salient and provide an important opportunity to shift gears when this is needed to deliver the task. The power of temporal structuring through the use of deadlines and other temporal markers has been underlined in other studies. For example, Lindkvist et al. (1998) revealed how tight deadlines for new product delivery at Ericsson stimulated the firm to develop a novel mode of temporal structuring (the "fountains model") in which key activities were scheduled in parallel rather than sequentially. This project management innovation subsequently spread and has contributed to speeding up product development.

In a study of large-scale transformation efforts, Söderlund (2010) confirms the power of deadlines and milestones in stimulating participants to engage in knowledge integration at key moments in order to deliver results. Similarly, Söderlund and Pemsel (2022) investigated the introduction of digital design methods to a construction firm and revealed how a form of temporal structuring based on deadlines and a rigid "no design time" window created greater temporal consciousness among participants, enabling them to organize future work as a function of past progress, current needs, and upcoming temporal milestones. Yet the study also revealed how the success of this initiative also required the creation of new managerial roles dedicated to ensuring coordination and conformity to novel temporal structures.

Temporal closure enacted in deadlines and milestones clearly orient project behavior, often in positive ways, as shown by many of these studies. And yet, various contingencies may make them difficult to meet, suggesting a need for flexibility. Vaagasar (2020) points out that as deadlines approach, temporal shifts in the organization of activities become increasingly difficult to make. This suggests a need for continued attention to situated temporal orientations among participants as a project evolves, rather than a rigid focus on implementing preconceived plans.

Along these lines, one might ask what happens when projects are complex and time spans become extended, albeit still with essentially immutable deadlines. The planning of regularly scheduled events such as international exhibitions, academic conferences, or the Olympic games fall into this category. The evidence tends to suggest that the management of large and complex mega-events with fixed deadlines can often be highly problematic, with a tendency toward large cost overruns (Müller, 2015; Flyvbjerg et al., 2021). For example, for the Olympic games, Flyvbjerg et al. (2021) note that uncertainties caused by long lead-times, combined with the inexorability of deadlines, and the limited possibility of adjusting the quality of deliverables (task inflexibility) create severe cost pressures leading to an average cost overrun of 172 percent. Within such long time lines, unexpected contingencies are likely to derail tightly formulated plans and may well require budgetary adjustments.

Moreover, as deadlines approach, contractors are able to exploit their power position to obtain large premiums to finish on time (Müller, 2015). These effects are enhanced by the irreversibility of many such commitments (Flyvbjerg et al., 2021). Indeed, Ross and Staw (1986) refer to Vancouver's organization of Expo 86 as a "prototype of escalation" reflecting the way in which politicians and civil servants became increasingly locked in to holding the exhibition no matter what: social, psychological, and institutional factors made it impossible to back out, despite exploding costs. This is the case for many event-based projects.

In the face of such complexity and uncertainty, classic approaches to project management based on detailed preconceived plans and time lines may appear inadequate and almost bound to be disrupted as soon as they are formulated. Yet how else might projects be organized to deliver on time? In a study of an infrastructure project associated with the Sydney Olympic games, Pitsis et al. (2003, p. 575) developed the notion of "future-perfect thinking" to describe how project managers built not so much on detailed pre-planned specifications but on a visualization of how they wanted the future endpoint to be ("a projection of ends"), and then worked with project partners in a collaborative process to determine in an ongoing way what exactly would have to be accomplished to achieve those ends, perceived "as an emergent rather than explicitly scripted strategy." This was guided by an ambitious endpoint that implied not only the respect of cost and scheduling targets but also goals related to safety, community, and environment.

Relatedly, in a study of the 2012 London Olympics, which were perceived as a success both in terms of delivery on time as well as within budget, Davies and Mackenzie (2014) revealed a mode of governance – referred to as a meta-system of integration – that enabled this complexity to be managed. Grabher and Thiel (2014) built on these findings and on their own research on the London Olympics to argue that a form of organizing based on "heterarchy" (multiple, tangled, and shifting hierarchies) rather than a pure "hierarchy" is more likely to enable the required degree of adaptability over time. Heterarchy is described as a form of organization that involves three features: ambiguity, redundancy, and loose coupling.

Ambiguity implies structuring organizational units involved in the project to ensure a balance between diverse goals (e.g., preparing for a successful event vs. contributing to future economic development). Redundancy has cognitive (e.g., openness to considering alternative options), organizational (e.g., scheduling buffers and contingency funds), and relational (informal trust-based relations allowing smooth adaptation) dimensions according to Grabher and Thiel (2014), which combined provide the slack needed to accommodate the unexpected. Loose coupling implies decomposing complex projects into components that may be managed relatively autonomously, with their own specific sets of plans and time lines that are nevertheless connected to the whole (Davies & Mackenzie, 2014).

Subproject autonomy may also allow the creative reformulation of certain task components as deadlines approach (Alioua & Simon, 2017), without undermining the whole. The heterarchical form of organization described by these authors, while enabling creativity and autonomy in the development of specific project components, is nevertheless oriented by higher level targets and milestones, accompanied by both scheduled and ad hoc forums for problem-solving and supported by a collaborative culture among different partners.

Overall, temporal structuring to meet deadlines clearly becomes more challenging and multifaceted as projects expand and diversify. Moreover, while larger and more complex projects clearly demand greater attention to formal temporal structuring involving temporal artifacts such as plans and time lines, the research suggests that these devices need to embed flexibility, modularity, and open-endedness to allow for adaptation and creative problem-solving, drawing on future-perfect thinking and heterarchical organizational forms.

A final question that might arise is what happens when formal temporal structuring devices are applied to creative projects that involve very short time lines. Interestingly, Lifshitz-Assaf et al. (2021) studied precisely this in the context of short 72-hour hackathons aimed at developing assistive technology solutions for disabled people. Comparing 13 separate hackathon teams, the authors found that those teams who attempted to import standard temporal structuring devices from their regular workplaces (e.g., involving upfront product design, planning, and "full coordination") were unable to generate viable working products because they found themselves channeled into a failing trajectory and unable to reorient in the face of setbacks. In contrast, those teams that engaged in minimal coordination involving only a high-level product design without clear focus on methods or materials were slightly more successful. However, it was only those teams who began with minimal coordination involving free experimentation around ideas, but then gradually developed their own temporal structures allowing adaptive coordination (e.g., by exchanging work and nudging each other forward), that were able to generate fully functioning products within the time constraint. This leads the authors to argue for the value of emergent temporal structuring for innovative projects.

Combined with the very different studies previously described, it appears that the adaptation of tasks to temporal constraints (whether long or short) is permeated by an ongoing tension between planning and emergence, where effective temporal coordination may require both in different doses depending on the setting and the repetitiveness or innovativeness of the task (Lundin & Söderholm, 1995; Kalff, 2022). It is not clear, however, that scholars have yet fully captured the implications of this tradeoff. Moreover, as we discuss next, some projects are naturally more temporally ambiguous and open-ended, begging the question of how temporal structuring might be organized in such circumstances.

Temporal Ambiguity: Negotiating Time and Task When Projects Are Open-Ended

While some project tasks and time frames are predefined, they may be more open-ended in other projects and need to be mutually negotiated over time, a situation we qualify as "temporal ambiguity." Various factors might contribute to temporal ambiguity: some are related to the inherent uncertainty about future events (Beckert, 2016) or about the nature of the task to be accomplished (Nachbagauer, 2022). Other projects may involve imagining desirable futures (Alimadadi et al., 2022), working back from this imagined future to establish what activities might be required and by when, without necessarily being able to clearly pin down precise time lines.

In addition, unpredictable events also often affect projects and disrupt plans (Nachbagauer, 2022). This is typical for entrepreneurial ventures. For example, as Berends et al. (2021) show, unforeseen events may lead entrepreneurs to reconsider their temporal commitments by deferring or reformulating their projects or may even lead them to pivot towards a new project entirely (Berends et al., 2021). Indeed, where deciding how to respond to unexpected events takes a long time, "dwindling time" reduces the chance of getting projects back on track (Vaagaasar et al., 2020).

Moreover, as imagined futures draw closer, people may change how they perceive tasks and time lines, becoming preoccupied with practical everyday concerns rather than ideal imagined futures (Trope & Liberman, 2003). A sense of urgency may lead to increasing closure in temporal structuring (Orlikowski & Yates, 2002) or a concern to prevent potentially undesirable futures from emerging (Alimadadi et al., 2022). Thus, plans that seemed desirable in the far future may even come to be seen as mistakes (Augustine et al., 2019; Trope & Liberman, 2003; Whyte & Nussbaum, 2020).

A particular form of temporal ambiguity may occur for what Gustavsson and Hallin (2015), refer to as "goal seeking" projects where it is principally the achievement of some goal or broad ambition, rather than the precise time line, that constitutes the project. Examples might include John F. Kennedy and NASA's ambition to put a man on the moon or the World Health Organization's projects to eradicate diseases such as smallpox and polio. In these cases, it is (in principle at least) the achievement of the goal that determines the end of the project, not a fixed date or time frame.

Brookes et al. (2017) point out that some megaprojects may actually be more open-ended and enduring than the surrounding organizations that they are related to, inverting the generally assumed relationship between the two. For example, they show how a project to develop a large wind farm evolved in the face of bankruptcies of the organizations that were involved in developing it, shifting partner roles, and the fuzzy boundaries between development, construction, and operations. In the end, the "project" was projected to continue for an imprecise period of 25–50 years that would include the delivery, operation, refurbishment, and eventual decommissioning of the wind farm. In these circumstances, the distinctiveness of project organization as compared with permanent organization (especially when many permanent organizations embed multiple projects) becomes fluid.

When projects are temporally open-ended, this begs the question of when and how they might ultimately come to be terminated. Whyte and Nussbaum (2020) focus on the temporal boundaries between megaproject completion and the operations that derive from them. They point out the need for a variety of mechanisms that are themselves fuzzy and overlapping in time. For example, they point out the role of specific artifacts and boundary objects, as well as distinctive temporally organized procedures for handover. They also refer to the notions of "soft landing" and testing implying progressively timed partial rather than immediate and full operation of delivered infrastructure accompanied by testing and adjustment over a long time frame. The transition itself thus requires its own forms of temporal structuring: almost a "project" in itself.

Engwall and Westling (2004) discuss the notion of "peripety" during R&D projects – a moment of sudden change in which a concrete shared conceptualization of a project mission emerges, enabling participants to move on from discussing ambiguous problems and goals to actively addressing them. Rather than happening at prescribed milestones, or project midpoints as Gersick (1988) suggests, Engwall and Westling (2004) find that peripety emerges when project participants have developed a common theoretical understanding of their mission, concrete experience of a potential solution, and have spent enough time together for the project to reach "maturity." This suggests that innovative breakthroughs tend to happen at the right "kairotic moment" (Garud et al., 2016) in a project, so projects need an open-ended time line to achieve their aims.

Yet project time line open-endedness can also lead to what might be called "creeping permanence" in the sense that some projects come to be continually renewed and routinized even though they may not be delivering results. There may also be ambiguity surrounding whether a "goal-seeking" task (such as eliminating a disease) has been accomplished or not, raising questions about whether and how the "project" should be disbanded. R&D projects that are slow to generate their expected breakthroughs may also run into this problem. In a study of such projects, Royer (2003) argues that just as the launching of new ideas may require dynamic and motivated project champions, their disbanding may require "stopping champions" who work in a similar manner to force the closure of projects that have taken on a life of their own.

Another kind of temporary organization that has an ambiguous open-ended character, despite the presence of temporal urgency (focused not on closed deadlines, but on event-based danger and risk) concerns disaster or crisis response. For example, Geiger et al. (2021) found firefighters using "temporal autonomy" to improvise and "perform temporal boundaries" (Bucher & Langley, 2016), uncoupling and recoupling temporal routines in response to temporal cues to realign collectively held temporal expectations and appropriately respond to evolving, potentially chaotic circumstances.

This echoes the work on megaprojects mentioned above where modularization of large projects enables subproject teams to adjust and draw upon the appropriate temporal structures to achieve tasks in ambiguous circumstances. Nachbagauer (2022) describes the importance of temporal work relating to timing in projects, highlighting the need at different times to stop dysfunctional momentum, interrupt, observe and reflect, wait, or quickly seize opportunities even under conditions of extreme urgency. Temporal structuring here is not just about scheduling and synchronizing but also about managing speed and rhythm.

Beyond the contextual uncertainties and ambiguities described so far, most importantly, project tasks and time lines may also be ambiguous due to the involvement of heterogenous stakeholders with different interests and temporal preferences who come together to pursue a common project for a limited period (Bakker, 2010; Dille et al., 2018; Stjerne et al., 2019; Dille et al., 2022). Aligning different interests and temporal preferences within the same project creates additional complexities in project behavior that may not always be fully recognized in advance.

For example, there may be temporal tensions between project and permanent organizations (Geraldi et al., 2020; Stjerne & Svejenova, 2016). Circumstances or how projects are viewed evolve, so stakeholders may wish to change the nature of their participation or no longer be involved in projects, which may result in the reopening of project aims and time lines (Bakker, 2016; Brookes et al., 2017). Drawing upon the example of a project to enhance a city's nightlife area, Hilbolling et al. (2022) also explain how collaborators' differing expectations of the project and of when its objectives would be achieved can change over time, creating reemerging temporal complexity that hampers project coordination.

Kaplan and Orlikowski (2013) argue that projects require temporal work to negotiate and agree to "temporal settlements" about project aims and time lines in order to productively move forward implementation. However, they also note that settlements among stakeholders are provisional and temporary, because contexts change, aims and time lines reopen to reinterpretation or break down, so ongoing temporal work is necessary for projects to make progress.

Along these lines, McGivern et al. (2018) showed how consultants, hired to assist a health care system in designing an efficiency savings program, mobilized an externally fixed deadline and imposed a rigid PowerPoint-based planning framework (conceptualized as a boundary object) on health care clinicians and managers. Clinicians and managers, for their part, engaged in passive resistance by going through the motions of filling out the framework without any intention to follow through on implementation. Here, the consultants' temporal orientation toward "blitzing and leaving" to optimize their profits conflicted fundamentally with managers and clinicians' orientation toward "taking the time to develop sustainable change." This resulted in a superficial temporal settlement that enabled the parties to meet the deadline but that ultimately unraveled after the consultants left (McGivern et al., 2018, pp. 1014–1015).

Indeed, divergent interests and interdependencies among different project participants may be influenced by the "shadow of the future" (Poppo, Zhou & Ryu, 2008; Ligthart et al., 2016; Swärd, 2016), particularly whether projects are seen as one off or to be repeated (Bakker et al., 2016). For example, studies have suggested that the shadow of the future may serve to promote the maintenance of trust and diffuse reciprocity among stakeholders in a project early in its life. However, this effect may become less influential as the project is coming to an end and is seen as one-off, when relations become more transactional and opportunistic (Das, 2006; Poppo et al., 2008; McGivern et al., 2018).

Projects may also be underpinned by "swift trust," based on "familiarity, shared experience, reciprocal disclosure, threats and deterrents, fulfilled promises, and demonstrations of non-exploitation of vulnerability" (Meyerson et al., 1996, p. 167), including temporal aspects linked to past, present, and future. Bechky (2006) shows how role expectations and interorganizational career progression structures underpinned trust coordination in temporary film projects. In simple terms, people working on temporary projects knew the roles they were expected to enact during film projects and enacted them well, because they knew that this would increase their chance of being invited to work on future projects and hence build careers in the film industry (see also Huemann et al., 2007).

Finally, studies have also suggested that forms of temporal coordination among project participants may be significantly affected by power dependencies among them. Thus, in their study of a consulting firm managing a complex construction project, Kremser and Blagoev (2021) show how internal deadlines and schedules were continually disrupted by temporal conflicts. Here, routines could not be carried out at scheduled times because of delays occasioned by higher status actors who prioritized other tasks. The result was that lower status individuals found themselves adapting the timing of their activities to those of higher status actors. This form of temporal structuring enabled external deadlines to be met but at the cost of long working hours and the invasion of private time. This reminds us that temporal work in project contexts overflows the workplace, with potentially unhealthy effects on certain people, notably those who are pressured into aligning their own temporal needs to the rhythms and demands of more powerful others (Ancona & Chong, 1996; Blagoev & Schreyogg, 2019).

Temporal Structuring and Project Behavior: Discussion and Future Agenda

Given the importance of deadlines and temporal closure in the very definition of what project management means, we began by reviewing the literature specifically focusing on deadline-based project behavior. We found that the importance of deadlines in orienting group attention and task activity at certain particular moments is clear (Gersick, 1988) and that the use of various temporal boundary objects and time lines to manage temporal constraints is deeply institutionalized (Yakura, 2002; Kalff, 2022). Yet, we also found that the literature dealing both with more complex megaprojects (Davies & Mackenzie, 2014; Grabher & Thiel, 2014) and with short-term initiatives (Lifshitz-Assaf et al., 2021) has emphasized the important role of temporal autonomy, flexibility, relational trust, and open-endedness, along with more formal temporal structuring devices for ensuring success.

In the second part of our review, we considered what happens when tight temporal constraints are relaxed, drawing attention to sources of temporal ambiguity, including uncertainties about when goals might be achievable (Gustavsson & Hallin, 2015), fuzziness around the boundaries and transitions between temporary and permanent organization (Brookes et al., 2017; Whyte & Nussbaum, 2020), event-based contingencies (Nachbagauer, 2022) and political dynamics (McGivern et al., 2018; Kremser & Blagoev, 2021). As we saw, these conditions augment the diversity of temporal structuring devices considered and illustrate forms of project behavior deviating from projects' formally espoused goals.

We note also that as project management research has become more sophisticated, there is increasing recognition of the need to view projects from a processual perspective that takes into account time and temporality, rather than from a more static variance-oriented perspective that has dominated the project management field in the past (Söderlund, 2013; Tryggestad et al., 2013; Brookes et al., 2017; Stjerne et al., 2019; Vaagaasar et al., 2020; Brunet et al., 2021; Dille et al., 2022). The attention to time and temporality has thus clearly increased in recent years and this is manifest in the rich insights we report on in this chapter. Yet several areas for development remain.

Notably, throughout our review, several different temporal structuring tensions and tradeoffs emerged as crucial to affecting project behavior. These include interrelated tensions between temporary and permanent organizations (Burke & Morley, 2016), detailed planning and adaptive emergence (Lifshitz-Assaf et al., 2021), past-oriented rigidity and future-oriented flexibility (Pitsis et al., 2003), autonomy and coordination (Grabher & Thiel, 2014; Geiger et al., 2021), acceleration to achieve quick results and slowing down to regroup and reorient (Nachbagauer, 2022), and time-based, sequence-based, and role-based forms of timing and synchronization (Kremser & Blagoev, 2021).

A first and obvious direction for future research would involve investigating further the temporal tensions and tradeoffs within projects and their effects on outcomes. Given the emphasis of much of the literature on the intertwined nature of the poles of these tensions, one could imagine both a contingency approach to considering them (i.e., identifying the conditions where different orientations would be desirable) or, perhaps more fruitfully, a paradox approach (Burke & Morley, 2016; Delisle, 2019; Geraldi et al., 2020; Smith & Lewis, 2011) that recognizes the value of both poles under most conditions.

A second important direction for research involves deepening analysis of the role of political dynamics in temporal structuring and project behavior. The papers reviewed here reveal how varying temporal assumptions among stakeholders (Dille et al., 2018; McGivern et al., 2018), power dependencies (Kremser & Blagoev, 2021), and trust relations (Bechky, 2006; Swärd, 2016) can orient the way in which tasks are negotiated and synchronized over time, with effects on individual lives and on mandated and unanticipated project outcomes (Burke & Morley, 2016). We also know that temporal boundary objects may have different meanings for different people (Yakura, 2002; Bechky, 2003; McGivern et al., 2018). There is room for further study of temporal negotiation and boundary-drawing among stakeholders in the context of projects.

A third area of study is to consider how the kinds of temporal structuring phenomena we described for individual projects influences broader organizational behavior in the context of ongoing trends toward "projectification" (Kremser & Blagoev, 2021), that is, efforts to increase the use of project organizing within nontemporary organizational settings in order to instigate desired change or to implement novel practices. Reflecting on temporality during participation in a project may enable reconceptualization of past, present, and future; facilitate wider organizational change (Soderlund & Pemsel, 2022); or refocusing on project activities (Lindkvist et al., 1998).

However, the political and interpersonal issues related to temporal structuring we noted above are likely to be intensified when individuals find that their time needs to be sliced across different projects that have different temporal demands. To the extent that people respond to the scheduling issues this creates for them by prioritizing the tasks that are of importance to higher status others as Kremser and Blagoev (2021) infer, the particular mix of projects people are involved in, as well as the power dependencies they imply, could have important consequences for the way in which organizations are managed and their capacity to successfully implement organizational change. Certain authors have begun to examine how change projects interfere with each other (Falkenberg et al., 2005; Kanitz et al., 2022) but have not done so using a temporality lens.

Fourth, and building on this, there has been little research that has considered the intersection of projects and of peoples' lives and careers. We have already mentioned how some forms of temporal structuring may create work-life balance problems for individuals, an endemic phenomenon, notably in professional service domains such as consulting (Blagoev & Schreyogg, 2019). Bechky (2006) describes how interorganizational career pathways, premised upon meeting role expectations during projects, ensure trust and coordination during one-off film projects.

Yet taking a longer term perspective, some project managers may choose to pursue tasks and time lines that reflect their own career trajectories, for example, aiming to produce quick wins to earn promotions to bigger and better projects, which may not benefit the project's or the organization's longer term success or sustainability (Tavory & Elisasoph, 2013). Kunisch et al. (2017) argue that individuals' professional lifecycles may influence the degree to which they may be willing to engage in change projects and the approaches they may take to them. Lives and projects intersect and there would be value in paying more attention to the consequences of this both for project behavior and human development.

Fifth, as Brunet et al. (2021) indicate, researchers who study projects may consider time and temporality from a variety of different perspectives depending on their onto-epistemological assumptions. Most of the research we have described here views time from a more objectivist perspective, although recognizing the potential for human agency to orient temporal structures. However, project management scholars drawing on a narrative perspective (Deuten & Rip, 2000; Pitsis et al., 2003; Sergeeva & Winch, 2021) have drawn attention to more subjectivist notions of time and the way temporality is both represented in participants' accounts of the past and drawn on to shape the future.

Moreover, Shipp and Jansen (2021) suggest that individuals' subjective notions of time – that is, sensemaking about past, present, and future expressed in narratives – itself evolves over objective time, with potentially important consequences. There is thus room to build further on a subjective time perspective to better understand how and why project participants' individual and collective narrative sensemaking evolves and contributes (perhaps along with material artifacts) to orienting behavior throughout the duration of projects.

Finally, projects are likely to play a role in attempts to develop sustainable future organizations and society. Yet the temporary nature of projects is logically incompatible with the long-term focus of sustainable development, so there is need to better understand how to focus on longer-term project deliverables, while working on shorter-term projects (Brookes et al., 2017; Huemann & Silvius, 2017).

Moreover, in the face of major societal and ecological upheaval involving "grand challenges" (Ika & Munro, 2022), such as global warming, wars, corruption (Lehtinen et al., 2022), pandemics, and rising health and social care demands, there is an increasing chance that large infrastructure projects may be difficult to insulate from turbulent contexts. Projects risk being overwhelmed by the unexpected (e.g., the "2020" Tokyo Olympics – postponed because of the Covid-19 pandemic and ultimately held in 2021). Corrupt politicians and officials may commission project where costs, benefits, and time forecasts are deliberately and systematically over-optimistic, expecting bribes and/or political support but leading to poor return and overruns (Lehtinen et al., 2022; Locatelli et al., 2017). Corruption may also undermine alternative projects that would have better addressed grand challenges.

It is therefore possible in some cases that complex projects focused on grand challenges may be overtaken by the very problems that they are intended to address. Understanding how to intervene in such areas through project organizing and yet maintain the ability to "manage" through some kind of temporal structuring over the longer-term seems likely to stretch project management capabilities. Tracking and explaining such processes into the future may therefore be an important research enterprise.

The key practical implication for project managers is that, when conceiving, initiating, and running projects, they should be critically mindful of predictable and unanticipated ways in which time and temporality, and their inter-relationship with project tasks, affect project behavior.

References

Alimadadi, S., Davies, A., and Tell, F. (2022). A palace fit for the future: Desirability in temporal work. *Strategic Organization*, *20*(1), 20–50.

Alioua, H., and Simon, F. (2017). Managing time pacing in organizations transitioning to a project-based mode-3 cases studies of two multinational companies. *International Journal of Project Management*, *35*(8), 1427–1443.

Ancona, D., and Chong, C.-L. (1996). Entrainment: Pace, cycle, and rhythm in organizational behavior. *Research in Organizational Behavior*, *18*, 251–284.

Augustine, G. L., Soderstrom, S., Milner, D., and Weber, K. (2019). Constructing a distant future: Imaginaries in geoengineering. *Academy of Management Journal*. https://doi.org/10.5465/amj.2018.0059.

Bakker, R. M. (2010). Taking stock of temporary organizational forms: A systematic review and research agenda. *International Journal of Management Reviews*, *12*(4), 466–486.

Bakker, R. M. (2016). Stepping in and stepping out: Strategic alliance partner reconfiguration and the unplanned termination of complex projects. *Strategic Management Journal*, *37*(9), 1919–1941.

Bakker, R. M., Boroş, S., Kenis, P., and Oerlemans, L. A. (2013). It's only temporary: Time frame and the dynamics of creative project teams. *British Journal of Management*, *24*(3), 383–397.

Bakker, R. M., DeFillippi, R., Schwab, A., and Sydow, J. (2016). Temporary organizing: Promises, processes, problems. *Organization Studies*, *37*(12), 1703–1719.

Bansal, P., Reinecke, J., Suddaby, R., and Langley, A. (2022). Temporal work: The strategic organization of time. *Strategic Organization*, *20*(1), 6–19.

Bechky, B. A. (2003). Object lessons: Workplace artifacts as representations of occupational jurisdiction. *American Journal of Sociology*, *109*(3), 720–752.

Bechky, B. A. (2006). Gaffers, gofers, and grips: Role-based coordination in temporary organizations. *Organization Science*, *17*(1), 3–21.

Beckert, J. (2016). *Imagined futures*. Harvard University Press.

Berends, H., van Burg, E., and Garud, R. (2021). Pivoting or persevering with venture ideas: Recalibrating temporal commitments. *Journal of Business Venturing*, *36*(4), 106126.

Blagoev, B., and Schreyogg, G. (2019). Why do extreme work hours persist? Temporal uncoupling as a new way of seeing. *Academy of Management Journal*, *62*(6), 1818–1847.

Brookes, N., Sage, D., Dainty, A., Locatelli, G., and Whyte, J. (2017). An island of constancy in a sea of change: Rethinking project temporalities with long-term megaprojects. *International Journal of Project Management*, *35*(7), 1213–1224.

Brunet, M., Fachin, F., and Langley, A. (2021). Studying projects processually. *International Journal of Project Management*, *39*(8), 834–848.

Bucher, S., and Langley, A. (2016). The interplay of reflective and experimental spaces in interrupting and reorienting routine dynamics. *Organization Science*, *27*(3), 594–613.

Burke, C. M., and Morley, M. J. (2016). On temporary organizations: A review, synthesis and research agenda. *Human Relations*, *69*(6), 1235–1258.

Das, T. K. (2006). Strategic alliance temporalities and partner opportunism. *British Journal of Management*, *17*, 1–21.

Davies, A., and Mackenzie, I. (2014). Project complexity and systems integration: Constructing the London 2012 Olympics and Paralympics Games. *International Journal of Project Management*, *32*(5), 773–790.

Delisle, J. (2019). Uncovering temporal underpinnings of project management standards. *International Journal of Project Management*, *37*(8), 968–978.

Deuten, J. J., and Rip, A. (2000). Narrative infrastructure in product creation processes. *Organization*, *7*(1), 69–93.

Dille, T., Hernes, T., and Vaagaasar, A. L. (2022). Stuck in temporal translation? Challenges of discrepant temporal structures in interorganizational project collaboration. *Organization Studies*. https://journals.sagepub.com/doi/full/10.1177/01708406221137841.

Dille, T., Söderlund, J., and Clegg, S. (2018). Temporal conditioning and the dynamics of inter-institutional projects. *International Journal of Project Management*, *36*(5), 673–686.

Engwall, M., and Westling, G. (2004). Peripety in an R&D drama: Capturing a turnaround in project dynamics. *Organization Studies*, *25*(9), 1557–1578.

Falkenberg, J., Stensaker, I. G., Meyer, C. B., and Haueng, A. C. (2005). *When change becomes excessive research in organizational change and development*. Emerald Group.

Flyvbjerg, B., Budzier, A., and Lunn, D. (2021). Regression to the tail: Why the Olympics blow up. *Environment and Planning A: Economy and Space*, *53*(2), 233–260.

Garud, R., Gehman, J., Kumaraswamy, A., and Tuertscher, P. (2016). From the process of innovation to innovation as process (pp. 451–466). In A. Langley and H. Tsoukas (eds.). *The SAGE handbook of process organization studies*. Sage.

Geiger, D., Danner-Schröder, A., and Kremser, W. (2021). Getting ahead of time – performing temporal boundaries to coordinate routines under temporal uncertainty. *Administrative Science Quarterly*, *66*(1), 220–264.

Gemino, A., Reich, B. H., and Serrador, P. M. (2021). Agile, traditional, and hybrid approaches to project success: Is hybrid a poor second choice? *Project Management Journal*, *52*(2), 161–175.

Geraldi, J., Stjerne, I., and Oehmen, J. (2020). Acting in time: Temporal work enacting tensions at the interface between temporary and permanent organisations (pp. 81–103). In T. Braun and J. Lampel (eds.). *Tensions and paradoxes in temporary organizing (Research in the xociology of organizations, vol. 67)*. Emerald.

Gersick, C. J. (1988). Time and transition in work teams: Toward a new model of group development. *Academy of Management Journal*, *31*(1), 9–41.

Gersick, C. J. (1989). Marking Time: Predictable transitions in task groups. *Academy of Management Journal*, *32*(2), 274–309.

Grabher, G., and Thiel, J. (2014). Coping with a self-induced shock: The heterarchic organization of the London Olympic Games 2012. *Social Sciences*, *3*(3), 527–548.

Gustavsson, T. K., and Hallin, A. (2015). Goal seeking and goal oriented projects – trajectories of the temporary organisation. *International Journal of Managing Projects in Business*, *8*(2), 368–378.

Hassard, J. (1991). Aspects of time in organization. *Human Relations*, *44*(2), 105–125.

Hilbolling, S., Deken, F., Berends, H., and Tuertscher, P. (2022). Process-based temporal coordination in multiparty collaboration for societal challenges. *Strategic Organization*, *20*(1), 135–163.

Huemann, M., Keegan, A., and Turner, J. R. (2007). Human resource management in the project-oriented company: A review. *International Journal of Project Management*, *25*(3), 315–323.

Huemann, M., and Silvius, G. (2017). Projects to create the future: Managing projects meets sustainable development. *International Journal of Project Management*, *35*(6), 1066–1070.

Ika, L. A., Love, P. E., and Pinto, J. K. (2022). Moving beyond the planning fallacy: The emergence of a new principle of project behavior. *IEEE Transactions on Engineering Management*, *69*(6), 3310–3325.

Ika, L. A., and Munro, L. T. (2022). Tackling grand challenges with projects: Five insights and a research agenda for project management theory and practice. *International Journal of Project Management*, *40*(6), 601–607.

Kalff, Y. (2022). Managing projects as a mode of temporal ordering. Performative organising of time and temporality in projects. *International Journal of Managing Projects in Business*, *15*(1), 82–101.

Kanitz, R., Huy, Q. N., Backmann, J., and Hoegl, M. (2022). No change is an island: How interferences between change initiatives evoke inconsistencies that undermine implementation. *Academy of Management Journal*, *65*(2), 683–710.

Kaplan, S., and Orlikowski, W. (2013). Temporal work in strategy making. *Organization Science*, *24*(4), 965–995.

Kremser, W., and Blagoev, B. (2021). The dynamics of prioritizing: How actors temporally pattern complex role-routine ecologies. *Administrative Science Quarterly*, *66*(2), 339–379.

Kunisch, S., Bartunek, J. M., Mueller, J., and Huy, Q. N. (2017). Time in strategic change research. *Academy of Management Annals*, *11*(2), 1005–1064.

Lehtinen, J., Locatelli, G., Sainati, T., Artto, K., and Evans, B. (2022). The grand challenge: Effective anti-corruption measures in projects. *International Journal of Project Management*, *40*(4), 347–361.

Lifshitz-Assaf, H., Lebovitz, S., and Zalmanson, L. (2021). Minimal and adaptive coordination: How hackathons' projects accelerate innovation without killing it. *Academy of Management Journal*, *64*(3), 684–715.

Ligthart, R., Oerlemans, L., and Noorderhaven, N. (2016). In the shadows of time: A case study of flexibility behaviors in an interorganizational project. *Organization Studies*, *37*(12), 1721–1743.

Lindkvist, L., Soderlund, J., and Tell, F. (1998). Managing product development projects: On the significance of fountains and deadlines. *Organization Studies*, *19*(6), 931–951.

Locatelli, G., Mariani, G., Sainati, T., and Greco, M. (2017). Corruption in public projects and megaprojects: There is an elephant in the room! *International Journal of Project Management*, *35*(3), 252–268.

Lundin, R., and Söderholm, A. (1995). A theory of the temporary organization. *Scandinavian Journal of Management*, *11*(4), 437–455.

McGivern, G., Dopson, S., Ferlie, E., Fischer, M., Fitzgerald, L., Ledger, J., and Bennett, C. (2018). The silent politics of temporal work: A case study of a management consultancy project to redesign public health care. *Organization Studies*, *39*(8), 1007–1030.

Meyerson, D., Weick, K. E., and Kramer, R. M. (1996). Swift trust and temporary groups (pp. 166–195). In R. M. Kramer and T. R. Tyler (eds.). *Trust in Organizations: Frontiers of Theory and research.* Sage.

Müller, M. (2015). The mega-event syndrome: Why so much goes wrong in mega-event planning and what to do about it. *Journal of the American Planning Association*, *81*(1), 6–17.

Nachbagauer, A. (2022). Synchronous and diachronic timing: Insights into managing projects from disaster management and fast-response organizations. *Project Management Journal*, *53*(2), 146–160.

Okhuysen, G. A., and Waller, M. J. (2002). Focusing on midpoint transitions: An analysis of boundary conditions. *Academy of Management Journal*, *45*(5), 1056–1065.

Orlikowski, W. J., and Yates, J. (2002). It's about time: Temporal structuring in organizations. *Organization Science*, *13*(6), 684–700.

Pitsis, T. S., Clegg, S. R., Marosszeky, M., and Rura-Polley, T. (2003). Constructing the Olympic dream: A future perfect strategy of project management. *Organization Science*, *14*(5), 574–590.

Poppo, L., Zhou, K. Z., and Ryu, S. (2008). Alternative origins to interorganizational trust: An interdependence perspective on the shadow of the past and the shadow of the future. *Organization Science*, *19*(1), 39–55.

Project Management Institute. (2017). *A guide to the project management body of knowledge (PMBOK® Guide)*. 6th ed. Project Management Institute.

Ross, J., and Staw, B. M. (1986). Expo 86: An escalation prototype. *Administrative Science Quarterly*, 274–297.

Royer, I. (2003). Why bad projects are so hard to kill. *Harvard Business Review*, *81*(2), 48–56, 123.

Sergeeva, N., and Winch, G. M. (2021). Project narratives that potentially perform and change the future. *Project Management Journal*, *52*(3), 264–277.

Shipp, A. J., and Jansen, K. J. (2021). The "other" time: A review of the subjective experience of time in organizations. *Academy of Management Annals*, *15*(1), 299–334.

Smith, W. K., and Lewis, M. W. (2011). Toward a theory of paradox: A dynamic equilibrium model of organizing. *Academy of management Review*, *36*(2), 381–403.

Söderlund, J. (2010). Knowledge entrainment and project management: The case of large-scale transformation projects. *International Journal of Project Management*, *28*(2), 130–141.

Söderlund, J. (2013). Pluralistic and processual understandings of projects and project organizing: Towards theories of project temporality (pp. 117–135). In N. Drouin, R. Müller, and S. Shankar (eds.). *Novel approaches to organizational project management research: Translational and transformational*. Copenhagen Business School Press.

Söderlund, J., and Pemsel, S. (2022). Changing times for digitalization: The multiple roles of temporal shifts in enabling organizational change. *Human Relations*, *75*(5), 871–902.

Stjerne, I. S., Söderlund, J., and Minbaeva, D. (2019). Crossing times: Temporal boundary-spanning practices in interorganizational projects. *International Journal of Project Management*, *37*(2), 347–365.

Stjerne, I. S., and Svejenova, S. (2016). Connecting temporary and permanent organizing: Tensions and boundary work in a series of film projects. *Organization Studies*, *37*(12), 1771–1792.

Swärd, A. (2016). Trust, reciprocity, and actions: The development of trust in temporary inter-organizational relations. *Organization Studies*, *37*(12), 1841–1860.

Tavory, I., and Elisasoph, N. (2013). Coordinating futures: Towards a theory of anticipation. *Americal Journal of Sociology*, *118*(4), 908–942.

Trope, K., and Liberman, N. (2003). Temporal construal. *Psychological Review*, *110*(3), 403–421.

Tryggestad, K., Justesen, L., and Mouritsen, J. (2013). Project temporalities: How frogs can become stakeholders. *International Journal of Managing Projects in Business*, *6*(1), 69–87.

Vaagaasar, A. L., Hernes, T., and Dille, T. (2020). The challenges of implementing temporal shifts in temporary organizations: Implications of a situated temporal view. *Project Management Journal*, *51*(4), 420–428.

Waller, M. J., Zellmer-Bruhn, M. E., and Giambatista, R. C. (2002). Watching the clock: Group pacing behavior under dynamic deadlines. *Academy of Management Journal*, *45*(5), 1046–1055.

Whyte, J., and Nussbaum, T. (2020). Transition and temporalities: Spanning temporal boundaries as projects end and operations begin. *Project Management Journal*, *51*(5), 505–521.

Yakura, E. (2002). Charting time: Timelines as temporal boundary objects *Academy of Management Journal*, *45*(5), 956–970.

CHAPTER 5

Managing Project Complexity and Uncertainty through Dynamic and Systemic Stakeholder Modeling

FRAN ACKERMANN

Introduction

Project Stakeholder Management has seen, over the last two decades, tremendous growth in research activity reflecting an increasing awareness of the impact stakeholders can have on the well-being of projects. However, while this research has revealed important insights, projects still experience stakeholder challenges. Why is this the case? This question has been noted by others, for example, Jepsen and Eskerod (2009); Eskerod et al. (2015b), and touches on issues relating to uncertainty (that is, *who* to involve) and complexity (for example, *how* to involve them, and involve them effectively, and *when* to involve them).

This chapter seeks to reflect on these three questions (*who*, *how*, and *when*) regarding project stakeholders before moving on to consider some of the complexities emerging from seeking to resolve the questions. Complexities relating to process (recognizing the sociopolitical considerations), complexities relating to content management (dealing with the extensive, interconnected, and often competing issues and values), and dynamic complexity (reflecting the shifts in personnel and norms). The questions and complexities are considered by reflecting on projects including large public sector–oriented initiatives. One of the drivers for this necessity comes from a subset of projects today requiring a social license to operate – and thus engagement with the public is increasingly being seen as a necessary activity, a point reinforced by researchers, for example, Amadi et al. (2018).

Consideration of these three stakeholder management questions suggests that part of the complexity may be due to there being a potentially paradoxical element to them. Paradoxes, "persistent contradictions between interdependent elements" (Schad et al., 2016), comprise both positive and negative consequences at the same time – implying managerial challenges. Paradoxes can be seen as a continuous process that requires active learning about the paradox by the parties involved and the need for balancing the moments of stability with moments for change (Raisch et al., 2018). Paradoxes pervade much of managerial life and recently have received considerable attention in the management literature (Schad et al., 2016; Jarzabkowski et al., 2019). For example, Jarzabkowski et al. (2019) note that paradoxes are likely to emerge when people work across organizational boundaries, a phenomenon often experienced by projects. The use of the paradox lens in project management is not new, paradoxes are normal in projects (Brady & Maylor, 2010). As learning is a key requirement when managing paradoxes, researchers have noted that it is important to take a collaborative stance (Luscher & Lewis, 2008) to avoid experiencing friction. Gaim and et al. (2022) echo this need to attend to collaboration when managing paradoxes. They note, when discussing the Sydney Opera House project, "a both/and approach to managing paradoxes strives to see and nurture unique aspects of contradictory tensions, striving to devise collaborative constituencies of interest and strategies to solder solidaristic actions" (p. 398). This view also provides elements of creativity and innovation to the components of collaboration, cross-boundary operations, and a willingness to learn and combines both processual and content-oriented elements.

One such paradox pertaining to project stakeholder management is the view that "it seems essential, yet in some ways illegitimate, to orient corporate decisions by ethical values that go beyond strategic stakeholder considerations to multi-fiduciary ones" Goodpaster (1991, p. 63) – touching on the question of *who* to involve and widening the scope of attention to move beyond a predominately cost-oriented mindset. This view is elaborated upon by Dalcher (2020) who comments on the paradoxical position of either "business without ethics or ethics without business" (p. 3). This could be construed as a signal reflecting a changing societal impetus for wider engagement as reflected in the increasing attention given to Corporate Social Responsibility (a field that has seen considerable research into stakeholder engagement) and more recently ESG. Both are changing business models (Freeman et al., 2020), which, in turn, it could be surmised, will change the management practices on projects.

This chapter commences with a short review of the extant literature about stakeholder management and projects before considering the questions of who, how, and why in detail. This is followed by a consideration of the process, content, and dynamic complexities – what do they constitute and how can organizations navigate them? The chapter concludes with some reflections touching on the potential paradoxes and the need to take a systemic approach.

A Brief Review of the Literature

Given the first question regarding *who* to involve, understanding who is "a stakeholder" is an important consideration. Examination of the literature reveals that there are many definitions. That said, there are several common themes that transect them. Starting with one of the earliest (and probably best known) authors on stakeholders and stakeholder theory, Ed Freeman defines stakeholders as "any group or individual who can affect or is affected by the achievement of the organization's objectives" (1984, p. 46). A more recent definition of who is a stakeholder, drawing on the project management literature, is "any individual or group of individuals that is directly or indirectly impacted by a project" (Sutterfield et al., 2006). As can be seen, there is a clear overlap between the definitions with the difference being the focus (organizational objectives versus project – and it can be argued that projects themselves are the means to achieve organizational objectives).

As such, stakeholder theory recognizes the importance of taking different stakeholder perspectives into account (Freeman, 1984; Freeman et al., 2007; Lapulme et al., 2008). Much of the early (and ongoing) work builds off work in the strategy field with Ed Freeman's work (1984) being continuously cited along with that of Mitchell, Agle, and Wood (1997) and Donaldson and Preston (1995) to mention a few. Moving to the project management field, researchers such as Cleland (1986), Littau et al. (2010), Eskerod et al. (2015a, 2015b), and Winch (2017) have highlighted the importance of attending to stakeholders when embarking on projects. Other project management researchers have sought to understand stakeholders' roles and to create, develop, and maintain good relationships with project stakeholders for improving project performance (Winch, 2017). The project management research effort includes studies relating to stakeholder identification (Ackermann & Eden, 2011; Aapaoja & Haapasalo, 2014), stakeholder influence (Olander & Lander, 2005), stakeholder engagement (Lehtinen & Aaltonen, 2020), stakeholder inclusiveness (Eskerod et al., 2015a), stakeholder analysis (Jepsen and Eskerod, 2009), stakeholder theory (Littau et al., 2010) and stakeholder disengagement (Lehtinen et al., 2019). This increasing attention to project management stakeholders has also been recognized in the industry "toolkits" such as the Project Management Institute's PMBOK Guide (2017) and the Association for Project Management APMBOK guide (APM, 2019).

However, reflecting on this breadth of work reveals a tension for project managers – returning to the presence of paradoxes. For example, by recognizing the diversity of stakeholders (noting research in stakeholder identification and inclusiveness) and thus reducing uncertainties around "who is who in the zoo," project managers are confronted with increasing project complexity (Winch, 2004) – whom to include or not to include and how. As such, the resolution of uncertainty appears to result in complexity.

As such, the chapter now considers the three questions focusing first on *who*, before moving to *how* and *why*. In doing this, the chapter seeks to keep in mind the twin challenges of uncertainty and complexity, as they are important considerations. For example, in understanding *who* to engage with (and thus reduce uncertainty on one front), we also need to consider issues around processual complexity, that is, understanding *how* to engage; and when reflecting on engagement, there are considerations surrounding content complexity (the management of the range of contributions). Finally, when considering *when* to engage, we touch on dynamic complexity. Managing across these different forms of complexity has elements of permeability – that is, when thinking about process complexity it is difficult to separate this from content complexity – however, when managing both together, it is possible to accrue multiplier effects (Eden, 1990).

The Three Questions

Who to Engage?

As noted in the Introduction, considering *who* to engage is one of the questions facing project managers. This question touches on a further question, namely, *why* engage with the latter question providing some help in resolving the question of who. As noted earlier, there has been considerable research undertaken (both in the project management field and strategy) in terms of stakeholder identification, inclusiveness, and analysis. However, one of the issues that emerges from exploring the stakeholder landscape is the challenge relating to the overwhelming number of stakeholders. Mitchell et al. have noted that working with a considerable number of stakeholders can be "bewilderingly complex for managers" (1997, p. 857) and provided a stakeholder analysis model incorporating three attributes, namely, power, legitimacy, and urgency. This model – a Venn diagram – allows for managerial action to be tailored depending on which of the three attributes the stakeholder is perceived to have. For example, a stakeholder who is perceived to have both power and urgency may be viewed as dangerous and management actions will be tailored accordingly. This model takes a resource-based approach reflecting the costs (in terms of time and money) required to manage a full suite of stakeholders. Researchers have noted the rationality of not attending to non-salient stakeholders (Eskerod, et al., 2015a). This, however, can be vulnerable to change (dynamic complexity) as stakeholders over time can gain salience (through new alliances being created, new capabilities being developed, legislative changes, etc.)

Other means of both identifying and managing the wealth of stakeholders can be through the power interest matrix (Mendelow, 1981), where project team members are encouraged to surface a wide range of stakeholders and then position these on the matrix. Stakeholders are placed into one of four quadrants with each quadrant having management activities associated. For example, those stakeholders in the high-power high-interest quadrant are seen as key players, those in the high-power low-interest are seen as kept informed. Using this helps take a broader view of stakeholders – a position argued by many (Eskerod et al., 2015a; Meynhardt et al., 2016).

This matrix has been further developed by Ackermann and Eden (2011), where additional considerations have been introduced to allow for further consideration of who to involve. These additions include encouraging the disaggregation of stakeholders to the level of management, for example, considering specific ministers or departments rather than "the government" or mentioning by name key suppliers that need specific management attention from suppliers in general. A second addition is to overlay dispositions, namely, which stakeholders are likely to be positive, negative, and neutral in relation to the project. Finally, building on social network analysis (Rowley, 1997), adding the formal and informal relationships between stakeholders onto the matrix allows for forms of soft power and influence to be identified and considered.

Simon (1977) recommends the four stages of decision-making, namely, intelligence, design, evaluation, and implementation, and warns of the dangers of moving to evaluation too quickly.

Stakeholder identification fits solidly in the intelligence stage with the power interest matrix and/or stakeholder analysis model enabling the structuring of data (design) and helping with the analysis for evaluation. Each of the activities not only helps in reducing uncertainty – as all the models/matrices act as dialectics teasing out additional information – but also with the complexity through the structuring properties. The analysis also assists with evaluation – helping to reveal which of the stakeholders requires attention and when. This is important; as Warren Bennis commented, "All claims deserve consideration, but some claims are more important than others" (2011). Determining who to involve or not has resource implications – a point noted by Lethtinen et al., when they state "the reason for this exclusion was to eliminate the need for complex negotiation and bargaining processes among external stakeholders with conflicting interests and to avoid the uncertainties, instability and progress delays that could arise from overly complex organizational arrangements" (2019, p. 66)

Activities such as understanding the power and interest of stakeholders, carrying out social network analysis, and developing stakeholder webs (Ackermann & Eden, 2011) can help in determining which stakeholders to focus on and why. The stakeholder webs help explore in more depth the bases of power and interest allowing a more nuanced appreciation of the stakeholder to be gained. An example of this is nuclear power projects. Licensees can become frustrated with regulatory inspectors when they examine proposed changes or a new build, in what appears to the licensee to be excessive detail that results in considerable delay. However, on understanding better the underlying rationale for this behavior, namely, that each inspector is personally liable for any project they sign off on, the behavior became more understandable and a more collaborative stance becomes possible. This deeper understanding resonates with a quote attributed to Abraham Lincoln, namely, "I don't like that man; I must get to know him better." Helping project managers understand not just what a stakeholder can do but also why (their objectives) is likely to increase the chance of effective management.

Returning to the point made in the Introduction, spending time throughout the life of a project actively considering who are stakeholders and which need to be attended to can be challenging both from the perspective of time (and therefore cost) and competencies (which will be explored further when considering process and content complexity).

How to Engage?

How to engage encompasses several decisions – including the role the stakeholder might play (Winch 2017), the benefits accrued, and the form of engagement, for example, interviews, workshops, and surveys. Project managers are faced with a range of different engagement options – with the choice influenced by issues relating to governance, values, and dynamism (Lehtinen & Aalonen, 2020). Deciding on how to engage requires determining whether it is one way – project team to stakeholders, stakeholders to the team, or both ways, that is, stakeholders to stakeholders and team. Project managers can decide between the "management *of*" stakeholders versus management *for* stakeholders (Freeman et al., 2007). The "management *of*" focus seeks to attend to those who can withhold resources (and thus either enable or impede the project's progression) whereas the "management *for*" activity considers legitimacy and that these stakeholders are inherently valuable. Undertaking the power-interest matrix can provide some help in making this decision. An alternative, when considering public engagement, is Rowe and Frewer's three chronological elements, namely, "public community," "public consultation," and "public participation" (2005).

When considering different engagement options, factors such as enhancing social learning (Pasquier et al., 2020), facilitating the arrival of a consensual view (Newton & Elliott, 2016), and increasing trust and social cohesion to reduce conflicts (van Leeuwen et al., 2014) must be considered. These are all valuable factors and touch on the need to attend to learning and collaboration. However, when considering how to engage, managers also need to be careful to avoid complaints regarding stakeholder fatigue (van Leeuwen et al.,

2014; Bracken et al., 2015; Newton & Elliott, 2016; Pasquier et al., 2020), tokenistic engagement (Eskerod & Huemann, 2013; van Leeuwen et al., 2014), and that the engagement is lacking representation/credibility (Gramberger et al., 2015). A further factor is expectation alignment (Eskerod, et al. 2015a).

Depending on how managers wish to engage with stakeholders, the forms of engagement vary. Often, in large public-oriented projects, there is a tendency to use surveys to gather data from a wide range of stakeholders. However, there are challenges with this, as surveys/questionnaires do not allow for "deeply held beliefs" (Green & Sergeeva, 2019) to be identified and provide little chance for stakeholders to expand on their beliefs (Lupton, 1993). That said, surveys are relatively easy to administer and analyze. Workshops provide another mode of engagement – allowing for stakeholders to have a voice, piggyback off one another, and learn but require facilitation from both a processual and content management perspective and take time. The choice of how to engage is therefore inextricably linked with both process and content complexities.

When to Engage?

Returning to the strategy field, early work saw stakeholders being considered either in the initial stages of strategic planning as part of analyzing the environment (for example, industry analysis) or when considering the implementation of the strategy. However, more recently, there is an increasing sense that engaging with stakeholders is an ongoing process. This shift toward continual consideration is reflected in the project management literature. For example, Amadi et al. (2018) argue for early and constant engagement. Likewise, Aaltonen et al. (2015) show how proactive influence strategies consisting of active dialogue and early stakeholder engagement shifted the opposing external stakeholders into neutral ones. Continual engagement can provide benefits.

Furthermore, Aaltonen and colleagues noted that proactive engagement provided early indications of how the use of stakeholder management strategies may change over time – reflecting a dynamic stakeholder landscape. "Managing the inherent stakeholder dynamics of inter-organizational projects – that is, the constantly changing interactions between internal and external stakeholders" (Lehtinen & Aalonen, 2020) adds to the project management challenges. This then requires looking at stakeholders in a systemic (rather than discrete) manner as illustrated by Eskerod et al. reflecting on Ackoff's suggestion that "stakeholders should be seen as elements of a system" 2015b, p. 8). Project managers are faced with navigating the compounding series of actions and reactions by individuals as they interact with each other throughout the engagement process (Chinyio & Olomolaiye, 2010; Eskerod & Vaagaasar, 2014; Eden & Ackermann, 2021).

To assist in managing this, Lehtinen et al. (2019) present a processual model that encompasses four stages, namely, framing, legitimating, maintaining, and reflecting on different activities over time. Reflecting on this dynamic nature of the stakeholder landscape, Lehtinen et al. propose the role of disengagement alongside that of engagement, particularly in the early life cycle phases of projects (2019, p. 68) further touching on variations over time. Tung (2020) examined the critical paths of decommissioning projects and, based on analysis of existing cases and interview data, developed a set of stakeholder-oriented critical paths revealing when it was critical to engage.

But knowing who, when, and how demands knowing how to manage the complexities surrounding stakeholder engagement processes and resultant content in an effective manner.

Managing Process Complexity

As noted in the Introduction, one consequence of seeking to reduce uncertainties, particularly in the realm of project stakeholder management is that it generates process and content complexities requiring managerial attention. As such, project managers will need to ensure that they have an even broader range of competencies (Cha & Maytorena, 2019) attending to both technical and relational competencies (Eskerod & Vaagaasad, 2014). While technical competencies typically are well known and seen as a necessary part of a project managers toolkit, relational or social competencies are less so, and yet "project managers must become skilled at managing and resolving conflict between various project stakeholders while keeping the project on time and within budget" (Sutterfield, 2006, p. 32), illustrating one of the many relational competencies required.

Many of these process complexities can be seen as akin to facilitation skills where managing power, politics, personalities, and other sociopolitical considerations are paramount. For example, it is argued that to succeed in managing these issues, project managers are encouraged to engage with stakeholders – that is, to undertake practices "to involve stakeholders in a positive manner in organizational activities" (Greenwood, 2007, p. 315). When viewed through the stakeholder project management lens, issues relating to encouraging involvement, gaining a social licence to operate, managing conflict, and facilitating negotiation appear as critical competencies.

Encouraging involvement is seen as a challenge both from the perspective of the organization managing its stakeholders and from the stakeholders themselves. Taking the focal organization's perspective first, there are few descriptions of how stakeholder management "ideas" are implemented in practice and of what value this brings to organizations (De Gooyert et al., 2017). This can have an impact on engagement as organizations can be wary of expending resources on managing stakeholders. For example, when faced with tight deadlines, spending time on stakeholder management risks may be put to one side or given superficial attention (leading to the claims of tokenism). There is also a concern that involving stakeholders may lead to expectation escalation (and the potential for disappointment) and delays in a project. Moreover, encouraging involvement may result in increased inclusiveness and thus carries increased risks of loss of focus on key stakeholders as noted by Smith and Love (2004) and Eskerod et al. (2015a) – touching on the uncertainty challenges relating to who and how.

Likewise, there are also competing pressures on the stakeholders that focal organizations are seeking to manage and engage. These may include time pressures but also uncertainties about the implications of being involved. Are they representing their entire organization, their industry, how they are expected to engage, etc? For example, a project seeking to understand the key questions regarding the different decommissioning options available (namely, leave in situ, totally remove, partially remove) sought the views of a range of different cohorts but struggled to be able to encourage participants to engage. This reticence is not new – many stakeholders experience stakeholder fatigue (van Leeuwen et al., 2014; Bracken et al., 2015; Newton & Elliott, 2016; Pasquier et al., 2020). Consequently, getting the right people to attend is challenging – partly through being clear *who* are the right people and, secondly, convincing them to engage.

Moreover, having got the stakeholders to engage, *how* to engage raises itself as an issue (returning to the uncertainty consideration). In some instances, conformity pressures can inhibit openness, and there can be instances where air time is not equally spread between members potentially resulting in important considerations being missed (having both content and process implications). As such, project managers must attend to issues relating to procedural justice (Kim & Mauborgne, 1995) as well as procedural rationality (Simon, 1957). Attending to the design of engagement becomes a key competency and both Malhotra et al. (2017) and Luedicke et al. (2017) highlight the fact that effectiveness in inclusion relies on a range of practices, for example, controlled agenda-setting and issue-framing to manage the risk of dysfunctional escalation of openness. They also note the need to watch for the excessive promotion of individual interests and manage problems of information overload (touching on the content complexity consideration).

When considering projects that are in the public arena, for example, the construction of a new port, there are demands on project managers to include a very wide range of stakeholders to *gain a social license* to operate. Designing effective engagement practices to attend to these broad constituencies highlights another competency, one that is important given the increasing appetite to meet CSR/ESG requirements. In a recent article by McKinsey, it is noted that "although valid questions have been raised about ESG, the need for companies to understand and address their externalities is likely to become essential to maintaining their social licence" (Perez et al., 2022). When this is not attended to, problems can occur, however, when done well, engagement and ownership can result. "Studies have shown that taking stakeholders into account often improves organizational performance, mainly through improved reputation, increased trust from stakeholders, an improved 'license to operate'" (De Grooyert et al., 2017, p. 404).

One of the key justifications for engaging stakeholders is to *avoid conflict and challenges* in projects (Olander & Landin, 2005). Project managers naturally seek to avoid problems relating to adverse consequences – for cost, time, reputational damage, etc. reasons. However, while this sounds intuitively obvious, and well covered in both the academic and professional literature, there are still many instances where insufficient consideration of stakeholders (potentially through either not recognizing a stakeholder's significance or not even identifying a stakeholder) sees projects being significantly affected. This is illustrated in the well-known example of Brent Spar and a more recent situation focusing on the destruction of Jukkan Gorge (Wensing, 2021). As such, effective engagement is critical to gain social license (Moffat et al., 2016).

A related consideration in relation to avoiding conflict and challenges is attending to political considerations. Public projects are particularly subject to this as evidenced through the design and build of the Scottish Parliament building and many others. Political interests can be fickle, with support being initially provided and later withdrawn (as different ministers transition in and out of roles). An example of this is the Sydney Opera house project (Gaim et al., 2022) and the Municipality case by Eskerod et al. (2016). Being alert to this possibility adds to the process complexity competencies, as well as touching on dynamic complexity.

Finally providing project managers with *negotiation skills* is an important process competence. The need to ensure alignment of goals has been seen to be critical for effective project management for some considerable time (Christensen & Walker, 2003) but little assistance is given in terms of how this might be achieved (de Gooyert et al., 2017). Understanding the different stakeholder values in detail provides valuable insights and can be informed by using management webs. Designing opportunities for stakeholders to surface their goals and their underlying rationale and explore these in a "safe" environment (managing the earlier mentioned conformity pressures, etc.) can facilitate alignment. Having the skills "to combine, contrast and aggregate the different priorities and positions in order to balance the diverse claims and fuse the fragmented set of interests into a collective notion of a wider common good" (Dalcher, 2020, p. 4) illustrates the need for negotiation competencies as does the demand "to seek win-win solutions rather than trade-offs" (Eskerod et al., 2015, p. 10).

Managing Content Complexity

One of the consequences of attending to the uncertainties relating to *who* and *how* along with managing the process complexity is the resultant content management complexity. In seeking to engage stakeholders, it is inevitable that the *volume of information* surfaced increases. Techniques such as causal mapping can help (Edkins et al., 2007; Maytorena et al., 2007; Ackermann and Alexander, 2016). Causal maps not only allow for the breadth of contribution to be managed but additionally provide analytical features thus helping with the management of the resultant complexity. In addition, they also help in enhancing communications as stakeholders can see each other's views in context (returning to the need for deeper understanding and learning) and issues relating to cognitive overload can be reduced (Malhotra et al., 2017; Luedicke et al., 2017). Dalcher argues that "integrating different perspectives requires engagement, appreciation, understanding and rich interpretation" (2020, p. 4). Other forms of visualization that assist with content management are stakeholder circles (Bourne & Walker, 2005).

A specific example of an increase in information is in the plurality of goals – as already noted (when considering process complexity), particularly in relation to gaining a social license to operate. For example, the shift from a predominant focus on shareholder value to one that encompasses wider social, environmental, and governance goals – seeking to develop strategies that attend to the "common good" (Bryson et al., 2021) – is gaining traction in both the strategy and project management arenas. Moving beyond the iron triangle to acknowledge and respond to micro and macro (strategic) objectives (Lim & Mohamed 1999) or values (Lehtinen & Aaltonen 2020) becomes an important consideration. Goodpaster et al. (2002, p. 98) note, "It seems essential, yet problematic, to guide corporate decisions by a view of common good arrived at by simply aggregating separate stakeholder costs and benefits." Thus, identifying and managing the content as well as negotiating is critical.

Moreover, it is not just the plurality of values that need to be considered but also their impacts on one another – in essence building a goal system – that is critical *to identifying and managing goals/values*. Bryson et al. (2016) reflect on the need to attend to a goals system that comprises both project goals and organizational goals when embarking upon a new power generation project. The project goals centered on goals such as "ensuring facilities are safe, reliable and secure" and "build quality better than existing." These goals (and associated actions), however, were within the context of both the licensee and regulator's own organizational goals – for example, "build facilities to cost and create a viable export market" (licensee goal) and "develop greater public confidence in the regulator" (regulator goal). Thus, when considering actions to help achieve the project goals, these were evaluated against the entire goals system rather than just project goals, increasing the likelihood of implementation. This recognition of the two potential sets of goals has been identified by others (Lehtinen & Aaltonen, 2020). Designing interventions that allow for the surfacing and structuring of the goals provide a structure for negotiation – managing process and content complexity.

Managing both process and content helps *increase creativity and innovation*. By enabling stakeholders (internal or external) to be able to effectively engage and surface contributions, new ways forward can be co-created through the generation of new options (Fisher & Ury, 1981). Gaim et al. also reflect on this role of creativity and managing the process considerations, noting, "From our analysis, two forms of voice were apparent: blended, where multiple voices were allowed to interpenetrate compared with singular voices, in which individual voices dominated" (2022, p. 408). Designing engagement attending to both process and content considerations allows for structured conversations – enabling polyphony through being able to "fuse their perspectives to some extent while sustaining the uniqueness of their individual perspectives" (Baxter, 2004, p. 191).

Finally, a further benefit of managing content complexity is that the increased range of views helps in *reducing bias* (Tversky & Kahneman, 1974) and narrowness of vision. For example, an energy company, seeking to develop a new energy solution for a remote set of islands was considering smart grids (enabling the integration of wind, waste burning, and oil-generated power). While conducting risk workshops involving stakeholders such as the island council as part of their engagement process, a hitherto unforeseen risk – namely, the challenge of retaining someone to manage the smart grid in such an isolated area – came to light. It had never occurred to the energy company.

Managing Dynamic Complexity

Adding to process and content complexity is dynamic complexity, which adds to the uncertainties experienced by project managers and can take several aspects. One aspect is that stakeholders cannot be considered discrete entities. Project managers need to consider the actions and reactions made by stakeholders as they interact with each other throughout the project (Lehtinen et al., 2019; Eden & Ackermann, 2021) as reflected in Chow and Leringer's comment that "managing stakeholders involves managing compounding series of actions and reactions by individuals as they interact with each other throughout the engagement process" (2020, p. 25).

The second aspect of dynamic complexity is that, over time, projects experience changes such as (a) stakeholders come and go, (b) external events occur (e.g. new regulations, pandemics, etc.), and (c) new relationships are built. This can result in goals or objectives changing over the course of a project particularly when they are lengthy projects (Bourne & Walker, 2005). An example of this is the earlier mentioned example of the Sydney Opera House project.

The third aspect of dynamic complexity stems from needing to consider the objectives of future stakeholders (Silvius & Schipper, 2014) – particularly for projects taking decades to complete. This has been found to be much more challenging as anticipating the values of future stakeholders is incredibly difficult to predict.

Conclusion

To summarize, there are several interacting uncertainties facing project managers including those about who, how, and when to engage. Moreover, when attempts are made at resolving these uncertainties, the resulting outcomes may add to the complexities facing project managers. This is reflected in Figure 5.1

Moreover, three potential paradoxes emerge, namely:

- *Paradox 1 – project managers seeking to manage uncertainty risk increasing the complexity of the project.*
- *Paradox 2 – project managers when engaging to reduce dissent and tap into creativity can experience time delays, and scope changes.* Engaging stakeholders raises expectations and can surface demands that may lead to changes in scope and can require managerial time (a finite resource). As noted by Eskerod and Vaasaagar, "the project management team only has limited resources (seen in a very broad sense in terms of money, time, management attention, and so forth) to spend on project stakeholder interactions" (2014, p. 72) and "we do not have unlimited resources to generate benefits for the stakeholders, but at the same time we can only sustain support if our stakeholders are not negatively surprised" (Eskerod et al., 2015).

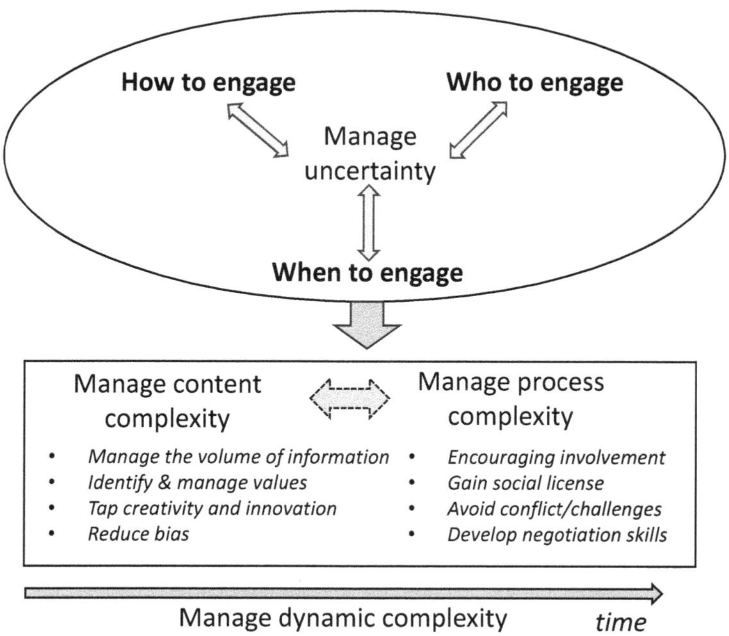

Figure 5.1 The interactive nature of project uncertainties and complexities.

- *Paradox 3 – project managers seeking to engage stakeholders may experience a loss of control over decision making.* Touching on earlier considerations engaging stakeholders reduces speed and flexibility over the decision-making processes (Rowe et al., 2005).

These paradoxes and the proposed model need careful consideration, particularly as "paradoxes presumed solved by closing off consideration of one side of the contradiction will be resolved only in the short term" (Gaim et al., 2022, p. 397). By being aware of them, project managers can develop the necessary competencies for managing process and content complexity, allowing for more collaborative and learning-rich engagements.

Returning to the strategy literature, project managers also may find value in exploring some of the practices being proposed for Open Strategy (Mack & Szulanski, 2017). Open strategy can provide insights into the dilemmas of process, commitment, disclosure, empowerment, and escalation (Hautz et al., 2017). As such, this work can help managers in clarifying the purpose of engagement (attending to determining who, when, and how) and will help with both the management of process (procedural justice) and content (procedural rationality) complexity. Finally, recognizing that projects comprise a flow and a rhythm of engagement and disengagement (Lehtinem et al., 2019), a systemic approach is necessary.

References

Aapaoja, A., and Haapasalo, H. (2014). A framework for stakeholder identification and classification in construction projects. *Open Journal of Business and Management*, *2*(1), 43–55.

Ackermann, F., and Alexander, J. (2016). Researching complex projects: Using causal mapping to take a systems perspective. *International Journal of Project Management*, *34*, 891–901.

Ackermann, F., and Eden, C. (2011). Strategic management of stakeholders: Theory and practice. *Long Range Planning*, *44*(3), 179–196.

Aaltonen, K., Kujala, J., Havela, L., and Savage, G. (2015). Stakeholder dynamics during the project front-end: The case of nuclear waste repository projects. *Project Management Journal*, *46*, 15–41.

Amadi, C., Carrillo, P., and Tuulie, M. (2018). Stakeholder management in PPP projects: External stakeholders' perspective. *Built Environment and Project Asset Management* *8*(4), 403–414.

APM (2019). *APM body of knowledge*, 7th ed., R. Murray-Webster and D. Dalcher (eds.). Association of Project Management.

Baxter, L. (2004). A tale of two voices: Relational dialectics theory. *Journal of Family Communication*, *4*(3–4), 181–192.

Bourne, L., and Walker, D. H. T. (2006). Visualizing stakeholder influence – two Australian examples. *Project Management Journal*, *37*(1), 5–21.

Bracken, L. J., Bulkeley, H. A., and Whitman, G. (2015). Transdisciplinary research: Understanding the stakeholder perspective. *Journal of Environmental Planning and Management*, *58*(7), 1291–1308.

Brady, T., and Maylor, H. (2010). The improvement paradox in project contexts: A clue to the way forward? *International Journal of Project Management*, *28*(8), 787–795.

Bryson, J. M., Ackermann, F., and Eden, C. (2016). Discovering collaborative advantage: The contributions of goal categories and visual strategy mapping. *Public Administration Review*, *76*(6), 912–925.

Bryson, J. M., Barberg, B., Crosby, B. C., and Patton, M. Q. (2021). Leading social transformations: Creating public value and advancing the common good. *Journal of Change Management*, *21*(2), 180–202.

Cha, J., and Maytorena, E. (2019). Prioritising project management competences across the software project lifecycle. *International Journal of Managing Projects in Business*, *12*(4), 961–978.

Chinyio, E., and Olomolaiye, P. (2010). Introducing stakeholder management (pp. 1–12). In E. Chinyio and P. Olomolaiye (eds.). *Construction stakeholder management*. Wiley-Blackwell.

Chow, V., and Leiringer, R. (2020). The practice of public engagement on projects: From managing external stakeholders to facilitating active contributors. *Project Management Journal*, *51*(1) 24–37.

Christensen, D., and Walker, D. H. T. (2003). Vision as a critical success factor to project outcomes. 17th World Congress on Project Management, Moscow, Russia, June 3–6.

Cleland, D. I. (1986). Project stakeholder management. *Project Management Journal, 17*(4), 36–44.

Dalcher, D. (2020). In whose interest? Repositioning the stakeholder paradox, advances in project management series, *PM World Journal, 9*(9), 1–9.

De Gooyert, V., Rouwette, E., Van Kranenburg, H., and Freeman, E. (2017). Reviewing the role of stakeholders in operational research: A stakeholder theory perspective. *European Journal of Operational Research, 262*(2), 402–410.

Donaldson, T., and Preston, L. (1995). The stakeholder theory of the corporation: Concepts, evidence, and implications. *Academy of Management Review, 20*(1), 65–91.

Eden, C. (1990). The unfolding nature of group decision support: Two dimensions of skill (pp. 48–52). In C. Eden and J. Radford (eds.). *Tackling strategic problems: The role of group decision support.* Sage.

Eden, C., and Ackermann, F. (2021). Modelling stakeholder dynamics for supporting group decision and negotiation: Theory to practice. *Group Decision and Negotiation, 30*(5), 1001–1025.

Edkins, A. J., Kurul, E., Maytorena-Sanchez, E., and Rintala, K. (2007). The application of cognitive mapping methodologies in project management research. *International Journal of Project Management, 25*(8), 762–772.

Eskerod, P., and Huemann, M. (2013). Sustainable development and project stakeholder management: What standards say. *International Journal of Managing Projects in Business, 6*(1), 36–50.

Eskerod, P., and Vaagaasar, A. L. (2014). Stakeholder management strategies and practices during a project course, *Project Management Journal, 45*(5), 71–85.

Eskerod, P., Huemann, M., and Ringhofer, C. (2015a). Stakeholder inclusiveness: Enriching project management with general stakeholder theory. *Project Management Journal, 46*(6), 42–53.

Eskerod, P., Huemann, M., and Savage, G. (2015b). Project stakeholder management – past and present. *Project Management Journal, 46*(6), 6–14.

Fisher, R., and Ury, W. (1981). *Getting to yes: Negotiating agreement without giving in,* 1st ed. Houghton Mifflin.

Freeman, R. E. (1984). *StrategimManagement: A stakeholder approach.* Pitman.

Freeman, R. E., Harrison, J. S., and Wicks, A. C. (2007). *Managing for stakeholders: Survival, reputation, and success.* Yale University Press.

Freeman, R. E., Parmar, B. L., and Martin, K. (2020). *The power of and: Responsible business without trade-offs.* Columbia University Press.

Gaim, M., Clegg, S., and Cunha, M. P. (2022). In praise of paradox persistence: Evidence from the Sydney Opera House project. *Project Management Journal, 53*(4), 397–415.

Goodpaster, K. E. (1991). Business ethics and stakeholder analysis. *Business Ethics Quarterly,* 53–73.

Goodpaster, K. E., Maines, T. D., and Rovang, M. D. (2002). Stakeholder thinking: Beyond paradox to practicality. *Journal of Corporate Citizenship,* 7, 93–111.

Gramberger, M., Zellmer, K., Kok, K., and Metzger, M. J. (2015). Stakeholder integrated research (STIR): A new approach tested in climate change adaptation research. *Climatic Change, 128*(3), 201–214.

Green, S. D., and Sergeeva, N. (2019). Value creation in projects: Towards a narrative perspective. *International Journal of Project Management, 37*(5), 636–651.

Greenwood, M. (2007). Stakeholder engagement: Beyond the myth of corporate responsibility. *Journal of Business Ethics, 74,* 315–327.

Hautz, J., Seidl, D., and Whittington, R. (2017). Open strategy: Dimensions, dilemmas, dynamics. *Long Range Planning, 50*(3) 298–309.

Jarzabkowski, P, Bednarek, R, Chalkias, K, et al. (2019). Exploring inter-organizational paradoxes: Methodological lessons from a study of a grand challenge. *Strategic Organization, 17*(1), 120–132.

Jepsen, A. L., and Eskerod, P. (2009). Stakeholder analysis in projects: Challenges in using current guidelines in the real world. *International Journal of Project Management, 27*(4), 335–343.

Laplume, A. O., Sonpar, K., and Litz, R. A. (2008). Stakeholder theory: Reviewing a theory that moves us. *Journal of Management, 34*(6), 1152–1189.

Lehtinen, J., and Aaltonen, K. (2020). Organizing external stakeholder engagement in inter-organizational projects: Opening the black box. *International Journal of Project Management,* 38, 85–98.

Lehtinen, J., Aaltonen, K., and Rajala, R. (2019). Stakeholder management in complex product systems: Practices and rationales for engagement and disengagement. *Industrial marketing management, 79,* 58–70.

Lim, C., and Mohamed, M. Z. (1999). Criteria of project success: An exploratory re-examination. *International Journal of Project Management, 17*(4), 243–248.

Littau, P., Jujagiri, J., and Adlbrecht, G. (2010). 25 years of stakeholder theory in project management literature (1984–2009). *Project Management Journal, 41*(4), 17–29.

Luedicke, M. K., Husemann, K. C., Furnari, S., and Ladstaetter, F. (2017). Radically open strategizing: How the premium cola collective takes open strategy to the extreme. *Long Range Planning, 50*(3), 371–384.

Lupton, D. (1993). Risk as moral danger: The social and political functions of risk discourse in public health. *International Journal of Health Services, 23*(3), 425–435.

Luscher, L. S., and Lewis, M. W. (2008). Organizational change and managerial sensemaking: Working through paradox. *Academy of Management Journal, 51*(2), 221–240.

Mack, D. Z., and Szulanski, G. (2017). Opening up: How centralization affects participation and inclusion in strategy making. *Long Range Planning, 50*(3), 385–396.

Malhotra, A., Majchrzak, A., and Niemiec, R. M. (2017). Using public crowds for open strategy formulation: Mitigating the risks of knowledge gaps. *Long Range Planning 50*(3), 397–410.

Maytorena, E., Winch, G. M., Freeman, J., and Kiely, T. (2007). The influence of experience and information search styles on project risk identification performance. *IEEE Transactions in Engineering Management, 54*(2), 315–326.

Mendelow A. (1981). Environmental scanning: The impact of stakeholder concept. In Proceedings of the Second International Conference on Information Systems, December.

Meynhardt, T., Chandler, J. D., and Strathoff, P. (2016). Systemic principles of value cocreation: Synergetics of value and service ecosystems. *Journal of Business Research, 69*(8), 2981–2989.

Mitchell, R. K., Agle, B. R., and Wood, D. J. (1997). Toward a theory of stakeholder identification and salience: Defining the principle of who and what really counts. *The Academy of Management Review, 22*(4), 853–886.

Moffat, K., Lacey, J., Zhang, A., and Leipold, S. (2016). The social licence to operate: A critical review. *Forestry. An International Journal of Forest Research, 89*(5), 477–488.

Morris, B. (2011). Interview with Bob Morris. Bobmorris.biz. https://Bobmorris.Biz/Warren-g-Bennis-an-Interview-by-Bob-Morris.

Newton, A., and Elliott, M. (2016). A typology of stakeholders and guidelines for engagement in transdisciplinary, participatory processes. *Frontiers in Marine Science, 3*, 230.

Olander, S., and Lander, A. (2005). Evaluation of stakeholder influence in the implementation of construction projects, *International Journal of Project Management, 23*, 321–328.

Pasquier, U., Few, R., Goulden, M. C., Hooton, S., He, Y., and Hiscock, K. M. (2020). "We can't do it on our own!" – integrating stakeholder and scientific knowledge of future flood risk to inform climate change adaptation planning in a coastal region. *Environmental Science & Policy, 103*, 50–57.

Perez, L., Hunt, V., Samandari, H., Nuttall, R., and Biniek, K. (2022). Does ESG really matter – and why? *McKinsey Quarterly*, August, 1–9.

Polanyi, M. (1966). *The tacit dimension*. Doubleday and Company.

Puranam, P. (2017). When will we stop studying innovations in organizing, and start creating them? *Innovation, 19*, 5–10.

Raisch S, Hargrave, T. J., and van de Ven, A. H. (2018). The learning spiral: A process perspective on paradox. *Journal of Management Studies, 55*(8), 1507–1526.

Rowe, G., Horlick-Jones, T., Walls, J., and Pidgeon, N. (2005). Difficulties in evaluating public engagement initiatives: Reflections on an evaluation of the UK GM Nation? Public debate about transgenic crops. *Public Understanding of Science, 14*(4), 331–352.

Rowley, T. J. (1997). Moving beyond dyadic ties: A network theory of stakeholder influences. *Academy of Management Review, 22*, 887–910.

Schad, J., Lewis, M. W., Raisch, S., et al. (2016). Paradox research in management science: Looking back to move forward. *Academy of Management Annals, 10*(1): 5–64.

Silvius, A. J. G., and Schipper, R. P. J. (2014). Sustainability in project management: A literature review and impact analysis. *Social Business, 4*(1), 63–96.

Simon, H. A. (1977). *The New science of management decision*, 3rd rev. ed.; 1st ed. (1960). Prentice-Hall.

Smith, J., and Love, P. E. D. (2004). Stakeholder management during project inception: Strategic needs analysis. *Journal of Architectural Engineering*, *10*(1), 22–33.

Smith, W. K., and Lewis, M. (2011). Toward a theory of paradox: A dynamic equilibrium model of organizing. *Academy of Management Review*, 36(2), 381–403.

Sutterfield, J. S., Friday-Stroud, S. S., and Shivers-Blackwell, S. L. (2006). A case study of project and stakeholder management failures: Lessons learned. *Project Management Journal*, *37*(5) 26–35.

Tung, A. (2020). Design and analysis of stakeholder-oriented critical paths for offshore decommissioning projects in the United Kingdom and Australian landscape using mixed-methods. Offshore Technology Conference, May.

Tversky, A., and Kahneman, D. (1974). Judgement under uncertainty: Heuristics and biases. *Science*, *185*(4157), 1124–1131.

van Leeuwen, J., Raakjaer, J., van Hoof, L., van Tatenhove, J., Long, R., and Ounanian, K. (2014). Implementing the marine strategy framework directive: A policy perspective on regulatory, institutional and stakeholder impediments to effective implementation. *Marine Policy*, *50*, 325–330.

Wensing, E. (2021). The destruction of Juukan Gorge: Lessons for planners and local governments. *Australian Planner*, *56*(4): 241–248.

Winch, G. M. (2004). Managing project stakeholders (pp. 321–339). In P. W. G. Morris and J. K. Pinto (eds.). *The Wiley guide to managing projects*. Wiley.

Winch, G. M. (2017). Megaproject stakeholder management (pp. 339–361). In Flyvbjerg, B. ed. *The Oxford handbook of megaproject management*. Oxford University Press.

PART II

Deviating from Plans

How Complexity and Uncertainty Affect Project Behavior

CHAPTER 6

Averaging Out Divergent Project Behavior

An Unintended Consequence of Project Structures

KIM VAN OORSCHOT, THERESE F. DILLE, and JONAS SÖDERLUND

Introduction

A central tenet of any large-scale project is the decomposition of the overall task into several smaller modules and sub-tasks whose development is allocated to different teams (Sosa et al., 2004). In effect, each team works on a work package or sub-problem, of which work is supervised by a sub-project manager who reports to the overall project manager. The role of the project manager is to coordinate sub-project activities and to support sub-project managers when problems arise – although obviously without knowing all the details of each sub-project. Although both programs and projects can be decomposed into smaller modules, in this chapter we focus on projects rather than programs. According to the PRINCE2 definition (PRINCE2, 2023), a project is a temporary organization that is created for the purpose of delivering one or more business products (content) according to a specified business case within a strict deadline, whereas a program is usually long term, without a fixed deadline, more aimed at delivering outputs that benefit the entire organization (context).

However, several boundary conditions have been identified in previous research pertaining to the effectiveness of such decompositions or hierarchical structures (e.g., Anderson & Brown, 2010), not to mention its negative consequences on information processing and decision-making (e.g., Dilts & Pence, 2006; Mihm et al., 2010). An underlying reason is that these decompositions establish a perceptual frame that may activate certain kinds of cognitive biases, which run the risk of impairing the quality of decision-making (Tversky & Kahneman, 1974). There are many different cognitive biases, see, for example, Flyvbjerg's overview of the top ten behavioral biases in project management (2021), but social comparison biases are particularly important in the context of hierarchy (Foss & Weber, 2016). Therefore, it is important to understand how such structures influence the ability of project managers to pay attention to the different parts of a hierarchy (e.g., sub-projects in a project) (Jacobides, 2007) and how this, in turn, affects project behavior. We refer here specifically to the behavior *of* projects, as opposed to the behavior *in* projects which is more aligned to organizational behavior (Unterhitzenberger, 2022). We aim to study how projects work or behave or take different and complex turn-outs (Ika et al., 2022). This has motivated our research question: *How do project structures influence the decision-making quality of a project manager and consequently, project behavior?*

To answer this question, we develop a process model that indicates that project structures – like the project hierarchy examined in this chapter – trigger categorical thinking. When the behavior of sub-projects is viewed as either good or bad, positive or negative, these diverging behaviors tend to be averaged out, which leads to overestimation of overall project performance. Overestimation of performance, we argue, can explain why projects run into trouble. We show that this is an unintended, negative, consequence of project structures that require further scrutiny in future research.

Theoretical Background

The core principle of an organizational hierarchy is that a task is decomposed into sub-tasks so that, once each sub-task has been solved, the original task will be completed. It is important to group smaller tasks that are similar, tightly coupled, or interdependent and to separate those tasks from others with respect to which they are but loosely coupled or even independent (Zhou, 2013). The execution of tasks at lower levels in the hierarchy is coordinated by higher levels. Such coordination consists mainly of three components: information processing, communicating, and decision-making (Tushman & Nadler, 1978; Zhou, 2013).

Complexity has led most contemporary large-scale projects to be undertaken not by a single project team but rather by several project teams that are highly interdependent (Shenhar, 2001), grouped under a common large-scale integrative project under the supervision of an overall project manager who heads the project hierarchy (Hoegl et al., 2004; Hoegl, 2005). The manager at the top of the hierarchy does not require detailed information about the behavior and performance of each sub-unit. This manager's primary role is not to "know everything" but instead to coordinate across sub-units, prioritize among sub-units, and oversee system-wide performance (Galbraith, 1973). The hierarchy thus serves the following purposes (Cyert & March, 1963; Jacobides, 2007): the design of problem decomposition, exception management for cognition (by helping frame and reframe problems), and actions or decision-making (by checking routine responses).

Many researchers have focused on problem decomposition – that is, on how to best divide a large-scale task or project into smaller sub-tasks or sub-projects. Previous research has addressed the nature and coordination of sub-task interdependencies (Smith & Eppinger, 1997; Ethiraj & Levinthal, 2004b), the manager's span of control (Keren & Levhari, 1979; Radner, 1992), and on performance differences of different hierarchical structures (Visser, 2000; Christensen & Knudsen, 2010; Mihm et al., 2010; Ingvaldsen & Rolfsen, 2012). In addition, several studies have examined the role of hierarchies in cognitive framing and decision-making.

Cognitive frames are heuristics that allow humans with limited processing capacity to make sense of their complex world (Gigerenzer, 2003; Foss & Weber, 2016). Organizational structures, like hierarchies, can act as so-called frames. They are attention-focusing devices (Jacobides, 2007). Rhee et al. (2019) have analyzed how cognitive accessibility, or the ease of information recall, influences the probability that a particular stimulus will be attended to by higher levels in the hierarchy. This can create a paradox at these higher levels.

Solutions to problems often reside at the lowest levels of an organization, but top level attention to the hierarchy's overall performance may impede the realization of those lower level solutions (Gaba & Joseph, 2013). Foss and Weber (2016) posit that different hierarchical forms facilitate specific cognitive frames and biases. More specifically, they point to biases in project hierarchies that can prompt an overestimation of individual abilities and claim greater contribution or success than warranted.

Hierarchical project structures usually reflect the product architecture, which means that there are more task dependencies within than between the sub-units of the project (Ethiraj & Levinthal, 2004b; Sosa et al., 2004). However, there is still a need to coordinate and integrate the activities of teams working on different sub-projects (Cheng, 1984; Ethiraj and Levinthal, 2004a). Therefore, on the one hand, hierarchies help managers by decomposing the problem and delegating the parts to other units or teams in the organization. As lower levels filter and compress information for the higher levels, detail is removed and order added (Thompson & Wildavsky, 1986), thereby protecting managers from an overload of too much detailed information (Simon, 1962). However, on the other hand, because of cognitive frames induced by organizational structures like hierarchies, information may get lost as it travels up the hierarchy. Hierarchies can therefore be both functional and dysfunctional (Bunderson et al., 2016). As such, we should consider how project decompositions (von Hippel, 1994) impact the ability of project managers to pay attention to the parts and, as a result, how this will influence their search for solutions (Jacobides, 2007). In fact, poor decision-making quality can be a logical consequence of organizational structures. Being unaware of the influence of such structures on decision-making can be an impediment of desirable behavior (Sterman, 2000). Project behavior consists of successes and failures, systematic veerings from preassigned paths, and propensities toward specific difficulties or payoffs (Hirschman, 1967). Therefore, it is crucial to understand how hierarchies affect managerial decision-making and consequently project behavior to fully comprehend the conflicting effects (both functional and dysfunctional) of hierarchies (Bunderson et al., 2016; Keum and See, 2017). As such, we focus on how the project as a whole behaves (as a system), not how the individual project manager and the sub-project managers within that particular project behave (Ika et al., 2022).

Research Methodology

We adopt a processual perspective (Langley, 1999) to acknowledge the complexity of the world and to examine relationships between project structures, managerial decision-making, and project behavior. Thus, our process study intends to address "the temporal order and sequence of change events based on a story or narrative" (Van de Ven, 2007, p. 196). As such, we first followed the narrative strategy for sensemaking, which involved the construction of a detailed story from the raw data (Step 1 of our approach). We then complemented the narrative strategy with the quantification (Step 2) and temporal bracketing strategy (Step 3). Based on the results of these three research steps, we developed a process model to explain our findings.

Research Context

The project studied in this chapter ("InfoTech") was a large and complex information systems project at Alpha Telecom (a pseudonym) with a total budget exceeding €100 million. The new system replaced several obsolete systems and would make it possible to improve the integration of administrative support and information across Alpha Telecom's three business units (BUs). These BUs were distributed over a large geographical area and problems with communicating within and across the BUs had been an ongoing issue for several years. The new system was therefore considered a business-critical investment. Hence, one of the project's main goals was to improve collaboration across Alpha Telecom's separate BUs, which until then had operated more or less autonomously.

InfoTech was initiated in 2007, and our research was launched approximately one year after that. InfoTech's initial period encompassed working out its finances, selecting the main sub-contractor, specifying requirements for the new information system, and establishing interfaces among the three business units. At this time, the project was not structured as a hierarchy involving three sub-projects. Although project activities had been divided into modules, so far there was only one project manager and no sub-project managers.

After this initial period, focus shifted from the generic overall project to the three BUs and the management team decided to structure the project as a hierarchy with three separate sub-projects – one for each BU – by which those unit-specific requirements would be addressed. Large parts of the firm's current IT system were similar for all three BUs; some parts of the new system were developed with reference to each BU's specific requirements concerning, for example, the user interface, integration with local IT systems, and required level of information security. BU1 was the largest business unit consisting of multiple local departments with specific requirements specifications. BU2 and BU3 had about the same level of complexity and challenges. To coordinate the activities within each sub-project, three sub-project managers were hired. In terms of team size: directly involved in each sub-project were one responsible sub-project manager and 8–10 additional members of staff for each sub-project.

All three sub-projects were to be executed in parallel, and all had the same due date because of the need for a synchronized transition to the new

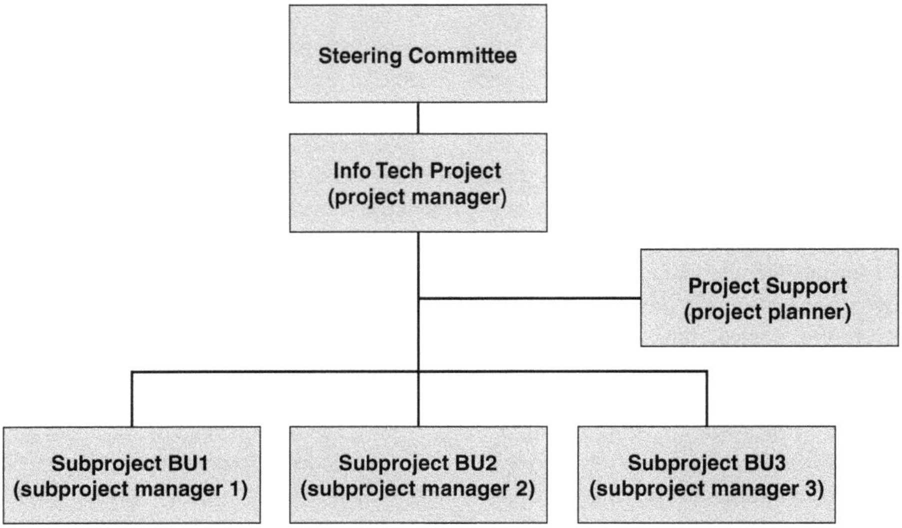

Figure 6.1 The project hierarchy of InfoTech.

system. A synchronized and well-coordinated sequential approach was considered essential for success in developing, implementing, and testing the new system. The main software development was outsourced to an international sub-contractor that had considerable experience working on similar projects for other organizations around the world.

The management team consisted of a project manager and a project planner as well as three sub-project managers, each responsible for one of the three sub-projects. The project manager reported regularly to the organization's steering committee, which comprised a small group of top managers and line managers. The project hierarchy is depicted in Figure 6.1.

Data Collection

We followed the project in real time through participant observations and interviews. One of the authors was invited to attend the project management meetings for a period of nine months. The observation period coincided with the project's most critical phase: the months when the system's development was being planned and implementation of a pilot project was taking place.

In addition, and to maximize our understanding of the project *in vivo*, we also conducted interviews covering what was happening at several different times (Van de Ven, 2007). Prior to the observation period, 21 interviews were held so that we would better understand the project's background and its initiation phase. We also conducted 8 interviews during the observation period and 11 interviews after the final project management meeting; these last interviews sought to characterize how the project ended and to clarify and expand on themes discussed at the observed meetings. Interviewees included the project manager, sub-project managers, staff members, top managers, and selected significant stakeholders. Most interviews were recorded and transcribed; in addition, detailed comments were written during and immediately after the interview. Each interview lasted approximately two hours. We also had regular informal meetings with the project manager about the project's progress and the content of reports that were sent to the steering committee.

Findings and Analysis

Step 1: The Narrative

Following the new implementation approach with sub-project managers, InfoTech entered the first of two phases. Phase 1 was to culminate in a pilot implementation – namely, development and small-scale rollout of the new system in one of Alpha Telecom's main business regions. Upon completion of that phase, the system would be thoroughly evaluated before determining the design and structure to be used for the organization-wide rollout (Phase 2). Both the change to a project hierarchy and the phased time schedules were generally viewed as successful. As the project manager explained in an interview: "We have appointed sub-project managers for each BU. This has had very positive consequences – obvious things, like being able to follow up each individual BU in a better way. We are closer to them, and our relationship is much better . . . I would also say this has allowed us to make the progress we've made . . .. The BUs are also satisfied with this new way of managing the project."

During the first four project meetings that we observed, the overall atmosphere was positive. The project manager began the meeting with a brief introduction that updated important project activities and core problems. After this introduction, each sub-project manager presented a brief status report and summarized any problems currently encountered; these presentations lasted for about 20 minutes each. Figure 6.2 presents an overview of the types of problems that were discussed during the meetings. For example, in meeting #1, a little over 60 percent of the problems were related to time, around 30 percent of the problems were related to costs, and around 10 percent were related to synchronization of the three sub-projects. In the period that spanned these first four meetings, synchronization problems became more dominant. BU1 had more specific requirements than the other two sub-projects, causing administrative work and delays. BU3 had relatively few problems in ensuring that its requirements were integrated into the system and executed on time. As the BU3 sub-project manager expressed it in a meeting: "We need to establish a plan on how activities should be coordinated in Phase 2 . . .. Now, everything for the BU3 is in place. Meanwhile, BU1 has just started the integration process." Although BU2 experienced some delays, they were less serious than the problems encountered by BU1.

Toward meeting #5, the situation turned. There seemed to be two factors driving this change. First, the approaching due date for the pilot created an urge to speed up activities in both BU1 and BU2 – that is, so their progress would be sufficient to gain approval for an organization-wide rollout in all business regions. The second factor was that, as the start of Phase 2 approached, the project manager's attention was diverted from Phase 1 toward the planning of Phase 2; of course, the sub-project managers were also involved and provided input for this task. As the project manager expressed in one of the meetings: "We have to get them started on Phase 2 planning, and we have to make sure that they meet the Phase 1 deadline. We have to make this work . . .. That means, we need to prioritize, and we have to meet this final milestone." The due date of Phase 1 was also communicated to the top management of the company and also to the

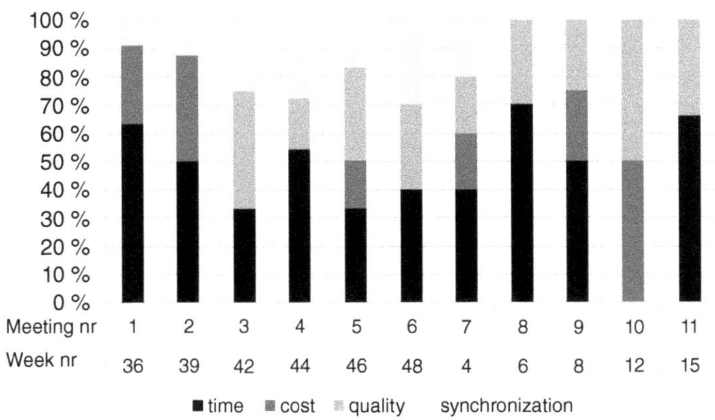

Figure 6.2 Relative distribution of types of problems discussed in monthly project meetings.

project's steering committee. This made it even more critical to meet the final milestone and begin preparing Phase 2.

Planning for Phase 2 was especially difficult for BU1, which needed all its time and energy to complete its pilot activities on time. In contrast, BU3 was ready for Phase 2, and BU3's sub-project manager emphasized repeatedly that any delay would damage momentum of the sub-project team. Potentially, a delay in this process could cause a major hold-up of the overall implementation process. The project manager seemed to follow the pace of BU3 and began focusing more on the future (Phase 2) than on current issues in the other sub-projects. This resulted in confusion and unanswered questions in the meetings: "We have many parallel activities now. Who should do what and how should we coordinate all this? How do we handle all these issues?" (BU1 sub-project manager).

Despite that sub-project managers of BU1 and BU2 repeatedly stated that Phase 1 completion was problematical, the project manager focused more and more on preparing for Phase 2. In particular, the sub-project manager representing BU3 emphasized the importance of starting the preparation of Phase 2: "BU3 is not satisfied, they have been waiting for a long time and their motivation is decreasing. We need to establish an honest plan on how activities should be coordinated in Phase 2. There have been so many problems in Phase 1, so we have to be trustworthy and realistic."

The focus on BU3's requirements affected the overall atmosphere in the meetings and the sub-project managers representing BU1 and BU2 felt that they were not being heard, as exemplified by the following quotes. BU1 sub-project manager: "What is happening? The plan for Phase 2, what is it based on?" BU2 sub-project manager: "There are no common principles. BU3 has been leading this process; they have had time to prepare this, they have their own lists. It should be the same for everyone." BU1 sub-project manager: "BU1 and BU2 have not gotten sufficient experience yet to prepare this [Phase 2]."

While the project manager and BU3's sub-project manager synchronized their preparations for the second phase, BU1 lagged farther and farther behind schedule on Phase 1. This was challenging for BU1's sub-project manager. In the meetings, he urged the others to focus more on the ongoing activities in the first phase: "It is important that we help [BU1] in this process. [BU1] has a long way to go. They are delayed on all parts in Phase 1, we can add several months on their schedule."

Despite attempts to coordinate project activities and allocate more resources, the problems in the first phase remained. The problems appeared both too many and too large. The lack of support and information from the project manager became even more pressing as the deadline approached.

Eight months after the start of Phase 1, it became apparent that the three sub-projects could not synchronize their pilot activities. This is also reflected in Figure 6.2, as problems regarding synchronization disappear from the meetings. As the project manager explained later, "Problems of synchronizing activities were undoubtedly one of the most crucial issues in the project." If the pilot tests were delayed, then BU3 would be disappointed because they were on schedule and would be "punished for working hard." However, if the pilot tests were not delayed then BU1 would suffer greatly because nonstop work would be required to get back on schedule. One project member expressed his frustration in an interview: "We've gotten into a situation where we have major problems with BU1. We have to recognize that that's where we are. It's difficult, but we just have to continue doing the job on a practical level."

The only way to resolve this situation was to de-synchronize implementation. After this decision, the meetings began to focus more on restructuring the project than on discussing current problems. Ten months after the start of Phase 1, the steering committee decided that the envisioned synchronized implementation and transition to the new system across sub-projects could be abandoned.

Although this de-synchronized implementation was viewed as the best way to proceed, it required the hierarchical project structure to change. The new mandate given by the steering committee empowered the sub-project managers, who now took more control of their respective sub-projects, while relegating the project manager to the role of facilitator who would provide guidance and support to each sub-project as needed. Hence, project management activities and decisions became more decentralized at the sub-project level, reducing the need for traditional project management meetings. The sub-project managers could focus more on implementing the new system as separate projects in their own BUs and less on synchronization problems. This new implementation strategy also meant that the technical interfaces between the BUs had to be solved on a local level when each of the units were ready to start using the new system. While this created a number of new coordination challenges, it was considered to be the most efficient way to organize the project.

Each sub-project team managed to finish Phase 1 before 2012 – although not at the same time. The result was a delay of approximately one year as compared with the initial plan.

Step 2: Quantification of Problems

The project hierarchy put the project manager in the driver's seat, while the sub-project managers oversaw their respective sub-projects. The project manager collected the status information received from the sub-project managers, processed it into an evaluation of InfoTech as a whole and acted accordingly. Thus, the project manager was precisely following the rules of an organizational hierarchy. Still, almost a year elapsed before the project manager realized that the project's hierarchy, initially embraced as an instrument for synchronizing activities, was not working at all.

To analyze the project's dynamics and how the project hierarchy functioned, we coded our qualitative data (meeting notes and quotes). The core concept for our research concerned exceptional events that happened during the execution of sub-projects: problematic project behavior, or for short: *problems*. A problem reflects any (potentially) negative event that a sub-project faces and must be resolved in order not to compromise the overall project plan's time, quality, and cost requirements – that is, conventional success criteria for projects of this kind. After all, it is a critical task of the project management team to identify and structure the most important problems threatening the project. In the meetings, problems can be mentioned by any of the three sub-project managers, followed by a response from the project manager. When the project manager acknowledges the problem, provides guidance, offers solutions, or notes that he will take further action after the meeting, the problem is *escalated* to the project level. Each time problematic sub-project behavior was mentioned by one of the sub-project managers, we coded the incident with the number 1 for the respective BU. Every time such a problem was escalated to the project level, we also coded the incident with the number 1 at the project level (so this incident would have a number 1 at both the BU level and at the project level). Problems that were ignored by the project manager or not discussed any further were not given a number at the project level. As such, for each problem we know where it occurred, when it was mentioned (which meeting), and whether it was escalated to the project manager (leading to a decision made by the project manager). Table 6.1 displays some sample quotes, taken from the management team meetings. To check for inter-coder reliability (Miles & Huberman, 1994), another individual – not otherwise connected to the study – was asked to code the total set of events. There was 82.3 percent agreement on the coding, which exceeds the 80 percent threshold for reliability suggested by Miles and Huberman. Yet to improve that reliability further, the research team reexamined all the events that had been coded differently and agreed on the final coding.

The quantitative codes enabled us to see how problems evolved over time. Figure 6.3 plots the behavior of the number of problems discussed in each meeting at different levels. Stacked columns represent the problems at the BU level; a solid line represents the problems at the project level. (Note that during the first two meetings, the number of problems at the project level exceeds the sum of all problems at the BU level. This happened because the project manager discussed generic problems that were equally relevant to all BUs.)

Figure 6.3 illustrates two remarkable findings. First, it clearly shows that the sub-projects varied widely in terms of the number of problems they faced. BU1 (black columns) was the most

Table 6.1 Coding examples

Week	Incident	Problem owner BU1	BU2	BU3	Project
6	Sub-project manager BU1: "There are problems with 'going live' for one of our sub-systems. The due date is critical." Project manager: "We will discuss this with the sub-contractor. It is important to define which tasks need to be ready before going live and the [sub-contractor] has to take responsibility for finishing these tasks in time. This is not your fault."	1			1
11	Sub-project manager BU2: "Some of the software deliveries are flawless, which is good, but we have also discovered some flaws in other deliveries. This requires rework and this will create delays." Project manager: (no response)		1		
13	Sub-project manager BU1: "We still have 33 open issues, problems that have not been solved. We have to solve them before we can move on." Project manager: (no response)	1			

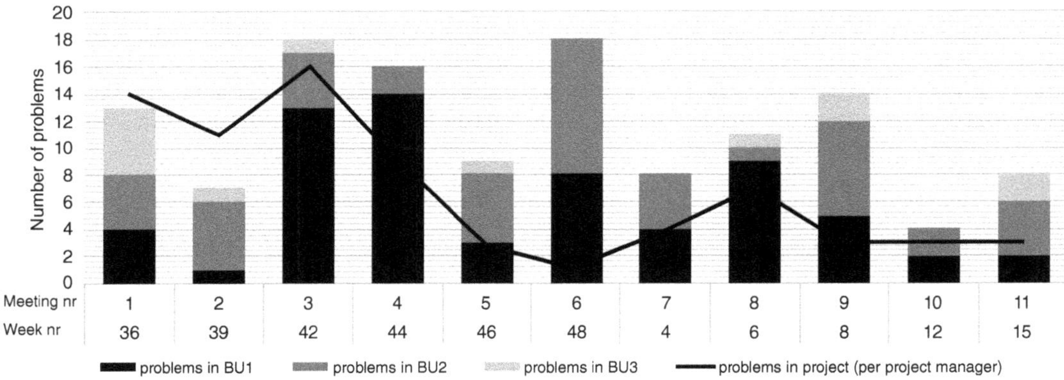

Figure 6.3 Project and sub-project problems over time.

problematic project, whereas BU3 (light gray) had the fewest problems. BU2 (dark gray) usually exhibited fewer problems than BU1 but more than BU3 – an observation generally supported by our interviews. Second, from the perspective of the overall project (black solid line), there were many problems in the beginning and yet, from meeting #5 onward, the situation was seemingly more under control. This trend is striking when one considers that two of the three sub-projects, BU1 and BU2, still had many difficulties in that period. Figure 6.3 also confirms that meetings #10 and #11 evinced little concern for current problems. Instead, these meetings focused on a new project structure with a de-synchronized approach, both of which were approved by the steering committee after meeting #11.

Step 3: Temporal Bracketing

In the next step of our analysis, we examined the number of problems, mentioned by the sub-project managers, from a different angle. We calculated both their sum (additive rule) and their average (averaging rule) and then compared the resulting numbers with the problems that were acknowledged by the project manager. The results are shown in Figure 6.4. In Figure 6.4, the black solid

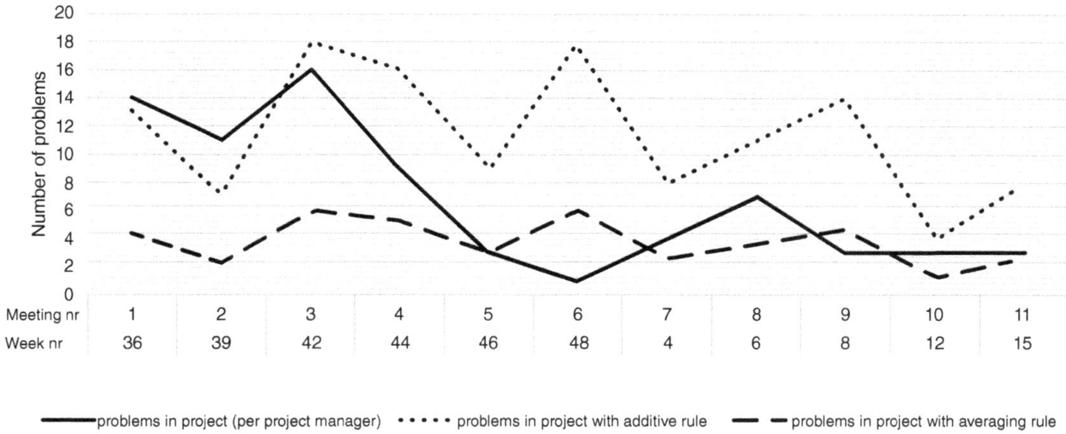

Figure 6.4 Additive versus averaging rule over time.

line plots the number of problems discussed by the project manager (this line is the same as in Figure 6.3), and the dotted (resp. dashed) line plots the sum (resp. average) of problems in the three sub-projects. During the first three meetings, there seems to be a certain continuity in the number of problems at the project manager's level: this number is best approximated by the additive rule. From the fifth meeting onward, another period of continuity appears. Now, the averaging rule shows a better fit. Meeting #4 appears to be representing a transition from the additive to the averaging rule (period of discontinuity). These results indicate that, during the first three meetings, the project manager attended to the problems brought up by the sub-project managers. In particular, he either offered suggestions on how to solve each problem or decided to pursue the matter himself. The overall status of InfoTech (number of problems the project manager addressed) could be derived simply by adding up the sub-projects' respective problems. After the fourth meeting, however, the project manager's behavior changed. He began to focus less on the problems of sub-project managers and instead spoke in more general terms about progress of InfoTech, as the following quote (from meeting #7) illustrates, "We have received good feedback from [Quality Assurance] regarding Phase 2. I thank [the project planner] for a good job. The QA was very pleased with the plans. This is very promising for Phase 2." Yet in BU1 the perception was quite different. According to one of that business unit's key stakeholders: "There has been a focus on overall project progress only, but the underlying problems have not been solved. These problems have been pushed forward .... The [project manager] has only solved the 'symptoms' of the problems .... The fundamental problems have not been addressed."

The overall status of the project during this period (i.e., meetings 5–11), as proxied by the number of problems that the project manager had to deal with, would perhaps be more accurately reflected by the average, and not the total number, of sub-project problems. As viewed from the top of the hierarchy, then, the project was not in such bad shape after all. Averaging out the number of sub-project problems could have caused InfoTech's project manager to be optimistic about the project's progress and consequently, to continue the commitment to the project and the way in which it was structured. This attitude is well illustrated by the following statement made by the project manager in February 2011: "The last months of 2010 have been OK. All [BUs] have been able to progress more or less with sufficient tempo." If the project manager believed that sub-projects' problems did not threaten the overall project's performance, then why should he have wasted precious time discussing those issues? Moreover, why would he decide anything other than continuing the project and its hierarchical structure? In the next section, we will discuss potential causes for using an additive rule first for a certain period, followed by an averaging rule in the following period.

A Process Model of the Averaging Bias in Project Hierarchies

The Averaging Bias

Our findings suggest that a particular cognitive bias likely to be activated in a hierarchical project structure is what we refer to as the *averaging bias*. Averaging bias stems from the general propensity of humans to engage in categorical thinking and rely on compensatory decision-making. Some have gone so far as to claim that the mind cannot think without the aid of categories (Allport, 1954). These categories are the basis for normal prejudgment and sensemaking. The process of categorical thinking cannot be avoided and is, in fact, fundamental for all kinds of managerial decisions (Bowker & Star, 1999). It has the advantage of promoting efficiency, increased ease in solving problems, and streamlined decision-making.

Notwithstanding these positive effects of categorical thinking, they may also have the negative effect of introducing biases into the decision-making process that skew the results in often unintended ways (Sadler-Smith & Shefy, 2004; Seo & Barrett, 2007; Fenton-O'Creevy et al., 2011). For instance, categorical thinking in combination with difficult goals leads to reduced performance in dynamic environments because of oversimplification, tunnel vision, and high levels of stress (Drach-Zahavy & Somech, 1999). Those findings are highly relevant to the management of information technology projects, which are typically implemented in settings characterized by ambitious and ambiguous goals and dynamism (Engwall & Westling, 2004; Gregory et al., 2013).

This type of bias has been observed in the context of estimating the calorie content of a combination of healthy and unhealthy food (Chernev & Gal, 2010), assessing the monetary value of a combination of one expensive item and one inexpensive item (Brough & Chernev, 2012), and estimating the environmental impact of a set of environmentally friendly and less friendly actions (Holmgren, et al. 2018). As such, the averaging bias is a more general pattern of decision-making that can be observed in contexts that involve humans evaluating combinations of options that have been classified into opposite categories (Chernev and Gal, 2010).

Returning to InfoTech, one sub-project (BU1) had many problems, one (BU3) had few problems, and one (BU2) was somewhere in between. The project manager's reasoning seemed to run as follows: if the situation was one bad, one mediocre, and one good sub-project then, *on average*, the overall project was doing satisfactorily – or at least much better than BU1. That conclusion is biased because, in an interdependent project like the one studied here, the overall project is only as good as its worst performing sub-project (Tushman, 1978), especially when synchronization is crucial for overall task completion (Benbya & McKelvey, 2006). Thus, a delay in any one sub-project will necessitate an overall project delay, from which it follows that progress-related sub-project problems should never be ignored by the project manager.

Transition from Additive to Averaging Rule

Our results provide evidence that initially the additive rule but later the averaging rule could account for the project manager's behavior. Still, we were curious why his behavior changed during the project, or why the averaging bias suddenly appeared.

Prior research has attributed the averaging bias to a dual-level judgment process. When estimating the calorie content of combinations of food items, for instance, people's quantitative estimates were affected by their qualitative evaluations of those items (Chernev & Gal, 2010). When the food items were classified into opposite categories (broccoli good, hamburger bad), respondents tended to balance out their evaluations and so used an averaging rather than an additive rule; yet when respondents estimated the total calories in combinations of food items in the same category (e.g., a hamburger and a cookie), no averaging bias was observed (Chernev

& Gal, 2010). Finally, the experiments showed that the averaging bias increased on par with the *difference* between the good and bad items.

In the context of InfoTech's hierarchical project management, the project manager's knowledge of problems at the sub-project level was limited to information received from lower-level managers. His first evaluation of each sub-project may have been a qualitative one. The three sub-projects reported similar progress at meetings #1 and #2 (of the 11 meetings that we observed). Each sub-project manager mentioned several problems, but no BU distinguished itself for better or worse. The units struggled with similar problems of comparable severity and had about the same number of problems – a situation in which the averaging bias did not arise because all items/sub-projects were essentially in the same category. By meeting #4, however, there were evident differences between the three sub-projects. BU1 suffered from many problems whereas BU3 encountered hardly any. As the difference between the progress of these two sub-projects increased, BU1 could be viewed as the "bad" sub-project and BU3 as the "good" one. It is likely that this categorical labeling was the precursor of the averaging bias.

Toward a Process Model

Following earlier process-oriented studies (e.g., Mähring & Keil, 2008; Keil & Mähring, 2010; Gregory et al., 2013), we argue that our observations can be captured by a sequence of three primary stages. These stages presuppose a hierarchical project structure featuring sub-projects controlled by sub-project managers and strong interdependencies among tasks. Our case study evidence matches up well with the first, *uniform behavior* stage in that similar sub-project behavior was observed among the InfoTech sub-projects. In this stage, there were (a) no significant deviations between planned and actual performance and (b) only small differences in behavior among sub-projects. Hence, the project manager relied on the *additive* rule and generally perceived the project's overall performance accurately.

The second stage, the *diverging behavior* stage, is triggered by emerging differences in behavior among sub-projects. Managers generally became more aware of problems in the project. However, they evaluate projects through a qualitative categorization of sub-projects' behavior into good or bad. In that respect, they rely on categorical thinking to make sense of the situation. The assessment of the project's overall performance is now based on the *averaging* rule (i.e., the average number of sub-project problems). The events in the project (diverging behavior between sub-projects) force the project manager to focus on control, on reducing ambiguity and complexity. Using an averaging rule reduces ambiguity and complexity, at least, in the short term. However, the averaging rule also leads to a misperception of project performance because the rule leads to an underestimation of the number of unresolved problems.

It is well-known that when problems are underestimated, they do not get sufficient attention. Focusing on what comes easily to mind may therefore result in an accumulation of problems (Tversky & Kahneman, 1974). This is the third stage in our process model: *aggravation of problems*. In this stage, management realizes that sub-projects' behavioral differences are only increasing, and the project cannot be completed following the set course. Managers realize the need for preventive action. Based on our findings, we hypothesize two alternative outcomes from this experience. Alternative 1 is illustrated by our case. This alternative represents a turnaround of the project that includes measures to significantly reduce the reliance on the averaging rule for evaluations. Here, as our case indicates, it is important to avoid simplified categorizations of sub-project behavior, which can be accomplished by revising the hierarchical project structure and/or reducing the interdependence between sub-projects. More precisely, in Alternative 1, as our case demonstrates, management realized that the project hierarchy was dysfunctional, which caused a change of this structure to turn the project around. From a theoretical angle, Alternative 1 could be an example of the so-called Fifth Hand identified by Ika et al. (2022) by which a project manager gradually understands the project's evolving context and learns from experience

Table 6.2 Process model of the averaging bias in project hierarchies

Antecedent conditions	Stage and sensemaking	Triggering conditions	Decisions	Consequences
• Hierarchical project structure (project consisting of multiple sub-projects) • Sub-projects controlled by sub-project managers who report to overall project manager • Interdependence between sub-projects	Stage 1: Uniform sub-project behavior	• No large deviations between planned and actual performance • Limited difference among sub-projects' behavior	• Qualitative evaluation of sub-projects in similar categories (good/good) • Application of additive rule	• Project manager has an accurate perception of project performance • Project manager provides support and helps where necessary
	Stage 2: Diverging sub-project behavior	• Emerging differences between behavior and performance of sub-projects	• Qualitative evaluation of sub-projects in opposing categories (good/bad) • Application of averaging rule	• Project manager overestimates project performance (misperception) • Project manager ignores problems of troubled sub-project(s)
	Stage 3: Aggravation of problems	• Increased behavior and performance differences among sub-projects • Clear sign that the overall project is in trouble • Common view among decision makers that the project is in trouble	• Alternative 1: Drastic project turnaround through piecemeal evaluation of sub-projects • Alternative 2: Termination of the project	• Alternative 1: A new project structure (e.g., dissolving the hierarchy and/or reducing the interdependence among sub-projects) • Alternative 2: Resources are assigned to other projects

to implement measures to ensure the project progresses satisfactorily.

In contrast, Alternative 2 is far more drastic: simply terminate the project (Ewusi-Mensah & Przasnyski, 1991). Such measures have been identified in a range of studies highlighting what decision-makers should do when projects drift away or come to complete standstills. In that respect, this is a decision that represents the exit alternative in Hirschman's classic writings (Hirschman, 1970). Indeed, this might be the best decision if the sub-project problems are so severe that they outweigh the overall project's potential benefits or if one or more sub-projects have problems that are considered unresolvable. In Alternative 2, management realizes that the project is dysfunctional but potentially without discovering the role the hierarchical project structure played in this. Alternative 2 could thus be an example of "The Passive Hand" in which a project manager is aware that the project structure is not working but still thinks that the complexity of the project requires such a structure (Anheier, 2016). In other words, in Alternative 2, managers do not learn that the hierarchical structure is the underlying problem but take measures that target the project's underlying rationale rather than its organizational structure.

In short, our process model of averaging bias comprises three main stages and zeroes in on two very different alternatives of underlying problem solving in a complex project. The model is summarized in Table 6.2.

Implications and Further Research

Our findings contribute to theory in different ways. First, we show that hierarchical structures may affect project behavior. Project behavior is about how projects work and take different and complex out-turns (Ika et al., 2022). Our study suggests that hierarchical structures impact how managers interpret information received from lower levels in the hierarchy and that this is compromised by various cognitive biases such as the averaging bias. As a result, information visibility in project management is reduced, which is known to negatively impact project performance (Bendoly & Swink, 2007). A hierarchical structure may therefore prompt project managers to evaluate sub-projects according to categorical thinking into good/bad categories. A focus on such categorization leads them to evaluate the overall project in a compensatory way, such that the good sub-project averages out the bad sub-project. When that happens, our study indicates, the hierarchical structure impairs rather than supports decision-making and consequently project behavior. When sub-projects are dependent on each other, the good cannot compensate for the bad and therefore we need to analyze the behavior of the project as a whole, which is difficult to deduce from understanding the individual parts (Unterhitzenberger, 2021). Although we do not focus on specific decisions made by the project manager and the quality of these decisions, our findings do suggest that the averaging bias could cause the project manager to ignore or neglect certain problems of sub-projects. Ignoring problems can of course be viewed as a decision (the decision not to do anything), and in hindsight, this decision seemed to be of poor quality. Thus, our identification of an averaging bias in project management augments prior research that calls for examining how cognitive architectures evolve from the organization's particular decomposition of tasks and labor (Jacobides, 2007). It also corroborates previous findings by Bendoly & Swink (2007) about how limited local information visibility in project management is insufficient in the pursuit of performance of the project as a whole.

Second, a combination of sub-projects performing well and poorly is associated with categorical thinking and thus overestimation of the overall project performance. In other words, the combination of a good sub-project and a bad one makes it more difficult for a project manager to evaluate overall project behavior. These asymmetrical findings of positive (resp. negative) perceptions and negative (resp. positive) outcomes are consistent with previous research (Storbeck & Clore, 2005; Lindebaum & Fielden, 2011).

Our results may also help explain the large number of troubled projects (Kappelman et al., 2006; Nelson, 2007) that go wrong because errors in one sub-project cause a chain reaction that spreads throughout the entire project yet is not detected by upper management until too late (Mähring & Keil, 2008). Thus, the difficulty of detecting errors early on (Kappelman et al., 2006) could be related to the averaging bias in decision-making. By demonstrating how the project structure can shape cognitive biases, we add to the literature on escalation of commitment and erroneous decision-making in large-scale and complex projects (van Oorschot et al., 2013). More specially, our process model shows the dynamic relationship between hierarchical structures, information processing, and (erroneous) decision making. It thereby highlights the resulting need to change the hierarchy and provides answers to various calls for more research on the influence of organizational structure on framing and biases (Jacobides, 2007; Sleesman et al. 2012; Keum & See, 2017).

Finally, our findings provide support for the hierarchical erosion effect (Gibson et al. 2019). Hierarchical erosion implies that perceptions about higher-level (organization-wide) practices become *less* favorable the *lower* one goes in the hierarchy. Our research shows that erosion can also work in the opposite direction: perceptions about lower-level practices (i.e., sub-projects) become *more* favorable the *higher* one goes in the hierarchy. Interestingly, Gibson et al. (2019) wonder whether empowerment of employees could resolve erosion. This is precisely what happened in the project we studied: when the project failed to meet objectives, the hierarchical project structure was dismantled and sub-project managers were empowered, as they became project managers.

Our research also offers several managerial implications. Staying clear of hierarchical structures is an obvious but unrealistic solution for project managers. Seeking to eliminate (or at least reduce) the averaging bias will usually be a better solution for project managers than sacrificing the project hierarchy. One approach is to curb categorical thinking, especially classifying in terms of good or bad. This approach can be implemented by having sub-project managers explicitly write down the number of unresolved problems – that is, rather than only talking about them in meetings. Such a recommendation is consistent with researchers who suggest that providing explicit (quantitative) information minimizes the effects of the averaging bias (Chernev & Gal, 2010). Another way to circumvent the averaging bias is for decision-makers to make only piecemeal evaluations of the sub-projects and not holistic evaluations of the entire project. The steering committee (or hierarchical level to which the project manager reports) could certainly handle piecemeal information processing; it could ask the project manager to report only on each sub-project's performance and major problems, forgoing that manager's evaluation of the project as a whole. Separate meetings with each sub-project manager would facilitate such unit-by-unit evaluations.

Although we offer no statistically significant evidence for the averaging bias in the project we examined, our empirical findings and theoretical elaborations do raise a "reasonable doubt" as regards the widely held belief that hierarchical project structures help project managers make informed decisions about the status and performance of the overall project. Future research could refine our results for the existence of the averaging bias in hierarchies. It would be interesting to explore in more depth how much of the behavior of project managers can be attributed to the averaging bias versus other causes, such as an external pressure from the steering committee to report satisfactory performance. One might design an experiment, situated in a project management context, to see whether the project manager's overall evaluation is affected by the status of sub-projects. Another interesting avenue for further exploration is to analyze the averaging bias in different kinds of industries or organizational hierarchies. Large organizations are usually divided in divisions or business units, such as the multi-divisional firm (Gaba & Joseph, 2013; Foss & Weber, 2016). How does the CEO of such a large organization evaluate its overall performance when one unit is performing below target while another one is above or on target? In what settings might the averaging bias surface and create problems? The answers to these questions are most definitely worth pursuing. Finally, we call for more research on project behavior, that is, the behavior *of* projects. Our study shows that although it makes sense from a project management perspective to divide a large project in smaller sub-projects, such division could be dysfunctional when it reduces the visibility of how the project works (that is: project behavior) as a whole. Future research should focus more on how the interplay between the parts (sub-projects) and the whole (the project) influence project behavior.

References

Allport, G. W. (1954). *The nature of prejudice*. Addison-Wesley.

Anderson, C., and Brown, C. E. (2010). The functions and dysfunctions of hierarchy. *Research in Organizational Behavior*, *30*, 55–89.

Anheier, H. K. (2016). Of hiding hands and other ways of coping with uncertainty: A commentary. *Social Research: An International Quarterly*, *83*(4), 1005–1010.

Benbya, H., and McKelvey, B. (2006). Toward a complexity theory of information systems development. *Information Technology & People*, *19*(1), 12–34.

Bendoly, E., and Swink, M. (2007). Moderating effects of information access on project management behavior, performance and perceptions. *Journal of Operations Management*, *25*(3), 604–622.

Bowker, G. C., and Star, S.L. (1999). *Sorting things out: Classification and its consequences*. MIT Press.

Brough, A. R., and Chernev, A. (2012). When opposites detract: Categorical reasoning and subtractive valuations of product combinations. *Journal of Consumer Research*, *39*(2), 399–414.

Bunderson, J. S., Van der Vegt, G. S., Cantimur, Y., and Rink, F. (2016). Different views of hierarchy and why they matter: Hierarchy as inequality or as cascading influence. *Academy of Management Journal*, *59*(4), 1265–1289.

Cheng, J. L. C. (1984). Organizational coordination, uncertainty, and performance – an integrative study. *Human Relations*, *37*(10), 829–851.

Chernev, A., and Gal, D. (2010). Categorization effects in value judgments: Averaging bias in evaluating combinations of vices and virtues. *Journal of Marketing Research*, *47*(4), 738–747.

Christensen, M., and Knudsen, T. (2010). Design of decision-making organizations. *Management Science*, *56*(1), 71–89.

Cyert, R. M., and March, J. G. (1963). *A behavioral theory of the firm*. Prentice Hall.

Dilts, D. M. and Pence, K. R. (2006). Impact of role in the decision to fail: An exploratory study of terminated projects. *Journal of Operations Management*, *24*, 378–396.

Drach-Zahavy, A., and Somech, A. (1999). Constructive thinking: A complex coping variable that distinctively influences the effectiveness of specific difficult goals. *Personality and Individual Differences*, *27*(5), 969–984.

Engwall, M., and Westling, G. (2004). Peripety in an R&D drama: Capturing a turnaround in project dynamics. *Organization Studies*, *25*(9), 1557–1578.

Ethiraj, S. K., and Levinthal, D. (2004a). Bounded rationality and the search for organizational architecture: An evolutionary perspective on the design of organizations and their evolvability. *Administrative Science Quarterly*, *49*(3), 404–437.

Ethiraj, S. K., and Levinthal, D. (2004b). Modularity and innovation in complex systems. *Management Science*, *50*(2), 159–173.

Ewusi-Mensah, K., and Przasnyski, Z. H. (1991). On information systems project abandonment: An exploratory study of organizational practices. *MIS Quarterly*, *15*(2), 67–80.

Fenton-O'Creevy, M., Soane, E., Nicholson, N., and Willman, P. (2011). Thinking, feeling and deciding: The influence of emotions on the decision making and performance of traders. *Journal of Organizational Behavior*, *32*(8), 1044–1061.

Flyvbjerg, B. (2021). Top-ten behavioral biases in project management: An overview. *Project Management Journal*, *52*(6), 531–546.

Foss, N. J., and Weber, L. (2016). Moving opportunism to the back seat: Bounded rationality, costly conflict, and hierarchical forms. *Academy of Management Journal*, *41*(1), 61–79.

Gaba, V., and Joseph, J. (2013). Corporate structure and performance feedback: Aspirations and adaptation in M-form firms. *Organization Science*, *24*(4), 1102–1119.

Gibson, C. B., Birkinshaw, J., McDaniel Sumpter, D. and Ambos, T. (2019). The hierarchical erosion effect: A new perspective on perceptual differences and business performance. *Journal of Management Studies*, *56*(8), 1713–1747.

Gigerenzer, G. (2003). Why does framing influence judgment? *Journal of General Internal Medicine*, 18, 960–961.

Gregory, R. W., Beck, R. and Keil, M. (2013). Control balancing in information systems development offshoring projects. *MIS Quarterly*, *37*(4), 1211–1232.

Hirschman, A. O. (1967). *Development projects observed*. Brookings Institution.

Hoegl, M. (2005). Smaller teams – better teamwork: How to keep project teams small. *Business Horizons*, *48*(3), 209–214.

Hoegl, M., Weinkauf, K., and Gemuenden, H. G. (2004). Interteam coordination, project commitment, and teamwork in multiteam R&D projects: A longitudinal study. *Organization Science*, *15*(1), 38–55.

Holmgren, M., Andersson, H., and Sörqvist, P. (2018). Averaging bias in environmental impact estimates: Evidence from the negative footprint illusion. *Journal of Environmental Psychology*, *55*, 48–52.

Ika, L. A., Love, P. E. D., and Pinto, J. K. (2022). Moving beyond the planning fallacy: The emergence of a new principle of project behavior. *IEEE Transactions on Engineering Management*, *69*(6), 3310–3325.

Ingvaldsen, J. A., and Rolfsen, M. (2012). Autonomous work groups and the challenge of inter-group coordination. *Human Relations*, *65*(7), 861–881.

Jacobides, M. G. (2007). The inherent limits of organizational structure and the unfulfilled role of hierarchy: Lessons from a near-war. *Organization Science*, *18*(3), 455–477.

Kappelman, L., McKeeman, R., and Zhang, L. (2006). Early warning signs of IT project failure: The dominant dozen. *Information Systems Management*, *23*(4), 31–36.

Keil, M., and Mähring, M. (2010). Is your IT project turning into a black hole? *California Management Review*, *53*(1), 6–31.

Keren, M., and Levhari, D. (1979). The optimum span of control in a pure hierarchy. *Management Science*, *25*(11), 1162–1172.

Keum, D. D., and See, K. E. (2017). The influence of hierarchy on idea generation and selection in the innovation process. *Organization Science*, *28*(4), 653–669.

Langley, A. (1999). Strategies for theorizing from process data. *The Academy of Management Review*, *24*(4), 691–710.

Lindebaum, D.a, nd Fielden, S. L. (2011). 'It's good to be angry': Enacting anger in construction project management to achieve perceived leader effectiveness. *Human Relations*, *64*(3), 437–458.

Macrae, C. N., and Bodenhausen, G. V. (2000). Social cognition: Thinking categorically about others. *Annual Review of Psychology*, *51*, 93–120.

Mähring, M., and Keil, M. (2008). Information technology project escalation: A process model. *Decision Sciences*, *39*(2), 239–272.

Mihm, J., Loch, C. H., Wilkinson, D., and Huberman, B. A. (2010). Hierarchical structure and search in complex organizations. *Management Science*, *56*(5), 831–848.

Miles, M. B., and Huberman, M. (1994). *Qualitative data analysis: A sourcebook of new methods.* 2nd ed. Sage.

Nelson, R. (2007). IT project management: Infamous failures, classic mistakes and best practices. *MIS Quarterly Executive*, *6*(2), 67–78.

PRINCE2. (2023). Projects versus programmes. www.prince2.com/eur/blog/project-vs-programme.

Radner, R. (1992). Hierarchy: The economics of managing. *Journal of Economic Literature*, *30*(3), 1382–1415.

Rhee, L., Ocasio, W., and Kim, T.-H. (2019). Performance feedback in hierarchical business groups: The cross-level effects of cognitive accessibility on R&D search behavior. *Organization Science*, *30*(1), 51–69.

Sadler-Smith, E., and Shefy, E. (2004). The intuitive executive: Understanding and applying 'gut feel' in decision-making. *Academy of Management Executive*, *18*(4), 76–91.

Seo, M. G., and Barrett, L. F. (2007). Being emotional during decision making – good or bad? An empirical investigation. *Academy of Management Journal*, *50*(4), 923–940.

Simon, H. A. (1962). The architecture of complexity. *Proceedings of the American Philosophical Society*, *106*(6), 467–482.

Sleesman, D. J., Conlon, D. E., McNamara, G., and Miles, J. E. (2012). Cleaning up the big muddy: A meta-analytic review of the determinants of escalation of commitment. *Academy of Management Journal*, *55*(3), 541–562.

Smith, R. P., and Eppinger, S. D. (1997). Identifying controlling features of engineering design iteration. *Management Science*, *43*(3), 276–293.

Sosa, M. E., Eppinger, S. D., and Rowles, C. (2004). The misalignment of product architecture and organizational structure in complex product development. *Management Science*, *50*(12), 1674–1689.

Sterman, J. D. (2000). *Business dynamics: Systems thinking and modeling for a complex world.* Irwin McGraw-Hill.

Storbeck, J., and Clore, G. L. (2005). With sadness comes accuracy; with happiness, false memory: Mood and the false memory effect. *Psychological Science*, *16*(10), 785–791.

Thompson, M., and Wildavsky, A. (1986). A cultural theory of information bias in organizations. *Journal of Management Studies*, *23*(3), 273–286.

Tushman, M. L. (1978). Technical communication in R&D laboratories: The impact of project work characteristics. *Academy of Management Journal*, *21*(4), 624–645.

Tushman, M. L., and Nadler, D. A. (1978). Information processing as an integrating concept in organizational design. *Academy of Management Review*, *3*(3), 613–624.

Tversky, A., and Kahneman, D. (1974). Judgment under uncertainty: Heuristics and biases. *Science*, *185*(4157), 1124–1131.

Unterhitzenberger, C. (2021). Special issue on project behavior. *Project Management Journal*, *52*(6), 527–530.

Van de Ven, A. (2007). *Engaged scholarship: A guide for organizational and social research.* Oxford University Press.

Van Oorschot, K. E., Akkermans, H., Sengupta, K., and Van Wassenhove, L. N. (2013). Anatomy of a decision trap in complex new product development projects. *Academy of Management Journal*, *56*(1), 285–307.

Visser, B. (2000). Organizational communication structure and performance. *Journal of Economic Behavior and Organization*, *42*(2), 231–252.

von Hippel, E. (1994). "Sticky information" and the locus of problem solving: Implications for innovation. *Management Science*, *40*(4), 429–439.

Zhou, Y. M. (2013). Designing for complexity: Using divisions and hierarchy to manage complex tasks. *Organization Science*, *24*(2), 339–355.

CHAPTER 7

Intra- and Inter-Organizational Governance and the Behavior of Projects

RALF MÜLLER

Introduction

Governance is known for providing the framework within which (project) managers do their work. This includes not only the ways managers are controlled but also defines their sphere of authority, level of autonomy, and relationships with stakeholders and institutions. Governance transfers the values managers work for and influence and provides libraries of methods, techniques, processes, and other "tools of the trade" for managers. In other words, governance goes far beyond the often found cliché of being solely a control instrument (Müller, 2017). Through that, governance also provides the framework to evaluate the performance of these managers (OECD, 2001). Definitions of governance are manifold and often differ by the particular perspectives of the author. For example, definitions from an economic perspective differ substantially from those taking an ethics or management perspective. The literature often describes this as problematic, but it is an advantage in practice because a complex concept like governance is unlikely to be explained with just one (single-minded) definition. Imagine we as human beings would be defined by just one definition. What would this be? A psychological, physical, chemical, or economic definition? Whatever we pick, it would just describe one of the many facets of the phenomenon called a human being. The same applies to governance. The variety of existing definitions provides a good chance to find a suitable definition for the particular lens we take when looking at governance, be it economic, managerial, or something else.

Among the most popular definitions are those emphasizing that governance provides the structures, processes, policies, and value system for the governed entity, as well as the means and control methods required to set and accomplish the objectives of this entity (e.g., Turner, 2022). This applies equally to permanent organizations, like firms, and temporary organizations, like projects.

Within organizations such as corporations, the governance of projects is executed at several levels of the organizational hierarchy (see Figure 7.1). The accountabilities, responsibilities, and scope differ by position in the hierarchy. Typically they include:

Corporate governance: At the corporate level, the business goals are defined along with the means to pursue them. This is communicated via strategy, objectives, policies, and ethical principles. From a project perspective, this governance can be seen as setting the ground rules for project-related governance in the company. This is known as metagovernance, or governance of governance (more on this later).

Board-level governance: This refers to the part of the business executed through projects. Here the board defines the role of project management in the organization, the need for strategic project management offices (PMOs), and other project-related governance institutions, such as portfolio steering committees, etc..

Governance of projects: This relates to the governance level of project selection into portfolios and/or groups for programs. The commonalities in the governance of the projects in these groups are defined and governed here. This includes project execution standards/methodologies, reporting standards, and performance measures to achieve transparency and comparability of the projects in these programs and portfolios.

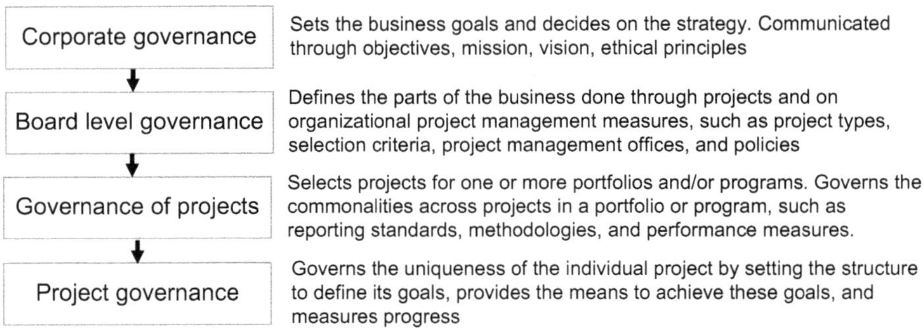

Figure 7.1 Intra-organizational governance of projects.

Project governance: This relates to the governance of the individual project. Here the goal of each project is defined, the resources provided to achieve the goals, and the project's progress is controlled.

Hence, *project governance* is mainly concerned with governing the particularities of the project at hand, while *governance of projects* addresses cross-project commonalities in programs or portfolios of projects. The context for this sets *board-level governance* by defining the scope of project work and its management in the organization, whereas metagovernance is executed through *corporate governance*.

Each of the governance layers has a profound impact on project behavior because they vary in their application of governance standards and governance paradigms. Further on in this chapter, this is explained in detail, along with related examples.

Governance Principles

The axiom of governance is the separation of ownership of a task from the control of its execution. For example, the separation of the project management task owned by the project manager and the control of this execution by the project steering committee. Recent decades have shown numerous examples where a violation of this "ground rule" has caused severe damage. Among the most visible is the global financial crisis in 2008, where the insufficient control of task execution of investment bankers led to a chain of bankruptcies, resulting in a global economic downturn. As such, it is an example of how the behavior of individual projects (like that of investment bankers) impacts the wider society.

The Organization for Economic Cooperation and Development (OECD) and the World Bank (OECD, 2001) jointly developed four principles of good governance, which should underly every governance system. Interpreted in the context of projects, these are:

Transparency: The provision of accurate and timely information from the project managers to the governing institutions, such as steering committees or project management offices. Project owners' and other stakeholders' confidence in the project depends on this information, which should be delivered clearly, consistently, and in a comparable manner.

Accountability: Unambiguous definition of roles, rights, and answerabilities within and across organizations. This includes escalation procedures for issue handling. In projects, the steering group typically holds the project manager accountable to the project owner for achieving the project objectives. Simultaneously, the steering committee is accountable to upper management for accomplishing the project's business case.

Responsibility: Using socially accepted standards for task execution. This includes professional working standards and training, education, and potential certification to achieve the required qualification levels to implement these standards.

Fairness: Equal, fair, and ethical treatment of persons and institutions inside and outside the organization. With this goes protection against illegal actions.

The OECD recently added a fifth principle, that of *Sustainability*. Due to its conceptual proximity, sustainability is often perceived as a subset of the fairness principle, assuming that sustainability means being fair to humankind and the planet. The same is done in this chapter.

The Intra-Organizational View

Governance Approaches in Practice Standards

Governance has become a popular topic in the professional and academic literature in project management. For example, professional organizations make the concept accessible, usable, and popular in practitioner circles by issuing practice standards. These standards differ in their approaches from prescriptive to non-prescriptive, mirroring particular governance practices of the countries they originate from. Prescriptive standards apply so-called rule-based approaches to governance, with clearly defined tasks, processes, roles, and responsibilities. Their execution is enforced, and deviations are sanctioned. These standards are typically "bottom-up" developed extensions of equally prescriptive project management methodologies or standards, which elevate the attitudes toward process compliance and continuous control from the project management to the project governance level. This approach is also known as "comply or get punished" in the corporate governance literature. The *PMI Practice Guide for Governance of Portfolios, Programs, and Projects* (PMI, 2016) is an example of these types of standards.

Non-prescriptive or principles-based approaches to governance provide a series of principles for setting up a governance structure without prescribing tasks or processes. Instead, they point out the most crucial aspects to be considered in the design of a governance system. Examples of this are principles like: "The board has overall responsibility for the governance of project management" or "the organisation fosters a culture of improvement and of frank internal disclosure" (APM, 2011, pp. 9–10). These standards are typically developed "top-down" from a corporate governance perspective, thereby preserving the awareness of non-delegable accountabilities at the top of the organization without limiting the delegation of responsibilities to lower levels of the corporate echelon. The corporate governance literature refers to this approach as "comply or explain." A typical example of this is the *APM Guide for the Governance of Project Management* (APM, 2011).

In between these two extremes are hybrid approaches, like ISO 21505 Standard for *Project, Programme and Portfolio management – Guidance on Governance* (ISO, 2017). These types of standards provide both skeletons of processes and tasks and principles so that organizations can apply the most appropriate approach, given their industry, company size, and project management maturity.

The implications of this diversity of standards for project behavior are significant. Assume an organization whose corporate governance policy does not allow to engage in projects with clients using fixed-price contracts. If the project manager does it anyway, he or she will face severe disciplinary measures in cases of organizations applying the "complain or get punished" approach. In contrast, the same project manager will have a chance to explain the reasons for doing so in a "comply or explain" environment, potentially being praised for the oversight that led to this decision.

Governance Paradigms

A more academic perspective is that of governance paradigms, which emerge as the link between corporate governance and project governance. Governance paradigms provide the framework for selecting and executing project management tasks. To that end, the paradigm combines corporate-level and program/portfolio-level governance information to a particular paradigm that governs project execution. Corporate governance provides thereby the information on the raison d'être of the organization. That is, does the organization predominantly exist to create value for its shareholders (i.e., has a shareholder orientation), or does it exist to provide value for many different stakeholder groups, of which one is the shareholders (i.e., has a

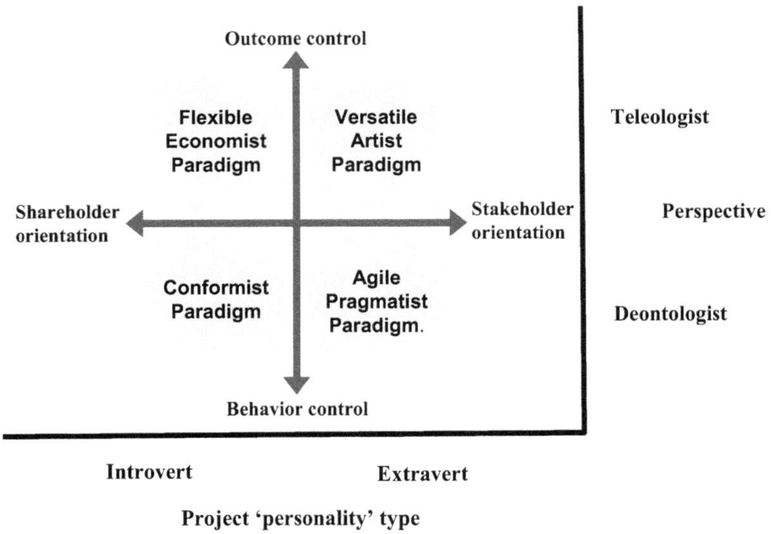

Figure 7.2 Project governance paradigms and project behavior (based on Müller, 2009).
Reproduced with permission of The Licensor through PLSclear.

stakeholder orientation)? In shareholder-oriented organizations, decisions are governed by the desire to maximize share price and dividends for shareholders. In stakeholder-oriented organizations, benefits are balanced across the various stakeholder groups with often conflicting objectives. Overlaying this corporate governance information with the control approach chosen in the particular portfolio a project belongs to identifies four different governance paradigms, each fostering a specific project behavior (see Figure 7.2).

Control is hereby measured on a continuum from behavior control, such as control through strict process compliance, to outcome control, such as control through the comparison of deliverables against defined specifications.

The inner four sections of Figure 7.2 depict the four resulting governance paradigms (Müller & Lecoeuvre, 2014). The outer part shows the resulting behavioral characteristics of projects governed by these paradigms. Four types of behavioral characteristics are shown:

- *Introvert* is a psychological concept developed by the twentieth-century Swiss psychiatrist Carl Jung. It describes a person (in this case a project) whose interest is generally directed inward toward their own feelings and thoughts (Britannica.com, 2022). Decisions in these projects are made from an inward perspective, typically to safeguard the company's economic goals in the best interest of the company owners. Examples include meeting certain profit thresholds for being selected in a portfolio, or changes to the project being predominantly evaluated on their economic impact on company results
- *Extravert* describes a person (here a project) whose attention is directed toward other people and the outside world (Britannica.com, 2022). Decisions in these projects are made from an outward perspective. Attention is given to the company's market or context. Projects and changes to them are evaluated on their contribution to a variety of goals, such as sustainability, profitability, market growth, and/or corporate social responsibility.
- *Teleologists* are focused on the consequences or outcomes of their actions, rather than the correctness of the means to achieve these outcomes (Vitell & Davis, 1990). In the realm of project behavior, this refers to projects that focus primarily on meeting the product or service specifications of the final product, at the risk of compromising existing processes or policies. From this perspective, "the end justifies the

means" and flexibility prevails in methodology selection.

- *Deontologists* are predominantly focused on the correctness of the actions rather than their consequences (Vitell & Davis, 1990). The behavior of these projects is characterized by process and policy compliance. This is often found in high-risk industries, where the trust in the process is higher than the trust in the capabilities of the individuals. In this perspective, "the means justify the end" and flexibility prevails in the details of the final deliverables and their timing.

The differences in project behavior described above stem from the four paradigms' particular framework for decision-making they impose on a project, each behavior is underpinned by a different governance paradigm.

Introvert deontological behavior is fostered by the *conformist paradigm*, which emphasizes adherence to strict time and cost priorities in decision-making and process compliance in project execution. This assumes cost efficiency by using existing management processes and/or methodologies. The strong emphasis on "following the process" at the cost of a devaluation of project management to an administrative task in the overall management process is assumed to be supportive of the economic goal accomplishment of a process-oriented organization. However, it can have severe consequences for the projects therein. Too strong a process and cost orientation hinder innovation and delivery according to customer needs and expectations. Examples are smaller and medium-sized engineering companies focusing on delivering their standard product, potentially with very little tailoring for their customers, or a large producer of bulk goods with little or no experience in projects. In both cases, the enforcement of process compliance can foster behaviors that cause unintended costs and/or problems with the project outcomes.

Introverted teleologist projects are underpinned by the *flexible economist paradigm*, which prioritizes the accomplishment of shareholder value through projects whose managers are controlled by the project's outcomes. This paradigm assumes that cost efficiency is accomplished by empowering project managers to self-decide on the most efficient way to run their projects. Project managers are perceived as experts based on their experience and former success. They are often supported by project management offices (PMOs) as consultants in adjusting project management to the particularities of their projects. These projects' characteristics include a focus on the deliverables, process flexibility, and state-of-the-art project management methods, tools, and techniques. This paradigm is typical for organizations with customer transactions done through projects that satisfy internal economic criteria.

Extraverted teleologist behavior is reinforced by the *versatile artist paradigm*, which prioritizes creating value for multiple stakeholder groups, while project managers are controlled by their project outcomes. The paradigm suggests that project managers identify the possible balance of benefits over the different stakeholder groups and their diverse objectives. That is because they are closest to the different stakeholder groups. Managers of these projects are typically senior experts in both project management and the project's particular industry, often supported by PMOs. The behavior of these projects is characterized by versatility and flexibility, mainly in the processes leading to the deliverables. These senior experts often develop a project-specific methodology based on their prior experience, which allows integration of the different stakeholder requirements. This paradigm is often found in organizations that are mature in project management, such as major vendors or consulting companies, and organizations adjusting to new market needs or customer groups.

Extraverted deontologist behavior of projects is driven by the *agile pragmatist paradigm*, which prioritizes creating value for multiple stakeholder groups while enforcing process compliance. This paradigm suggests that splitting projects into small task groups (aka *sprints*), and managing this through a repetitive process, provides for fast incremental delivery. The project sponsor defines the balance of benefits for the different stakeholder groups. Characteristic of the behavior of these projects is their incremental provision of smaller units of deliverables that eventually add up to a larger final deliverable. Not all project deliverables can be delivered this way, which limits this paradigm in applicability. Other behavior characteristics include extreme flexibility in scope, outcome, or other changes and early availability of subsets of the final deliverable at the expense of difficulties in defining a definitive delivery date upfront.

The differences in project behavior described above stem from the four paradigms' particular framework for decision-making they impose on a project. Governance paradigms that emphasize, for example, shareholder return on investment typically prioritize economic results over stakeholder satisfaction. This clearly signals the project's behavior toward their different stakeholder groups.

Paradigms may vary over the different project portfolios, such as more conformist governance for projects in maintenance departments and agile pragmatist paradigms for software development departments. In contrast, a versatile artist paradigm might govern projects in the engineering or marketing department. Hence, different paradigms may be found in different parts of a larger organization, all contributing to the accomplishment of strategic goals under the umbrella of corporate governance.

A specific impact on project behavior has the governance paradigm applied at the start of a project. Research has shown a correlation between stakeholder orientation and project success. The higher the stakeholder orientation, the higher the chances for success (Joslin & Müller, 2016). Outcome-oriented paradigms are based on trust in the project manager to deliver as intended. In contrast, behavior-oriented paradigms prioritize trust in the process over trust in the project manager. So projects starting under the versatile artist paradigm have the advantage that the steering committee trusts the project manager at the outset. If the project starts to compromise goal accomplishment, it may shift slightly toward more control, but if it recovers, it is back in the trustful versatile artist paradigm, and the project manager enjoys managerial freedom in decision-making.

In more practical terms, this means project managers should strive for a trust-based relationship with their steering committee from the beginning of their project (i.e., start by applying a versatile artist paradigm). This provides for the highest levels of freedom in decision-making and lowest levels of control, and with it, the best chances to finish the project successfully. If the project starts deviating from the plan, measures to secure the original trust level should be taken quickly by the project manager, such as early information about upcoming issues, root-cause analysis, development of contingency measures, plan and budget updates, etc. to show transparency, accountability, and responsible work practices. This prevents the steering committee's governance from shifting to control-oriented paradigms, such as the conformist paradigm (within which success rates are much lower). Such a shift is typically indicated when the steering committee increases the reporting frequency (e.g., from monthly to weekly and then to daily) and asks for more physical meetings, reviews, audits, and a broader set of data to be reported. In these cases, the efforts should be directed toward both the recovery of the project and the improvement of the collaboration with the steering committee. Research has shown that the best project results are accomplished at the highest levels of collaboration between project managers and steering committees and medium levels of control (i.e., the project manager should have sufficient freedom to fulfill his/her task) (Turner & Müller, 2004). Hence, trust-building measures are an important lever in managing which governance paradigm the steering committee applies.

This is different in, for example, government projects with only one stakeholder group, the public. By being the only stakeholder group, the public takes on the role of the shareholders in the model in Figure 7.2. Here the project manager has to show that the taxpayer's money is spent wisely (i.e., introvert behavior). This is done by following the processes and policies of the government (i.e., deontological behavior). So the initial starting point of these projects is typically the conformist paradigm, enforcing economic results through behavior control. The requirement for introvert behavior by showing the sensibility for taxpayers' money through process compliance will prevail throughout the project. Even if the project progresses better than planned, it will not leave this paradigm of continuous control. Even worse, when the project compromises performance objectives, control increases, typically in the form of more reporting, reviews, and other internal control methods. This leads to what the German sociologist Max Weber called the "iron cage of bureaucracy," which aims for maximizing efficiency by increasing rational calculation and control (Guzman & Hill, 2017). It enforces rules and laws (Ashworth, Boyne & Delbridge, 2009), which, through their rigidity, foster the dehumanization of individuals (Elwell, 2022).

This vicious circle of ever more control makes it impossible for the project to leave this governance paradigm for more trustful ones, where the project manager could take true recovery measures rather than monotonously following the organizational processes and policies, no matter whether they are appropriate or not. The case of Berlin Brandenburg Airport (FBB) in Germany exemplifies this. The case is described later in this chapter.

So far, this chapter has described some of the basic tenets of governance, such as the principles underlying good governance, and used practice standards as examples for the most popular governance approaches, such as rule-based and principles-based, and their implications for project behavior. Then the focus turned to project governance paradigms, which link the corporate level of governance with its project-level counterpart to define the particular type of governance for a given project. The discussion showed that the direction given by governance paradigms significantly influences project behavior.

The above discussion has taken an intra-organizational perspective on project governance by outlining the governance layers of an organization like a corporation, the roles of these layers in governing projects, and their impact on project behavior. However, not all projects are internal to an organization. Some, especially large and complex projects, require the collaboration of many different firms and other organizations over an extended period of time. These projects are often delivered through networks of organizations that repeatedly work together over time in some but not all of their projects. These networks also require governance, which, in turn, impacts project behavior. For example, some firms engaged in the public FBB airport project mentioned above might occasionally work together in private-sector projects, such as in building private homes. Here the governance exercised by the project owner is typically less process-oriented than that of the Berlin government in the FBB case. Private-sector sponsors tend to be more outcome-oriented and give more freedom to their network of firms in the setup of the network, the procedures to use, and empowerment in decision-making. Thus, these projects are likely to show an extraverted teleologist behavior, as opposed to the introverted deontologist behavior of public projects.

The Inter-organizational View

Inter-organizational networks for the delivery of projects are formed by three or more partner organizations to maximize their joint performance in project delivery. Like any other organization, such a network needs governance to set the framework for its managers. The governance of an inter-organizational network for the delivery of a particular project is known as *network governance*, which is "the use of formal and informal institutions to allocate resources and coordinate joint action in a network of organizations" (Kapucu & Hu, 2020, p. 5). Network governance differs from network management, which addresses "planning, organizing, leading, and controlling ... conditioned by continuous interaction and adaptation among autonomous actors" and situation-specific tasks (Järvensivu & Möller, 2009, p. 659).

As said earlier, collaborations in these networks are often not limited to a single project but continue over several projects simultaneously and over time. This leads to groupings (or say portfolios) of networks that interface, interact, and collaborate to deliver their joint projects. As described above for projects, this network of networks requires governance, called the *Governance of Networks*. This level of governance steers the many different networks a project investor organization (like the government or large-scale private sector investors) is part of. This includes networks of companies bidding together for projects, networks of companies jointly executing projects, or networks of companies providing education, training, or certification for the other networked organizations to achieve required qualification levels.

However, both network governance and governance of networks require a set of "ground-rules" that define the most basic criteria for governance, such as which projects/networks are prioritized, how networks are formed, and partners are selected, etc. This is done through *metagovernance*, a function of the investor with the aim to avoid governance failure at the other governance levels.

The following presents a three-layered model of metagovernance, governance of networks, and network governance, developed by Müller et al. (2024) and validated by Unterhitzenberger et al. (2022). For each of these layers, the governance elements are discussed and examples of the impact on project behavior are given. Figure 7.3 shows the model.

The development of the model was inspired by the work of Peter Morris (1994) on *The Governance of Projects,* which outlined, among others, the need to understand the distinct characteristics and challenges at the early stages of projects. The model described here transcends this into the realm of inter-organizational networks for projects and aims to help develop a more comprehensive understanding of this particular type of governance.

Metagovernance

In metagovernance (aka governance of governance), public government organizations or large-scale private investors issue (semi)permanent norms and principles through policies and guidelines to set the stage for the governance of networks to be established, which, in turn, governs the setup of the project-specific networks. Metagovernance aims to avoid failure at lower governance levels, which often emanate from coordination problems and insufficient understanding of the circumstances for governance. Therefore, metagovernance steers and directs the

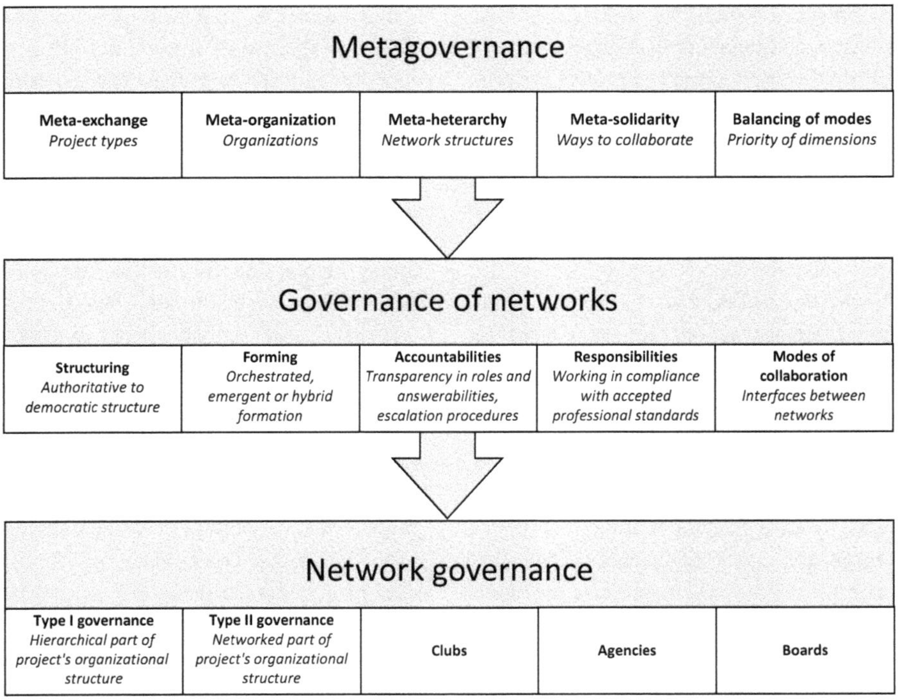

Figure 7.3 Layers and elements for the governance of inter-organizational networks for projects (after Müller et al., 2024).

networks by setting boundaries for their self-governance (Jessop, 2015).

Metagovernace comprises four reflexive modes of governance and a fifth to direct them. Reflexive is hereby the careful design and situational contingent decisions that consider circumstances and expectations. It starts with *meta-exchange*, the reflexive design of markets, and the subdivisions they include. In a project context, this refers to market-level decisions investors make, such as the investments outlined in the investors' project portfolio list, hence, the decision of what particular projects to pursue. The second mode is *meta-organization*, the decision on which organizations, intermediate organizations, and ecologies of organizations to allow – for example, only local or international suppliers, the authorization of special purpose vehicles (SPVs), the preferences for hierarchical or networked structures, etc. The third mode, *meta-heterarchy,* addresses the level of self-regulation of the networks in terms of their formation. Emergent formation allows networks to form by "knowing someone who knows someone," which typically leads to democratic structures with distributed authority. This approach dominates the private sector. Orchestrated formation requires following strictly defined processes and criteria to identify qualified potential network partners. This typically leads to more authoritative structures and is more often found in the public sector. The preference for one or the other reflects the investor's attitude toward avoiding governance failures either through combined knowledge of the participating organizations or through formal control structures.

Meta-solidarity is the fourth mode and addresses enabling opportunities for collaboration among actors, as deemed appropriate by the investor. These include bidder meetings, knowledge-sharing workshops, or training and certification programs to advance qualification levels. The emphasis for particular modes varies over time and requires adjustment to circumstances. Hence, the fifth mode, *balancing*, addresses the particular mix for emphasizing the four modes depending on the circumstances.

An example for metagovernance and its impact on project behavior is the Berlin Brandenburg Airport (FBB) in Germany (as described by Teworte & Albeniz, 2015; Fiedler & Wendler, 2016), which became well known for overspending and delays. Initially, meta-exchange aimed to have the airport built by a construction firm. However, the proposals sent in by the bidding companies were all approximately €1 billion fixed price for turnkey delivery. The governing body suspected collusion among the bidders and turned down all offers. In their mistrust toward bidders, they decided to govern the project themselves. They broke the project into 5 lots, which later became 50, which increased the scope and complexity of the governance of networks layer significantly. Subsequently, countless issues and delays forced shifting the opening date from 2012 to 2020. Moreover, instead of trusting the construction firms and paying a one-time sum of €1 billion for the airport to a construction firm, the governance body, through countless reworks and delays, created a loss of €1 billion per year between 2012 and 2020. In summary, the cost of mistrust in meta-exchange amounted to €7 billion of taxpayer money.

Meta-organization decisions in the FBB project included the exchange of main contractors that failed to meet performance criteria and forming new organizational entities, such as PMOs when the need emerged. Meta-heterarchy decisions included the restructuring of the network of networks for FBB from a megaproject (with one final deliverable) to a program that bundled the tasks necessary to accelerate achieving operational use of the airport. Examples include the additional projects to cope with the increased passenger load over the years because of the delay in airport opening, such as the expansion of the airport's train station from one track to several tracks. In other words, the megaproject's behavior turned the entire undertaking from a project into a semi-permanent program of airport building and continuous extension.

Examples of meta-solidarity in the FBB project include forming an on-site program office to improve communication between internal and external experts from various disciplines, such as FBB managers, construction firms, external consultants, and general planners. Metagovernance's balancing was evident by emphasizing meta-exchange at the early stages of the project, such as during planning and bidding. Meta-organization was emphasized both early on and when needed in later stages. Meta-heterarchy and meta-solidarity were emphasized when issues needed to be resolved.

Metagovernance in the FBB example contrasts with that of more successful megaprojects, such as the 2010 EXPO in Shanghai, which opened on time and encountered only a very small cost overrun. Zhai et al. (2017) describe the structures, values, and principles applied by the government for metagoverning this project. The most apparent difference between the FBB and EXPO projects is the level of trust among the partners. Contrary to the mistrust shown by FBB's governance institutions, the governance institutions in the EXPO case trusted their bidders. Zhai et al. (2017, p. 45) quoted the deputy director of the Construction Headquarter, saying, "We trust them [the main contractor]. We gave SCG [the main contractor] the permanent projects through bidding and authorized them to lead onsite." Hence, while FBB started under a *conformist* paradigm emphasizing process compliance and introvert/deontology behavior, the EXPO project started under a *versatile artist* paradigm, emphasizing outcome control and empowerment, fostering extravert/teleological behavior, with participants' freedom to act in the project's best interest. This resembles the discussion above on the importance of the initial governance paradigm for project performance and success.

Meta-exchange in the EXPO case avoided direct project governance by the government. Two nongovernmental governance institutions, the Construction Headquarter and the Bureau of EXPO Coordination, acted as mediators between the government and the project. This provided for indirect steering by the government and decision-making authority lying with industry professionals.

The meta-organizational approach fostered working with long-standing partner organizations, like the Shanghai Construction Engineering Division (SCG), as the main contractor with a track record of more than 50 years of joint successful landmark projects. Significant efforts went into making the process of contractor selection transparent for all involved parties. Meta-heterarchy for self-regulation of the governed entities was pursued through contractual and psychological commitments by the contractors, combined with trust and empowerment. This included a value system fostering "priority for efficiency" (Zhai et al., 2017, p. 44) and commitment by all stakeholders.

Meta-solidarity was characterized by flexible arrangements, such as coordination and other meetings held only when considered necessary. However, the minutes of these meetings were legally binding.

Overall, the EXPO case description by Zhai et al. (2017) shows the presence of high levels of trust among the parties, framed by unambiguous contractual agreements, personal commitment to deliver, and long-term relationships. Visibility of governance principles includes transparency in processes, management, supervision, and relationships. Accountabilities were unambiguously assigned and "key project officials were held personally accountable to the government for the success of the project" (p. 41), while the interviewees in Zhai et al's case study stress their leaders' responsible way of working.

Many writers have outlined the context contingency of governance in megaprojects and the resulting uniqueness of the related governance structures (e.g., Miller & Hobbs, 2005). Hence, the above discussion of different metagovernance approaches should not be understood as recommending a single 'best' governance structure. Instead, it should be understood as two examples of different levels of contextual fit of a particular governance approach.

Governance of Networks

Governance of networks addresses how the different inter-organizational networks for the investor's projects are governed as one network. It provides the framework for setting up networks, thereby balancing long- and short-term objectives. Governance focuses hereby predominantly on the formation, structure, accountabilities, responsibilities, and modes of collaboration among networks:

Structuring extends the meta-heterarchy requirement from the metagovernance layer into the governance of networks layer by emphasizing either more authoritative or more democratic network structures. This has direct implications for project behavior as these preferences typically reach through to the project level and influence the project structure and culture. Examples of networks activated at this layer include training and knowledge-sharing networks whose events are organized between projects, or, alternatively, information-sharing networks for potential collaborator organizations whose events are part of the tendering process for projects. Governance of networks coordinates these diverse activities and avoids clashes or omissions among the events by governing through defining formation, structuring, accountabilities, responsibilities, and modes of collaboration within the network of networks.

Formation extends meta-organization and meta-solidarity from metagovernance into the governance of networks layer. Public sector examples include official calls for tender, where defined selection criteria for potential bidders ensure transparency and neutrality in selecting participating organizations. This typically leads to orchestrated networks (a meta-organization requirement), supported by bidder conferences (a meta-solidarity requirement). Private sector examples include formal calls for proposals to a few selected companies and information meetings leading to emerging networks, thereby following more relaxed requirements from metagovernance. As described in the paragraph above, these formation approaches have an impact on the project and, with it, the behavior of the project.

Accountabilities are defined to provide transparency through a clear definition of the roles of networks, their answerabilities, and escalation procedures. The different accountabilities should be closely aligned with the purpose of the network. An example of the impact on project behavior is the training organization accountable for the certification of all network members for certain safety standards at the time of an infrastructure project launch. This certification project will be more authoritarian and demanding if the accountability is clearly defined and communicated in the network, as in the case of unclear accountabilities.

Responsibilities are defined to ensure task execution in the network meets expected quality levels. This ensures compliance with accepted professional working standards, such as ISO 21505 for the governance of projects, programs, and portfolios. Several studies have shown the positive impact of both certification and professional working standards in project management on project success and therefore project behavior. Examples include studies showing the link between methodology use and success (e.g., Joslin & Müller, 2015), as well as studies showing that certified project managers can be found in projects of all success levels, but the most successful projects were significantly more often managed by certified project managers (Müller & Turner, 2007)

Modes of collaboration define the interfaces between networks and their ways of collaboration. Setting up digital infrastructure in a construction project through the collaboration of execution networks and education networks exemplifies this. As shown in this example, the modes of collaboration enable projects to behave in specific ways.

Network Governance

Network governance is the governance of one network for one project. Studies on the structures of these networks showed that they are well explained through Multi-Level Governance Theory (MLG), as originally developed by Hooghe and Marks (2001) and later adapted to the realm of inter-organizational networks for projects by Unterhitzenberger et al. (2022). These networks are characterized by a mix of hierarchical and networked structures. To explain these complex settings, MLG distinguishes between:

- *Type I* governance, which addresses the hierarchical part of the network. This is typically the hierarchy of owner/sponsor, possible temporary client organization (SPEs), and the Tier One

Suppliers. Governance is institutionalized through clearly defined structures, roles, and responsibilities and explained through existing governance theories, such as agency theory, stewardship theory, or transaction costs economics for projects

- *Type II* governance, which addresses the non-hierarchical parts of the network. This includes the complex interaction between the many suppliers that engage in the project in the short and long term. Their interaction is governed by the desire to apply knowledge and experience to develop the project's deliverables. This may include overcoming sudden issues through informal, noninstitutionalized mutual support, irrespective of formal structures, roles, or responsibilities. Democratic governance theory (Skelcher, 2005) explains the relationships between these organizations.

Splitting networks in Type I and Type II governed entities raises the question of how the two governance approaches interact. For example, how are Type I governance (e.g., main contractor) items, such as policies to respect or methods to be used, forwarded to Type II governance entities (e.g., Tier 4 suppliers), and their implementation controlled? Three types of organizational units are used for this, which vary in their formality, authority, and staffing:

- *Boards* are the most formal and authoritative of these entities, typically overseeing the overall correctness of project execution for both internal and external governance of the project and its network. The scope of their tasks is broader than that of clubs and agencies and often spans the entire lifetime of a project or beyond.
- *Agencies* are formal organizational units set up to meet regularly, typically devoted to a particular aspect of the project, like changes, safety, or quality. They are often headed by prime contractor's representatives and staffed with suppliers' representatives.
- *Clubs* are informal and ad-hoc collaborations of volunteers in solving issues. They form based on mutual trust in jointly solving the problem at hand. Examples include machines not working, deliverables that do not fit their purpose, etc.

This is depicted in Figure 7.4 with examples from Scandinavia, as described by (Šimkonis et al., 2021). A board for legal, financial, and technical matters, enforcing process and policy compliance by addressing Type I and Type II governance issues simultaneously, as in a school construction project. Agencies are set up for specific themes (e.g., safety) in a railway construction project, thereby linking the hierarchically organized Type I institutions with the networked suppliers (Type II organizations). Clubs are formed by representatives of supplier firms to solve unexpected problems and issues, as in almost all projects.

The setup of the network governance structure has implications for project behavior in terms of

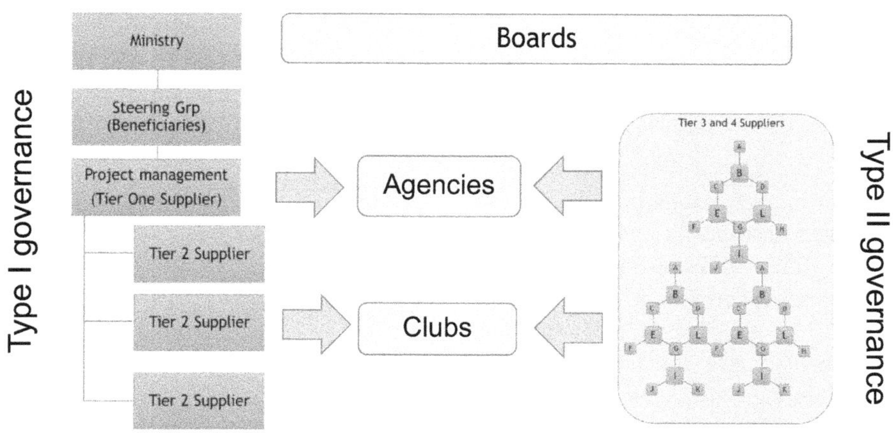

Figure 7.4 Linking Type I and II governance through boards, agencies, and clubs.

interaction among actors and project results. Unterhitzenberger et al. (2022) show that fostering Type II governance provides more democratic structures and flexibility in the network and the project. In addition, networks that emphasize Type II governance generally accomplish higher success levels than those governed mainly through Type I organizations. In other words, the flexibility of Type II leads to more successful behavior of the projects.

Moreover, in their studies on the interaction of the layers described above, they show how the setting of clear accountabilities and responsibilities at the governance of network layer mediates the impact of metagovernance on Type I governance at the network governance level, that is, substituting for missing guidance from metagovernance. This exemplifies one of the many different influences a project is exposed to, which affects project behavior.

The three-layer model described above and shown in Figure 7.3 represents a complex form of governance with multiple centers of decision-making, each of which operates with some degree of autonomy, which qualifies it as a polycentric system in the sense of Carlisle and Gruby (2019). Translated in the realm of projects, polycentricity is a design choice for the governance of inter-organizational networks for large and mega projects by creating "collaborative structures to achieve system goals in a pluralistic setting" as outlined by Gil and Pinto (2018, p. 730). The implications of that include the variety of governance influences on a project and the resulting complexity for its execution, all of which impact what projects do, that is, the behavior of projects.

Conclusions

This chapter described the interaction of governance and project behavior, first from an intra-organizational and then from an inter-organizational governance perspective. For that, the chapter introduced governance basics, practice standards, principles, and the resulting behavior of projects. Practical examples were given to guide practitioners in implementing these concepts in practice.

The alignment of a cognitive perspective (i.e., governance paradigm) and a psychological (i.e., introvert/extravert and ethical) perspective described in this chapter sheds light on the interaction between governance settings and the behavior of projects. In other words, the back-and-forth influences of the cognitive and psychological elements culminate in forming a particular "project personality type" with its particular behavior. Moreover, the chapter showed the potential triggers for and measures of how the governance paradigm and the "project personality type" steer and shape each other.

The chapter contributes to the discussion on project behavior, which Unterhitzenberger (2021) categorizes into (a) behavior *in* projects, which addresses the behavior of people, ranging from the individual to groups to organizational environments, and (b) behavior *of* projects, typically building on a systems dynamics and systems behavior tradition. The present chapter belongs to and extends the latter category, as it goes beyond the rational systems view by using the analogy of project personality and psyche to describe the project as a cumulative mind of its governance and management institutions. In other words, the chapter addressed the behavior *of* projects through the lens of behavior *in* projects. An approach that Geraldi and Söderlund (2018, p. 58) describe as the "broadening of levels of analysis" to develop alternative frames for conceptualizing practices. Herein, the interaction of governance and project behavior.

References

APM. (2011). *Directing change: A guide to governance of project management.* Association for Project Management.

Ashworth, R., Boyne, G., and Delbridge, R. (2009). Escape from the iron cage? Organizational change and isomorphic pressures in the public sector. *Journal of Public Administration Research and Theory, 19*(1), 165–187. https://doi.org/10.1093/jopart/mum038.

Britannica.com. (2022). Introvert and extrovert. www.britannica.com/science/introvert.

Carlisle, K., and Gruby, R. L. (2019). Polycentric systems of governance: A theoretical model for the commons. *Policy Studies Journal*, *47*(4), 921–946. https://doi.org/10.1111/psj.12212.

Elwell, F. (2022). The sociology of Max Weber. https://academic.udayton.edu/RichardGhere/POL307/weber.htm.

Fiedler, J., and Wendler, A. (2016). Berlin Brandenburg Airport (pp. 1–206). In G. Kostka and J. Fiedler (eds.). *Large infrastructure projects in Germany: Between ambition and realities*. Springer International.

Geraldi, J., and Söderlund, J. (2018). Project studies: What it is, where it is going. *International Journal of Project Management*, *36*(1), 55–70. https://doi.org/10.1016/j.ijproman.2017.06.004.

Gil, N., and Pinto, J. K. (2018). Polycentric organizing and performance: A contingency model and evidence from megaproject planning in the UK. *Research Policy*, *47*(4), 717–734. https://doi.org/10.1016/j.respol.2018.02.001.

Guzman, S., and Hill, J. (2017). *An analysis of Max Weber's The Protestant Ethics and the Spirit of Capitalism*. Macat International.

Hooghe, L., and Marks, G. (2001). Types of multi-level governance. *European Integration Online Papers*, *5*(11), 9163–9170. https://doi.org/10.1039/c9sm90238d.

ISO. (2017). *Project, programme and portfolio management: Guidance on governance*. ISO Copyright Office.

Jessop, B. (2015). From governance to governance failure and from multi-level governance to multi-scalar meta-governance (pp. 625–646). In I. Bache and M. Flinders (eds.). *Multi-level governance: Essential readings I.* Edward Elgar.

Joslin, R, and Müller, R. (2016). The relationship between project governance and project success. *International Journal of Project Management*, *34*(4), 613–626.

Joslin, Robert, and Müller, R. (2015). Relationships between project methodology and success in different governance contexts. *International Journal of Project Management*, *33*(6), 1377–1392.

Miller, R., and Hobbs, B. (2005). Governance regimes for large projects. *Project Management Journal*, *36*(3), 42–51.

Morris, P. W. G. (1994). *The management of projects*. Thomas Telford.

Müller, R. (2009). *Project governance*. Gower.

Müller, R. (2017). Organizational project governance (pp. 11–24). In R. Müller (ed.), *Governance and governmentality for projects: Enablers, practice and consequences*. Routledge.

Müller, R., and Lecoeuvre, L. (2014). Operationalizing governance categories of projects. *International Journal of Project Management*, *32*(8). https://doi.org/10.1016/j.ijproman.2014.04.005.

Müller, R., Alix-Séguin, C., Alonderienė, R., Bourgault, M., Chmielauskas, A., Drouin, N., Ke, Y., Minelgaite, I., Pilkienė, M., Šimkonis, S. and Unterhitzenberger, C., 2024. Vaagaasar, A.L., and Zhu, F. A (meta) governance framework for multi-level governance of inter-organizational project networks. Production Planning & Control, *35*(10), 1043–1062.

Müller, R, and Turner, J. R. (2007). The influence of project managers on project success criteria and project success by type of project. *European Management Journal*, *25*(4), 289–309.

Müller, R. (2009). *Project governance*. Gower.

OECD. (2001). *Governance in the 21st Century. OECD*. OECD. http://www.oecd.org/futures/17394484.pdf.

PMI. (2016). *Governance of portfolios, programs, and projects: A practice guide*. Project Management Institute, USA. www.pmi.org/~/media/PDF/learning/portfolio-program-project-governance-practice-guide.ashx.

Šimkonis, Š., Müller, R., Alonderienė, R., Chmieliauskas, A., and Pilkienė, M. (2021). Multi-level governance in inter-organizational project settings (pp. 1–20). In *Proceedings of the British Academy of Management (BAM) Conference in the Cloud, October 31 to September 2, 2021, Lancaster University, UK*.

Skelcher, C. (2005). Jurisdictional integrity, polycentrism and the design of democratic governance. *Governance*, *18*(1), 89–111.

Teworte, V., and Albeniz, V. M. (2015). *Berlin Brandenburg International Airport*. ES617P-1142-E, IESE.

Turner, J. R. (2022). Using principal–steward contracting and scenario planning to manage megaprojects. *Project Management Journal*, *53*(1), 8–16. https://doi.org/10.1177/87569728211061836.

Turner, J. R., and Müller, R. (2004). Communication and co-operation on projects between the project owner as principal and the project manager as agent. *European Management Journal*, *22*(3). https://doi.org/10.1016/j.emj.2004.04.010.

Unterhitzenberger, C. (2021). Special issue on project behavior. *Project Management Journal*, *52*(6),

527–530. https://doi.org/10.1177/87569728211054716.

Unterhitzenberger, C., Müller, R., Vaagaasar, A. L., Ke, Y., Alonderienė, R., Minelgaite, I., Pilkiene, M., Wang, L., Zhu, F., Drouin, N., Chmieliauskas, A., Simkonis, S., and Mongeon, M. (2022). A multi-level governance model for inter-organizational project networks. *Project Management Journal*, *54*(1), 88–105.

Vitell, S. J., and Davis, D. L. (1990). Ethical beliefs of MIS professionals: The frequency and opportunity for unethical behavior. *Journal of Business Ethics*, *9*(1), 63–70. https://doi.org/10.1007/BF00382565.

Zhai, Z., Ahola, T., Le, Y., and Xie, J. (2017). Governmental gGovernance of megaprojects: The case of EXPO 2010 Shanghai. *Project Management Journal*, *48*(1), 37–50. https://doi.org/10.1177/875697281704800103.

CHAPTER 8

Strategic Alignment, Uncertainties, and Realignment of Project Portfolios

MIIA MARTINSUO and SIIRI TUOMINEN

Introduction

Organizations typically have several innovation projects in their project portfolio, since they need to develop multiple products and services for different markets in parallel and prepare for alternative futures. Some innovation projects may be planned to follow the organization's official strategy and process, while some projects may emerge in an unplanned manner (Loch, 2000; Kopmann et al., 2017; Globocnik et al., 2022). In project portfolio management (PPM), project portfolios and their single projects are expected to fit the organization's strategy, and projects are often assessed in terms of strategic alignment to prioritize them for selection (Cooper et al., 1997; Archer & Ghasemzadeh, 1999; Dye & Pennypacker, 1999; Englund & Graham, 1999). Similarly, strategic alignment is often treated as a success criterion, when evaluating the project portfolio's performance (Cooper et al., 1999; Jonas et al., 2013; Kock et al., 2016; Kopmann et al., 2017; Kock & Gemünden, 2019). Between the beginning of projects and the periodic assessment of project portfolio success, however, anything can happen.

Projects and portfolios face uncertainties both from projects and the environment, and managers may need to readjust, realign, and reconfigure the project portfolio to fulfill the strategic aspirations. Uncertainty is very commonly experienced both concerning single projects and the project portfolio as a whole, so there is a need to understand any uncertainty sources that affect project portfolios and the consequent managerial actions taken for realignment. Some previous research has already mapped the types of uncertainties experienced in project portfolios and related managerial responses (Petit & Hobbs, 2010; Petit, 2012; Korhonen et al., 2014; Martinsuo et al., 2014; Teller et al., 2014; Kock & Gemünden, 2016). While such research acknowledges the consequent reconfiguration of the project portfolio, to adjust and realign it either with the earlier or with a completely new strategy, this realignment will deserve more attention.

Here, project behavior is understood as the behavior *of* projects, which should also include considerations of behavior *in* projects (Unterhitzenberger, 2021) within a portfolio of multiple projects. When organizations strive for strategic alignment in their project portfolios, behavior in projects and external uncertainties may either drive or threaten that alignment. Behavior in projects is susceptible to various assumptions, heuristics, and biases in thinking, stemming from incomplete and uncertain information and potentially leading to project misperformance (Ika et al., 2022). Some (organizational and environmental) uncertainties may reside completely outside of managers' own control, but also they may require mitigation and coping in terms of new project behaviors. Thereby, behavior *in* projects is expected to be connected with behavior *of* projects in various ways (Unterhitzenberger, 2021). There is a need to understand these connections underlying the behavior of projects.

The goal of this chapter is to reveal the sources of uncertainties firms face in their innovation project portfolios and characterize their approaches to strategic realignment as means to resolve the uncertainties. We generally assume that organizations pursue strategic alignment both in their project and portfolio selection and as a performance criterion and they also experience uncertainty stemming from both project behavior and the surrounding context. We seek answers to the following questions:

Table 8.1 Overview to empirical examples used in this chapter

	Industry	Turnover M€	Number of employees	Number of project portfolios
Large firms, data: 12 interviewees				
ForestCo	Forest industry	>1,800	>2,000	2
MechaniCo	Mechanical engineering	>3,000	>10,000	>3
AutomatiCo	Automation and mechanical engineering	>1,500	>10,000	>3
Medium-sized firms, data: 8 interviewees				
SoftwareCo	Software solutions	>60	>900	2
MachineryCo	Heavy machinery	>600	>1,700	2

1. From where, which sources, do uncertainties emerge in innovation project portfolios? In particular, how do firms of different sizes differ in their uncertainty experiences?
2. How, through what kinds of phases, do managers realign the portfolios with strategy when responding to uncertainty?

The next section characterizes the organizations' common pursuit of strategic alignment in their project portfolios. We then introduce the necessity to acknowledge the environment, organizational complexity, and single projects as possible sources of uncertainty for project portfolios. We explain the need for managers to monitor the events surrounding the project portfolio, to be able to take action upon uncertainties and to strategically realign the project portfolio, when needed. We report empirical evidence and examples from qualitative, interview-based case studies in five industrial firms representing somewhat different sizes and industries and each managing at least two innovation project portfolios (based on Tuominen, 2020; Anttila, 2021; Martinsuo & Tuominen, 2021; Martinsuo & Anttila, 2022). Table 8.1 summarizes the contexts of the studied firms (labeled with pseudonyms to retain anonymity).

We use empirical examples from some of the studied companies concerning the pandemic-induced chaos that generated a flood of uncertainties to highlight the steps leading to the project portfolios' strategic realignment. As conclusions, we reveal some firm size–related differences in the uncertainty sources, map the managers' cognitive process of project portfolio's strategic realignment, and advocate perceiving project behavior not just as a source of uncertainty, but as a mechanism for reaching strategic realignment in a project portfolio.

The Pursuit of Strategic Alignment in Project Portfolios

Innovation projects represent organization's means to develop new products and services and establish new revenue streams. Because firms may operate on multiple different markets and serve different market segments, they need to be involved in multiple parallel innovation projects and organize the projects into project portfolios. Similarly, they need to prepare for alternative futures with different projects, because the future is unknown.

The compilation of innovation projects is typically guided by the firm's business or innovation strategy that communicates choices concerning key markets, technologies, channels, and capabilities. Firms' strategies differ clearly from each other, but the suitability of the project portfolio is often assessed in very generic terms merely as *strategic alignment* (Martinsuo & Geraldi, 2020). Next to value maximization and portfolio balance, strategic alignment or fit is typically considered as a key goal for PPM (Cooper et al., 1997). Also exploitation of synergies and average project or product success may occasionally be considered as goals and success criteria in PPM (Jonas et al.,

2013; Kock et al., 2016; Kopmann et al., 2017; Kock & Gemünden, 2019). While any of these measures may be used as episodic success criteria in evaluating the project portfolio performance, they are also considered carefully when screening and assessing projects and proposing, prioritizing, and selecting projects to the portfolio (Cooper et al., 1997; Archer & Ghasemzadeh, 1999; Dye & Pennypacker, 1999; Englund & Graham, 1999). Projects, thereby, are reviewed strategically and often treated as vehicles or mechanisms of strategy implementation.

A single project's strategic alignment requires that the project and its goals, benefits, and ways of operating are planned with the strategy in mind (Englund & Graham, 1999). This strategic pursuit may be challenging and paradoxical in the context of innovations. On the one hand, innovations are expected to drive renewal in the firm and potentially enable the emergence of completely new strategies (Loch, 2000; Kopmann et al., 2017). On the other hand, if the strategy already communicates such renewal intentions, then the strategy is expected to guide projects' goal setting and planning directly (Cooper et al., 1997; Englund & Graham, 1999). This intent of innovation project portfolios to serve both strategy implementation and renewal may be reflected in the types of practices used for PPM (Kopmann et al., 2017). Firms may even use different project portfolios to implement different strategies, for example, concerning incremental vs. radical innovations (Loch, 2000).

The five example companies all had specified strategies to guide the project portfolios, which were derived from a more general business or innovation strategy. As they all had two or more project portfolios, each portfolio served a somewhat different innovation strategy, for example, differentiated by the incremental vs. radical nature of innovations or dedicated to specific business areas or product segments (e.g., oriented toward specific customer markets or hardware vs. software). Regardless of this division, all companies considered their innovation strategies to be integral parts of the organization's high-level strategy serving ultimately the same purpose. All the firms had some routines and practices in place, to ensure the alignment of their innovation projects with such strategies, ranging from the use of strategic evaluation criteria to comprehensive PPM systems. Informants in our study acknowledged quite well that strategies and circumstances change and that also the project portfolios evolve over time, when facing uncertainty.

Uncertainty in Project Portfolios

Even if all projects are planned so that they and the project portfolio are aligned with strategy originally, they are susceptible to changing circumstances and surprising events. PPM research already acknowledges that managers need to pay attention to their uncertain environments (Petit & Hobbs, 2010; Petit, 2012), ensure that new information is brought into the social decision-making events (Blichfeldt & Eskerod, 2008; Christiansen & Varnes, 2008), and use information on uncertainties in managing the project portfolios (Korhonen et al., 2014). Where risks are known occurrences that can be assessed in terms of their probability and impact and affect the project performance positively or negatively (Chapman & Ward, 1997; Knight, 2006), uncertainties are such occurrences that cannot necessarily be known and whose outcomes cannot be anticipated (De Meyer et al., 2002). In innovation projects, various uncertainties are prevalent, but organizations cope with them and reduce them by accessing new information and preparing for alternative outcomes during the innovation process (De Meyer et al., 2002; Pich et al., 2002). Managing uncertainty does not deal with managing threats, opportunities, and their implications only, but with understanding the sources of uncertainty, already before starting to plan any responses to such uncertainty (Ward & Chapman, 2003)

This study considers uncertainty in project portfolios, where portfolio uncertainties may stem from any occurrences, changes, and deviations arising from within the projects or the context. Project portfolio managers face uncertainty from three main types of sources: the environment, parent organization's complexity, and single projects (Korhonen et al., 2014; Martinsuo et al.,

2014). We mapped the sources of uncertainty experienced by project portfolio managers in the studied five firms into these three categories. Martinsuo et al., (2014) suggest that through understanding these sources of uncertainties, the managers frame the uncertainties into the categories of threats, neutral, and opportunities, which will consequently affect how they potentially respond to the uncertainties.

Sources of Uncertainty in the External Environment

External environment is broadly considered as a substantial source of project portfolio uncertainty (Petit & Hobbs 2010; Petit 2012; Voss & Kock 2013; Korhonen et al., 2014; Kock & Gemünden, 2016; Hoffmann et al., 2020; Kaufmann et al., 2021). Various external uncertainty sources seem to affect PPM regardless of the organizations' industry and size. For instance, *changing customer needs* are often considered a significant source of portfolio uncertainty, as they provide inputs and direction to new innovation projects and may change in an unforeseen manner (Petit & Hobbs, 2010; Petit, 2012; Voss, 2012; Korhonen et al., 2014; Kock & Gemünden, 2016; Hoffmann et al., 2020). Customer needs, therefore, demand continuous business intelligence activities and external monitoring as part of PPM. Another common portfolio uncertainty is *technology* (Voss & Kock, 2013; Korhonen et al., 2014; Hoffmann et al., 2020), as novel technologies may spark ideas for new product development projects, evolve in an unknown pace, and also cause changes to existing technology choices. New technologies have been positively associated with portfolio innovativeness and therefore eventual portfolio success (Kaufmann et al., 2021). Continuous technology monitoring and scouting offer important information for PPM.

In addition to uncertainty sources in the closest business environment of firms, also broader societal issues may appear as relevant for innovation project portfolios. Some studies have identified *legislation and regulations* as an influential source of portfolio uncertainty (Petit 2012; Korhonen et al., 2014; Hoffmann et al., 2020), along with the company's *competitors* (Petit, 2012; Korhonen et al., 2014; Kock & Gemünden, 2016). Changes in legislation and regulations may drive new innovations or cause pressures to existing projects, and competitors' actions are typically monitored carefully, to ensure timely responses. Some studies have mentioned various *third parties*, that is, other organizations within or nearby the company's supply chain, as a source of portfolio uncertainty (Petit & Hobbs, 2010; Korhonen et al., 2014). Lastly, Petit and Hobbs (2010) have recognized *global economy* as another source of portfolio uncertainty not belonging to any of the categories described above but still important to be considered when practicing PPM.

The findings of case studies conducted in large and medium-sized companies in different industries offer evidence of how portfolio managers experienced the sources of external uncertainty in their innovation project portfolios. Figure 8.1 summarizes sources of uncertainty in the external environment, as experienced in the studied firms. In this and the next figures, the significance of the uncertainty source was assessed by the frequency of expressions in the interview data. *High significance* indicates that the majority of the interviewees mentioned portfolio uncertainties arising from such a source, whereas *low significance* indicates that the uncertainty source was mentioned merely by a single interviewee. *Moderate significance* then falls between these two categories with the frequency of expressions between high and low significance.

Managers in both the large and medium-sized firms experienced *customers*, *technology*, and *competitors* as the most significant uncertainty sources affecting PPM. The expectations of customers vary and change over time, the actions of competitors may be surprising, and the emergence, pace, and direction of new technologies is perceived as uncertain. Some of our informants characterized these issues more generally, as part of the industry domain in which they operated: certain industries are more fast-paced and uncertain than others. Particularly, the digitalization trend has been experienced in all firms and had influenced decisions concerning innovation project portfolios, too.

Company size	Large	Medium
Industries / Uncertainty source	Automation, manufacturing, forestry	Software solutions, machinery
Customers	● ● ●	● ● ●
Technology	● ● ●	● ● ●
Competitors	● ● ●	● ● ●
Legislation and regulation	● ● ●	● ● ○
Third parties	● ○ ○	● ● ●
Other external uncertainty	● ● ○	● ○ ○
Significance ● = Low ● ● = Moderate ● ● ● = High		

Figure 8.1 Sources and significance of portfolio uncertainties stemming from the external environment.

On top of these three sources, *legislation and regulations* were seen as a significant source of uncertainty in large companies and moderate in medium-sized companies. Informants in large companies experienced legislation and regulations both as a driver to change the strategic direction and as a source of operative requirements throughout the supply chain, consequently filtered to innovation project portfolios. The pace of changes in legislation might be slow, but the large firms had to be sensitive to regulatory changes on different market areas and customer industries in their global operations and the implications on innovation strategies and portfolios appeared as more influential. As the medium-sized companies had more restricted markets and industry domains and a more agile way of operating to begin with, the regulatory evolution was not equally visible as in the large firms.

Third parties were experienced as a significant source of project portfolio uncertainty more in medium-sized companies, and less so in large companies, even if third-party cooperation is used in innovation projects in both types of firms. Such uncertainties dealt with access to suppliers and partners, start-up cooperation, and research cooperation, and it enabled (or disabled) access to relevant information that guides the innovation projects. The difference between firms of different sizes may be explained through the differences in portfolio size and hierarchies of decision-making. It is likely that third-party cooperation is handled at the project level and will be reflected onto the portfolio level better in smaller portfolios with lower decision hierarchies. Alternatively, large companies may have better internal access to critical resources and capabilities, whereas medium-sized companies might need to rely on external resources more frequently in their projects, which could increase the significance of third party–related portfolio uncertainties in them. Additionally, some *other external uncertainties* such as the turbulence caused by the COVID pandemic and the influence of labor unions were identified in both large and medium-sized companies. The medium-sized firms were studied in the early phase of the pandemic (when the effects were not yet fully seen) and large firms were studied in the middle of the pandemic and additionally emphasized the influence of labor unions (both in their own firms and in customer firms), which could explain their difference better than the difference in the industry or company size.

Sources of Uncertainty from Organizational Complexity

Organizational complexity concerns strategies, structural arrangements, resources and responsibilities, and culture and power within the organization, as the parent organization's internal surroundings in which the project portfolios are located. It, too, is a significant and well-understood source of uncertainty for project portfolios (Petit & Hobbs, 2010; Petit, 2012; Teller et al., 2012; Voss & Kock, 2013; Korhonen et al., 2014; Kock & Gemünden, 2016; Hoffman et al., 2020; Kauffman et al., 2021). As such, organizational sources of uncertainties seem to influence companies regardless of their size and industry.

Many studies have emphasized the company's *resource availability* as a significant source of portfolio uncertainty (Petit 2012; Korhonen et al., 2014; Kock & Gemünden, 2016; Hoffman et al., 2020), as resource limitations often guide the prioritization decisions during portfolio reconfiguration (Hoffman et al., 2020). Specifically concerning human resources, the *company's employees*, their competences, roles, and responsibilities, have an impact on PPM (Teller et al., 2012; Korhonen et al., 2014; Hoffman et al., 2020). Ways of allocating resources between projects and specifying the roles and responsibilities of individuals may change over time, and this has implications on the project portfolio. Also actions to promote employees' motivation and well-being may have an influence (Hoffmann et al., 2020), particularly if the objectives are ambitious and if employees need to prioritize between different projects in their daily work. Generally, it is important to consider *organizational culture* as a source of portfolio uncertainty (Petit, 2012; Teller at al., 2014; Hoffmann et al., 2020; Kaufmann et al., 2021), so that processes and portfolio management mechanisms can be developed to fit the organization's norms (Hoffmann et al., 2020). For example, the organization's norms, processes, and ways of operating may vary between very simple and highly complex, and the extent of intra-organizational complexity may be reflected in various degrees of uncertainty tolerance vs. uncertainty avoidance.

Portfolio structure has been mentioned as a significant source of portfolio uncertainty in multiple studies (Petit & Hobbs, 2010; Petit, 2012; Voss & Kock, 2013; Korhonen et al., 2014; Hoffman et al., 2020; Kaufmann et all, 2021). For instance, Hoffmann et al. (2020) identified the risk of portfolio's strategic misalignment and ultimately failure, if new projects are constantly added without considering their implications on the portfolio and if PPM does not handle project prioritization and approval in a timely manner. Some portfolio uncertainties might emerge from the general *organizational structure*, where structural changes might occur and require actions in the project portfolio (Petit & Hobbs, 2010; Korhonen et al., 2014). Structural changes might mean adding or deleting a new organizational unit, or allocating new responsibilities for a specific unit, and any of such changes could cause pressures to change the location or composition of project portfolios. According to Petit and Hobbs (2010), however, such uncertainties stemming from organizational structure seemed to have only a minor impact on the portfolio level. Similarly, changes in *organization's strategy* are assumed to have an impact on portfolio's strategic alignment (PMI, 2008; Petit & Hobbs, 2010), but such uncertainties have not been observed widely in previous studies.

Companies of different sizes and industries in our empirical exploration differed in their perceptions of organizational complexities as sources of uncertainty. This difference can be seen in Figure 8.2.

In the medium-sized companies, the most significant source of uncertainty stemming from organizational complexity concerned the companies' *resources*, whereas larger companies deemed the resource-related uncertainties less significant. This could be explained by the availability of resources, as medium-sized companies may hit the resource capacity limit quicker compared to larger organizations. In the larger firms, *organizational culture* was seen as the most significant source of organizational complexity, particularly in terms of the historical legacy in technical systems and somewhat rigid ways of operating, whereas cultural uncertainties were not discussed

Company size	Large	Medium
Industries / **Uncertainty source**	Automation, manufacturing, forestry	Software solutions, machinery
Resource availability	● ● ○	● ● ●
Portfolio structure	● ● ○	● ● ○
Culture	● ● ●	○ ○ ○
People	● ○ ○	● ● ○
Organizational structure	○ ○ ○	○ ○ ○
Strategy	○ ○ ○	○ ○ ○
Significance ● = Low ●● = Moderate ●●● = High		

Figure 8.2 Sources and significance of portfolio uncertainties stemming from organizational complexity.

in the medium-sized companies. This difference in perception could be explained by potentially more conservative and stable organizational cultures in larger organizations, which might imply reduced flexibility compared to more agile smaller companies.

People, especially in terms of their competences, roles, and responsibilities, were expressed as a source of portfolio uncertainty in both large and medium-sized companies, for example, concerning the allocation of certain competences to innovation projects and risk of losing critical competences. In medium-sized companies, the significance of this uncertainty source was seen as greater compared to larger organizations. This difference could be related to the access to the right types of competences and capabilities in light of the job demands, where medium-sized companies might have fewer employees with key competences compared to larger organizations. Alternatively, larger organizations may have more established procedures concerning the allocation of roles and responsibilities, whereas medium-sized companies might have to assign key employees to multiple different roles at the same time especially when resources are scarce.

During the study period, uncertainties rising from *organizational structure* or *strategy* were not discussed in the target firms due to such adjustments being relatively rare and due to our informants representing those involved in PPM (not the general top management). The lack of observations does not mean that such changes should be overlooked in PPM; rather, it is likely that such sources of uncertainty are experienced elsewhere in the organization and that the informants experienced strategies and structures as clear, not causing particular uncertainty at the moment.

Sources of Uncertainty in Individual Projects

Uncertainties and their sources have been widely studied at the single project level (Ward & Chapman, 2003), but they also have clear implications at the level of the project portfolio. These uncertainties can be classified into three different categories, where the most common source of project uncertainty is related to *project parameters*: time, cost, and quality (Ward & Chapman 2003; Petit & Hobbs, 2010; Korhonen et al., 2014). Such uncertainty may mean that issues concerning time, cost, or quality are for some reason unknown or

Company size	Large	Medium
Industries **Uncertainty source**	Automation, manufacturing, forestry	Software solutions, machinery
Project parameters	● ● ●	● ● ●
Assessment quality	○ ○ ○	● ● ●
Project complexity	○ ○ ○	○ ○ ○
Significance ● = Low ● ● = Moderate ● ● ● = High		

Figure 8.3 Sources and significance of portfolio uncertainties stemming from single projects.

that these parameters are sensitive to changes due to how they are managed. The *assessment quality* on these parameters has also been suggested as a source portfolio uncertainty (Ward & Chapman, 2003; Petit & Hobbs, 2010). This deals with deficient estimations concerning the project parameters and causes uncertainty, as poor project planning might be reflected on the portfolio level and multiply due to project interrelations. Lastly, *project complexity*, including project characteristics and scope, has been highlighted as a source of portfolio uncertainty stemming from single projects (Petit & Hobbs, 2010; Korhonen et al., 2014). While many of the single-project sources of uncertainty may be monitored and resolved at the single-project level, they may also have ramifications at the project portfolio level due to projects' interdependencies and competition for resources, and they therefore require some monitoring and consideration in the portfolio, too.

Figure 8.3 shows how the single-project uncertainties appeared in the portfolios of the five studied firms. Uncertainties stemming from *project parameters* were apparent in both large and medium-sized companies. In fact, interviewees in all companies reported uncertainties related to project schedule, budget, or quality and their implications at the level of the project portfolio. When single projects stretch their schedules or budgets or fail to produce expected innovation outcomes, it appears in a need to rearrange resources and budgets for other projects. In turn, uncertainties related to *assessment quality* were only discussed in the medium-sized companies, where multiple instances of insufficient estimations of projects' resource need, schedule, quality, and budget were reported and caused changes and pressures to the portfolio level. It may be that large organizations considered such assessment quality uncertainties to be embedded in project parameters, and therefore they were not reported separately. Project complexity as a separate uncertainty source was not observed in either large or medium-sized companies, potentially due to the fact that different types of projects were divided into separate portfolios, each with their processes and guidelines.

Tackling Uncertainty through Strategic Realignment

The above overview to the sources of uncertainty in innovation project portfolios has drawn attention to the managers' need to monitor events and changes and take action to ensure that the portfolio stays on its course over time. If managers notice that the project portfolio is insufficiently strategy-aligned, they should engage in *strategic realignment*, which means making the necessary portfolio-level changes to regain the pursued balance and alignment between the portfolio and the innovation strategy. Strategic realignment may occur on a regular interval, such as annual or semi-annual portfolio review meetings, episodically following a more significant event that has caused turmoil in the portfolio, or also in the micro-level actions of managers, when reallocating resources or prioritizing between projects in a sub-portfolio. Petit (2012) discusses reconfiguring, that is, changes in the portfolio in terms of what is done and how resources are allocated. He also acknowledges the possibility to transform the portfolio management processes, due to the experienced changes.

Excessive monitoring is not necessary or even desired for project portfolios, even if some processes of uncertainty and risk identification and management are needed. A study concerning the formalized aspects of risk management in project portfolios revealed that redundant risk monitoring may even have a negative effect on project portfolio success (Teller & Kock, 2013). Another study on managers' uncertainty handling approaches suggests that unnecessary control may damage organizational learning and communication (Martinsuo et al., 2014). Due to this, some flexibility needs to be present in effective PPM especially in a highly dynamic context (Martinsuo et al., 2014). In our view, managers just need to stay alert to the sources of uncertainty and be prepared to act on them upon need.

In order to understand how strategic realignment takes place, we explored our five case companies for such very topical occurrences where managers had to respond to an episodic turmoil and go through strategic realignment. We noticed that all the studied companies had experienced the COVID-19 pandemic as a source of external uncertainty, influencing many other uncertainties and causing a necessity for managers to reconsider the project portfolio's strategic alignment. This can be considered as an extreme event, demonstrating the interconnectedness of multiple different uncertainties and, thereby, enabling pattern discovery in companies' responses to the uncertainties.

Chaos Emerging through Interlinked Uncertainties

When the COVID-19 pandemic emerged, companies around the globe and across industries were hit by a shock. The uncertainties rising from the external environment and country-specific lockdowns were so severe that customers temporarily stopped using the solutions supplied by the studied firms for weeks or months, these process interruptions occurred at different times on the different market areas, and the companies had to stall recruitment processes, spare resources, and slow down investments. Instead of investing into innovations for the longer-term future, the firms we studied had to concentrate more on resolving crises and problems, alongside their day-to-day operations.

The changes permeated through the supply chains broadly and quickly. As a result, uncertainties concerning organizational complexity and single projects also started to surface. Resources had to be rearranged, responsibilities had to be reconsidered, and project parameters faced new unknowns, and all these movements required consideration also at the portfolio level. The snowball effect led to complete chaos, that is, unforeseen events with high severity (De Meyer et al., 2002), where a series of severe and unforeseen events started to invalidate innovation project portfolios' previously planned objectives.

During the early phases of the pandemic, the core project portfolio actors in three companies MechaniCo, SoftwareCo, and MachineryCo, started to behave in an interestingly similar manner when practicing their PPM. After noticing the chaos, they first became alarmed about it, which triggered managerial action, then began considerations on refocusing the portfolio through drastic reconfiguration, and finally completed a strategic realignment in the project portfolio. We describe these phases below, in how it appeared in these firms.

Alarms Triggering Managerial Action

COVID-19 was experienced in the firms both as a "shock," "heavy blow," and "misty outlook," and all these metaphors acted as alarms that the firms needed to take seriously. Particularly, the larger firm MechaniCo started seeing signs of uncertainty immediately after China's first lockdowns in the form of canceled customer orders, difficulties in getting components from the suppliers, and remote monitoring systems informing the reduced or stalled use of their equipment in customers' processes. As one manager reported: "It is fortunate that we have access to remote data on our systems in customer's processes. We could see the reduction in equipment use rather fast, and in just one or two months we were in a totally different mode of operating [as a response to the identified uncertainty]." In SoftwareCo, the focus of the innovation project portfolios changed drastically due to COVID-19, as the company's customers were facing completely new challenges in the quickly transforming and unpredictable environment. At the same time, MachineryCo was struggling with similar uncertainties in their own, completely different industry and market. The rapidly emerging new requirements and demands from customers, suppliers, and various partners alerted the firms to a new situation: their innovation project portfolios were no longer appropriate, and they could not handle the innovation project portfolios with the resources that they possessed.

These distressing alarms rising from the external environment forced the companies to stall recruitment as a precaution. In a global research and development organization, lockdowns required remote work arrangements, which was challenging to handle as all employees do not have personal laptops and remote connections from home. These resource-related issues meant that the resources for innovation projects began to suffer. As an unexpected consequence, new uncertainties began to emerge from organizational complexity and single projects. In the middle of changing customer needs, pressing resource limitations, and distorted project plans, the companies had to try and understand the nature of these alarms (i.e., uncertainties that required immediate responses) and their impact on the innovation project portfolios.

Management Teams Reconfiguring the Portfolios

After identifying and assessing the uncertainty, the project portfolio actors in MechaniCo, SoftwareCo, and MachineryCo had to develop adequate responses to the various uncertainties quickly and efficiently in order to realign the portfolio toward the new and constantly changing strategic objectives. According to one manager, the chaotic circumstances required dramatic actions: "Well, our actions were rather significant, in response to the misty outlook. We did not have much insight into whether we would sell anything at all, for a while. So we had to switch our spending to such a [lower] level, too, and really fast." In the companies, the portfolios were heavily reconfigured during the pandemic, for example, by adding and deleting projects, rearranging resources between them, and changing project scopes, schedules, and budgets. It also meant a momentary scale-down of some portfolios and projects and shifting managers' day-to-day attention to even very minor details within the portfolios. In SoftwareCo, portfolio reconfiguration was carried out by the product council, as explained by one of the company's portfolio managers:

> We did a lot of reconfiguration during the spring, as the focus points changed drastically when the markets were hit by the shock. One thing that was previously deemed important was not as crucial anymore, and even if we did not necessarily terminate an initiative, we might have put some things on hold or on a lower priority. At the same time, if we recognized some other projects that we wanted to push forward, we increased their priority and reallocated resources to those initiatives. Due to that, we of course had to then lower the priority of some other projects, so we would get more resources out of it.

The reconfiguration actions in MachineryCo were very similar, as the company was also trying to realign the project portfolio with the company's renewing strategic objectives, while the strategy was being reconsidered to match the new circumstances in the business environment. During this portfolio refocusing, the portfolio components were reprioritized, resources reallocated, new projects added, and some projects were backlogged.

Achieving Strategic Realignment

During heavy reconfiguration and refocusing the portfolios, new projects had been added to serve the reformed customer needs, redundant projects had been terminated or backlogged to free resources, projects had been reprioritized to respond to the new demands, and resources were reallocated according to the new prioritization. As a result, innovation project portfolios in the companies were more responsive to the identified uncertainties rising from the external environment, organizational complexity, and single projects, and again realigned with the companies' renewed strategies. Particularly at the later phase of our research, the firms had already "returned back to almost normal" and adjusted their innovation projects to prepare for the future after the pandemic, as one manager explained: "Last summer we had to adjust various things quite a bit, but then we could turn the knobs [readjust the portfolio] to a more ordinary position."

The strategic alignment of an innovation project portfolio is a moving target, and the future after pandemic appears as different from the future anticipated before the pandemic. Therefore, a portfolio's strategic alignment requires continuous monitoring of portfolio uncertainties and frequent reconfiguration, as explained by one of the portfolio actors in MachineryCo:

> We have a huge number of projects, even a bit too many. In that sense, the spring [2020] and COVID-19 pandemic was a good time to pause and seek for focus again. We should remember that during the good times as well, that we should sit down for a bit and review the things that are ongoing in the portfolio.

Conclusions

We have portrayed PPM as a pursuit of strategic alignment and, yet, a sensitive endeavor facing various uncertainties. In response to the first research question, we mapped sources of uncertainties stemming from the surrounding environment, organizational complexity, and single projects. In our study, project behavior in the form of performance criteria, assessment quality, and complexity is only one uncertainty dimension, with the other sources of uncertainties faced at the project portfolio level. Our exploration of five firms indicates that the influence of behavior in projects stemming from single-project uncertainties toward the project portfolio is minor compared to uncertainties from the environment and organization. It is likely that the majority of project-level uncertainties are treated within the projects and only rarely accumulate to such concerns that should be considered at the project portfolio level. However, changes in project behavior become necessary as ways to respond to and mitigate the uncertainties stemming from the environment and organizational complexity, as project portfolio decisions need to be implemented in the affected projects, too. Thereby, we portray project behavior both as a possible source of uncertainty and as a way to mitigate uncertainty to achieve strategic realignment.

While the various uncertainty sources have been covered in different ways in earlier research, our study offers novel information on the differences potentially stemming from different firm sizes (and industries). In our interpretation, the differences may result from a combination of portfolio positioning, organizational history, and industry clockspeed, as these differentiate the large firms from the medium-sized firms. *Portfolio positioning* deals with the portfolio's span and centrality or hierarchical location in the organization. In the large firms (particularly MechaniCo and AutomatiCo), there were several portfolios and portfolios were distributed at the different levels of the organization, whereas in the medium-sized firms (also ForestCo) there were just two main portfolios located centrally. This positioning may be reflected in access to dedicated resources and competences, sensitivity to project-level assessment quality, and need for third-party support, in particular. *Organizational history* concerns the legacy built over time, reflected both in developed technologies and related knowledge and competences. In the larger firms, this history appeared in considerations of culture as a source of both domain-specific knowledge and slowness, in the attention to slower-paced legislation changes, and in the sensitivity with regard to labor union's actions. In the medium-sized firms, the history of development was shorter and such concerns were barely mentioned. *Industry clockspeed* concerns the general pace of changes and technology development in the industry field. In the larger firms, with more mature industries, the clockspeed was slower in general and PPM routines thereby less frequent. However, the larger firms were also already familiar with the faster clockspeed concerning digital technologies. In the medium-sized firms, the pace was faster and responses to some external pressures were built into more frequent PPM routines. These identified differences and factors may explain other differences in PPM implementation and performance, too, and should potentially be taken into account in forthcoming research.

To respond to the second research question, we selected an extreme event faced by all companies in the past years, namely the COVID-19 pandemic, to discover how managers realigned their innovation project portfolios with strategy in response to environmental uncertainty. While the pandemic is generally viewed as something affecting individuals and their lives, also industrial firms have experienced severe consequences, due to the chaos and turmoil that emerged. This is also what our exploration of five firms revealed. We reported four main phases that switched the firms from a state of strategic alignment through to a new state of strategic realignment, namely: experiencing the emerging chaos including multiple interlinked uncertainties, paying attention to alarms that trigger managerial action, using the ordinary management team routines to reconfigure the project portfolio, and moving to a new state of strategic realignment, different from the original idea of strategic alignment. Thereby, our findings offer a project portfolio example concerning the chaos-type uncertainty (De Meyer et al., 2002).

This extreme case by no means reflects all types of strategic realignment in organizations. As described earlier, some strategic realignment appears quite routinely and regularly and on the different levels of the organization. However, our examples draw attention to the fact that all project portfolios may occasionally face multiple different uncertainties simultaneously and then they need to consider strategic realignment holistically, not just one uncertainty at a time. Our findings complement previous research that has covered the various responses to portfolio uncertainties (Petit & Hobbs, 2010; Petit, 2012; Korhonen et al., 2014), particularly through revealing the cognitive process for managers to initiate and go through their portfolio's strategic realignment holistically, acknowledging the compilation of uncertainties surrounding them at the given moment.

As a key contribution of our study, the actions required for the portfolio's strategic realignment draw attention back to project behavior. Behavior in projects is not merely a source of uncertainty, but managers and project personnel use it as a central mechanism to respond to environmental and organizational uncertainties. The findings offer a portfolio-centric view to the behavior *of* projects and reveal its two-way connection to behavior *in* projects, thereby responding to an earlier call for context-sensitive research on project behavior (Unterhitzenberger, 2021). The findings revealed that managers clearly adjust and redirect project behavior on purpose, to cope with and overcome uncertainties in the innovation project portfolio. This demonstrates that they have agency in their decisions and actions and they can "make best of the evolving context" (cf. Ika et al., 2022) also in the face of severe uncertainty. We showed that new projects were needed, projects had to be terminated or delayed, resources had to be released to new activities, and reprioritization occurred between projects, when refocusing the project portfolios toward the renewed strategic alignment. While our study revealed evidence concerning responses to the pandemic, organizations adjust project behavior through these different decisions constantly, not just in selecting projects and not just once a year. Thereby, project behavior is not only a source of uncertainty but a prospective solution to the need of strategic realignment. Forthcoming research should increasingly consider alternative portfolio decisions such as selecting, delaying, terminating, and reprioritizing projects together, as complementary and combined approaches to project portfolios' strategic alignment.

References

Anttila, R. (2021). Strategiakytkentä sekä epävarmuuden hallinta suuryritysten innovaatioprojektisalkuissa (Strategic linkage and uncertainty management in the innovation project portfolios of large companies). Master's thesis,

Tampere University. https://urn.fi/URN:NBN:fi:tuni-202110287960.

Archer, N., and Ghasemzadeh, F. (1999). An integrated framework for project portfolio selection. *International Journal of Project Management, 17*(4), 207–216.

Blichfeldt, B. S., and Eskerod, P. (2008). Project portfolio management: There's more to it than what management enacts. *International Journal of Project Management, 26*(4), 357–365.

Chapman, C., and Ward, S. (1997). Project risk management. Wiley.

Christiansen, J. K., and Varnes, C. (2008). From models to practice: Decision making at portfolio meetings. *International Journal of Quality and Reliability Management, 25*(1), 87–101.

Clegg, S., Killen, C. P., Biesenthal, C., and Shankaran, S. (2018). Practices, projects and portfolios: Current research trends and new directions. *International Journal of Project Management, 36*, 762–772.

Cooper, R. G., Edgett, S. J., and Kleinschmidt, E. J. (1997). Portfolio management in new product development: Lessons from the leaders – I. *Research Technology Management, 40*(5), pp. 16–28.

Cooper, R., Edgett, S., and Kleinschmidt, E. (2001). Portfolio management for new products, 2nd ed. Basic Books.

De Meyer, A., Loch, C. H., and Pich, M. T. (2002). Managing project uncertainty: From variation to chaos. *MIT Sloan Management Review, 43*(2), 60–67.

Dye, L., and Pennypacker, J. (eds.) (1999). *Project portfolio management. Selecting and prioritizing projects for competitive advantage*. Center for Business Practices.

Elonen, S., and Artto, K. (2003). Problems in managing internal development projects in multi-project environments. *International Journal of Project Management, 21*(6), 395–402.

Engwall, M. (2003). No project is an island: Linking projects to history and context. *Research Policy, 32*(5), 789–808.

Globocnik, F., Häufler, B. P., and Salomo, S. (2022). Organizational antecedents to bootlegging and consequences for the newness of the innovation portfolio. *Journal of Product Innovation Management*, 39, 717–745.

Hoffmann, D., Ahlemann, F., and Reining, S. (2020). Reconciling alignment, efficiency, and agility in IT project portfolio management: Recommendations based on a revelatory case study. *International Journal of Project Management, 38*, 124–136.

Ika, L. A., Love, P. E., and Pinto, J. K. (2020). Moving beyond the planning fallacy: The emergence of a new principle of project behavior. *IEEE Transactions on Engineering Management, 67*(2), 221–230.

Jerbrant, A., and Karrbom Gustavsson, T. (2013). Managing project portfolios: Balancing flexibility and structure by improvising. *International Journal of Managing Projects in Business, 6*(1), 152–172.

Kester, L., Griffin, A., Hultink, E. J., and Lauche, K. (2011). Exploring portfolio decision-making processes. *Journal of Product Innovation Management, 28*(5), 641–661.

Kester, L., Hultink, E. J., and Lauche, K. (2009). Portfolio decision-making genres: A case study. *Journal of Engineering and Technology Management, 26*(4), 327–341.

Kester, L., Hultink, E. J., and Griffin, A. (2014). An empirical investigation of the antecedents and outcomes of NPD portfolio success. *Journal of Product Innovation Management, 31*(6), 1199–1213.

Kock, A., and Gemünden, H. G. (2016). Antecedents to decision-making quality and agility in innovation portfolio management. *Journal of Product Innovation Management, 33*(6), 670–686.

Kock, A., Heising, W., and Gemünden, H. G. (2016). A contingency approach on the impact of front-end success on project portfolio success. *Project Management Journal, 47*(2), 115–129.

Kopmann, J., Kock, A., Killen, C. P., and Gemünden, H. G. (2017). The role of project portfolio management in fostering both deliberate and emergent strategy. *International Journal of Project Management, 35*, 557–570.

Korhonen, T., Laine, T., and Martinsuo, M., (2014). Management control of project portfolio uncertainty: A managerial role perspective. *Project Management Journal, 45*(1), 21–37.

Loch, C. (2000). Tailoring product development to strategy: Case of a European technology manufacturer. *European Management Journal, 18*(3), 246–258.

Martinsuo, M. (2013). Project portfolio management in practice and in context. *International Journal of Project Management, 31*(6), 794–803.

Martinsuo, M., and Anttila, R. (2022). Practices of strategic alignment in and across innovation project portfolios. Paper presented at EURAM

European Academy of Management Conference, June, 15–17, Winterthur, Switzerland.

Martinsuo, M., and Geraldi, J. (2020). The management of project portfolios: Relationships of project portfolios with their contexts. *International Journal of Project Management, 38*(7), 441–453.

Martinsuo, M., Korhonen, T., and Laine, T. (2014). Identifying, framing and managing uncertainties in project portfolios. *International Journal of Project Management, 32*(5), 732–746.

Martinsuo, M., and Lehtonen, P. (2007). Role of single-project management in achieving portfolio management efficiency. *International Journal of Project Management, 25*(1), 56–65.

Martinsuo, M., and Tuominen, S. (2021). Reconfiguring the innovation project portfolio: Responding to strategic uncertainties in a dynamic context. Paper presented at the 28th IPDMC Innovation and Product Development Management Conference, June 6–8, Milan, Italy.

Midler, C. (2013). Implementing a low-end disruption strategy through multiproject lineage management: the Logan case. *Project Management Journal, 44*(5), 24–35.

Petit, Y. (2012). Project portfolios in dynamic environments: Organizing for uncertainty. *International Journal of Project Management, 30*(5), 539–553.

Petit, Y., and Hobbs, B. (2010). Project portfolios in dynamic environments: Sources of uncertainty and sensing mechanisms. *Project Management Journal, 41*(4), 46–58.

Pich, M. T., Loch, C. H., and De Meyer, A. (2002). On uncertainty, ambiguity, and complexity in project management. *Management Science, 48*(8), 1008–1023.

Röth, T., Spieth, P., and Lange, D. (2019). Managerial political behavior in innovation portfolio management: A sensegiving and sensebreaking process. *Journal of Product Innovation Management, 36*(5), 534–559.

Stettina, C. J., and Hörz, J. (2015). Agile portfolio management: An empirical perspective on the practice in use. *International Journal of Project Management*, 33, 140–152.

Teece, D. J. (2007). Explicating dynamic capabilities: the nature and microfoundations of (sustainable) enterprise performance. *Strategic Management Journal*, 28, 1319–1350.

Teller, J., and Kock, A. (2013). An empirical investigation on how portfolio risk management influences project portfolio success. *International Journal of Project Management, 31*, 817–829.

Teller, J., Kock, A., and Gemünden, H. G. (2014). Risk management in project portfolios is more than managing project risks: A contingency perspective on risk management. *Project Management Journal, 45*(4), 67–80.

Teller, J., Unger, B. N., Kock, A., and Gemünden, H. G. (2012). Formalization of project portfolio management: The moderating role of project portfolio complexity. *International Journal of Project Management, 30*(5), 596–607.

Tuominen, S. (2020). Continuous reconfiguration: Managing innovation project portfolio uncertainty. Master's thesis, Tampere University. https://urn.fi/URN:NBN:fi:tuni-202012118764.

Unterhitzenberger, C. (2021). Editorial. Special issue on project behavior. *Project Management Journal, 52*(6), 527–530.

Vedel, J. B., and Geraldi, J. (2020). A 'stranger' in the making of strategy: A process perspective of project portfolio management in a pharmaceutical firm. *International Journal of Project Management, 38*, 454–463.

Voss, M., and Kock, A. (2013). Impact of relationship value on project portfolio success: Investigating the moderating effects of portfolio characteristics and external turbulence. *International Journal of Project Management, 31*(6), 847–861.

Ward, S., and Chapman, C. (2003). Transforming project risk management into project uncertainty management. *International Journal of Project Management, 21*(2), 97–105.

CHAPTER 9

Stakeholder Perceptions and Project Performance

KATE DAVIS, LIZ MACHTYNGER, and FRANCESCO DI MADDALONI

Introduction

This chapter explores stakeholders as a key element in understanding project behavior within a project. Stakeholder identification and management is an integral part of project behavior because it helps project managers to understand the needs and expectations of all individuals and groups who can impact or be impacted by a project (Unterhitzenberger, 2021). Stakeholders can have a variety of motivations, including financial, ethical, legal, and social concerns. It is important for project managers to understand the motivations of stakeholders in order to effectively manage their expectations and build successful relationships (Ika et al., 2022).

Projects have become for many organizations the centerpiece of their strategy and the way they drive change and, in some instances, how they drive their operations (Nieto-Rodriguez, 2021). As a result, the role of stakeholders and stakeholder management has become central to the success of projects. Existing literature presents individual stakeholder views that are recognised as contributing to project success, but limited studies have assimilated the views of different stakeholders or stakeholder groups. There is a widely held belief that a single stakeholder group, usually project managers, is sufficient to judge project performance (Andersen et al., 2004; Morris et al., 2011) and mainstream management research continues to reproduce a managerialist bias by implicitly foregrounding organizational elites as decision-makers who act in the best interest of all stakeholders (Scherer & Palazzo, 2007; Miles, 2017), without challenging the limits of this taken-for-granted assumption.

Phillips et al. (2003) state that the neo-classical view of the firm leads to unchanged assumptions in maximizing shareholder wealth or value, rather than optimizing collective value among the broader network of stakeholders, since they are the main priority of the focal organization. Nonetheless, for stakeholder theory, attention to the interests and well-being of some non-shareholders is obligatory for more than the prudential and instrumental purposes of wealth maximization of equity shareholders. Accordingly, the "stakeholder capitalism" movement (Freeman, 1994; Freeman et al., 2007), reinforces the need for a strategic and systematic approach to achieving organizational purpose and goals by fostering the proactive involvement and harmonizing the interests of all stakeholders. Differing from the resource-dependence view, the normative stance in stakeholder theory has acknowledged that business is always "moral in nature," where the focal organization should gather input from all the affected parties (Jensen & Sandström, 2013).

Stakeholder theory is concerned with who has input in decision-making as well as with who benefits from the outcomes of such decisions. This may be for either instrumental reasons (e.g., achieving "buy in") or for normative reasons – the organization has a moral obligation to its stakeholders requiring that they have input into how the organization is run. In this regard, Wateridge (1998) noted that organizations should use shared stakeholders success criteria to achieve the best outcomes. This view is supported by the work of McLeod et al. (2012, p. 72), who stated that "project outcomes are subjectively perceived by different stakeholders" and further reported that failing to consider one group's view may taint the project's overall outcome. Turner and Zolin (2012) and Turner (2014a, 2014b) added to this, suggesting that the perceptions of multiple stakeholders are critical to the success of a project and that failure to evaluate the success criteria with each group could lead to poor decision-making, demotivation of employees, and an unproductive organizational culture.

Stakeholder Theory Background

In the context of this chapter, a stakeholder is defined as an individual or group that has an interest or concern in something, especially a business. They can be internal stakeholders, such as employees or managers, or external stakeholders, such as customers or suppliers.

The dominance of the instrumental formulation of stakeholder theory is well recorded in both management and project studies (Bondy & Charles, 2018; Derakhshan et al., 2019). This perspective sees stakeholders as resource providers for the organization and categorizes them based on their potential ability to help or harm the organization (Eskerod & Huemann, 2013). This approach sees stakeholders as resource providers to the organization, based on their interests (Salancik & Pfeffer, 1978; Clarke, 2004). When there is a conflict of interest, trade-offs must be made, and whenever there is the need for a trade-off, prioritization is inevitable.

To identify and prioritize stakeholders among different and competing claims, Mitchell et al. (1997) developed the stakeholder "salience model" based on three attributes of power, legitimacy and urgency. This classification system indicates the amount of attention that project managers should give to stakeholders needs and perceptions of value from project outcomes (Mitchell et al., 1997). However, although many scholars cite this model in their work, important methods such as the "power/interest matrix" (Johnson et al., 2005) and "stakeholder circle methodology" (Bourne & Walker, 2005) were developed from Mitchell et al's (1997) work reflecting the instrumental perspective of stakeholder theory. The model represents a somewhat static picture of stakeholders rather than the more dynamic changing attitudes that tend to occur through the different phases of the project lifecycle (Olander, 2007) and it does not reflect that the resources, or the organizational positions of stakeholders can be considered static (Pajunen, 2006). The obvious implication is that project organizations face the very real conundrum of managing for value even in the face of transitory or shifting perceptions of what stakeholders seek from the project.

The "New Stakeholder Theory" relies primarily on economic and legal arguments that stakeholders will sustain their connection to an organization only if they expect and ultimately receive appropriate returns on their contributions (McGahan, 2021). Therefore, the challenge of delivering value in a project is mirrored by the concomitant challenge of identifying, understanding, and developing strategies for managing project stakeholders based on their interests and perceptions of benefits to be realized. Literature shows growing attention to stakeholder attitudes toward a project; and the model proposed by McElroy and Mills (2000) distinguishes whether a stakeholder is an advocate or adversary of the project in five levels of "active opposition," "passive opposition," "not committed," "passive support," and "active support." Olander (2007) and Nguyen et al. (2019) propose a quantitative approach ("stakeholder impact index") to assess stakeholder impact integrating more variables from Mitchell et al. (1997), McElroy and Mills (2000), and Bourne and Walker (2005). Moreover, a social network approach (Rowley, 1997) has been applied in stakeholder analysis for a small infrastructure project by Yang et al. (2011), which considers the interaction among multiple stakeholders by examining their simultaneous influence to forecast the corresponding responses and organizational strategies (Rowley, 1997).

Klein et al. (2019) explore the concept of organizational governance adaptation and its impact on the distribution of value among stakeholders. They argue that organizations must adapt their governance (systems and processes used to manage and control an organization) in response to changes in the external environment, such as changes in technology, regulation, or market conditions, in order to create and sustain value. They suggest that organizational governance adaptation involves three main components: inclusion, exclusion, and value distribution. Inclusion refers to the process of bringing new stakeholders into the governance system, such as new shareholders, customers, or suppliers. Exclusion refers to the process of removing existing stakeholders from the governance system, such as by buying out minority shareholders or terminating contracts with suppliers. Value distribution refers to the process of allocating the benefits and costs of the governance system among stakeholders. The organizational governance adaptation has important implications for the distribution of value among stakeholders. The process of inclusion and exclusion can lead to changes in the distribution of ownership and control, which in turn can affect the distribution of value. Klein et al. (2019) also argue that the process of value distribution can lead to conflicts and bargaining among stakeholders, which can affect the overall performance and stability of the organization.

Gil and Fu (2022) explore the concept of megaprojects as large-scale, complex projects involving multiple stakeholders that have a significant impact on society and the environment. They argue that while megaprojects can create value for stakeholders, they also pose significant risks and challenges in terms of performance, value creation, and value distribution. They suggest that organizational governance plays a critical role in determining the success or failure of a megaproject. Effective organizational governance must take into account the diverse interests and perspectives of the various stakeholders involved in the project and must balance the need to create value with the need to manage risk and uncertainty. They go on to highlight the importance of understanding the value distribution among stakeholders, which can be affected by the governance system and the decision-making processes used in megaprojects and argue that the governance system must ensure that the value created by the megaproject is distributed fairly among stakeholders, to ensure their support and engagement.

Based on an infrastructure project in Hong Kong, Li et al. (2012) consolidated a list of 17 stakeholder interests and different priorities in megaprojects of major stakeholder groups. What emerged is that in many cases stakeholders seek to prevent their vested interest from being jeopardized and an issue that is very important to one stakeholder group may be the lowest priority of another group (Li et al., 2012). Some scholars focus on the link between spatial dynamics and stakeholder impact. This concept has been applied in the context of infrastructure planning by Dooms et al. (2013), which examine that stakeholder structure and interests vary with their spatial distance from the project, with stakeholders gaining higher salience as they become geographically closer to the project. However, although conceptual frameworks and analytical models have been suggested by stakeholder theory scholars, managerial priorities and concerns have been focused almost exclusively on those primary stakeholders important to the project's economic interests (Hart & Sharma, 2004; Aaltonen and Kujala, 2010). In this way, project managers keep their dominant position as decision-makers who act in the best interest of all stakeholders (e.g., Eskerod & Huemann, 2013; Derakhshan et al., 2019), leading to instrumentally prioritize some actors, for example, clients or suppliers over others local communities.

The protection of interests could be seen as a zero-sum game where one person or group's gain is directly proportional to another person or group's loss. This means that the total value or resources available in the project is fixed, and any gain by one stakeholder must come at the expense of another stakeholder (von Neumann & Morgenstern, 1944). For example, in a project where the budget is fixed, if one team or department gets additional resources, it means that another team or department has to make do with less. Similarly, if one stakeholder can negotiate a larger share of the project's benefits, it means that the other stakeholders will have to accept a smaller share. In a zero-sum game, the project manager must manage the competing interests of stakeholders and make decisions that balance the needs and goals of each stakeholder. This can be challenging, particularly in multi-phase projects where the stakeholders evolve, and this often involves trade-offs and difficult choices. It also requires good communication and negotiation skills, as the project manager must be able to explain the reasons behind decisions and find mutually beneficial solutions. Additionally, it is important to note that in practice, most projects are not zero-sum games, and it is possible to create value for multiple stakeholders simultaneously, by using the available resources efficiently and creatively. Therefore, a project manager should not just focus on the zero-sum perspective but should also be able to find ways to create additional value for the stakeholders.

Classifying Stakeholders

Scholars have mainly distinguished primary stakeholders from secondary stakeholders and classified them using the literature's prevailing stakeholder salience model proposed by Mitchell et al. (1997). Primary stakeholders are characterized by contractual relationships with the project, such as customers or suppliers, or have a direct legal authority over the project, such as governmental organizations. Secondary stakeholders do not have a formal contractual bond with the project or direct legal authority over the project (Eesley & Lenox, 2006), but they can influence the project (Clarkson, 1995). According to Aaltonen et al. (2008), while actors of such interest include community groups, lobbyists, environmentalists and other non-governmental organizations, if secondary stakeholders are excluded by project managers, they may engage in a set of actions to advance their claims, with negative consequences to direct operational costs and to the reputation of the focal organization (Eesley & Lenox, 2006; Nguyen et al., 2019).

Much of the knowledge about stakeholder analysis practices has been from the stakeholder impact perspective, especially on the impact that primary stakeholders can exert on project outcomes. In fact, most prior project research has focused on the management of those primary stakeholders important to the project's resources. Secondary stakeholders seek a claim for a legitimate role in project decision-making (Olander & Landin, 2008; Di Maddaloni & Davis, 2017; Derakhshan et al., 2019) and therefore, more time should be spent at the front end of a project (Pinto & Winch, 2016) and developing a stakeholder engagement plan that includes a broader range of stakeholders (Eskerod et al., 2015; van den Ende & van Marrewijk 2018).

The generic list of project stakeholders is often homogenously presented; however, decision-making is often confounded by stakeholder groups having their own perspective and policy for decision-making. Stakeholders can be classified based on their level of power or interest in the decisions to be made and how involved they are in the project. Typical types of stakeholders can be found in Table 9.1. This list is not exhaustive and can vary depending on the type of organization and its operations.

Evolution of the Inclusion of Stakeholder Perceptions

The inclusion of different stakeholder group perceptions of projects has evolved throughout time. In Figure 9.1, Davis (2016, p. 27) illustrates this and notes that the perception of project success in the twenty-first century was defined by more than just the project manager, and therefore, other stakeholder expectations needed to be managed. In the figure there was a focus on stakeholder satisfaction and a move towards examining the project owner's perception of success. The importance of senior management commitment throughout the project is reiterated as crucial to provide the link between the organizational mission and project objectives. However, a majority of studies concentrated on the project manager's view of success and not those of other internal/external stakeholders of an organization (e.g., senior management, business departments such as finance and marketing, or the external environment) at one point in the project life cycle (for example, the initiation stage).

It is important to note that Figure 9.1 is not a fully comprehensive model and has moved on since this to include additional aspects such as sustainability or "green" success. "Green" success in projects is a concept that has been written about by many experts in various fields such as engineering, environmental science in the field of project management and

Table 9.1 Typical stakeholder types

Stakeholder	Role
Communities	External stakeholders who are affected by the organization's operations. They are concerned with issues such as environmental impact, job creation, and community development.
Creditors	This could be individuals or organizations that have extended credit to the project by lending money or providing goods or services on credit. For example, banks, suppliers, and bondholders. Creditors are entities that have financial claim on the project and expect to be repaid at some point in the future.
Customers / clients / members	External stakeholders who purchase the organization's products or services. They are concerned with issues such as product quality, customer service, and pricing.
Employees	Internal stakeholders who are directly impacted by the organization's policies and decisions. They are concerned with issues such as wages, benefits, and working conditions. Roles include supervisory, managerial and technical.
Government/government agencies	An external stakeholder, government is concerned with issues such as taxes, regulation, and compliance with laws and regulations. They can have a significant impact on projects by setting regulations and guidelines that must be followed, providing funding or other resources and having the authority to approve or deny project proposals. They can also affect projects by enforcing laws and policies related to the environment, public safety, and other areas that may impact the project. Additionally, they may be involved in the planning and oversight of projects to ensure they are completed on time and within budget. Overall, the level of impact can vary depending on the specific agency and the nature of the project.
Media	Strong media relationships lead to better brand recognition.
Non-governmental organizations	External stakeholders who are interested in the organization's impact on society and the environment.
Owners	Typically, high-level managers or executives who have the authority to make decisions about the project and allocate resources. They may also be the ones accountable for ensuring that the project is completed on time, within budget, and to the satisfaction of all stakeholders. In some organizations, the project owners may be the same as the organizational owners, but in other cases, they may be separate individuals or groups.
Shareholders/investors	Have a financial interest in the organization and are concerned with its financial performance and profitability.
Suppliers/vendors	External stakeholders who provide the organization with the goods and services it needs to operate. They are concerned with issues such as payment terms and delivery schedules.
Trade unions	Organizations that represent the interests of workers, and their involvement in projects can vary depending on the nature of the project and the specific union.

sustainability. In projects, this refers to the ability of a project to meet its objectives while minimizing its negative impact on the environment and promoting long-term environmental, social, and economic well-being (Giammalvo, 2010). This includes reducing the use of natural resources, minimizing waste and pollution, and promoting social and economic equity. In practice, achieving sustainability or "green" success in projects involves incorporating sustainable practices and principles into project planning, design, and execution. This can include using environmentally friendly materials and technologies, incorporating energy efficiency and renewable energy, reducing waste, and promoting biodiversity (Parker, 2016). It also involves engaging and collaborating with stakeholders, including the local community and other interested parties, to ensure that their needs and concerns are taken into account in the project planning and execution (Fridjonsson & Palsson, 2018, Di Maddaloni & Sabini, 2022). This can include assessing the potential environmental and social impacts of the project and developing strategies to mitigate or avoid them. In addition, sustainable success also involves the use of project management methodologies, such as Life Cycle Assessment and

	Technical era 1970-1979	Critical success factor list era 1980-1989	Framework era 1990-1999	Stakeholder era 2000+
View of Success	"Iron triangle" (time, cost, quality) Initial identification of success factors	Project relationship with client organisation Success factor lists, not categorised	CSF frameworks, categorising lists	Success linked to short term rather than long term organisational goals The need to include senior management commitment, the external environment
Project Stage	Implementation stage	Implementation stage	Implementation stage	Multiple stages
Stakeholder	Project manager perception	Stakeholder identified as important but not defined	Success linked to internal and external stakeholders	Multiple stakeholder view
Measurement	Surveys, subjective and objective measurement	Lists created intuitively, not based on research findings. Cross sectional	Formal quantitative and qualitative studies	Quantitative and qualitative studies, suggest longitudinal
Gap	Lacked empirical work and did not examine the post implementation stage Lacked work on stakeholders other than project manager	Omitted the planning stage Failure to link PM to strategic management	Omitted the planning stage Reproducing CSF lists, not extending them	Does not mention the board, programme or portfolio director, plus other organisational stakeholders (e.g. Business departments)

Figure 9.1 Time line of success development.

Environmental Impact Assessment to identify the environmental impacts of a project and developing strategies to reduce them (Viswanath & Narasimhan, 2009; Aguilar-Soto, 2018).

Identifying Stakeholders and Managing Engagement

It is important to identify and address the interests of different stakeholder groups for project success. The primary and secondary stakeholder groupings may well be developed into more specific groupings in order to be more specific in understanding their different needs and expectations. Some may have a direct decision-making or resourcing input, others may have influence or investment capability. There will inevitably be stakeholders who will actively prevent the mission of the project. Carrying out stakeholder mapping will enable the project manager to set out strategies for managing and responding to these groups.

The idea of marginalizing secondary stakeholders, or those stakeholders who have limited power and influence in a project, can be a challenge for project managers (di Maddaloni & Davis, 2018). These stakeholders may be difficult to identify, as they may not be directly involved in the project or may not have a clear or direct impact on its outcome. However, their support or opposition can still have a significant impact on the project's success.

One of the challenges in identifying these types of stakeholders is that they may be "invisible" until they make themselves visible or powerful, for example, by starting to oppose the project at some stage. This can make it difficult for project managers to anticipate and manage potential conflicts or issues that may arise with these stakeholders (Mitchell et al., 1997). Another challenge is that secondary stakeholders may not have the same level of interest or engagement in the project as primary stakeholders and may not be as responsive to communication and engagement efforts. This can make it difficult to build and maintain relationships with these stakeholders and to address their concerns or needs effectively. To overcome these challenges, project managers can take a proactive approach to identifying and engaging secondary stakeholders. This may involve conducting research to identify potential stakeholders and their interests, as well as monitoring the project environment for potential stakeholders who may become more visible or powerful over time. Additionally, project managers can develop communication and engagement strategies that are tailored to the specific needs and concerns of secondary stakeholders and can involve them in decision-making processes to the extent possible.

Lehtinen and Aaltonen (2017) discuss the importance of engaging external stakeholders in inter-organizational projects, as well as the challenges that can arise in doing so. They argue that previous research on stakeholder engagement has focused primarily on internal stakeholders and that there is a need for more research on engaging external stakeholders in inter-organizational projects. Their framework for organizing external stakeholder engagement in inter-organizational projects includes identifying key stakeholders, understanding their interests and expectations, and developing strategies for engaging them throughout the project.

However, one limitation stems from stakeholder identification and efforts taken to address "Who are the stakeholders?" and "What are their roles and rights?" Eskerod and Larsen (2018) elucidate that stakeholders are essentially identified and encountered based on their assigned roles (e.g., suppliers, end users, local community). This is more evident in instrumental management approaches towards stakeholders where the attribute of "power" represents the basis of their prioritization and salience (e.g., Mitchell et al., 1997; Bourne & Walker, 2005; Johnson et al., 2005). This approach has resulted in marginalization of secondary stakeholders in many projects (Derry, 2012; Teo & Loosemore, 2017; Di Maddaloni et al., 2025) and "makes it easy to separate decision-making from those stakeholders who are affected by decisions" (McVea & Freeman, 2005, p. 60).

Another limitation stems from the methodological and practical approaches taken to build knowledge from the demands, concerns and beliefs of stakeholders, thus posing the question, "How should the roles and rights of stakeholders be identified?" In the prevalent theoretical approaches, the priorities and demands of stakeholders are largely determined by the perspective of the organization (e.g., Friedman & Miles, 2002; Derakhshan et al., 2019). This organization-centric approach results in a dyadic, independent stakeholder relationship (Frooman, 1999; Eskerod et al., 2015; Eskerod & Larsen, 2018), as well as an "unbalanced perspective in which the stakeholder voice is under-represented and remains a limitation of stakeholder theory" (Miles, 2017, p. 448). The experiences and interests of many stakeholder groups are only distantly rationalized, without questioning how the stakeholders themselves perceive their entitlement to the conditions of the project (Bondy & Charles, 2018).

In fact, in formal project scenarios, stakeholders may be formalized and given a specific role and there may be regulations set out by the institution for who may need to be involved in some projects, for example, in data management scenarios there may be the need to include a data controller. In some project scenarios where there is the need for more innovative and future focused development, it may be wiser for project managers to open out the stakeholder base to drive more creative thought or challenge. This is particularly the case, for instance, in new product/service design projects. In these scenarios, it is important for the project manager to review the stakeholder base at different stages of the project, as ideas evolve new stakeholders may emerge. Further, as a project reaches completion, there needs to be a considered plan to hand over stakeholder management to the project recipient.

Examples of Perception of Benefits in Practice

As previously discussed, new stakeholder theory is a relatively recent development in the field of stakeholder management, which emphasizes the importance of considering the interests and needs of all stakeholders in a project or organization, not just shareholders or investors. This theory recognizes that a wide range of stakeholders, including employees, customers, suppliers, and the local community, can have a significant impact on a company's success and must be taken into account in decision-making.

Once the interests are identified, we must consider managing the benefits for all stakeholders. Benefits management is opposite to new stakeholder theory as it is a systematic approach to identifying, planning, delivering, and realizing the benefits of a project or program. It involves establishing clear objectives, identifying the stakeholders who will benefit from the project, and planning how to deliver and measure the benefits. Effective benefits management can help ensure that a project delivers the intended results and that stakeholders are satisfied with the outcome (Thorpe & Holt, 2005). Both new stakeholder theory and benefits management are important for ensuring that projects are aligned with the needs and interests of all stakeholders and that they deliver the intended results. By considering the needs of all stakeholders and planning for the delivery and realization of benefits, organizations can increase the chances of project success and build strong relationships with stakeholders.

To illustrate, the Thames Barrier was "priced at £110.7 million in October 1973 (compared with initial estimates of £13–18 million) [and] was ultimately delivered at a cost of £440 million" (Dalcher, 2012, p. 648). Further, it took just under twice the estimated four years because of delays during the preconstruction phase. However, regardless of the delays, it is considered a great engineering achievement with the value of preventing floods and saving lives (Morris & Hough, 1987). On the other hand, Heathrow Terminal Five was completed successfully within time and cost constraints; however, British Airways had minor commissioning issues relating to check-in procedures for oversized baggage, leading to the later public and customer perception that the project was not able to deliver the promised benefits with consequent damage to the reputation of British Airways (Brady & Davies, 2009, 2010a, 2010b; Brady & Maylor, 2010). This raises the question of whether a better focus on benefits realization is required, especially for complex projects whose value is not immediately obvious at completion.

Another well-known example is the construction of the Sydney Opera House in Australia. The project began in the 1950s with a design competition, and a relatively unknown architect, Jørn Utzon, submitted the winning design. However, as the project progressed, the costs began to escalate, and the construction schedule began to slip. Many stakeholders, including government officials, the public, and the media, began to question the value of the project and criticized the project team for the delays and cost overruns. The project team struggled to manage the negative perception of the project and to communicate the value of the project to stakeholders. Despite these challenges, the project was eventually completed in 1973, and the Sydney Opera House is now considered one of the most iconic and recognizable buildings in the world. The project serves as an example of how perception can impact a project and how effective communication with stakeholders can be critical to project success (Parkinson, 1994).

These examples highlight how perception is a dynamic concept that can change over time and that stakeholders' perception of the project might change as the project progresses, when they see the final product and further into the future (Di Maddaloni & Derakhshan, 2023).

Managing Conflicts of Interest through Governance

There are often reported conflicts of interest between primary stakeholder groups in projects, this can cause major tensions for the project. It is important therefore for the project manager to identify what these interests and priorities are early on and ensure that the correct set of project objectives and measures are agreed on by all parties before the project progresses. In developing new customer propositions, for example, it could be the case that the delivery of the product and pricing for one product would contradict that of another product for the same customer group. This may then leave different product managers with trade-offs and agreements to be made about a middle ground in order to satisfy the customer need or market urgency. It can sometimes mean delays to the initiation of a project to iron out differences; but in the long run, it is crucial to the successful outcome for the project.

Further conflict arises with the "NIMBY" movement, or "Not-in-my-backyard," which refers to a phenomenon where individuals or groups oppose the development of a project or facility in their local community, even though they may support the project in general or in a different location. The term "NIMBY" is often used to describe opposition to the construction of landfills, power plants, highways, and other types of infrastructure projects. The reasons for NIMBY opposition can vary but often include concerns about the potential impact on property values, the environment, public health and safety, and quality of life. This often occurs when a project is exactly replicated in a new environment on the assumption that all needs/constraints are the same and stakeholders are not consulted.

Many NIMBY opponents argue that the negative impacts of a project should be borne by others, rather than their own community. NIMBYism can have significant impact on a project as it can delay or stop the project from being completed, increase the cost of the project, and create public relations challenges for the organization (Davidoff & Bowman, 1996; Gold, 1991; Smith, 1993). To address the NIMBY movement, organizations may use a variety of strategies, such as conducting community engagement, providing information on the benefits of the project, addressing concerns, and offering incentives to the community.

The governance structure can be designed to ensure that the interests and needs of all stakeholders are taken into account. Collaboration is a key aspect of successful project management; by working together, organizations and stakeholders can share ideas, resources, and expertise and develop a shared vision and goals for the project. Collaboration can also help to build trust and understanding among stakeholders, which can be critical for addressing complex issues and achieving lasting impact. Early stakeholder engagement can help to identify potential issues and concerns early in the project and develop strategies to mitigate them. Effective collaboration requires clear communication, shared decision-making, and a willingness to compromise and work towards common goals. It also requires the ability to identify and manage conflicts that may arise between stakeholders.

A governance structure can be created to encourage collaboration and will include systems and processes that allow stakeholders to have a say in decision-making, provide clear and effective communication channels to ensure that all stakeholders are kept informed of project progress and establish a framework for resolving conflicts that may arise between stakeholders. By considering the needs of all stakeholders and planning for the delivery and realization of benefits, organizations can increase the chances of project success and build strong relationships with stakeholders. In managing stakeholder conflicts, project governance plays a key role in the following ways:

1. Identifying stakeholders: helps to identify all stakeholders who have an interest in the project and to understand their needs, expectations, and concerns.
2. Communication: establishes clear and effective communication channels to ensure that all stakeholders are kept informed of project progress, changes, and any issues that arise.
3. Decision-making: provides a framework for decision-making that ensures that all stakeholders' views are taken into account and that decisions are made in the best interests of the project.
4. Conflict resolution: provides a framework for resolving conflicts that may arise between stakeholders. This may include establishing a dispute resolution process, appointing a neutral third party to mediate, or involving senior management to make a final decision.
5. Continuous improvement: includes a system of continuous improvement to review and monitor project performance, identify and resolve issues, and make necessary adjustments.

Guidance for Project Managers

For project managers, it is crucial to consider the type of project and the need for stakeholder engagement when managing stakeholders (Aaltonen et al., 2024). The approach to stakeholders should be tailored to the specific project, taking into account factors such as project duration and the scope of the impact on stakeholders. The context of the project will play a significant role in determining the appropriate stakeholder engagement strategy. Further, the engagement strategy can be paired with a relational governance approach that emphasizes building and maintaining relationships with stakeholders. A few suggestions for project managers to achieve this are to:

1. Identify stakeholders: The first step in setting up a stakeholder management approach is to identify all stakeholders who have an interest in the project. This includes internal stakeholders, such as employees, and external stakeholders, such as customers, suppliers, and the local community. This should include any enfranchized external/secondary stakeholders who have a vested interest in the project but are not directly involved in its execution. This includes, but is not limited to, the community, local government and the environment. They should be included in the decision-making process and their views should be considered throughout the lifetime of the project.
2. Analyze stakeholders: Once the stakeholders have been identified, analyze them to understand their needs, expectations, and concerns. This will help to prioritize which stakeholders to engage with and how to engage with them.
3. Set multi-party contractual arrangements: Multi-party contractual arrangements involve multiple stakeholders and organizations working together under a formal agreement to achieve project goals. These agreements should be clear, concise, and legally binding and should clearly define the roles, responsibilities, and expectations of each stakeholder.
4. Enfranchized External/ Secondary Stakeholders: Enfranchized external/secondary stakeholders are those who have a vested interest in the project but are not directly involved in its execution. This includes, but is not limited to, the community/potential new community (where the community is not established or known), local government and the environment. They should be included in the decision-making process and their views should be considered.
5. Develop a stakeholder engagement plan: Based on the analysis of stakeholders, develop a plan that outlines how to engage with each stakeholder group. This should include details on the communication channels to be used (for example, language, diversity and inclusion), the frequency of engagement, and the key messages to be conveyed.
6. Communicate effectively and collaborate: Clear and effective communication is essential for building trust and understanding among stakeholders, and is key to relational governance. Project managers (or those who have the appropriate relationship) should establish regular communication channels and ensure that stakeholders are kept informed of project progress, changes, and any issues that arise. They should also encourage stakeholders to share ideas, resources, and expertise and work together to achieve shared goals.
7. Build relationships: Building relationships with stakeholders is critical for stakeholder management. Project managers should work to build trust and understanding with stakeholders and be responsive to their needs and concerns.
8. Transparency and accountability: Relational governance requires transparency and accountability from all stakeholders. Project managers should ensure that stakeholders are aware of the project's goals, progress, and any issues that arise. They should also be willing to accept feedback and criticism and be held accountable for their actions.
9. Manage conflicts: Conflicts will inevitably arise during the project, and project managers should have a framework in place for identifying and resolving conflicts. This may include establishing a dispute resolution process, appointing a neutral third party to mediate, or involving senior management to make a final decision.
10. Monitor and review: Stakeholder management is an ongoing process, and project managers should continuously plan, monitor and review their stakeholder engagement plan. This includes evaluating the effectiveness of communication and engagement efforts and adjusting as needed.
11. Continual improvement: Relational governance is an ongoing process, and project managers should continuously monitor and review their stakeholder engagement plan.

We must emphasize the importance of building strong relationships and trust among stakeholders through relational governance. This focuses on creating a collaborative and inclusive environment in which stakeholders can work together to achieve shared goals.

Guidance for Scholars

Academics seeking to study the perceptions of success among stakeholders could consider investigating the following:

1. Examining how different stakeholders may have different definitions and expectations of project success, such as how stakeholders from different organizations, industries, or communities may have different priorities and values.
2. Investigating the factors that contribute to alignment or misalignment of stakeholders' perceptions of project success, such as how communication, leadership, or project management practices may affect the alignment of stakeholders' perceptions of project success.
3. Analyzing the impact of stakeholder perceptions of project success on project outcomes, such as how stakeholder perceptions of project success may affect project performance, satisfaction, and sustainability.
4. Identifying strategies for managing stakeholder perceptions of project success, such as how to effectively communicate project goals and objectives, how to involve stakeholders in the project planning and decision-making process, and how to address and resolve conflicts and disagreements among stakeholders.
5. Examining the role of power and influence in shaping stakeholders' perceptions of project success, such as how different stakeholders may have different levels of power and influence in shaping the project goals and objectives and how this may affect the alignment of stakeholders' perceptions of project success.
6. Investigating the relationship between stakeholder perceptions of project success and project governance, such as how stakeholders' perceptions of project success may affect the project governance structure and how it may impact the project success.
7. Exploring how stakeholder perceptions of project success may change over time and how it may impact the project outcome.

By understanding the different perceptions of project success among stakeholders, academics can help practitioners to better understand and manage stakeholder expectations, align project goals and objectives with stakeholders' priorities and values, and ultimately improve project outcomes.

Chapter Summary

Project behavior and stakeholder management are closely linked because the behavior of stakeholders can have a significant impact on the success of a project (Unterhitzenberger, 2021). Project managers must understand the behavior of stakeholders in order to effectively manage their expectations and build strong relationships (Ika et al., 2022). This can include:

- Identifying the motivations and expectations of stakeholders, which can include financial, ethical, legal, and social concerns.
- Assessing the level of influence and interest of stakeholders in the project, which can help to prioritize their needs and expectations.
- Communicating effectively with stakeholders to manage expectations, resolve conflicts, and build strong relationships.
- Addressing stakeholder concerns proactively, which can help to prevent potential issues from escalating into major problems.
- Foster a sense of collaboration and engagement among stakeholders, which can lead to increased commitment and support for the project.

The key to success in delivering projects is gaining a strong sense of stakeholder needs and priorities in order to drive out a shared view of the project objectives from the beginning. Setting up stakeholder plans carefully from the project initiation can take time but will ensure a project with stronger connection and more beneficial impact in the long run. Stakeholders will have differing positions, needs and priorities and these often challenge and refine the intended strategy and context for the project. Conflicts of interest and opinion can arise despite strong planning and these need to be carefully monitored and managed through a stakeholder plan.

To ensure strong support and effective decision-making throughout a project, it is essential for project managers to focus on the benefits that the project will bring and how they align with the priorities and interests of stakeholders. This requires close management and regular adjustments to the stakeholder engagement plan throughout the project delivery.

By understanding the behavior and effectively managing stakeholders, project managers can make informed decisions to improve the likelihood of project success and minimize the risk of project failure. Additionally, effective stakeholder management can help to build a positive reputation for the organization, which can lead to increased support for future projects. Project behavior and stakeholder management are therefore inextricably linked and must be carefully managed to ensure the success of a project.

References

Aaltonen, K., and Kujala, J. (2010). A project lifecycle perspective on stakeholder influence strategies in global projects. *Scandinavian Journal of Management*, *26*, 381–397.

Aaltonen, K., Kujala, J., and Oijala, T. (2008). Stakeholder salience in global projects. *International Journal of Project Management*, *26*, 509–516.

Aguilar-Soto, J. A. S. (2018). Sustainability in project management: A review of the literature and a proposed framework. *Journal of Cleaner Production*, *216*, 658–678.

Andersen, E. S., Grude, K. V., and Haug, T. (2004). *Goal directed project management*. Kogan Page.

Bondy, K., and Charles, A. (2018). Mitigating stakeholder marginalisation with the relational self. *Journal of Business Ethics*, 1–16.

Bourne, L., and Walker, D. (2005). Visualising and mapping stakeholder influence. *Management Decision*, *43*(5/6), 649–660.

Brady, T., and Davies, A. (2009). They think it's all over, it is now: Heathrow terminal 5. The Proceedings of EURAM 2009, The 9th Conference of The European Management Review, UK, May. University of Liverpool, Liverpool, UK.

Brady, T., and Davies, A. (2010a). From hero to hubris: Reconsidering the project management of Heathrow's Terminal 5. *International Journal of Project Management*, *28*(2), 151–157.

Brady, T., and Davies, A. (2010b). Learning to deliver a mega-project: The case of Heathrow Terminal 5 (pp. 190–212). In N. Caldwell and M. Howard (eds.). *Procuring complex performance: Studies of innovation in product-service management*. Routledge.

Brady, T., and Maylor, H. (2010). The improvement paradox in project contexts: A clue to the way forward? *International Journal of Project Management*, *28*(8), 787–795.

Clarke, T. (2004). Theories of corporate governance. *The Philosophical Foundations of Corporate Governance, Oxon*, *12*(4), 244–266.

Clarkson, M. (1995). Stakeholder framework for analyzing and evaluating corporate social performance. *Academy of Management Review*, *20*(1), 92–117.

Dalcher, D. (2012). The nature of project management, *International Journal of Managing Projects in Business*, *5*(4), 643–660.

Davidoff, M., and Bowman, J. R. (1996). Not in my backyard: A review of the literature and suggestions for future research. *Journal of Planning Literature*, *11*, 3–24.

Davis, K. (2016). Reconciling views of project success: A multiple stakeholder model. Doctoral Thesis. Kingston University London.

Derekhshan, R., Mancini, M., and Turner, J. R. (2019). Community's evaluation of organizational legitimacy: Formation and reconsideration. *International Journal of Project Management*, *1*, 73–86.

Di Maddaloni, F., and Davis, K. (2017). The influence of local community stakeholders in megaprojects: Rethinking their inclusiveness to improve project performance. *International Journal of Project Management*, *35*(8), 1537–1556.

Di Maddaloni, F., and Davis, K. (2018) Project manager's perception of the local communities' stakeholder in megaprojects. An empirical investigation in the UK. *International Journal of Project Management*, *36*(3), 542–565.

Di Maddaloni, F., and Sabini, L. (2022) Very important, yet very neglected: Where do local communities stand when examining social sustainability in major construction projects? *International Journal of Project Management*, *40*(7), 778–797.

Di Maddaloni, F., and Derakhshan, R. (2023) Stakeholders' perception of organization: an attribution and fairness perspective. *International Journal of Managing Projects in Business*, *17*(1), 27–49.

Aaltonen, K., Derakhshan, R., Di Maddaloni, F. and Turner, R. (2024) Stakeholder engagement: Theoretical and methodological directions for project scholarship *International Journal of Project Management, 42*(7), 102649.

Di Maddaloni, F., Meira, L. H., de Andrade, M. O., de Melo, I. R., Castro, A., and Locatelli, G. (2025) The dark legacy of megaprojects: A case of local disengagement, missed opportunities, and social value dissipation. *International Journal of Project Management, 43*(1), 102676.

Derry, R. (2012). Reclaiming marginalized stakeholders. *Journal of Business Ethics, 111*(2), 253–264.

Dooms, M., Verbeke, A., and Haezendonck, E. (2013). Stakeholder management and path dependence in large-scale transport infrastructure development: The port of Antwep case (1960–2010). *Journal of Transport Geography, 27*, 14–25.

Eesley, C., and Lenox, M. J. (2006). Firm responses to secondary stakeholder action. *Strategic Management Journal, Strategic Management*, 27, 765–781.

Eskerod, P., and Huemann, M. (2013). Sustainable development and project stakeholder management: What standards say. *International Journal of Managing Projects in Business, 6*(1), 36–50.

Eskerod, P., Huemann, M., and Ringhofer, C. (2015). Stakeholder inclusiveness: Enriching project management with general stakeholder theory. *Project Management Journal, 46*(6), 42–53.

Eskerod, P., and Larsen, T. (2018). Advancing project stakeholder analysis by the concept "shadow of the context." *International Journal of Project Management, 36*, 161–169.

Freeman, R. E. (1994). The politics of stakeholder theory: Some future directions. *Business Ethics Quarterly*, 409–421.

Freeman, R. E., Harrison, J. S., and Wicks, A. C. (2007). *Managing for stakeholders: Survival, reputation, and success*. Yale University Press.

Fridjonsson, G., and Palsson, E. (2018). *Green project management: Achieving sustainable business goals*. Taylor and Francis.

Friedman, A. L., and Miles, S. (2002). Developing stakeholder theory. *Journal of Management Studies, 39*(1), 1–21.

Frooman, J., (1999). Stakeholder influence strategies. *Academy of Management Review, 24*(2), 191–205.

Giammalvo, P. D. (2010). Green project management: A practical guide to sustainable business success. J. Ross.

Gil, N. A., and Fu, Y. (2022). Megaproject performance, value creation, and value distribution: An organizational governance perspective. *Academy of Management Discoveries, 8*(2), 224–251.

Gold, J. R. (1991). The not-in-my-backyard syndrome: A review of the literature and its implications for planning. *Journal of Planning Literature*, 6, 18–30.

Hart, S. L., and Sharma, S. (2004). Engaging fringe stakeholders for competitive imagination. *Academy of Management Executive, 18*(1), 7–18.

Ika L. A., Love P. E., Pinto J. K. (2022). Moving beyond the planning fallacy: The emergence of a new principle of project behavior. *IEEE Transactions on Engineering Management, 67*(2), 221–230.

Jensen, T., and Sandström, J. (2013). In defence of stakeholder pragmatism. *Journal of Business Ethics*, 114(2), 225–237.

Johnson, G., Scholes, K., and Whittington, R. (2005). *Exploring corporate strategy: Text and cases*, 6th ed. Prentice Hall.

Klein, P. G., Mahoney, J. T., McGahan, A. M., and Pitelis, C. N. (2019). Organizational governance adaptation: Who is in, who is out, and who gets what. *Academy of Management Review, 44*(1), 6–27.

Lehtinen, J., and Aaltonen, K. (2017). Organizing external stakeholder engagement in inter-organizational projects: Opening the black box. *Journal of Business & Technical Communication, 31*, 1–31.

Li, T. H. Y., Ng, S. T., Skitmore, M. (2012). Public participation in infrastructure and construction projects in China: From an EIA-based to a whole-cycle process. *Habitat International, 36*, 47–56.

McElroy, B., and Mills, C. (2000). Managing stakeholders (pp. 757–775). In R. Turner (ed.). *People in project management*. Gower.

McGahan, A. M. (2021). Integrating insights from the resource-based view of the firm into the new stakeholder theory. *Journal of management, 47*(7), 1734–1756.

McLeod, R., Kruger, P., and Howells, J. (2012). *Project management for construction*. Pearson Higher Education.

McVea, J. F., and Freeman, R. E. (2005). A names-and-faces approach to stakeholder management: How focusing on stakeholders as individuals can bring ethics and entrepreneurial strategy together. *Journal of Management Enquiry, 14*(1), 57–69.

Miles, S. (2017). Stakeholder theory classification: A theoretical and empirical evaluation of definitions. *Journal of Business Ethics*, *142*(3), 437–459.

Mitchell, R. K., Agle, B. R., and Wood, D. J. (1997). Toward a theory of stakeholder identification and salience: Defining the principle of who and what really counts. *Academy of Management Review*, *22*(4), 853–886.

Morris, P. W. G., and Hough, G. H. (1987). *The anatomy of major projects: A study of the reality of project management*. John Wiley & Sons.

Morris, P. W. G., Pinto, J. K., and Söderlund, J. (2011). *The Oxford handbook of project management*. Oxford Handbooks Online.

Nguyen, T. H. D., Chileshe, N., Rameezdeen, R., and Wood, A. (2019). External stakeholder strategic actions in projects: A multi-case study. *International Journal of Project Management*, *37*(1), 176–191.

Nieto-Rodriguez, A. (2021). The project economy has arrived. Spotlight series / Better project management. *Harvard Business Review*. https://hbr.org/2021/11/the-project-economy-has-arrived?utm_medium = email&utm_source = newsletter_perissue&utm_campaign = bestofissue_activesubs_notdigital&deliveryName = DM156050.

Olander, S., and Landin, A. (2008). A comparative study of factors affecting the external stakeholder management process. *Construction Management and Economics*, *26*, 553–561.

Olander, S. (2007). Stakeholder impact analysis in construction project management. *Construction Management and Economics*, *25*, 277–287.

Pajunen, K. (2006). Stakeholder influences in organizational survival. *Journal of Management Studies*, *43*(6), 1261–1288.

Parker, G. A. (2016). *Project management for environmental, construction, and manufacturing engineers*. John Wiley & Sons.

Parkinson, R. (1994). *The Sydney Opera House: The making of an iicon*. ABC Books.

Phillips, R., Freeman, R. E., and Wicks, A. C. (2003). What stakeholder theory is not. *Business Ethics Quarterly*, *13*(4), 479–502.

Pinto, J. K., and Winch, G. (2016). The unsettling of "settled science." The past and future of the management of projects. *International Journal of Project Management*, *34*, 237–245.

Rowley, T. J. (1997). Moving beyond dyadic ties: A network theory of stakeholder influences. *Academy of Management Review*, *22*(4), 887–910.

Salancik, G. R., and Pfeffer, J. (1978). A social information processing approach to job attitudes and task design. *Administrative Science Quarterly*, 224–253.

Scherer, A. G., and Palazzo, G. (2007). Toward a political conception of corporate responsibility: Business and society seen from a political perspective. *Journal of Management Studies*, *32*(4), 1096–1120.

Smith, R. K. T. (1993). The not-in-my-backyard syndrome and the theory of externalities. *Environmental Values*, *2*, 113–134.

Teo, M., and Loosemore, M. (2017). Understanding community protest from a project management perspective: A relationship-based approach. *International Journal of Project Management*, *35*(8),1444–1458.

Thorpe, D., and Holt, G. D. (2005). The relationship between project management and benefits management. *International Journal of Project Management*, *23*(6), 455–461.

Turner, J. R. (2014a). *Gower handbook of project management*. 5th ed. Gower.

Turner, J. R. (2014b). *The handbook of project-based management*. McGraw-Hill.

Turner, J. R., and Zolin, R. (2012). Forecasting success on large projects: Developing reliable scales to predict multiple perspectives by multiple stakeholders over multiple time frames. *Project Management Journal*, *43*(5), 87–99.

Unterhitzenberger, C. (2021). Special issue on project behavior. *Project Management Journal*, *52*(6), 527–530.

van den Ende, L., and van Marrewijk, A. (2018). Teargas, taboo and transformation: A neo-institutional study of community resistance and the struggle to legitimize subway projects in Amsterdam 1960–2018. *International Journal of Project Management*, *37*(2), 331–346.

Viswanath, C., and Narasimhan, R. (2009). Green project management: A framework and a case study. *Journal of Cleaner Production*, *17*, 1381–1390.

von Neumann, J., and Morgenstern, O. (1944). *Theory of games and economic behavior*. Princeton University Press.

Wateridge, J. (1998). How can IS/IT projects be measured for success? *International Journal of Project Management*, *16*(1), 59–63.

Yang, L., Huang, C., and Wu, K. (2011). The association among project manager's leadership style, teamwork and project success. *International Journal of Project Management*, *29*(3), 258–267.

CHAPTER 10

Governance Shifts and Short-term Performance

MAUDE BRUNET

Introduction

It is well established that governance is important in managing projects. At the turn of the millenium, Miller and Lessard (2000) concluded that shaping flexible institutional arrangements was one of the keys to assuring project performance. While the dynamic notions of governance and performance remain understudied in project scholarship, there are signs of growing interest (Song et al., 2022). Governance is a key element in understanding project behavior, as it can shape how people interact, make decisions, and attribute critical resources over a project. The type of governance adopted for a specific project shapes the incentives to collaborate toward success and might improve accountability of the project actors. Project governance attracts scholars interested in a wide array of topics. A review by Song et al (2022) identifies the main themes explored in a recent literature: contractual complexity, opportunistic behavior, PPP projects, organizational design, project investment success, portfolio management, institutional complexity, relational governance, and partnering flexibility. They argue that most of these subjects are studied in a somewhat static way and not as processes. While an increasing number of studies embrace the idea of "project governing," notably from a practice-based and contingency-based theoretical perspective, Song et al. (2022) suggest that further and deeper inquiry is needed and that some areas remain under-investigated. This chapter looks at what is known about project governance and its impact on project performance. I first explain different types of governance and the concept of governance shift (turning point), which provides a dynamic perspective. I then examine governance phenomena through the methodological and theoretical lens of actor network theory (ANT) as a promising complement to practice-based views. I find that the dynamic view of governance remains understudied and that two major perspectives can lead to significantly different impacts, based on a reactive or a proactive view. Lastly, I describe certain limitations to this study and propose avenues for future research.

Project Governance

Project governance is a vast topic, which grew as a distinct subfield within project management (Söderlund, 2011). Musawir et al. (2020) define it broadly as "the management of project management ... a system that exists at a higher level than, and provides oversight of, the project management system." It involves the structure, processes, decisions-making, and actors that make sure a project (or group of projects) runs smoothly and obtains adequate resources and helps to reduce constraints and optimize performance. Project governance ensures that the overarching scheme for undertaking a project, including contractual arrangements, is in line so that the project is delivered successfully (Sirisomboonsuk et al., 2018). It differs from project control, which aims at attesting to what extent the project conforms to the quality metrics, either internally (by the project team or client) or externally (via external audits) (Winch, 2014; McGrath & Whitty, 2015). Several researchers have investigated the topic of project governance in depth, and one author in particular stands out. Ralf Müller provided a thorough definition of governance in his 2009 book, clearly distinguished project governance from corporate governance, and argued that it should become a core concept. Ahola et al. (2014) reinforced this point, and Söderlund (2011) even suggested that

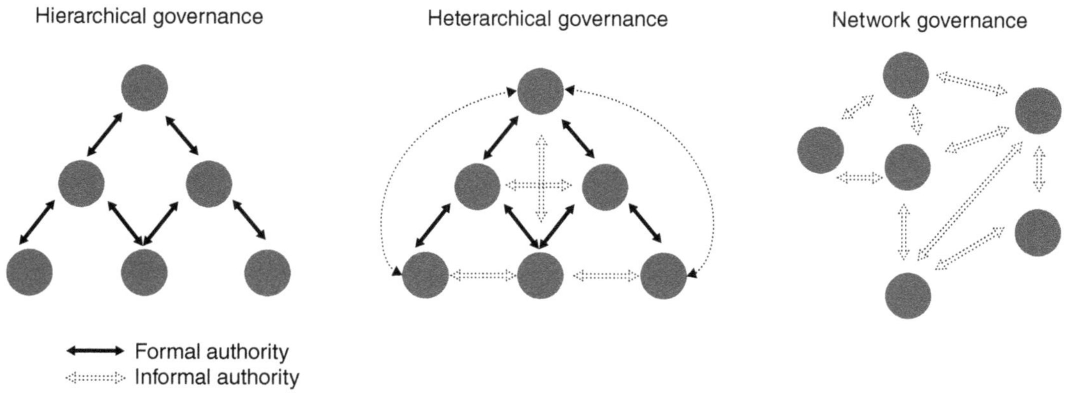

Figure 10.1 Simplified representation of the three types of project governance.

project governance constitutes a distinct school of thought in project studies. Researchers in public management explored governance frameworks for public infrastructure projects (Williams et al., 2010; Brunet & Aubry, 2016). While it is generally acknowledged that project governance applies to projects, with main features being its shareholder–stakeholder orientation and efforts at behavior-outcome control (Müller & Lecoeuvre, 2014), project governance also involves multiple layers within and outside organizations (Müller et al., 2019). Project governance is dependant on the context and should be designed considering the multiple possibilities surrounding a project (Adami & Verschoore, 2018). A project can be within the realm of a single organization, that is, intra-organizational, or may imply several organizations, and in this case will be inter-organizational, leading to different decisions regarding the design of its overall governance (Ahola et al., 2014). A concept related to governance that has been investigated in recent years in project studies is governmentality, inspired by the work of Foucault (Clegg, 2019). It can be defined as "the mentalities, rationalities, and ways of interaction, chosen by the governance roles to implement, maintain, and change the governance structure" (Müller, 2016, p. 20). It is an integrative concept that harks back to attitudes and the way that governing unfolds in different types of governance and the level at which they operate – project, organization, or institution (Müller et al., 2015). In this chapter, the aim is not to systematically review the literature on project governance but, in line with the notion of governmentality, to present three types of governance that are often overlooked or taken for granted. The three types are presented below, and Figure 10.1 offers a simplified illustration to highlight the main differences.

Hierarchical Governance

Hierarchical governance is how governance is conceived in the traditional, classical sense, as the direct application of authority, hierarchy being defined as "a system in which people or things are arranged according to their importance" (Cambridge Dictionary). Based on the seminal work of Williamson (1975), governance is conceived as being either anchored within the market, exercised as a hierarchy within organizations, or assuming a hybrid form (Ezzamel & Reed, 2008). Given that project governance is often defined in distinction to corporate governance, researchers also question its relationship with the overall organizational hierarchy. For example, Aubry et al. (2014) reveal the paradoxical tensions between the requirements of the project and hierarchical governance. The work of Ruuska et al. (2011) suggests that for multi-firm projects, prevalent governance approaches that rely on market, hierarchy, or hybrid forms are inadequate, and they propose adopting a type of governance based on the project network. Clegg et al. (2006) suggest that for projects, a clear hierarchy enables decisions to be made, responsibilities to be assumed, and disputes to be settled quickly. Classical project governance structures allow for a clear understanding of the roles each party plays and instigates a way to resolve issues from the bottom up as well as from top down (Volden & Andersen, 2018).

Network Governance

At the other end of the spectrum, lays a decentralized and polyphonous type of governance, named network governance. Jones et al. (1997, p. 913) define it as "interfirm coordination that is characterized by organic or informal social systems, in contrast to bureaucratic structures within firms and formal contractual relationships between them." When discussing network governance in the context of projects, this can be a real challenge. DeFillippi and Sydow (2016) highlight three characteristics that make governing project networks complex: (1) no single actor may act as a legitimate authority for the network as a whole, (2) there are no definite criteria by which the boundary of the network may be identified and controlled, and (3) each project is temporally limited and dynamically changing and (partially) reconstructed from one project to the next. For example, Adami and Verschoore (2018) show how supply, contractual, and information networks influence the governance of project networks. However, network governance might promote a collaborative culture that is open and favors a competitive advantage, as it "involves a select, persistent, and structured set of autonomous firms (as well as nonprofit agencies) engaged in creating products or services based on implicit and open-ended contracts to adapt to environmental contingencies and to coordinate and safeguard exchanges. These contracts are socially – not legally – binding" (Jones et al., 1997, p. 914). With the increase in project network organizations, considerations regarding their governance types, mechanisms, and outcomes need to be investigated (DeFillippi & Sydow, 2016; Manning, 2017). In particular, the important link with knowledge management should be addressed, as individuals in projects learn and are reconfigured more largely in the network as projects dissolve and others begin (Grabher, 2004).

Heterarchical Governance

Heterarchical governance is increasingly recognized as a specific type of governance, which typically applies to megaprojects but is also relevant to other inter-organizational projects (Brunet & Cohendet, 2021). The definition lies between hierarchy and network: "a system with multiple, tangled and shifting hierarchies" (Grabher and Thiel 2014, p. 531). It is not quite as decentralized as a network and builds on hierarchy to provide some of the decentralized features of the network. Stephenson (2009) argues that heterarchy brings several distinctive advantages over hierarchies and networks. Brunet and Cohendet (2021) also argue that this type of governance applies especially well to megaprojects as: (1) stakeholders are diverse and fluctuate over the course of a project and (2) the current digital transformation in construction, and more largely in project organizing (see Winch et al., 2023), fosters an enabling environment for heterarchical forms of organizing. Some advantages are highlighted by Clegg et al. (2006), for example, encouraging creativity, co-learning, motivation, and communication. However, this type of governance is very difficult to manage, and an optimal equilibrium point between all actors might be challenging to sustain over the long term. Some characteristics that might help reap the benefits of this type of governance are to establish clear governance rules, carefully define assigned roles that enable shared leadership, and build on learning (Brunet & Cohendet, 2021). Studies of heterarchical governance and megaprojects are still in their infancy, and more investigation should be undertaken in upcoming years and decades on this topic. A similar concept, which is gaining recognition in project studies, is polycentric governance (Gil & Pinto, 2018). According to Gil & Pinto (2018, p. 717), organizations adopting polycentric governance "supplement their internal hierarchical decision-making structures with egalitarian, local structures in order to encourage collaboration with legally independent stakeholders." This concept of polycentric governance can be thus complementary to hierarchical governance and might constitute an intermediate step in enabling a project to progress to a larger cooperation in joint local value-creation activities (Gil & Fu, 2022).

Dynamic Governance as a Common Yet Understated Characteristic

Projects unfold through a series of macro and micro processes, with distinctive temporalities and shifting objectives and intertwining actors and power relations. It is now commonly understood that governance structures, mechanisms, and actors require some flexibility to allow smooth progression of the project, adapting to circumstances and obstacles that appear along the way (Pitsis et al., 2014). Miller and Hobbs (2005, p. 42) question why project governance is mostly studied from a static perspective, suggesting that "governance regimes must adapt to the specific project and context, deal with emergent complexity, and change as the project development process unfolds." Recent studies conducted with the lenses of practice studies, contingency theories, and processual theories help deepen our understanding of these dynamics, as they enable a deep dive into micro activities and the way project activities and governance mechanisms are articulated through actors (Song et al., 2022). Although still immature as a field of study, and expected to make more significant contributions in future years, this approach brings to the fore the importance of considering governance as an evolving and dynamic concept. In his insightful essay about project tragedies, Bröchner (2022, p. 468) builds on Aristotle and peripeties to examine the way process is treated in project management research, for example, as "a turning point, where the course of events in a play transforms into another state." He suggests that "turning point" might be a good choice of words meaning "a point where a decisive change takes place," as several related concepts have been used without a clear-cut definition between them (for example, change, converging moment, freezing point, inflection point, metamorphosis, realignment, reframing, revolution, shift, state-change, tipping point, transformation, transition, and turnaround) (Bröchner, 2022). In his words: "Turning points seem a good choice with a reasonable chance of being understood, but only if it is spelled out what goes before and after the turning point." (p. 469) This is of importance for the discussion, as the study of specific turning points through the lens of ANT allows for a better understanding of the unfolding of a project and its governance. But before proceeding, a brief detour is needed to look at the idea of project performance as it relates to the type of governance adopted.

Project Performance

Project performance figures prominently in project studies and is a topic practitioners value for its practical relevance: How to make things better and achieve project objectives? Ika and Pinto (2022) find that project success is often blurred with other concepts such as efficiency, effectiveness, and performance. They argue that these are, in effect different with project success constituting "the end point or the achievement of the goal the organization and related stakeholders seek to reach through a temporary endeavor," while project performance "measures the extent to which the management processes and practices used to deliver the project are likely to help meet the project's planned targets and stakeholder expectations" (Ika & Pinto, 2022, p. 837). Aside from classical performance on cost, other criteria may include planning, funding, scope, contract, challenges/issues, and benefits (Love et al., 2021). While a review of the literature on this topic is beyond the scope of this chapter, it is of interest to highlight that a few studies have attempted to address the connections between governance and trust and how they affect performance (Vukomanović et al., 2021). Some find that project governance has a positive impact on project performance (Biesenthal and Wilden, 2014; Sirisomboonsuk et al., 2018). However, as stated previously, project governance must be dynamic, not static, to respond to the dynamic process of the project and its interaction with other organizational structures and actors (Floricel et al., 2011). Project governance structures enable greater performance when they allow for flexibility in the institutional setup at the organizational level, in the transfer of authority to the project level, and in the development of a project team mindset as self-responsible and self-organizing (Müller et al, 2015). However, adapting project governance to context remains challenging, as little is known about how to ensure that the structure and mechanisms in place are optimal for a given set of circumstances and actors, which often causes tensions in complex environments (Aubry et al., 2014). For example, Martinsuo and Ahola (2022) suggest that the performance of an inter-organizational project is mostly shaped by the quality of the relationships among project actors, its strategy, resources, and governance adopted. Studying the performance of project portfolios, Müller et al. (2008) found that control had a direct effect on performance, while the type of governance acted as a moderator. First, a review of a few studies conducted with ANT in project studies is conducted, and second is explored how ANT might be used to investigate governance shifts and their impact on project performance.

Actor-Network Theory

This section presents Actor-Network Theory (ANT) as a theoretical and methodological perspective and describes some of its important features along with an important variant of this perspective, translation studies, to then look at empirical research in management and project management that mobilizes ANT. Then, Table 10.1 summarizes a few suggestions of how to tackle project governance and performance using the ANT perspective.

ANT emerged in the 1980s as an extension from strategic analysis (Rouleau, 2007). It is categorized as a contemporary and political approach, which introduces a pluralist representation of organizations, considers organized action, and proposes inductive methods to understand behaviors. Basically, ANT is a constructivist method for studying associations (Latour, 2005; Akrich et al., 2006). According to Latour (2005, p. 147), its main tenet is “that actors themselves make everything, including their own frameworks, their own theories, their own contexts, their own metaphysics, even their own ontologies.” Callon and Latour developed, from the 1980s onwards, a sociology of translation (also called ANT), which draws mainly on an anthropology of sciences and techniques (Vinck, 2007).

An influential book edited by Akrich, Callon, and Latour brings together the founding texts of this sociology of translation (Akrich et al., 2006). Some important themes and concepts developed include (1) translation, both as a process and as a result; (2) chains of translation, translation centres, and critical junctions; (3) the role of materiality as actant, as boundary object for translation; and (4) negotiations and controversies. It is also relevant to highlight that narratives and descriptions are very important for ANT, as they tend to reveal chains of translation as they are constructed and deconstructed by actants (both human and nonhuman).

Table 10.1 Project governance and performance through ANT

Type of governance	Focal point using ANT	Potential impacts on performance	Dynamic aspects
Hierarchical governance	– the organization as actant (project embedding) – formal relations	– traces of organizational and project artifacts (project progress report, information systems, etc.)	– evolution of the governance through time, within and across project phases
Heterarchical governance	– the project as an actant, intertwined within the organizational context – the associations of power and main actors – informal ties	– how suppliers, contractual and information are shared and enacted – digital technologies used – build on learning and adaptation mechanisms	– translation of clear governance rules (which may evolve), roles enabling shared leadership – tracing accountability mechanisms
Network governance	– the project as an actant in itself – the multiple stakeholders, their associations – main network nodes	– how collective and socially binding contracts and information are shared, controlled and enacted – traces the inherent quality of the collaborative culture	– construction and reproduction of knowledge, within and between projects

Latour's seminal work (2005) describes ANT in more detail. His aim is to "redefine the notion of social by going back to its original meaning and making it able to trace connections again" (p. 1). For Latour, this tracing of associations is the unit of analysis, and he postulates that "there is no society, no social realm, and no social ties, but there exist translations between mediators that may generate traceable associations" (Latour, 2005, p. 108). The first part of his book maps out controversies around the social realm, and five sources of uncertainty are presented that arise from those controversies: (1) the nature of groups, which are never fixed and thus cannot be studied on their own; rather, it is the process of making and unmaking that is to be studied, which leaves many traces; (2) the nature of actions and agency: an "actor" may in fact be an individual or a network, since action is in fact dislocated; (3) the nature of objects, which have agency: extending the notion of the word "social" means that in order to trace associations, anything that modifies a state of affairs is an actor, be it a person, a network, or an object; (4) the nature of facts: what differentiates a fact from a concern? According to ANT, the difference is in the making and thus must be studied accordingly; and (5) the writing of research accounts, which are also mediators.

The second part of Latour's (2005) book explains how to render associations traceable and proposes to "flatten" the landscape of the social by performing three main moves. The first is to localize the global by "realizing that there is no 'global', but only a chain of connected localities" (Czarniawska, 2006, p. 1555), which forces the researcher to recognize that what is "global" is actually many connected times and places. The second move is to redistribute the local. A local interaction is "the assemblage of all the other local interactions distributed elsewhere in time and space" (Latour, 2005, p. 194). This symmetric operation is important because neither the global nor the local has a concrete existence. Rather, it is the "connectors" that are important and that have to be brought to the fore. Thus, an actor-network is "what is made to act by a large star-shaped web of mediators flowing in and out. It is made to exist by its many ties: attachments are first, actors are second" (Latour, 2005, p. 217). The third move is to connect sites, "now conceived as actors-networks – and to investigate the stabilization of the social" (Gubert, 2007, p. 606). The global is made of many connected times and places, and the local is a product of many connected times and places. What are the connectors, and how are these sites connected? What makes those connections stable? Only by observing those three moves can the researcher grasp the "topography of the social" (Latour, 2005, p. 165).

These three moves are thus a means of tracing associations and translations, yet veer away from a conventional classification of micro, meso, and macro: "The solution explored by ANT ... has nothing to do with offering still another compromise between micro and macro, actor and system – and even less with pushing the swing so forcefully that it circles through some dialectic circles" (Latour, 2005, p. 170). For Latour (2005, p. 185), "scale is the actor's own achievement," and thus it does not fall to the researcher to define the level of analysis.

Thus, ANT offers an interesting perspective to study projects, their governance, and how actants are connected and intermediated. This perspective, which shares a similar ontological position to the practice perspective (Brunet & Aubry, 2018), has been mobilized in general management and project studies, yet remains marginal. Pollack and Clegg (2023) offer a comprehensive review of the main studies carried out in the field of project management. One early work is Blackburn's (2002), which takes the project manager as the central point. Later studies diversify the conceptualization of actants: from a project status report (Aubry, 2011), an information system (Pollack et al., 2013; Missonier & Loufrani-Fedida, 2014), an accountability system (Burga & Rezania, 2017), and primordial stakeholders such as nature or frogs (Tryggestad et al., 2013), to digital technologies (Voordijk, 2021). Yet, if researchers have long highlighted that ANT is important to study project networks (Grabher, 2004), there is plenty of room to develop this approach further, especially to study the governance surrounding projects. While reviewing the (thin) literature on projects and ANT, only a few papers seem to look closely at governance. For example, Aubry (2001, p. 438) asks: "How do project management networks interface with the organisation's hierarchy?" Burga and Rezania (2017) also investigate the role of an accountability system within the larger governance of projects.

It is paradoxical that there has been so little work on the project as a central, powerful actant. In their review, Pollack and Clegg (2023) suggest that "Projects, as deliberately temporary forms of organisation, undergo significant change throughout the project lifecycle, being formed through new associations between people, processes, materialities and technologies, temporarily stabilised in networks to be deliberately sundered on delivery." However, the authors do not present studies that use ANT to explore a project as a whole system of associations, as could be expected based on the early work of Porsander (2000). Latour's (1993) seminal work appears as an exception and provides us an interesting example to build upon. Thus, ANT offers a useful theoretical and methodological lens to understand projects as actants and trace governance shifts and their impact on performance. Table 10.1 sums up potential focal points, impacts, and dynamic aspects depending on the types of governance. It is simplified and not exhaustive. As it will be argued in the following discussion, we should not only pay attention to the types of governance individually and how they might impact performance, but also how a project might switch from one type to another one during its course, through the study of particular turning points.

Discussion: Shifts in Governance

I have thus far argued that project governance is widely recognized as dynamic in essence but that little is known about the "turning points" that create shifts in governance and how these impact on project performance. Vaagaasar et al. (2020) studied temporal shifts in projects from a situated viewpoint and found that they highlight challenges for organizations. Song et al. (2022) advocate mobilizing additional theories that help to better understand the notion of governing, such as practice and contingency approaches. They do not explicitly talk about ANT as a way forward, but reading between the lines one can easily relate ANT to the strength of this approach to "encourage more researchers to join the practice turn to diversify our understanding of the project governance phenomenon and discover how the roles of actors and materials, the relationships among stakeholders, unanticipated deviations, and even the criteria of success evolve and are enacted during the governing process" (Song et al., 2022, p. 342). A few intuitive examples are offered here, which hopefully will be pursued in the coming years to help uncover the dynamics of governance shifts and their impact on project performance. There are also challenges related to this suggested avenue, as we need to perhaps reconceptualize the notion of project performance to include broader measures of benefits realization (Zwikael & Smyrk, 2015; Ika & Pinto, 2022).

Reactive versus Proactive Turning Points

It would be interesting to investigate how an organization goes about making governance shifts. Empirical examples suggest that if a crisis leads to a reactive response in order to change governance, for example, to account for social acceptability or other environmental imperatives, this can lead to enhanced short-term performance, as it eases immediate tensions and allows a project to continue. One illustration is the Metropolitan light train megaproject, which has prompted government to take over from the original promoter following several controversial decisions that reduced social acceptability and led to contestation (Ben Abdallah et al., 2022). There are obvious gains in the short term, but reactive shifts might not generate many benefits over the long run. A counterexample is presented by Di Maddaloni and Derakhsan (2022). The Italian Apennine highway project "Variante di Valico" proactively adapted its governance to allow for a more inclusive approach, resulting in a substantial change in stakeholders' perceptions of fairness. The performance that can be attained with this proactive governance shift warrants scrutiny in future research, yet one can assume that it might genuinely lead to better short- and long-term improvements.

Turning Points: From One Type of Governance to Another

Another topic worth investigating is related to the types of governance described above: hierarchical, network, and heterarchical. Governance shifts might imply moving from one type to another, either abruptly or through a slow adaptation as the project evolves. How these turning points might impact the performance of a project remains unknown, yet again the literature offers some insights. Li et al. (2018) argue that the World Expo 2010 project in China was a success notably because it adopted evolutionary governance. Gil and Fu (2022) suggest that governance and cost adaptations lead to higher project performance, notably regarding social value. It would be interesting to investigate governance shifts in several cases, where shifts lead to centralizing (closing down) or decentralizing (opening up) governance, and assessing how these shifts impact short-term and long-term performance. As project governance seeks to frame and incentivize behavior, understanding more finely underlying values behind the adopted scheme is of interest to academics as well as practitioners, for example, considering not only legitimacy, accountability, and efficiency but also fairness (Unterhitzenberger & Moeller, 2021). As governance evolves and might shift during a project, it is important to understand how it might contribute to shape project actors' behaviors, for the good or for the bad.

Conclusion

This chapter presents three different types of governance: hierarchical, network, and heterarchical. It then examines the dynamic but under-developed and under-researched dimensions of governance, where governance shifts constitute turning points. Whereas practice-based approaches and contingency theories have been proposed as ways to study this important phenomenon, I suggest that ANT should also be considered. It allows the project itself to be considered as a powerful actant, which mobilizes actors and resources in a specific context and temporality. Project governance assembles and disassembles as the project evolve, through the power plays of actors, outside events that create shocks and other circumstances. Turning points provide a good starting point, as they lead to shifts in governance. These shifts may be proactive, reactive, radical, or evolutionary, and in some cases imply changing from one type of governance to another. How they impact the performance of projects is still an open question, which will hopefully interest some of us in the near future.

References

Adami, V. S., and J. R. Verschoore (2018). Implications of network relations for the governance of complex projects. *Project Management Journal*, *49*(2), 71–88.

Ahola, T., Ruuska, I., Artto, K., and Kujala, J. (2014). What is project governance and what are its origins? *International Journal of Project Management*, *32*(8), 1321–1332.

Akrich, M., Callon, M., and Latour, B. (2006). *Sociologie de la traduction: Textes fondateurs*. École des mines de Paris.

Aubry, M. (2011). The social reality of organisational project management at the interface between networks and hierarchy. *International Journal of Managing Projects in Business*, *4*(3), 436–456.

Aubry, M., Richer, M. C., and Lavoie-Tremblay, M. (2014). Governance performance in complex environment: The case of a major transformation in a university hospital. *International Journal of Project Management*, *32*(8), 1333–1345.

Ben Abdallah, S., El–Boukri, S., Floricel, S., Hudon, P.–A., Brunet, M., Petit, M.–C., Aubry, M. (2022). A process-oriented framework to measure development performance and success of megaprojects. *International Journal of Project Management*, *40*(6), 685–702.

Biesenthal, C., and Wilden, R. (2014). Multi-level project governance: Trends and opportunities. *International Journal of Project Management*, *32*(8), 1291–1308.

Blackburn, S. (2002). The project manager and the project-network. *International Journal of Project Management*, *20*(3), 199–204.

Bröchner, J. (2022). Project tragedies. *International Journal of Project Management*, *40*(5), 467–470.

Brunet, M., and Aubry, M. (2016). The three dimensions of a governance framework for major public projects. *International Journal of Project Management*, 34(8), 1596–1607.

Brunet, M., and Aubry, M. (2018). The governance of major public infrastructure projects: The process of translation. *International Journal of Managing Projects in Business*, *11*(1), 80–103.

Brunet, M., and Cohendet, P. (2021). Transforming construction: Heterarchical megaproject ecologies and the management of innovation. *Construction Management and Economics*, 1–14.

Burga, R., and Rezania, D. (2017). Project accountability: An exploratory case study using actor–network theory. *International Journal of Project Management*, 35(6), 1024–1036.

Clegg, S. (2019). Governmentality. *Project Management Journal*, 50(3), 266–270.

Clegg, S. R., Tyrone, P., Marosszeky, M., and Rura-Polley, T. (2006). Making the future perfect: Constructing the Olympic dream (pp. 265–293). In D. Hodgson and S. Cicmil (eds.). *Making projects critical*. Palgrave.

Czarniawska, B. (2006). Book review: Bruno Latour: *Reassembling the social: An introduction to actor-network theory. Organization Studies*, *27*(10), 1553–1557.

DeFillippi, R., and Sydow, J. (2016). Project networks: Governance choices and paradoxical tensions. *Project Management Journal*, *47*(5), 6–17.

Di Maddaloni, F., and Derakhshan, R. (2022). Towards a conceptual framework for unfolding stakeholder's perceptions." Presented at the European Academy of Management, June, Winterthur.

Ezzamel, M., and Reed, M. (2008). Governance: A code of multiple colours. *Human Relations*, *61*(5), 597–615.

Floricel, S., Piperca, S., and Banik, M. (2011). *Increasing project flexibility: The response capacity of complex projects*. Project Management Institute.

Gil, N., and Fu, Y. (2022). Megaproject performance, value creation, and value distribution: An organizational governance perspective. *Academy of Management Discoveries*, *8*(2), 224–251.

Gil, N., and Pinto, J. K. (2018). Polycentric organizing and performance: A contingency model and evidence from megaproject planning in the UK. *Research Policy*, *47*, 717–734.

Grabher, G. (2004). Learning in projects, remembering in networks? Communality, sociality, and connectivity in project ecologies. *European Urban and Regional Studies*, *11*(2), 103–123.

Gubert, L. (2007). Book review: Reassembling the social: *An introduction to actor-network-theory*. By Bruno Latour. *Critical Sociology*, *33*(3), 603–607.

Ika, L. A., and Pinto, J. K. (2022). The "re-meaning" of project success: Updating and recalibrating for a modern project management. *International Journal of Project Management*, *40*(7), 835–848.

Jones, C., Hesterly, W. S., and Borgatti, S. P. (1997). A general theory of network governance: Exchange conditions and social mechanisms. *Academy of Management Review*, *22*, 911–945.

Latour, B. (1993). *Aramis ou l'amour des techniques*. La Découverte.

Latour, B. (2005). *Reassembling the social: An introduction to actor-network theory*. Oxford University Press.

Li, Y., Lu, Y., Ma, L., and Kwak, Y. H. (2018). Evolutionary governance for mega-event projects (Meps): A case study of the World Expo 2010 in China. *Project Management Journal*, *49*(1), 57–78.

Love, P. E. D., Ika, L. A., Matthews, J., and Fang, W. (2021). Large-scale transport infrastructure project performance: Generating a narrative of context and meaning. *IEEE Transactions on Engineering Management*, *70*(10), 3637–3652.

Manning, S. (2017). The rise of project network organizations: Building core teams and flexible partner pools for interorganizational projects. *Research Policy*, *46*(8), 1399–1415.

Martinsuo, M., and Ahola, T. (2022). Multi-project management in inter-organizational contexts. *International Journal of Project Management*, *40*(7), 813–826.

McGrath, S. K., and Whitty, S. J. (2015). Redefining governance: From confusion to certainty and clarity. *International Journal of Managing Projects in Business*, *8*(4), 755–787.

Miller, R., and B. Hobbs (2005). Governance regimes for large complex projects. *Project Management Journal*, *36*(3), 42–50.

Miller, R., and Lessard, D. (2000). *The strategic management of large engineering projects: Shaping institutions, risks, and governance*. MIT Press.

Missonier, S., and Loufrani-Fedida, S. (2014). Stakeholder analysis and engagement in projects: From stakeholder relational perspective to stakeholder relational ontology. *International Journal of Project Management*, *32*(7), 1108–1122.

Müller, R. (2009). Governance of project management. *Project governance*. Gower.

Müller, R. (2016). Organizational project governance (pp. 11–24). In R. Müller (ed.). *Governance and governmentality for projects: Enablers, practice and consequences*. Routledge.

Müller, R., Drouin, N., and Sankaran, S. (2019). Modeling organizational project management. *Project Management Journal*, *50*(4), 499–513.

Müller, R., and Lecoeuvre, L. (2014). Operationalizing governance categories of projects. *International Journal of Project Management*, 32(8), 1346–1357.

Müller, R., Martinsuo, M., and Blomquist, T. (2008). Project portfolio control and portfolio management performance in different contexts. *Project Management Journal*, *39*(3), 28–42.

Müller, R., Pemsel, S., and Shao, J. (2015). Organizational enablers for project governance and governmentality in project-based organizations. *International Journal of Project Management*, *33*(4), 839–851.

Musawir, A. u., Abd-Karim, S. B., and Mohd-Danuri, M. S. (2020). Project governance and its role in enabling organizational strategy implementation: A systematic literature review. *International Journal of Project Management*, *38*(1), 1–16.

Pitsis, T. S., Sankaran, S., Gudergan, S., and Clegg, S. R. (2014). Governing projects under complexity: Theory and practice in project management. *International Journal of Project Management*, *32*(8), 1285–1290.

Pollack, J., and Clegg, S. (2023). Uncovering the role of non-human actors in projects (pp. 117–126). In G. M. Winch, M. Brunet, and D. Cao (eds.). *Research handbook on complex project organizing*. Edward Elgar.

Pollack, J., et al. (2013). Applying actor–network theory as a sensemaking framework for complex organisational change programs. *International Journal of Project Management*, *31*(8), 1118–1128.

Porsander, L. (2000). Translating a dream of immortality in a (con)temporary order. *Journal of Organizational Change Management*, 13(1), 14–29.

Rouleau, L. (2007). *Théories des organisations: Approches classiques, contemporaines et de l'avant-garde*. Presses de l'Université du Québec.

Ruuska, I., Ahola, T., Artto, K., Locatelli, G., and Mancini, M. (2011). A new governance approach for multi-firm projects: Lessons from Olkiluoto 3 and Flamanville 3 nuclear power plant projects. *International Journal of Project Management*, *29*(6), 647–660.

Sirisomboonsuk, P., Gu, V. C., Cao, R. Q., and Burns, J. R. (2018). Relationships between project governance and information technology governance and their impact on project performance. *International Journal of Project Management*, *36*(2), 287–300.

Söderlund, J. (2011). Pluralism in project management: Navigating the crossroads of specialization and fragmentation. *International Journal of Management Reviews*, *13*(2), 153–176.

Song, J., Song, L., Liu, H., Feng, Z., and Müller, R. (2022). Rethinking project governance: Incorporating contextual and practice-based views. *International Journal of Project Management*, *40*(4), 332–346.

Tryggestad, K., Justesen, L., and Mouritsen, J. (2013). Project temporalities: How frogs can become stakeholders. *International Journal of Managing Projects in Business*, *6*(1), 69–87.

Unterhitzenberger, C., and Moeller, D. (2021). Fair project governance: An organisational justice approach to project governance. *International Journal of Project Management*, *39*(6), 683–696.

Vaagaasar, A. L., Hernes, T., and Dille, T. (2020). The challenges of implementing temporal shifts in temporary organizations: Implications of a situated temporal view. *Project Management Journal*, *51*(4), 420–428.

Volden, G. H., and Andersen, B. (2018). The hierarchy of public project governance frameworks: An empirical study of principles and practices in Norwegian ministries and agencies. *International Journal of Managing Projects in Business*, *11*(1), 174–197.

Voordijk, H. (2021) Technical mediation and digital technologies in construction practice. *Architectural Engineering and Design Management*, *19*(2) 1–15.

Vukomanović, M., Cerić, A., Brunet, M., Locatelli, G., and Davies, A. (2021). Editorial: Trust and governance in megaprojects. *International*

Journal of Project Management, *39*(4), 321–324.

Williams, T., Klakegg, O. J., Magnussen, O. M., and Glasspool, H. (2010). An Investigation of governance frameworks for public projects in Norway and the UK. *International Journal of Project Management*, *28*(1), 40–50.

Williamson, O. E. (1975). *Markets and hierarchies: Analysis and antitrust implications*. The Free Press.

Winch, G. M. (2014). Three domains of project organising. *International Journal of Project Management*, *32*, 721–731.

Winch, G. M., Brunet, M., Cao, D. (eds.). (2023). *Research handbook on complex project organizing*. Edward Elgar.

Zwikael, O., and Smyrk, J. (2015). Project governance: Balancing control and trust in dealing with risk. *International Journal of Project Management*, *33*(4), 852–862.

CHAPTER 11

Maximum Feasible Project Failure

The German Reform of Money Laundering Prevention

WOLFGANG SEIBEL and KATHARINA EßMEYER

Complexity and Complexity Reduction as a Challenge for Project Management

Complexity and unpredictability are being characterized in the literature as crucial challenges of project management (Baccarini, 1996; Bakhshi, Ireland & Gorod, 2016; Marle & Vidal, 2016). The notion of complexity and the unforeseen or unforeseeable is also essential for the concept of project behavior (Ika et al., 2020; Ika et al., 2022; Ika & Pinto 2022). Projects can develop their own dynamics and lifecycle far beyond the intentions and control of those officially in charge – individuals, organizations, regulators. Quite paradoxically though, one driver of project behavior autodynamics is not complexity per se but complexity reduction inherent to organizations and decision-making (cf. Simon, 1962; March, 1991). The near decomposability (H. A. Simon; cf. Egidi & Marengo, 2004) of hierarchical systems in the form of departmentalization mitigates the bottleneck problem of information processing at the top of the hierarchy. Routines and standard operating procedures, often connected to professional standards and identities, make decisions easier by reducing the burden of calculating pros and cons. By the same token, however, departmentalization increases the risk of silo thinking and miscoordination while routines and standard operating procedures reduce agility and adaptability. Put another way: What strengthens resilience under the regular conditions of managerial reality may weaken managerial coping under the exceptional conditions of project management.

Skillful project managers will anticipate precisely this. Temporarily reintegrating otherwise siloed organizational units and harmonizing divergent professional identities can be an essential part of project management. This has been referred to as temporary hybridization (Matinheikki et al., 2019; cf. also Seibel, 2015). Temporality also implies a provisional managerial style, based on wisdom and experience rather than textbook knowledge – much in the sense of Michael Polanyi's (1966, p. 4) characterization of tacit knowledge ("we can more than we can tell"). Skilled project managers understand the peculiarities and idiosyncrasies of the entities and identities that need to be coordinated and/or harmonized, and they are aware that managerial success can depend critically on using system knowledge without making it explicit.

Grand challenge projects involving public authorities represent a prominent case in point. What Ika and Munro (2022) define as "grand challenge" is a situation in which the objectives of a project are clear but the techniques for achieving them are unclear. This can happen when policymakers are faced with previously unknown but identifiable problem-solving needs, or when known techniques for known problems prove ineffective. In both scenarios, the balance between politics and administration is disrupted. And so is the established combination of flexibility and routine. Run-of-the-mill projects in the public sector are routine and therefore typically managed by professional bureaucracies that operate below the radar of public attention and perceived political relevance. By contrast, grand challenge projects in the public sector necessitate even greater involvement of government experts while simultaneously engaging politicians as generators of resources, power, and public attention. A carefully calibrated use of political influence – either from within or from outside the respective political-administrative sub-system – can serve as an effective problem-solving mechanism when it comes to tackling complex challenges, as evidenced by Pinto's (2000) observations (cf. also Wynn, Smith & Killen, 2021). However, the durability and consistency of this approach, as well as its alignment with the project's core objectives, cannot be taken for granted. The reason is that selective politicization of administrative problem-solving may easily suspend the very mechanisms of complexity reduction on which the stability and effectiveness of the relevant administrative sub-system is based. Those who hold the tacit knowledge needed to smoothly change established patterns of governance and problem-solving tend to be nonpolitical experts in the rank-and-file structure of public agencies, while those wielding power and influence are the ones who, according to the classic definition by Karl W. Deutsch, are "able to afford not to learn" (Deutsch, 1966, p. 111). This makes bureaucratic self-management (Martela, 2019) especially relevant. It requires boundary spanners as quasi-entrepreneurs (cf. the seminal paper by Tushman & Scanlon, 1981, and, for an overview, Tang et al., 2018), that is, individuals who possess an understanding of the logic of both the political and the administrative realms and are sufficiently adept at navigating their interaction. High-ranking appointed officials or members of parliament with administrative experience are typical candidates for this role pattern (cf. Brierley et al., 2023). The emergence of boundary spanning activity is a non-routine pattern of action in a bureaucratic environment, however. Accordingly, its emergence cannot be taken for granted either.

In terms of project behavior, this implies that projects whose very nature requires the involvement of government experts while simultaneously engaging politicians also involve higher risks of self-inflicted vulnerability. When self-management remains insufficient and boundary spanning across multiple jurisdictions is weak or absent, the influence of political actors, who inevitably lack "system knowledge" and can "afford not to learn," can easily be counterproductive. Politicized project management can degenerate into a mere unsorted stream of choice opportunities for various participants to get rid of selected problems and supposed solutions, like throwing garbage into a trash can, as identified by Cohen et al. (1972) as a standard pathology of organizational behavior.

This is what the following case study illustrates. The project in question concerns the fight against money laundering as an integral part of the fight against organized crime and terrorism. The creeping crisis of the German anti-money laundering system led in 2017 to a reform project that exacerbated the crisis instead of alleviating it. This paradoxical effect was triggered by the political decision to transfer the responsible administrative unit from the jurisdiction of the Federal Ministry of the Interior to the jurisdiction of the Federal Ministry of Finance. As a result, the complex system of cooperation between criminological and financial experts was disrupted. Warnings were ignored by political decision-makers in the government and parliament. High-ranking civil servants were directly involved as potential boundary spanners. However, they did not make use of their tacit knowledge of the political and administrative logic of the reform project but left its implementation to the respective rank and file bureaucrats who themselves lacked the formal responsibilities and incentives to make the reform work effectively. The project became an avoidable failure with serious consequences. At the beginning of 2019, tens of thousands of suspected money laundering cases remained unprocessed, including more than 2,000 cases related to possible terrorist financing.

A Case in Brief

In the Summer of 2022, then German Finance Minister Christian Lindner announced a profound reorganization of the fight against money laundering in Germany (BMF, 2022). The Finance Minister's statement was an indirect admission of the failure of a project that began in 2015, designed to overcome notorious deficiencies in the fight against money laundering and organized crime. The project's key component, implemented in 2017, was the transfer of the authority for combating money laundering, known in English as the Financial Intelligence Unit (FIU), from the jurisdiction of the Federal Criminal Police Office (Bundeskriminalamt, BKA) and thus from the portfolio of the Federal Ministry of the Interior to the General Customs Directorate, a federal authority in the portfolio of the Federal Ministry of Finance (Doc. 26). The fact of the matter was that a major and challenging reform project was initiated by elected and appointed officials who made no effort to acknowledge the project's intricate nature, which in turn left the experts in the ministerial bureaucracy without guidance. The absence of political guidance could have been compensated for by bureaucratic self-management part of which would have necessarily involved boundary spanning action of high-ranking officials. No such countervailing initiatives took place though. What was intended as an improvement of law enforcement, however, resulted in administrative disaster with the consequence of tens of thousands of cases of suspected money-laundering remaining unprocessed among which, as of early 2019, are more than 2,000 cases of financing terrorism (De Masi, 2019).

Dismantled Expertise

The establishment of Financial Intelligence Units within the framework of the Financial Action Task Force (FATF) affiliated with the Organization for Economic Co-ordination and Development (OECD) dating back to 1989 was designed to ensure the integration of criminal and financial intelligence in the fight against money laundering and to facilitate the investigation of transnationally organized crimes (FATF, 2012). This involves combating the most serious crimes in the form of terrorism, illegal arms trafficking, drug-related crime, human trafficking, and forced prostitution (FATF, 2012, p. 121). Combating money laundering is thus a crucial issue of domestic security and human rights policy. Removing the German FIU from the Federal Criminal Police Office (BKA) to the Directorate General of Customs implied the opposite, namely, to split rather than integrate the criminological and the finance-related expertise in the fight against money laundering, thereby weakening rather than strengthening law enforcement. Which leads to the question of how a project of a profoundly counterproductive nature could have been conceived in the first place.

At the beginning, there were accurate diagnoses of implementation deficiencies. Until 2017, one undisputed problem of the German FIU model was the dependence on the criminal investigation offices in the 16 federal states and their heterogeneous administrative structures. That was virtually incompatible with what had been intended as the establishment of a coherent organizational structure of the combat against money-laundering in the OECD world (FATF, 2010). In Germany, however, it was the consequence of the constitutional arrangements according to which policing is delegated to the federal states while jurisdiction of the BKA is limited to law enforcement in cases of a cross-state character and, specifically, designed to assist state-level criminal police through advanced investigative technology (Doc. 03, p. 1466). The basic idea behind the transfer of the FIU from the BKA to the portfolio of the Federal Ministry of Finance was therefore to transfer responsibility to a central federal agency with a coherent administrative substructure, namely, the customs administration (Doc. 18). German customs has specific law enforcement competences ranging from supervising legal employment of foreign workforce on construction sites to combating transnational drug-trafficking (Zoll, 2022). Yet, by its very nature, the customs service lacks in-depth knowledge of the nature and structure of organized crime and, thus, of combating money-laundering as the financial dimension of intensive criminal activity with severe consequences.

Still, the inevitable downside of the new model could have been neutralized if at least data exchange between the FIU and the criminal investigation offices of the federal states would have been secured. That, however, was not the case (Doc. 3, p. 2959). The new FIU, now affiliated with customs administration, was to forward only relevant ("valuable") suspicious cases to the law enforcement agencies, an assessment that would have required the expertise of seasoned criminal investigators (Doc. 18). Instead, the state criminal investigation offices did not even have access to corresponding data files of the FIU (Doc. 03, p. 3411). Consequently, the use of criminal investigation competence as the very basis of fact-finding and investigations on sectors, products, and criminal individuals or groups in which money laundering offenses typically occur was blocked.

The negative consequences of splitting what should have been integrated criminal and financial competences through the 2017 reorganization of the FIU were highlighted by experts from the very beginning (Doc. 03, p. 1466; Doc. 03, p. 92). This leads to the more specific question of why the warning voices were not heeded.

Pathological Learning

As early as 2010, an evaluation report by the OECD-related Financial Action Task Force (FATF) identified serious weaknesses in the German anti-money laundering system (FATF, 2010). In particular, the FATF criticized the fact that the actual task of a FIU, namely, the evaluation of Suspicious Activity Reports (SARs), was not performed by the German FIU itself but by the criminal investigation offices of the 16 federal states (FATF, 2010, p. 105). According to FATF assessment, this made the transmission of crime-relevant information and the initiation of prosecution measures cumbersome and correspondingly slow and hindered international cooperation in the prosecution of cross-border crimes (FATF, 2010, p. 106). As a consequence of the report, the enactment of the European Union's Fourth Money Laundering Directive in May 2015 became a critical fork in the road since its implementation had to be completed by June 2017, thus requiring substantial steps toward improved FIU performance (Doc. 17).

At the time, a glaring shortage of staff at the FIU, still part of the Federal Criminal Police Office (BKA), was widely acknowledged (Doc. 03, p. 93). There was talk of 150 additional posts being needed to upgrade the FIU (Doc. 03, pp. 279 and 266). This was a political issue in itself, as the Federal Minister of the Interior, who was responsible for the FIU, would have had to submit a proposal to the Federal Minister of Finance to increase staff by this amount, and the President of the Federal Criminal Police Office would have had to lobby for it. Approaches to this were in place, but they proved unsustainable. Since May 2015, the state secretaries of the Ministry of Finance and the Ministry of the Interior discussed the matter, a series of consultations between the technical officials of both ministries followed (Doc. 3). The proposal to transfer the FIU from the Federal Criminal Police Office to the General Directorate of Customs was the result of these same consultations (Doc. 03, p. 1023) – the outcome of a process that may be denoted as pathological learning.

In a memo of May 11, 2015, the responsible Public Security Division II 1 of the Federal Ministry of the Interior referred to the fundamental division of labor between the Ministry itself and the Federal Ministry of Finance in the fight against money laundering, terrorism, and organized crime and to the fact that "according to initial assessments, the installation of the FIU in the portfolio of the Federal Ministry of the Interior . . . could run counter to an effective evaluation of suspicious activity reports and ... could lead to essential indications and references to the aforementioned areas of crime remaining undetected" (Doc. 3, p. 120). In the course of detailed statements both from the bureaucracy of the Federal Ministry of the Interior and from the BKA and the FIU emphasizing both the indispensable integration of criminal investigation expertise and the understaffing of the FIU, the quantitative and structural personnel issues ultimately developed into the key criterion for a profound reorganization (Doc. 03, p. 92).

What was indispensable as an objective description of the problem turned out to be an argumentative advantage for the Federal Ministry of Finance in the course of deliberations with the Federal Ministry of the Interior. After all, the statements from the FIU, still part of the BKA and the jurisdiction of the Ministry of the Interior, seemed to confirm the weakness of the existing institutional arrangement. It would therefore have been all the more important for the management of the FIU and the Federal Ministry of the Interior to resolutely represent the professional interests of the FIU and the BKA. To all appearances, that support did not materialize (Doc. 03, p. 400). This must have strengthened the inclination of the leadership of the Ministry of the Interior, including the then Minister of the Interior himself, to get rid of a chronic problem with the FIU while at the same time to avoid a conflict with the Ministry of Finance. On November 2, 2015, the responsible state secretaries Emily Haber (Interior, or BMI) and Werner Gatzer (Finance, or BMF) reached the agreement to transfer the FIU to the BMF's portfolio (Doc. 03, p. 1023). State Secretary Haber also ensured that the written agreement in question included the assurance that the transfer of competencies would not entail any loss of information to the detriment of police investigations into suspected money laundering cases. In retrospect, however, this proved to be an inconsequential severability clause.

Harmful Political Self-commitment

The political self-commitment of the Federal Ministry of the Interior as a result of the agreement reached by the state secretaries of the BMI and BMF in November 2015 inevitably became a source of internal contradictions. The need to integrate the criminal police expertise and to ensure full data exchange with the future FIU would have required the participation of police experts in the decision-making processes for the transfer of the FIU to the BMF's portfolio. However, in the responsible working group only three experts of the state criminal investigation departments and one from the BKA were admitted –as advisory guests (Doc. 03, p. 2334). A separate working group of the state criminal investigation offices and the BKA drew up a 63-page statement in February 2016 criticizing the project of a FIU transfer to the Ministry of Finance as ill-conceived from the very outset (Doc. 03, p. 1466).

At this point, however, the proverbial point of no return had already been passed. On December 2, 2015, shortly after the terrorist attack on the Bataclan vaudeville theater in Paris on November 13, German Minister of Finance Wolfgang Schäuble had announced at a joint press conference with his French counterpart Michel Sapin in Berlin that Germany and France would jointly intensify the fight against terrorism and that the reorganization of the fight against money laundering with a transfer of the Financial Intelligence Unit to the portfolio of the Federal Minister of Finance would play an important role in this (BDZ, 2015). While the intra-administrative act of the State Secretary Agreement of November 2, 2015, had naturally remained publicly invisible and basically reversible, the FIU reorganization project became a matter of prestige with Schäuble's official announcement, not only for the Federal Minister of Finance, but for the federal government as a whole, and on an international level as well. The gap between intensive politicization of the relevant decision-making process and a lack of integration of the technical expertise of operational crime fighting thus became almost unbridgeable. Changes could still have been made during the actual legislative process. But this was not to happen either.

The key legislative process began in October 2016, with the implementation of the Fourth EU Money Laundering Directive being the key legislative issue (Doc. 18). This also meant that the time frame was fixed, as implementation had to take place by June 2017 (Doc. 17). Notwithstanding the fact that the political impetus for reorganizing the FIU came from an agreement between the two CDU federal ministers of finance and the interior, Schäuble and de Maizière, the parliamentary deliberations were characterized by great unity among the parties of the then grand coalition of CDU, CSU, and SPD. This was already expressed at the first reading of the bill in the Bundestag on March 23, 2017 (Doc. 19). The German government had to deal with a more critical constellation in the Bundesrat, the upper house of the German parliament, where the bill was first debated on March 31, 2017 (Doc. 20, p. 191f.). In the responsible committee of the Bundesrat, the concerns of the state criminal investigation offices were taken up, and the request to the federal government was

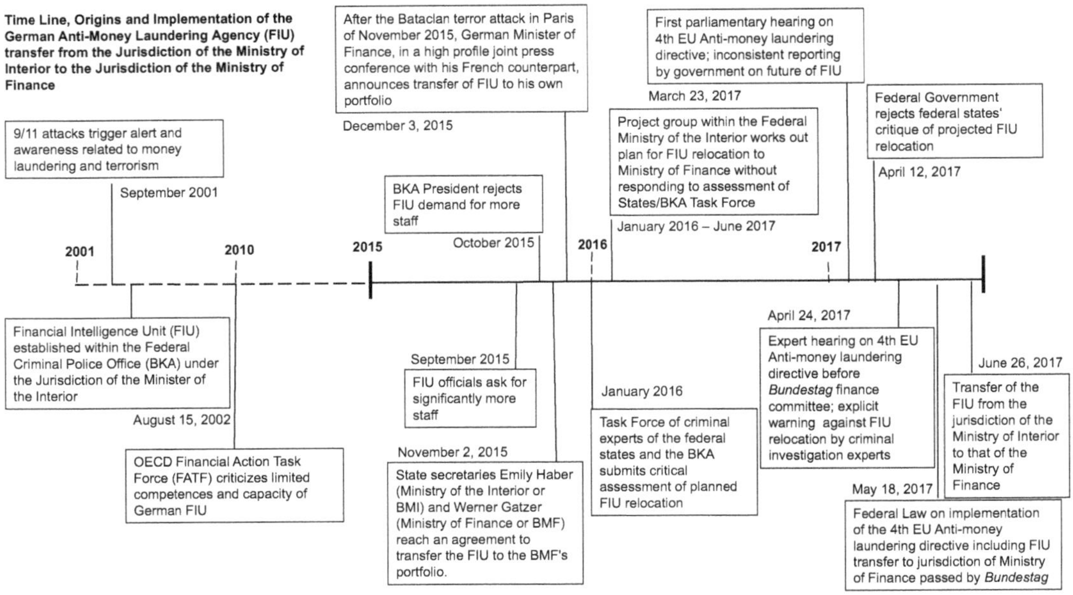

Figure 11.1 Time line, origins, and implementation of the German Anti-Money Laundering Agency (FIU) transfer from the jurisdiction of the Ministry of Interior to the jurisdiction of the Ministry of Finance.

that the legislative project be halted (Doc. 21, p. 11f.). This was rejected by the federal government in a statement dated April 12, 2017 (Doc. 21, p. 25). In this statement, the federal government emphasized, on the basis of a submission by the Federal Ministry of Finance, that the FIU would in future be assigned a filter function in the portfolio of the Federal Ministry of Finance, which would ensure that only cases significant to the fight against crime would be forwarded to the prosecution authorities and that this would ultimately also serve to relieve the burden on the state criminal investigation offices. Furthermore, the planned expansion of the staff of the new FIU in the General Directorate of Customs was emphasized.

On April 24, 2017, the draft bill was discussed by the Bundestag's Finance Committee (Doc. 22). The committee heard from various experts and association representatives, including the chairman of the Association of German Criminal Police Officers (BDK), Sebastian Fiedler, who commented on the draft law in detail and critically (Doc. 22, pp. 25–26). The BDK chairman referred, in line with the original line of argumentation of the specialist officers in the Federal Criminal Police Office, to the completely inadequate staffing levels in the current FIU, which is so dramatic that the colleagues involved in processing around 50,000 SARs per year see themselves placed in a situation "that takes them close to the edge of obstruction of justice in office" (Doc. 22, p. 25). He also pointed out that the customs administration lacks the expertise to perform the so-called filter function, as the future FIU was now supposed to do, and that this expertise could not be developed there in the short term (Doc. 22, p. 26).

The "Act on the Implementation of the Fourth EU Money Laundering Directive, the Implementation of the EU Money Transfer Regulation and the Reorganization of the Central Financial Transaction Investigation Authority" was passed by the Bundestag on May 18, 2017, and the transfer of the Financial Intelligence Unit to the portfolio of the Federal Ministry of Finance was completed on June 26, 2017 (Doc. 26). At the time of the transfer from the BMI to the BMF, the FIU was, according to the assessment of at least the Federal Ministry of the Interior, not operational in the form required by law (Doc. 5, p. 617). For its part, the Federal Ministry of Finance admitted that the final document of the steering group set up between the two ministries had not included the proposals of the Federal Criminal Police Office, where the FIU had been located until then (Doc. 5, p. 596). The planned software for data transmission could not initially be set up at the new FIU, and those required to report in the retail and banking sectors still had to submit SARs by fax (Doc. 05, p. 603). The steering group's final document comprised two volumes, only one of which was accepted by the representatives of the BMI and BKA, while the other was merely "taken note of" (Doc. 05, p. 616).

Immediately after the transfer of the FIU from the BKA to the General Customs Directorate and thus to the portfolio of the Federal Ministry of Finance, there was a massive decline in the number of money laundering reports submitted by the FIU to the state criminal investigation offices for further police processing (De Masi, 2019). Likewise, according to the assessment of the state criminal investigation offices, the quality of the reports had deteriorated significantly (De Masi, 2019). Federal states continued to complain that the SARs forwarded to them by the FIU were incomplete and sometimes unusable for the state criminal investigation offices, but above all that they were received significantly too late, so that crimes were subsequently concealed and perpetrators were able to evade prosecution all the more easily (Diehl, 2017). The state of Bavaria decided to review the SARs as a matter of principle and, if necessary, to conduct follow-up investigations (LT-Drucks. 18/4494, 2020, p. 2). Eighteen months after the FIU's transfer to the Federal Ministry of Finance was completed, as of January 31, 2019, a backlog of 22,281 unprocessed SARs had built up at the FIU. Of these, 2,795 related to suspected cases of terrorist financing (De Masi, 2019).

Conclusion: Lessons to Be Learned from Politicized Project Management

The German anti-money laundering reform is a borderline case of project behavior. It changed its character in the course of the project, not in the form of learning and increased adaptability but, on the contrary, as a case of counterproductive path dependency. The project could have been successful either on the basis of bureaucratic self-management below the radar of political attention or as a political project with sustainable guidance and hierarchical control. In the end, the project was neither. While the project itself was triggered by obvious deficiencies diagnosed by both national and international institutions, no assessment of root causes took place. Those causes were primarily connected to the vertical division of labor between the law enforcement authorities at the state and at the federal level. The creeping crisis in the fight against money laundering was mainly due to the inadequate staffing of the Financial Intelligence Unit at the Federal Criminal Police Office (BKA) within the jurisdiction of the Ministry of the Interior. Otherwise, however, the institutional unity of diverse but related tasks – combating organized crime and controlling illegal cash flows – was guaranteed. A significant increase in the FIU's workforce would have been the appropriate solution, which was precisely what the criminal investigation experts suggested. However, none of their superiors took the initiative for the unpopular measure of a large increase in personnel at a federal authority. Instead, the Ministry of Finance, which received the brunt of the criticism for the slowness of Germany's anti-money laundering efforts at the international level within the EU, promoted the project of relocating the FIU to its own jurisdiction. The BKA president, against the explicit warning of the agency's criminal investigation experts, did not object since he was going to get rid of a unit that had always been a source of trouble. When, in December 2015, German Minister of Finance Wolfgang Schäuble, in a joint press conference with his French counterpart Michel Sapin, announced the transfer of the Financial Intelligence Unit to his own portfolio, the point of no return was passed.

Relocating a highly specialized branch of criminal investigation from one ministry to another was a profoundly challenging yet manageable project. Its implementation would have required proactive boundary spanning by senior officials under the gentle pressure of knowledgeable political leadership. This, however, did not happen either. The lack of awareness of what was at stake was evident at both the political and bureaucratic levels. Money laundering is not just another type of tax fraud but the financial framework of most serious crimes connected with brutal violence and human rights violations. What the correspondence and emails between the Federal Ministry of Finance and the Federal Ministry of the Interior reveals, though, is that human safety concerns and the effectiveness of law enforcement remained entirely unaddressed in the relevant discussions (Doc. 1, p. 15). The same applies to parliamentary deliberations in the actual legislative process (Doc. 16, p. 26).

The consequence was systematic de-professionalization of the project. Turf struggles between the Federal Ministries of the Interior and Finance were settled through a consensus based on the lowest common denominator. Both ministries wanted to keep legislation low-key in order to circumvent a possible veto by the second legislative chamber, the Bundesrat, as the representative body of the Federal States, the *Länder*. It is at the state level, however, where law enforcement expertise on organized crime is located. Yet, law enforcement officials of the *Länder* were deliberately excluded from planning the project since their participation would have indicated that the *Länder* were indeed affected by the reform that would have made their formal consent in the Bundesrat indispensable. Thus, the absence of professional expertise in the planning phase paved the way for amateurism in the implementation phase. As a result, the relocation of the Financial Intelligence Unit disrupted the necessary integration of criminological and financial expertise in the fight against money laundering. Politicized project management did indeed degenerate into a mere unsorted stream of choice opportunities for various participants to get rid of selected problems and supposed solutions, as identified by Cohen et al. (1972), but the real problem was the absence of a policy entrepreneur who, according to John Kingdon's (1984) agenda setting theorem, was willing and capable to recouple the various streams to a problem-solving outcome.

From which follows: Just like any other type of strategic management, public project management requires a systematic connection between the project goal and the nuts and bolts of operational control (cf. Slevin & Pinto, 1987). This means that, contrary to what the mainstream literature suggests (see Ika et al., 2022, for an overview), the challenge of "grand challenge" project management (Ika & Munro, 2022) is not complexity per se. A necessary, yet not sufficient, condition for success is a common understanding of the project's mission among the stakeholders and a communication strategy that stimulates the spirit of a common cause. What challenges the necessary stakeholder consensus in public sector projects is the fact that the rationality of politicians and the rationality of administrative experts familiar with the task at hand are subject to different logics. Politicians need constituency support while experts need to maintain professional identity. When the German Finance Minister finally presented the project of a new federal authority to combat money laundering in autumn 2023 (BMF, 2023), the institutional integration of criminological and the finance-related expertise in the fight against money laundering remained unaddressed. Yet Germany managed to get the European Parliament's and Council's approval for hosting the seat of the EU's new Anti-Money Laundering Authority (AMLA) to be located in Frankfurt (BMF, 2024).

This suggests that the fundamental uncertainty in public sector project management is not due to a lack of knowledge but rather to the fact that the will of political actors to disregard existing expert knowledge is as unpredictable as their ability to get away with it through skillful communication. After all, as Henderson (2004) has pointed out, the difference between communicative encoding and decoding is an important aspect of project management. Encoding conveys more or less plausible messages, while decoding explains the meaning and purpose of messages. According to Henderson's results, encoding correlates clearly with sense making and satisfaction, while decoding correlates more strongly with the performance of project participants. This implies that a project's weak performance may be eclipsed by an erroneous but plausible narrative or encoded message, so that the need for positive identification and satisfaction prevents sober and realistic decoding – a variant of successful project failure (Seibel, 2023) that may remain viable as long as the message of alleged success remains uncontested.

References

Andrews, M. (2018). Public policy failure: "How often?" and "What is failure, anyway?" (CID Working Paper No. 344). Harvard University, Center for International Development (CID).

Baccarini, D. (1996). The concept of project complexity – a review. *International Journal of Project Management*, *14*(4), 201–204. DOI:10.1016/0263-7863(95)00093-3.

Bakhshi, J., Ireland, V., and Gorod, A. (2016). Clarifying the project complexity construct: Past, present and future. *International Journal of Project Management*, *34*(7), 1199–1213. DOI:10.1016/j.ijproman.2016.06.002.

Brierley, S., Lowande, K., Potter, R. A., and Toral, G. (2023). Bureaucratic politics: Blind spots and opportunities in political science. *Annual Review of Political Science*, *26*, 271–290. https://doi.org/10.1146/annurev-polisci-061621-084933.

BDZ. (2015). Terrorismusfinanzierung: Schäuble stärkt den Zoll. Stellungnahme zur Verkündung der Kompetenzübertragung der FIU durch Schäuble. Deutsche Zoll- und Finanzgewerkschaft. December 4. www.bdz.eu/medien/nachrichten/detail/news/terrorismusfinanzierung-schaeuble-staerkt-den-zoll.html.

BMF. (2022). Voller Einsatz gegen Finanzkriminalität. Bundesministerium der Finanzen. August 23. www.bundesfinanzministerium.de/Content/DE/Downloads/Internationales-Finanzmarkt/Geldwaesche/eckpunkte-schlagkraeftigere-bekaempfung-von-finanzkriminalitaet.pdf?__blob = publicationFile&v = 8.

BMF. (2023). Stepping up the fight against financial crime. Bundesministerium der Finanzen. October 11. www.bundesfinanzministerium.de/Content/EN/Standardartikel/Topics/Priority-Issues/Financial-Crime/fight-against-financial-crime.html.

BMF. (2024). Success for the European financial centre Frankfurt: Germany wins the race to host the EU's Anti-Money Laundering Authority (AMLA). Joint press release by the Federal Ministry of Finance, the Hessian state government and the city of Frankfurt. Bundesministerium der Finanzen. February 22. www.bundesfinanzministerium.de/Content/EN/Pressemitteilungen/2024/2024-02-22-european-financial-centre-frankfurt.html.

Cohen, M. D., March, J. G., and Olsen, J. P. (1972). A garbage can model of organizational choice. *Administrative Science Quarterly*, *17*, 1–25.

De Masi, F. (2019). Dauerkrise in der Geldwäschebekämpfung. April 16. www.fabio-de-masi.de/de/article/2293.dauerkrise-in-der-geldw%C3%A4schebek%C3%A4mpfung.html.

Deutsch, K. W. (1963). *The nerves of Government: Models of political communication and control*. The Free Press.

Diehl, J., and Siemens, A. (2020). Verdacht auf Strafvereitelung: Ermittler gehen gegen Zoll-Spezialeinheit vor. *Spiegel Panorama*. July 14. www.spiegel.de/panorama/justiz/verdacht-auf-strafvereitelung-ermittler-gehen-gegen-zoll-spezialeinheit-fiu-vor-a-8d657c7f-f570-4a16-85c0-82134da79905.

Diehl, J. (2017). Kritik an Schäubles BKA-Umbau: Risiko für die innere Sicherheit. *Spiegel Online*. April 26. www.spiegel.de/panorama/justiz/wolfgang-schaeuble-und-der-geplante-bka-umbau-risiko-fuer-die-innere-sicherheit-a-1144980.html.

Egidi, M., amd Marengo, L. (2004). Near-decomposability, organization, and evolution: Some note's on Herbert Simon's contribution (pp. 335–350). In M. Augier and J. G. March (eds.). *Models of a man. Essays in memory of Herbert A. Simon*. MIT Press.

FATF (2010). Mutual Evaluation Report Germany: Anti-Money Laundering and Combating the Financing of Terrorism. Financial Action Task Force. February 19. www.fatf-gafi.org/media/fatf/documents/reports/mer/MER%20Germany%20full.pdf.

FATF (2012). International Standards on Combating Money Laundering and the Financing of Terrorism & Proliferation. The FATF Recommendations. Financial Action Task Force, amended March 2022. www.fatf-gafi.org/media/fatf/documents/recommendations/pdfs/FATF%20Recommendations%202012.pdf.

FATF (2022). Mutual Evaluation Report Germany: Anti-Money Laundering and Counter-Terrorist Financing Measures. Financial Action Task Force. August 25. www.fatf-gafi.org/media/fatf/documents/reports/mer4/Mutual-Evaluation-Report-Germany-2022.pdf.

Henderson, L. S. (2004). Encoding and decoding communication competencies in project management – an exploratory study. *International Journal of Project Management*, *22*(6), 469–476.

Ika, L. A., Söderlund, J., Munro, L. T., and Landoni, P. (2020). Cross-learning between project management and international development: Analysis and research agenda. *International Journal of Project Management*, *38*(8), 548–558. https://doi.org/10.1016/j.ijproman.2020.10.005.

Ika, L. A., and Munro, L. T. (2022). Tackling grand challenges with projects: Five insights and a research agenda for project management theory and practice. *International Journal of Project Management*, *40*(6), 601–607. https://doi.org/10.1016/j.ijproman.2022.05.008.

Ika, L. A., and Pinto, J. K. (2022). The re-meaning of project success: Updating and recalibrating for a modern project management. *International Journal of Project Management*, *40*(7), 835–848. https://doi.org/10.1016/j.ijproman.2022.08.001.

Ika, L. A., Love, P. E. D., and Pinto, J. K. (2022). Moving beyond the Planning Fallacy: The emergence of a new principle of project behavior. *IEEE Transactions on Engineering Management*, *69*(6), 3310–3325. DOI:10.1109/TEM.2020.3040526.

Kingdon, J. W. (1984). *Agendas, alternatives and public policies*. Little, Brown & Co.

March, J. G., with the assistance of C. Heath (1991). *A primer on decision making: How decisions happen*. The Free Press.

March, J. G., and Simon, H. A. (1958). *Organizations*. Wiley.

Marle, F., and Vidal, L.-A. (2016). *Managing complex, high risk projects: A guide to basic and advanced project management*. Springer.

Martela, F. (2019). What makes self-managing organizations novel? Comparing how Weberian bureaucracy, Mintzberg's adhocracy, and self-organizing solve six fundamental problems of organizing. *Journal of Organization Design*, *8*(23). DOI:10.1186/s41469–019-0062-9.

Matinheikki, J., Aaltonen, K., and Walker, D. (2019). Politics, public servants, and profits: Institutional complexity and temporary hybridization in a public infrastructure alliance project. *International Journal of Project Management*, *37*(2), 298–317. https://doi.org/10.1016/j.ijproman.2018.07.004.

Pinto, J. K. (2000). Understanding the role of politics in successful project management. *International Journal of Project Management*, *18*(2), 85–91.

Polanyi, M. (1966). *The tacit dimension*. Routledge & Kegan Paul.

Seibel, W. (2015). Studying hybrids. Sectors and mechanisms. *Organization Studies*, *36*(6), 697–712.

Seibel, W. (2023). Successful failure (pp. 137–146). In A. Mica, M. Pawlak, A. Horolets, and P. Kubicki (eds.). *Routledge international handbook of failure*. Routledge.

Simon, H. A. (1962). The architecture of complexity. *Proceedings of the American Philosophical Society*, *106*(6), 467–482.

Slevin, D. P., and Pinto, J. K. (1987). Balancing strategy and tactics in project implementation. *Sloan Management Review*, 29(1), 33–41.

Tang, R. W., Qiu, X., and Zhang, M. W. (2018). Spanning the boundary of organisations. A systematic review of the inter-organisational boundary-spanning literature (pp. 181–217). In M. Zhang (ed.). *Trust building and boundary spanning in cross-border management*. Taylor & Francis.

Tushman, M. L., and Scanlon, T. J. (1981). Boundary spanning individuals: Their role in information transfer and their antecedents. *The Academy of Management Journal*, *24*(2), 289–305. https://doi.org/10.2307/255842.

Wynn, C., Smith, L., and Killen, C. (2021). How power influences behavior in projects: A theory of planned behavior perspective. *Project Management Journal*, *52*(6), 607–621. https://doi.org/10.1177/87569728211052592.

Zoll (2022). Aufgaben des Zolls. Generalzolldirektion. www.zoll.de/DE/Der-Zoll/Aufgaben-des-Zolls/aufgaben-des-zolls_node.html.

Documentation through German Freedom of Information Request (Informationsfreiheitsgesetz, IFG)

Doc. 01: IFG (2021a). Anfrage nach Informations freiheitsgesetz: *Neuorganisation FIU* (#2786). ÖS II 1 – 50004-9-15. Geldwäsche-Gesetzgebung, Umsetzung 4. Geldwäsche-Richtlinie. Ministry of the Interior and Community. 14.06.2016-20.07.2017.

Doc. 02: IFG (2021b). Anfrage nach Informations freiheitsgesetz: *Neuorganisation FIU* (#2786). ÖS II 1 – 50004-45-6. Geldwäsche – FIU Financial Intelligence Unit, AG Kripo. Ministry of the Interior and Community. 02.12.2016-20.06.2017.

Doc. 03: IFG (2021c). Anfrage nach Informations freiheitsgesetz: *Neuorganisation FIU* (#2786). ÖS II 1 – 50004-45-10 Geldwäsche – FIU Financial Intelligence Unit, Ausgliederung der FIU. Ministry of the Interior and Community. 08.05.2015-28.07.2017.

Doc. 04: IFG (2021d). Anfrage nach Informations freiheitsgesetz: *Neuorganisation FIU* (#2786). ÖS II 1 – 50004-45-14. Geldwäsche – FIU Financial Intelligence Unit, Projektgruppe FIU-Verlagerung. Ministry of the Interior and Community. 13.05.2016-20.07.2017.

Doc. 05: IFG (2021e). Anfrage nach Informations freiheitsgesetz: *Neuorganisation FIU* (#2786). ÖS II 1 – 50004-45-15 Geldwäsche – FIU Financial Intelligence Unit, Lenkungsausschuss FIU-Verlagerung. Ministry of the Interior and Community. 25.05.2016-13.06.2017.

Doc. 06: IFG (2021f). Anfrage nach Informations freiheitsgesetz: *Informationen zur Zentralstelle für F inanztransaktionsuntersuchungen (FIU).* Anhang 1 4_Dok. 2015_1107920. Ministry of Finance. 30.11.2015; 16.12.2015.

Doc. 07: IFG (2021g). Anfrage nach Informations freiheitsgesetz: *Informationen zur Zentralstelle für F inanztransaktionsuntersuchungen (FIU).* Anhang 2 11_Dok. 2015_1180761. Ministry of Finance. 14.12.2015.

Doc. 08: IFG (2021h). Anfrage nach Informations freiheitsgesetz: *Informationen zur Zentralstelle für F inanztransaktionsuntersuchungen (FIU).* Anhang 3 17_Dok. 2016_0319896. Ministry of Finance. 15.01.2016; 09.03.2016.

Doc. 09: IFG (2021i). Anfrage nach Informations freiheitsgesetz: *Informationen zur Zentralstelle für F inanztransaktionsuntersuchungen (FIU).* Anhang 4 20_Dok. 2016_0319923. Ministry of Finance. 2016.

Doc. 10: IFG (2021j). Anfrage nach Informations freiheitsgesetz: *Informationen zur Zentralstelle für F inanztransaktionsuntersuchungen (FIU).* Anhang 5 35_Dok. 2016_0321029. Ministry of Finance. 2016.

Doc. 11: IFG (2021k). Anfrage nach Informations freiheitsgesetz: *Informationen zur Zentralstelle für F inanztransaktionsuntersuchungen (FIU).* Anhang 6 36_Dok. 2016_0321029. Ministry of Finance. 09.02.2016.

Doc. 12: IFG (2021l). Anfrage nach Informations freiheitsgesetz: *Informationen zur Zentralstelle für F inanztransaktionsuntersuchungen (FIU).* Anhang 7 43_Dok. 2016_0321082. Ministry of Finance. 2016.

Doc. 13: IFG (2021m). Anfrage nach Informations freiheitsgesetz: *Informationen zur Zentralstelle für F inanztransaktionsuntersuchungen (FIU).* Anhang 8 44_Dok. 2016_0321082. Ministry of Finance. 21.03.2016

Doc. 14: IFG (2021n). Anfrage nach Informations freiheitsgesetz: *Informationen zur Zentralstelle für F inanztransaktionsuntersuchungen (FIU).* Anhang 9 46_Dok. 2016_0321094. Ministry of Finance. 2016.

Doc. 15: IFG (2021o). Anfrage nach Informations freiheitsgesetz: *Informationen zur Zentralstelle für F inanztransaktionsuntersuchungen (FIU).* Anhang 10 44_Dok. 2016_0321094. Ministry of Finance. 2016.

Public Documents

Doc. 16: BR-Drucksache 217/02 (2002). Bundesrat, 15 March 2002. https://dserver.bundestag.de/brd/2002/0217-02.pdf.

Doc. 17: Directive (EU) 2015/849 of the European Parliament and of the Council of 20 May 2015 on the prevention of the use of the financial system for the purposes of money laundering or terrorist financing, amending Regulation (EU) No 648/2012 of the European Parliament and of the Council, and repealing Directive 2005/60/EC of the European Parliament and of the Council and Commission Directive 2006/70/EC (Text with EEA relevance) OJ L 141, 5 June 2015, p. 73–117. http://data.europa.eu/eli/dir/2015/849/oj.

Doc. 18: BR-Drucksache 182/17 (2017). Bundesrat, 23 February 2017. https://dserver.bundestag.de/brd/2017/0182-17.pdf.

Doc. 19: BT-Drucksache 18/11555 (2017). Deutscher Bundestag, 17 March 2017. https://dserver.bundestag.de/btd/18/115/1811555.pdf.

Doc. 20: BR-Plenarprotokoll 956 (2017). Bundesrat, 31 March 2017. https://dserver.bundestag.de/brp/956.pdf.

Doc. 21: BT-Drucksache 18/11928 (2017). Deutscher Bundestag, 12 April 2017. https://dserver.bundestag.de/btd/18/119/1811928.pdf.

Doc. 22: BT-Plenarprotokoll 18/110 (2015). Deutscher Bundestag, 12 June 2015. https://dserver.bundestag.de/btp/18/18110.pdf.

Doc. 23: BT-Drucksache 18/12405 (2017). Deutscher Bundestag, 17 May 2017. https://dserver.bundestag.de/btd/18/124/1812405.pdf.

Doc. 24: BT-Plenarprotokoll 18/234 (2017). Deutscher Bundestag, 18 May 2017. https://dserver.bundestag.de/btp/18/18234.pdf.

Doc. 25: BR-Drucksache 389/17. Bundesrat, 19 May 2017. https://dserver.bundestag.de/brd/2017/0389-17.pdf.

Doc. 26: Drucksache 389/17 (2017). Bundesrat, 19 May 2017. https://dserver.bundestag.de/brd/2017/0389-17.pdf.

LT-Drucks. 18/4494 (2020). Bayerischer Landtag, 14 February 2020. www1.bayern.landtag.de/www/ElanTextAblage_WP18/Drucksachen/Schriftliche%20Anfragen/18_0004494.pdf.

CHAPTER 12

Project Misbehavior in Infrastructure Projects

Mega-Projects for Mega-Corruption

REGIS SIGNOR and PETER E. D. LOVE

Introduction

> "If we fail to do all that in us lies to stamp out corruption, we cannot escape our share of responsibility for the guilt." Theodore Roosevelt, in his third annual message to the Senate and House of Representatives. (December 7, 1903)

This chapter contributes to the ongoing discourse of project behavior by making sense of the realities of corruption and collusion by uncovering their presence in real-life projects. Hirschman (1967) refers to project behavior as an explanation and anticipation of the "successes and failures and understanding systematic veerings from pre-assigned paths, propensities toward specific difficulties and opportunities for special payoffs" of projects (p. 4). Simply put, project behavior is about "how projects work," "behave," or "take different and complex out-turns" (Ika et al., 2022, p. 3311). The Hiding Hand principle of Hirschman (1967) underpins this view of project behavior. Still, it is assumed that it arises due to misjudgments, ignorance and "offsetting underestimations of knowledge and creativity" (Ika et al., 2022, p. 3317).

But corruption and collusion in the public procurement of infrastructure projects do not arise out of ignorance or "offsetting knowledge and complexity." Instead, they occur due to willful and criminal decisions and actions taken to deceive and exploit processes for monetary gain. Their causes vary due to contextual factors within different countries (Ika et al., 2022, p. 8). So, within the context of the four principles of project behavior (i.e., Hiding, Protecting, Malevolent, and Passive Hands) identified by Anheier (2016), corruption and collusion are both aligned with the notion of the Malevolent Hand (i.e., willful and deceitful acts), which forms an integral part of Flyvbjerg's (2018) *Planning Fallacy* explanation of "how projects work" and is also considered by Ika et al. (2022) in their proposed *Fifth Hand* principle of project behavior.

The presence of corruption is a sign that public officials have abandoned the rule of law and indicates illegitimacy and instability within the entire governing system (Garcia-Rodríguez et al., 2022; Pontes & Anselmo, 2022; Signor et al., 2023). In fact, corruption is a dishonest or criminal act that "erodes trust, weakens democracy, hampers economic development, and further exacerbates inequality, poverty, social division and environmental" degradation (Transparency International, 2022). Corruption is an immoral abuse of power, not simply the neglect or omission of expected or required actions, typically associated with failure. So, within the context of this chapter, we associate corruption with "project misbehavior" to reinforce its nefarious rackets of organized crime.

Collusion "involves a horizontal relationship between bidders in a public procurement" that "conspire to remove the competition from the process," typically through bid rigging (OECD, 2010, p. 9). In this instance, the bidders (i.e., cartel) determine who will win an auction. Then in future auctions, they rotate the winner between themselves. While "corruption and collusion are distinct problems with public procurement, they frequently occur in tandem in construction and have mutually reinforcing effects. They are best viewed, therefore, as concomitant threats to the integrity of public procurement" (OECD, 2010, p. 9).

Within the project management literature, limited empirical research exists examining corruption and collusion due to their clandestine existence and the difficulties associated with obtaining robust and reliable data to prove their existence (Signor et al., 2023). However, interest is growing in this area as measures to deal with corruption and collusion effectively have been ineffective in construction (Lehtinen et al., 2022). As for governments, the problem is proving the presence of corruption and collusion (Signor et al., 2019; Garcia-Rodríguez et al., 2022; Signor et al., 2023).

This chapter uses a case study approach to unearth the interplay and nuances of corruption and collusion that came to light from two police investigations (i.e., our unit of analysis) that examined the construction of several mega-projects in Brazil. The underlying rationale for selecting these cases is twofold: (1) the global attention that they have received from the media and their negative impact on the economic and social well-being of Brazil and (2) the projects were "sold" to the people of Brazil by the incumbent government as agents of change with promises of improved economic prosperity and the strengthening of Brazil's hegemony in soccer.

Mega-Projects for Mega-Corruption

We use the framing of "mega-projects for mega-corruption" to present our cases to emphasize the sheer magnitude of the immorality that occurred and how the Malevolent Hand played out in the two cases we present. Affording a context within which Malevolent Hand operates provides the understanding required to develop robust mechanisms for identifying and dealing with corruption, which has been missing from the project management literature.

The first case we examine is Petróleo Brasileiro SA, better known as Petrobras, Brazil's state-owned multi-national corporation, which was almost bankrupted from four of its commissioned mega-projects due to corruption. Then, we consider several soccer stadiums built for the Federation Internationale de Football Association (FIFA) 2014 World Cup in the second case. From the evidence provided below and drawing on the works of Pontes and Anselmo (2022), we conclude that such stadiums were constructed for no reason other than to channel millions of dollars in bribes into the pockets of politicians from construction companies who solicited contracts to build them. Examples of the evidence used to support the presence of corruption are presented in Table 12.1.

We now examine the corruption stemming from Petrobras' projects and police investigation known as "Operation Car Wash" (*Operação Lava Jato* in Portuguese), which has received global media attention and is the subject of a film entitled *Federal Police: No One is Above the Law* (*Polícia Federal: A Lei é para Todos*) and a mini-series called *The Mechanism* available on Netflix.

The Failure of a State-Owned Multi-national Corporation

A group of 16 leading national construction companies formed a cartel known as the "League of 16" and decided to collude and divide a series of mega-projects delivered by Petrobras. The inaugurated collusive scheme that unfolded has been identified as the world's largest-ever global foreign bribery case (US Department of Justice, 2016; Pontes & Anselmo, 2022). The corruptive scheme was initially revealed by the Brazilian Federal Police's Operation Car Wash investigation.

As the investigation gained momentum, the extent and ramifications of the corruption began to unfold, involving several countries in Latin America and Africa, reaching public officials at all levels, including several presidents (Moro, 2021). The scheme involved financial transactions in more than twenty nations (Dallagnol, 2017), including the United States, where the Brazilian construction company Odebrecht and one of its subsidiaries pleaded guilty to conspiracy to violate anti-bribery provisions of the US Foreign Corrupt Practices Act. Consequently, Odebrecht agreed to

Table 12.1 Case comparison of evidence

Evidence	Petrobras	FIFA World Cup
Circumstantial	Disregard of the stage-gate investment decision process led to economically unviable refineries (negative NPV)	Construction of unnecessary stadiums in cities without major soccer teams
Internal documents/ confessions	Executive 1 accelerated the schedule for completing COMPERJ, resulting in procurement commencing, in some cases, without sufficient technical designs and providing the bribe-paying contractors with lucrative contracting opportunities (US DOJ, 2018, p. A-8) With downstream returns globally subdued even for cost-competitive projects due to the immense oversupply in the refining market, we strongly believe Petrobras' new refineries are uneconomical. (Brasil, 2018a, p. 87)	In the understanding of the Signatories, due to the size [of specific] stadiums to be built and/or renovated for the [FIFA] World Cup, these sports facilities would not attract enough patrons to cover their maintenance and administration costs and generate profits after the event; that is, even when regional and/or national championships are held at them. (Brasil, 2016, p. 79)

pay at least US$3.5 billion in global penalties (US Department of Justice, 2016). For example, in several countries in the Americas, this case is called the "Odebrecht Case" (Durand, 2019; Campos et al., 2021; Yuhui, 2021).

In the Beginning: An Accidental Discovery

In the early 2000s, Petrobras began planning four mega-projects to expand its refining capacity: (1) the Rio de Janeiro Petrochemical Complex (COMPERJ), (2) the Abreu e Lima Refinery (RNEST), and (3) the Premium I and II refineries. As these ventures progressed, the budget allocated for these four projects increased from US$12 billion to a staggering US$80 billion between 2007 and 2015 (Brasil, 2018a). But, since the budget increase made the economic projections of the refineries unviable, it can be concluded that the costs of these projects did not necessarily increase due to technically justifiable scope changes but something sinister – corruption (Brasil, 2018a; Pontes & Anselmo, 2022).

The unveiling of corruption in these mega-projects happened accidentally. In 2013, the Brazilian Federal Police began investigating an illicit money laundering network operating from a car wash, hence the coining of Operation Car Wash (Netto, 2016). During this investigation, it was discovered that a former Petrobras director had been gifted a luxury armoured car by the scheme's head money changer (Dallagnol, 2017). As the investigation continued, a complex web of criminal activity began to unfold, which led to corruption at Petrobras being unearthed and brought to the attention of the Brazilian people.

The Investigation: Confessions and Scientific Evidence

The corruption in Petrobras' mega-projects was largely confirmed through investigations, confessions, and scientific evidence (US Department of Justice, 2016, 2018; Dallagnol, 2017; Signor et al., 2017, 2019, 2020; Vallim, 2018). Documents seized by the Brazilian Federal Police show that the level of organization within the colluding group was such that they even drafted regulations for the division of the "loot" (Pontes & Anselmo, 2022). The criminal nature of the activity led these regulations to be codified, simulating sports championships and games such as "soccer," "tennis," or "bingo." The cartel decided among themselves who would be the "winners" and prepared spreadsheets for the division of projects ("prizes"). An extract from an anti-trust leniency agreement between company executives and the Administrative Council for Economic Defense (CADE) is partially reproduced in Table 12.2 (Brasil, 2015, 2017a).

When more than one construction company wanted to secure the same project, or when it was necessary to include outsiders appointed by corrupt politicians or who could jeopardize the scheme, the

Table 12.2 Extract from the contract division worksheet

Final Settlement Proposal for Bingo in Rio de Janeiro [COMPERJ]		
No.	**Prize**	**Players [winners]**
1	UDA + UDV [Atmospheric and vacuum distillation unit]	Consortium SK/PRO/VX
2	Coque + Arm. Coque [Production and storage of petroleum coke]	Consortium TC/AG
3	02 HDTs [two hydrotreatment units]	Consortium QG/IE/GAL
4–13	. . .	. . .
14	ETDI [Industrial waste treatment station]	Consortium CC/SCH

Note: From the secret meeting held between the collusive contractors on 25 April 2009.

solution of the colluders was often the formation of consortia between them. For each mega-project auction, the company or consortium selected to win would provide an overpriced bid value. Then, this value would be communicated to other bidders, who provided cover bids (i.e., higher values). In Odebrecht's words (US Department of Justice, 2016):

> As part of the scheme, ODEBRECHT participated in a series of meetings with other construction companies to evaluate and divide up future contracts for Petrobras projects among the companies (together, the Cartel Companies). Once it was determined which company or companies should be responsible for a certain project, as well as the price that Petrobras felt was appropriate for the particular project, it was agreed that only the pre-determined company would present a qualifying bid and that the other Cartel Companies would present proposals that would ensure the predetermined company's winning bid. In this manner, the Cartel Companies rotated the available Petrobras contracts between them. (p. 13)

The absence of any vestige of competition enabled contractors to adopt an energetic strategy to boost overpricing. Petrobras' procurement process was based on a Pre-Tender Estimate (PTE) calculated by its engineering department. During the auctioning phase, bids that exceeded the PTE by more than 20 percent were summarily disqualified. Knowing this, all the collusive contractors presented bids far above this limit, forcing Petrobras to increase its PTE and carry out new bidding rounds until the pre-determined company was finally declared the auction's winner by an artificially overestimated amount.

Table 12.3 exemplifies one of these cases in which, according to a winner, after this artifice had been used twice, the company ended up being contracted for the negotiated value of US$1.113 billion,[1] still 25 percent higher than Petrobras' initial PTE (Brasil, 2017a; Signor et al., 2017). The coordinated and repeated actions by the colluders resulted in an overall increase in Petrobras' auction prices.

Proving Collusion

Signor et al. (2017) analyzed 77 Petrobras' projects tendered during the cartel's operation period. For the 22 rigged auctions, the relationship between the 73 collusive bids and their respective PTEs followed a normal distribution with parameters ($\bar{x}$ = 0.357; s = 0.232). Contrastingly, for the 55 competitive auctions, the relationship between the 439 honest bids and their respective PTEs followed a normal distribution ($\bar{x}$ = 0.082; s = 0.192) (Figure 12.1).

The averages of the two groups of bids are different, as shown by the t-test, indicating that it is practically impossible for the distributions to

[1] When the source documents do not express the amounts in US$, exchange rates in this chapter shall be referred to December 31st of the year in question, in accordance with Petrobras' respective financial statements.

Table 12.3 Bid and rebid for the "Prize 2" of Table 12.2

Bidders	Bid (July 17, 2009) (in millions)	Re-bid (September 22, 2009) (in millions)	Contract (direct negotiation) (in millions)
Consortium TC/AG	R$2,878 US$1,653	R$2,488 US$1,429	R$1,938 US$1,113
Consortium CN/UT/MJ	R$2,952 US$1,695	R$2,598 US$1,492	–
Contractor VX	R$3,356 US$1,928	–	–
Consortium QG/GAL/IE	–	R$2,771 US$1,592	–
Petrobras PTE	**R$1,552** **US$891**	**R$1,680** **US$965**	–

Note: The production and storage of petroleum coke at COMPERJ had previously been allocated to the consortium formed by the construction companies TC and AG.

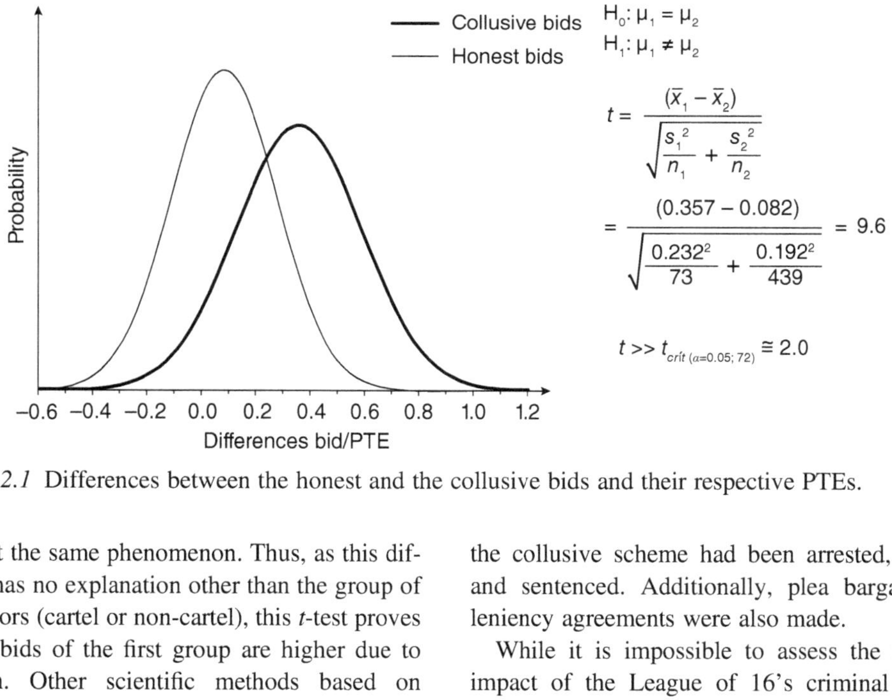

Figure 12.1 Differences between the honest and the collusive bids and their respective PTEs.

represent the same phenomenon. Thus, as this difference has no explanation other than the group of competitors (cartel or non-cartel), this *t*-test proves that the bids of the first group are higher due to collusion. Other scientific methods based on "econometric" and "order statistics" analysis have also proved this collusive behavior (Signor et al., 2019, 2023).

Despite the inherent inertia within the Brazilian judicial process, the trials resulting from the Operation Car Wash investigation were urgently met due to the seriousness of the criminal acts committed. By 2022, many people involved in the collusive scheme had been arrested, trialled, and sentenced. Additionally, plea bargains and leniency agreements were also made.

While it is impossible to assess the financial impact of the League of 16's criminal actions, forensic reports by the Brazilian Federal Police in 2016 estimated that Petrobras directly lost R$19.9 billion (US$6.1 billion) in dozens of its contracts due to collusion alone. As a result, the Brazilian Public Prosecution's Office filed criminal proceedings in April 2018 to recover this stolen money. When writing this chapter, Criminal Action Number 5028838-35.2018.4.04.7000 was still awaiting sentence in the Thirteenth Federal Criminal Court of Curitiba, where the main cases of Operation Car Wash were tried.

The Aftermath and Unearthing of Strategic Misrepresentation and Willful Misconduct

Strategic misrepresentation (i.e., deception), a key component of the Planning Fallacy, arose during the investment decision-making process of Petrobras' four mega-projects enabling corruption to manifest. In essence, *strategic misrepresentation* is the tendency to deliberately and systematically distort or misstate information for strategic purposes (Jones & Euske, 1991).

After discovering and proving that collusion had occurred, it was realized that there was never any technical or economic justification for Petrobras to procure the four mega-projects and double its refining capacity. While demand for fuel had not been forecasted to double until 2030, Petrobras' administrators systematically distorted the justification process to ensure projects were procured to meet this requirement by 2015 (Brasil, 2018a). The ensuing mismatch between demand and supply meant that the new refineries would operate below their installed capacity resulting in a negative net present value (NPV) for these projects. Put simply, the mega-projects were planned and constructed to make a loss! (Brasil, 2018a; Pontes & Anselmo, 2022). As a result, Petrobras' net debt exceeded one hundred billion dollars in 2015 (more than five times the earnings before interest, taxes, depreciation and amortization), leading to the need to divest assets to reduce its indebtedness (Petrobras, 2015).

Faced with the realization of such debt, the Brazilian Court of Accounts began to examine the recklessness of this decision-making behavior that threatened the financial viability of Brazil's state-owned multi-national company. The investigation of the company's administrators' decisions revealed that they failed to fulfill their fiduciary duties in a continuous series of commissive and omissive acts. The errors were so gross and insistent that the Brazilian Court of Accounts even classified the decisions of those responsible for four mega-projects as "willful misconduct" as was stated (Brasil, 2018a):

> The members of Petrobras' Board of Directors were fully aware of the high possibility of adverse results, but even so, they took the risk of carrying out bold business plans, compromising the company's perpetuity. (p. 102)

Decision-making and the Manifestation of Project Misbehavior

Aiming to help better understand how corruption manifested in the four mega-projects coming to life, a chronological analysis of relevant facts and successive decisions taken by Petrobras is presented in Figure 12.2 and explained below. These decisions involved managers of all levels, the Petrobras' board of directors, executive board and administrative council, and high-ranked politicians (Brasil, 2018a; US Department of Justice, 2018). Naturally, both global shareholders and Brazilian taxpayers were disadvantaged stakeholders.

As mentioned above, in 2006, Petrobras announced that it planned to invest US$12 billion to increase its oil processing capacity. In the same year, the company processed approximately 1,700k barrels per day (bpd), corresponding with the expected demand of the Brazilian market.

Anticipating the growth of this market, the company arranged to increase its processing capacity to around 2,900k bpd by 2020 (an increase of 1,200k bpd or 70 percent). It so happens that, in 2007, the Brazilian Energy Research Company projected that the increase in demand would take place at a slower rate, and thus, this 70 percent increase in refining capacity would only be necessary for 2030, meaning that Petrobras was advancing a massive investment by about ten years (Brasil, 2018a).

In 2008, the US mortgage crisis led to expectations of lower growth in the world economy. Petrobras detected the reversal of the upward trend in the price of oil. Given the prediction of lower global growth, the oil price fell in the second half of the year, from US$93.89 per barrel at the end of 2007 to US$41.76 per barrel at the end of 2008, a 56 percent fall (Petrobras, 2008). However, to make things worse, in the same year, Petrobras launched a new investment plan that was inexplicably more aggressive than its previous one: the

Year	Facts
2004	• Petrobras began planning the expansion of its refining capacity.
2006	• Petrobras plans to increase its oil processing capacity by 70% by 2020, at a cost of US$ 12 billion.
2007	• The Brazilian Energy Research Company projected that this 70% increase in refining capacity would only be needed for 2030.
2008	• US mortgage crisis; • Drop in oil prices; • Petrobras' investment plan brought forward to 2015.
2009	• The four mega-projects' budget rises to US$60 billion; • An independent consultancy contracted by Petrobras claims that the new refineries are uneconomical; • The Brazilian Federal Court of Accounts recommends the interruption of the works (Petrobras ignores the recommendation).
2010	• Petrobras closes a global public offering raising nearly US$70 billion in capital from the Brazilian, US and international markets; • Credit Suisse publishes a report stating that Petrobras' new refineries were uneconomical.
2013	• Operation Car Wash begins its initially secret investigation.
2014	• Operation Car Wash becomes public and starts raids; • Petrobras recognizes a loss due to corruption of almost US$50 billion.
2015	• Petrobras abandons the construction of Premium I and Premium II refineries due to debt accumulation.
2016	• Brazilian Federal Police estimates a direct loss of US$ 6.1 billion in dozens of Petrobras contracts due to collusion alone; • Odebrecht agrees to pay at least $3.5 billion in global fines; • Petrobras' market value drops by almost 90% compared to 2008.
2017	• The Brazilian Court of Accounts points the 'willful misconduct' of the Petrobras' Board of Directors; • The company recognizes the corruption in an US lawsuit.

Figure 12.2 Summary of relevant facts.

1,200k bpd increase in refining capacity was brought forward to 2015. In Petrobras' own words (Petrobras, 2008):

> The 2009–2013 Business Plan provides investments of US$174.4 billion; an increase of 55% compared to the previous […]. Despite the international economic crisis and instability in oil prices, Petrobras has ambitious goals for growth, since it has a portfolio of well-structured projects and high return. (p. 7)

Petrobras' administrators disrespected the company's investment proceedings to implement these ambitious growth goals. They disregarded its stage-gate investment decision process (i.e., identification of the opportunity, conceptual design, basic design, execution and closing), even though it had been demonstrated that the four mega-projects faced a risk of negative NPV. This five-year anticipation generated cost increases and led to other technical errors, such as the advance purchase of critical equipment that was never used (Brasil, 2018a, 2020, 2021). Here is the caveat that Petrobras itself admitted in its "Statement of Facts" (US Department of Justice, 2018):

> Executive 1, Executive 2, and Manager 1 also each received millions of dollars in bribes from contractors that obtained business from Petrobras in association with the COMPERJ project. In exchange, among other things, Manager 1 leaked confidential information regarding certain projects that were used to review bid proposals, and Executive 1 accelerated the schedule for completing COMPERJ, resulting in procurement commencing, in some cases, without sufficient technical designs, and providing the bribe-paying contractors with lucrative contracting opportunities. (p. A-8)

In 2009, the budget of the four mega-projects was already approaching US$60 billion, and their unitary refining capital expenditure (CAPEX) was considered excessively high. An independent consultancy contracted by Petrobras in 2009 made the following comment (Brasil, 2018a):

> With downstream returns globally subdued even for cost-competitive projects, due to the immense oversupply in the refining market, we strongly believe Petrobras' new refineries are uneconomical. (p. 87)

Fittingly, the Brazilian Court of Accounts recommended the stoppage of work on these contracts (Brasil, 2018a, 2020). Despite the negative NPV and the recommendation to stop work on these projects, Petrobras still proceeded to procure them.

In 2010, Petrobras announced that it would invest US$224 billion in several projects between 2010 and 2014 (Petrobras, 2010). To finance these mega-projects, the company offered equity securities to investors. As a result, Petrobras became the world's third-largest energy company by market capitalization (Petrobras, 2010). When providing evidence to the US Department of Justice (2018) about the raising of capital investment, Petrobras commented:

> In or around September 2010, Petrobras closed on a global public offering of equity securities, raising nearly US$70 billion in capital from the Brazilian, US, and international capital markets [...]. The primary goals of the 2010 Offering were to (1) finance the purchase of pre-salt exploration and production rights in the Brazilian pre-salt basin; and (2) finance a portion of Petrobras's planned investment program. (p. A-11)

However, this investment program was not planned wisely. Table 12.4 provides an analysis after Petrobras' capitalization, when a global investment company also warned the market about the high CAPEX of the planned projects. As can be seen, the CAPEX of the new Brazilian refineries averaged US$40,725/bpd, which was more than double the global average and over four times the approximate US$9,000/bpd of the most efficient refineries (Brasil, 2018a).

The significant increases in future expenditures led to questions about this aggressive investment policy by Petrobras, both by the investment market and by some participants of the company's board of directors. The increase in the costs of these mega-projects and the economic scenario made it clear that these projects could be uneconomical. However, despite some in-house dissonant voices, the bases of investment policy were maintained until, in 2014, Operation Car Wash unveiled the scandal that would send a shock throughout Brazil and the world.

According to Petrobras' documentation, in 2014, the company was well aware that the high levels of investment in new projects had significantly increased the company's net debt by 52 percent. In January 2015, Petrobras abandoned the construction of its Premium I and Premium II refineries due to debt accumulation. This decision resulted in a charge of US$1.2 billion recognized in other expenses to write off all capitalized costs with respect to those mega-projects alone (Petrobras, 2014). As a general result, Petrobras'

Table 12.4 Extract of refining costs in different projects worldwide by CAPEX

Refinery	Country	Company	Startup	Capacity (kbpd)	Cost (million US$)	CAPEX per bpd (US$)
1. Jamnagar	India	Reliance	2008	660	6,000	9,091
2. Qingdao	China	Sinopec	2008	200	1,875	9,375
3–10	...	...	...	...	...	...
12. Sandino-Bolivar	Nicaragua	PDVSA/Petronic	2012	150	4,000	26,667
Global average						**18,199**
Premium I	Brazil	Petrobras	2014	600	19,800	33,000
Premium II	Brazil	Petrobras	2017	300	11,100	37,000
Abreu e Lima	Brazil	Petrobras	2012	230	12,000	52,174
Petrobras' average						**40,725**

financial statements recognized that the differences between the "book value" and the "fair value" of the assets affected by corruption represented an aggregate loss of almost fifty billion dollars for the company (Petrobras, 2014).

The Politics of Corruption and Rules of the Game

In addition to the money stolen by corruption, the waste of valuable resources due to poor investment decisions contributed to plunging Petrobras' market value, from nearly R$500 billion (US$214 billion) in 2008 to R$73 billion (US$22 billion) in 2016. In successive years, in which the accounting results were negative, there was no dividend distribution to shareholders among the Brazilian population (Brasil, 2018a). The former federal judge Sergio Moro, who tried most of the Operation Car Wash cases, made the following comment (Moro, 2021):

> [Corruption] destroys competition and distorts the investment of public and private money. Public investments in a system of corruption are directed to projects and services that generate opportunities for the payment of bribes. The famous "cathedrals in the desert" appear, that is, pharaonic works or investments that do not make sense from the point of view of economic or social efficiency. Companies, in turn, neglect investment in innovation and productivity since what is important is "crony capitalism," that is, proximity to public administration through non-republican relationships to get business. (p. 76)

In a similar vein, the public prosecutor who led the Operation Car Wash team made the following remark (Dallagnol, 2017):

> The bribes distort public policies, which become inefficient. Corruption directs the government to acquire products and services that provide private gains – even if more costly or unnecessary. (p. 44)

Apart from the direct financial losses incurred by corruption, other serious related problems include the loss of efficiency and quality, increased waste, and loss of reliability (Locatelli et al., 2017). Moreover, corruption represents an institutionalized attack on democracy, mainly when politicians' election campaigns are financed by organizations that expect their interests to be served if elected to public office (Netto, 2016; Pontes & Anselmo, 2022). This situation was found to have arisen during the Operation Car Wash investigation.

According to one of the construction companies involved in the League of 16 "it is a great fallacy to say that there are donations for [political] campaigns in Brazil. In fact, they are real loans to be charged at high interest when they [politicians] are in office" (Netto, 2016, p. 64). As a matter of fact, contractors contributing to Brazil's ruling-party legislative winners saw their average "contribution/investment" return between 14 and 39 times in government contracts (Boas et al., 2014).

Once in government, politicians realize that the bigger the projects, the bigger the bribes and contributions from corrupt contractors in the next elections. Campaign donations can "buy" policy outcomes, and policy outcomes can "buy" campaign donations. This scheme's strength is such that Odebrecht was even called "the company that captured governments" (Durand, 2019).

Naturally (and unfortunately), this vicious circle is fueled by impunity. The track record of Brazilian justice against white-collar crimes is inconsequential, and examples of criminal convictions are rare (Dallagnol, 2017; Moro, 2021; Pontes & Anselmo, 2022). The engagement or not of politicians and contractors in corruption is a rational choice, where these actors weigh up the costs and benefits of this immoral action. While the fear of legal punishment is a discouraging factor in white-collar crimes (Edelhertz, 1970; Gottschalk, 2020), it did not exist for Petrobras' administrators and the League of 16 (Signor et al., 2022) as corruption was considered a cultural norm (i.e., the way we get things done) and the "rule of the game" (Moro, 2018).

Despite the role of dishonest politicians and contractors in cases of corruption involving public infrastructure, it is important to point out that they cannot act alone. Most countries require that trained professionals such as architects and engineers sign off on documents related to design and construction. Thus, it can be said that there would be no corruption in these projects without these professionals' actions and/or omissions. It is important to reflect on this, even considering the political system usually protects itself and blames those who signed technical documents such as designs, budgets and invoices.

During the Operation Car Wash investigation, the engineers involved in the Petrobras projects were the first to be arrested. Engineers confessed to their crimes to reduce their sentences, as the evidence presented was irrefutable. Additionally, they were required to return hundreds of millions of dollars in bribes hidden in personal accounts in Brazil and offshore (Pontes & Anselmo, 2022). In fact, one engineer alone returned nearly US$100 million, an amount impossible to be saved from their Petrobras salary.

The collusion between politicians, contractors and construction professionals has resulted in unsustainable losses for Petrobras; two mega-projects were canceled, one was postponed, and one is only partially operating. Operation Car Wash prevented Petrobras from haemorrhaging an additional US$50 billion in expenditure on these mega-projects. Explicitly, the Malevolent Hand, writ very large, was at play in Petrobras' project procurement processes. The Malevolent Hand again comes to the fore in the next case we examine.

2014 World Cup Soccer Stadiums

Ronaldo Luís Nazário de Lima, the former Brazilian striker who scored twice against Germany to give Brazil its fifth world trophy in 2002, when answering questions raised by protesters angry at the Brazilian government for spending billions on hosting the 2014 World Cup instead of developing the country's much needed social infrastructure (e.g., hospitals) declared:

> The World Cup is not made with hospitals, you have to build stadiums, or there won't be the [2014 FIFA] World Cup.

When preparations were made to host the 2014 World Cup, questions were raised in the media about the incumbent government's priorities and motives for holding the event, as the health system needed urgent attention and investment (Rosenthal & Cardoso, 2015). Ronaldo recognized the insensitivity of his comment and apologized to the Brazilian people. But this apology should not distract attention away from the fact he was cast as a member of the board of directors of the Local Organizing Committee of the 2014 FIFA World Cup, lending his name to the tournament's credibility.

The Award: A Case of "It's Just Too Good to Be True"

Brazil was the sole bidder for hosting the 2014 World Cup and thus was crowned the winner.

Interestingly, being the only bidder immediately eliminated the possibility of corruption at face value, unlike the 2016 Olympic Games, where Brazil bought votes from International Olympic Committee members to ensure its selection as the host (Pontes & Anselmo, 2022). In the case of the World Cup, there was no need to buy votes from FIFA officials, as was the case of South Africa and possibly others (US Department of Justice, 2015; Boudreaux et al., 2016). Moreover, with no other nation willing to host the World Cup, a single candidate can leverage and not have to provide additional commitments over and above the minimum required by FIFA (Ledsom, 2007).

Deception and Delusion

The Brazilian government deliberately deceived the public when they promised no public money would be used to support the tournament – but this was not the case (Nobre, 2017). Moreover, the Brazilian government gave FIFA a host of tax exemptions as a reward, which riled the public (Mitra, 2015). The total amount of public money spent to host the World Cup is difficult to determine. Still, the estimates converge at around US$11.6 billion (Rapoza, 2014), with the likelihood that these funds were diverted from those allocated to social infrastructure projects (e.g., hospitals and schools). A significant part of the estimated US$11.6 billion was spent on constructing mega-projects that were neither required nor wanted (Brun & Gomez, 2022).

There was an expectation from FIFA for eight soccer stadiums to host the eight groups of the tournament so that national teams could establish themselves in the host cities, minimize their travel, and enable them to acclimatize to the prevailing conditions (Chade, 2014). Surprisingly, the Brazilian bid foresaw the construction of twelve stadiums, with some in remote locations where there were not even soccer teams that could maintain the facilities after the World Cup – a sense of delusion prevailed. An example is the Arena Amazônia in Manaus, deep in the Amazon rainforest. The stadium is now empty requiring millions of dollars of public funding each year to maintain the facility (Dantas, 2019; Pontes & Anselmo, 2022). The lessons to be learned from hosting the 2014 World Cup went unheeded by the Brazilian government as the same fate of squandered spending as a result of the 2016 Olympics has left an "albatross of high debt and sustained maintenance costs" for stadiums that are not being used (Bray, 2011, p. 100; Mcbride & Manno, 2021).

Tourism Promotion and Infrastructure Legacy: Broken Promises

The government's justification for building so many "new" stadiums was somewhat noble at face value, albeit shortsighted: the intention was to promote tourism and leave a legacy of infrastructure in the host cities. These two plans were only partially achieved. Rio de Janeiro and the country's financial capital São Paulo have famous stadiums and are renowned tourist destinations. But other cities (i.e., Belo Horizonte, Brasília, Cuiabá, Curitiba, Fortaleza, Manaus, Natal, Porto Alegre, Recife, and Salvador) were relatively unknown tourist destinations (Brasil, 2014). To stimulate tourism, the government promised to improve each city's transport systems and networks (e.g., airports, rail, and roads) and social infrastructure. However, stadiums were constructed or refurbished at a significant cost using public money, with some being among the most expensive in the world (Chade, 2014; Mitra, 2015; Nobre, 2017). A case in point undercovered during a police investigation is the Brasília National Stadium, which we will now examine.

The Case of Brasília's National Stadium

Hosting an international sporting event, such as the World Cup, "can sometimes be a useful development tool, but economic gains come only from meticulous financial management and planning, use of existing stadiums and sports facilities and investment focused (on) essential internal infrastructure" (Bray, 2011, p. 101). While there is a desire to host mega-sporting events due to their prestige, they can also be a financial burden, as Brazil is experiencing years after the 2014 World Cup and 2016 Olympic Games.

Intentionally Constructed to Support Corruption

As mentioned, eight soccer stadiums were required to meet FIFA's technical and safety standards. Despite being "the country of soccer" and having thousands of facilities spread across its territory, Brazil surprisingly did not have any stadium that met FIFA's specifications when it applied to host the tournament. Fortunately, two privately funded stadiums meeting FIFA's requirements began to be built and refurbished: the Grêmio and Palmeiras stadiums, which were inaugurated in 2012 in Porto Alegre and 2014 in São Paulo. However, these newly built privately funded stadiums were not selected. Instead, the government decided to refurbish an old stadium in Porto Alegre (Estádio Beira-Rio) and build an entirely new one in São Paulo (Arena de São Paulo, also known as Arena Corinthians) using public money. In addition, ten more cities were chosen to host the games, some without any soccer teams. Undoubtedly, some stadiums were intentionally constructed to financially benefit politicians and their co-conspirators (Pontes & Anselmo, 2022).

Among the chosen cities was Brasília, which despite being the country's capital, never had a team in the first division of Brazilian soccer. However, the existing 45,000 seating capacity stadium was transformed into a 72,777 mega-stadium, Brasília's National Stadium, at the cost of approximately US$1.0 billion. We can compare Brasília's National Stadium with Wembley Stadium in London (United Kingdom, UK) to highlight the significant difference in relative costs between them.

Wembley stadium was completed in 2007 at "around" £800 million (~US$1.6 billion) for a capacity of 90,000 seats (The Football Association, 2022). While the absolute costs of Wembley were higher than Brasília's new stadium, Wembley's relative costs were significantly smaller when considering the wealth of the two nations. For example, in Table 12.5, a seat at Wembley represents a small proportion of the minimum wage in the United Kingdom (UK). Contrastingly the cost of a seat at Brasília's stadium is significantly higher as a proportion of a person's minimum wage.

Table 12.5 Comparative costs of Wembley and Brasília's national stadiums

Stadium	Wembley	Brasília
Total cost (US$ billion) (a)	1.6	1.0
Seats (b)	90,000	72,777
Seat cost (US$) (c) = b/a	17,778	13,741
Real minimum wages (US$/year) (in 2020 constant prices at 2020 US$ exchange rates) (d)	18,799	2,051
Seat cost / real minimum wage (year) (e) = c/d	0.9	6.7

Note: Data on minimum wages (OECD, 2022).

Premeditated Cost Increase and the Construction of a "White Elephant"

The planning for Brasília's National Stadium commenced in 2010, its budget was R$700 million (US$400 million), but through successive contract additives, this significantly increased to R$1.7 billion (Distrito Federal, 2017a, 2017b). The cost increases were not due to ill-informed decisions, optimism bias or errors. The cost increase to the stadium was premeditated and began early in the procurement process. The contractor who built Brasília's National Stadium signed a leniency agreement (Brasil, 2016) stating that:

> After the official confirmation that Brazil would host the 2014 FIFA World Cup on October 20, 2007, preliminary discussions and negotiations began between representatives of the construction companies about the possible cities that would host the World Cup games. Such discussions intensified in 2008 when negotiations began for a preliminary market division.

According to the contractor, agreements were made to (1) fix prices, conditions, advantages and abstentions from bidding between competitors and (2) divide the market and allocate projects through the formation of a cartel, the suppression of proposals, the presentation of cover bids and the promise of future subcontracting.

Another contractor that signed a collaboration agreement stated that the collusive group acted to deter honest competitors from entering the auction. The entry deterrence was made possible by inserting restrictive and overly specific requirements into the qualification documents that only one contractor could meet. For example, prior experience constructing sports facilities projects with at least 20,000 seats was required (Brasil, 2017b, 2018b).

The contractor also confessed to the widespread payment of bribes to politicians while the stadiums were being constructed (Brasil, 2017b, 2018b). But again, apart from the politicians' behavior, we would like to highlight the construction professionals' role in this corruption. A governmental control agency pointed out several issues, which included: (1) the payments for services not performed, (2) prices above the market rate, (3) quality problems, (4) periodic price adjustments, and (5) other irregularities in the construction of the Brasília's National Stadium (Distrito Federal, 2016, 2017a, 2017b). The losses in public funds due to these professionals' corrupt practices cost Brazilan taxpayers hundreds of millions of dollars (Brasil, 2017b; Distrito Federal, 2017a). More alarmingly, taxpayers are now left with a stadium that needs to be maintained for years to come but is seldom used. The Brazilian people have unnecessarily been gifted a "White Elephant" (Bray, 2011; Alm et al., 2014).

What Can We Glean from These Brazilian Cases?

The more we know and understand about the nature of corruption, "the better we can decide which policy instruments to use to combat" its occurrence (De Graaf, 2007, p. 39). But no one-size-fits-all instrument can address corruption as it is complex, and its tentacles are often far-reaching in projects. Indeed, corruption is context-specific, requiring an understanding of its motives and reasons within the various micro, meso, and macro levels within which it manifests before measures can be determined to deal with its occurrence (De Graaf, 2007). Noting the difficulty in determining the causes of corruption, Caiden (2001) suggests that "just as there are many varieties of corrupt behavior, so there are multitudinous factors contributing to corruption. So many explanations [as to the causes of corruption] are offered that it is difficult to classify them in any systematic way" (p. 21). Determining what anti-corruption methods work best under specific circumstances is challenging for project procurement as we know little about what corruption controls work best and most efficiently. The cases we have examined in this chapter provide a much-needed context to understand better that corruption in infrastructure procurement is multifaceted, reaching far beyond the immediate project involving many stakeholders.

When Operation Car Wash commenced in 2014, it initially focused on investigating drug dealers who were money laundering through one person. However, as the investigation progressed, allegations of corruption at Petrobras began to unfold involving politicians, the largest construction companies in Brazil and many business leaders. The convictions of powerful Brazilian politicians made the headlines worldwide, sending a message that "no one was above the law."

The money laundering and the consequences of corruption revealed by Operation Car Wash reached the US. As a result, Petrobras and the largest collusive contractor (Odebrecht) signed leniency agreements with US authorities (US Department of Justice, 2016, 2018). Similarly, several other construction companies signed similar agreements with the Brazilian authorities, and these agreements exposed other cases of corruption, such as the soccer stadiums destined for the 2014 FIFA World Cup (Brasil, 2016). These new revelations spawned Operation Car Wash spin-offs, such as Operation Panathenaic (*Panatenaico* in Portuguese). They showed that the collusive contractors' modus operandi was practically the same: division of the market among a group of colluders, bid rigging, and widespread payment of bribes to politicians.

Theoretical Implications

The procurement and construction of infrastructure projects have provided a breeding ground for corruption and collusion for centuries. The lack of attention to the context within which corruption arises in projects and examination of specific cases where it has occurred has resulted in only "predisposing causes" being identified instead of the "triggers" (De Graaf, 2007, p. 62; Signor et al., 2022). Aligning corruption and collusion within the framing of the Malevolent Hand provides the contextuality to understand how misbehavior in the form of strategic misrepresentation during the investment justification process of projects, willful misconduct, bribery, and delusion were uncovered once collusion had been suspected and identified. In our cases, we demonstrate the importance of context by providing a narrative linking the evidence discovered from police investigations.

The project management literature lacks a theoretical explanation of the causes of corruption. Understanding the dynamics within single cases can provide a rich picture of the behaviors, motives, and reasons for corruption. Our cases provide motivation for developing a causal theory of corruption, enabling policymakers to make headway toward developing anti-corruption methods that work in projects under specific conditions and circumstances.

We hasten to note there are subtle differences between collusion, corruption and strategic misrepresentation that will require exploration to understand why and how they manifest in projects. For example, those who collude tend to conceal information and transact with bribes, making the "separation of powers ineffective in providing checks and balances" (D'Souza, 2009, p. 17). By way of contrast, corruption is not necessarily a product of a culture of greed or wrong policies per se. Instead, it is caused by the "inherent design of non-market institutions set up to promote the social good" (D'Souza, 2009, p. 17). Strategic misrepresentation is a false statement "deliberately created by someone to intentionally deceive others; deception requires justification" (Love & Ahiaga-Dagbui, 2018, p. 365). There needs to be a motivation to enact the lie, though it is invariably driven by self-interest.

Practical Implications

The cases of mega-corruption at Petrobras and the FIFA World Cup stadiums originated long before project practitioners (e.g., project managers and engineers) became aware of its presence and were able to take action. As abundantly demonstrated, unscrupulous politicians' decisions were the genesis of mega-projects whose planning and procurement aimed to generate bribes rather than provide taxpayers with assets that would benefit the economy and society. The corruption that ensued goes beyond the planning and procurement process of projects. Although some practitioners warned that Petrobras' refineries would have negative NPV and several stadiums would be economically unviable after the World Cup, such warnings were unheeded by the politicians who held the final decision on the progress of these projects. Moreover, some practitioners served as instruments to the decision-making, enabling and sanctioning overpriced budgets, unnecessary charges and substandard and cheaper materials than specified.

From a policy perspective, forming an independent body of practitioners to advise governments on the viability and benefits of projects would go some way to overcoming strategic misrepresentation and willful misconduct. This would ensure public funds are directed toward those delivering the best outcomes for taxpayers. Additionally, establishing a whistleblowing policy could potentially act as a corruption deterrent. In this instance, practitioners involved in procuring infrastructure projects can feel safe identifying and calling out misbehavior in the public interest, which can detrimentally impact taxpayers.

Conclusion

As Robert Zoelick, the eleventh president of the World Bank, insightfully points out, "corruption is a cancer that steals from the poor, eats away at governance and moral fibre and destroys trust." Corruption in Brazil has stymied its economic and social development. The two notable cases we present in this chapter, Petrobras and the 2014 World Cup stadiums, have adversely impacted the economic and social well-being of Brazil. The immoral and willful acts of dishonest politicians, construction companies and professionals to intentionally design mega-projects for mega-corruption brought to the fore the need for Brazilian authorities to act swiftly to engage in legal proceedings and convict, where possible, perpetrators involved in the corruption.

The search for convictions, indictments and plea bargains was effective in the short term in Brazil, but currently, Operation Car Wash has been dismantled, convictions have been annulled and contractor fines have not been paid. Thus, mitigating corruption involves reinforcing the political and legal systems and the vigilance of practitioners, who are also important stakeholders in procuring public infrastructure.

Proving corruption in the procurement of infrastructure is difficult. Still, it is only through providing a context and sharing knowledge and experiences that we can understand how the Malevolent Hand operates and contributes to project behavior. After all, this context has been missing from the project management literature.

References

Alm, J., Solberg, H., Storm, R., and Jakobsen, T. (2014). Hosting major sports events: The challenge of taming white elephants. *Leisure Studies*, *35*(1), 1–19.

Anheier, H. K. (2016). Of Hiding Hands and other ways of coping with uncertainty: A commentary. *Social Research International Quarterly*, *83*(4), 1005–1010.

Boas, T. C., Hidalgo, F. D., and Richardson, N. P. (2014). The spoils of victory: Campaign donations and government contracts in Brazil. *The Journal of Politics*, *76*(2), 415–429.

Boudreaux, C. J., Karahan, G., and Coats, M. (2016). Bend it like FIFA: Corruption on and off the pitch. *Managerial Finance*, *42*(9), 866–878.

Bray, E. (2011). The curse of good hospitality: Why developing countries shouldn't host international sporting events. *The SAIS Review of International Affairs*, *31*(1), 99–102.

Brasil (2014). Caracterização e dimensionamento do turismo internacional no Brasil (2010–2014) – Relatório Descritivo. Brasília: Ministério do Turismo. www.dadosefatos.turismo.gov.br/2016-02-04-11-54-03/demanda-tur%C3%ADstica-internacional/item/download/702_7dd6fcbac8dbb5ef39348da6bdd2147a.html.

Brasil (2015). Histórico da Conduta da Construções e Comércio Camargo Corrêa S.A.. Brasília: Conselho Administrativo de Defesa Econômica (CADE). https://sei.cade.gov.br/sei/modulos/pesquisa/md_pesq_documento_consulta_externa.php?DZ2uWeaYicbuRZEFhBt-n3BfPLlu9u7akQAh8mpB9yNujxYamZFUzrxMQKDi2WzTGgANhDb2Plzp_4Qt5mIXyCwbuZmhwM5jGSyd4trcY-GRO15Hx_tXH9nplvvhlvnZ.

Brasil (2016). Histórico da Conduta (Estádios de Futebol). Brasília: Conselho Administrativo de Defesa Econômica (CADE). https://sei.cade.gov.br/sei/modulos/pesquisa/md_pesq_documento_consulta_externa.php?mYbVb954ULaAV-MRKzMwwbd5g_PuAKStTlNgP-jtcH5MdmPeznqYAOxKmGO9r4mCfJ1TXxQMN01pTgFwPLudA0W_LdtF3sGOU_wjQEVeX0sEioFi2hOz_FpTktHQYRhY.

Brasil (2017a). Histórico da Conduta da Andrade Gutierrez Engenharia S.A. Brasília: Conselho Administrativo de Defesa Econômica (CADE). https://sei.cade.gov.br/sei/modulos/pesquisa/md_pesq_documento_consulta_externa.phpDZ2uWeaYicbuRZEFhBt-n3BfPLlu9u7akQAh8mpB9yPBLPf1PbYQnnw-XDJT85UIqrfGC6sfn1dX7wUDRb_ZsFQKUa-SxircpjUlHniUIDjx92oKHasHVt-Ca60juSOK.

Brasil (2017b). Relatório Final da Operação Panatenaico. Brasília: Polícia Federal. https://static.poder360.com.br/2017/08/PANA.pdf.

Brasil (2018a). Acórdão n° 1839/2018. Plenário. Relator: Ministro José Múcio Monteiro. Sessão de 08/08/2018. Brasília: Tribunal de Contas da União (TCU). https://pesquisa.apps.tcu.gov.br/#/redireciona/acordao-completo/%22ACORDAO-COMPLETO-2303835%22.

Brasil (2018b). Denúncia relativa ao Inquérito Policial n° 1095/2016 (autos n° 7161-85.2017.4.01.3400). Brasília: Ministério Público Federal (MPF). www.mpf.mp.br/df/sala-de-imprensa/docs/denuncia-nucleo-politico-arruda.

Brasil (2020). Acórdão n° 2750/2020. Plenário. Relator: Ministro Benjamin Zymler. Sessão de 14/10/2020. Brasília: Tribunal de Contas da União (TCU). https://pesquisa.apps.tcu.gov.br/#/redireciona/acordao-completo/%22ACORDAO-COMPLETO-2360631%22.

Brasil (2021). Acórdão n° 784/2021. Plenário. Relator: Ministro Vital do Rêgo. Sessão de 07/04/2021. Brasília: Tribunal de Contas da União (TCU). https://pesquisa.apps.tcu.gov.br/#/redireciona/acordao-completo/%22ACORDAO-COMPLETO-2394204%22.

Brun, E. E., and Gomez, C. (2022). Politics and geopolitics in staging the FIFA World Cup: What is at stake for the hosting nations? (pp. 47–60). In S. Chadwick, P. Widdop, C.

Anagnostopoulos, and D. Parnell (eds.). *The business of the FIFA World Cup*. Routledge.

Caiden, G. (2001). Corruption and governance (pp. 15–38). In G. Caiden, O. Dwivedi, and J. G.Jabbra, (eds.). *Where corruption lives*. Kurmarian Press.

Campos, N., Engel, E., Fischer, R. D., and Galetovic, A. (2021). The ways of corruption in infrastructure: Lessons from the Odebrecht case. *The Journal of Economic Perspectives, 35*(2), 171–190.

Chade, J. (2014). *A Copa como ela é: A história de dez anos de preparação para a Copa de 2014*. Companhia das Letras.

Dallagnol, D. (2017). *A luta contra a corrupção*. Primeira Pessoa.

Dantas, M. (2019). Arena da Amazônia atinge custo mensal de R$ 1 milhão, o maior de sua história. https://ge.globo.com/am/futebol/noticia/arena-da-amazonia-atinge-custo-mensal-de-r-1-milhao-por-mes-o-maior-de-sua-historia.ghtml.

De Graaf, G. (2007). Causes of corruption: Towards a contextual theory of corruption. *Public Administration Quarterly, 31*(1/2), 39–86.

Distrito Federal (2016). Informação nº 22/16 – NFO. Brasília: TCDF, Núcleo de Fiscalização de Obras e Serviços de Engenharia. https://etcdf.tc.df.gov.br/?a = documento&f = downloadPDF&iddocumento = 1559116.

Distrito Federal (2017a). Auditoria de Regularidade – Relatório Final. Estádio Nacional de Brasília – 3ª Etapa. Brasília: TCDF, Núcleo de Fiscalização de Obras e Serviços de Engenharia. https://etcdf.tc.df.gov.br/?a = documento&f = downloadPDF&iddocumento = 1684186.

Distrito Federal (2017b). Auditoria de Regularidade – Relatório Final. Execução dos serviços de reforma e ampliação do Estádio Nacional de Brasília – Mané Garrincha (4ª Etapa da Fiscalização) (Processo nº 29.565/2013). Brasília: TCDF, Núcleo de Fiscalização de Obras e Serviços de Engenharia. https://etcdf.tc.df.gov.br/?a = documento&f = downloadPDF&iddocumento = 1674583.

D'Souza, E. (2009). Collusion in government and corruption. *Journal of Interdisciplinary Economics, 21*(1), 17–33.

Durand, F. (2019). *Odebrecht: La empresa que capturaba gobiernos*. Pontificia Universidad Católica del Perú; Oxfam.

Edelhertz, H. (1970). *Nature, impact and prosecution of white-collar crime*. National Institute of Law Enforcement and Criminal Justice.

Flyvbjerg, B. (2018). The fallacy of beneficial ignorance: A test of Hirschman's hiding hand. *World Development, 84*, 176–189.

Gottschalk, P. (2020). *Convenience dynamics and white-collar crime*. Routledge.

García-Rodríguez, M. J., Rodríguez-Montequín, V., Ballesteros-Pérez, P., Love, P. E. D., and Signor, R. (2022). Collusion detection in public procurement auctions with machine learning. *Automation in Construction, 133*, 104047.

Hirschman, A. O. (1967). *Development projects observed*. The Brookings Institution.

Ika, L. A., Love, P. E. D., and Pinto, J. K. (2022). Moving beyond the Planning Fallacy: The emergence of a new principle of project behaviour. *IEEE Transactions on Engineering Management, 69*(6), 3310–3325

Jones, L. R., and Euske, K. J. (1991). Strategic misrepresentation in budgeting. *Journal of Public Administration Research and Theory, 1*, 437–460.

Ledsom, M. (2007). FIFA ends World Cup rotation policy. www.reuters.com/article/uk-soccer-FIFA-rotation-idUKL2941735420071029.

Lehtinen, J., Locatelli, G., Sainati, T., Artto, K., and Evans, B. (2022). The grand challenge: Effective anti-corruption measures in projects. *International Journal of Project Management, 40*(4), 347–361.

Locatelli, G., Mariani, G., Sainati, T., and Greco, M. (2017). Corruption in public projects and megaprojects: There is an elephant in the room! *International Journal of Project Management, 35*(1), 252–268.

Love, P. E. D., and Ahiaga-Dagbui, D. (2018). Debunking fake news in a post-truth era: The plausible untruths of cost underestimation in transport infrastructure projects. *Transportation Research A: Policy and Practice, 113*, 337–368.

McBride, J., and Manno, M. (2021). The economics of hosting the Olympics. Council on Foreign Relations. www.cfr.org/backgrounder/economics-hosting-olympic-games#:~:text = In%20Brazil%2C%20the%20first%20South,shouldering%20at%20least%20%2413%20billion.

Mitra, A. (2015). An ethical analysis of the 2014 FIFA World Cup in Brazil. *Law and Business Review of the Americas, 21*(1), 3–19.

Moro, S. F. (2018). Preventing systemic corruption in Brazil. *Daedalus, 147*(3), 157–168.

Moro, S. F. (2021). *Contra o sistema da corrupção*. Primeira Pessoa.

Netto, V. (2016). *Lava Jato: O juiz Sergio Moro e os bastidores da operação que abalou o Brasil*. Primeira Pessoa.

Nobre, E. A. C. (2017). The 2014 FIFA World Cup in Brazil: Hosting a sport mega-event in a BRIC Context (pp. 1–23). In E. A. C. Nobre (ed.). *Sports mega-events and urban legacies: The 2014 FIFA World Cup, Brazil*. Palgrave Macmillan.

Organization for Economic Co-operation and Development (2010). Policy Roundtables: Collusion and Corruption in Public Procurement. www.oecd.org/competition/cartels/46235884.pdf.

Organization for Economic Co-operation and Development (2022). Dataset: Real Minimum Wages. https://stats.oecd.org/index.aspx?DataSetCode = RMW.

Petrobras (2008). Annual Report of Activities 2008. www.investidorpetrobras.com.br/en/investor-services/download-center/.

Petrobras (2010). 2010 Annual Report. www.investidorpetrobras.com.br/en/investor-services/download-center/.

Petrobras (2014). Petróleo Brasileiro SA – Petrobras – Consolidated Financial Statements as of December 31, 2014, 2013, and 2012 with Report of Independent Registered Public Accounting Firm. www.investidorpetrobras.com.br/en/investor-services/download-center/.

Petrobras (2015). Management Report 2015. www.investidorpetrobras.com.br/en/investor-services/download-center/.

Pontes, J., and Anselmo, M. (2022). *Operation Car Wash: Brazil's institutionalized crime and the inside story of the biggest corruption scandal in history*. Bloomsbury Academic.

Rapoza, K. (2014). Bringing FIFA to Brazil equal to roughly 61% of education budget. www.forbes.com/sites/kenrapoza/2014/06/11/bringing-fifa-to-brazil-equal-to-roughly-61-of-education-budget/?sh = 274aac4436d6.

Rosenthal, B., and Cardoso, F. (2015). "There will not be a World Cup": The Kratophanous power of the FIFA 2014 World Cup in Brazil. *Consumer Culture Theory*, *17*(1), 367–399.

Signor, R., Love, P. E. D., Olatunji, O., Vallim, J. J. C. B., and Raupp A. B. (2017). Collusive bidding in Brazilian infrastructure projects. *Proceedings of the Institution of Civil Engineers: Forensic Engineering*, *170*(3), 113–123.

Signor, R., Love, P. E. D., Vallim, J. J. C. B., Raupp, A. B., and Olatunji, O. (2019). It is not collusion unless you get caught: The case of "Operation Car Wash" and unearthing of a cartel. *Journal of Antitrust Enforcement*, *7*(2), 177–202.

Signor, R, Love, P. E. D., Belarmino, A. T. N., and Olatunji, O. (2020). Detection of collusive tenders in infrastructure projects: Learning from operation car wash. *ASCE Journal of Construction Engineering and Management*, *146*(1), 05019015.

Signor, R., Love, P. E. D., and Ika, L. A. (2022). White collar crime: Unearthing collusion in the procurement of infrastructure projects. *IEEE Transactions on Engineering Management*, *69*(5), 1932–1943.

Signor, R., Ballesteros-Pérez, P., and Love, P. E. D. (2023). Collusion detection in infrastructure procurement: A modified order statistic method for uncapped Auctions. *IEEE Transactions on Engineering Management*, *70*(2), 464–477.

The Football Association (2022). The History of the FA. www.thefa.com/about-football-association/what-we-do/history.

Transparency International (2022). What is corruption? www.transparency.org/en/what-is-corruption.

US Department of Justice (2015). Sixteen additional FIFA officials indicted for racketeering conspiracy and corruption. Press Release (Updated December 7, 2015). www.justice.gov/usao-edny/pr/sixteen-additional-fifa-officials-indicted-racketeering-conspiracy-and-corruption.

US Department of Justice (2016). Odebrecht and Braskem plead guilty and agree to pay at least $3.5 billion in global penalties to resolve largest foreign bribery case in history. Press Release Number: 16-1515 (Updated October 3, 2017). www.justice.gov/opa/pr/odebrecht-and-braskem-plead-guilty-and-agree-pay-least-35-billion-global-penalties-resolve.

US Department of Justice (2018). Non-prosecution agreement and statement of facts. www.justice.gov/opa/press-release/file/1096706/download.

Vallim J. J. C. B. (2018). *Engenharia forense: Metodologias aplicadas na Operação Lava-Jato*. Juruá.

Yuhui, S. (2021). El cáncer de la corrupción en Latinoamérica: El caso Odebrecht. *Gestión y política pública*, *30*(3), 237–265.

PART III

Practical Tips

How to Shape Project Behavior and Curb Project Misbehavior

CHAPTER 13

Setting Realistic Project Goals

OFER ZWIKAEL, ALICIA GILCHRIST, and JACK MEREDITH

Introduction

The purpose of a project is to achieve a specified goal (Shenhar et al., 2007), defined as an "object or aim of an action" (Locke & Latham, 2012, p. 4). Further, project goals are set by the entity funding the project (i.e., the funding or owner organization) during the front-end stage of a project. These goals are then included in the project's business case (Zwikael & Meredith, 2022). However, research argues that project goals are commonly unrealistic, which negatively impacts decision making during the front-end and has ramifications for the project throughout its life (Zwikael et al., 2018; Asadabadi & Zwikael, 2024). Project goals are considered unrealistic when they have been underestimated prior to a project's commencement (e.g., project lifecycle cost) and/or overestimated beyond the values that independent experts would find realistic (e.g., target benefits; Zwikael & Meredith, 2019). Yet senior executives continue to set and accept unrealistic project goals for various reasons, such as ambition, a lack of knowledge, uncertainty, the planning fallacy, cognitive bias, errors, invalid assumptions, political pressure, and strategic misrepresentation (Atkinson et al., 2006; Love et al., 2011; Jayatilleke & Lai, 2018; Asadabadi et al., 2020).

Literature is unclear about the key factors contributing to unrealistic project goal setting and effective approaches managers in the project owner organization can use to mitigate these factors. These research gaps are important because setting unrealistic project goals during the project front-end can have a negative impact on project investment decision making. For example, project proposals with unrealistic goals are more likely to be inappropriately approved at the expense of proposals with more realistic goals. To address these research gaps, we adopt a project behavior perspective to learn how incidences of unrealistic goal setting can be identified and reduced to ensure future project investment decision making is based on realistic estimates and thus more likely to result in the selection of not only the "best" project from the available options but the project most likely to succeed. As major projects typically suffer the greatest consequences of unrealistic goals in terms of cost and years, we constrain the focus of this chapter to major projects (Denicol et al., 2020; Wynn et al., 2021). Major projects differ from other types of projects, as they are often of high monetary value, subject to a high level of public and political scrutiny, defined by effect rather than solution, and are characterized by high levels of complexity, uncertainty, ambiguity, and/or a large number of stakeholders (Mazur et al., 2014; Major Projects Association, 2020).

In this chapter, we examine project goals set by the project owner organization. Further, we constrain our focus on project failure to "not meeting project goals." The aim of this chapter is to enhance our knowledge of the behavioral factors that cause project funders, owners, champions, and planners in the project owner organization to set unrealistic project goals. We first review the project goal-setting literature and investigate how project behavior can impact goal setting. Next, we analyze the failure of seven major projects and empirically assess which behavioral factors contributed the most to unrealistic goal setting. Finally, we propose 10 practical recommendations to help managers set more realistic project goals. These recommendations analyze the goal-setting process holistically and hence are grouped into best practices of goal setting, goal appraisal, and project appraisal.

Behavioral Factors Contributing to Unrealistic Goal Setting in Projects

Project Behavior

Project behavior has been studied comprehensively in the project management literature (Unterhitzenberger, 2021; Ika et al., 2022; Love et al., 2022). Project behavior concerns decisions made by managers to resolve project difficulties or seek opportunities for payoffs (Love et al., 2022). In this chapter, we also view unrealistic goal setting as a project behavior issue. As a result, we contribute to this growing body of research by focusing our investigation into the behavioral causes of unrealistic goal setting by managers in the project owner organization, such as the project funder, project owner, and project champion (Zwikael & Meredith, 2018), to be referred to as "managers in the project owner organisation" or "managers," in short, in this chapter. Behavioral factors warrant further investigation as they have been found to contribute to projects completed over budget and experiencing benefits shortfalls (Ika et al., 2022).

Two well-known theories of project behavior that may explain poor project outcomes are the Planning Fallacy and the Hiding Hand. The Planning Fallacy occurs when managers are overly optimistic about the project's cost, benefits, and/or the time it will take to complete the project (Flyvbjerg, 2016). Alternatively, the Hiding Hand suggests that ignorance can be beneficial during the project front-end, as the underestimation of costs and overestimation of benefits can increase the likelihood of projects being attempted and the development of creative solutions to address unforeseen problems (Ika et al., 2022).

To reconcile the differences between the two conflicting theories, Ika et al. (2022) offer a third theory – the Fifth Hand – which views projects as more complex and nuanced than either the Hiding Hand or the Planning Fallacy account for on their own. The Fifth Hand "construes planners and managers as plural and paradoxical, optimistic and pessimistic, and prone to both bias and error, but with the agency to make the best of the evolving context and draw and learn from experience in the face of complexity and uncertainty" (Ika et al., 2022, p. 14). All three theories indicate project behavior can impact project goal setting.

Project Goal Setting

The project front-end "begins with a problem or an opportunity formulated into a business case, and ends when it is approved or rejected by a funding entity" (Zwikael & Gilchrist, 2022, p. 43). Project goals are set during the front-end by the project proposal development team (e.g., Zwikael & Bar-Yoseph, 2004) prior to the submission of a business case for funding consideration (Zwikael & Meredith, 2019). Doran's (1981) goal-setting theory states that goals should be SMART - specific, measurable, attainable, relevant, and time-bound. To tailor goal-setting theory (Doran, 1981) to the project front-end context, Zwikael et al. (2018) suggested target benefits need to be specific, attainable, and comprehensive to be effective. Effective goal setting enhances project investment decision making, project outcomes, and organizational performance (Pinto & Slevin, 1988; Serra & Kunc, 2015).

Unrealistic Goal Setting

Research on how project goals are developed and set, and the conceptual frameworks practitioners use to guide best practice, is scarce. Without an appropriate goal-setting framework, goals are often vague, unrealistic, and lacking evidence (Samset et al., 2014). Literature has identified factors that can trigger managers to set unrealistic project goals. Some of these factors are at the project level, such as a lack of planning or project management capabilities (Zwikael et al., 2006; Feris et al., 2017), and other factors relate to the environmental level in which the project organization operates, such as political bargaining and external events (Gil & Pinto, 2018).

Another set of factors are at the individual level. According to Huber and Power (1985, p. 172), at this level, managers are likely to set unrealistic project goals for one of four reasons: "1. They are motivated to do so; 2. Their perceptual and cognitive limitations result in inadvertent errors; 3. They lack crucial information about the event of interest; and 4. They have been questioned with an inappropriate data elicitation procedure."

Behavioral Factors Impacting Unrealistic Goal Setting

This chapter focuses on behavioral factors that impact the setting of unrealistic project goals. One such behavioral factor is cognitive bias, defined as cases where "human cognition reliably produces representations that are systematically distorted compared to some aspect of objective reality" (Haselton et al., 2015, p. 968). The term "cognitive bias" involves an interpretative judgment that the response is unfair, illegitimate, or unjustifiable, in the sense that it goes beyond the objective requirements or evidence of the situation (Hewstone et al. 2002; Steinel & De Dreu, 2004).

Although managers are most often well-educated professionals trained to work through complex problems and make correct decisions quickly and efficiently, they are still susceptible to universal cognitive limitations (Huber & Power, 1985). Research suggests that one of the primary reasons project goals are not achieved stems from cognitive biases via the setting of unrealistic goals. For instance, Shore (2008) examined systematic cognitive biases in human decision making and ways they can be used as a lens for understanding and diagnosing project failure. Shore first identified nine systematic cognitive biases in the decision-making literature. Twenty-two business professionals then examined eight project failure case studies. All but one of the cognitive biases was thought to "best explain" why one or more of the projects failed. In addition, McCray, Purvis, and McCray (2002) related 16 "heuristics and cognitive biases" to project management processes. For illustrative purposes, how cognitive biases may potentially trigger managers to unintentionally set unrealistic project goals is discussed using three well-known cognitive biases – optimism bias, the endowment effect, and anchoring.

Optimism bias assumes people are unrealistically optimistic about the future (Kahneman, 2011). Whereas it has some positive effects on people, such as increased happiness (Gilbert, 2005) and job performance (Youssef & Luthans, 2007), it also contributes to ignoring a threatening reality. As a result, managers who are too optimistic can tend to underestimate risks, leading to the overestimation of a project's expected benefits and the underestimation of its costs – thereby setting unrealistic project goals (Flyvbjerg, 2014). The UK government (2011, p. 29) found that "there is a demonstrated, systematic, tendency for project appraisers to be overly optimistic." For example, optimistic (and also pessimistic) behavior by project managers was observed in their reporting on the status of projects during project execution (Kaufmann & Kock, 2023). The UK government further clarifies that "This is a worldwide phenomenon that affects both the private and public sectors. Many project parameters are affected by optimism – appraisers tend to overstate benefits, and understate timings and costs, both capital and operational." Optimism bias undermines the likely success of a project to achieve its goals, often leading to substantial cost overruns, delays in completion, and failure to deliver the target benefits.

The *endowment effect* assumes individuals assign objects that they own higher values than their real market value (Kahneman et al., 1991). Similarly, the endowment effect can cause managers to feel ownership in a project, hence valuing it more than its real worth, and accordingly setting unrealistic goals (Feris et al., 2017). The feeling of ownership in a project may be felt by the manager who came up with the idea for, or who proposed, the project, or when a senior executive adopts the project as their own personal possession (Zwikael et al., 2008).

The third example of a cognitive bias is *anchoring*, which is thought to occur when an individual relies too heavily on an initial piece of information when making a decision (Lovallo et al., 2023). In projects, managers rely on market research, historical projects, and other external information to set goals for a new project. However, using a specified and pre-selected piece of information as an anchor for a new project may lead to setting unrealistic goals.

Table 13.1 Behavioral factors contributing to unrealistic goal setting in projects

Behavioral factors	Definition	Example
1. Strategic misrepresentation	The deliberate distortion of information to achieve a strategic outcome.	Inflating target benefits on a project proposal for the purpose of making the proposal appear more attractive and win the bid.
2. Optimism bias	Overestimating the likelihood of positive events occurring or underestimating the likelihood of negative events occurring.	Calculating the likelihood of a positive project outcome as being greater than an objective assessment of the available data would indicate.
3. Uniqueness bias	Viewing a project as unique when it is not.	Treating a project as though it is more complex than other similar projects and thereby inflating its costs unnecessarily, or treating it as less complex than other similar projects and thereby reducing its costs unrealistically.
4. The planning fallacy	Underestimating project costs while overestimating project benefits.	Planning to complete a project with less funding than the project requires and anticipating that the project will produce greater benefits than is feasible.
5. Overconfidence bias	Being confident about a project or some aspect of a project without sufficient evidence to support that level of confidence.	Being overly confident that a project will be delivered on time.
6. Hindsight bias	The belief by a person that they had predicted a past event.	Believing they can predict a similar project outcome in the future.
7. Availability bias	Making a decision based on a past project that comes readily to mind even though it may not be the best project to base the decision on. Believing that the project is more representative than it actually is.	Making a project decision based on a well-known example of project success or failure when it is not the most appropriate comparison.
8. The base rate fallacy	Ignoring averages and focusing instead on one-offs or outliers.	Basing a project decision on a past project that was unusual or rare.
9. Anchoring	Placing too much emphasis or 'anchoring' on one particular piece of information when making decisions.	Continuing a project because there was strong public support when it commenced despite multiple indications that such public support no longer exists.
10. Escalation of commitment	Increasing commitment to a project as a result of previous investment in the project while ignoring evidence that indicates the increase in commitment is not the best course of action.	Increasing funding for a failing project based on significant prior investment in the project.

Flyvbjerg (2021) identifies nine cognitive biases as the most significant within a project context: (1) optimism bias, (2) uniqueness bias, (3) the planning fallacy, (4) overconfidence bias, (5) hindsight bias, (6) availability bias, (7) the base rate fallacy, (8) anchoring, and (9) escalation of commitment. In addition to cognitive bias, Flyvbjerg (2021) also discusses strategic misrepresentation, defined as the deliberate distortion of information to achieve a strategic outcome through planned, systematic distortion or misstatement of fact (Jones & Euske, 1991). Table 13.1 defines and illustrates these ten behavioral factors.

Methodology

In this section, we introduce the project cases and our analysis approach to evaluate the extent to which each of the 10 behavioral factors discussed in Table 13.1 contribute to setting unrealistic goals. For this purpose, we selected seven well-known cases of project failure to understand why projects fail to achieve their official goals. We use secondary data of major projects, which have been comprehensively reported in the literature.

Case Selection

Our selection criteria for the inclusion of the cases are as follows: (1) the case has been analyzed in multiple research outlets independently, (2) the case is well known globally, (3) the project failed to achieve its goals, (4) sufficient reliable information about the case's goal setting process is available, and (5) it qualifies as a "major" project.

The seven major projects that were selected as cases are: (1) The Hubble Space Telescope, (2) Boeing 787 Dreamliner, (3) Denver International Airport, (4) Sydney Opera House, (5) Green Meadow's Utility Outage, (6) Biogen, Inc. rBeta Interferon, and (7) Copenhagen Metro. Each project's type, country, budget, and duration (from conception to completion) is presented in Table 13.2.

Case and Data Analysis

We analyzed the relative impact of each of the 10 behavioral factors (see Table 13.1) on the setting of unrealistic goals in each project case. The three research team members and a highly experienced program manager independently rated the level of impact of each behavioral factor in each project case on a scale of zero to three using the following criteria:

- No impact. No evidence for the behavioral factor was present in the project. Calculated as zero points in the total impact.
- Slight impact. There was evidence for slight impact of the behavioral factor in the project. Calculated as one point in the total impact.
- Moderate impact. There was evidence for moderate impact of the behavioral factor in the project. Calculated as two points in the total impact.
- Substantial impact. There was evidence for substantial impact of the behavioral factor in the project. Calculated as three points in the total impact.

Inter-rater reliability between the four raters was determined using the Intraclass Correlation Coefficient (ICC) in IBM SPSS 29.

Results

This section analyzes the seven project cases qualitatively, then presents the results of a quantitative analysis to identify the relative frequency of the various behavioral factors investigated.

Case Qualitative Analysis

In this section, we provide a summary of each project, an analysis of the behavioral factors that appear to have contributed to the setting of the project's unrealistic goals, and consider how they may have contributed.

Table 13.2 Project type, country, budget, and duration

Project	Project type	Country	Budget ($US)	Conception to completion
1. The Hubble Space Telescope	Aerospace	United States	$16 billion	1940s to 1990
2. Boeing 787 Dreamliner	Aerospace	United States	$32 billion	2002 to 2011
3. Denver International Airport	Construction	United States	$4.9 billion	1980s to 1995
4. Sydney Opera House	Construction	Australia	$102 million	1956 to 1973
5. Green Meadow's Utility Outage	Utilities	United States	$1.6 million	1989
6. Biogen, Inc. rBeta Interferon	Pharmaceutical	United States	Unknown	1990 to 1996
7. Copenhagen Metro	Construction	Denmark	$2.3 billion	1990 to 2002

1. The Hubble Space Telescope. The telescope was produced, delivered, and implemented with a distinct spherical aberration in the telescope's primary mirror (Shenhar & Holzmann, 2017). The resulting need for space shuttle crews to make repairs caused schedule and budget overruns in the operation of the telescope. In contrast, the perspective of the astronomy community (NASA included) is that the images generated by the telescope have been of incalculable scientific value (Dunar & Waring, 1999). For example, it has helped determine the age of the universe, the identity of quasars, and the presence of dark energy (NASA, 2018). The actual long-term results from the project were reduced and delayed, due to the poor performance of a NASA contractor, yet the decision to fund the project was justified.

NASA has a strong innovative culture, which also enhances optimism: "This culture is essential to overcoming the extraordinary technological challenges inherent in the development of unique, first-of-their-kind space systems. However, this same optimism can sometimes prevent managers and leaders from making critical assessments of . . . what a project can realistically accomplish within a set budget and timetable" (Martin, 2012, p. iv).

This optimism contributed to NASA relying on a specialist external contractor to build the telescope to specifications, a risk they had not anticipated. The poor risk analysis in the Hubble Telescope project has been confirmed by NASA as a culture of "underestimating technical complexity" (Martin, 2012). Underestimating risks was also triggered by a term later coined as "Hubble psychology" (Charette, 2017) – "an expectation among NASA personnel that projects that fail to meet cost and schedule goals will receive additional funding and that subsequent scientific and technological success will overshadow any budgetary and schedule problems" (Martin, 2012, p. vi).

Finally, there was an "ownership" effect operating here, as would be expected with all their high-visibility launches. For example, the inspector general for NASA (Martin, 2012, p. 3) notes that "NASA ... is justifiably proud of its numerous scientific discoveries and technological innovations" and confirms this with the statement by the former NASA chief of safety and mission assurance: "If it's been a while since our last failure, people who are looking to us to do great things sometimes forget how hard this work is to do" (p. 1).

2. Boeing 787 Dreamliner. The development of this plane ran into a myriad of problems, from its subcontracting approach to its highly technical features such as its use of composites and lithium batteries. The first plane was delivered over three years late (Shenhar et al., 2016, p. 62), its development cost was 10 times its $5 billion estimate, and the cost per plane (excluding engines and custom interiors) by 2016 was over twice its $40 million estimate (Ostrower & Viswanatha, 2016, p. B2).

With this project, Boeing completely changed the way they developed and manufactured planes – moving toward widely scattered outsourcing of not just manufacturing but also component development (called "build to performance"). This new approach introduced major amendments to their process, such as three-day assembly by snap-fitting the plane's fuselage sections, using carbon fiber instead of aluminum for critical structures, assuming employee acceptance of substantial outsourcing, promising four-year delivery to their customers instead of the usual eight, and promising a reduced fuel burn of 20 percent (Kotha et al., 2005). However, despite introducing all these substantial changes in one project, Boeing remained extremely optimistic that everything would go well due to confidence in their past successful record and the capabilities of their untested suppliers (Shenhar et al., 2016).

In addition, Boeing felt strong "ownership" in this project since it was their primary response to Airbus' recent surge in building competing and even bigger planes. As a result, they misjudged the extreme complexity of the project and conducted only a minimal risk analysis, which was largely confined to a few relatively minor technical issues, such as higher cabin pressurization, wingspan lengths, and large diameter engine offsets (Kotha, et al., 2005; Shenhar et al., 2016).

3. Denver International Airport. As air traffic expanded beyond the capacity of Denver's Stapleton airport in the 1990s, and even more was expected in the future, the city of Denver decided to build a new airport on a large tract of land northeast of the city. In the process of developing the airport, costs and schedules escalated substantially beyond the business case, primarily due to the failure of a high-tech baggage system that United Airlines insisted on for their own terminal, but which the airport planners then decided to extend to the entire airport (Szyliowicz & Goetz, 1995). The solution developed by all the stakeholders to the continuing failure was to deescalate the project by letting United Airlines use the high-tech system for their own terminal but revert to a simpler, lower-tech baggage system for the rest of the airport, thereby resulting in an overall successful investment (Montealegre & Kell, 2000).

The airport's planners were optimistic that if United Airlines could get such an advanced technology system to work for their terminal, then it would be easy to extend to the remainder of the airport because any bugs in the system would have been remedied for United Airlines' terminal. The Denver aviation director confessed they were too optimistic: "We had a project that should have taken seven years and we tried to do it in four years" (Schloh, 1996, p. 9). In addition, high passenger forecasts based on the assumption that three airlines would be hubbing at Denver turned out to be wrong (Goetz & Szyliowicz, 1997).

The added length of the baggage system, additional transition points, new technology, and additional equipment compounded the complexity of the system. The planners recognized this risk but felt that the vendor would handle those issues. When they realized that it was the additional complexity of the system that was causing the problems, they reverted to the lower-tech cart and manual labor system for the rest of the airport.

4. Sydney Opera House. The construction of the Sydney Opera house project exceeded its estimated four-year construction time by 10 years and its $7 million budget by $95 million (Zwikael & Smyrk, 2012). However, since its completion, it has become an iconic building, which has attracted many tourists to Sydney and become a UNESCO World Heritage Site (Colbert, 2003). Zwikael and Smyrk (2012, p. 18) conclude that "despite the project management failure, as an overall venture the Sydney Opera House appears to have been a successful investment for the state government."

The initial project budget was low-balled, as the NSW premier's "deliberate deception about the cost" in Parliament (Flyvbjerg, 2014, p. 13) was designed for project approval before the coming elections. In addition, the project administrators were optimistic about the project (Von Bergen & Bressler, 2011; Makridakis & Moleskis, 2015) as the premier made the project "his personal priority" (Flyvbjerg, 2005, p. 54). Later analysis concluded that the Sydney Opera House was "built on lies" (Flyvbjerg et al., 2018, p. 184) and as a result, no effective risk analysis on this high-visibility project was conducted.

5. Green Meadow's Utility Outage. B&W Nuclear Services (BWNS) won a contract to perform a routine refueling outage and steam generator inspection for one of its long-time utility customers under a fixed-price contract of approximately US$500,000 (Filliben & Colley, 1993; Meredith et al., 2018). However, due to technical issues, customer delays, and policy changes introduced by the customer, the project was late, and the costs rose to US$1,600,000, yet both were approved by the customer's apparent representatives. Although the project provided a short-term gain in the sense that BWNS made a profit on the project, in the long term it was considered a failure since the funder then refused to do further business with BWNS.

BWNS was optimistic about the success of this project since they had a successful working relationship with this customer over many years, which had become rather informal. This optimism was based on their assumption that the customer would deliver the parts on time as specified in the contract, as they usually did. However, "the problem leading to the large overrun was the delay in the utility's relinquishment of the generators" (Meredith et al., 2018, p. 417). Another indication was their assumption that the customer would pay their bill since their representatives had approved the changes, but in a rebuke to BWNS, Green Meadow said that they "would not pay any more money toward the $1.6 million [BWNS] said it owed" (Meredith et al., 2018, p. 417).

Although BWNS felt some ownership in the project, they did not overvalue it, in fact worrying that the increased cost and time would not be approved by the customer, although it was (they thought). BNWS had conducted many projects like this before and knew where the technical risks laid, which in fact surfaced during the project – yet again, the customer approved the cost and time increases. However, their optimism based on their prior experience with this customer caused them to underestimate the managerial risks of this project.

6. Biogen, Inc. Beta Interferon. This well-known biotechnology firm was initiating a major change in their drug development business model, having decided to move beyond simply developing and licensing their successful drugs to other manufacturers and instead producing the drugs themselves. However, their first project, manufacturing a new interferon drug, was an initial failure, running late and over budget. A project evaluation conducted near the project's due date found many serious weaknesses in their project management process, yet noted "the perception among senior managers that it was acceptable to be late if the 'real' issues were being discussed and worked on, and progress was being made" (Wheelwright, 1996, p. 9). From this description of the senior managers' perspective on the project, it appears that they knew the goals of the project were unrealistic and misrepresented at the outset but wanted to see what the organization could achieve toward those goals. Of course, they recognized there were plenty of risks with the project, but this effort would surface the main ones for them to consider in their future planning for this new direction, so there was no point in conducting a risk analysis.

7. Copenhagen Metro. The first phase of the metro (subway) project was opened in 2002, followed by phase 2 in 2003. In addition to major cost overruns, the expected number of passengers was not achieved in the first five years of operation, hence failing to realize the business case's goals. However, since 2007, the number of passengers has significantly increased and even exceeded the original objectives in the business strategy. Together with international "best metro" awards, "operational reliability, the speed of the new line to the airport, the system's safety level, and the growing passenger rating" (OECD, 2009, p. 151), the project is now considered a long-term investment success. Since the phase 2 project was based on the success and experience obtained in phase 1, the need for an exhaustive and time-consuming risk analysis was considered unnecessary. As a result, the project suffered from unrealistic financial goals that were challenged by many in the community (Andersen & Hovgaard, 2003).

Case Quantitative Analysis

Table 13.3 summarizes the results using a rating of the level of impact of each behavioral factor in each project case on a scale of zero (-), through to slight (+), moderate (++) and substantial (+++). The total impact for each behavioral factor has then been added up across all cases. The table also presents the inter-rater reliability for each of the behavioral factors.

Our findings indicate that all behavioral factors gained some level of support across the seven project cases. The impact of the 10 behavioral factors on the projects, from highest to lowest (total calculated impact in parentheses), is as follows: optimism bias (18), overconfidence bias (15), planning fallacy (12), escalation of commitment (12), hindsight bias (10), uniqueness bias (9), strategic misrepresentation (7), base rate fallacy (7), availability bias (6), and anchoring bias (6). Further, in all seven cases, we found that when optimism bias occurred, so did overconfidence bias. We also found that the planning fallacy was the only cognitive bias to occur in all seven projects. Strategic misrepresentation was only observed as having a substantial impact (+++) in two well-reported projects (Sydney Opera House and Biogen) and no effect at all in four other projects.

The inter-rater reliability for eight of the behavioral factors was moderate (>.75) to strong (>.90) and significant, indicating ICC level between the four raters has been achieved. For the other two behavioral factors (planning fallacy and anchoring bias), the ICC was not significant, suggesting agreement between the four independent raters had not been fully reached.

Discussion

Ika et al. (2022) state that even if costs are underestimated and benefits overestimated, projects

Table 13.3 An analysis of the project case studies – behavioral factors impacting unrealistic project goal setting

Case title \ Behavioral factor	SM	OPB	UB	PF	OVB	HB	AB1	BRF	AB2	EC
1. The Hubble Space Telescope	-	+++	+++	++	+++	+	-	-	-	++
2. Boeing 787 Dreamliner	+	+++	+++	++	+++	+++	-	-	+	+++
3. Denver International Airport	-	+++	-	++	+++	-	-	+	+	+
4. Sydney Opera House	+++	+++	+++	++	++	-	++	++	++	+++
5. Green Meadow's Utility Outage	-	+++	-	+	+	+++	+	+	+	-
6. Biogen, Inc. rBeta Interferon	+++	-	-	+	-	-	-	+	-	+
7. Copenhagen Metro	-	+++	-	++	+++	+++	+++	++	+	++
Inter-Rater Reliability	.98**	.77*	.83**	.25	.79*	.96**	.84**	.79*	.40	.76*
Total Impact	**7**	**18**	**9**	**12**	**15**	**10**	**6**	**7**	**6**	**12**

Notes: Abbreviations for the 10 behavioral factors (see Table 13.1) are (1) Strategic misrepresentation (SM), (2) Optimism bias (OPB), (3) Uniqueness bias (UB), (4) Planning fallacy (PF), (5) Overconfidence bias (OVB), (6) Hindsight bias (HB), (7) Availability bias (AB1), (8) Base rate fallacy (BRF), (9) Anchoring bias (AB2), and (10) Escalation of commitment (EC); $^{**}p = 0.05$; $^{**}p<0.01$.

may still achieve success. However, the setting and acceptance of unrealistic project goals can contribute to poor project investment decision-making, such as selecting the wrong project because the goals in its business case were set unrealistically (Meredith & Zwikael, 2019). In this chapter, we examined 10 common behavioral factors that could trigger a manager to set unrealistic project goals. For this purpose, we analyzed seven case studies of well-known project failures to determine which behavioral factors appear to contribute to unrealistic goal setting the most. Our findings indicate that of the 10 behavioral factors, optimism bias, overconfidence bias, the planning fallacy and escalation of commitment had the highest levels of impact on these seven projects, while anchoring bias and availability bias had the lowest level of impact.

Optimism and overconfidence bias were found to be the top two behavioral factors that impact the setting of unrealistic project goals. Optimism bias was a defining factor in all of the seven projects that have failed to achieve their goals except one – Biogen, Inc. rBeta Interferon. Availability bias and anchoring bias were rated as having the lowest impact on the projects.

Inter-rater reliability between the four independent raters was assessed and found to be present for all the behavioral factors except two – planning fallacy and anchoring bias. It is possible that this lack of agreement is a result of the popularity of the planning fallacy. One or more of the raters may have been biased in thinking it is more prevalent than it actually is. Planning fallacy may also be viewed as vague or broad and therefore thought to be present more often than it is. The poor inter-rater reliability for the anchoring bias may be a result of the raters' lack of "insider" knowledge to more confidently assess the extent it was a factor in the setting of unrealistic project goals.

The researchers also noted the impact of other behavioral factors outside of the 10 identified in Table 13.1. This finding suggests that the 10 behavioral factors (Flyvbjerg, 2021) are not comprehensive and additional key factors should also be empirically analyzed in future research. For example, knowledge deficits played a key role in The Hubble Space Telescope's difficulties – human error and accidental use of faulty technology. In addition, The Sydney Opera House was substantially affected by the endowment effect (Kahneman et al., 1991), which can cause managers to feel ownership in a project, hence valuing it more than its real worth, and accordingly setting unrealistic goals (Feris et al., 2017). A final example is the Boeing 787 Dreamliner, which was impacted by "risk underestimation," which can occur when a person does not account for or consider a known risk when setting project goals. It should be noted here, that while our research shows some behavioral factors appear to occur more frequently than others, due to the nature of our research design, our findings are not necessarily generalizable to other projects and can only be used for illustrative purposes.

Practical Recommendations for Setting Realistic Project Goals

We propose practical recommendations for managers to increase the occurrence of realistic project goal setting (Table 13.4). These practices were derived from our cases, the academic literature, and leading organizations' project practices. The proposed 10 practices are grouped into 3 major goal setting processes that occur during a project's front-end: (1) effective goal setting – this includes the identification, definition, and setting of target values for project goals; (2) effective goal appraisal – this process includes the presentation of the project goals to a group of stakeholders, beneficiaries, and independent experts to comment on their appropriateness; and (3) effective project appraisal – this process includes the presentation of the proposed project (usually as part of a business case) to a potential funder for final approval and funding.

In Table 13.4, we have also included which of the 10 behavioral factors examined in this chapter can be directly affected from implementing each of the practical recommendations. For example, practical recommendation 1 (Reliable Data) may be able to reduce the impact of optimism bias by providing the decision-maker with the best available data. This is because we anticipate that it is likely to be more difficult to overestimate the likelihood of positive events occurring or of underestimating the likelihood of negative events occurring when reliable data are available. Conversely, we anticipate that it is easier to overestimate the likelihood of positive events occurring or of underestimating the likelihood of negative events occurring when reliable data are *not* available.

An example of why we chose to exclude some behavioral factors from the practical recommendations in Table 13.4 is as follows: Possessing reliable data is unlikely to reduce the escalation of commitment bias. Indeed, we anticipate that a decision-maker, who has decided to ignore evidence that indicates increase in commitment is not the best course of action, by definition, possesses reliable data – and is increasing commitment anyway. Thus, possession of reliable data is unlikely to reduce the occurrence of this bias.

The practices suggested in Table 13.4 are common in major projects. Although it may seem sensible to implement these recommendations in all projects, few organizations actually follow them. For example, how many organizations proposing projects use outside auditors to review their proposals? Or include a budget for mitigating risks? Or adjust challenging goals based on the history of the organization in achieving similarly challenging goals in the past? What *is* surprising is that managers who know better and should be following these recommendations do not bother with them and instead fall into the cognitive traps we have described here – and not just once but repeatedly.

Table 13.4 also offers some direct responses to the behavioral factors discussed earlier in the chapter. For example, to deal with optimism bias, the UK government (2018) suggests correction and adjustments in response to the level of uncertainty in the data, assumptions used, and project type. The maximum corrections in costs and benefits will be made in cases of uncorroborated expert judgment and data older than five years, whereas no corrections are required in cases of independently audited data conducted in the past year. All of the behavioral factors have been linked to at least one practical recommendation.

Our findings lend support to Ika et al.'s (2022, p.14) Fifth Hand theory, as they indicate planners and managers can be influenced by multiple cognitive biases at the same time when setting project goals and thus can be "plural and paradoxical, optimistic and pessimistic, and prone to both bias and

Table 13.4 Practical recommendations for setting realistic project goals

Practical recommendation	Description	Example of best practice organization	Reference	Behavioral factors impacted
Effective Goal Setting				
1. Reliable data	Use the best available data for estimates by comparing them with evidence from past or similar projects elsewhere	Australian government	Kahneman, 2011; Australian government, 2018	OPB PF UB AB1
2. Valid assumptions	Ensure a transparent understanding of the assumptions underpinning the estimation processes	Australian government; UK government	Australian government, 2016; Samset & Volden, 2016; UK government, 2018	OPB PF OVB AB2
3. Risk costs	Include the costs of mitigating and managing risks in the project cost	UK government	Australian government, 2016	SM OPB PF OVB AB1
4. Confidence levels	Set intervals for estimates	NASA	Martin, 2012	OPB PF OVB
Effective Goal Appraisal				
5. Sensitivity analysis	Test the robustness of results through sensitivity testing by analyzing the effect of changing key input variables	UK, Australian governments	Australian government, 2016	SM OPB PF OVB
6. Independent auditors	Use external auditors to confirm that goal setting is realistic	Norwegian, Western Australian, Australian Federal governments	Williams et al., 2010; Flyvjberg, 2014; Australian government, 2016; Caffieri et al., 2018	SM OPB PF
7. Reference class forecasting	Compare the risk level with previous, similar projects and make goal adjustments accordingly	Edinburgh Tram, London's Crossrail project	Flyvbjerg, 2008	SM UB PF OVB HB AB BRF AB2
8. Adjustments for optimism bias	Adjust goals based on an organization's own evidence, expert analysis, and data analysis	UK government; UK Department for Transport	De Reyck et al., 2017; Asadabadi & Zwikael, 2024	OPB PF
Effective Project Appraisal				
9. Project quality assurance	Evaluate projects at various gateways	Norwegian government	Williams et al., 2010; Samset & Volden, 2016	SM PF EC
10. A portfolio selection approach	Proposals should not be independently evaluated	UK, Norwegian governments	Williams et al., 2010; Merikhi & Zwikael, 2017	UB EC

Note: Abbreviations for the 10 behavioral factors (see Table 13.1) are (1) Strategic misrepresentation (SM), (2) Optimism bias (OPB), (3) Uniqueness bias (UB), (4) Planning fallacy (PF), (5) Overconfidence bias (OVB), (6) Hindsight bias (HB), (7) Availability bias (AB1), (8) Base rate fallacy (BRF), (9) Anchoring bias (AB2), and (10) Escalation of commitment (EC).

error." We provide practical recommendations for reducing cognitive bias and setting realistic goals as we also believe project practitioners have the "agency to make the best of the evolving context and draw and learn from experience in the face of complexity and uncertainty" (Ika et al., 2022, p. 14).

Conclusions

Unrealistic project goals have major implications for project selection, management, and evaluation. Projects with unrealistic goals are likely to be prioritized over other projects with more realistic (but less attractive) goals. Such poor investment decisions result in wasted resources and time, lost benefits, inappropriately funded projects, falling behind competitors, missed opportunities, discouraged employees, and ultimately, project failure, as the approved projects fail to achieve their inflated goals (Zwikael, 2016). To reduce cases of unrealistic project goal setting, this chapter analyzes key behavioral factors that can trigger managers in the project owner organization to set unrealistic project goals and identifies those that affected major projects the most. Following the analysis, the chapter proposes practical recommendations for setting realistic goals in major projects to overcome the impact of the behavioral factors – best practice goal setting, goal appraisal, and project appraisal. Project practitioners can reduce unrealistic goal setting through the application of these recommendations during the project front-end.

Our contribution in this chapter is twofold. Theoretically, we suggest which of the various behavioral factors proposed in the literature (e.g., Flyvbjerg, 2021; Lovallo et al. 2023) contribute the most to unrealistic goal setting. Practically, we propose 10 recommendations to help managers set more realistic project goals.

Implications are for future researchers by directing their attention to the most common behavioral factors and ensuring not all are treated as equal. Further, implications are also for practitioners to ensure training programs focus on those behavioral factors likely to cause the most harm for their projects and organizations. We recommend future research continues to identify additional behavioral factors that can impact goal setting at the individual, team, and organizational levels and tests the impact of goal setting best practice on the resulting goals. Last, we recommend future research investigate these factors across a range of different project types and sizes, including those with varying degrees of political influence.

References

Andersen, J., and Hovgaard, G. (2003). Welfare and urban planning in transition: A Copenhagen case study. *Research Papers/Department of Social Sciences*, *8*(58), 1399–1396.

Asadabadi, M. R., Chang, E., Zwikael, O., Saberi, M., and Sharpe, K. (2020). Hidden fuzzy information: Requirement specification and measurement of project provider performance using the best worst method. *Fuzzy Sets and Systems*, *383*, 127–145.

Asadabadi, M. R., and Zwikael, O. (2024). Unrealistic project goals: Detection and modification. *Journal of Construction Engineering and Management*, *150*(3), 04023166.

Atkinson, R., Crawford, L., and Ward, S. (2006). Fundamental uncertainties in projects and the scope of project management. *International Journal of Project Management*, *24*(8), 687–698.

Australian government – Australian Transport Assessment and Planning (ATAP). (2016). Australian transport assessment and planning guidelines on optimism bias. Australian Transport Assessment and Planning, Canberra, ACT, Australia.

Australian government – Department of Infrastructure, Regional Development and Cities. (2018). Ex-post economic evaluation of national road investment orojects. Report 145, vol. 1. Canberra, ACT, Australia.

Bingham, C. B., and Eisenhardt, K. M. (2011). Rational heuristics: The "simple rules" that strategists learn from process experience. *Strategic Management Journal*, *32*(13), 1437–1464.

Brockner, J. (1992). The escalation of commitment to a failing course of action: Toward theoretical progress. *Academy of Management Review*, *17*(1), 39–61.

Caffieri, J. J., Love, P. E. D., Whyte, A., and Ahiaga-Dagbui, D. (2018). Planning for production in construction: Controlling costs in major capital projects. *Production Planning and Control, 29*(1), 41–50.

Charette, R. N. (2017). Low clearance ahead: Can predictable IT crashes be avoided? *Computer, 50*(10), 86–91.

Denicol, J., Davies, A., and Krystallis, I. (2020). What are the causes and cures of poor megaproject performance? A systematic literature review and research agenda. *Project Management Journal, 51*(3), 328–345.

De Reyck, B., Grushka-Cockayne, Y., Fragkos, I., Harrison, J., and Read, D. (2017). Transport optimism bias study recommended adjustments to optimism bias uplifts. Prepared for the UK Department of Transport.

Doran, G. (1981). There's a SMART way to write management's goals and objectives. *Management Review, 70*(11), 35–36.

Dunar, A. J., and Waring, S. P. (1999). The Hubble Space Telescope (ch. 12) In *Power to Explore – History of Marshall Space Flight Center 1960–1990*. US Government Printing Office.

Feris, M., Zwikael, O., and Gregor, S. (2017). QPLAN: Decision support for evaluating planning quality in software development projects. *Decision Support Systems, 96*, 92–102.

Filliben, E., and Colley, J. L., Jr. (1993). The project manager/customer interface. Case UVA-OM-0739-PER, Charlottesville, VA: Darden Graduate Business School Foundation.

Flyvbjerg, B. (2005). Design by deception: The politics of megaproject approval. *Harvard Design Magazine*, Spring/Summer, *22*, 50–59.

Flyvbjerg, B. (2008). Curbing optimism bias and strategic misrepresentation in planning: Reference class forecasting in practice, *European Planning Studies, 16*(1), 3–21.

Flyvbjerg, B. (2014). What you should know about megaprojects and why: An overview. *Project Management Journal, 45*(2), 6–19.

Flyvbjerg, B. (2016). The fallacy of beneficial ignorance: A test of Hirschman's hiding hand. *World Development, 84*, 176–189.

Flyvbjerg, B. (2021). Top ten behavioural biases in project management: An overview. *Project Management Journal, 52*(6), 531–546.

Flyvbjerg, B., Ansara, A., Budzier, A., Buhl, S., Cantarelli, C., Garbuio, M., Glenting, C., Holm, M.S., Lovallo, D., Lunn, D., Molin, E., Rønnest, A., Stewart, A., and van Wee, B. (2018). Five things you should know about cost overrun. *Transportation Research Part A, 118*, 174–190.

Gil, N., and Pinto, J. K. (2018). Polycentric organizing and performance: A contingency model and evidence from megaproject planning in the UK. *Research Policy, 47*(4), 717–734.

Gilbert, D. (2005). *Stumbling on happiness*. Vintage Books.

Goetz, A. R., and Szyliowicz, J. S. (1997). Revisiting transportation planning and decision making theory: The case of Denver International Airport. *Transportation Research Part A, 31*(4), 263–280.

Haselton, M. G., Nettle, D., and Murray, D. R. (2015). The evolution of cognitive bias (pp. 1–20). *The handbook of evolutionary psychology*. Wiley.

Hewstone, M., Rubin, M., and Willis, H. (2002). Intergroup cognitive bias. *Annual Review of Psychology, 53*(1), 575–604.

Huber, G. P., and Power, D. J. (1985). Retrospective reports of strategic-level managers: Guidelines for increasing their accuracy. *Strategic Management Journal, 6*(2), 171–180.

Ika, L. A., Love, P. E., and Pinto, J. K. (2022). Moving beyond the planning fallacy: The emergence of a new principle of project behavior. *IEEE Transactions on Engineering Management, 69*(6), 3310–3325.

Jayatilleke, S., and Lai, R. (2018). A systematic review of requirements change management. *Information and Software Technology, 93*, 163–185.

Jones, L. R., and Euske, K. J. (1991). Strategic misrepresentation in budgeting. *Journal of Public Administration Research and Theory, 1*(4), 437–460.

Kahneman, D. (2011). *Thinking, fast and slow*, 1st ed. Farrar, Straus and Giroux.

Kahneman, D., Knetsch, J. L., and Thaler, R. H. (1991). The endowment effect, loss aversion, and status quo bias: anomalies. *Journal of Economic Perspectives, 5*(1), 193–206.

Kaufmann, C., and Kock, A. (2023). The performance effects of optimistic and pessimistic project status reporting behavior. *International Journal of Project Management, 41*(7), 102514.

Kotha, S., Olesen, D. E., Nolan, R., and Condit, P. M. (2005). Boeing 787: The Dreamliner, Harvard Business School Case 9-305-101, Boston, MA.

Locke, E. A., and Latham, G. P. (2012). Goal setting theory (pp. 23–40). In *Motivation: Theory and research*. Routledge.

Lovallo, D., Cristofaro, M., and Flyvbjerg, B. (2023). Governing large projects: A three-stage process to get it right. Academy of Management Perspectives.

Love, P. E., Ika, L. A., and Pinto, J. K. (2022). Homo heuristicus: From risk management to managing uncertainty in large-scale infrastructure projects. *IEEE Transactions on Engineering Management.* DOI: 10.1109/TEM.2022.3170474.

Love, P. E., Edwards, D. J., and Irani, Z. (2011). Moving beyond optimism cognitive bias and strategic misrepresentation: An explanation for social infrastructure project cost overruns. *IEEE Transactions on Engineering Management, 59*(4), 560–571.

Major Projects Association. (2020). Project terminology. https://majorprojects.org/project-terminology/.

Makridakis, S., and Moleskis, A. (2015). The costs and benefits of positive illusions. *Frontiers in Psychology, 6*, 859.

Martin, P. K. (2012). NASA's challenges to meeting cost schedule and performance goals, audit report no. IG-12-021. Office of Inspector General. National Aeronautics and Space Administration.

Mazur, A., Pisarski, A., Chang, A., and Ashkanasy, N. M. (2014). Rating defence major project success: The role of personal attributes and stakeholder relationships. *International Journal of Project Management, 32*(6), 944–957.

McCray, G. E., Purvis, R. L., and McCray, C. G. (2002). Project management under uncertainty: The impact of heuristics and biases. *Project Management Journal, 33*(1), 49–57.

Meredith, J. R., Shafer, S. M., and Mantel, S. J., Jr. (2018). *Project management: A strategic managerial approach*, 10th ed. John Wiley and Sons.

Meredith, J., and Zwikael, O. (2019). When is a project successful? *IEEE Engineering Management Review, 47*(3), 127–134.

Merikhi, E., and Zwikael, O. (2017). Customizing modern portfolio theory for the project portfolio selection problem. The Academy of Management Annual Meeting, Atlanta, GA.

Montealegre, R., and Kell, M. (2000). De-escalating information technology projects: Lessons from the Denver International Airport. *MIS Quarterly, 24*(3), 417–447.

NASA. 2018. Hubblesite.http://hubblesite.org/the_telescope/hubble_essentials/.

OECD. (2009). OECD Territorial Reviews: Copenhagen, Denmark. ISBN Number: 9789264060029.

Ostrower, J., and Viswanatha, A. (2016). Boeing's unique accounting helped lift profit. *Wall Street Journal*, October 4, p. B2.

Pinto, J. K., and Slevin, D. P. (1988). Critical success factors across the project life cycle. Project Management Institute, Drexel Hill, PA.

Samset, K., Andersen, B., and Austeng, K. (2014). To which extent do projects explore the opportunity space? A study of conceptual appraisals and the choice of conceptual solutions. *International Journal of Managing Projects in Business, 7*(3), 473–492.

Samset, K., and Volden, G. H. (2016). Front-end definition of projects: Ten paradoxes and some reflections regarding project management and project governance. *International Journal of Project Management, 34*(2), 297–313.

Schloh, M. (1996). *Analysis of the Denver International Airport baggage system.* California Polytechnic State University.

Serra, C. E. M., and Kunc, M. (2015). Benefits realisation management and its influence on project success and on the execution of business strategies. *International Journal of Project Management, 33*(1), 53–66.

Shenhar, A., and Holzmann, V. (2017). The three secrets of megaproject success: Clear strategic vision, total alignment, and adapting to complexity. *Project Management Journal, 48*(6), 29–46.

Shenhar, A., Holzmann, V., Melamed, B., and Zhao, Y. (2016). The challenge of innovation in highly complex projects: What can we learn from Boeing's Dreamliner experience? *Project Management Journal, 47*(2), 62–78.

Shore, B. (2008). Systematic biases and culture in project failures. *Project Management Journal,* 39(4), 5–16.

Steinel, W., and De Dreu, C. K. (2004). Social motives and strategic misrepresentation in social decision making. *Journal of Personality and Social Psychology, 86*(3), 419.

Szyliowicz, J. S., and Goetz, A. R. (1995). Getting realistic about megaproject planning: The case of the new Denver International Airport. *Policy Sciences, 28*, 347–367.

UK government. (2011). The Green Book: Appraisal and evaluation in central government, treasury guidance. HM Treasury.

UK government. (2018). The Green Book: Central government guidance on appraisal and evaluation. HM Treasury.

Unterhitzenberger, C. (2021). Special issue on project behavior. *Project Management Journal, 52*(6), 527–530.

Von Bergen, C. W., and Bressler, M. S. (2011). Too much positive thinking hinders entrepreneur success. *Journal of Business and Entrepreneurship, 23*(1), 30–52.

Wheelwright, S. C. (1996). Biogen Inc.: rBeta interferon manufacturing process development. Harvard Business School Case 9-696-083, Boston, MA.

Williams, T., Klakegg, O. J., Magnussen, O. M., and Glasspool, H. (2010). An investigation of governance frameworks for public projects in Norway and the UK. *International Journal of Project Management, 28*(1), 40–50.

Wynn, C., Smith, L., and Killen, C. (2021). How power influences behavior in projects: A theory of planned behavior perspective. *Project Management Journal, 52*(6), 607–621.

Youssef, C. M., and Luthans, F. (2007). Positive organizational behavior in the workplace the impact of hope, optimism, and resilience. *Journal of Management, 33*(5), 774–800.

Zwikael, O. (2016). Editorial. Special issue on project benefit management. *International Journal of Project Management, 34*(4), 734–735.

Zwikael, O., and Bar-Yoseph, B. (2004). Improving the capabilities of project team management using the Gestalt cycle of experience. *Team Performance Management, 10*(7), 137–144.

Zwikael, O., Chih, Y., and Meredith, J. (2018). Project benefit management: Setting effective target benefits. *International Journal of Project Management, 36*, 650–658.

Zwikael, O., Cohen, Y., and Sadeh, A. (2006). Non-delay scheduling as a managerial approach for managing projects. *International Journal of Project Management, 24*(4), 330–336.

Zwikael, O., and Gilchrist, A. (2022). The logic of the project front end (pp. 43–68). In T. Williams, K. Samset, and G. Holst Volden (eds.). *The front-end of large public projects: Paradoxes and ways ahead.* Routledge Taylor & Francis Group.

Zwikael, O., and Levin, G., Rad, P. (2008). Top management support – the project friendly organization. *Cost Engineering Journal, 50*(9), 22–30.

Zwikael, O., and Meredith, J. R. (2019). How can comprehensive goal setting enhance project investment decisions? *IEEE Transactions on Engineering Management, 69*(6), 2781–2790.

Zwikael, O., and Meredith, J. R. (2019). The role of organizational climate in setting project goals. *International Journal of Operations & Production Management, 39*(12), 1281–1294.

Zwikael, O., and Meredith, J. R. (2022). How can comprehensive goal setting enhance project investment decisions? *IEEE Transactions on Engineering Management, 69*(6), 2781–2790.

Zwikael, O., and Smyrk, J. (2012). A general framework for gauging the performance of initiatives to enhance organizational value. *British Journal of Management, 23*, S6–S22.

CHAPTER 14

At the Brink of a Project

Heuristics to Block Potential Project Disasters during the Early Project Opportunity Screening

JOANA GERALDI, VERENA STINGL, and MAXIMILIAN SCHRIEWERSMANN

Introduction

> The good ones go into your pot – the bad ones go into your crop —Cinderella, The Grimm Brothers

Large construction and infrastructure projects are shaped by a chain of decisions (Rolstadås et al., 2015). Understanding how these decisions *are* formed – beyond the notion of how they *should* be formed – is essential to understand project behavior, that is, to explain, anticipate, and cope with challenges and opportunities in the course of projects (Hirschman, 1967). Project scholars turned to cognitive and behavioral psychology concepts to explain how individuals and groups make these decisions under high uncertainty (Stingl & Geraldi, 2018). However, psychology-inspired studies have been mostly confined to the school of heuristics and bias (e.g., Flyvbjerg, 2006, 2021), which investigates heuristics as systematic, yet flawed cognitive short-cuts in the capturing and processing of cues used in decision-making (Kahneman, 2010). Accordingly, its basic rationale is to idolatrize rationality portrayed in economic theories, lament human deviations from it, and develop approaches to de-bias decisions, by, for example, increasing accuracy in project estimations through the reference-class forecasting method and thereby hope to curb planning fallacy and, ultimately, cost overruns and benefit shortfalls (Flyvbjerg, 2016).

However, this approach fails to explain the range of project behaviors experienced in practice (Ika et al., 2022). The consequence is that the literature on project behavior appears to be stuck in a debate between error vs. lie, and the benevolent or detrimental effects of the hiding hand (Ika, 2018). Ika et al. (2022) suggested reconciling these two positions through a different perspective, dubbed the Fifth Hand. This perspective builds on German psychologist Gerd Gigerenzer's critique of Kahneman's notion of heuristics – simple decision rules that only rely on a subset of the available information – as inherently biased (Gigerenzer & Brighton, 2009; Gigerenzer & Gaissmaier, 2011). Specifically, Gigerenzer and colleagues introduced the notion of fast-and-frugal heuristics as potentially both effective and efficient decision strategies (Gigerenzer & Goldstein, 1996). Their key argument is that these heuristics are not biased per se, as posited by Kahneman's heuristics and biases school (Tversky & Kahneman, 1974) and the Planning Fallacy theory. Instead, heuristics can be ecologically rational (Gigerenzer & Gaissmaier, 2011), that is, appropriate or inappropriate for a given decision context. Consequentially, Gigerenzer argues, such heuristics can be the smart strategy for decision-making under uncertainty – an argument to which Ika et al. (2022) connect when developing their Fifth Hand proposition. Following their argument, Ika et al. (2022) suggest to "empower [project planners and managers] with simple rules of thumb and above all help them learn and draw from experience" (p. 3320).

However, most research on heuristics in project studies falls into the heuristics and biases school, addressing behaviors like optimism bias and escalation of commitment (Stingl & Geraldi, 2017). Such research frames heuristics as inherently bad and suggests debiasing techniques and "rational" tools to avoid commonly experienced cost overruns and benefit shortfalls (Flyvbjerg, 2008). There is some research on fast-and-frugal heuristics in other real-life settings, for example, judges (Dhami, 2003), burglars and policemen (Garcia-Retamero & Dhami, 2009), or real estate investors (Berg, 2014). However, the settings represent highly simplified (or highly repetitive) decisions. In project contexts, where uncertainty and complexity are high, empirical research on heuristics as practitioners' fast-and-frugal strategies – and the effectiveness thereof – exists (e.g., Oliver & Jacobs, 2007; Davies et al., 2017; Eriksson and Kadefors, 2017) but remains thin and mostly disconnected from the cradle of simple heuristics research programs (Stingl & Geraldi, 2021).

Moving forward, however, we have to ask how these practitioners develop their specific heuristics in light of their context (Simon, 1991). This is important because simple heuristics require contextual sensitivity. Accordingly, Ika et al. (2022) call for further exploration of the workings of the Fifth Hand and to empower managers in the use of *smart* heuristics. To follow this call, we require additional empirical insights into the use and role of heuristics in project front-end decision-making. For this research, we thus adopt the perspective of simple heuristics in projects (Stingl & Geraldi, 2021; Love et al., 2022).

We have chosen to conduct an empirical study on heuristics used by senior managers of a large and international engineering consultancy firm to screen and select which of the tendering opportunities of large infrastructure projects to pursue. The early stage bid/no bid decisions has been extensively studied, yet mostly from an operations management perspective (e.g., Ahmad, 1990; Han & Diekmann, 2001; Lin & Chen, 2004; Egemen & Mohamed, 2007; de Araújo et al., 2021) and not yet a project behavior one. Yet the decision context is appropriate to study heuristics, as decisions are individual, frequent, and quick decisions based on fuzzy cues and hence, heuristics can be developed and applied successfully (Gigerenzer & Gaissmaier, 2011). However, the investigated decisions are "messy" problems, characterized by, for example, ambiguity, psychological and political influence, and turbulence (Williams & Samset, 2010). Such problems are hard to study with the current methodological toolkit of simple heuristics, designed for well-defined decision problems with an unambiguous understanding of success and well-structured (yet incomplete) information (Stingl & Geraldi, 2021). Therefore, the bid/no bid decision offers an opportunity to apply qualitative methods from the naturalistic decision-making program (NDM), such as Cognitive Task Analysis (Lipshitz et al., 2001). Such a method is appropriate to identify how practitioners structure messy informational contexts through heuristics, as suggested by Stingl and Geraldi (2021).

The chapter contributes to project studies by providing empirical findings on the role of simple heuristics in project behavior in the front-end phases of infrastructure projects. Specifically, we present a decision strategy based on heuristics, which we termed *thresholding*, which distills rich experience and interpretation of fuzzy contextual information into a binary decision suited to avoid disastrous project engagements. We thereby also add a fresh perspective to the bid/no-bid literature. Complex modeling currently dominates the literature yet is not widely used in practice (Drew et al., 2001; Bagies & Fortune, 2006). Our work takes the actual decision practice as a point of departure and shows how the decisions are *actually* done, namely, through thresholding. Finally, we discuss the implications of the findings to issues related to the Planning Fallacy debate.

Empirical Context: Screening Project Opportunities

For a project-based firm, tender opportunities emerge from the environment, typically presenting themselves individually and often sequentially. As such, the decision-maker must repeatedly judge which opportunity to consider and which to reject before allocating further resources to the development of the opportunity. This early stage decision is referred to as the bid/no-bid decision.

The bid/no-bid decision is a critical decision for any project-based organization. If decision-makers reject an opportunity, they may increase the risk of not having enough projects in their portfolio or missing out on strategically important opportunities. Yet developing too many bids may bind significant organisational resources with a highly uncertain outcome (Davies & Hobday, 2005). Moreover, winning too many projects can strain the company's resources with adverse effects on quality, reputation, and profits, whereas winning the wrong projects, those that lead to financial losses or other adverse effects, can damage the whole organization. Therefore, designing the portfolio of opportunities upfront has high strategic relevance to the project-based firm, as it shapes the firm's profile in the long term (Brady & Davies, 2004).

Given the high associated stakes, bid/no-bid decisions have garnered interest from research, particularly in operations research, and practice, exploring contractors' bidding behavior (e.g., Chen et al., 2015; Chisala, 2017; Zaqout et al., 2022), and developing decision support tools for bid/no-bid decision (e.g. Ahmad, 1990; Han & Diekmann, 2001; Lin & Chen, 2004). This research has afforded an exhaustive list of factors to predict contractors' bidding behavior. The body of research adheres to rationality as an ideal and proclaims guiding "the contracting organizations in reaching *'strategically correct'* bid/no bid decisions" (Egemen & Mohamed, 2007, p. 1373). Specifically, the literature aims to support their bid/no-bid decisions and to determine the appropriate mark-up level, such as current workload and tendering conditions by identifying critical factors (Egemen & Mohamed, 2007; de Araújo et al., 2021) and developing bid/no-bid decision-support tools for PBOs, especially in the construction sector. The tools range from balanced scorecards (Ahmad, 1990; Han & Diekmann, 2001) to substantially more complex fuzzy set approaches (Lin & Chen, 2004; Marzouk & Mohamed, 2018; de Araújo et al., 2021) or other probabilistic approaches (e.g., Gunduz & Al-Ajji, 2020; Li et al., 2020), which consider a wide and diverse range of criteria. The underlying rationale of these approaches is to determine the value or worth of an opportunity beforehand (Ahmad, 1990) informed by factors that contribute to probabilistic value expectations and base the bid/no-bid decision on this prospective value. Despite extensive research over decades, bid/no-bid decisions were not yet studied from a project behavior in general and heuristics angle.

Indeed, taking the perspective of simple heuristics, this increased complexification of the bid/no-bid decision to anticipate the value of an opportunity might not be suitable. Owing to the early, information-deficient stage of the project, the bid/no-bid decision is characterized by substantial uncertainty when it comes to assessing the value of the project in terms of financial or other gains (Li et al., 2020). The individual factors or circumstances that may lead to a successful or failing project are arguably complex and dynamic, and hence, difficult, if not impossible, to be modeled comprehensively. Moreover, overly complex stochastic models risk overfitting the data, that is, they are excessively tailored to fit the specific empirical data used, and thereby lose their ability to generalize well to new or unseen data, reducing their predictive power (Goldstein & Gigerenzer, 2009). Finally, following the argument of the simple heuristics research, in such contexts of high uncertainty, simple heuristics may be just as effective – if not even more effective – than complex stochastic models (Goldstein & Gigerenzer, 2009).

The increased complexification of bid/no-bid decision support tools raises a further point of concern, as it means that substantial efforts are required to apply these tools and feed them the numerous bits of information that they require. As such, they become increasingly resource-demanding and closer to tasks related to bid preparation, going against the intention of using bid/no-bid decisions as a quick screening step to avoid waste of resources. Additionally, the effortful engagement with the opportunity may trigger an escalation of commitment, complicating the decision to abandon the opportunity.

Finally, contrary to the suggestions of the literature, practitioners often do not rely on these complicated tools (Drew et al., 2001; Bagies &

Fortune, 2006) and rather refer to the bid/no-bid decision as essentially driven by experience and intuition (Ahmad, 1990). Only recently, a small stream of research in the area recognizes the relevance of subjective evaluation and risk propensity (Chen et al., 2015). Yet such challenges were addressed within the same paradigm, attempting to minimize subjective judgment and increase modeling complexity. The actual bid/no bid decision-making behavior remains underexplored.

Following these limitations of the bid/no-bid literature, we explore the actual decision-making behavior through the lens of simple heuristics. Specifically, our research investigates bid/no-bid decisions as individual deliberations reliant on heuristics. We do so for two reasons. First, in the studied organizations, these decisions are formal decisions taken by appointed individuals, the managers of specific business units. While we acknowledge the complex social processes shaping the narrative around an opportunity, these decision-makers need to structure the information provided through the social context as a rationalized and explicit decision. Second, these decision types are both frequent – managers are presented with opportunities several times a month – and are taken quickly with very limited information about the opportunity. Thus, they provide a context in which simple heuristics can thrive and in which the decision-makers are likely to distill their own experience into decision rules, given the absence of suitable analytical methods.

For this study, we follow Stingl and Geraldi's (2021, p. 8) framework for studying heuristics in managerial decision-making, asking not only which cues inform the decision and how but also what decision-makers understand as the task during the bid/no-bid decision-making. We use these building blocks to discuss aspects of ecological rationality for the identified heuristics in the decision process.

Theoretical Frame: Simple Heuristics

Heuristics – as phenomena in cognitive psychology – are decision strategies that use only a part of the available information. Traditionally, heuristics have been researched from a presumption of bias (Tversky & Kahneman, 1974), as the use of heuristics deviates from rational decision models. However, this view has been challenged by the simple heuristics research program (Gigerenzer et al., 2011; Gigerenzer & Gaissmaier, 2011). Table 14.1 provides a systematic and concise comparison between the two programs of work.

Simple heuristics research frames heuristics as natural, fast, and potentially effective decision strategies in contexts of high uncertainty (Todd & Gigerenzer, 2012). A central idea of the research is the concept of *ecological rationality*, which posits that rationality should be evaluated based on how well the decision strategy aligns with the structure of the environment (Todd & Gigerenzer, 2012),

Table 14.1 Onto-epistemological differences between the "heuristics-and-biases" and the "adaptive heuristics" programs

	Heuristics and biases	Simple heuristics
Ontology (worldview)		
Concept of heuristics	Deviation from the rational process, that introduces error.	In the right context ("ecology"), useful and accurate tools for predictions and choices.
Concept of rationality	Assumption of a universal rationality	Assumption of ecological rationality
Epistemology (scientific method)		
Modeling detail	As-is model (only output)	Rigorous process modeling
Aim of research	Descriptive	Descriptive and normative
Contribution to practice	De-biasing methods	Formalized heuristics with criteria for ecological rationality

rather than adhering to a universal definition of rationality, following an abstract ideal of reasoning, as suggested by the heuristics and biases program.

The simple heuristics research program (Gigerenzer et al., 2011) aims to identify, describe, and compare individual strategies in decision-making. This approach has resulted in abundant structural descriptions of heuristics, as well as insights into their formation and contexts in which they are appropriate (Gigerenzer & Gaissmaier, 2011). One of the most prominent examples of such simple heuristics is satisficing, a strategy to choose the first encountered option that fulfills a minimum requirement of predefined cues instead of aiming to identify the most optimal option. Such a strategy can be ecologically rational in the context of quickly disappearing options, such as real estate (Berg, 2014) or mating choices (Todd & Miller, 1999).

The simple heuristics research is concerned with developing a typology of different heuristics and insights into how individuals intuitively or deliberately apply these heuristics based on the specific decision context (Gigerenzer & Gaissmaier, 2011). The difference between strategies concerns how information is processed as individual "cues." Cues here are understood as structured pieces of information "that are probabilistically related to the to-be-judged dimension" (Pachur & Bröder, 2013, p. 665) – for example, price as a (potentially misleading) cue indicating the quality of a product. A variety of cue-based strategies have been collected and reported as explicit heuristics in a body of work referring to an "adaptive toolbox" (Gigerenzer & Brighton, 2009). Typologies of heuristics classify these strategies according to three basic building blocks: search, stopping, and decision rules. The search rule defines how the decision-maker searches for information and transforms them into cues, which are used in the judgment process, for example, the project budget, the project location, etc. The stopping rules explain when decision-makers stop the search for cues. Finally, the decision rules explain how these cues inform a judgment or decision (Todd & Gigerenzer, 2012). The notion of building blocks indicates that the elements are separate and, thus, can be recombined to create new heuristics. By changing one of the elements, heuristics are adapted and made applicable to a new situation – a process of adaption to context usually through experience (e.g., Summers et al., 2004; Garcia-Retamero and Dhami, 2009; Pachur and Marinello, 2013). We adopt these building blocks as a guiding frame for our data analysis.

However, as discussed by Stingl and Geraldi (2021), using this theoretical lens also requires adaptations. Despite the increasing attention to heuristics as a theoretical frame to study managerial cognition and decision-making (Mousavi & Gigerenzer, 2014; Artinger et al., 2015; Loock & Hinnen, 2015), this body of work is mostly developed in contexts of operations with recurrent decisions taken in well-structured and often abundant information environments (e.g., Cianci & Kaplan, 2010; Bauer et al., 2013; Berg, 2014; Luan et al., 2019). However, most decisions in projects are messier, less repetitive, and marked by uncertainty and less-structured information environments (Love et al., 2022, 2023). Moreover, given that a project is a unique undertaking, even repetitive decisions take place in unique contexts, challenging the quantitative assessment of a heuristic's ecological rationality (Stingl & Geraldi, 2021).

Thus, despite the potential relevance of heuristics to project decision-making, very few empirical studies have used simple heuristics to investigate decisions in projects to date. Exceptions are studies on organizational or group-level heuristics that identified simple heuristics as guiding principles embedded in narratives (Oliver & Jacobs, 2007), shared mantras or catchphrases (Eriksson & Kadefors, 2017), or simple rules (Bingham & Eisenhardt, 2011; Davies et al., 2017). Table 14.2 provides an overview of empirical studies that evoke, implicitly or explicitly, simple heuristics.

These studies highlight both the potential to use heuristics as a theoretical frame to expose cognitive strategies (e.g., Winch & Maytorena, 2009; Stingl & Geraldi, 2023) and to evaluate heuristics as "ecologically rational" decision strategies (e.g., Albar & Jetter, 2011; Van Oorschot et al. 2011). However, the showcased diversity of approaches also

Table 14.2 Overview of literature on simple heuristics in project studies

	Explicitly positioned as simple heuristics research?	Aim of study	Research topic and methodology
(Albar & Jetter, 2011)	Yes	Prescriptive	Evaluation of different heuristics in their performance to support project portfolio selection at the front end (quantitative case study)
(Eriksson & Kadefors, 2017)	Yes	Descriptive	Simple heuristics as a developing phenomenon for organizing complex technical projects (qualitative case study)
(Hartono & Yap, 2011)	Yes	Descriptive	Description of heuristics guiding mark-up decisions in the construction industry (quantitative experiment)
(Mathews, 2010)	Yes	Descriptive	Description of constructed "Fast-and-Frugal" type heuristic for early-stage screening of innovation projects in an organization (qualitative case report)
(Maytorena et al., 2007)	No	Descriptive/ Prescriptive	Information search strategies for risk identification in construction projects (simulation experiment with mixed-method analysis)
(Van Oorschot et al., 2011)	No	Descriptive/ Prescriptive	(i.a.) heuristics for interventions in new product development projects (quantitative hypothesis testing)
(Winch & Maytorena, 2009)	No	Descriptive	(cf Maytorena et al., 2007)
(Stingl & Geraldi, 2023)	Yes	Descriptive	Heuristics as strategies to identify and formulate project risks and opportunities (simulation experiment with mixed-method analysis)

illustrates the difficulty of studying heuristics in project contexts. While acknowledging the importance and potential of simple heuristics in project studies, we contend that some project scholars are prone to oversee its potential onto-epistemological clashes, as discussed in Stingl & Geraldi (2021). Our study thereby proposes an alternative approach, which allows us to stay closer to the framing of the simple heuristics research program as proposed by Gigerenzer and colleagues.

Research Design

The presented research follows a single case study design (Yin, 2009), investigating senior managers' cognitive strategies as the unit of analysis embedded in a shared organizational context. Case studies are of paramount importance in theorizing as they offer detailed and context-specific insights into complex phenomena (Yin, 2018). Case studies enable the examination of complex and multifaceted phenomena, particularly in the realm of human behavior, by capturing the richness of qualitative data (Flyvbjerg, 2006). This in-depth contextual understanding is crucial for the study of heuristics, as the context plays a crucial role in explaining the origin, structure, and appropriateness of simple heuristics (Stingl & Geraldi, 2021). By focusing on individual decision cases, researchers can gain detailed insights into the cognitive processes and mental shortcuts individuals employ when making choices. This examination of specific decisions allows for a nuanced understanding of how simple heuristics are used in real-world contexts, shedding light on the underlying structures and mechanisms at play. The analysis of decision cases provides empirical evidence that can be used to validate, refine, or generate theoretical frameworks concerning cognitive heuristics.

Research Context: Case Company and Early Opportunity Screening

The organizational context of this case is a leading engineering consultancy firm, subsequently referred to as EC. The case company employs over 10,000 employees across several countries, with their headquarters located in Denmark. EC is active in a wide variety of engineering business sectors, such as construction, transport, and energy and serves both private and public clients.

Two characteristics are critical to defining EC's context in the screening decision. First, decision-makers need to implement strategy "with their hands tied," as tendering opportunities are *externally generated*, limited, emerge consecutively, and are often available to the main competitors. Second, through implementing the stage-gate process, EC has established a risk-oriented approach to opportunity screening, to avoid major project failures experienced in their recent past.

Data Sources

The empirical data involved in this study consists of structured interviews to elicit cognitive strategies supplemented by an ethnographic study to capture the organizational context. The structured interviews were based on the Applied Cognitive Task Analysis (ACTA; Militello & Hutton, 1998) method, which is presented in detail below. The ethnographic study used an insider-outsider approach (Bartunek & Louis, 1996). One of the authors, the insider, conducted a six-month-long ethnographically inspired study (Fetterman, 2010) at EC, between January and June 2017. He was part of the company's milieu, made friendships and developed social relationships, and had access to the intranet, project-related documents, and other company generic information. During this time, he discussed the context, opportunity screening, and project review through exploratory interviews and written communication with key organizational actors. Findings and impressions of the organization were discussed periodically with the other two coauthors (outsiders).

Choice of Interviewees

The literature on the development of cognitive strategies of expert decision-makers (Shanteau, 1992) suggests that expertise requires experience, sometimes for several years. Following theoretical sampling, we chose high-ranking senior managers with at least ten years of experience in project work and currently engaging in opportunity screening decisions regularly. Our interviewees suggested that this experience threshold is required to understand the context and have exposure to several projects, as opportunities do not emerge daily, and as EC's complex engineering projects have a long duration. The required high level of experience capped the number of individuals that were both relevant and available for the structured data collection in the organization to six. Yet the sample covers most senior managers in the organization who meet the 10-year criteria. Moreover, as EC is a global company active in multiple sectors, our sample covers various geographical regions (Denmark, United Kingdom, Middle East/Asia), industry sectors (buildings, transport, aviation, harbors), and managerial positions, thus capturing the multifaceted dimensions present within the case context and reducing potential interviewee biases (Eisenhardt & Graebner, 2007). Throughout the interviews, shared decision cues and cognitive strategies emerged, which indicates that the sample reached theoretical saturation (Eisenhardt, 1989).

Data Collection Method

The structured data collection followed an adaptation of the Applied Cognitive Task Analysis (Militello & Hutton, 1998). ACTA aims to expose cognitive strategies experts use to accomplish a given task by identifying cues and cue processing at use (Crandall & Hoffman, 2013). The data collection instrument included: (1) a task diagram interview, (2) a knowledge audit, and (3) a cognitive demand table (Militello & Hutton, 1998). ACTA affords a verbal report of the screening decision through a think-aloud protocol, completed through probing based on specific examples and accompanied by a visual documentation of the interviewee's statements. The knowledge audit was supplemented by aspects of the Critical Decision Method (CDM), whereby the interviewer solicits examples of screening choices and scrutinizes the examples in progressive deepening through probing questions regarding the "interviewees" used cues and decision strategies (Hoffman, 1998).

This structured interview guide was developed based on six piloting interviews that allowed testing and familiarization of the researcher with the method. The interviews took place during the second half of the ethnographic study, between March and May 2017, lasting between 60–90 minutes. The interviews were recorded and transcribed. We photographed the drawings developed during the interviews.

Data Analysis

To understand whether and how the interviewees used heuristics, we started the analysis with the practitioners' perceptions of their context and task. We focused on the perceived challenge of the task, the formulation of the task, and the expressed criteria for good task delivery. Then, to identify the heuristics of the practitioners, we coded the transcripts for the three building blocks of heuristics: (1) How did practitioners search for cues and what *cues* and *patterns of cues* they considered? (*search rules*), (2) When did the practitioner stop looking for cues? (*stopping rules*), (3) How did the cues inform the screening decision (*decision rules*)? Finally, we analyzed the influence of project context on the development of these heuristics.

The third author (insider) developed the initial coding, which was subsequently validated and discussed with the other authors. Finally, we validated the emerging findings through discussion with practitioners within the organization. This process reduced the bias of the researcher (Bartunek & Louis, 1996), increasing validity and reliability.

Findings: Simple Heuristics to Avoid Major Disasters

Our data revealed two findings that challenge and expand our understanding of bid/no-bid decisions. First, senior managers prioritize eliminating potential project disasters over selecting excellent opportunities. As a result, the bid/no-bid decision is framed around evaluating risks rather than assessing value. Second, they do so through a fast and efficient strategy reliant on various combinations of heuristics, which we call *thresholding*. Given the current methodological impossibility of observing the actual cognitive process, conclusions are inferred based on theoretical concepts and can never claim to reflect the "true" cognitive processes beyond doubt (Dhami, 2003). Therefore, we discuss our findings in light of the literature and hence front-load the discussion of the findings.

The Objective of the Decision: Elimination of Potential Disasters

While the literature on bid/no bid predominately focuses on selecting good opportunities, practitioners in our study framed the purpose of the screening decision as the early elimination of "bad projects," that is, projects that were perceived as too risky or obviously not fitting their portfolio. They screened for risks and critical showstoppers – not asking, "How good is the opportunity?" but "How bad is it?" For example, the regional director's key concern was to make the right, timely call for deselecting opportunities that would otherwise waste time and resources:

> Sometimes ... I am in two minds whether we should, or not. And I've said "Okay, we'll give it a go," and I regret it halfway through and wished we hadn't .... And you burn your fees.

The common rationale for early elimination was the difficulty of "killing" a bid that had already received a "go-ahead" at an earlier stage:

> Once we have set our target on a project, it is very difficult to get people out of it ... we kind of get blind and think we can solve it and then we have this optimism that we will solve it. We get carried away.

As another interviewee remarked: "This is not about saying yes to everything; this is about saying no to some things." Thus, senior managers understood the screening task as a strategy to deselect unfavorable bid opportunities timely, avoiding waste of resources and subsequent risk of escalation of commitment. Hence, senior managers were aware of the danger of escalation of commitment and used these early sifts to safeguard the company from major failures.

Signal-Detection Theory (Luan et al., 2011) provides a suitable theoretical angle to explain this finding. First, according to Luan et al., the signal-noise ratio or sensitivity of a cue determines whether a cue should be considered early or late in the decision process. Two aspects of competitive bidding are significant here: first, the client's behavior and the management of the project will shape the opportunity after the project-based firm has won the bid. Hence, the signal-noise ratio of cues is assumed to be weak: a specific indication at the time of the screening may just as likely be shaped into a success as into a failure. Yet the risk-oriented cues consider aspects that are unlikely to be substantially modified and shaped at later stages. Hence, critical risk factors identified at the screening stage will exhibit a significantly stronger and more dependable signal and are thus more valid cues at this stage. The project review practices and stage gate meetings further reinforce the focus and learning of risk-oriented cues, as they draw managers' attention to the identification and discussion of individual aspects (cues) for salient problems within running or concluded projects.

Second, failing by deselecting potentially excellent projects is significantly less critical than failing by selecting potentially disastrous opportunities. Hence, the observed risk orientation is highly suitable. The risk-oriented cue formulation allows the identification of opportunities with little to no chance of success, thus supporting the rejection of opportunities that do not pass the minimum threshold. Conversely, as any opportunity that eventually can be shaped into a potential success should ideally pass the screening, there is no value in ranking the opportunities regarding their potential upsides at this stage. Hence, in this context, cues concerned with the benefits of the opportunity have little informative value for the screening decision.

The Practice of Thresholding: Using Heuristics to Separate the Bad from the Potentially Good

Senior managers relied on a range of simple heuristics to decide on opportunities to select (or deselect). The decision to select, in this case, means that the opportunity for tendering entered EC's stage-gate governance model for further scrutiny. Deselection meant that the opportunity would be no further pursued.

Senior managers described the decision as going through a mental checklist concerned with several explicit single aspects of the opportunity they evaluated. They experienced the decision as relatively undemanding. This suggests that they translated fuzzy contextual information into an *unambiguous binary decision.*

For example, according to a regional director, the screening "doesn't take a lot of time . . .. I don't need a piece of paper or a spreadsheet to work that out; I just look at it and . . . decide 'Yeah, this is for us.' or 'Yeah, this is not for us.'" Similarly, another participant described the screening task as a sequence of "some basic sifts that we go through" to identify those projects they would like to select. Moreover, senior managers described the screening decision as an essentially binary task. As one head of department encapsulated, the decision is "just a lot of information that you need to boil down to a Yes or No," reflecting a cognitive filtering of available information to arrive at inferences, which defines heuristics. While arriving at this binary decision is also the purpose of the complex bid/no-bid decision tools (e.g., Ahmad, 1990; Han & Diekmann, 2001; Chisala, 2017), and the factors considered are similar to the critical factors identified in the bid/no bid literature (e.g., Egemen & Mohamed, 2007; de Araújo et al., 2021), the approach used by the senior managers was significantly different compared to the quantitative decision tools.

To filter and process the information, they relied on a set of complementary heuristics organized in a practice we term thresholding. While the concrete cues and heuristics varied between the managers, the structure of heuristics used followed an overarching one-reason decision pattern across all interviewees and used nested heuristics to generate the cues for these decisions.

One-reason decisions are "a class of heuristics that bases judgments on one good reason only, ignoring other cues" (Gigerenzer & Gaissmaier, 2011, p. 463). Such a class of decisions involves either the use of the same one-reason for all decisions, like "we only hire from Harvard," or "the

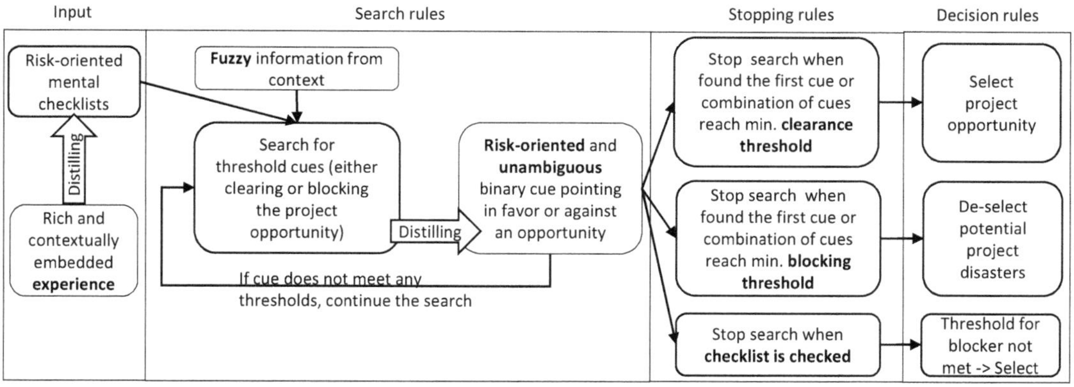

Figure 14.1 Structure for thresholding practice: A nested heuristics approach.

sequential search through cues, and it may search for more than one cue but also bases its decision on only one" (p. 463). Such sequential search was the approach that managers in our sample found most effective and efficient. They searched for individual cues and stopped when they found a cue that by itself could serve to justify their screening decision – typically a single reason to deselect an opportunity, which we call a blocking threshold.

However, owing to the complexity of the decision task (relative to past studies on heuristics), the identification and formulation of the cues were not always straightforward and required additional strategies to move from fuzzy information to explicit cues. We observed that to achieve this, the managers followed a cognitive strategy that resembled nested heuristics. In other words, the practitioners first used heuristics to transform complex information into cues, which informed the following one-reason heuristic. We called the entire process thresholding practice.

Figure 14.1 portrays the thresholding practice according to the three building blocks of heuristics (Todd & Gigerenzer, 2012). We describe the apparent cognitive processes and iterative processes for selecting and applying concrete heuristics involved in thresholding in the following sections.

Input: Distilling Rich Experience into a Mental Checklist

Our findings suggest that a mental checklist of one-reason heuristics guided the bid/no-bid decision. Decision makers curated their checklist individually, distilling factors based on a rich and contextually embedded experience. Specifically, we identified 51 distinguishable cues in 10 categories, which could serve as cues for one-reason decisions (see Table 14.3).

The checklist was exogenous to the decision process and developed through their experience managing and governing major projects in the organisation.

Only 6 of the 51 cues occurred in all interviews, and 22 of them were mentioned by less than half of the participants. This topical variety reflects the diversity of EC's businesses, where units of the organization exhibit significant differences in project size, project numbers, geographical markets, industries, customer types, etc., pointing to the relevance of contextual experience in the development of these mental checklists. Hence, while the cues resemble the critical factors identified in the bid/no bid literature (e.g., Egemen & Mohamed, 2007; de Araújo et al., 2021), the actual mental checklist of each decision-maker was colored by their prior experience and tailored to their context.

The mental checklist distilled complex and fuzzy experiences into binary questions, which are simple to apply and serve as one-reason heuristics. For example: "Will we be able to find the right partners?," 'Is the country on the No-Go list?," or "Is it going to earn us enough money? Some questions were formulated open-endedly, for example, "What is the competition?," "Who are the partners?," or "Where is the money coming

Table 14.3 List of cue categories and examples of cues (the numbers in brackets indicate the total number of cues per category)

Category	Example of cue criteria
Strategy (2)	Does the project fit the strategy?
Size (2)	Is the complexity adequate for the organisation?
Competition (1)	Can we beat the competition?
Time (2)	Is there sufficient time to develop a tender proposal?
Location (4)	Does global compliance prohibit the 'project's location?
Client (11)	Does the client want to work with our organisation? Is the 'client's funding source reliable?
Contract (4)	Is the commercial risk bearable?
Organisation (11)	Does our organisation have the right capabilities for the project? Is the role in the project attractive?
Colleagues (2)	Do other colleagues see the project as worthwhile?
Partners (13)	Can we find a suitable (local) partner to deliver the project? Is the 'partner's reputation favourable?

from?" Yet, upon probing, senior managers typically restated or connected the open questions as one or several closed questions. For example, a regional director explained why he would consider the type of relationship with the client (an open-ended question) as follows:

> We are not interested in projects where we are a sub-consultant to a sub-consultant. We want to be ideally the lead consultant where we are in direct interaction with the client.

In another example, a country market director specified that he needs to know the details of the required services to answer the binary question, "Can we deliver this?"

Search Rules: Looking for Unambiguous Blockers or Clearances

Our data suggest that senior managers went through their checklists when examining an opportunity for tender, searching for unambiguous answers in a fuzzy and uncertain information context of the tendering opportunity. The answers became cue values, that is, the information used in the decision process. The search had two interesting characteristics.

First, senior managers did not search sequentially through the checklist. Instead, they searched for cues that would amount to a threshold to *block* potential disastrous projects or to give *clearance* to obviously relevant project opportunities. Typically, these would start with cues that require relatively little effort to generate from the available information. If the answer to a question (or question series) would not amount to a threshold, they continued addressing another question on their mental checklist. Although senior managers managed both clearance and blockers cues, the expressed cues in the structured interviews were predominantly concerned with possible *critical risk factors*, with only very few expressed cues related to project benefits, such as long-term strategic value, cross-selling opportunities, or reputational gain. Individuals who mentioned benefit-related cues recalled them significantly later in the interview than risk-oriented cues. Moreover, aspects typically associated with benefits, such as the long-term strategic importance of clients and industries, were typically mentioned in direct relation to pre-formulated strategies. Additionally, the practitioners considered the financial side of the opportunity – if at all – typically only through the risk lens, for example, regarding the client's budget expectation as too low, again reinforcing the risk-oriented approach to the decision.

Another essential characteristic of this step was that practitioners developed *unambiguous, binary* cues pointing either in favor or against the pursuit of the opportunity. Curating unambiguous cues was straightforward for cues related to objective properties. These cues typically referred to criteria established in organizational documents, such as strategy formulation or compliance guidelines. Most of the practitioners formulated cues such as "[Is] the client named in our business plan as a strategic client?" or "Have we got an office nearby?"

Most cues, however, required subjective assessment through the practitioner. Through probing, three approaches – aligned with the three types of heuristics described by Gigerenzer and Gaissmaier

(2011) – explain how practitioners transformed subjective judgments into binary cues. The first approach related to self-defined acceptable limits using one-reason heuristics. For example, a country market director evaluated the criterion: "Can we beat the competition?" as: "[If] There are maybe only two or three competitors [it is fine]. If there had been 10, I would say: 'Forget it!'"

The second approach followed the structure of trade-off heuristics, considering several informational aspects together to generate a binary cue. For example, one manager would deselect opportunities based on a low probability of winning the tender. To generate the cue, he would consider several cues for which "you look at the tick-boxes to say: 'Yes, we got a very good chance of getting this job.'"

The third approach was recognition-based heuristics, to generate binary cues based on a holistic consideration of available information. Here, practitioners typically consulted intuition based on experience or a feeling for "what it should be." Examples of such approaches related to high-level cues such as "Is the client interested to work with us?" or "Is the level of complexity appropriate for us?" In these cases, a general impression from documents or interactions with the client informed the evaluation of the binary, abstract cues.

Stopping and Decision Rules: Select the Mandatory, Discard the Potential Disasters

Our data suggest three stopping rules and following decision rules (see Figure 14.1).

Clearance thresholding: A few of the opportunities for tendering were considered obvious opportunities to pursue and were quickly selected. Hence, senior managers stopped the search and selected the opportunity as soon as they met the first cue or a combination of cues (usually not more than two), pointing to the obvious need to pursue the opportunity, which we called clearance thresholding. For example, an interviewee explained that there are projects "that ... we know this is something we need to bid on [... which] would typically be big projects on our home markets." Another interviewee supports this by stating, "There are some projects where you don't even need to think about whether to bid or not. It is just mandatory that we do so because it is our home market or with a client, we have worked a lot with ...." Another senior manager specified: 'We got good relationships with 15 architects and ... we have them listed down and then we know probably 20 end-clients, whom we either work with or aspire to work with, so if an inquiry comes in from one of those architects or an inquiry comes in from one of those clients, because they are on our list of preferred clients, it's a high probability that we gonna go for the job." This heuristic ensured that the company would not miss projects with strategic significance.

Blocking thresholding dominated the decision process of most interviewees. Several participants described searching for a single cue or a combination of usually not more than two cues that pointed to significant potential risks, which we termed blocking threshold. When that threshold was met, they stopped the search and decided to deselect the opportunity. For example, a country market director stated this in a manner exemplary for his peers: "If there is not enough time, if you can't compete ... a lot of stuff .... So I think it could be a no-go for any of these."

In some cases, they decided by *balancing* compensatory cues, that is, by compensating individual negative cue-criterion relations with other, positive cue-criterion relations. Here, two or more cues could offset each other. In these cases, practitioners also typically implied the weights of the different cues. For example, as a country market director recalled,

> [The unfavorable] location of the project was not so important, because it was more [... that] the client was an international contractor.

This cue processing strategy is similar to the compensatory cue-abstraction strategy (Pachur & Bröder, 2013), whereby the relationship between cues is considered. Accordingly, these strategies allow for compensation of individual negative cue-criterion relations through other, positive cue-criterion relations. The Minimum Requirement heuristic is a classic example of such strategies (Hu & Wang, 2014). It involves collecting information on a predefined set of cues and deciding based on the tally, that is, all cue values taken together. This kind of cognitive strategy is still simple yet cognitively more complex than one-reason decisions mentioned above. Yet, the overall thresholding logic is maintained; that is, as soon as the connected cues meet a threshold, the opportunity will be selected or deselected.

Finally, senior managers stopped the search and selected the opportunity if they went through their checklists and could not find reasons to block the opportunity.

Discussion and Conclusion

Our research addresses Ika et al.'s (2022) call for a more nuanced understanding of project behavior that is not blind-sighted by an exclusively negative view of heuristics. The simple heuristics perspective – integrated into Ika et al.'s proposed Fifth Hand – considers heuristics as building blocks of our cognition, which can be adaptively deployed depending on the decision context. If used wisely, they can be fast and frugal. Our study contributes to project studies in three main ways. Firstly, we offer an empirical examination of simple heuristics in a complex decision-making context, and thereby the study provides an approach to bridge simple heuristics and project studies. Secondly, it uncovers decision practices that differ from traditional bid/no bid models. Lastly, it offers a fresh perspective on the Hiding Hand debate. Overall, our research enhances our understanding of decision-making in projects.

First, our study offers a fresh perspective on the bid/no bid literature. The literature so far has approached bid/no bid decisions mainly through an Operations Research perspective, aiming at the development of complex decision support tools that are disconnected from organizational practice (e.g. Ahmad, 1990; Egemen & Mohamed, 2007; Chen et al., 2015; Chisala, 2017; Marzouk & Mohamed, 2018; Gunduz & Al-Ajji, 2020; Li et al., 2020; de Araújo et al., 2021; Zaqout et al., 2022). By investigating the actual practice of these decisions, through the perspective of simple heuristics, we were able to describe the thresholding practice that is both in intent and execution substantially different from complex bid/no-bid decision support tools. While decision-makers in our empirical work considered similar factors to those identified in the literature – for example, competition, contact, and availability of resources (e.g., Egemen & Mohamed, 2007; de Araújo et al., 2021), their purpose and decision practice were different. Current literature focuses on methods and factors to select the best opportunities; however, our study suggests that practitioners rather *deselect* the potential disasters through thresholding. Thresholding starts as senior managers use their intuition and experience to distill complex and fuzzy considerations into a binary and risk-oriented mental checklist that they then use to *deselect* potential project disasters. Such an approach is smart in the context of decisions where resources for investigation are scarce, uncertainty abounds, and decision-makers are torn between the risk of too few projects and too many bad projects. Thus, it illustrates the Fifth Hand's balance between simple rules of thumb and statistical analysis, as Ika et al. (2022) suggested. Our empirical findings indicate that potential project disasters are tentatively curbed not by avoiding heuristics but by using them wisely. Doing so does not guarantee the elimination of potential disasters, nor will it solve project cost overruns and benefit shortfalls, but it avoids at least the obviously "bad projects."

The findings also contribute to the debate on the Hiding Hand. Our discussion of thresholding adds to the debate by not being concerned with what is hidden, why it is hidden, and how to unhide; instead, it points to the importance of looking for what *can be known* with confidence in the early fuzzy front end of projects. Accordingly, senior managers were not looking to foresee which projects would give the most value – which is widely unforeseeable. Instead, they captured and focused their decisions on high-validity cues that pointed to project disasters; that is, they looked for cues that could predict problems with a high level of confidence and only looked for those cues, not others. In doing so, thresholding accommodates both Hirschman's belief in the human ability to overcome problems and transform opportunities into successful projects at the end and Flyvbjerg's call for some scrutiny at the front end of projects to avoid catastrophic projects that start on the wrong premises.

The approach also gives credence to agency, as it only deselects disasters but keeps many potential alternatives in the portfolio. The remaining options are offered time and space to mature until further evaluation. Therefore, it allows project actors to transform potential opportunities into potentially "good projects," which Kreiner (2020) termed project management as a pursuit.

Finally, bridging disciplines is a well-known challenge, yet critical (Knudsen, 2003; Raasch et al., 2013). In our case, the challenge lies in the need to balance a sensitivity to the nature of project context and to the onto-epistemological traditions of simple heuristics, as detailed in Stingl and Geraldi (2021). Simple heuristics are traditionally applied to well-structured decisions and often abundant information environments (e.g., Cianci & Kaplan, 2010; Bauer et al., 2013; Berg, 2014; Luan et al., 2019). We exemplified how simple heuristics can be applied to more complex decision problems, through a careful choice of decision problem and methodology. We searched for and identified a decision problem that is critical to projects, with a literature that is dominated by a rational approach through complex modeling, yet disconnected from the actual decision-making practices. Moreover, bid/no bid decisions are individual, frequent, and quick, and therefore likely to draw on simple heuristics and can be studied from a simple heuristics perspective with some adaptations, as discussed in Stingl and Geraldi (2021). We hope our study offers inspiration to future studies on simple heuristics in project contexts, calibrating researchers' gaze to appropriate decision problems and research methods.

Although pointing to interesting implications, our study is exploratory and has limitations. First, it is an in-depth but single case study with a small sample of interviewees within a single organization. This limits drawing conclusions for cognitive processes in competitive bidding in general. Further studies could explore cognitive processes in other competitive bidding contexts, such as architectural competitions, and compare the findings. Second, our methodology bears the limitations of any interview-type method, that is, the possibility of biased statements, in particular triggering a (post-)rationalization of decisions. A validation of the verbally described approach through experimentation in a simulation interview or through observation provides a way around this limitation. Yet, in the present study, such a validation was not possible through the stereotypically limited availability of senior managers. Apart from the classic methodological solutions within positivist paradigms, future studies could attempt to triangulate the findings through other qualitative methods, such as the observation of steering committee meetings followed by, and complemented with, interviews. Linguistic analysis of the data could also provide interesting insights into the way arguments are shaped in such meetings, connecting the cognitive strategies with sensemaking. Third, the methodology only allowed collecting indications of the used cognitive strategies, by proxy of individual information search behavior. Yet, given the current methodological impossibility to observe the actual cognitive process, any such conclusion can only be measured in accordance with its predictive capability to the observed behavior and can never claim to reflect the "true" cognitive processes beyond doubt (Dhami, 2003). Fourth, the findings only report the strategies practitioners select, and make no assumptions regarding the suitability or effectiveness of these strategies given the specific context. Hence, this research remains in the domain of descriptive studies with yet limited implication for practice. However, the gained insight on the set of applied strategies, and the role of organizational behavior in encouraging the selection of some strategies over others, opens up for future research to formalize, test, and improve screening and feedback practices for competitive bidding. Finally, future studies could test the effectiveness of thresholding in different contexts and thereby contribute to more robust theorizing about the environmental conditions in which this approach and its underlying heuristics are ecologically rational. More generically, our study suggests a reconciliation of Hirschman's and Flyvbjerg's aspirations. We hope our work inspires fellow scholars to take decision-makers and their complex context as a point of departure for their inquiries.

References

Ahmad, I. (1990). Decision-support system for modeling bid/no-bid decision problem. *Journal of Construction Engineering and Management, 116*(4), 595–608.

Albar, F. M., and Jetter, A. (2011). An investigation on Fast and Frugal Model for new project screening. PICMET: Portland International Center for Management of Engineering and Technology, Proceedings.

Bagies, A., and Fortune, C. (2006). Bid/no-bid decision modelling for construction projects (pp. 511–521). In *Proceedings of the 22nd annual ARCOM conference*. ARCOM.

Bartunek, J. M., and Louis, M. R. (1996). Insider/outsider team research. In *Insider/outsider team research*. SAGE.

Berg, N. (2014). Success from satisficing and imitation: Entrepreneurs' location choice and implications of heuristics for local economic development. *Journal of Business Research, 67*(8), 1700–1709.

de Araújo, M. C. B., Alencar, L. H., and de Miranda Mota, C. M. (2022). Classification model for bid/no-bid decision in construction projects. *International Transactions in Operational Research, 29*(2), 1025–1047.

Chen, Y. Q., Zhang, S. J., Liu, L. S., and Hu, J. (2015). Risk perception and propensity in bid/no-bid decision-making of construction projects. *Engineering, Construction and Architectural Management, 22*(1), 2–20.

Chisala, M. L. (2017). Quantitative bid or no-bid decision-support model for contractors. *Journal of Construction Engineering and Management, 143*(12), 04017088.

Crandall, B. W., and Hoffman, R. R. (2013). Cognitive task analysis (pp. 1–19). In J. D. Lee and A. Kirlik (eds.). *The Oxford handbook of cognitive engineering*. Oxford Univeristy Press.

Dhami, M. K. (2003). Psychological models of professional decision making. *Psychological Science, 14*, 175–180.

Drew, D., Skitmore, M., and Lo, H. P. (2001). The effect of client and type and size of construction work on a contractor's bidding strategy. *Building and Environment, 36*(3), 393–406.

Egemen, M., and Mohamed, A. N. (2007). A framework for contractors to reach strategically correct bid/no bid and mark-up size decisions. *Building and Environment, 42*(3), 1373–1385.

Eisenhardt, K. M. (1989). Building theories from case study research. *The Academy of Management Review, 14*(4), 532–550.

Eisenhardt, K. M., and Graebner, M. E. (2007). Theory building from cases: Opportunities and challenges. *Academy of Management Journal, 50*(1), 25–32.

Eriksson, T., and Kadefors, A. (2017). Organisational design and development in a large rail tunnel project: Influence of heuristics and mantras. *International Journal of Project Management*, in press. https://doi.org/10.1016/j.ijproman.2016.12.006.

Fetterman, D. M. (2010). *Ethnography: Step-by-step*, 3rd ed. SAGE.

Flyvbjerg, B. (2008). Curbing optimism bias and strategic misrepresentation in planning: Reference class forecasting in practice. *European Planning Studies, 16*(1), 3–21. https://doi.org/10.1080/09654310701747936.

Flyvbjerg, B. (2016). The fallacy of beneficial ignorance: A test of Hirschman's Hiding Hand. *World Development, 84*, 176–189.

Garcia-Retamero, R., and Dhami, M. K. (2009). Take-the-best in expert-novice decision strategies for residential burglary. *Psychonomic Bulletin & Review, 16*, 163–169.

Gigerenzer, G., and Brighton, H. (2009). Homo heuristicus: Why biased minds make better inferences. *Topics in Cognitive Science, 1*(1), 107–143.

Gigerenzer, G., and Gaissmaier, W. (2011). Heuristic decision making. *Annual Review of Psychology, 62*(1), 451–482.

Gigerenzer, G., and Goldstein, D. G. (1996). Reasoning the fast and frugal way: Models of bounded rationality. *Psychological Review, 103*(4), 650–669.

Gigerenzer, G., Hertwig, R., and Pachur, T. (eds.). (2011). *Heuristics: The foundations of adaptive behavior*. Oxford University Press.

Goldstein, D. G., and Gigerenzer, G. (2009). Fast and frugal forecasting. *International Journal of Forecasting, 25*(4), 760–772.

Gunduz, M., and Al-Ajji, I. (2022). Employment of CHAID and CRT decision tree algorithms to develop bid/no-bid decision-making models for contractors. *Engineering, Construction and Architectural Management, 29*(9), 3712–3736.

Han, S. H., and Diekmann, J. E. (2001). Making a risk-based bid decision for overseas construction projects. *Construction Management and Economics*, *19*(8), 765–776.

Hartono, B., and Yap, C. M. (2011). Understanding risky bidding: A prospect-contingent perspective. *Construction Management and Economics*, *29*(6), 579–593.

Hirschman, A. O. (1967). *Development projects observed*. Brookings Institution Press.

Hoffman, R. (1998). Use of the critical decision method to elicit expert knowledge: A case study in the methodology of cognitive task analysis. *Human Factors*, *40*(2), 158–170.

Ika, L. A. (2018). Beneficial or detrimental ignorance: The straw man fallacy of Flyvbjerg's test of Hirschman's Hiding Hand. *World Development*, *103*, 369–382.

Ika, L. A., Love, P. E. D., and Pinto, J. K. (2022). Moving beyond the Planning Fallacy: The emergence of a new principle of project behavior. *IEEE Transactions on Engineering Management*, *69*(6), 3310–3325.

Kahneman, D., and Tversky, A. (1979). Prospect theory: An analysis of decision under risk. *Econometrica*, *66*(3), 497–527.

Knudsen, C. (2003). Pluralism, scientific progress, and the structure of organization theory (pp. 262–288). In H. Tsoukas and C. Knudsen (eds.). *The Oxford handbook of organization theory*. Oxford University Press.

Li, G., Zhang, G., Chen, C., and Martek, I. (2020). Empirical bid or no bid decision process in international construction projects: Structural equation modeling framework. *Journal of Construction Engineering and Management*, *146*(6), 04020050.

Lin, C.-T., and Chen, Y.-T. (2004). Bid/no-bid decision-making – a fuzzy linguistic approach. *International Journal of Project Management*, *22*(7), 585–593.

Lipshitz, R., Klein, G., and Orasanu, J. (2001). Focus article: Taking stock of naturalistic decision making. *Journal of Behavioural Decision Making*, *352*, 331–352.

Love, P. E. D., Ika, L. A., and Pinto, J. K. (2022). Homo heuristicus: From risk management to managing uncertainty in large-scale infrastructure projects. *IEEE Transactions on Engineering Management*, 1–10.

Luan, S., Schooler, L., and Gigerenzer, G. (2011). A signal-detection analysis of fast-and-frugal trees. *Psychological Review*, *118*(2), 316–338.

Mathews, S. (2010). Innovation portfolio architecture. *Research Technology Management*, *53*(6), 30–40.

Marzouk, M., and Mohamed, E. (2018). Modeling bid/no bid decisions using fuzzy fault tree. *Construction Innovation*, *18*(1), 90–108.

Maytorena, E., Winch, G., Freeman, J., and Kiely, T. (2007). The influence of experience and information search styles on project risk identification performance. *IEEE Transactions on Engineering Management*, *54*(2), 315–326.

Militello, L. G., and Hutton, R. J. (1998). Applied cognitive task analysis (ACTA): A practitioner's toolkit for understanding cognitive task demands. *Ergonomics*, *41*(11), 1618–1641.

Pachur, T., and Bröder, A. (2013). Judgment: A cognitive processing perspective. *Wiley Interdisciplinary Reviews: Cognitive Science*, *4*(6), 665–681.

Raasch, C., Lee, V., Spaeth, S., and Herstatt, C. (2013). The rise and fall of interdisciplinary research: The case of open source innovation. Research Policy, *42*(5), 1138–1151.

Rolstadås, A. a A., Pinto, J. K. b J. K., Falster, P. c P., Venkataraman, R. b R., Rolstadås, A. a A., Pinto, J. K. b J. K., Falster, P. c P., and Venkataraman, R. b R. (2015). Project decision chain. *Project Management Journal*, *46*(4), 6–19.

Shanteau, J. (1992). Competence in experts: The role of task characteristics. *Organizational Behavior and Human Decision Processes*, *53*, 252–266.

Stingl, V., and Geraldi, J. (2021). A research agenda for studying managerial decision making through the lenses of simple heuristics. *Technological Forecasting and Social Change*, in press.

Stingl, V., and Geraldi, J. (2023). Imagining futures: Cognitive processes of desirable or undesirable project prospections. *Technological Forecasting and Social Change*, in press. https://doi.org/10.1016/j.techfore.2023.122701.

Todd, P. M., and Gigerenzer, G. (2012). What is ecological rationality? (pp. 3–30). In P. M. Todd, G. Gigerenzer, and ABC Reserach Group (eds.). *Ecological rationality: Intelligence in the world*. Oxford University Press.

Todd, P. M., and Miller, G. F. (1999). From pride and prejudice to persuasion: Satisficing in mate search (pp. 287–308). In G. Gigerenzer, P. M. Todd, and The ABC Research Group (eds.). *Simple heuristics that make us smart*.Oxford University Press.

Tversky, A., and Kahneman, D. (1974). Judgment under uncertainty: Heuristics and biases. *Science*, *185*(4157), 1124–1131.

Van Oorschot, K. E. a, Langerak, F. b, and Sengupta, K. c. (2011). Escalation, de-escalation, or reformulation: Effective interventions in delayed NPD projects. *Journal of Product Innovation Management*, *28*(6), 848–867.

Williams, T., and Samset, K. (2010). Issues in front-end decision making on projects. *Project Management Journal*, *43*(2), 84–100.

Winch, G. M., and Maytorena, E. (2009). Making good sense: Assessing the quality of risky decision-making. *Organization Studies*, *30*(2–3), 181–203.

Yin, R. K. (2009). *Case study research: Design and methods*, 2nd ed. Sage.

Zaqout, I. S., Islam, M. S., Hadidi, L. A., and Skitmore, M. (2022). Modeling bidding decisions and bid markup size for construction projects: A fuzzy approach. *Engineering Applications of Artificial Intelligence*, *113*, 104982.

CHAPTER 15

The Roles of Governance Mechanisms to Manage Misbehaviors in the Project Front-End

JOSEPH W. HARRISON, JENS K. ROEHRICH, and MICHAEL A. LEWIS

Introduction

The project front-end (PFE) has long been understood as a phase critical to overall project success (Edkins et al., 2013; Lewis et al., 2023). Several studies have explored the notion of the PFE in its role in helping to combat common project misbehaviors (e.g., Samset & Volden, 2016). Prior PFE studies have highlighted that for projects to perform optimally, in that they deliver the desired social, economic, and/or environmental outcomes, the PFE needs to be "well executed," in that misbehaviors need to be avoided and/or swiftly addressed (Williams et al., 2022). As argued by PFE scholars, it is in the PFE where strategic project success or failure is determined (Williams et al., 2019). Despite the increasing number of PFE research studies, there still remains several common issues surrounding misbehaviors in this project phase (McClory et al., 2017). Thus, this chapter focuses on investigating the roles of governance mechanisms to help manage and address misbehaviors.

Before addressing "misbehavior" (its meaning, consequences, and interaction with the PFE) it is necessary to define what "project behavior" is (Unterhitzenberger, 2021). Ika et al. (2022, p. 3311) defined project behavior to mean "the study of how projects work or behave or take complex out-turns [and this involves], explaining and anticipating successes and failures, systematic veerings from preassigned paths, propensities toward specific difficulties as well as opportunities for special payoffs." Recent project behavior research has specifically aimed to understand why projects behave the way they do as well as illustrating ways to control and guide the behavior of projects (Flyvbjerg, 2021; Shafi et al., 2021; Wang et al., 2021; Wynn et al., 2021). This chapter contributes to project behavior research by focusing on the "veerings from preassigned paths" and "propensities towards specific difficulties" elements of the project behavior definition. Specifically, this chapter aims to shed light on how (and why) projects (mis-)behave in the PFE phase and how (relational and contractual) governance mechanisms can be used to manage such behavior.

"Misbehavior" is a wide-ranging term encompassing factors that could relate to a vast array of different (project-related) activities and processes (Love et al., 2019). Misbehavior can be defined as "bad behaviour, or behaviour that breaks a rule" (Cambridge Dictionary, 2021). However, the difficulty in defining what, in a project context, is "bad" or "breaks a rule" is often a highly subjective endeavor, especially in the open, flexible, and (often) unaccountable space that is the PFE (Morris, 2009). While prior studies have mentioned and investigated some examples of misbehavior in the PFE that are evidently "bad" such as "corruption in the tender process" (Locatelli et al., 2017, p.257), other commonly cited misbehaviors – for example, misrepresentation, are somewhat more contestable (Kreiner, 2020). This is especially so considering one of the most seminal works in the field of project studies addresses the contestable theme of misbehavior in the PFE. The principle of the "hiding hand" argues that in order for projects to be commissioned the true cost and obstacles to be faced must not be known at the point of commissioning (Hirschman, 1967, 2014). This is because, if they are known, such projects may never be commissioned, as the true cost reflects that projects can routinely be over 40 percent late or overbudget (Davies, 2017). Hirschman's work, and this argument, is not without critique (e.g., Ika & Söderlund, 2016; Flyvbjerg, 2017; Kreiner, 2020), however, such a seminal and widely disseminated idea leads us to evaluate the varied roles of misbehaviors in the PFE and what might be done to address them (Ika et al., 2022).

To help address misbehaviors in the PFE, appropriate governance in the form of contractual and relational governance mechanisms (Cao & Lumineau, 2015; Roehrich et al., 2020; Roehrich & Kivleniece, 2022) have long been cited as being critical in ensuring optimal project outcomes are achieved (Williams et al., 2019). Contractual governance can be defined as the use of (mainly written and detailed) contracts to manage relationships, whereas relational governance refers to governing using informal means such as through trust and social norms (including the organization's cultural norms) (Poppo & Zenger, 2002; Roehrich et al., 2020). In studying the role of governance mechanisms in addressing misbehaviors, the PFE is particularly interesting, as the traditional study of project governance has mostly neglected this project phase (Samset & Volden, 2016). There have been several studies involving the examination of project governance during the in-progress project phase such as Biesenthal and Wilden (2014) and Klakegg et al. (2016) since Müller's (2009) call highlighting the opportunity and need for more research in this area. Some prior studies have highlighted weak or ineffectual front-end governance as being commonplace in differing institutional contexts (Shiferaw et al., 2012) or have been more concerned about the generic discussion and evaluation of the PFE (Samset & Volden, 2016). The common theme, however, surrounds a lack of a strong understanding of PFE governance and its role in mitigating/addressing misbehavior. In this chapter, we contribute to the theme of this book by evaluating the roles of contractual and relational governance mechanisms in the PFE for addressing misbehaviors. In doing so, the following research question is addressed: *How can contractual and relational governance mechanisms be used in the front-end of projects to manage misbehaviors?*

The remainder of this chapter is structured as follows. The next section considers prior studies of the PFE and introduces the reader to project misbehaviors. This is followed by a brief overview of prior studies on contractual and relational governance mechanisms (with application to the PFE). Examples are then detailed for how PFE misbehaviors can be managed through governance mechanisms. The final section offers some concluding thoughts and a future research agenda.

The Project Front End and Project Misbehaviors

Building on the literature review of PFE studies by Williams et al. (2019), the PFE starts at the point at which the initial idea/concept/solution for a project is evoked in the mind of a project stakeholder and ends at the point at which the project is transferred to the delivery organization ready for execution (i.e., the project is ready to start) (Williams & Samset, 2010). The PFE encompasses every intermediate process within these boundaries. Table 15.1 unpacks these main PFE processes.

The PFE matters in the context of a project because it is the point at which strategic success or failure for the project is set (Morris, 2009). More specifically, it is in the PFE that resources are allocated, (resource/financial) support is given, and the plan for the project is devised (Matinheikki et al., 2016). It is where the "project will typically lock in many aspects of what will be the final project configuration" (Levitt & Scott, 2017, p. 107). In other words, the PFE is "where" most aspects of the project will be "frozen" (or at least strict bounding of measurements/acceptance will be determined) as key requirements are taken forward into execution (Lewis et al., 2023). Despite the importance of the PFE, its conceptualization is often still vague and imprecise, lacking formal rules (Edkins et al., 2013). For example, the PFE process is key in the exploration of alternative project options. However, Samset and Volden (2016) found that biases (both internal – Pinto, 2000 – and external – Williams & Samset, 2012) and election cycles influence selected options in numerous (large-scale) projects (Flyvbjerg, 2021). More broadly, however, and

Table 15.1 Processes at the PFE (based on Edkins et al., 2013; Williams et al., 2019)

Main PFE Processes	Brief Description	Exemplar Studies
Emergence of initial ideas	• An idea for a project occurs in the mind of a project stakeholder based upon a problem/opportunity identified	• Williams et al. (2019)
Estimates of costs and benefits	• As projects are a function of the costs (to be imposed) and benefits (to be gained), initial estimations are made to decide whether further consideration of the idea for the project should occur • Consideration of aspects such as complexity, uncertainty and underlying problems are also made	• Olsson and Magnussen (2007) • Frishammer et al. (2010) • Welde and Odeck (2017)
Development of conceptual alternatives/options	• As the estimates of costs and benefits occur, stakeholder preferences become clearer (and sometimes conflicting) • Because the project is beginning to become clearly realized in the minds of stakeholders, such voices can become distorted • Multiple options are explored usually in the form of the composition of multiple business cases	• Edkins et al. (2013) • Lessard and Miller (2013) • Samset and Volden (2016) • Zwikael and Meredith (2019)
Option selected	• A decision is made about which project option to allocate resource to (doing nothing is also an option) • Final planning for option selected	• Williams and Samset (2010)
Project ready to commence	• Project begins with resources employed and realized (unless the option to do nothing has been selected)	• Morris (2009)

linking to our subsequent discussion, misbehaviors in the PFE can cause serious problems and cultivate the conditions that may "breed" project misbehaviors in later project phases if the PFE is not executed well and misbehaviors are not addressed sufficiently during this important project phase (Aaltonen et al., 2015). It is also important to note, however, that this characterization of the PFE as a structured and linear process holds true for what can be termed "traditional" or "waterfall" projects but for some alternative forms of project organizing (i.e., agile), this process may slightly differ (Serrador & Pinto, 2015).

We now briefly review project misbehaviors that may occur in the PFE or at later project life-cycle stages if not addressed in the PFE. While we highlight a range of different misbehaviors, this overview is by no means all-encompassing but should be considered as guidance only. A selection of misbehaviors that may occur across three key levels of analysis – macro (project level), meso (project team level), micro (individual level) – in a project are discussed.

Macro: Common examples of misbehaviors at the project level in the PFE phase include *corruption* in the composition of government expenditure to fund projects (Mauro, 1998; Locatelli et al., 2017), *front-end project option misrepresentation* in the pursuit of economic growth (Mo, 2001), and *strategic project misrepresentation* in the deliberate attempt of *understating costs and risks* and *overstating benefits* in an attempt to get a project (or a particular project option) selected (Flyvbjerg, 2006). Equally, PFE misbehaviors because of a *lack of employment of adequate front-end resource* (Miller & Lessard, 2000) has in many instances become so normalized in projects that many each year *fail to ensure ethical employment practices and policies* are in place (van Wee, 2013). This failure in the PFE can then cultivate the necessary conditions for *modern slavery and exploitation* to occur (Crane, 2013).

Meso: Misbehaviors can, and often do, also occur at the meso level such as within project teams or project functions (Ashforth & Anand, 2003). For instance, Pinto (2014) highlighted the *normalization of deviance* within project teams as a critical misbehavior building upon a rich sociological history of deviant behavior within groups (Vaughan, 1996). Applying this to the PFE can be exemplified through the NASA challenger space incident in 1986 where PFE misbehavior (*lack of planning* to understand how different components perform under different weather conditions) was a primary cause of the disaster that led to seven fatalities among crew members (Vaughan, 2004).

Micro: Misbehaviors at the micro level can also be evidenced (Buvinić, 1986). For example, Pinto and Patanakul (2015, p. 1181), found that *narcissistic behavior traits* at the level of the individual (particularly in the context of project directors/ owners) "have the potential of severely affecting projects ... [including the] selection of viable options to pursue." This therefore provides evidence of how one individual's misbehavior (especially if they hold a position of power within the project) could cause disruptions (Breese et al., 2020). Equally, misbehaviors by individuals outside the immediate boundary of core project functions could also be problematic (Cicmil et al., 2006). Samset and Volden (2016) highlighted that intervention by political figures *distorting best value options and preferences* as a misbehavior (at the level of the individual) can have a large impact on project outcomes.

Table 15.2 provides an overview of further additional misbehaviors identified by prior studies across levels of analysis.

This discussion of PFE misbehaviors raises many scholarly and practically relevant points. It is evident that misbehaviors in the PFE occur and manifest in many ways (Sagie et al., 2003). Misbehaviors may also occur on a macro, meso, or micro level (Li et al., 2019). The relative extent of misbehaviors as well as the extent of the impact of misbehaviors also vary in that (subjective?) interpretations of what misbehavior is differ among both scholars and practitioners (Buvinić, 1986; Hajikazemi et al., 2020). For example, is it acceptable to deliberately misrepresent projects by

Table 15.2 More misbehaviors in projects across the levels of analysis

Level of analysis	Unit of analysis	Exemplifications of misbehavior	Exemplar studies/ works	Exemplar stakeholders
Macro Level	Project	• Corruption (in the tender process) • Front-end project option misrepresentation • Strategic project misrepresentation • Failure to ensure governance structures are in place • Fraud within the boundary of the project	• Mauro (1998) • Miller and Lessard (2000) • Mo (2001) • Locatelli et al. (2017)	• Government • Government department(s) • Political parties • Multinational corporations
Meso Level	Project Team	• Normalization of deviance within project teams • Bullying and/or intimidation of differing project teams • Collective departure from agreed project strategy by project teams • Unsafe and/or dangerous working practices by project teams	• Pinto (2014) • Ashforth and Anand (2003) • Vaughan (1996, 2004)	• Project leadership teams • Project function teams • Project working/ steering groups • Contractor groups • Informal groups
Micro Level	Individual	• Narcissistic behavior traits at the level of the individual • Distortion of best value options and preferences • Bullying and/or manipulation at the level of individual • "Turning a blind eye" with respect to not reporting others misbehavior • Deliberate sabotage of the selected project option	• Cicmil et al. (2006) • Pinto and Patanakul (2015) • Samset and Volden (2016) • Breese et al. (2020)	• Senior owner(s). • Project director(s) • Project manager(s) • Project practitioner(s) • Politician(s)

understating costs/risks and overstating benefits (in the knowledge that significant emergent [but as yet unknown] benefits are likely to be generated) (Hirschman, 2014)? The next section considers the role of governance mechanisms, specifically addressing what they are, why they are important, and how they can be used to manage misbehaviors in the PFE.

Contractual and Relational Governance

The PFE exists *before* project boundaries are crafted at a time where there *are* "governing processes at play" but, typically, no, or at least limited, "plans nor formal contracts to govern the actions and relationships of the parties involved" (Hellström et al., 2013, p. 712). With project stakeholders recognizing that an emphasis on improved front-end management is likely to pay off in a wider project life cycle (Miller & Lessard, 2000), we now explore the roles that governance mechanisms may play in the PFE.

Building on prior strategy and operations and supply chain management (OSCM) studies, governance mechanisms are considered the formal and informal rules of exchange between organizations (Vandaele et al., 2007; Roehrich et al., 2020). As a reminder, formal rules refer to contractual governance mechanisms involving the use of (mainly written and detailed) contracts to manage relationships, whereas informal rules refer to relational governance mechanisms such as trust and social norms (Poppo & Zenger, 2002; Cao & Lumineau, 2015). These governance mechanisms can be used individually or in combination to govern relationships in projects (Cao & Lumineau, 2015; Aben et al., 2021). More recently, prior governance studies have shown that governance mechanisms have inherent functions of control and coordination (e.g. Schepker et al., 2014; Schilke & Lumineau, 2018; Engelhart et al., 2023). We argue that by building on prior governance studies from strategy and OSCM fields, we can help to increase our understanding of managing (i.e., control and coordinate) PFE misbehaviors.

Prior governance literature has distinguished between two functions inherent in both contractual and relational governance mechanisms, namely, control and coordination. Control has been defined as "any phenomenon or attribute that helps ensure that the other in a relationship will perform in accordance with one's desires or expectations" (Salbu, 1997, p. 332). Coordination has been defined as the "deliberate and orderly alignment or adjustment of partners' actions to achieve jointly determined goals" (Gulati et al., 2012, p. 12). Within the PFE, more than any other phase of the project lifecycle, characterized by high complexity and uncertainty as well as limited information (Williams et al., 2019; Aben et al., 2021), governance mechanisms' functions of coordinating activities and resources as well as controlling (mis-) behaviors are important. For instance, complexity (e.g., structural or dynamic – Brady & Davies, 2014) introduce control and coordination tensions between different project stakeholders and the various interdependent activities and resource needs. Similarly, uncertainty, arising from unforeseeable events with unpredictable consequences (Pich et al., 2002; Davies & Mackenzie, 2014), needs to be managed in this project phase. Here, control tensions exist in rapidly changing environments (e.g., due to changing market and technology requirements) (Shenhar & Dvir, 2007).

On one hand, control focuses on specifying roles and responsibilities to manage (mis-)behaviors (Mellewigt et al., 2007; Schepker et al., 2014) which is vital to reach project goals and objectives (Dahlgren & Söderlund, 2010). The control function helps to safeguard parties against potential opportunism (Schepker et al., 2014; Kapsali et al., 2019). For instance, contracts designed with an emphasis on control would orient the need for processing information pertaining to the monitoring of partners' activities (Provan & Skinner, 1989). Prior research demonstrated that effective cooperation is dependent on the adoption of appropriate control mechanisms and studied the phenomena through contract completeness and/or the degree of trust/norms present in the relationships (Das & Teng, 2001; Li et al., 2010). The assumption of complete contracts and social control is that it can constrain opportunistic behavior (a form of misbehavior) in the other party (Jayaraman et al., 2013). This can be exemplified in practice in Kalra et al. (2021) in their evaluation of control and coordination failures in a major project (cf., the British Royal Air Force and BAE Systems). Following this stream of research, scholars have investigated the interplay of contractual and relational control (Li et al., 2010; Huang et al., 2014) and its influence on performance (Jayaraman et al., 2013). For example, a study by Liu et al. (2009) showed that contractual and relational control have different impacts on performance. They argue that while contractual control is more effective in mitigating opportunism, relational control is more effective in improving relationship performance.

On the other hand, the importance of coordination in projects (across life cycle phases) arise because of the necessity to organize effectively, for instance, tasks, activities, meetings, and labor (Gulati et al., 2012). From a contractual governance perspective, it includes outlining formal communication for reporting requirements, conflict resolution, and decision-making (Lumineau & Henderson, 2012). Coordination based on relational governance (Caldwell et al., 2017; Oliveira & Lumineau, 2017) refers to informal information sharing (providing information that helps the other party, exchanging information informally that is not included in the prespecified agreement), flexibility (i.e., requesting alterations due to change in circumstances, adjusting to changes in the ongoing relationship), and solidarity (joint problem solving, improving the relationship as a whole) (Mesquita & Brush, 2008). Coordination is especially of importance in projects and inter-organizational relationships that experience high uncertainty and/or task complexity (Schepker et al., 2014; Roehrich et al., 2023) because it can simplify exchange structures and thus mitigate the risk of misunderstandings between exchange parties (Salbu, 1997). Coordination concerns the pooling of resources, division of labor, and bringing together disperse activities (Hoetker & Mellewigt, 2009), and thus addresses possible project misbehaviors.

It should be noted that drafting detailed contracts to reduce uncertainty is costly and time consuming and these clauses are often difficult to enforce and monitor due to asymmetric information between partnering organizations (Aben et al., 2021; Karaba et al., 2022). The study by Roehrich and Lewis (2014) showed that while most organizations seek to reduce complexity and uncertainty in projects by increasing the number of contractual clauses, more effective arrangements use more simplified governance mechanisms. Roehrich et al. (2020) argued that if contracts are incomplete and unspecified ex ante, contracting parties might consider ex post bargaining and renegotiation to increase contractual safeguards and/or coordination clauses. Gaps in contracts are often filled by parties building up relational governance mechanisms (Zheng et al., 2008), but this might also be resource/time-consuming (Larson, 1992) and is often hindered by a lack of prior joint working experience. Coordination tensions and failures arise as uncertainty requires organizations to adapt to incomplete and sometimes asymmetric information (Kalra et al., 2021) across project life cycle phases.

When considering the PFE, governance mechanisms that are available for organizations and managers to use during the delivery phase of a project will not always be present in the front-end phase. For instance, contracts for the project will not have been (fully) drawn up yet and partnering organizations may not have had the time to develop relational governance as they may have not previously worked together. While these governance mechanisms may not have been formalized (as contract negotiation for the project has not taken place yet), organizations may rely on contract templates (as part of contractual governance) with boilerplate terms that are accepted as industry standards (Roehrich et al., 2020). Also, organizations may rely on individual boundary-spanners (as part of relational governance) who are organizations' knowledge holders whose role is central to the transfer of knowledge to other organizations (Sarafan et al., 2022). Both governance mechanisms may help at the PFE to achieve agreement in terms of project objectives as prior studies have pointed out the importance of achieving agreement (Samset et al., 2014). For instance, Youker (1989) concluded that a lack of agreement on project objectives was one of the biggest problems facing international development projects. In this early project phase, counteracting uncertainty (e.g., due to missing information) and achieving agreements may rely more heavily on relational governance through personal connections and ties among organizations.

Addressing PFE Misbehaviors through Governance Mechanisms

Having considered the roles and definition of the PFE and project misbehaviors and briefly reviewed governance mechanisms, we now synthesize our findings by considering how some PFE misbehaviors can be addressed through governance mechanisms. We do not seek to produce a comprehensive list of how different governance mechanisms (and their respective functions) might be used to address a host of different PFE misbehaviors but have rather carried through examples of three specific misbehaviors (across three levels) and detailed how they may be addressed.

Macro: Strategic Project Misrepresentation

Strategic misrepresentation (at the level of the project) is a commonly cited PFE misbehavior (e.g., Flyvbjerg, 2006; Næss et al., 2015). Traditional governance utilized to address this problem has revolved around the use of formal contractual and control mechanisms due to the vast sums of money invested as well as the power such (large) projects may have (Lumineau & Henderson, 2012). Formal contractual mechanisms are not the only way that project professionals can address this misbehavior. Governing through relational means, especially within established project delivery organizations, has been cited as being the key to addressing this challenge (Brady & Davies, 2004). This is because it is harder to develop an unrealistic depiction of benefits/costs for colleagues and partner organizations (with whom a preexisting relationship exists) (Roehrich et al., 2020). The relational and tacit knowledge developed over long time periods has the potential to address, unpack, and ultimately prevent any strategic misrepresentation before it occurs (Davies et al., 2009). The development of rigorous, objective, peer-led and mutually reinforceable standards of behavior is likely to be impactful in preventing such misrepresentation. Thus, the role of governance to help address strategic misrepresentation in the PFE (such as through the use of inter-project learning and integrated project teams) is highlighted (Davies et al., 2019; Roehrich et al., 2019).

Meso: Normalization of Deviance within Groups

The normalization of deviance within project groups is another common project (and PFE) misbehavior (Hajikazemi et al., 2020). Pinto (2014) highlighted five steps to counter this misbehavior: (i) process analysis (identification of deviance), (ii) education of organizational members, (iii) clarification of standards of appropriate behavior, (iv) ensuring transparency throughout the organization, and (v) reward compliance with new standards. We posit that this well-cited and rigorous governance process is not well suited to the PFE, however. This is because of the transitory nature of organizational members in the PFE (Williams et al., 2019). Deviant behaviors have the potential to become quickly normalized within groups, but because of the high turnover of group members (Parker & Skitmore, 2005), such a relational governance mechanism is fundamentally flawed in this project phase. Relational governance processes would still be preferred over contractual governance to allow for the full and unrestricted execution of the PFE phase, however (Müller et al., 2014). Regular formal and informal reviews of behavior(s) for the direction of individual groups would be preferred over a retrospective and remedial correcting analysis of such behavior(s) when they have clearly manifested as a problem. Such regular preemptive (coordinating) governance is likely to be even more important because project teams and groups, as a collective, are acutely aware that repercussions and accountability for deviant behavior are likely to be minimal due to teams being contracted to differing projects often on a fixed term basis (Edkins et al., 2013). The use of regular, highly visible, and overt relational governance to prevent misbehavior before it occurs is therefore recommended (Borg & Scott-Young, 2022).

Micro: Narcissistic Behavior Traits at the Level of the Individual

One example of a misbehavior in a project context that occurs at the level of the individual is narcissistic behavior (Pinto & Patanakul, 2015). Relational governance (governing through trust and social norms) would be the preferred option to help ensure projects (and people within those projects) do not suffer from individuals misbehaving by using narcissistic behavior. This is why projects have a clearly defined hierarchical organizational structure from project delivery professionals within teams up to project managers and senior responsible owners (Kloppenborg et al., 2014). To prevent narcissistic behavior, using relational governance mechanisms may be beneficial in such circumstances because of the project phase (PFE) being undertaken. The PFE is widely accepted as a creative process, which, where possible, should be free from too many restrictive rules (Maier & Branzei, 2014). The imposition of too much rigidity (by using multiple formal contractual governance mechanisms) is likely to stifle such creativity and generate boilerplate, inflexible project options lacking any innovative potential (Cantarelli & Genovese, 2021).

Equally, narcissistic leaders can plague otherwise "healthy" projects and it is important to have strong contractual governance mechanisms in place to control such behavior if coordinating relational mechanisms fail to have the desired impact (Liu et al., 2010; Lumineau & Henderson, 2012). This could include clear systems of escalation and contractual clauses (within employment and consultancy contracts) to remove individuals from the project and/or project teams who display narcissistic behavioral traits (e.g., placing unreasonable demands on colleagues or insisting that "their" project delivery strategy be chosen) (Campbell et al., 2011). It is also important to do this in a timely manner as it is positioned that narcissistic individuals would have a potential greater adverse impact in the PFE due to this being the phase where the path to strategic success or failure is chosen (Williams et al., 2019). Furthermore, it is important to note that contractual governance solutions do not exclusively have to appear in the contract(s) for the project. It is something of a misnomer to suggest that *no* contracts exist in the front-end. Employment contracts, scoping contracts, and consultancy contracts all exist in this phase and can, and should, be used to address misbehavior where appropriate.

A Future Research Agenda and Concluding Thoughts

This chapter has considered the role of contractual and relational governance in addressing misbehaviors in the PFE. This chapter has found that because of the open and flexible nature of the PFE, governing this project phase is often a difficult endeavor. We draw out the role that contractual and relational governance mechanisms could perform in this phase. This research contributes to existing project behavior scholarship through the provision of what (to the best of the authors' knowledge is) the first dedicated scholarly investigation of misbehavior in the PFE phase. To further our understanding of PFE misbehaviors, Table 15.3 provides an overview of future research opportunities across the three levels of analysis (macro, meso, micro). Table 15.3 has been carefully crafted based upon gaps evident in existing scholarship and opportunities identified within this chapter.

We hope that further studies will conceptually extend and empirically investigate different types and functions of governance mechanisms (e.g., control and coordination functions) in the PFE with the specific aim of addressing project misbehaviors. The PFE possesses markedly unique features compared to other project phases (e.g., in terms of flexibility, uncertainty, innovation potential), so we contend that the logical starting point for further research would be a comprehensive empirical investigation to first consider the applicability of existing governance research to the PFE phase.

There also exists a clear opportunity to study how (groups of) actors at different analytical levels (macro/meso/micro) respond to misbehavior. Considering that individuals may perceive and interpret misbehavior differently as well as the fact that a key feature of the PFE is that it lacks accountability (Williams & Samset, 2010), it therefore poses an impactful and timely opportunity to empirically evaluate how project professionals within differing

Table 15.3 A future research agenda for project misbehaviors in the PFE

	Macro	Meso	Micro	All Levels
Levels of analysis	• Project	• Project team	• Individual	• Project, project team, and individual
Potential research questions	• Should preventing misbehavior be a core project objective/ target? • How are organizational structures created and refined to prevent misbehavior? • Do projects need to use more relational governance to stop misbehavior (at the level of the project)?	• How do teams identify and respond to misbehavior in the PFE? • Is misbehavior contagious? For example, if one team misbehaves does this encourage other teams to misbehave? • Are certain project teams/ functions more likely to misbehave than others?	• How do project directors/owners ensure misbehavior does not occur in the PFE? • Do any project directors/owners encourage misbehavior in certain circumstances? • What incentives can make individuals care about preventing misbehavior?	• What are the different types and severities of misbehavior that exist (in the PFE)? • Do any misbehaviors interact to form more severe misbehaviors (in the PFE)? • To what extent is misbehavior more or less likely in the PFE phase than in later project phases?

(social) project context(s) address misbehaviors. Furthermore, there exists a strong opportunity to consider the processual and temporal dynamics/evolution of PFE misbehavior. For example, it would be useful for scholars and practitioners to understand whether front-end project phases where specific attention is given to preventing and addressing misbehavior then go on to experience fewer misbehaviors in later project phases.

Furthermore, in the absence of a typology of project misbehaviors (which we argue would be a strong further research contribution) additional theoretical and empirical investigation should be completed to illustrate how misbehaviors can manifest in various shapes/forms/degrees with some being potentially more damaging/impactful/extreme than others. To illustrate this point, misbehavior through a single minor contravention of a safe working practice by a project team member is not comparable to corruption in the project tender process, for example.

To summarize, we hope that this chapter will stimulate further research and inform business practices and policy interventions to augment our understanding of misbehaviors and the use of governance mechanisms to manage them in the PFE. We have highlighted that the PFE is unique in respect to the governance mechanisms required and hope subsequent research studies will further elaborate on this challenge. While there has not been the space available to evaluate all future research opportunities here, we encourage readers to critically consider the gaps presented in Table 15.3 to further build on what is an important and emerging topic in both academia and practice alike.

References

Aaltonen, K., Kujala, J., Havela, L., and Savage, G. (2015). Stakeholder dynamics during the project front-end: The case of nuclear waste repository projects. *Project Management Journal*, *46*(6), 15–41.

Aben, T, Van der Valk, W., Roehrich, J. K., and Selviaridis, K. (2021). Digital transformation in public-private relationships: The role of inter-organisational governance in managing information asymmetry. *International Journal of Operations and Production Management*, *41*(7), 1145–1191.

Ashforth, B., and Anand, V. (2003). The normalization of corruption in organizations. *Research in Organizational Behavior*, *25*(1), 1–52.

Biesenthal, C. and Wilden, R. (2014). Multi-level project governance: Trends and opportunities. *International Journal of Project Management*, *32*(8), 1291–1308.

Borg, J., and Scott-Young, C. (2022). Contributing factors to turnover intentions of early career project management professionals in construction. *Construction Management and Economics*, *40*(10), 835–853.

Brady, T., and Davies, A. (2004). Building project capabilities: From exploratory to exploitative learning. *Organization Studies*, *25*(9), 1601–1621.

Brady, T., and Davies, A. (2014). Managing structural and dynamic complexity: A tale of two projects. *Project Management Journal, 45*(4), 21–38.

Breese, R., Couch, O., and Turner, D. (2020). The project sponsor role and benefits realisation: More than "just doing the day job." *International Journal of Project Management, 38*(1), 17–26.

Buvinić, M. (1986). Projects for women in the third world: Explaining their misbehavior. *World Development, 14*(5), 653–664.

Caldwell, N., Roehrich, J. K., and George, G. (2017). Social value creation and relational coordination in public-private collaborations. *Journal of Management Studies, 54*(6), 906–928.

Campbell, W., Hoffman, B., Campbell, S., and Marchisio, G. (2011). Narcissism in organizational contexts. *Human Resource Management Review, 21*(4), 268–284.

Cantarelli, C., and Genovese, A. (2021). Innovation potential of megaprojects: A systematic literature review. *Production, Planning and Control, 34*(10), 1350–1370.

Cao, Z., and Lumineau, F. (2015). Revisiting the interplay between contractual and relational governance: A qualitative and meta-analytic investigation. *Journal of Operations Management, 33*(1), 15–42.

Cicmil, S., Williams, T., Thomas, J., and Hodgson, D. (2006). Rethinking project management: Researching the actuality of projects. *International Journal of Project Management, 24*(8), 675–686.

Crane, A. (2013). Modern slavery as a management practice: Exploring the conditions and capabilities for human exploitation. *Academy of Management Review, 38*(1), 49–69.

Dahlgren, J., and Söderlund, J. (2010). Modes and mechanisms in multi-project organisations: The R&D case. *International Journal of Technology Management, 50*(1), 1–22.

Das, T., and Teng, B. (2001). Trust, control, and risk in strategic alliances: An integrated framework. *Organization Studies. 22*(2), 251–283.

Davies, A., Gann, D., and Douglas, T. (2009). Innovation in megaprojects: Systems integration at London Heathrow Terminal 5. *California Management Review, 51*(2), 101–125.

Davies, A., and Mackenzie, I. (2014). Project complexity and systems integration: Constructing the London 2012 Olympics and Paralympics games. *International Journal of Project Management, 35*(4), 773–790.

Davies, A. (2017). *Projects: A very short introduction.* Oxford University Press.

Davies, A., MacAulay, S., and Brady, T. (2019). Delivery model innovation: Insights from infrastructure projects. *Project Management Journal, 50*(2), 119–127.

Edkins, A., Geraldi, J., Morris, P., and Smith, A. (2013). Exploring the front-end of project management. *Engineering Project Organization Journal, 3*(2), 71–85.

Engelhart, J., Roehrich, J. K., and Squire, B. (2023). Governing inter-organisational relationships in large projects: A review and future research agenda (pp. 213–222). In G. Winch, M. Brunet, and D. Cao (eds.). *Research handbook on complex project organizing*. Edward Elgar.

Flyvbjerg, B. (2006). From Nobel Prize to project management: Getting risks right. *Project Management Journal, 37*(3), 5–15.

Flyvbjerg, B. (2017). Did megaproject research pioneer behavioural economics: The case of Albert O. Hirschman (pp. 155–193). In B. Flyvbjerg (ed.). *Oxford Handbook of Megaproject Management.* Oxford University Press.

Flyvbjerg, B. (2021). Top ten biases in project management: An overview. *Project Management Journal*, 52(6), 531–546.

Frishammar, J., Florén, H., & Wincent, J. (2010). Beyond managing uncertainty: Insights from studying equivocality in the fuzzy front end of product and process innovation projects. *IEEE Transactions on Engineering Management, 58*(3), 551–563.

Gulati, R., Wohlgezogen, F., and Zhelyazkov, P. (2012). The two facets of collaboration: Cooperation and coordination in strategic alliances. *Academy of Management Annals, 6*(1), 531–583.

Hajikazemi, S., Aaltonen, K., Ahola, T., Aarseth, W., and Andersen, B. (2020). Normalising deviance in construction project organizations: A case study on the collapse of Carillion. *Construction Management and Economics, 38*(12), 1122–1138.

Hellström, M., Ruuska, I., Wikström, K., and Jåfs, D. (2013). Project governance and path creation in the early stages of Finnish nuclear power projects. *International Journal of Project Management, 31*(5), 712–723.

Hirschman, A. (1967). *Development projects observed.* Brookings Institution Press.

Hirschman, A. (2014). *Development projects observed.* Brookings Institution Press.

Hoetker, G., and Mellewigt, T. (2009). Choice and performance of governance mechanisms: Matching alliance governance to asset type. *Strategic Management Journal, 30*(1), 1025–1044.

Huang, M., Cheng, H., and Tseng, C. (2014). Re-examining the direct and interactive effects of governance mechanisms upon buyer–supplier cooperative performance. *Industrial Marketing Management, 43*(4), 704–716.

Ika, L., and Söderlund, J. (2016). Rethinking revisited: Insights from an early rethinker. *International Journal of Managing Projects in Business, 9*(4), 931–954.

Ika, L., Love, P., and Pinto, J. (2022). Moving beyond the planning fallacy: The emergence of a new principle of project behavior. *IEEE Transactions on Engineering Management, 69*(6), 3310–3325.

Jayaraman, V., Narayanan, S., Luo, Y., and Swaminathan, J. (2013). Offshoring business process services and governance control mechanisms: An examination of service providers from India. *Production and Operations Management, 22*(2), 314–334.

Kalra, J., Lewis, M., and Roehrich, J.K. (2021). Manifestation of coordination failures in service triads. *Supply Chain Management: An International Journal, 26*(3), 341–358.

Kapsali, M., Roehrich, J. K., and Akhtar, P. (2018). Effective contracting for high operational performance in projects. *International Journal of Operations and Production Management, 39*(2), 294–325.

Karaba, F., Roehrich, J. K., Conway, S., and Turner, J. (2022). Information sharing in public-private relationships: The role of boundary objects in contracts. *Public Management Review, 25*(11), 2166–2190.

Klakegg, O., Williams, T., and Shiferaw, A. (2016). Taming the "trolls": Major public projects in the making. *International Journal of Project Management, 34*(2), 282–296.

Kloppenborg, T., Tesch, D., and Manolis, C. (2014). Project success and executive sponsor behaviours: Empirical life cycle stage investigations. *Project Management Journal, 45*(1), 9–20.

Kreiner, K. (2020). Conflicting notions of a project: The battle between Albert O. Hirschman and Bent Flyvbjerg. *Project Management Journal, 51*(4), 400–410.

Larson, A. (1992). Network dyads in entrepreneurial settings: A study of the governance of exchange relationships. *Administrative Science Quarterly, 37*(1), 76–104.

Lessard, D., and Miller, R. (2013). The shaping of large engineering projects (pp. 34–56). In H. Priemus, and B. van Wee (eds.). *International handbook on megaprojects.* Edward Elgar.

Levitt, R., and Scott, R. (2017). Institutional challenges and solutions for global megaprojects (pp. 96–117). In B. Flyvbjerg (ed.). *Oxford handbook of Megaproject Management.* Oxford University Press.

Lewis, M., Harrison, J., and Roehrich, J. K. (2023). Its all a bit fuzzy? The front-end in project and innovation management (pp. 101–124) In A. Davies, S. Lenfle, C. Loch and C. Midler (eds.). *Handbook of Innovation and Project Management.* Edward Elgar.

Li, Y., Xie, E., Teo, H., and Peng, M. (2010). Formal control and social control in domestic and international buyer–supplier relationships. *Journal of Operations Management, 28*(4), 333–344.

Li, Y., Lu, Y, Cui, Q., and Han, Y. (2019). Organizational behaviour in megaprojects: Integrative review and directions for future research. *Journal of Management in Engineering, 35*(4), 1–11.

Liu, Y., Luo, Y., and Liu, T. (2009). Governing buyer-supplier relationships through transactional and relational mechanisms: Evidence from China. *Journal of Operations Management, 27*(4), 294–309.

Liu, Y., Li, Y., and Zhang, L. (2010). Control mechanisms across a buyer-supplier relationship matrix. *Journal of Business Research, 63*(1), 3–12.

Locatelli, G., Mariani, G., Sainati, T., and Greco, M. (2017). Corruption in public projects and megaprojects: There is an elephant in the room. *International Journal of Project Management, 35*(3), 252–268.

Love, P., Ika, L., and Ahiaga-Dagbui, D. (2019). On de-bunking "fake news" in a post truth era: Why does the planning fallacy explanation for cost overruns fall short? *Transportation Research Part A: Policy and Practice, 126*(1), 397–408.

Lumineau, F., and Henderson, J. (2012). The influence of relational experience and contractual governance on the negotiation strategy in buyer-supplier disputes. *Journal of Operations Management, 30*(5), 382–395.

Maier, E., and Branzei, O. (2014). "On time and on budget": Harnessing creativity in large scale projects. *International Journal of Project Management, 32*(7), 1123–1133.

Matinheikki, J., Artto, K., Peltokorpi, A., and Rajala, R. (2016). Managing inter-organizational networks for value creation in the front-end of projects. *International Journal of Project Management, 34*(7), 1226–1241.

Mauro, P. (1998). Corruption and the composition of government expenditure. *Journal of Public Economics, 69*(2), 263–279.

McClory, S., Read, M., and Labib, A. (2017). Conceptualising the lessons-learned process in project management: Towards a triple-loop learning framework. *International Journal of Project Management, 35*(7), 1322–1335.

Mellewigt, T., Madhok, A., and Weibel, A. (2007). Trust and formal contracts in interorganizational relationships – substitutes and complements. *Managerial and Decision Economics, 28*(8), 833–847.

Mesquita, L., and Brush, T. (2008). Untangling safeguard and production coordination effects in long-term buyer-supplier relationships. *Academy of Management Journal, 51*(4), 785–807.

Miller, R., and Lessard, D. (2000). *The strategic management of large engineering projects: Shaping institutions, risks, and governance*. MIT Press.

Mo, P. (2001). Corruption and economic growth. *Journal of Comparative Economics, 29*(1), 66–79.

Morris, P. (2009). Implementing strategy through project management: The importance of managing the project front-end. In T. Williams, K. Samset, and K. Sunnevåg (eds.). *Making essential choices with scant information: Front-end decision making in major projects*. Palgrave Macmillan.

Müller, R. (2009). *Project governance*. Gower.

Müller, R., Turner, R., Andersen, E., Shao, J., and Kvalnes, Ø. (2014). Ethics, trust, and governance in temporary organizations. *Project Management Journal, 45*(4), 39–54.

Næss, P., Andersen, J., Nicolaisen, M., and Strand, A. (2015). Forecasting inaccuracies: A result of unexpected events, optimism bias, technical problems, or strategic misrepresentation? *Journal of Transport and Land Use, 8*(3), 39–55.

Oliveira, N., and Lumineau, F. (2017). How coordination trajectories influence the performance of interorganizational project networks. *Organization Science, 28*(6), 1029–1060.

Olsson, N. O., & Magnussen, O. M. (2007). Flexibility at different stages in the life cycle of projects: an empirical illustration of the "freedom to maneuver". *Project Management Journal, 38*(4), 25–32.

Parker, S., and Skitmore, M. (2005). Project management turnover: Causes and effects on project performance. *International Journal of Project Management, 23*(3), 205–214.

Pich, M., Loch, C., and De Meyer, A. (2002). On uncertainty, ambiguity, and complexity in project management. *Management Science, 48*(8), 1008–1023.

Pinto, J. (2000). Understanding the role of politics in successful project management. *International Journal of Project Management, 18*(2), 85–91.

Pinto, J. (2014). Project management, governance, and the normalization of deviance. *International Journal of Project Management, 32*(3), 376–387.

Pinto, J., and Patanakul, P. (2015). When narcissism drives project champions: A review and research agenda. *International Journal of Project Management, 33*(1), 1180–1190.

Poppo, L., and Zenger, T. (2002). Do formal contracts and relational governance function as substitutes or complements? *Strategic Management Journal, 23*(8), 707–725.

Provan, K., and Skinner, S. (1989). Interorganizational dependence and control as predictors of opportunism in dealer-supplier relations. *Academy of Management Journal, 32*(1), 202–212.

Roehrich, J. K., and Lewis, M. (2014). Procuring complex performance: Implications for exchange governance complexity. *International Journal of Operations and Production Management, 34*(2), 221–241.

Roehrich, J. K., Davies, A., Frederiksen, L., and Sergeeva, N. (2019). Management innovation in complex products and systems: The case of integrated project teams. *Industrial Marketing Management, 79*(1), 84–93.

Roehrich, J. K., Selviaridis, K., Karla, J., Van der Valk, W., and Fang, F. (2020). Inter-organizational governance: A review, conceptualisation, and extension. *Production Planning and Control, 31*(6), 453–469.

Roehrich, J. K., and Kivleniece, I. (2022). Creating and distributing sustainable value through public-private collaborative projects (pp. 474–500). In G. George, M. Hass, H. Joshi, A. McGahan, and P. Tracey (eds.). *Handbook on the business of sustainability: The organization, implementation, and practice of sustainable growth*. Edward Elgar.

Roehrich, J. K., Kalra, J., Squire, B., and Davies, A. (2023). Network orchestration in a large inter-organizational project. *Journal of Operations Management, 69*(7), 1078–1099.

Sagie, A., Statshevsky, S., and Koslowsky, M. (2003). *Misbehaviour and dysfunctional attitudes in organizations*. Springer.

Salbu, S. (1997). Evolving contract as a device for flexible coordination and control. *American Business Law Journal*, *34*(1), 329–384.

Samset, K., Andersen, B., and Austeng, K. (2014). To which extent do projects explore the opportunity space? A study of conceptual appraisals and the choice of conceptual solutions. *International Journal of Managing Projects in Business*, *7*(3), 473–492.

Samset, K., and Volden, G. (2016). Front-end definition of projects: Ten paradoxes and some reflections regarding project management and project governance. *International Journal of Project Management*, *34*(2), 297–313.

Sarafan, M., Lawson, B., Roehrich, J. K., and Squire, B. (2022). Knowledge sharing within project-based supply networks. *International Journal of Operations and Production Management*, *42*(6), 852–874.

Serrador, P., and Pinto, J. (2015). Does agile work? A quantitative analysis of agile project success. *International Journal of Project Management*, *33*(5), 1040–1051.

Schepker, D., Oh, W., and Poppo, L. (2014). The many futures of contracts: Moving beyond structure and safeguarding to coordination and adaptation. *Journal of Management*, *40*(1), 193–225.

Schilke, O., and Lumineau, F. (2018). The double-edged effect of contracts on alliance performance. *Journal of Management*, *44*(7), 2827–2858.

Shafi, M, Iqbal, R., Shahzad, K., and Unterhitzenberger, C. (2021). The mediating role of project citizenship behavior in the relationship between organizational justice dimensions and project success. *Project Management Journal*, *52*(6), 547–562.

Shenhar, A., and Dvir, D. (2007). *Reinventing project management: The diamond approach to successful growth and innovation*. MIT Press.

Shiferaw, A., Klakegg, O., and Haavaldsen, T. (2012). Governance of public investment projects in Ethiopia. *Project Management Journal*, *43*(4), 52–69.

Unterhitzenberger, C. (2021). Special issue on project behavior. *Project Management Journal*, *52*(6), 527–530.

Van Wee, B. (2013). Ethics and the ex-ante evaluation of megaprojects (pp. 356–378). In H. Priemus and B. van Wee (eds.). *International Handbook on Megaprojects*. Edward Elgar.

Vandaele, D., Rangarajan, D., Gemmel, P., and Lievens, A. (2007). How to govern business services exchanges: Contractual and relational issues. *International Journal of Management Reviews*, *9*(3), 237–258.

Vaughan, D. (1996). *The challenger launch decision: Risky technology, culture, and deviance at NASA*. University of Chicago Press.

Vaughan, D. (2004). Organizational rituals of risk and error (pp. 33–66). In B. Hunter and M. Power (eds.). *Organization encounters with risk*. Cambridge University Press.

Wang, L., Müller, R., Zhu, F., and Yang, X. (2021). Collective mindfulness: The key to organizational resilience in megaprojects. *Project Management Journal*, *52*(6), 592–606.

Welde, M., Odeck, J. (2017). Cost escalations in the front-end of projects–empirical evidence from Norwegian road projects. *Transport Reviews*, *37*(5), 612–630.

Williams, T., and Samset, K. (2010). Issues in front-end decision making on projects. *Project Management Journal*, *41*(2), 38–49.

Williams, T., and Samset, K. (2012). *Project governance: Getting investments right*. Palgrave Macmillan.

Williams, T., Vo, H., Samset, K., and Edkins, A. (2019). The front-end of projects: a systematic literature review and structuring. *Production Planning and Control*, *30*(14), 1137–1169.

Williams, T., Samset, K., and Volden, G. (2022). *The front-end of large public projects: Paradoxes and ways ahead*. Routledge.

Wynn, C., Smith, L., and Killen, C. (2021). How power influences behaviour in projects: A theory of planned behavior perspective. *Project Management Journal*, *52*(6), 607–621.

Youker, R. (1989). Managing the project cycle for time, cost and quality: lessons from World Bank experience. *International Journal of Project Management*, *7*(1), 52–57.

Zheng, J., Roehrich, J. K., and Lewis, M. (2008). The dynamics of contractual and relational governance: Evidence from long-term public-private procurement arrangements. *Journal of Purchasing and Supply Management*, *14*(1), 43–54.

Zwikael, O., and Meredith, J. (2019). The role of organizational climate in setting project goals. *International Journal of Operations and Production Management*, *39*(12), 1281–1294.

CHAPTER 16

Coping with Changes to the Plan

Dealing with Twists and Turns in Projects

ASHWIN MAHALINGAM

Introduction

I just built a house. Or rather, I project managed the construction of a residential facility. While the intention behind constructing this facility was not to study it, I realized over the course of the project that this offered an excellent site for an ethnographic study of project behavior. After all, I was a part of the group that both initiated and executed this project, and what better way then to understand the deviation between the two. Furthermore, although I have spent most of my academic career studying the organization and behavior of large engineering projects, most of my data (and that of many other scholars in this field) has either been from interviews or project documents – both of which only provide secondary accounts of what actually happens on projects. While these data points are in some cases supplemented by direct field observations, the geographical and temporal spread of projects and the dynamic nature of project processes and project organizations really does not do justice to all the events that happen. I seized upon this chance to actually observe and live in the life cycle of a project, small as it may be. Finally, in order to provide insights to practitioners, it was highly advantageous to be able to transition into a practitioner myself for a brief period, experience the challenges from a project behavioral perspective, and to think through potential ideas that might be helpful to someone with boots in the field. This chapter is therefore a story of my experiences in the field, the insights I gained into project behavior, and what practitioners can take away from my story.

The fact that construction projects all over the world face time and cost overruns is very well documented (e.g., Flyvjberg et al., 2002, 2003, 2018). The key project behavioral question has therefore been "why does this happen?" – a question toward which much thought has been dedicated and several theories abound. Many news articles and published papers typically study this phenomenon on large infrastructure projects such as roads, bridges, and so on (Flyvjberg et al., 2003, 2018). However, the literature suggests that smaller facilities such as residential projects are equally susceptible to cost and time overruns, although the reasons for these may differ from larger projects and the scale of these impacts is often far lower (Kaushki & Kartam, 2004, Alshihri et al., 2022). In this chapter, I propose to dive deep into how projects in the residential construction sector behave. Indeed, construction projects retain an element of similarity irrespective of scale and geography – they go through similar phases of design, estimation, planning and construction, and involve the integration of a fragmented supply chain of vendors, contractors, and consultants. They suffer from similar vicissitudes such as client-induced changes midway in the project, the need to deal with uncertainties on quantities and price, and so on. Therefore, while I do not intend to equate the behaviors of large and small projects in this chapter – the multitude of stakeholders involved in larger, more complex projects might lead to dynamics (such as protests by special interest groups) that are way beyond the scope of smaller projects – I posit that some of these learnings that are presented here may also apply to the behavior of larger projects.

The outline of this chapter is as follows. In the next section, I discuss some of the relevant literature that currently attempts to explain project behavior. Next, I describe the research setting, as it were, as well as the methodology by which data was collected. Following this, I present a quantitative picture of project performance and show data on how the project actually progressed in the "Observations" section. In the next section, titled "How Did This Project Behave," I analyze the drivers behind the way the project progressed and describe the evolution of the project by classifying my observations into three temporal phases. Finally, I review these findings and attempt to theorize the project behavior that I observed. The chapter concludes with some thoughts on project behavior and its consequences that might be of use to academics and practitioners.

Explaining Project Behavior

While considerable literature exists on time and cost overruns and their underlying causes, these broadly fall into two key schools of thought. The first is sometimes referred to as the Planning Fallacy Theory (Love et al., 2022), the governance paradigm (Love & Ika, 2022), or simply the "bias" school. Proponents of this school suggest that psychological constructs such as overconfidence in expectations at the start of a project (an Optimism bias) or an even more nefarious intent to suppress or manipulate the true nature of project outcomes in order to obtain stakeholder buy-in for a project (Strategic Misrepresentation) are reasons for systematic cost and time overruns (Jones and Euske, 1991; Flyvjberg et al., 2002). Optimism bias often leads to forecasts of project schedules and costs being "unrealistically close to best-case scenarios" (Ika et al,. 2022), a phenomenon referred to as the Planning Fallacy, as plans thus made are unlikely to be realized. Proponents of the optimism and strategic misrepresentation views argue that since divergence in project outcomes is almost always skewed toward the negative side of project performance (underestimates that lead to cost and time overruns that are often seen as indicators of project failure as opposed to overestimates that could lead to underruns and perceptions of efficient project management), this is not mere chance happenstance. In other words, deviations between expected and observed project behavior are not emergent but are pre-ordained. This is supported by data from several megaprojects (Flyvbjerg et al., 2002). Optimism bias, for instance, has been noted in estimates that small groups of people present (Kahneman, 2017), and is therefore likely to be a driver of behavior in residential construction projects, which, while fragmented, feature a relatively smaller set of stakeholders and decision makers.

While this Planning Fallacy–based view was one of the main theoretically supported explanations on time and cost overruns, it has been accused of lacking empirical support and has in recent times been heavily contested by an alternative viewpoint – the "error" school or the project management paradigm (Love & Ika, 2022). Proponents of this school such as Love and Ahiagu-Dagbui (2018) debunk the methodological underpinnings of some of the Planning Fallacy arguments. Mak and Raftery (1992) suggest that professional competence must count for something and that estimators cannot be systematically incorrect all the time. Indeed, in a study of risk attitude and systematic biases in private projects, they find no evidence for the existence of optimism biases, at least on large projects (Mak & Raftery, 1992). Ika et al (2022) argue that the inability to predict numerous uncertainties in infrastructure projects can also lead to cost overruns. Gil and Pinto's (2018) views support this thesis where they argue that projects evolve over time. Project overruns are not really a case of projects not going according to plan (budget) but the other way round – plans not going according to the project. They suggest that as the project evolves, new stakeholders who have an interest in the project emerge – landholders, utilities, subcontractors, vendors, and the like. As these stakeholders supply accurate information on their own spheres of influence to the project, well after the start, the actual costs of the project become more apparent and initial estimates become overruns. Gil and Pinto (2018) thus attribute cost overruns to this polycentric governance system prevalent in construction, where no single party controls all the information flow on the project. Ahiaga-Dagbui and Smith (2014) also suggest that deviations in project outcomes can be attributed to scope changes, managerial or technical difficulties, risk and uncertainty, ground conditions, and price fluctuations. Other related explanations of time and cost overruns that fit within this school point to projects being extremely fragmented, with complex supply chains whose parameters are non-transparent (Meng 2012; Subramani et al., 2014), and incomplete information at the bidding stage of a project (Rosenfeld, 2014) as reasons that prevent the process of estimating project outcomes from becoming an exact science.

In recent times, a rather heated debate on "error" *or* "bias" has given way to a more inclusive view that points to "error" *and* "bias" influencing project behavior (Ika et al., 2022; Love et al., 2022; Love & Ika, 2022; Ika et al., 2023). What is well known is that projects do not behave as planned. There is growing acceptance that this is now partially due to the Planning Fallacy where estimators are too optimistic (Kahneman & Tversky, 1977; Flyvbjerg, 2016), while allowing for the fact that Hirschman's principle of the "Hiding Hand" (Hirschman, 1967), where in some cases errors in estimation may fuel creativity and positive project benefits, may also play a role (Ika et al., 2022).

This attempt to merge the two traditions relies on the idea of a set of invisible "hands" that guide the project. Anheier (2016) proposes several "hands" – the Hiding Hand, the Malevolent Hand, the Protecting Hand, and the Passive Hand. The Hiding Hand is of course Hirschman's idea that unexpected jolts to a project may trigger creative and innovative processes and outcomes, while the Malevolent Hand is the "evil twin" of the Hiding Hand as averred by Flyvbjerg and Sunstein (2016), where project outcomes are deliberately underestimated. The "error" school has traditionally supported the presence of the Hiding Hand, whereas the "bias" school has long been a proponent of the Malevolent Hand.

However, two more hands exist. Under the aegis of the Protecting Hand, project proponents take into account the presence of incomplete information and uncertainty and therefore overestimate cost and time requirements for the project. The Passive Hand is a close cousin of the Protecting Hand, where despite the lack of uncertainty, project proponents employ a conservative mindset, perhaps in the expectation that "unknown unknowns" will occur and persist with overestimating project costs and durations. In summary, the Hiding and the Malevolent hands often lead to an underestimation of project costs and benefits – the former due to a lack of knowledge and the latter due to a desire to manipulate information for gain. The Protecting and Passive hands often overestimate project costs and durations – with the protecting hand performing "a manifest function of addressing ignorance with risk management and a planning approach that assumes worst-case outcomes" (Anheier, 2016) and the passive hand often veering toward inaction and risk avoidance.

Recent scholarship in project behavior proposes a "fifth hand" that integrates all four hands described here and notes that a combination of all four could be at play on projects (Ika et al., 2022; Love et al., 2022). However, as Ika et al. (2022) note, the theory of the "fifth hand" needs considerable development. A large part of the limitation here, thus far, appears to be methodological. While the planning fallacy proponents have often relied heavily on statistical analysis (at least with regard to the effects), the "error" school too has relied on macro data over long time spans on large infrastructure megaprojects. Neither of these approaches allows us to understand "what is going on" in projects from the micro-perspective of the actual practices adopted that influence project behavior. In contrast, an ethnographic approach, on smaller projects such as residential construction – which have also been known to suffer from cost and time overruns but have largely been ignored by both schools and have therefore been subject to analysis through other, typically more quantitative lenses (e.g., Shehu et al., 2014; Taha et al., 2022) – may be better suited to providing complementary insights on project behavior. Although some studies in the ethnographic tradition exist (see, for instance, Oswald & Dainty [2020] for a review), they are few and far between, perhaps due to the inherent challenges in observing the variegated facets of large projects that are typically taken up for study. In this chapter, we focus on an alternative to megaprojects – a smaller residential construction project – and use an in-depth quasi ethnographic approach as described in the next section to unpack the "complex out-turns" (Ika et al., 2022) that the project takes over its lifetime. The objective is to see if we can shed more light on the interplay of the various hands across project phases and to add to our understanding of exactly how project duration and cost estimates evolve over a project's lifetime.

The Methods and the Site

The project observed was a single-story residential structure built in a small village called Konnaiyur in the interior of the state of Tamil Nadu, India. The choice of project was directed purely by convenience. As a civil engineer, I was asked if I could see this project through to completion. Having been offered a rare opportunity to practice what I preach, I accepted. Consequently, the unmitigated access I had to this project made it an ideal candidate for analysis on project behavior. Figures 16.1a and 16.1b provides the architects drawings and rendering of the project.

The structure was not particularly complex – the structural engineers decided to provide a continuous foundation made of rubble masonry on which stood load bearing brick walls supporting a single story. Two beams – one at the level of the plinth and another at the level of the ceiling held the structure together. While the eastern and western wings of the house were covered with traditional flat ceiling slabs, the central portion sported a feature traditional to the region – an inward sloping roof with an opening at the center for air circulation, called a "mittam."

As is the case with construction projects of virtually any scale, the project organization was fragmented. While a lead contractor was in charge of most of the structural works that required concreting or brickwork, an "asari" or a master-guildsman was in charge of the woodwork – the mittam, sun-shades, interior cabinetry, doors, and windows. Another master guildsman, who specialized in manufacturing an indigenous variety of tiles known as "Athangudi tiles" (after a nearby village of the same name), was in charge of the

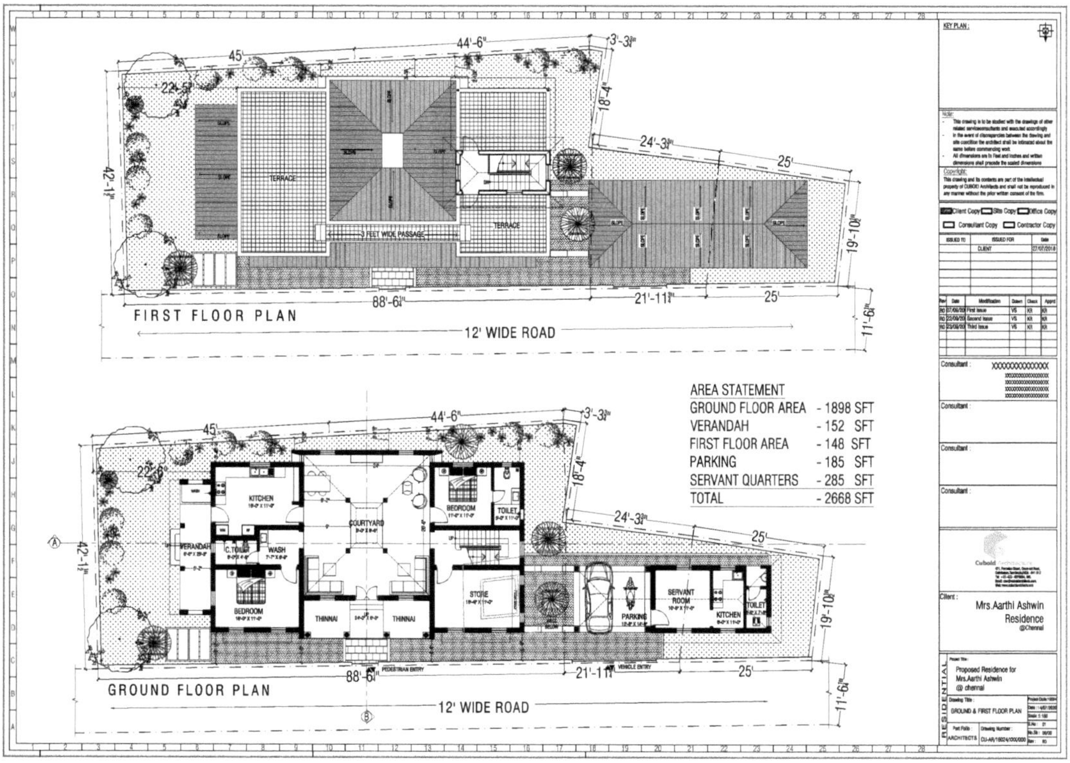

Figure 16.1a Plan of the house.

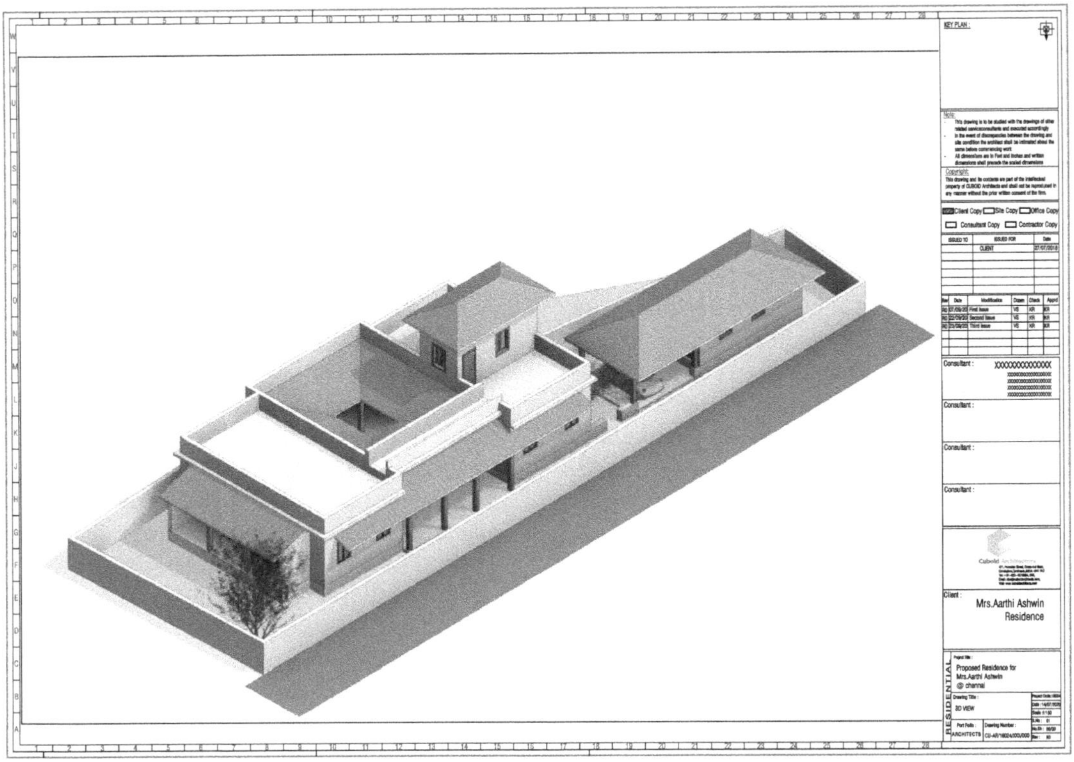

Figure 16.1b Isometric view of the house.

flooring, and, of course, specialized plumbing and electrical sub-contractors were involved. While I project managed the project, a conservation architect specializing in such traditional structures also monitored the project to ensure that the finished version reflected the original design intent – the design resembled those of traditional homes in this region and not contemporary ones, necessitating the presence of this architect to ensure that the heritage design intent was met. The client also had relationships with several suppliers who supplied cement, aggregates, steel, bricks, and a variety of other building materials and these were procured directly and brought to site. Independent labor contractors were also engaged to provide local labor in some cases.

My research methods were necessarily mixed but resembled those of a participant ethnographer. Very often researchers cite time and access constraints as well as the vast temporal and spatial spread of construction projects and argue for the need to conduct "intense" ethnographies, combining data from interviews with a variety of observations (Pink et al., 2010; Oswald & Dainty, 2020). In contrast, my methods here were more traditional and relied on observations over the design and construction phases. While I was not at the site full-time, every visit I made (20 in all) yielded a summary report on the progress of the project, activities to be completed, reasons for delays, the views of the project participants, and so on. I had a diary in which my observations and experiences each time I visited the site were recorded (2–3 pages per visit). In addition, while away from the site, the project team and I continued to be connected on WhatsApp where continuous conversations were held, primarily on the progress of the project. The WhatsApp group also served as a repository of key decisions that were made over the course of the project and therefore served as a useful source of data for ex-post analysis of project performance and behavior.

In terms of analysis, I was able to undertake some quantitative analysis of the project's adherence to time and cost targets based on the various updates I had made to the schedule after each of my visits, as well as from a detailed project cost control spreadsheet that I maintained. This spreadsheet contained every single expense incurred on the project as well as the date of occurrence, and this data could be compared with the initial project estimates as well as the initial project schedule. This analysis allowed me to develop a preliminary account of project behavior on this project.

This was then supplemented by qualitative analysis that I undertook on the WhatsApp conversations, as well as my own reflections on how the project behaved. Specifically, I was able to import the WhatsApp transcript of the entire project into a .txt file, which had 4,795 independent lines of text, not counting images, attachments, and other artifacts. This document along with my field notes were subjected to an open-coding exercise. Codes were generated that related to delay or cost-overrun causing events as well as reasons for these and were subsequently connected through an axial coding exercise. Where possible, I had recorded some quotes from other project participants in my diary as well as my own reflections, which were also coded. These codes were then analyzed longitudinally over time in order to identify higher order constructs that related to how the project behaved at various stages in the construction phase. Taken together, I attempted to paste the qualitative experiences on to the quantitative data to identify inflection points where cost and time estimates changed dramatically and to subsequently identify causes for why the project behaved in such a manner. For instance, where the quantitative data showed a sudden increase in cost or time estimates, I went back to the qualitative data to understand key dynamics that occurred on the project just preceding this event. The quantitative data provided trigger points around which I queried the qualitative data for patterns. My observations are now presented.

Observations

The project was a disaster as far as meeting the initial time and cost estimates were concerned. The project started in June of 2021 and was expected to finish in December of 2021, based on a macro-level schedule that was drawn. Final substantive completion was in October of 2022 representing a time overrun of close to 150 percent. The initial budget was INR 8,063,369 (approximately USD 100,000) but the project came in at INR 11,144,752 (approximately USD 139,000) representing a cost overrun of nearly 40 percent. Much like contemporary observations on projects, this project did nothing to assuage the thinking that time and cost overruns on projects are not the exception but the norm. So, what exactly happened? Let us take a closer look at the data.

Figure 16.2 shows how the project's estimated end-date varied over time. In June of 2021, the project was expected to be completed in six months (i.e, in December 2021). However, as project reviews were held and as the project was constantly rescheduled, the proposed end-date kept increasing. In July, the project had already been pushed back by a month. Between July and November, the project's expected completion date remained relatively static and was shifted back only by a month or so. The project was expected to finish in January. However, post November 2021, the volatility in the proposed end date increased dramatically. Between November and January, the project's end date was pushed back to April 2022. Beyond January, the project witnessed an almost monotonic increase in the proposed end date, with each subsequent review pushing this date further and further away, at a uniform pace, until the actual completion of the project caught up with the planned completion during the final review in October of 2022!

An analysis of project costs provides us with a different, complementary picture. Figure 16.3 below shows the monthly and cumulative spending in INR through the course of the project. While not quite a traditional "S' curve, the cumulative cost curve shows a somewhat monotonic increase over time, subject to a few kinks, indicating a somewhat constant rate of spend on the project barring a few months where the spending was negligible or excessive. In small projects of this nature, costs are sometimes spent before or after they are actually incurred. Mobilization advances, for instance,

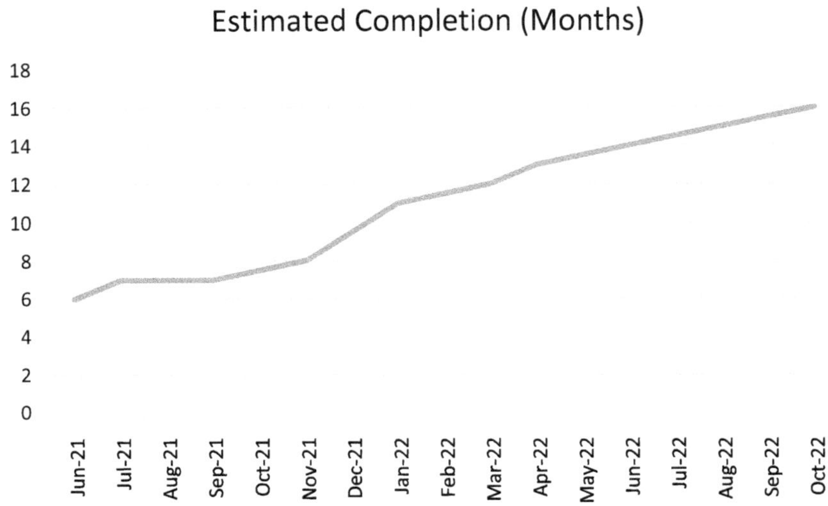

Figure 16.2 Project's estimated end date.

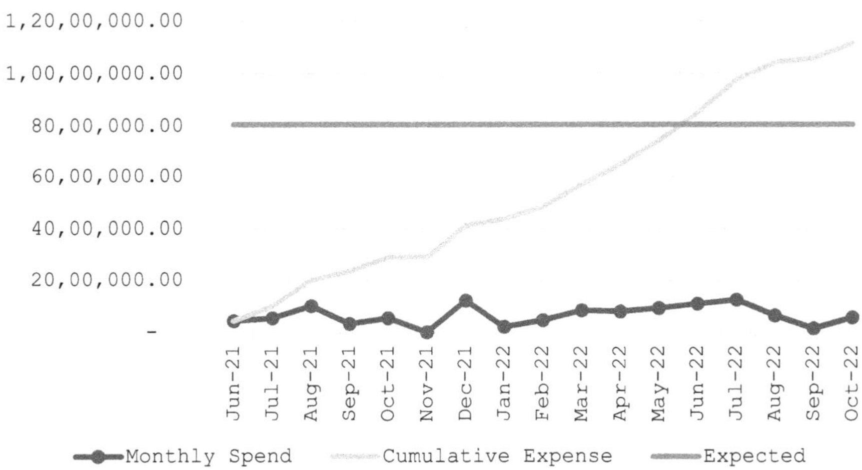

Figure 16.3 Project expenditure.

are given prior to work starting, while payments are occasionally paid against milestones that represent payments against actual costs incurred earlier or later. This graph tells us that the original budgeted estimate of approximately INR 8 million was breached in May 2022.

Perhaps more telling is an analysis of a metric known as the cost performance index (CPI). The CPI is part of a larger analysis technique known as "earned value analysis" – a technique that is commonly used in construction project management. Earned value analysis attempts to identify the extent to which a project conforms to its budgeted cost and time estimates at *intermediate* stages of the project. The advantage of this technique is that if project slippages can be identified earlier rather than later, corrective mechanisms can be employed to bring the project back on track. Indeed, this aligns with the "Plan-do-check-act" philosophy espoused by traditional project management scholars, with the earned value technique being the fulcrum of the "check" function in this cycle.

Very often, in order to gauge a project's cost performance, the expenditure of actual costs at intermediate stages are compared to the planned expenditure schedule of budgeted costs. If actual spending is faster or slower than budgeted spending, conclusions are drawn with regard to whether the project is on budget or not. This analysis is erroneous as it disregards the amount of actual work performed. A project that is spending money faster than budgeted may still be on track to meet its cost estimates provided work is also being done faster than planned. The earned value method deals with this issue through the creation of the CPI. The CPI as an index is a ratio of two parameters – the budgeted cost of the work performed (BCWP) or the earned value (from where the technique gets its name) and the actual cost of the work performed (ACWP) or the actual spending (often denoted simply as actual cost). Simply put, the BCWP is the amount that a contractor can invoice based on both work done as well as the value of that work as agreed upon in the contract. CPI is calculated as: $\text{CPI} = \text{BCWP}/ACWP$

As can be intuitively seen from this formula, when the earned value (BCWP) matches with the amount that is spent (ACWP), the CPI is 1. In this case budgeted spending and actual spending match each other and therefore a CPI value of 1 indicates that the project is on track to meet its estimated budget. If the earned value of work done is greater than the actual cost spent, this implies that cost-saving mechanisms have been employed and the project is likely to finish under budget. Consequently, a CPI value greater than 1 indicates a potential within-budget completion. On the other hand, a CPI value less than 1 implies that actual costs spent for a unit of work are greater than the budgeted cost for the performance of the same piece of work. The ACWP in this case is greater than the BCWP indicating that the project is likely to overrun its cost estimates. The extent to which the CPI deviates from 1 is an indicator of the magnitude of potential cost overruns/underruns. As CPI is a measure that is to be computed during the course of the project, Figure 16.4 shows how the CPI varied on this project over time, on a monthly basis.

As the figure shows, the project started off with a CPI greater than 1 in the first month – more work was achieved than what was paid for. However, this is neither surprising nor noteworthy as the initial stages of the project involve trivial exercises such as marking out the layout and so on. Post the first month, the CPI can be seen to dip, mainly on account of some unintended expenses that I will presently discuss as well as several mobilization advances that were paid to various project entities, which represent payments made ahead of work undertaken. However, by around November, once these early blips had settled, the CPI made its way back to just below 1 (0.98). Post November, the CPI began to fall – dramatically in December, then rose marginally in January and February before falling steadily thereon. A minor correction toward

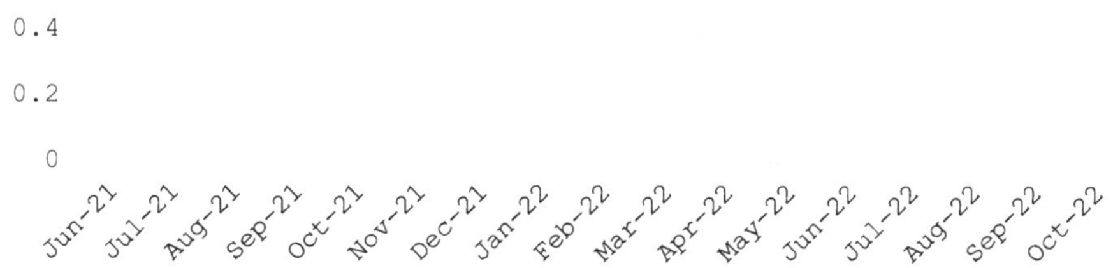

Figure 16.4 Monthly CPI variation.

the end ensured that the CPI moved from an all-time low of 0.68 to finish at 0.72. This trend is indicative of how the project behaved over time and where exactly cost overruns first started to manifest.

Before discussing these trends in detail, I present one final set of quantitative data. While estimating the project, the work was divided into 5 "packages" – (a) civil works that included the foundation, concreting of the plinth and edge beams, as well as the construction of brick walls and the roof slabs on the east and west sides of the main building; (b) mechanical, electrical, and plumbing (MEP) works for the house; (c) joinery works or works related to woodwork including roofs on both the main and annex buildings, doors, windows, and interior cupboards and shelves; (d) finishing works that included polishing, flooring, painting, and miscellaneous landscaping works; and (e) other costs that include temporary structures that needed to be erected, monies paid to a variety of consultants, miscellaneous support expenses, and so on. Figure 16.5 presents a comparison of budgeted and expected costs for each of these packages.

As we can see from this analysis, the estimates for civil works were almost spot on! There was a mild variance in the cost of MEP works but this came down to a choice of a more expensive set of electrical fixtures by the client than was originally envisaged. The major deviation was in the joinery works (a cost increase of upwards of 200 percent), while the finishes and other cost packages featured lesser but nonetheless nontrivial cost overruns.

Having presented these quantitative snapshots of how the project performed over time, I now attempt to juxtapose these with qualitative reflections to shed more light on the project's behavior.

How Did This Project Behave?

Taken together, the qualitative and quantitative data point to three distinct phases with distinct project behaviors – the teething troubles phase, the honeymoon phase, and the nightmare phase. I describe each of these below.

Teething Troubles

The first phase occurred right at the start of the project, lasted for about a month, and can be termed as the "teething troubles" phase. At the end of this phase, the project's CPI had dropped below 1 and the overall schedule had already been extended by 45 days. The chief dynamic here was the emergence of information that the project team was unaware of as they started the project. As an example, it is well known that construction requires quite a bit of water particularly to create concrete and mortar mixes. Since piped water supply was unavailable in Konnaiyur, alternative

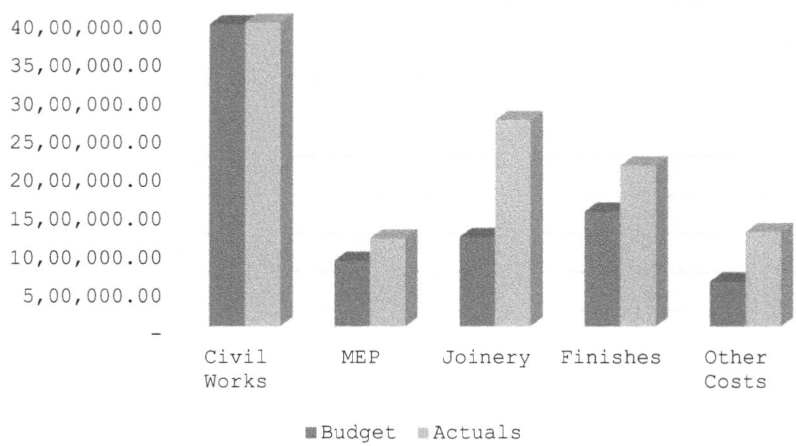

Figure 16.5 Deviations in package costs.

sources for water needed to be found. The original footprint of the site contained an old well, a remnant from the previous structure that stood on this site. The initial construction plan was to draw water from this well – initial investigations indicated sufficient water availability. Furthermore, another well existed barely a few hundred meters from the site. This too appeared to hold copious quantities of water. The project team decided to go ahead with the construction believing that they had a reliable water supply source as well as a backup source, increasing the redundancy. Unfortunately, their hopes were dashed rather quickly. Construction started in June of 2021 – in the peak of the Indian summer and the well on site ran dry within the first week. The team shifted their water pipeline to the second well. On the first day, we received reports of how the water surpassed drinking quality. By the seventh day, this well too was starting to dry up.

Faced with this lack of water, the client was presented with two options – procure water through water tankers throughout the duration of the project or dig a borewell to tap into an underground aquifer. The latter was a far more expensive proposition but had long-term implications since the borewell could be used to supply water to the house even after construction. The client therefore chose the latter option, bringing the project to a temporary halt while a borewell contractor was identified, initial sounding studies were conducted to identify an appropriate borewell location, and the borewell was actually drilled and constructed. Such events led to both an increase in project costs as well as delays in expected completion times.

Another example pertains to the construction of the foundation. Despite conducting geotechnical investigations where soil samples were drawn from various portions of the site, the actual soil conditions along the footprint of the foundation turned out to be different from the conditions that were used as the basis for foundation design. Consequently, the structural system of the foundation was changed to what is known as a rubble-masonry footing. The depth of the foundation was also increased. Procuring the stones required to construct this foundation was a challenge since this material was not readily available locally. The project team spent a few days before they could identify a reliable supplier.

Such challenges are part and parcel of most projects. Actual soil conditions often differ from expected ones and these issues are often captured as a part of differential site conditions clauses on large contracts. Other preparatory works (provision of water and electricity, setting up of a temporary facility to store materials, housing for workers etc.) are also known to take up time and in this case led to a few delays during this phase of the project, pushing back time and cost estimates. Some of these issues can be attributed to inadequate planning (for instance, costs of setting up a temporary storage facility are often just not added to project estimates in a precise manner), while other issues can be attributed to the presence of inadequate information (such as the need to arrange for a borewell for water). In the bias vs. error debate (Love et al., 2019; Ika et al., 2022) the overruns observed in this phase seem to fall into the error side of the ledger. Consistent with Gil and Pinto's (2018) views, delays did not seem to result from biased or overoptimistic estimates. Rather, the original estimates of time and cost for the work done during this phase were achievable. It was the emergence of new information, particularly geotechnical, that led to errors in the original plans and the consequent reorganization of work that led to the observed outcomes.

Honeymoon

After the end of this first phase, the project entered its second or "honeymoon" phase. This phase lasted from the months of July to the middle of November 2021, constituting nearly 75 percent of the project's originally planned duration. In this phase, the primary activities undertaken were from the civil works package. Multiple layers of the foundation were laid. A reinforced concrete plinth beam was then laid on top of the foundation to balance the structural load uniformly onto the foundation. This was followed by the construction of load-bearing brick walls for the exterior and interior walls first up to the level of the lintels and subsequently up to the level of the roof.

An edge beam was laid on the roof once again to uniformly distribute the roofing loads, and roof slabs for the east and west wings of the main building were poured using reinforced concrete. The lead contractor – a civil mason – and his crew performed all of this work.

During this period, the overall progress as can be seen in Figures 16.2 and 16.4 stayed largely on target. For the first three months, there were no delays to the schedule and the target completion date continued to be pegged at January of 2022. This was then pushed back by a month toward the end of this period primarily due to a mild decrease in productivity due to excessive rainfall in the region in 2021 (Konnaiyur receives rainfall primarily from October to December due to India's North-West Monsoon. In 2021, the monsoon set in a bit early with a higher-than-expected intensity of rainfall leading to frequent stoppages of work, as laborers were still working in the open prior to casting the roof.) By the end of November, the CPI, which had initially dipped, had also made its way back almost to the ideal figure of 1 (0.98).

As mentioned earlier, the initial dip in CPI was due to mobilization advances given to the contractor as well as to unexpected expenses such as the digging of the borewell. However, once these advances had been worked off and payments started getting linked to milestones, the spending on the project started matching the budgeted costs leading to a rise in the CPI. Since the contractor had complete access to the workfront, control over his crew and no inter-dependency at this stage, work proceeded at a good pace. Reliable links were set up with material suppliers, some of whom gave a discount on their prices, allowing the project to compensate for the extra expenses incurred in the first phase. The contractor also had good visibility on the progress of the work and could precisely anticipate the rate of consumption of materials as well as the requirement for additional materials. Once they got to know the average lead times of supply from the respective vendors (none of which were particularly lengthy) they were able to efficiently plan for the ordering and receipt of materials on site. Thus, the lack of qualified labor, the nonavailability of drawings, work front or material – oft-cited excuses for project delay – were conspicuous by their absence during this phase. During this phase, the project team fully expected to finish the project on budget and with a mild delay.

The experiences in this phase support Mak and Raftery's (1992) views that experienced personnel do know a thing or two about estimating and planning. The plans made were realistic and more often than not, targets were achieved on a monthly basis.

Nightmare

Toward the end of November, the project transitioned from the honeymoon phase into what can be termed as the "nightmare" phase. The wheels of the well-oiled machine rolled off rather spectacularly. As Figure 16.2 showed us, the expected project duration increased dramatically over the first few months of this phase and continued to consistently increase after each review meeting. Similarly, the CPI fell steeply in the initial months and, notwithstanding a minor resurrection, continued to fall steadily month after month. In other words, time and cost performance steadily worsened after each monthly review. What exactly went on in this phase?

This phase featured activities with quite a bit of interdependencies between them as well as a number of agencies that had to simultaneously work on the project. Part of the roofs were made of wooden rafters with tiles mounted on them. A carpenter (the artisan mentioned earlier) and his crew therefore started working. Simultaneously, the mechanical contractor started laying his pipes and the electrical contractor started fixing switchboards and installing the wiring (the MEP activities had been enabled by the civil contractor who had provided conduits for these in accordance with the drawings). A special variety of handmade, cement-based flooring tiles called the Athangudi tiles, named after a nearby village from which they are globally sourced were used. These were specially crafted and laid by a separate contractor. The main contractor, having finished most of the civil works also took on other finishing activities such as plastering and painting of the walls, building septic tanks for waste collection, building the compound wall, and so on.

This presence of multiple agencies led to reciprocal dependencies that now necessitated much more careful planning of the work. The flooring artisan wanted to come in as late as possible and wanted the plastering of the walls to be done first. The finishing contractor, however, wanted to wait till the completion of the flooring to apply the final coat of paint and close out the project. In between, the electrical contractor had to both complete the wiring and install the fixtures. This constant need for movement of various trades in and out of the workspace led to scheduling challenges. In addition, most contractors wanted to optimize their efforts on the project and minimize the number of times that they would come to the site. They preferred to come for one contiguous period, complete their work, and leave. This strategy was fundamentally incompatible with the earlier requirement of having trades weave in and out of the site. Confusion resulted. The plumbing contractor was asked to come to finish the plumbing for the bathrooms in the main building. However, he chose to wait until the plumbing fixtures had arrived and until the outdoor water treatment infrastructure (septic tanks) were complete so as to maximize the amount of work his crew could undertake when they came to site. The ensuing delay in the plumbing works for the bathroom then delayed the finishing works here as well.

A second dynamic that led to cost overruns was associated with changes made by the client. Up until the completion of civil works, the client had very few inputs into the construction process. However, once the finishing and joinery activities commenced, a number of discussions took place. Some of the client's requests had no bearing on project duration and a mild impact on costs – a change in the color of the walls, for instance. Others led to the creation of complex activities that resulted in fundamental schedule changes. For instance, the initial vision for the parapet in the terrace was to have a solid wall. The client, however, changed their mind and requested grills. These grills had to be prefabricated in a casting yard, delivered to the site, and subsequently erected, leading to a much different sequence of work than previously envisaged.

Similarly, with regard to landscaping, the client wanted an intricate tile arrangement popularized by a Sri Lankan architect named Deshamanya Geoffrey Manning Bawa. This involved the procurement of a type of stone known as tandoor stone, cutting these stones into a series of different shapes, preparing a solid bed, laying these tiles in what might appear to be a random manner and grouting the joints in between. All of these activities were far more effort intensive than what had originally been envisaged for landscaping and also resulted in higher labor as well as material costs.

Another example arose as the kitchen was being built. The initial plan was to have open cupboards. However, upon seeing the partially built kitchen, the client changed their mind and asked for the cupboards to be closed, glazed, and painted. Similarly, a number of changes were suggested as the project came to life and as the client started to engage with a real three-dimensional (3D) facility and not a two-dimensional (or virtual 3D) rendering.

A third dynamic that resulted in time and cost overruns was due to an apparent lack of micro-planning when estimating the project. The architect had designed wooden sunshades on top of the windows – identical to the wooden roof that had been built. However, while the roof had been estimated in great detail, these sunshades had not, and their appearance added to the cost. Further, in order to erect them, temporary structures such as scaffolding had to be procured and erected. These were not planned for and this resulted in a frantic last-minute search for vendors, delaying these activities. In other cases, some elements such as light fittings, for instance, had just not been specified. A ballpark estimate had been provided. However, when a detailed lighting and ventilation analysis was done, leading to a selection of fixtures on both functional and aesthetic grounds, the costs of the fixtures were far higher than originally envisaged.

While all of these dynamics resulted in a spiralling out of time and cost, another issue surfaced. The project team, which until then had seemed to behave as a coherent unit started to bicker and complain internally. The joinery artisan complained to me about how the lead contractor doing the civil works had committed to infeasible dates that led to delays, in turn giving everyone else on the project a bad name. The lead contractor responded by arguing that the delays were due to the joinery artisan's lack of planning and resource mobilization. Both parties then resorted to sending voice messages on the project team WhatsApp group either notifying each other that a certain piece of work had been completed or requesting for some work to be done by the other party to enable them to proceed. In reality, these were trivial pieces of communication that were best done face-to-face on the site, but both parties felt the need to prove to the larger team that included the client and the architect that they were not the ones delaying the project. The team thus dissolved into a collection of individual entities, each looking after their own interests rather than the interests of the project. This is consistent with observations on most projects where the fragmented organizational structure of a project organization promotes goal incongruence (Thomsen et al., 2005).

As the project's end neared, work started proceeding more and more slowly. While a checklist was prepared and more frequent review meetings were held, items just did not get checked off and crews continued to putter about the site making incremental progress. This was also partially due to the fact that most of the vendors had obtained new projects to work on at this stage since they knew this project was coming to an end. Eager to make a good first impression with their new clients, they deployed their best manpower at these new sites, further handicapping our project. As the labor strength and productivity decreased, the project slowly limped over the finish line in October 2022.

This phase illustrates the notion that delays are not merely additive and independent. Rather, as already noted in the literature, a systems perspective provides a better understanding of how delays cascade from one cause to another and how dynamic feedback loops result wherein the combined impact of delays is far greater than their expected individual impact (Williams et al., 1995; Eden et al., 2000). For instance, when the plumber finally arrived on site to complete the installation of fixtures, electrical underground lines were already laid. The plumber inadvertently hit one of the electrical lines while digging, requiring repair work by the electrical contractor, which led to further delays and disruptions.

Several of the causes for delays and cost overruns are well known. The notion of project complexity and reciprocal dependencies (e.g., Eden et al., 1995) is not new. Neither is the "naughty customer" stereotype where clients cause changes post award of the contract, although as Love et al. (2019) note, these are "sanctioned changes" that are best considered as leading to cost increases rather than cost overruns. Such increases may also lead to additional benefits such as greater client satisfaction, improved utilization of the asset, and enhanced durability of the structure and should therefore not be treated as negative outcomes. Despite this, there was some evidence of the Planning Fallacy (Flyvjberg, 2016) in this phase, where initial forecasts were closer to best-case than to a realistic scenario, due to the inherent optimism on the part of the project team. The project team had clearly underestimated the coordination requirements associated with such a project and had proposed a highly optimistic project duration. The carpenter even confided with me saying that had he been the lead contractor, he would have never agreed to such an aggressive time line. On the cost side, however, infusion of new information by a stakeholder late in the process (client-induced changes in this instance) was chiefly responsible for cost increases, supporting Gil and Pinto's (2018) thesis on how actors and new information influence the project's cost and time estimates as it evolves.

What Have We Learned about Project Behavior?

The case study highlights a variety of behavioral issues that lead to time and cost overruns, some of which are well known – the uncertainties at the "fuzzy front end" (Miller & Lessard, 2001) and the coordination requirements between trades at the back end (Choo & Tommelein, 1999), to name a few. However, there are a few learnings from this case that are worth highlighting.

First, as noted earlier, the project went through three different phases – teething troubles, honeymoon, and nightmare – each with its own set of behaviors. The teething troubles phase jolted the project with some extraneous shocks leading to an immediate reconfiguration of the project's performance parameters. The honeymoon phase maintained a consistent rate of performance in line with the plan, while the nightmare phase applied a series of relatively weaker but more prevalent stresses as compared to the teething troubles phase, slowly worsening the condition of the project and drawing out the denouement, steadily lowering time and cost performance. A key insight here is that project behavior may not be constant throughout a project's lifecycle, and different phases of a project may show distinct types of behaviors. This is critical from a project management perspective, as project managers can break their project down into phases, attempt to predict the behavioral archetype of each phase, and then develop specific strategies at different points in time to combat the challenges anticipated in each phase, as opposed to adopting a one-size-fits all project governance framework.

The literature suggests several strategies for handling the "teething troubles" phase – using better (and increasingly automated) methods of information gathering to prevent surprises, network building and co-optation of stakeholders, and flexible project designs that can be changed based on initial site conditions (Miller & Lessard, 2001; de Neufville and Scholtes, 2011; Henisz et al., 2012) to name a few. The honeymoon phase is perhaps best managed by traditional project management and control techniques – the use of critical path schedules, earned value analysis, and so on to ensure project progress. These processes can also be digitally enabled.

The nightmare phase requires considerable effort to manage. Since coordination is one of the key challenges here, project managers are well advised to consider adopting collaborative techniques such as perhaps those in the lean construction playbook, during this phase (Koskela et al., 2002). Building on lean manufacturing ideas, lean construction posits that coordination challenges manifest in the form of a variety of "wastes" on construction sites leading to delays and cost overruns. A number of techniques exist to first identify these wastes (mapping the value stream, for instance) and then to organize construction sites to minimize these wastes (systems such as the Last Planner^{TM}). In essence, these techniques are systematic methods that enable better coordination between trades during this phase leading to better project outcomes.

Another critical challenge during this phase arose due to changes made to the scope of the project. Visualization tools can help provide immersive experiences earlier in the project that can in turn lead to a variety of issues being flagged at the front end and decisions that can be taken before work begins. Indeed, the science of virtual design and construction or VDC integrates digital products with project organizations and processes to serve as a decision-making aid (Kunz & Fischer, 2020). Such integrative approaches can ensure smoother progress during the nightmare phase.

Second, there has been considerable debate on the causes of project behavior, as we have mentioned earlier, that runs the gamut from strategic misrepresentation to incompetence to an inability of prevailing systems to deal with complexity. Analyzing the project from the perspective of the various guiding "hands" is telling. Table 16.1 tabulates the three observed phases and the project behaviors that were observed:

Consistent with contemporary ideas on why time and cost overruns occur, the data suggests that what we see on projects is not an "either-or" choice between "hands" but perhaps an amalgamation or even an entanglement between them, with multiple hands simultaneously driving project behavior particularly in the nightmare phase. For instance, I observed instances of both the Hiding Hand (in the case of the borewell that needed to be dug) as well as the Protecting Hand (that created enough buffers in the honeymoon phase to ensure that there was no deviation between planned and observed project outcomes). The presence of the Malevolent Hand can also not be ruled out as some of the increases in joinery costs, for instance, were unavoidable and by rights should have been foreseen earlier in the project. Researchers and practitioners may therefore benefit by acknowledging the presence of multiple guiding forces – perhaps both benign and malignant – that shape both the course and the behavior of such projects.

The type of hand that guides a project may also depend on the complexity of each phase of the

Table 16.1 Project behaviors across phases

Phase	Complexity	Observed "out turns"	Evidence of hands
1. Teething troubles	Low – only a few stakeholders involved: main contractor, architect, borehole provider, and so on	Costs and Time estimate increases due to unforeseen soil conditions, lack of groundwater	Some evidence of errors and the hiding hand that was used to find creative solutions – to the lack of water, for instance.
2. Honeymoon	Minimal	Hardly any. Project went according to plan	Some evidence of the protecting hand creating buffers for the project .
3. Nightmare	High – several stakeholders and interdependencies	Costs and time estimate increases due to coordination challenges between trades, client induced changes, and complications in task requirements.	Evidence of all four hands acting simultaneously. The malevolent hand led to optimistic estimates, the Hiding hand did not anticipate client changes, the Passive Hand led to the clients constantly trying to reduce the scope and the Protective Hand led to more planning and control meetings.

project. The initial phase of construction projects – the teething troubles phase in our case – is characterized by "unknown unknowns" – obtaining permits, especially in countries such as India is hardly a straightforward process and despite the best of engineering efforts, subsoil conditions throw up surprises more often than not. However, the number of actors that need to negotiate this phase is limited – often restricted to geotechnical consultants, the main contractor, and the client's team and coordination pathways are clear. Perhaps expectedly, we saw the prevalence of "errors" in estimates in this phase due to incomplete information and perhaps even a semblance of the Hiding Hand, as the main contractor worked with the client to find innovative solutions to issues such as the lack of water on the site.

As the project moved on to the honeymoon phase, we observe a further decrease in project complexity. The number of agencies involved in site work were few – chiefly the main contractor – instructions were available and work got done. In such an environment, we observe a bit of the Protecting Hand as project and risk management systems were put in place. The project resembled a well-oiled machine in this phase – material orders were placed with appropriate lead times time and the crew worked consistently and productively. Most of the guiding "hands" were conspicuous by their absence as the project hardly observed any out-turns in this phase.

However, the nightmare phase was perhaps the most complex in terms of stakeholder engagement, with a variety of subcontractors simultaneously executing work on the project. Here we observe all four hands working simultaneously on the project. Despite continual challenges, the main contractor constantly proposed an optimistic completion date that needed to be revised – providing some evidence of bias and the Malevolent Hand; clients induced changes in the plan and subcontractor sequencing was a challenge leading to errors in estimates. Both of these dynamics led to time and cost increases. In response, the client reacted by trying to impose more stringent project control systems, with more frequent meetings to try to anticipate and control risks – providing some evidence of the Protecting Hand. Furthermore, an attempt was made to simplify what remained of the project – apart from the Geoffrey Bawa–inspired tiling patterns, some more ambitious landscaping efforts were set aside in order to ensure project completion – evidence of the passive hand.

Based on these observations, I posit that project behavior is neither consistent across a project's lifetime, nor determined a priori. Rather, behavior changes across phases. While more complex projects may be categorized into more nuanced phases, project behavior is tied to the complexity of a phase, as determined by the number of stakeholders who need to be coordinated. The higher the complexity (typically in the "finishes" stage of a residential project but can be seen in other stages in more complex projects), the more likely we are to see a multiplicity of "hands" guiding the project. The Fifth Hand in this case is more of a balancing hand, as cost and time overruns caused by the Hiding or Malevolent hands are countered in part by the Passive and Protecting hands, all the while guiding the project toward completion.

Conclusion

The objective of this chapter was to shed light on project behavior in a manner that might provide learnings to both practitioners as well as academics. It was for this reason that I chose to analyze a real-world case study.

As mentioned in the previous section, the key contributions of this study are to highlight the key phases of the project from a behavioral perspective and to show, a la Ika et al., (2022) that there exists a duality (or indeed a multiplicity) rather than a dualism of guiding forces that shape project behavior – errors, biases, orientations toward risk, incomplete information, and uncertainty all interplay in determining how a project behaves over its construction life cycle. The case also shows how interconnected and systemic the causes of delays and overruns are, leading to project behavior perhaps being best conceptualized as a complex adaptive system. Furthermore, this system is embedded in a larger ecology of stakeholder networks, both internal and external (Grabher 2004; Ninan et al., 2019), as well as external force majeure influences, including in this case rainfall events that determined the availability of groundwater for construction.

While some of these elements, especially those relating to forces of nature, cannot be controlled, there is a case to be made that managing stakeholder inputs and requirements can positively influence project behavior. For instance, using building information models (BIM) to discern client requirements early on can lead to fewer client-induced changes and in turn fewer cascading delays between various trades that need to rescope and reschedule their work. I therefore posit that project behavior can indeed be shaped. If left unchecked, the error and bias combination will lead to significant time and cost overruns.

Project managers need to proactively counter these overruns through the use of strategies that exemplify the Passive and Protecting hands. Some of this was observed in the case and indeed tighter project control and a downward revision of scope prevented the nightmare phase from becoming an even greater nightmare. Yet these strategies were often used reactively and it is my submission that anticipating the need to balance the four hands and the proactive introduction of these strategies cannot only streamline project behavior but also lead to more beneficial project outcomes.

Another salient contribution of this study is to shed light on the dynamic nature of project behavior. In earlier formulations, the "front end" of a project plays a critical role and the causes for errors and biases are to be found here. This remains partially true. However, the project is not set upon a predetermined time and cost overrun trajectory based on the orientation in the front end. Rather, as the project's complexity waxes and wanes over various phases, time and cost overruns too may have a propensity to change and can in turn be balanced by Passive and Protecting hand strategies employed by project proponents. Project behavior is therefore shaped by internal and external forces on an ongoing basis.

There are, of course, limitations to case study–based research, the ability to generalize findings from a small (single) sample being the most often cited one. I would argue, however, that while the specifics vary from project to project, several of the observations, particularly with regard to the phases that the project went through, are likely to be observable across projects and thus qualify as more generic learnings. With regard to the specifics of this project, ironically the project had several enabling conditions that should have eased its path. Some of these were not mentioned earlier as they were tangential to the narrative but are worth mentioning now. Laborers were provided with good quality housing near the site for free. Labor retention was therefore not an issue and challenges that one observes on other sites where human resources are not available did not manifest. In addition, the client directly procured materials from most vendors. Contractors therefore primarily provided labor. One of the challenges on projects is that contractors typically work across multiple projects and shift funds between projects. When cashflow in one project is halted, this has a domino effect on other projects as well. By ensuring that material supply was not halted under any circumstances, the client ensured that the contractor would not face cashflow issues at least as far as this project was concerned. The project therefore had a variety of enabling boundary conditions, yet could not finish on time and on budget. The fate of other projects that do not have these advantages can only be contemplated.

In conclusion, this chapter has presented a deepdive into a specific residential project and has allowed us to understand project behavior in a micro-context. We remind ourselves that project behavior is the study of how projects work as a whole and the complex out-turns that they take throughout their lifetime. Project behavior is about "explaining and anticipating successes and failures, systematic veerings from pre-assigned paths, propensities toward specific difficulties, and opportunities for special payoffs" (Hirschman, 1967, p. 4). My intention in claiming the "micro perspective" is to emphasize that I have attempted to look "under the hood" to tease out specific dynamics such as those identified by Hirschman and others that then contribute to these outturns. In doing so, I find support for the notion of a "Fifth Hand" and attempt to unpack it in some small degree, recognizing that it may have balancing properties and that is likely to occur in phases of high project complexity. This study also shows that practitioners can proactively influence project behavior throughout the project through the use of a variety of management techniques and therefore shifts the debate toward what practitioners can do to influence project behaviors and outcomes, as opposed to merely analyzing the impacts of the cards that they have dealt with. I hope that this story has helped practitioners in particular obtain a better sense of the flavors and vicissitudes of project behavior, and in turn plays at least a small part in helping them better prepare for the project behavioral challenges that they will no doubt face on their projects.

References

Ahiaga-Dagbui, D. D, and Smith, S. D. (2014) Rethinking construction cost overruns: Cognition, learning and estimation. *Journal of Financial Management and Property Construction, 19*(1), 38–54.

Alshihri, S., Al-Gahtani, K., and Almohsen, A. (2022). Risk factors that lead to time and cost overruns of building projects in Saudi Arabia. *Buildings, 12*(7), 902.

Anheier, H. K. (2016). Of Hiding Hands and other ways of coping with uncertainty: A commentary. *Social Research, 83*(4), 1005–1010.

Barley, S. R., and Kunda, G. (2001). Bringing work back in. *Organization Science, 12*(1), 76–95.

Choo, H. J., and Tommelein, I. D. (1999). Parade of trades: A game for understanding variability and dependence. Construction Engineering and Management Program, Civil and Environmental Engineering Department. University of California, Berkeley.

De Neufville, R., and Scholtes, S. (2011). *Flexibility in engineering design*. MIT Press.

Eden, C., Williams, T., Ackermann, F., and Howick, S. (2000). The role of feedback dynamics in disruption and delay on the nature of disruption and delay (D&D) in major projects. *Journal of the Operational Research Society, 51*(3), 291–300.

Eden, C., Ackermann, F., and Williams, T. (2005). The amoebic growth of project costs. *Project Management Journal, 36*(2), 15–27.

Flyvbjerg, B., Holm. M., and Buhl, S. (2002). Underestimating costs in public works projects. *Journal of the American Planning Association, 68*(3), 279–295.

Flyvbjerg, B., Bruzelius, N., and Rothengatter, W. (2003). *Megaprojects and risk: An anatomy of ambition*. Cambridge University Press.

Flyvbjerg, B. (2016). The fallacy of beneficial ignorance: A test of Hirschman's Hiding Hand. *World Development, 84*, 176–189.

Flyvbjerg, B., and Sunstein, C. R. (2016). The principle of the malevolent hiding hand; or, the planning fallacy writ large. *Social Research: An International Quarterly, 83*(3), 979–1004.

Flyvbjerg,B., Ansar, A., Budzier, A., Buhl, S., Cantarelli, C., Garbuio, M., Glenting, C., Holm, M. S., Lovallo, D., Lunn, D., Molin, E., Rønnest, A., Stewart, A., and Van Wee, B. (2018). Five things you should know about cost overrun. *Transportation Research Part A: Policy and Practice*, *118*, 174–190.

Gil, N., and Pinto, J. (2018). Polycentric organizing and performance: A contingency model and evidence from megaproject planning in the UK. *Research Policy*, *47*(4), 717–734.

Grabher, G. (2004). Temporary architectures of learning: Knowledge governance in project ecologies. *Organization Studies*, *25*(9), 1491–1514.

Henisz, W. J., Levitt, R. E., and Scott, W. R. (2012). Toward a unified theory of project governance: Economic, sociological and psychological supports for relational contracting. *Engineering Project Organization Journal*, *2*(1–2), 37–55.

Hirschman, A. O. (1967). *Development projects observed*. Brookings Institution.

L. A. Ika, Love, P. E. D., and Pinto, J. K. (2022). Moving beyond the Planning Fallacy: The emergence of a new principle of project nehavior. *IEEE Transactions on Engineering Management*, *69*(6), 3310–3325.

Ika, L. A., Pinto, J. K., Love, P. E. D., and Pache, G. (2023). Bias versus error: Why projects fall short. *Journal of Business Strategy*, *44*(2), 67–75

Jones, L. R., and Euske, K. J. (1991). Strategic misrepresentation in budgeting. *Journal of Public Administration Research and Theory*, *1*(4), 437–460.

Kahneman, D. (2017). *Thinking, fast and slow*. Farrar, Straus and Giroux.

Kahneman, D., andTversky, A. (1977). *Intuitive prediction: Biases and corrective procedures*. Defense Advanced Research Projects Agency.

Koskela, L., Howell, G., Ballard, G., and Tommelein, I. (2002). The foundations of lean construction. *Design and Construction: Building in Value*, *291*, 211–226.

Koushki, P. A., and Kartam, N. (2004). Impact of construction materials on project time and cost in Kuwait. *Engineering, Construction and Architectural Management*, *11*(2), 126–132.

Kunz, J., and Fischer, M. (2020). Virtual design and construction. *Construction Management and Economics*, *38*(4), 355–363.

Love, P. E. D, and Ahiaga-Dagbui, D. (2018). Debunking fake news in a post-truth era: The plausible untruths of cost underestimation in transport infrastructure projects. *Transportation Research Part A: Policy and Practice*, *113*, 357–368.

Love, P. E. D., Pinto, J. K., and Ika, L. A. (2022). Hundreds of years of pain, with minimal gain: Capital project cost overruns, the past, present, and optimistic future. *IEEE Engineering Management Review*, *50*(4), 56–70.

Love, P. E. D., and Ika, L. A. (2022). Making sense of hospital project misperformance: Over budget, late, time and time again—Why? And what can be done about it? *Engineering*, *12*, 183–201.

Love, P. E. D., Ika, L. A., and Sing, M. C. (2019). Does the planning fallacy prevail in social infrastructure projects? Empirical evidence and competing explanations. *IEEE Transactions on Engineering Management*, *69*(6), 2588–2602.

Love, P. E. D., Sing, M. C. P., Ika, L.A., and Newton, S. (2019). The cost performance of transportation projects: The fallacy of the Planning Fallacy account. *Transportation Research Part A: Policy and Practice*, *122*, 1–20.

Mak, S., and Raftery, J. (1992). Risk attitude and systematic bias in estimating and forecasting. *Construction Management and Economics*, *10*(4), 303–320.

Meng, X. (2012). The effect of relationship management on project performance in construction. *International Journal of Project Management*, *30*(2), 188–198.

Miller, R., and Lessard, D. R. (2001). *The strategic management of large engineering projects: Shaping institutions, risks, and governance*. MIT Press.

Ninan, J., Mahalingam, A., and Clegg, S. (2019). External stakeholder management strategies and resources in megaprojects: an organizational power perspective. *Project Management Journal*, *50*(6), 625–640.

Oswald, D., and Dainty, A. (2020). Ethnographic research in the construction industry: A critical review. *Journal of Construction Engineering and Management*, *146*(10), 1–13.

Pink, S., Tutt, D., Dainty, A., and Gibb, A. (2010). Ethnographic methodologies for construction research: Knowing, practice and interventions. *Building Research Information*, *38*(6), 647–659.

Rosenfield, Y. (2014). Root-cause analysis of construction-cost overruns. *ASCE Journal of Construction Management*, *140*(1). DOI: 10 .1061/(ASCE)CO.1943-7862.0000789.

Shehu, Z., Endut, I. R., Akintoye, A., and Holt, G. (2014). Cost overrun in the Malaysian construction industry projects: A deeper insight. *International Journal of Project Management*, *32*(8), 1471–1480.

Subramani, T., Sruthi, P. S., and Kavitha, M. (2014). Causes of cost overrun in construction. *IOSR Journal of Engineering*, *4*(6), 1–7.

Taha, G., Sherif, A., and Badawy, M. (2022). Dynamic modeling for analyzing cost overrun risks in residential projects. *ASCE-ASME Journal of Risk and Uncertainty in Engineering Systems, Part A: Civil Engineering*, *8*(3). DOI: 10.1061/AJRUA6.0001262.

Thomsen, J., Levitt, R. E., and Nass, C. I. (2005). The virtual team alliance (VTA): Extending Galbraith's information-processing model to account for goal incongruency. *Computational & Mathematical Organization Theory*, *10*(4), 349–372.

Williams, T., Eden, C., Ackermann, F., and Tait, A. (1995). The effects of design changes and delays on project costs. *Journal of the Operational Research Society*, *46*, 809–818.

CHAPTER 17

Project Behavior, Disruptions, and the Antifragility Spectrum

JEFFREY K. PINTO and GREG USHER*

Introduction

As of late 2024, the world is slowly emerging from the combination of societal and healthcare crises and economic disruptions caused by the COVID-19 pandemic. While in many ways, the final chapter of this singular event is still to be written, countries and public and private organizations are coming to grips with the implications of COVID-19 and how quickly they can return to a sense of normalcy and predictability in social and economic systems. Within this broader context, organizational initiatives in the form of supporting ongoing projects and spearheading new ventures are having their call for reflection on the implications of such disruptions for future planning, project development, and project behavior (Trump & Linkov, 2020; Pinto, 2022).

Disruptions and subsequent responses form an important part of the broader concept of project behavior, as we try to understand sense-making when such disruptions occur and the spectrum of possible responses to such challenges. Similar to Flyvbjerg (2018), we understand project behavior to be "how projects work" and have adopted Ika et al.'s (2022) definition of project behavior as "explaining and anticipating successes and failures, systemic veering's from preassigned paths, propensities toward specific difficulties, as well as opportunities for special payoffs" (p. 4).

In this chapter, we will explore how Taleb's concept of antifragility (2012) provides a novel lens for understanding project behavior, particularly arising from disruptions, or "shocks or changes in the environment" (Oliveira et al., 2022 p. 361). Of particular interest in our discussion is the idea of "opportunities for special payoffs" contained in our project behavior definition. One of the core principles of Taleb's (2012) antifragility is that unexpected events, such as disruptions, can provide an opportunity to create new, unexpected value.

To explain how this is possible we view project behavior through Taleb's antifragility and highlight four types of behavior that projects can exhibit when faced with disruptions. These are (i) fragile, (ii) robust, (iii) resilient, and (iv) antifragile. Each behavior will produce different outcomes for a project, ranging from irretrievable value loss to considerable value gain. We will explore some preparatory and remedial strategies to ensure projects, at the very least, do not lose value when facing disruptions – but more importantly, how projects can be set up to gain value from disruptions.

The strong potential for project disruptions remains a common feature of ongoing projects of all sizes and in all industrial settings (Flyvbjerg et al., 2002; Oliveira et al., 2022). The way organizations and their actors identify and respond to these disruptions is critically important to their ultimate success. Achieving this success, despite disruptions, requires project managers to find a middle ground involving a "complexification" of project behavior combining theorizing and pragmatic problem-solving (Ika et al., 2022). We hope that this chapter moves us toward this middle ground.

Antifragility: Gaining from Disruptions

In 2014, *The International Journal of Project Management* issued a call for papers for a special

* Portions of this chapter were adapted from G. Usher, C. C. Cantarelli, K. Davis, J. K. Pinto, and N. Turner (2024). Managing sudden unexpected disruptions in complex projects: The antifragility hierarchy. *Production Planning & Control*, 1–18, doi.org/10.1080/09537287.2024.2433479.

issue on uncertainty, risk and opportunity, resilience and anti-fragility (Bredillet & Tywoniak, 2014). In this call, the editors explicitly sought to pursue a holistic view of risk by first noting, "To date, there has been mainly a predisposition for risk management to focus only on technical, contractual, and financial risks in an isolated way rather than those of a non-technical, strategic or systemic nature. This has hindered the effectiveness of risk management within the complex and uncertain context of major or mega projects." (Bredillet & Tywoniak, 2014, p. 363). Consequently, their goal with the special issue was to explicitly link a deeper understanding of project risk to resulting behaviors, including resilience and anti–fragility, governance, and decision-making.

Interestingly, of the six papers that formed the resulting special issue, the majority focused on themes of risk, uncertainty, and project complexity, as well as their governance. Only one directly linked these constructs to the idea of resilience (Thomé et al., 2016), while none addressed the implications of antifragility as a reactive theme within the broader context of project complexity and uncertainty (and their management). We see this as a significant missed opportunity to investigate the application of Taleb's (2012) theory of antifragility within the discipline of project management, particularly in how disruptions may present opportunities for project managers to create new benefits if they will only delay undertaking "knee-jerk" reactions to get the project back on track.

Thus, while the project literature has begun to address resilience, through special issues and increased submissions, the broader context that examines the spectrum of responses to disruption (up to and including antifragility) remains largely ignored. In our opinion, this leads to the potential for misinterpretation or a general failure to understand and apply these principles within the project context (in the broader organizational context, this spectrum is just beginning to be addressed, as per the recent work of Munoz et al., 2022). To demonstrate why we believe this to be true, we must first look at two significant shifts in modern project management thinking. The first is the shift from stable environments to VUCA environments. The second is the shift from project delivery to value creation.

VUCA Environments

The term "VUCA" refers to the acronym for volatility, uncertainty, complexity, and ambiguity and was coined by the US War College during the height of the Cold War to describe the nature of battlefield conditions in the future (Bennett & Lemoine, 2014). VUCA environments are fertile ground for the "shocks and changes" (i.e., disruptions) that can drive unexpected project behavior. Below we discuss each of these ideas and how they relate to projects.

Volatility: Volatility refers to a project's ability to change rapidly or unpredictably, which can result in "veering's from preassigned paths" (Ika et al., 2022). Volatility is not necessarily hard to understand, and in most cases, knowledge about the change itself is readily available. However, the instability or risks inherent in projects creates unpredictability. This unpredictability requires project managers to cope with changes that can be frequent, rapid, and go on for an unknown duration (Botjes et al., 2020). Moreover, the accelerating rate of change forces organizations to remain in an information scanning and processing mode.

Uncertainty: There is a strong tradition of literature on the principle of project uncertainty (cf. Winch & Maytorena, 2011). Uncertainty refers to a lack of clarity about present and future project behavior. It is also important to distinguish project uncertainty from risk; as Love et al. (2022) have noted, riskiness is usually associated with statistical probabilities, implying most risks are identifiable and therefore quantifiable. On the other hand, uncertainty within projects means that, even if the basic causal elements of the change are known in advance, there is a general lack of knowledge about whether the change will occur and how to accurately quantify the likelihood of such events. Uncertainty in an environment means that, while change is possible, it is not guaranteed. Alternatively, the uncertainty could be about the impact of the disruption. So, while the event leading to a disruption could be predicted, the impact of that disruption may not be able to be completely predicted (Love et al., 2022).

Complexity: Complexity refers to the multiplicity of decision variables, or factors, that influence decision-making (Baccarini, 1996). Complexity does not mean that there is insufficient information about the disruption but rather that the volume or nature of that information is too overwhelming to process (Botjes et al., 2020). This overabundance of information can lead to new complexities within the project and generate irreducible problems (Ika & Saint-Macary, 2023). Research on project-based work has observed that project settings are increasingly subject to higher and higher levels of complexity and have noted that whereas many projects are complicated, their management "is fairly predictable, and essentially linear, in terms of outputs such as cost, time and performance. By comparison complex projects consist of ambiguity and uncertainty, interdependency, non-linearity, unique local conditions, autonomy, emergent behaviours and unfixed boundaries" (Bakhshi et al., 2016, p. 1201) making it difficult, if not impossible, to predict their behavior.

Ambiguity: Ambiguity arises when causal relationships are unclear; that is, the structure of the project is not well-defined due to limited information about the situation (Wiewiora & O'Connor, 2022). This circumstance can occur because historical data is either lacking (as a point of reference) or is not definitive and subject to misinterpretation. As Wiewiora and O'Connor (2022, p. 921) noted: "Ambiguity is inherent to project management, because projects are often created to reduce ambiguity in some way, e.g. to solve 'messy' problems without a correct solution, and/or 'wicked' problems that seem impossible to solve (Walker et al., 2017)." When ambiguity is present, there is a fundamental lack of knowledge about cause and effect and hence no precedent for deciding how to manage or mitigate it. This lack of clarity regarding the problem that needs to be solved (i.e., the reason the project exists) can cause the project to behave in unexpected ways.

Ambiguity represents a significant challenge for projects because standard models for costing or managing projects in traditional linear ways are no longer applicable, making planning and ongoing status determination fuzzy and imprecise.

In commercial and organization settings, VUCA environments have been defined to refer to systems that are subject to the unforeseeable and, consequently, prone to disturbances, as various surface conditions (typified by the VUCA characterization) impact the organization and its operations. In this kind of environment, we see three major aspects that may impact project behavior (Mack et al., 2015):

(i) A move away from a stable vertically hierarchical structure toward more fluid, dynamic forms. This shift can lead to fully network-oriented structures, where traditional hierarchies and one-company approaches are replaced by a set of independent but closely interrelated organizations. (Mack et al., 2015)

(ii) The increasing awareness of the need to reintegrate human beings as important actors and active and intelligent process agents. Parameters linked to individuals, such as commitment, cooperativeness, or doubtfulness in actions are key drivers of project success. To deal with the increasing speed and dynamics, many companies need to do business in a more project-oriented way.

(iii) The need for a continuous adaptation and renewal of processes and structures in an organization. Understanding projects within their larger context – the VUCA environment – allows us to better address the complexity of project behaviors. Indeed this contextual view of projects, sometimes referred to as "project ecologies" (Grabher & Ibert, 2011; Usher, 2021) offers a lens for understanding both the causal factors (VUCA criteria) and subsequent effects (proclivity toward disruption and approaches for correction of the system). Likewise, Ika and Saint-

Figure 17.1 The five-step transformational production management model (from Usher, 2021).

Macary (2023) emphasized the management of "wicked problems" and complexity in project settings as a conjunctive exercise that is a necessary feature of successful project organizations. Research on VUCA environments and projects has, to date, emphasized a range of monitoring and corrective behaviors, including the need for crisis leadership (Alkhaldi et al., 2017), digital competences (Nowacka & Rzemieniak, 2022), project management methods (de Moura et al., 2023), risk management (Fridgeirsson et al., 2021), and systems integration (Mack & Jungen, 2016), to name just a few.

From Project Creation to Value Creation

In 2003, the UK's Engineering and Physical Sciences Research Council (EPSRC) funded the Rethinking Project Management research project. This project outlined a framework for future directions aimed at developing a research agenda to "inform and stimulate current and future research activity in developing the field of project management" (Winter et al., 2006. p. 638). From within that framework, five directions for future research were developed. Direction 3 in that framework is a move from project creation to value creation. Specifically, a move from concepts and methodologies which focus on product creation, "the development or improvement of a physical product, system or facility etc, to specification, cost and time," toward concepts and frameworks which focus on value creation as the prime focus of projects, programmes and portfolios (p. 644).

The need for projects to focus on value creation creates a direct link to the concept of antifragility, which Taleb (2012) defines as "things that gain from disorder." Historically, project management has been classified as a sub-set of production and operations management (Koskela, 2000), or more specifically, project management has evolved from the transformational production management body of knowledge (Koskela, 1999; Koskela & Ballard, 2006). According to this body of knowledge, value is created through a five-step process designed to satisfy customer or consumer needs. This process begins with a producer identifying a need in the market. This producer then gathers together all the necessary inputs (i.e., knowledge, labor, materials, etc). These inputs will move through a specific transformation process, to create a particular output. This output is then offered to the market in the hope that it will satisfy the need that was first identified by the producer. This process is shown in Figure 17.1.

Usher (2021) explores how this traditional classification has shaped the project management profession's understanding of value creation. He explains how the use of this linear model, linked with the traditional belief that project managers merely need to deliver projects to "the desired scope, on time and under budget" to claim that their project was a success, was originally derived from Adam Smith's concept of "exchange value" (Smith, 1950). According to Smith (1950), the value of an object is equal to whatever a person is willing to exchange for it. Traditionally, this exchange is money, however, it could be another commodity (i.e., bartering). Within the concept of "exchange value" is the core thought that value is tangible and tradable. If a person can obtain information about the cost of materials, the amount of labor to transform it, and the profit margin applied to a product, then it is possible to determine how much money (or otherwise) the purchaser should be willing to exchange for the product. Smith's perspective considers value to be *inherent in the product* and able to be assessed objectively (Usher, 2021)

An alternate perspective of value is the concept of representational value. This is the definition of value that Hegel et al. (1993) explore. From this perspective, value is created by the individual. Representational value is subjective (i.e., beauty is in the eye of the beholder). According to Hegel et al. (1993), this type of value is emotionally driven. It does not care how much an item costs to produce, and therefore, there is no value inherently linked to the product itself. The product only has value because of how it makes a person feel or how they believe it can be used to enhance their life. In other words, it has value because of what it represents.

Usher (2021) uses an example of an engagement ring to explain these two value perspectives. In this example, he shows that, although the ring itself can be produced for $1,000 this does not mean the wearer would be willing to sell it to you for $1,200, even though, based purely on Smith's concept of value, this would be a good exchange. The reason the sale would not occur is that, for the wearer, the representational value of the ring exceeds the exchange value.

This value dualism is crucial to understanding "how projects work" (Flyvbjerg, 2018) and particularly useful for "explaining and anticipating [project] successes and failures" (Ika et al., 2022, p. 4). As Laursen and Svejvig (2016) highlight, delivering a project "does not necessarily imply value creation" (p. 736). Usher and Whitty (2017b) argue that to achieve project success, both exchange and representational value must be delivered. However, they do note that this can create "two paradoxical phenomena within the project management construct" (p. 4), with each definition of value being understood through a different systemic discourse that uses "different codes and logic to derive meaning"(p. 4) and each "ruled by different regimes, untranslatable into the other" (Lyotard, 1993, p. 200). Thus, it is inherent in the role of project management that practitioners ensure these value systems "operate in parallel and stimulate one another" (p. 5) to manage their project's behavior.

The need to understand these two value perspectives in project management is now being recognized more formally. In 2021, the Project Management Institute released the PMBOK Guide, seventh edition. In this edition, we begin to see a shift in focus from project management for the purpose of project creation, to project management for the purpose of value creation. The previous edition of PMBOK was a process-driven publication, which sought to identify "processes that are considered good practice" (p. 2). However, the latest edition explores how "portfolios, programs, projects, products and operations. . .can be used individually and collectively to create value" (p. 8).

This shift in focus moves the practitioner's attention from a naïve belief that project success is simply a function of meeting the constraints of the iron triangle and instead acknowledges that projects exist within a larger social and organizational ecosystem, and their function is to create value for that ecosystem (Usher, 2021). In recognition of these two perspectives of value (exchange and representational), in this chapter, we have adopted the PMBOK (2021) definition, which is that value is "the worth, importance or usefulness of something" (p. 252).

Projects as Systems

Recently, researchers have begun to explore the idea of projects as a system (Thomas & Mengel, 2008; Edson, 2012; McEvoy et al., 2016). Applying this lens has provided new insights into project behavior. For example, we now know that projects "behave as bounded, complex adaptive systems. These systems create multiple pathways for reaching final objectives, and multiple stakeholder expectations ... [projects] develop nonlinear and non-sequential trajectories which must be simultaneously encouraged and controlled" (Usher 2019. p. 3)

Adopting this concept of "projects as a system" is crucial to a discussion on disruptions and the antifragility spectrum because it allows us to utilize a systems-thinking approach. Systems thinking "encourages us to look in a holistic way ... enabling patterns of change to be discerned as a spectrum rather than ... discrete elements" (McEvoy et al., 2016, p. 539). In our discussion on disruption and antifragility, we are interested to see "how the project system as a whole behaves, not how individuals, work groups or teams within the particular organisational contexts that are projects behave" (Ika et al., 2022, p. 3311).

Systems, such as projects, are recognizable due to the interconnectedness and interdependency between their constituent elements. This interconnectedness allows the elements within the system to continuously interact with one another in response to changes in their environment, and these changes can impact the behavior of the project in ways that were not planned or envisaged (Usher, 2021).

The only way to "manage" this behavior is through an "alertness to unintended benefits and unseen consequences" (McEvoy et al., 2016, p. 540), a trait that lies at the heart of antifragility. Antifragility is the ability to adapt, to "develop new capacities to respond to events that are outside the preconfigured design" (Rahi, 2019, p. 73). Systems, such as projects, can only become antifragile and develop these new capacities by adopting certain behavioral characteristics. As Nikookar et al. (2021, p. 3) have explained, systems become antifragile by developing optionality (Gorgeon, 2015; Russo & Ciancarini, 2017); creating redundancy (Derbyshire & Wright, 2014); weakening the links between nodes (Hole, 2016); imposing eustress (Taleb, 2012; Derbyshire & Wright, 2014; Dahlberg, 2015); adopting a barbell strategy (Taleb, 2012; Derbyshire & Wright 2014); allowing systems to fail fast (Hole, 2016); and conducting trial and error (Taleb, 2012; Derbyshire & Wright, 2014), effectuation (Derbyshire & Wright, 2014), and swarming (Jones, 2014).

Vulnerability and Disruptions

The focus of this chapter is on the nature of challenges that occur due to projects operating within complex and uncertain environments that inject a strong element of uncertainty and risk, coupled with the potential for disruptions. Recall that we are adopting the Love et al.'s (2023) conceptualization of uncertainty, which argues that it may be impossible to identify a priori all possible states (i.e., probabilities for likely occurrences or outcomes of threat, whereas under risk, the granular assumption of causes of disruptions is that they are knowable and, in their knowing, capable of being assigned probabilities). Or, as Knight (1921, p. 233) once observed: "The practical difference between the two categories, risk and uncertainty, is that in the former, the distribution of the outcome in a group of instances is known, while in the case of uncertainty, this is not true." In this section, we would like to further address the potential for disruptions to occur by first developing a deeper understanding of the nature of project vulnerabilities, which directly relates to the degree to which they are subsequently prone to disturbances and, potentially, catastrophic failure.

Vulnerability

The term "vulnerability" has several connotations for scholars and practitioners, though the most general way to understand vulnerability is the susceptibility of a system to harm. For example, within the IS field, a vulnerability may be related to a weakness in the system that leaves the potential for it to be the victim of malicious software or external hacking. For an organization's supply chain to be considered vulnerable, it would have to be exposed to disruptive external events or conditions, as in the case of COVID-19 upheavals that temporarily suspended key supply chains across numerous industries (Aleksić et al., 2014). Similarly, project vulnerabilities refer to the potential for projects, while under some stage of development, to be susceptible to a variety of external forces with the ability to disrupt the project, sometimes fatally.

Literature on disciplines as diverse as health care (e.g., Woods et al., 2005) and marketing (Brenkert, 1998; Lucan et al., 2017) have identified the existence of vulnerability, usually with regard to groups or individuals within specific settings (e.g., senior citizens or uninformed stakeholders). From this literature, we can distinguish between temporarily vulnerable and chronically vulnerable. For example, in the consumer behavior literature, temporary vulnerability is understood as

> a fluid state of powerlessness stemming from the inability of consumers to cope with the uncertainty and instability brought by sudden unforeseen

> disasters such as human-made disasters (e.g., war and terrorist attacks) and natural disasters (e.g., earthquakes, wildfires, tornadoes, hurricanes, etc.) that threaten lives and disrupt the functioning of a community or a society. Powerlessness occurs when consumers experience a lack of control and agency in consumption situations, which hinders their consumption goals, and ultimately, leads to a loss of consumer welfare. (Yap et al., 2021, p. 1241)

This temporary vs. chronic vulnerability can have an impact on a project's behavior. Projects can be impacted by disruptions that create a temporary "powerlessness" or inability to generate reasonable or effective countermeasures and can erode the value that the project is attempting to deliver. Chronic vulnerability, on the other hand, presumes a near-permanent (or extended) state of vulnerability, either due to significant weaknesses of critical systems or the VUCA environment in which the project is delivered. For example, a construction firm with historically shaky finances will repeatedly undertake projects that keep them in a high-risk state, due to their inability to secure more stable or longer-term financial support.

Project vulnerabilities arise from a range of complex issues, including:

(i) the myriad variables inherent in both the project and the delivery environment (i.e., VUCA settings and project complexity sharply ramp up the sources and types of pressures the project team and their organization faces);
(ii) shifting and changeable set of stakeholders that can result in the emergence of multiple, often-competing stakeholder groups and polycentric governance systems (Gil & Pinto, 2018);
(iii) the temporal (time-based) nature of threats across the stages of the project lifecycle. That is to say, projects may be more vulnerable to certain disruptions at certain times in their lifecycle, than at other times. One example could be during the hand-over between the contractor and the client organization at the end of construction when misunderstandings regarding commissioning protocols can lead to significant delays in completion. These disruptions can only occur at this specific stage of the project lifecycle.

In his literature review of project resilience research, Rahi (2019) noted that a common approach to vulnerability has been to emphasize risk reduction practices, though Crawford et al. (2013) criticize this approach as time-consuming and unnecessarily structured in the face of events requiring rapid response. The focus of resilience thinking, on the other hand, suggests the goal "should not only be on vulnerability reduction, but also on factors and conditions' identification that enables a successful response to disruptive events" (Rahi, 2019, p. 71). Alternatively, and importantly, other scholars argue that resilience itself should not be viewed through a normative lens as an attribute toward which the system should aspire (see Naderpajouh et al., 2020), arguing that negative or vulnerable attributes of a system may be equally "resilient," despite efforts to minimize or eliminate them.

Project Disruptions

Oliveira et al. (2022, p. 361) noted that: "'Disruptions' generally refer to shocks or changes in the environment in which the parties are transacting" such as a drastic change in conditions around which a project may be developing (a severe weather effect for construction, critical failure of technical component for IT or new product develop, and so forth). In most projects, however, the more fundamental challenge facing the firms involves not so much major shocks but more "mundane" disruptions: those that arise because of errors of inattention, misalignment of actions, or failure to apply full effort (Simon, 1973). While each disruption may have a relatively small effect on the cost of a project or the timeliness of its completion, the accumulation of many mundane disruptions may severely compromise the project delivery (Mishra & Sinha, 2016).

The idea that projects are at risk of a variety of disruptive events is hardly new. Considering the myriad of pressures, unforeseeable risks, and lingering uncertainty in which projects are delivered, disruptions should be considered inevitable. Hence, we take, as our starting position, the premise that all projects are subject to a variety of disruptions that can impact their behavior. Some will be relatively benign, such as a new software release midway through a firm's ERP implementation efforts. Others may be highly significant, such as a competitor launching a rival product ahead of us, while our project is still in development, creating the need for the project manager to undertake significant remedial action (See "Preparatory and Remedial Strategies" later in this chapter). Finally, there are other nearly catastrophic examples of disruptions, including severe weather-related impacts or critical safety site failures that result in significant delays or even project abandonment.

Disruption likelihood is also dependent on the types of projects being developed, the rapidity of change within the environment in which they are being delivered, the physical settings, and the environmental challenges associated with their development. For example, the development of the Indian government's Dulhasti hydro-electric power plant, hundreds of miles up in the Himalayan foothills, in a region that has seen unrest from separatist guerrillas, with uncertain regional government backing and highly complicated supply chains, would suggest a project that has a high likelihood of disruption (which, in the case of Dulhasti, was significant: 16-year-delayed completion and a final cost overrun of 2,532 percent) (Bhaskar, 2007).

Regardless of the source and nature of the disruption, one way to reflect on their impact on our projects is to first uncover the types of disruptions to which we may most be prone, as this process can help the firm develop effective scanning processes and subsequent solution strategies. One helpful way to understand project disruptions is to view them as either sudden or creeping (Shen & Ying, 2022).

Sudden Disruptions

Sudden disruptions usually occur due to the existence of preconditions in the environment or as the result of a decision, or sequence of decisions, that result in a catastrophic system failure. The sudden onset of the COVID-19 pandemic caught numerous firms wholly unprepared and scrambling to develop responses, secure supply chains, and address significant human resource health emergencies. Likewise, sudden disruptions can occur in projects through the deleterious effect of intervenor groups (Cleland, 1997), technical failures, economic or funding collapse (e.g., China's Evergrande bank failure), departures of key project champions, and so forth. The effect of sudden disruptions is often critical because they are rarely anticipated or adequately prepared for through project risk analysis. Sudden disruptions can result in significant loss of value, or in the worst cases, project termination. Sudden disruptions pose grave risks for projects because they are difficult to either anticipate or rapidly develop remedial strategies to address them.

Creeping Disruptions

In contrast to sudden disruptions, creeping disruptions are more insidious and often far harder to identify, because, rather than being the result of one specific act of disruption, creeping disruptions occur as a result of an accumulation of decisions that appear to have been reasonable at the time but end up eroding the project's value. As Mishra and Sinha (2016) noted, while each disruption may have a relatively small effect on the cost of a project or scheduled delivery date, the accumulation of many mundane disruptions can severely compromise the project's final success or value creation.

Creeping disruptions, per Shen and Ying (2022, p. 672), are "disruptions that have long incubation phases and emerge gradually as ongoing risks and uncertainties accumulate. For example, minor unchecked design variations that arise at different points of the component projects can accumulate to a wider mistake that could yield systemic failure to the program (Linkov & Trump, 2019)." In this sense, creeping disruptions share a common theme with the normalization of deviance behaviors, as suggested by Pinto (2014) and Davis and Pinto (2022), where the failure of governance and gradual accumulation of missteps, and post-hoc rationalizations, ultimately lead to a catastrophic event or significant disruption to the organizational system, brought about by their repeated disregard for appropriate procedural safeguards or militating practices.

Creeping disruptions are particularly dangerous to projects because it may be impossible to fully identify the latent conditions under which these disruptions germinate, forcing a completely reactive response to quickly assess and, if possible, resolve or mitigate a disruption for which no warning was received.

Fragility, Robustness, Resilience, and Antifragility

We noted previously that project-based organizations operating in VUCA environments are subject to a wide variety of potential and realized disruptions. These disruptions can create different outcomes in a project, ranging from irreparable loss of value (i.e., project termination) to opportunistic value creation (e.g., new features, functions, cost savings, etc.). Whether a project loses/gains value because of disruption depends on where the project sits on the antifragility spectrum. This spectrum ranges from fragile, to robust, to resilient, and then to antifragile. We will now explain these terms and illustrate the antifragility spectrum.

Fragility

As Taleb (2012) and other scholars define the idea of fragility, it bears important similarities to vulnerability but also offers some additional context. Vulnerability is "the manifestation of the inherent states of the systems that can be subjected to a natural hazard or be exploited to adversely affect that system" (Aven, 2011, p. 515), while fragility is "how a system suffers when it encounters disorder" (Taleb & Douady, 2011, p. 5). Thus, we see that it is the vulnerability of a system that allows disruptions to influence it. As we shall see, those disruptions can result in a range of outcomes from value loss (fragile) through to value creation (antifragile).

The fragile state is prone to damage. "The outcome of fragility is typically an irreversible loss of functionality . . .. Fragility is typically irreversible. Once broken the fragile cannot be readily restored to its original function" (Ansar et al., 2016, p. 5). In an engineering context, Jones (2014, p. 871) noted that: "Current systems are designed to be fragile to some degree: requirements for performance are specified and the system is designed to meet those requirements. If the system is stressed beyond the design requirements, it will fail." For projects, this fragility suggests that, because of underlying structural or process contradictions, a myriad set of factors can not only disrupt but ultimately cause the project to irreparably lose value – that is, to fail. Thus, in a project setting, we can deduce that, where fragility occurs, it is a failure of either the underlying project management systems or of identifying solutions to address the newly disrupted state to bring the project back to a viable undertaking or both.

Robustness

All systems, including projects, are expected to be able to perform or deliver value under a range of different circumstances and in the face of a variety of different challenges. A robust system can remain in a desired state and continue to deliver the desired value, regardless of the stress produced by a disturbance (Stelling et al., 2004; Kriete, 2013). As Johnson and Gheorghe (2013) note, the concepts of reliability and robustness are often confused in the literature, despite a critical difference. A system can be considered reliable if it can remain unchanged within the bounds of the established system limits. A system can be considered robust if it remains unchanged outside of the established system limits. In a simple project example, a price change for a supplier's component would not affect the project's bottom line, assuming that sufficient contingency was built into the contract. Hence, to be robust, a system must be capable of withstanding stress, have a lack of sensitivity to changes, and have a certain tolerance for impact. The broader the range of stress the system is capable of withstanding, the more stable the system, and therefore the more robust it is.

Therefore, we can see that central to the concept of robustness is the concept of resistance. Adger (2000) highlights that resistance is "the extent to which a disturbance is actually translated into impact." The robustness of a system is equal to its resistance to disruptions. That is, a system's robustness is equal to the system's ability to deflect the shock of a disruption, without losing any value in the process (Dahlberg, 2015).

Resilience

Resilience has become a popular concept in recent years in the project literature, with several authors noting that the philosophy of resilience relates well to project settings. Aven (2011) defines resilience as "the ability of the system to withstand a major disruption within acceptable degradation parameters and to recover within an acceptable time, and composite cost and risks" (p. 517). Additionally, Shen and Ying (2022) define resilience as the capability to prepare for and mitigate anticipated risks and respond and adapt to and recover from unexpected contingencies. In the face of system vulnerabilities due to multiple hazards, including carrying various vulnerability factors (physical, economic, institutional, etc.), resilience refers to the actor or project's attempt to transform, transfer, and rearrange them in time and space to achieve ongoing persistence (Sapountzaki, 2012).

The crucial elements within this characterization of resilience are the concepts of *adaptation* and *recovery*. Adaptation implies the system has emergent and potentially self-organizing capability (Anderson, 1999; Dahlberg, 2015). Recovery suggests that, although the system may initially lose value when impacted by a disturbance, the adaptation process ensures that this loss of value is not permanent and that the system will return to its original state and deliver the previous value (Nikookar et al., 2021). Resilience, then, can be thought of as the ability of a system to regain the desired value despite initially losing value after a disruption.

It is also useful to reflect that project resilience is grounded in a different understanding than other related disciplines, such as engineering, urban planning, or systems analysis. While these disciplines often assume that organizational systems may be designed a priori to be either robust or resilient (e.g., creating redundant systems), Piperca and Floricel (2023) note that resilience in project behavior scholarship suggests that enduring system properties such as governability result from behavioral responses to disrupted states, involving evolutionary processes like structuration and self-organization. Table 17.1 offers their perspectives involving three key viewpoints regarding resilience: strategic, complexity, and organization/structural. The first perspective, based on the assumption of strategy as a rational act, sees resilience as the ability to manage risks, given that projects face an uncertain and complex world. The complex systems view frames project resilience as a set of structural and cultural foci that

Table 17.1 Project resilience

	Perspectives on project resilience		
Aspect	**Strategic action**	**Complex system**	**Organizing process**
Origin of resilience	Designing technical, contractual, and organizational structures	Designed or evolved structural relations and potentialities	Relating to a network of actors with emerging goals and resources
Expected resilience	Robustness for anticipated risks	Reliable operation within a range of conditions	Endogenous response has regularly becoming
Facing major disruptions	Governability in facing unexpected events through legitimacy and signaling a clear vision of project objectives	Ability to rebound after limits are exceeded through partnerships, risk attitude, safety culture, proactive planning, and positive work relationships	Exceptional organizing episodes including flattened structure to facilitate communication and response time

Source: Geambasu, 2011; Piperca & Floricel, 2023

provide the organization with the ability to react to shocks or stresses beyond an expected range. Finally, the organizing process sees resilience as the response of creating rebound cycles and a flattened hierarchy that enables rapid response, creative problem-solving, and communication.

The various types of resilience – as they pertain to projects – have also been broken down by Naderpajouh, et al. (2020) as an interdisciplinary challenge that operates across multiple levels and units of analysis within the organization. In their review of the resilience literature, they were able to distinguish studies across a variety of organizational and broader industrial sector levels. These various levels provide a means to understand resilience as a personal characteristic and project-level phenomenon, all the way to the broadest, societal contexts. In this categorization, resilience can operate at the (1) psycho/social level, for project managers and team members; (2) at a project level to include concepts such as project resilience and vulnerability and uncertainty; (3) at the organization level; (4) at the inter-organizational network level, to address issues such as supply chain resilience or resilience of an industrial sector; and (5) at the societal level, with concern for business continuity, ecological resilience, social and political resilience, and engineering and institutional resilience.

Antifragility

Taleb (2012) introduced the term "antifragility" to explain his idea that the opposite of fragile is neither robust nor resilient. Taleb (2012, p. 3) contends that:

> Some things benefit from shocks, they thrive and grow. . .yet in spite of the ubiquity of the phenomenon, there is no word for the exact opposite of fragile. Let us call it antifragile. Antifragile is beyond resilience or robustness.

For this chapter, we have defined antifragility as the ability of a project to gain value (i.e., worth, importance, or usefulness) as a result of disruption. It is important to highlight that the focus of this definition is the end-state of the project, not the measure of value at the time the disruption occurs. It is possible, under this definition, that a project initially loses value as a result of the disturbance. However, provided that the project ultimately surpasses the original value, it can be considered antifragile.

In the project literature, we have seen examples of antifragility occurring typically within specific settings or disciplines. So, for example, the literature on Hiding Hand (Hirschman, 1967) was originally focused on infrastructure projects and argued that creative problem-solving was often a post hoc response to project systems that had initially "failed," through poor estimation or simply following rote plans. As Hirschman (1967, p. 13) suggests:

> The only way we can bring our creative resources fully into play is by misjudging the nature of the task, by presenting it to ourselves as more routine, simple, undemanding of genuine creativity than it will turn out to be.

Hirschman's (1967) Hiding Hand is a precondition for antifragility within projects. As Anheier (2016) notes, there are two dimensions to the Hiding Hand. The first is ignorance or underestimation of the complexity, challenges, and difficulties that the project is likely to encounter. The second is ignorance or underestimation of the planner's problem-solving capabilities. According to Anheier (2016), "both are necessary conditions for the likelihood of stumbling into success, for finding solutions to seemingly insurmountable problems, and for allowing creativity to take hold" (p. 1006). For antifragility to occur, it requires a disruption (which occurs as a result of ignorance or underestimation of the complexity, difficulties or challenges) plus a creative response in the face of this new uncertainty.

A summary of the systems in the antifragility spectrum is provided in Table 17.2. The antifragility spectrum can also be represented graphically as shown in Figure 17.2.

When represented graphically, it is easy to see the place that the antifragility spectrum has in any discussion on project behavior, as it provides a context for "explaining and anticipating successes and failures" as well as "opportunities for special payoffs" (Ika et al., 2022, p. 3311).

Table 17.2 Systems on the antifragility spectrum

System type	Description	Resultant impact on value	References
Fragile	Lose value when exposed to disturbances and never recover	-ve	(Taleb & Douady, 2011; Aven, 2015; Ansar et al., 2016; Santolini et al., 2021)
Robust	Able to withstand disturbances without losing value	Nil	(Stelling et al., 2004; Johnson & Gheorghe, 2013; Killen & Hunt, 2013; Kriete, 2013; Dahlberg, 2015)
Resilient	Lose value when exposed to disturbances but can regain that value.	Nil	(Dahlberg, 2015; Kutsch & Turner, 2016; Rahi, 2019; Botjes et al., 2020; Nikookar et al., 2021),
Antifragile	Lose value when exposed to disturbances but can gain additional value over time.	+ve	(Taleb, 2012; Bendell, 2019)

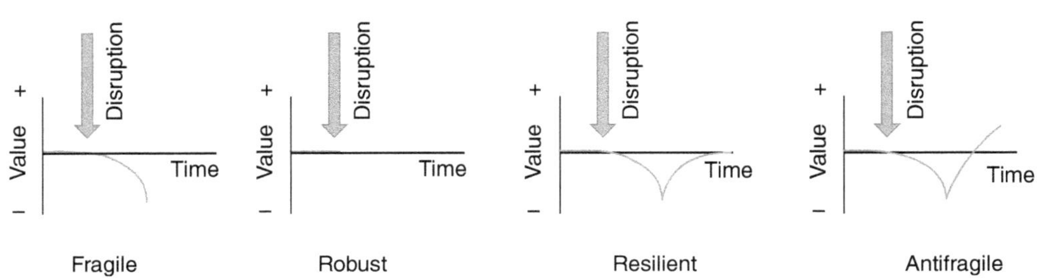

Figure 17.2 The antifragility spectrum.

Preparatory and Remedial Strategies

As we have already seen, PMBOK (2021) states that the sole purpose of a project is to create value. Ergo, any event or action that results in a loss of value runs contrary to a project's reason to exist. This presents a particular challenge for project managers because:

(a) VUCA environments contain a myriad of potential disruptions that can result in a value loss in the project;
(b) project managers often have very little warning of which of these potential disruptions may impact their projects; and
(c) even if a potential disruption could be forecast in advance, projects are complex systems (Usher, 2021), and complex systems resist detailed, predesigned resilience engineering processes (Dahlberg, 2015).

As Perrow (1999) highlights, the conditions above mean that disruptions are an inevitability for projects, and while it is impossible to eliminate disruptions, it is still the project manager's role to manage the impact of these disruptions to mitigate, or at least reduce, the impact these disruptions have on the value the project is tasked to deliver. At first, this may seem like an impossible task, however, there are a range of preparatory strategies that can be adopted to increase the probability of a project achieving antifragility, and several remedial actions that are available to project managers after a disruption has occurred. We will now look at these in more detail.

Preparatory Strategies

One might reasonably ask, "Why should we adopt preparatory strategies? Wouldn't we be better served by adopting preventative strategies?" The answer to this question has to do with the non-predictability of disruptions in a VUCA environment. As Taleb (2012, p. 7) explains "the rarer the event, the less tractable, and the less we know we know about how frequent its occurrence." For example, very few people in the financial sector predicted the Global Financial Crisis, however, in hindsight, countless strategies on "how it could have been prevented" were developed. These strategies relied on quantitative research drawn from datasets that do not exist until after the disruption has occurred; hence, the strategies are only relevant to the disruption that has just occurred and tell us nothing about the future disruption that could be just around the corner.

To develop "preventative" strategies, we would first need to have specific data about the causality of the event, the frequency of the event, and the duration of the event. None of these is available, for the simple reason that the disruption that creates the loss of value has not yet occurred. Ergo, we cannot develop prevention strategies, we can only implement preparation strategies that strengthen our systems "so that the shocking effects of the shocking events are not that shocking" (Aven, 2015, p. 476). This argument is based on the distinction drawn between "risk," which is generally accepted as consisting of known potential problems and which lend themselves to statistical probabilities, and "uncertainty," which covers "unknown-unknowns" and are therefore relatively immune to the conceit that it is possible to account for their occurrence (Love et al., 2022).

More Planning, Less Plans

Traditionally, project management is a discipline that has relied heavily on detailed planning and strong controls (Bryson & Bromiley, 1993; Baker et al.,1974). This detailed planning can make project managers and stakeholders *feel* confident that the project is in safe hands and under control; however, detailed planning in a VUCA environment is extremely fragile. At the first disruption, the plan loses value, in some cases to the point where the project itself must be abandoned (i.e., complete and irreparable loss of value). Thus, the project literature has long distinguished between the advantages of planning, while cautioning against the enduring value of "the plan" (Dvir & Lechler, 2004; Ika & Saint-Macary, 2023).

Taleb (2012, p. 170) argues that creating detailed plans requires the planner to make one major assumption, "[that] you know exactly where you are going and that knew where you were going in the past, and that others have succeeded in the past, by knowing where they were going." In demonstrating the fallacy of this critical assumption, he suggests a counterstrategy: when attempting to manage a complex system, such as a project, we move away from detailed planning, because "complex systems do not require complicated systems and regulations ... the simpler the better" (Taleb, 2012, p. 9).

According to Burnes (2005), one of the most significant findings of complexity theorists in recent history is that complex adaptive systems, such as a project, "operate from a limited number of order-generating rules, which permit limited chaos while providing relative order" (p. 3) This concept is echoed by Usher (2021) who argues that, because projects are dynamic and nonlinear, they are best "managed" through the use of broad order-generating rules that operate at either a systems level or local level, rather than detailed plans, which are susceptible to failure.

As Dwight Eisenhower, the 34th president of the United States, so aptly explains, "Plans are worthless, but planning is everything. There is a very great distinction because when you are planning for an emergency you must start with this one thing: the very definition of 'emergency' is that it is unexpected, therefore it is not going to happen the way you are planning" (Investigator, 2017). This distinction is crucial in any discussion on project behavior. Planning is the antifragile response to "veerings," and it begins with the question, "How can my project benefit from this?" Project success is not achieved by developing the perfect plan ex ante, rather, as Usher's (2017) Final State Convergence Model highlights, it is about progressively planning your way through multiple options in the face of disruptions.

Optioneering

Closely linked to the first concept of more planning but fewer plans is the concept of optioneering. As Taleb (2012, p. 171) argues, "the option is an agent of antifragility," explaining that less-detailed planning creates the opportunity to "benefit from the positive side of uncertainty, without the corresponding serious harm from the negative side." In other words, by planning less, we provide room to shift courses of action, without losing the value of the original plan.

Usher (2019) provides an example of how project value can be created by developing alternate options for sponsors and stakeholders to consider at key "decision nodes" in the schedule. His "Next Decision Node (NDN) Planning" paper explores how all projects are equifinal (i.e., multiple paths are available to achieve the same outcome) and how decisions need to be made at key nodes in the schedule to select the optimal path forward to the next decision node. Thus, if we return to our understanding of project behavior, which states, in part, that projects are prone to different and complex "out-turns" over their lifetime, requiring us to explain and anticipate systematic veerings from preassigned paths, or propensities toward specific difficulties, we can see that optioneering offers a means for real-time critical decision-making. The direction the project takes at one of these decision nodes is based on specific options that the project manager presents. For example, upon reaching the end of the design phase, the project manager may present three options: (a) bring the project in under budget, ahead of time, but with reduced scope; (b) retain the full scope, achieve the budget, but take longer than previously expected; or (c) retain the full scope, come in on time, but exceed the budget. The subsequent scheduling of the project will be determined by the option endorsed by the sponsor.

The challenge for project managers is that projects need to ensure they are creating value for the sponsors and stakeholders. Leaving a project "at large" in terms of potential options can erode that value and create a possible outcome where the project never achieves what it was created to do. Hence, leaving a project with a full and diverse set of options (i.e., "total options"), although creating complete antifragility, is unlikely to be a suitable preparatory strategy. To achieve the antifragility that we are seeking, while still ensuring the project generates the value for which it was created, we must find a balance between the art of the possible and the science of the required. Usher (2021) argues that project managers achieve this balance by filtering options so that only those options that propel the project toward its end goal are considered by stakeholders, while simultaneously removing options that will detract from the final objective. He calls this process "optioneering."

Optioneering impacts project behavior by selectively offering specific options for consideration the project manager can reduce the "veering's from preassigned paths" thereby increasing the chances of success (Ika et al., 2022, p. 3311).

Barbell Strategies

Originally drawn from Stoic philosophy, the concept of barbell strategies seeks to reduce the negative impacts of adverse disruptions, while simultaneously keeping the benefits of potential gains. The purpose of a barbell strategy is not to eliminate uncertainty; rather, it is to make sure that we "take full advantage of the benefits that it can provide while protecting ourselves from the potential for harm" (Baxter, 2017, p. 13). The philosophy here is very much in keeping with the challenge that we "embrace complexity" to understand the roots of much project behavior (Ika & Saint-Macary, 2023).

The essence of a barbell strategy is to avoid moderate or "average" risks and instead develop bimodal strategies that have a dual focus of extreme risk aversion in areas that can destroy (not erode) the value of a project and an extremely aggressive risk profile in areas that have potential upside. Thus, a barbell strategy is intended to promote the extremes in terms of resource allocation, and as Taleb (2012) has demonstrated, this bimodal approach consistently produces better outcomes in terms of creating value from disruptions (i.e., antifragility).

The concept of a barbell strategy is similar to Pareto's 80/20 rule and operates similarly from a decision-making perspective. For example, the project manager determines the minimal requirements the project must fulfill to survive (e.g., not to be terminated), and they allocate these resources (time, cost, human resources) to aggressively protect those minimum requirements. As we will demonstrate shortly, these "minimum requirements" will be project specific and aligned with the sponsor's and stakeholder's agreed project priorities. As Baxter (2017) highlights, these minimal requirements must be the absolute basic requirements for survival, "This minimum acceptable level must be defined carefully because if it is allowed to creep upward, it drives requirements that consume the entire budget and still cannot be achieved." Once the resources for the minimum requirements are allocated and aggressively protected, the remainder of the resources should be allocated in such a way as to create the most possible options for creating value (See Optioneering). Most of these experiments in value creation will fail (See Fail Fast), but some may produce exponentially large benefits in terms of the project value. Figure 17.3 provides a graphic representation of resource allocation based on a barbell strategy

Let us reflect on how a barbell strategy can work in a project setting. Suppose, for example, that in consultation with the project sponsor, you have agreed on the priorities for a project to develop a new mobile cell phone application. Based on Larsen's (2020) Constrain, Enhance and Accept model, the sponsor has advised that the performance of the application is the critical constraint, that speed to market is important and should be enhanced if possible, and thus, as a result of these decisions, the sponsor is willing to accept the overall cost of the project.

In adopting a barbell strategy for this project, the project manager would allocate sufficient resources (e.g., time, funds, human resources) to ensure the minimum performance standard is achieved. They would then apportion the remaining resources to developing innovative options for speed-to-market (i.e., multiple fast-tracked schedules, multiple schedule crashing options, experimenting with concurrent or simultaneous tasks in an attempt to find more speed), and allocate no resources to cost control. Adopting this strategy safeguards the project from termination (i.e., the minimum performance outcomes are met), provides the greatest opportunity for benefit by enhancing speed to market, and wastes no resources on the element that is accepted anyway.

Fail Fast

Closely linked to Taleb's (2012) concept of Barbell Strategies is the strategy of "fail fast." The concept of fail fast involves a process of experimentation, in which ideas are developed and tested quickly to determine their viability. Incorporating both Optioneering and Barbell strategies, failing fast reduces the negative impacts of disruption by rapidly (if possible, simultaneously) testing multiple remedial actions to identify which one has the best chance of creating additional value for the project. The fail-fast strategy is most easily recognized in the Agile methodology where multiple simultaneous project options, immediate feedback on interim technical results, and the cancelation of some project options to quickly divert resources to more promising ventures are commonplace (Khanna et al., 2016).

Three key features of an effective fail-fast strategy are:

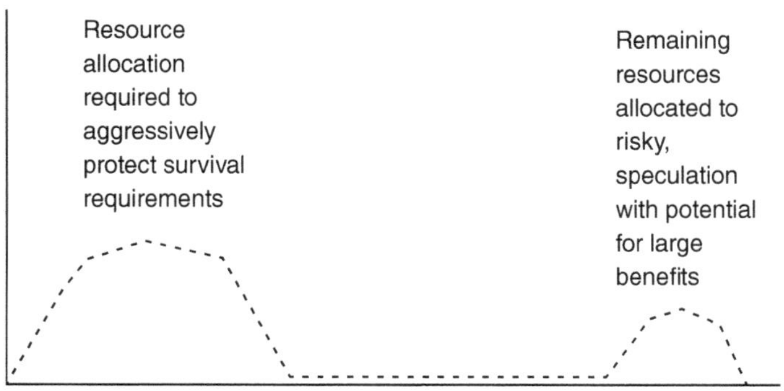

Figure 17.3 Resource allocation in a barbell strategy.

(i) a focus on market-fit ventures,
(ii) a focus on time-compressed scaling, and
(iii) a focus on aggressive scalability (Shankar & Clausen, 2020).

Assessing projects on these features allows firms to identify promising features in a set of new projects and not simply *absorb* but benefit from the inevitable disruptions of failed efforts by swiftly rechanneling energy and resources to more promising opportunities.

Remedial Actions

Regardless of the number or type of preparatory strategies that a project manager has enacted, disruptions may still impact their project. When this occurs, project managers need to be aware of the remedial actions that are available to them to gain from the disruptions where possible (i.e., antifragile), or at the very least ensure that value is not lost (i.e., fragile). In this research on project disruptions, Söderholm (2008) identified three types of actions that project managers adopt when disruptive events occur. These are fine-tuning, revision, and re-opening.

Fine-tuning

Söderholm (2008) does not provide a formal definition for "fine-tuning" in his research; however, he does explain that these types of actions are minor adjustments undertaken by a project manager to ensure that neither the project's prior planning nor the goal is impacted. Usher and Whitty (2017a: p. 782) state that "fine tuning is required due to the constant flow of information that occurs as a result of working in a dynamic environment" and go on to describe fine-tuning as "returning to the project's initial 'trajectory'" Additionally, Usher and Whitty (2017a) provide a graphical representation of fine-tuning (Figure 17.4). It is impossible not to notice a distinct similarity between their illustration of fine-tuning and our representation of resilience (Figure 17.2). Specifically, we see what Stochino et al. (2019) call the "resilience triangle." The distinctive shape of a system, which has lost value as a result of a disruption but regained it over time to ensure no long-term loss is realized.

Revisions

The second corrective action noted by Söderholm (2008) is "revisions." Project managers undertake

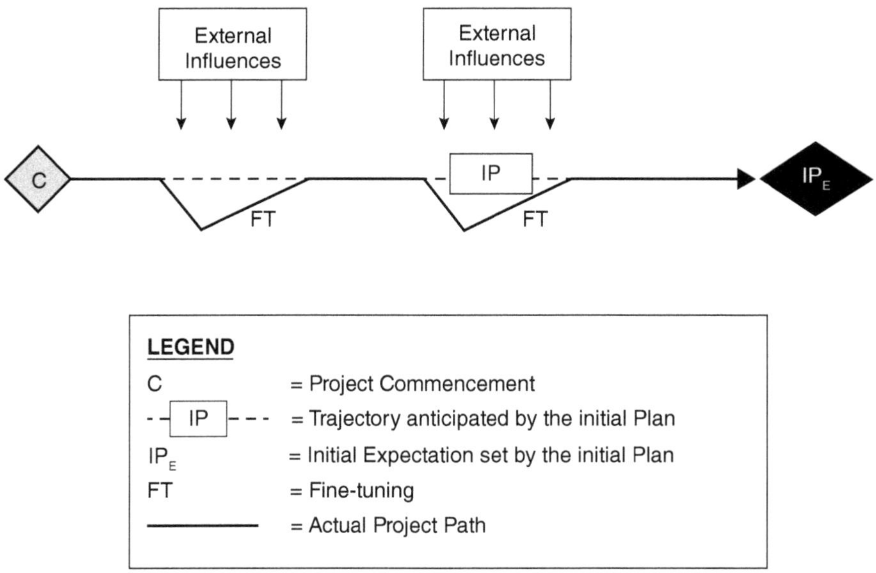

Figure 17.4 The impact of fine tuning a project
(from Usher & Whitty, 2017a).

revisions when dealing with a significant problem that may jeopardize the success of a project. According to Söderholm (2008), revisions involve replanning tasks and reallocating resources. Revision can be significant undertakings, as they can demand "the most innovation and on the spot action from project managers." Any revision is an attempt by the project manager to ensure the project can achieve its stated goal after a disruption has occurred. In the circumstances where these revision actions are successful, the result is to create resilience in the project.

Re-openings

The third and final corrective action is a "re-opening," described as opening the project to a new definition (Söderholm, 2008). This new definition could range from a decision to terminate the project (if the disruption is determined to have caused irreparable damage) through to a new direction that increases the value of the project by creating a new understanding of what could be achieved. The key differentiator between a revision and a re-opening is that revisions attempt to replan the project to achieve the originally stated outcomes (i.e., applying a resilience mindset), whereas a re-opening will result in either termination (i.e., the fragile state) or a new outcome, which should create more value based on the new information gleaned from the disruption (i.e., antifragile).

From the work of Söderholm (2008) and Usher and Whitty (2017a), we can now see where remedial actions align with the antifragility spectrum (Table 17.3). It should be noted that "robust" does not feature in the table reconciling the remedial actions with the antifragility spectrum because robust projects did not lose value because of disruptions, hence no remedial action is required.

Conclusions

Many projects operate in VUCA environments that serve as a precursor to subsequent (and sometimes regular) disruptions. While the degree to which such disruptions can occur varies, depending on the embedded vulnerabilities within the project itself, the net effect can be serious for a project's long-term viability. Key to the management of disruptions in projects is understanding they can result in a range of outcomes for the project. These outcomes can range from significant loss of value, if the project system is fragile, to significant value gain, if the project system is antifragile. Examining this issue from the perspective of project behavior, we understand that project managers can adopt preparatory strategies to increase the antifragility of their projects through strategies such as the reduction of detailed planning, deliberately developing options, barbell strategies aligned with project priorities, and experimentation through failing fast. After a disruption occurs, project managers can adopt remedial actions such as fine-tuning, revisions, and re-openings, to recover value that is lost (i.e., resilience), or better yet create or increase value as a result of the disruption (i.e., antifragility).

The inescapable fact is that, sooner or later, project managers who are managing complex value delivery systems in VUCA environments will face disruptions. The elimination of these disruptions should not be the project manager's goal, rather they should focus on creating systems that, at worst, do not lose value as a result of the disruption and, at best, gain from the disruption to create more value than was originally intended. We believe that the antifragility spectrum should be further explored in light of project behavior and in particular the tendency for projects to take

Table 17.3 How remedial actions align with the antifragility spectrum

Remedial action	Description	Antifragility spectrum
Fine-tuning	Minor adjustments to a project to regain original value	Resilience
Revision	Major adjustments to a project to regain original value	Resilience
Re-opening	Redefinition of a project based on new information from disruption	Fragile (if terminated) Antifragile (if new outcomes are created)

complex out-turns and deviate from plans. The spectrum offers both directions for organizations to orient their responses to disruptions (i.e., depending on the type and/or severity, alternate strategies might be considered, such as robust, resilient, or antifragile) as well as the broad tactical responses that characterize project behavior in the face of these complex out-turns.

References

Adger, W. N. (2000). Social and ecological resilience: are they related? *Progress in Human Geography*, *24*(3), 347–364.

Aleksić, A., Stefanović, M., Tadić, D., and Arsovski, S. (2014). A fuzzy model for assessment of organization vulnerability. *Measurement*, *51*, 214–223.

Alkhaldi, K. H., Austin, M. L., Cura, B. A., Dantzler, D., Holland, L., Maples, D. L., and Marcus, L. J. (2017). Are you ready? Crisis leadership in a hyper-VUCA environment. *Journal of Emergency Management*, *15*(3), 117–132.

Anderson, P. (1999). Complexity theory and organization science. *Organization Science*, *10*(3), 216–232.

Anheier, H. K. (2016). Of Hiding Hands and other ways of coping with uncertainty: A commentary. *Social Research*, *83*(4), 1005–1010.

Ansar, A., Flyvbjerg, B., Budzier, A., and Lunn, D. (2016). Big is fragile: An attempt at theorizing scale. *arXiv preprint*, 1603.01416.

Aven, T. (2011). On some recent definitions and analysis frameworks for risk, vulnerability, and resilience. *Risk Analysis: An International Journal*, *31*(4), 515–522.

Aven, T. (2015). The concept of antifragility and its implications for the practice of risk analysis. *Risk Analysis: An International Journal*, *35*(3), 476–483.

Baccarini, D. (1996). The concept of project complexity – a review. *International Journal of Project Management*, *14*(4), 201–204.

Baker, B. N., Murphy, D. C., and Fisher, D. ([1974] 2008). Factors affecting project success (pp. 902–919). In D. I. Cleland and W. R. King (eds.). *Project management handbook*. Van Nostrand Reinhold.

Bakhshi, J., Ireland, V., and Gorod, A. (2016). Clarifying the project complexity construct: Past, present and future. *International Journal of Project Management*, *34*(7), 1199–1213.

Baxter, L. (2017). *An antifragile approach to preparing for cyber conflict*. Air War College.

Bendell, T. (2019). Are projects and project managers fragile, robust or anti-fragile? (pp. 93–97). In D.Dalcher (ed.). *Managing projects in a world of people, strategy and change*, vol. 1. Routledge.

Bennett, N., and Lemoine, J. (2014). What VUCA really means for you. *Harvard Business Review*, *92*(1/2), https://ssrn.com/abstract=2389563.

Bhaskar, U. (2007). 16-year delays, 2,532% cost overrun shock house panel. Mint. www.livemint.com/Politics/c5jutT7SEK6KyIeViMm6HN/16year-delays-2532-cost-overruns-shock-House-panel.html.

Botjes, E., Mulder, H., and Nouwens, H. (2020). Defining antifragility and the application on organisation design. Master's thesis, Antwerp Management School.

Bredillet, C., and Tywoniak, S. (2014). Call for papers – special Issue on uncertainty, risk & opportunity, resilience & anti-fragility. *International Journal of Project Management*, *2*(32), 363–364.

Brenkert, G. G. (1998). Trust, morality and international business. *Business Ethics Quarterly*, *8*(2), 293–317.

Bryson, J. M., and Bromiley, P. (1993). Critical factors affecting the planning and implementation of major projects. *Strategic Management Journal*, *14*(5), 319–337.

Burnes, B. (2005). Complexity theories and organizational change. *International Journal of Management Reviews*, *7*(2), 73–90.

Cleland, D. I. (1997). Project stakeholder management (pp. 275–301). In D. I. Cleland and W. R. King (eds.). *Project management handbook*. John Wiley & Sons.

Crawford, L., Langston, C., and Bajracharya, B. (2013). Participatory project management for improved disaster resilience. *International Journal of Disaster Resilience in the Built Environment*, *4*(3), 317–333.

Dahlberg, R. (2015). Resilience and complexity: Conjoining the discourses of two contested concepts. *Culture Unbound*, *7*(3), 541–557.

Davis, K., and Pinto, J. K. (2022). The corruption of project governance through normalization of deviance. *IEEE Transactions on Engineering Management, 71*, 2447–2461.

de Moura, R. L., Carneiro, T. C. J., and Dias, T. L. (2023). VUCA environment on project success: The effect of project management methods. *Brazilian Business Review, 20*(3), 236–259.

Derbyshire, J., and Wright, G. (2014). Preparing for the future: development of an "antifragile" methodology that complements scenario planning by omitting causation. *Technological Forecasting and Social Change, 82*, 215–225.

Edson, M. C. (2012). A complex adaptive systems view of resilience in a project team. *Systems Research and Behavioral Science, 29*(5), 499–516.

Flyvbjerg, B. (2018). Planning fallacy or hiding hand: Which is the better explanation? *arXiv preprint*, 1802.09999.

Flyvbjerg, B., Holm, M. S., and Buhl, S. (2002). Underestimating costs in public works projects: Error or lie? *Journal of the American Planning Association, 68*(3), 279–295.

Fridgeirsson, T. V., Ingason, H. T., Jonasson, H. I., and Kristjansdottir, B. H. (2021). The VUCAlity of projects: A new approach to assess a project risk in a complex world. *Sustainability, 13*(7), 3808.

Geambasu, G. (2011). Expect the unexpected: An exploratory study on the conditions and factors driving the resilience of infrastructure projects. PhD dissertation, École Polytechnique Fédérale de Lausanne, Switzerland, Lausanne.

Gorgeon, A. (2015). Anti-fragile information systems. In T. A. Carte, A. Heinzl, & C. Urquhart (Eds.), *Proceedings of the 36th International Conference on Information Systems* (ICIS 2015) (pp. 1–19). Association for Information Systems.

Grabher, G., and Ibert, O. (2011). Project ecologies: A contextual view on temporary organizations (pp. 175–199). In P. W. G.Morris, J. K.Pinto, and J.Söderlund (eds.). *Oxford handbook of project management*. Oxford University Press.

Hegel, G. W. F., Burbidge, J., and Dickey, L. (1993). *The Cambridge companion to Hegel*. Cambridge University Press.

Hole, K. J., and Hole, K. J. (2016). Principles ensuring anti-fragility. In *Anti-fragile ICT Systems*. Springer. https://doi.org/10.1007/978-3-319-30070-2_4.

Ika, L., and Saint-Macary, J. (2023). *Managing fuzzy projects in 3D: A proven, multi-faceted blueprint for overseeing complex projects*. McGraw Hill Professional.

Ika, L. A., Love, P. E., and Pinto, J. K. (2022). Moving beyond the planning fallacy: The emergence of a new principle of project behavior. *IEEE Transactions on Engineering Management, 69*(6), 3310–3325.

Investigator, Q. (2017). Plans are worthless, but planning is everything. Quote Investigator. https://quoteinvestigator.com/2017/11/18/planning/.

Johnson, J., and Gheorghe, A. V. (2013). Antifragility analysis and measurement framework for systems of systems. *International Journal of Disaster Risk Science, 4*(4), 159–168.

Jones, K. H. (2014). Engineering antifragile systems: A change in design philosophy. *Procedia Computer Science, 32*, 870–875.

Khanna, R., Guler, I., and Nerkar, A. (2016). Fail often, fail big, and fail fast? Learning from small failures and R&D performance in the pharmaceutical industry. *Academy of Management Journal, 59*(2), 436–459.

Killen, C. P., and Hunt, R. A. (2013). Robust project portfolio management: Capability evolution and maturity. *International Journal of Managing Projects in Business, 6*(1), 131–151.

Koskela, L. (1999). *Management of production in construction: A theoretical view*. University of California Press.

Koskela, L. (2000). An exploration towards a production theory and its application to construction. Publication Number VTT Publications 408. Technical Research Centre of Finland, Helsinki.

Koskela, L., and Ballard, G. (2006). Should project management be based on theories of economics or production? *Building Research & Information, 34*(2), 154–163.

Kriete, A. (2013). Robustness and aging –a systems-level perspective. *Biosystems, 112*(1), 37–48.

Kutsch, E., and Turner, N. (2016). Project resilience – moving beyond traditional risk management (pp. 250–257). In D.Dalcher (ed.). *Further advances in project management: Guided exploration in unfamiliar landscapes*. Routledge.

Larsen, E. (2020). *Project mManagement: The manageral process*, 8th ed. McGraw-Hill Higher Education (International).

Laursen, M., and Svejvig, P. (2016). Taking stock of project value creation: A structured literature review with future directions for research and practice. *International Journal of Project Management, 34*(4), 736–747.

Linkov, I., and Trump, B. D. (2019). *The science and practice of resilience*. Springer.

Lucan, S. C., Maroko, A. R., Sanon, O. C., and Schechter, C. B. (2017). Unhealthful food-and-beverage advertising in subway stations: Targeted marketing, vulnerable groups, dietary intake, and poor health. *Journal of Urban Health, 94*, 220–232.

Lyotard, J.-F. (1993). Political writings. Trans. Bill Readings and Kevin Paul Geiman. UCL Press.

Mack, O., and Jungen, M. (2016). Program management in VUCA environments: Theoretical and pragmatical thoughts on a systemic management of projects and programs (pp. 41–57). In O. Mack, A. Khare, A. Krämer, and T. Burgartz (eds.). *Managing in a VUCA world.* Springer.

Mack, O., Khare, A., Krämer, A., and Burgartz, T. (eds.). (2015). *Managing in a VUCA world.* Springer.

McEvoy, P., Brady, M., and Munck, R. (2016). Capacity development through international projects: a complex adaptive systems perspective. *International Journal of Managing Projects in Business, 9*(3), 528–545.

Naderpajouh, N., Matinheikki, J., Keeys, L. A., Aldrich, D. P., and Linkov, I. (2020). Resilience and projects: An interdisciplinary crossroad. *Project Leadership and Society, 1*, 100001.

Nikookar, E., Varsei, M., and Wieland, A. (2021). Gaining from disorder: Making the case for antifragility in purchasing and supply chain management. *Journal of Purchasing and Supply Management, 27*(3), 100699.

Nowacka, A., and Rzemieniak, M. (2022). The impact of the VUCA environment on the digital competences of managers in the power industry. *Energies, 15*(1), 185.

Oliveira, N., Argyres, N., and Lumineau, F. (2022). The role of communication style in adaptation to interorganizational project disruptions. *Journal of Operations Management, 68*(4), 353–384.

Perrow, C. (1999). Organizing to reduce the vulnerabilities of complexity. *Journal of Contingencies and Crisis Management, 7*(3), 150–155.

Pinto, J. K. (2014). Project management, governance, and the normalization of deviance. *International Journal of Project Management, 32*(3), 376–387.

Pinto, J. K. (2022). No project should ever finish late (and why yours probably will, anyway). *IEEE Engineering Management Review, 50*, 181–192.

Piperca, S., and Floricel, S. (2023). Understanding project resilience: Designed, cultivated or emergent? *International Journal of Project Management, 41*(3), 102453.

PMI. (2017). *A guide to the project management body of knowledge (PMBOK® guide)*, 6th ed. Project Management Institute.

PMI. (2021). *A guide to the project management body of knowledge (PMBOK guide) and the standard for project management*, 7th ed. Project Management Institute.

Rahi, K. (2019). Project resilience: A conceptual framework. *International Journal of Information Systems and Project Management, 7*(1), 69–83.

Rue, L. W., and Ibrahim, N. A. (1998). The relationship between planning sophistication and performance in small nusinesses. *Journal of Small Business Management, 36*(4), 24–32.

Russo, D., and Ciancarini, P. (2017). Towards antifragile software architectures. *Procedia Computer Science, 109*, 929–934.

Santolini, M., Ellinas, C., and Nicolaides, C. (2021). Uncovering the fragility of large-scale engineering projects. *EPJ Data Science, 10*(1), 1–13.

Sapountzaki, K. (2012). Vulnerability management by means of resilience. *Natural Hazards, 60*, 1267–1285.

Shankar, R. K., and Clausen, T. H. (2020). Scale quickly or fail fast: An inductive study of acceleration. *Technovation, 98*, 102174.

Shen, W., and Ying, W. (2022). Large-scale construction programme resilience against creeping disruptions: Towards inter-project coordination. *International Journal of Project Management, 40*(6), 671–684.

Smith, A. (1950). *An inquiry into the nature and causes of the wealth of nations* (1776). Reprint. Random House (Modern Library), 1937.

Söderholm, A. (2008). Project management of unexpected events. *International Journal of Project Management, 26*(1), 80–86.

Stelling, J., Sauer, U., Szallasi, Z., Doyle III, F. J., and Doyle, J. (2004). Robustness of cellular functions. *Cell, 118*(6), 675–685.

Stochino, F., Bedon, C., Sagaseta, J., and Honfi, D. (2019). Robustness and resilience of structures under extreme loads. *Advances in Civil Engineering*, 4291703. https://doi.org/10.1155/2019/4291703.

Taleb, N. N. (2012). *Antifragile: Things that gain from disorder*, vol. 3. Random House.

Taleb, N. N., and Douady, R. (2011). A map and simple heuristic to detect fragility, antifragility, and model error. NYU-Poly working paper, SSRN.

Thomas, J., and Mengel, T. (2008). Preparing project managers to deal with complexity: Advanced project management education. *International*

Journal of Project Management, *26*(3), 304–315.

Trump, B. D., and Linkov, I. (2020). Risk and resilience in the time of the COVID-19 crisis. *Environment Systems and Decisions*, *40*(2), 171–173.

Usher, G. (2019). *Creating confidence amongst complexity: The "lived experience" of client-side project managers in the Australian construction sector*. University of Southern Queensland.

Usher, G. (2021). *Project management in the 21st century*. Springer Nature.

Usher, G., and Whitty, S. J. (2017a). The final state convergence model. *International Journal of Managing Projects in Business*, *10*(4), 770–795.

Usher, G., and Whitty, S. J. (2017b). Identifying and managing drift-changes. *International Journal of Project Management*, *35*(4), 586–603.

Usher, G., and Whitty, S. J. (2017c). Project management yinyang: Coupling project success and client satisfaction. *Project Management Research and Practice*, *4*, 5523–5523.

Usher, G. (2019). Next decision node (NDN) planning: An ambidextrous planning model. *International Journal of Managing Projects in Business*, *14*(2), 390–411.

Walker, D. H., Davis, P. R., and Stevenson, A. (2017). Coping with uncertainty and ambiguity through team collaboration in infrastructure projects. *International Journal of Project Management*, *35*(2), 180–190.

Wiewiora, A. M., and O'Connor, P. J. (2022). Not all project ambiguity is equal: A typology of project ambiguity and implications for its management. *International Journal of Project Management*, *40*(8), 921–933.

Winch, G. M., and Maytorena, E. (2011). Managing risk and uncertainty on projects: A cognitive approach (pp. 345–364). In P. Morris, J. Pinto, and J. Söderlund (eds.). *Oxford handbook of project management*. Oxford University Press.

Winter, M., Smith, C., Morris, P., and Cicmil, S. (2006). Directions for future research in project management: The main findings of a UK government-funded research network. *International Journal of Project Management*, *24*(8), 638–649.

Woods, S. P., Weinborn, M., Velnoweth, A., Rooney, A., and Bucks, R. S. (2012). Memory for intentions is uniquely associated with instrumental activities of daily living in healthy older adults. *Journal of the International Neuropsychological Society*, *18*(1), 134–138.

Yap, S. F., Xu, Y., and Tan, L. (2021). Coping with crisis: The paradox of technology and consumer vulnerability. *International Journal of Consumer Studies*, *45*(6), 1239–1257.

CHAPTER 18

Curbing Cost Increases and Benefit Shortfalls

MORTEN WELDE and GRO HOLST VOLDEN

Introduction

Projects are tools to achieve political objectives and strategic development in private and public sectors. Therefore, successful project delivery is essential for delivering political promises and meeting societal needs. The success of a project is often measured in terms of the ability to meet goals formulated in the business case that justified undertaking the project.

Project goals are formulated to operationalize project success – a concept that has attracted considerable attention and debate in the academic literature. Williams (2022) discussed different perspectives on success and suggested that the most basic level of success is project management success, while various strategic success criteria cover longer-term aspects. Samset (2010) argued that public project success has several dimensions, from the immediate project outputs through user benefits to wider and longer-term societal impacts.

Good goals are important for everyone involved in projects and provide an understanding of what the projects are to deliver. The goals ensure that all parties have the same understanding of the project and are used, among other things, to distribute responsibilities and as a basis for further planning. A project's goals provide information about why the project will be carried out, how much it will cost when it is completed, and the benefits/gains from its implementation. Time and cost are critical success criteria that are relatively unproblematic to measure. By contrast, measuring benefits can be more demanding, especially for projects in the public sector that deliver products that are not traded in markets. Common to all these success criteria is that the track record of projects, especially in the public sector, is mixed.

Costs matter. The investment cost usually attracts the most attention throughout the projects' front-end and implementation phases. It is suitable for making the responsible actors accountable, gauging progress and performance and assessing economic viability over time. However, the final cost of projects often turns out to be significantly higher than what was first announced to taxpayers and decision-makers. This is often referred to as cost overrun but, among others, Odeck and Welde (2021) argued that the term "cost overrun" should be distinguished from another related term, "cost escalation," which is used to express an anticipated growth in the estimated cost before the budget is set due to factors such as inflation or changes in societal needs.

Cost overruns, measured as the difference between actual costs and budgeted costs in real terms, can harm project progress, financial and social viability, and reputation. Because cost is a metric that can be measured with a high degree of accuracy, the list of studies of cost performance conducted by academics, auditors, and client organizations is extensive. Most of these studies have demonstrated that cost overruns are more prevalent than underruns. Odeck and Welde (2021) listed 48 studies of cost overruns in the transport sector worldwide from 1973 to 2012 and found that the weighted mean overrun (weighted by the number of projects in each study) across all of the studies was 40 percent. Flyvbjerg et al. (2018) claimed that 9 out of 10 transport projects worldwide experience a cost overrun. Similar results have been found in other sectors, such as ICT (Flyvbjerg & Budzier, 2011; Kashiwagi, 2018), the Olympic Games (Flyvbjerg et al., 2016), and defense acquisition (Hofbauer et al., 2011; Pfeifer & Warrel, 2021). However, even if many studies have documented that cost overruns are a problem, other authors have found more positive results with samples of projects below or close to budget (Odeck et al., 2015; Love et al., 2018; Love et al., 2019; Park, 2021; Welde & Klakegg, 2022). Love and Ahiaga-Dagbui (2018) and Love et al. (2022) therefore argued that the often repeated argument that "all" projects are prone to optimism bias is misleading and that there may be competing and equally plausible explanations as to why projects fall short of expectations. Therefore, improving cost performance should not be based only on failed projects. There may be more to learn from good practice than bad practice.

However, the purpose of carrying out projects is much broader than simply realizing a cost. Through achieving goals, we seek to realize positive effects for the users or the responsible organization, benefiting the wider society. The positive effects can relate to time or cost savings, a better quality of services, increased security, or better opportunities for value creation. Such benefits can be challenging to quantify ex ante, and it can be even more difficult to follow up on the benefits and determine whether or not they were achieved.

As noted by other authors (Cherns & Bryant, 1984; Zwikael & Smyrk, 2012), it is not the project manager's responsibility to achieve the higher-order goals in the business case. This is the project owner's responsibility. The easier-to-measure "iron triangle" and the project management perspective often receive the most attention in public projects. Samset and Volden (2016) referred to this as a paradox in project management and governance, as it can be argued that the strategic success perspective is inherently more important.

In general, benefits performance has been less studied than cost performance. Flyvbjerg et al. (2003) found that demand estimates were of poor quality in numerous transport projects, and the benefits were often overestimated. Moreover, environmental and other adverse side effects tended to be downplayed, while regional economic benefits were overestimated. Solberg and Preuss (2007) described how major sporting events are often justified by anticipated tourism-related and wider economic impacts but fail to realize such effects. Furthermore, many ICT projects do not meet the expectations of users and end up being abandoned or reworked (Cicmil & Braddon, 2012). However, as noted by Volden and Welde (2022), case studies tend to focus on projects for which there is already cause for concern, and there has been a striking lack of systematic ex post evaluation of public projects for learning purposes. Too little is known about whether citizens and taxpayers have reason to view public projects as successful in strategic terms.

The reasons why projects experience cost overruns or otherwise fail to meet the expectations of owners and stakeholders are many and have been discussed by different scholars, sometimes presenting wildly different theories ranging from strategic behavior bordering on criminal misbehavior to "honest" mistakes. In recent years, the academic debate has been characterized by disagreement about whether project underperformance is due to error or bias. The "error school" attributes cost overruns and benefit shortfalls to issues such as scope changes, increasing complexity, and marked issues (Ika et al., 2023). In contrast, the "bias school," often associated with the work by professor Bent Flyvbjerg and associates (Flyvbjerg & Gardner, 2023), suggests that the biggest risk in projects is human, or the inclination to ignore past project performance and instead focus on a particular case project. Sometimes, bias is intentional; other times, it is unintentional, but the results are the same. There have also been numerous publications, academic as well as from the consulting industry, that offer advice on how project behavior can be improved. Although projects are exposed to a range of external factors that may influence their outcomes, humans remain the most crucial resource for projects to be successful. Humans are, however, susceptible to different biases (Flyvbjerg, 2021). From a project behavioral perspective, the improvement in project performance from their initiation through their planning and implementation phases and to decades of operation thus relies on "soft" human factors and "hard" institutional arrangements. We must address both error and bias, and this chapter aims to advise both camps in the error vs. bias debate.

This chapter builds on research carried out by the Concept Research Program,[1] which the Norwegian Ministry of Finance tasks to research large government projects that undergo the ministry's project governance scheme. The scheme is, in turn, inspired by experiences and best practices identified in other countries, such as the UK, where a similar scheme exists (HM Treasury and Cabinet Office, 2011). Based on empirical data and theoretical studies, the research program gathers results and develops new knowledge about making sound decisions and governing major public projects. Trailing research and evaluation has the advantage of monitoring changes in project planning and delivery over time and continuously proposing avenues for improvement (Olsen & Lindøe, 2004). The program has operated since 2002 and has produced many research reports, papers, and project evaluations. In Norway, all government projects over a threshold value (currently c. EUR 100 million) must send the program all front-end reports regarding economic appraisal, cost estimation, and risk analysis. This creates rich data material on which to base research and evaluation. The content and advice in this chapter are based on the authors' experience working on the program. We refer to relevant research results based on empirical data and international literature where appropriate. The purpose is to provide practical advice based on experiences from past projects. The chapter concentrates on traditional project governance issues targeted at improving the performance of projects from the perspective of the owner or society. Project success does, however, rely on human beings. Our advice in the chapter is aimed at providing both an organizational and institutional context that both provide those working on planning and delivering projects with good tools and project owners with mechanisms that maximize the net benefit of projects.

The chapter proceeds as follows. The next section discusses the importance of the front-end phase and the early estimates of costs and benefits on which de facto project approval is often based. The following section constitutes the main part of the chapter, where we offer advice to improve the management of costs and benefits. The next section highlights ex post evaluation as a tool underused in learning and improvement, and the final section concludes the chapter.

[1] Concept Reasearch Program, www.ntnu.edu/concept.

The Importance of Projects' Front-End Phase

Research from the Concept Research Program has shown that we must distinguish between cost increase during projects' front-end phase (the period before the formal investment decision) and cost overrun after a formal budget is approved. Figure 18.1 illustrates a hypothetical development of a cost estimate in a project.[2]

Large projects are often based on a first initiative, idea, or vision. At this stage, very few details of a project are known. We may, for example, have a vision to connect an island to the mainland. Still, without further investigation, we will not know whether to build a bridge or a sub-sea tunnel, the standard and capacity of the new link, or whether we should opt for other measures to improve mobility. Cost estimates are typically low initially before more systematic attempts are made to estimate costs. During the front-end phase, the project evolves, often to accommodate user needs or compensate for potential adverse environmental or social impacts. In most projects, the project owner takes an active decision on whether to proceed with the project based on estimated costs and benefits throughout the front-end phase (illustrated by the blue dots in Figure 18.1). However, it is also during this stage, as Ahiaga-Dagbui and Smith (2014) argued, that the effects of human bias and strategic behavior are particularly heightened. Local promoters may feel they have little to lose and much to gain from an optimistic view of both costs and benefits. The estimation of benefits can have a similar development, with initial estimates

[2] In reality, most projects have more phases than those shown in Figure 18.1. The development in costs may differ between stages. The figure aims to illustrate that the biggest increase in costs is often during project development but before formal project approval.

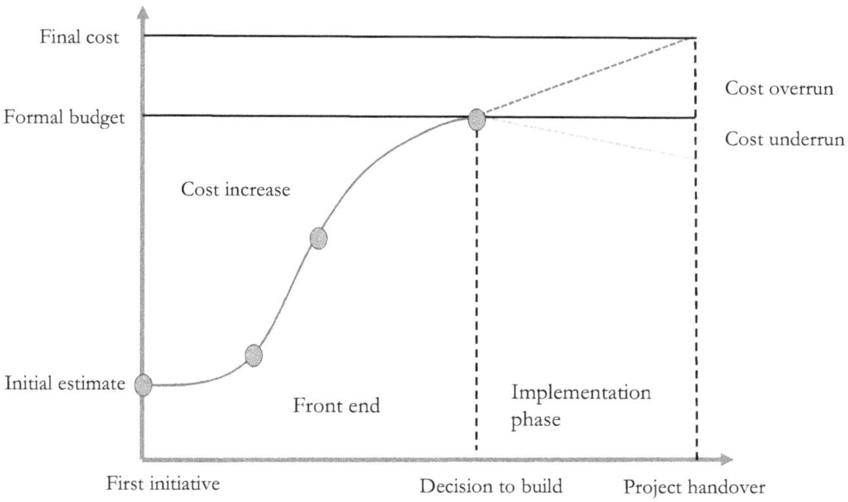

Figure 18.1 Development of a cost estimate in a project (based on Samset, 2010).
Note: Dots indicate potential decision points.

starting high (often including ambitious wider impacts for the community) and gradually becoming more realistic as the project takes shape.

Eventually, a formal budget is approved, and implementation/construction can start. The final cost may be higher or lower than the price-adjusted budget, but more often it is higher. Cost estimates evolve as the project matures and are inherently linked to the development of the project scope and schedule (Infrastructure and Projects Authority, 2021). A cost estimate is neither a budget nor a representation of actual expenditure. Unlike the budget, an estimate is not binding. Many projects experience a significant increase in cost estimates, yet they are never implemented. In other projects, the increased costs are justified on environmental, social, or economic grounds. One example is the 27 km-long E39 Rogfast tunnel currently under construction. It will reduce the journey time between Stavanger and Bergen, on the western coast of Norway, by 40 minutes. The first formal appraisal of the project was in 2002, when the construction cost was estimated at EUR 470 million. The estimate was based on average costs per meter of other sub-sea tunnels, which were all single tube at the time. This soon turned out to be unrealistic, considering the EU tunnel directive and traffic accidents in much shorter tunnels elsewhere. The revised design was based on a four-lane bidirectional tunnel and improved access roads on both sides. The final budget approved by parliament in 2020 was EUR 1.9 billion (first estimate and budget all in nominal values). The tunnel is still considered to have a positive net present value. Clearly, from both a safety and economic perspective, a single-tube tunnel almost 400 meters below the sea surface, carrying up to 10,000 vehicles per day, would be a terrible idea. The cost increase between 2002 and 2020 should not be considered an overrun but a modification to increased safety requirements and societal needs. Welde and Klakegg (2022) discussed the many definitions of overruns in the academic literature. They suggested that this was one of the reasons why the results of studies of cost overruns vary so much.

Figure 18.1 illustrates an extreme development in the estimated costs, but the research literature on cost estimation and quality during the front-end phase of projects is scarce (Edkins et al., 2013). Still, Andersen et al. (2016) showed that the increase in cost estimates from the first initiative to formal budget approval could amount to several multiples of 100 percent (and even over 1,000 percent). The same authors argued that many suboptimal projects are developed further from the first initiative because of unrealistically low first estimates. Early and unrealistically low cost estimates can significantly influence expectations, and as public projects gain momentum, they may be difficult to stop. Once politicians announce a project, they and the public tend to treat this as a commitment (Terrill, 2016).

The extent of cost escalation during the front end of projects depends on when the funding decision is taken. This may vary between countries. In Norway, the funding decision allows a budget to be allocated and the client to hire a contractor, that is, funds are allocated before procurement and detailed design. In the UK, the Infrastructure and Projects Authority (IPA) expects project maturity to be at >60 percent in the final business case for making a final investment decision (Infrastructure and Projects Authority, 2021). This level of maturity fits well with Norwegian cost estimates prepared for the final investment decision when funds are allocated.

Samset and Volden (2016) referred to the tendency to focus on getting the final estimate right while treating early cost estimates superficially as "the cost estimate paradox," and they argued that this could increase the risk of strategic failure. Therefore, efforts to improve project success should aim to improve cost estimation in both projects' front-end and implementation phases.

Improving the Success of Projects throughout Their Life Cycle

To improve the precision of cost estimates prepared at different stages, to prevent costs from blowing up, and to realize the intended goals of projects, we propose a set of advice that could be useful to project-based organizations. We distinguish between advice related to the governance of projects, that is, processes related to the initiation, selection, and organization of projects and advice related to traditional project management issues such as cost estimation, risk analysis, and project delivery. Finally, we offer some advice concerning the follow-up and documentation of benefits, which should continue after project completion (see Figure 18.2).

Develop a Cost-Effective Solution to the Problem

The first question should be whether we need a project at all. The question is not what, but why. Projects are often prepared on an ad-hoc basis, and often, the solution (the project) is selected before we adequately address which problem the project should solve (i.e., we end up with a project looking for a problem rather than the opposite). Politically, there is often pressure to "be seen to be doing something," which may lead to opting quickly for

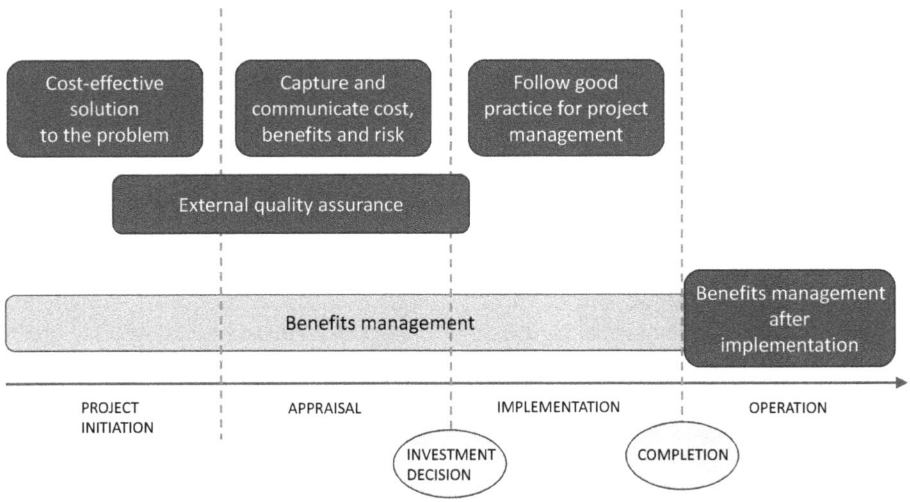

Figure 18.2 Activities to improve project success from project initiation to operation.

the seemingly best solution without exploring options (Zwikael & Gilchrist, 2022). The mandate for project appraisal is a formally initiating document in a chain of events. It gives instructions to start a review or appraisal to find the best and cost-effective solution to a problem. It should give investigators and relevant government agencies clear instructions to clarify the triggering problem, justify the need for change, why a project might be needed, and what the superior goal is (Samset & Welde, 2019). The mandate should also emphasize the strategic perspective and clarify the ambition level. It should always be clear that a do-nothing or a do-minimum alternative is an option throughout the appraisal process if the project is unviable in economic, social, and environmental terms.

Too often, appraisal and planning turn out to be a wish list of the needs and desires of different stakeholders to be met, which often results in spiralling costs while social benefits remain constant. Bakke et al. (2019) argued that many projects experience increasing costs from the estimated pre-design to the completion phase because of weak project mandates, poorly defined scopes, and unrealistic constraints. Active project ownership, starting with the mandate, is a condition to avoid that.

A piece of final advice on project mandates relates to who receives them. As Abraham Maslow formulated, if all you have is a hammer, everything looks like a nail (Wikipedia, 2022). For example, suppose you give a railway authority the task of investigating solutions to mobility problems between two cities. In that case, it is unlikely that improved road access will be the preferred option. For proper investigation of the opportunity space, the responsibility for the appraisal should not be given to an enterprise with a limited area of responsibility that may have an incentive to pursue one specific course of action.

Broad Overview of Consequences

A broad overview of alternatives' benefits, costs, and risks should be presented as part of the initial appraisal. As discussed above, few details are known at this stage and overoptimism regarding both costs and benefits can be a significant problem. This is because decision-makers often become de facto committed early on, and the political cost of turning the project down later can be high. Any efforts to improve the quality of early project appraisals should give good results.

A key issue is to ensure that all relevant consequences are considered. Experience shows that unintended consequences are often ignored, whereas intended costs and benefits are typically covered. Furthermore, while consequences that are easy to quantify receive much attention, unquantifiable consequences do not. This is especially true for some benefits and intangible costs, such as disturbances during construction and environmental costs. Political decision-makers care not only about the net benefits but often also about how benefits and costs are distributed across groups and regions. For example, suppose a particular group will have to bear a high negative consequence. In that case, knowing about this in advance will be crucial because otherwise the project will risk a high extra cost of compensatory measures later.

A broad, multidisciplinary appraisal of consequences should be presented to decision-makers early on. The needs of different stakeholders must be mapped, goals must be formulated, and conceptually different alternatives must be appraised before the financing party can decide whether to proceed with planning and eventually allocate a budget.

Capture and Communicate the Uncertainty of Estimates of Costs and Benefits

Early estimates of costs and benefits are inherently uncertain. For example, presenting a cost estimate as a single-point estimate at an early stage can obscure rather than clarify the likely cost of a scheme. Dysert (2006) thus argued that cost-estimate accuracy is an oxymoron or a contradiction in terms. Planners tend to forget, and decision-makers tend to be unaware, that an estimated cost or benefit is always a point on a probability distribution curve representing a range of potential outcomes. For example, the probability that the cost will be at or lower than a single-point deterministic estimate may be less than 30 percent. In such cases, we should expect cost overruns. Uncertainty arises from measured and unmeasured uncertainty ranges around defined elements and unknown uncertainties that are neither known nor understood. In the early stages of projects, a significant proportion of cost increase will come from unknown unknowns. The base case's inability to capture these is not "optimism bias" but is a natural part of most projects. An uplift or contingency to account for these unspecified risks should be added to the base estimate. Furthermore, the cost estimate should be presented as a range to account for the risk and uncertainty inherent in the project. The range should decrease as the project develops (Infrastructure and Projects Authority, 2021). If the accuracy range is expressed as a percentage, it is important to note whether it is around the estimate before or after contingency.

The literature on cost performance provides limited insight into what cost estimation methodologies are applied in different countries and industries, and to our knowledge, there are no reviews of which methods provide the best results. Welde and Klakegg (2022) argued that stochastic estimation coupled with Monte Carlo simulation and group processes can produce robust estimates. Total uncertainty can be better identified when a relatively large number of people provide input to the cost estimation and risk analysis process. Norway has used this method for large government projects for over two decades, and the results are good at the portfolio level (75 percent of projects within budget, n = 96). The Danish Road Directorate formerly employed a similar method but has since used budget uplifts based on different project maturity levels. There, the national auditor general has demonstrated that over 90 percent of projects are delivered within budget, leading to criticism that the budgets have been overly generous (Rigsrevisionen, 2019).

While it is increasingly accepted that cost estimates and budgets must include uncertainty and that presenting cost estimates with high precision is unrealistic, the estimation of benefits and their uncertainty is much less developed. Cost engineering for tangible assets has a long tradition, and estimates could be presented with increasing accuracy as the project develops. After completion, the costs can be summarized with 100 percent accuracy. However, the benefits are much fuzzier. Effects such as increased interaction between organizational units, increased well-being of individuals, and improved organizational quality are much more demanding to express accurately. In the transport sector, for example, where the practice of social cost-benefit analysis is well developed, benefits accruing from travel-time savings and traffic-safety improvements are often expressed to the nearest decimal point, yet most ex-post studies show that ex-ante estimates can be very inaccurate (Odeck & Kjerkreit, 2019; Hoque et al., 2022). The uncertainty of benefits cannot be planned or estimated away. Instead, we need to develop methods that express and visualize benefit success and, if possible, use probabilistic methods such as Monte Carlo simulation for benefits and costs (Salling & Leleur, 2011; Salci & Jenkins, 2016).

Develop Projects through a Stage-Gate Project Governance Model

It is gradually recognized that front-end activities like those above are best managed within a standardized project governance framework to ensure successful implementation and outcomes. Project governance refers to the processes, systems, and regulations the financing party must have to ensure that projects succeed (Volden & Samset, 2017). A governance framework, or a project governance model, is a collection of minimum requirements for how a project must be carried out from the idea phase to completion. It defines roles, concepts, and decision points between different phases. A stage-gate model requires cost estimates of increasing accuracy to make decisions to proceed to the next stage and eventually consent to implement the project and authorise project funding (Dysert & Elliott, 2020).

The most important aspects of a project governance model can be described as follows:

- Clear separation of project stages
- Decision points between stages
- Quality-assured basis for decisions
- Simplicity.

The purpose of decision points is to ensure that the participants in the decision process are aware of (1) when a decision is made, (2) what the decision is about, and (3) what the consequences of the decision are. At each decision point, the project can be terminated, changed, or continue as planned.

A standardized project governance model provides a structure for the preparation of projects and guides implementation. It increases the understanding of the purpose and content of the project and ensures that project participants have a common understanding of where they are in the decision-making process. In a democratic system, a project governance model also has another significant advantage: It ensures that projects are subject to effective political control and makes the participants accountable.

Take an Outside View of Plans and Estimates through External Quality Assurance

As mentioned above, quality assurance of estimates and other decision documents should be an integrated part of a project governance scheme. Individuals and groups can be susceptible to overoptimism, self-delusion, groupthink, and even willfull deception (Lovallo & Kahneman, 2003; Bénabou, 2013). As individuals, we are poor at assessing our performance, yet that bias is much less predominant when assessing the performance of others. A system of project controls that includes external quality assurance (QA) can help debias estimates and keep a project on track. QA is a system for ensuring a desired level of quality in the development, production, and delivery of products and services (Odeck et al., 2015). Independent and external peer reviews of forecasts and business cases can be a potential remedy for cost overruns and benefit shortfalls and improve the quality of front-end management by taking an "outside view" of planned actions (Flyvbjerg, 2013). QA can be performed between project stages and before final budget authorization. In 2000 (later extended in 2005), Norway introduced a system that requires external QA of cost estimates and business cases for large government projects. It is a gateway model that requires all large projects to go through two external reviews:

(1) QA1: Quality assurance of choice of concept before the government decision to start a pre-project.
(2) QA2: Quality assurance of cost estimates before the project is submitted to Parliament for approval and funding.

The results in terms of cost performance after formal budget approval are good. Odeck et al. (2015) and Welde and Klakegg (2022) demonstrated that most (75 percent) projects subjected to external QA have been completed within budget. But, the scheme has traditionally been less successful in curbing cost escalation in the front-end of projects (between QA1 and QA2 – before formal budget approval) (Welde & Odeck, 2017). However, in 2019, the Ministry of Finance introduced a formal requirement for all large government projects to maintain a change log of all changes in costs and scope during their front-end. Coupled with a stronger emphasis on a target cost after QA1, this will hopefully improve cost performance during the early phases of project development.

Align the Incentives of Project Stakeholders

Project or program benefits are rarely realized top-down but require buy-in from critical stakeholders. Stakeholder alignment (i.e., making the different parties that contribute to and benefit from a project agree on context, goals, and processes) is critical to controlling costs and realizing benefits. However, this task is challenging in projects in the public sector, where typically there is one financing party and several stakeholders set to benefit from the investment, often without financial contribution. Volden (2019) described such agency problems as "perverse incentives," which can occur especially when two preconditions are present: an underlying conflict of interest and information asymmetry.

Incentives to Initiate a Project

Perverse incentives can be a significant risk in the initiation phase of a public project. For local interest groups, project approval and funding are often non-discretionary; the alternative is to receive nothing.

The role of local interest groups is to provide the government with information about local needs and other conditions and to describe the suggested project and its results in a desirable manner. The cost is often assumed to be carried 100 percent by the government. This means that users may have an incentive to "gold-plate" investment, as they have little to lose and everything to gain by demanding solutions that benefit them but where the cost to society as a whole exceeds the total benefits. Even when there is a local contribution, for example, in the form of road tolls, the contribution of the individual user of the new facility will be negligible compared with the total cost of the facility. Sager (2016) suggested that perverse incentives are one of the reasons why the results of cost-benefit analyses in the Norwegian road sector have traditionally had little impact on project selection.

Volden (2019) argued that the absence of liabilities, such as local co-funding, is a risk factor that all project funders should be aware of. There is no quick fix for the misalignment of incentives. However, a thorough discussion of the terms of financing should be part of every project assessment. Furthermore, the government should base project selection on high-quality information about the problems, needs, benefits, costs, and risks. In this respect, external quality assurance and full data transparency results and decisions can play a role. Finally, in projects that require nondiscretionary funding, there should be a legal requirement for local financial contribution, and project selection should meet specific criteria, such as value for money.

Incentives to Realize the Planned Effects

A related problem to poor incentives for keeping costs down is the lack of incentives to realize the intended benefits (and costs) during and after construction. In the construction industry, it is increasingly recognized that traditional contract arrangements, such as unit price contracts where the client specifies the scope in detail in the description of works, may give unfortunate incentives to contractors to produce unrealistically low tenders (Ewerhart & Fieseler, 2003; Welde & Dahl, 2021). To align incentives in the delivery phase, many clients now use partnering and alliancing to achieve targeted costs (Walker et al., 2022).

Achieving the intended benefits may be more complicated as they do not happen automatically and will often depend on the efforts of a wide range of internal and external groups and individuals, some of whom may not have personal incentives to make such efforts. For example, assume that an organization introduces an ICT system to save time and eventually save costs. While this may be perfectly rational from a top management perspective, it may also imply that some employees will lose their jobs, and some department managers will receive a lower budget. If benefits realization depends on the same employees and department managers, we should not be surprised if they do not give their best effort. The situation is even more complex when more organizations are involved, which is often the case in public projects. The solution to this problem could be establishing an incentive scheme that allows those involved to keep a certain amount of the profits.

Follow Good Practices for Project Management

Much of the advice presented in the preceding sections relates to the projects' front-end and how this could be better managed and governed. There are good reasons to focus on the front-end phase, as there is solid empirical evidence to suggest that most projects that fail do so because of actions, or the lack of actions, taken before formal project sanctioning. However, this should not lead to the assumption that traditional project management activities are less important. Front-end loading can only improve cost performance to a certain extent before weaknesses in other practices become a constraint (Hollmann, 2002). Front-end activities such as risk analysis are carried out to support the subsequent delivery of the projects. Having the right skills to follow up on these pieces of advice is crucial for efficiently converting resources into results. The discipline of project management is far older than that of project governance, and there is a wealth of advice on managing projects efficiently (e.g., Project Management Institute, 2021).

Within the more than 300 large government projects that the Concept Research Program has been tasked to research, the risk analysis reports rank the most critical risk factors for the subsequent delivery. The risk factors that dominate the risk analyses are typically as follows:

- Project organization and human factors (e.g., skills within project organization, capacity, continuity, cooperation with contractor/supplier);
- Contract strategy (e.g., contract type, settlement terms, number and size of contracts, interface between contracts);
- Market issues (e.g., the number of bids and price offers compared with the client's estimate);
- Geotechnical conditions (e.g., soil carrying capacity, erodibility, compressibility, proportion of quick clay).

These issues should be identified along with strategies for managing them in the front-end, but they should also be managed during the project delivery stage. Efficient project delivery is a highly complex matter, and assuming that the problem of cost overruns and benefit shortfalls will be solved merely by having accurate estimates of costs and benefits is a somewhat naive approach.

Benefits Management Must Continue after Project Completion

Benefits management includes all processes and roles to (1) identify and structure benefits, (2) plans to realize them, 3) management of benefits during the implementation phase, and (4) documentation of realized benefits (Figure 18.3). In other words, benefits management requires continuous attention throughout the project life cycle.

Benefits management is still an immature area in the public sector. A study based on 23 Norwegian public digitalization projects found that, whereas benefits typically receive much attention in the early phases of projects, systematic benefits management practices are applied to a lesser extent during later phases of the project (Berg et al., 2021). Thus, as important as ensuring that the early estimates are of high quality, the main weakness in practice is the lack of follow-up activities during and after construction. Berg et al. (2021) found that the follow-up and documentation of effects were often superficial and brief, focusing only on a few quantifiable effects. Ex-post evaluations some years after the start of the operational phase were rare.

Berg et al. (2021) also found that although all the projects had a cost-benefit analysis as part of the business case, those analyses served mainly to secure project approval and financing. Project participants are eager to document a positive net present value ex ante. Still, they do not necessarily use the cost-benefit analysis actively to plan and manage benefits during the project.

We recommend paying more attention to the later phases of the benefits management cycles. Specifically, we advise the following:

- Use the cost-benefit analysis to plan how to realize the benefits (when, how, and who).
- In doing so, *benefits mapping* (see Figure 18.4, using an ICT project as an example) can visualize and communicate the project logic and planned benefits to internal and external stakeholders. The map in Figure 18.4 shows the relationships between deliveries and benefits and between benefits and strategic goals.
- Have personnel with responsibility for the realization of benefits.

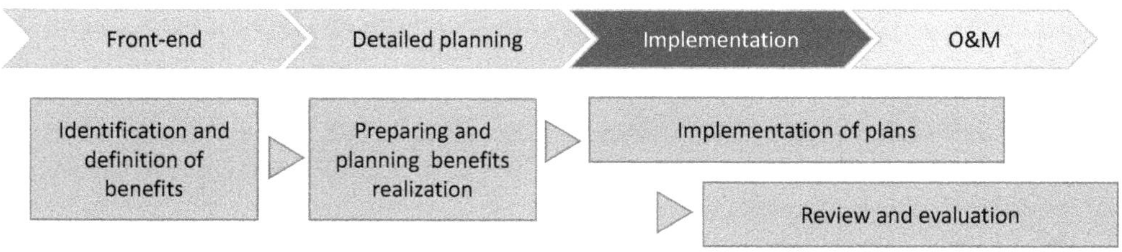

Figure 18.3 Benefits management through the project life cycle.

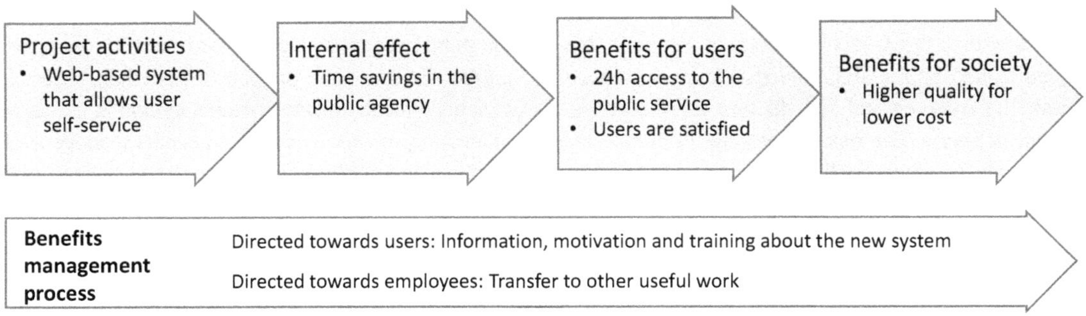

Figure 18.4 Benefits map, simplified example.

- Define processes for evaluating realized benefits, preferably through continuous monitoring and evaluation. Ensure that given benefits can be both evaluated and managed. Not all benefits can be quantified directly, but they can be evaluated using, for example, indicators or surveys.
- Improved mechanisms for sharing experiences from benefits management across projects and organisations.

Learn from Past Mistakes and Successes through Ex-Post Evaluation

The challenges experienced by many projects in terms of cost performance and benefits realization may seem a paradox based on the large number of projects carried out annually. According to some estimates, the total world annual expenditure on projects is USD 10 trillion (Williams et al., 2022). Ideally, this should create experiences facilitating learning and improving practices in future projects. Nevertheless, there is a tendency for projects to replicate the mistakes of the past. The skills and experiences of individuals within organizations may be considerable, yet the link from individual learning to organizational knowledge is often weak. Beste and Klakegg (2022) recommended that project-based organizations should use a wide range of efforts, including "hard" actions such as courses, databases with previous experiences, and extending the project governance model with more mandatory points, as well as "soft" actions that facilitate networks and encourage project members to share experiences.

Ex-post evaluation – the assessment of whether a specific intervention was justified, whether it achieved its objectives and why, and whether it had any unintended consequences – is rarely conducted as a systematic activity but instead takes the form of ad-hoc investigations of projects that have gone wrong (Worsley, 2015; Samset & Christensen, 2017). To the extent that some countries require ex-post evaluation of investment projects, it is typically restricted to the transport sector, with the main focus on economic aspects (Volden & Welde, 2022). Knowledge of projects' actual value for money, effectiveness, and sustainability may be limited. This contrasts with the extensive ex-ante evaluations that most organizations require before sanctioning large projects. Despite the considerable uncertainty at the time of the investment decision, it is assumed a priori that the intended effects will materialize within the proposed budget.

As discussed in the preceding section, there is a tendency for projects to perform comprehensive assessments of intended benefits upfront and then not follow up to find out whether or not the effects materialized. While the final cost will usually be disclosed one way or another, the actual benefits will often remain unknown. A requirement (from the financing party) to document benefits is crucial for benefits management and should be introduced in every project. In addition, broad ex-post evaluations should be conducted on a selection of projects as a means for learning and improvement in future projects. Such evaluations should focus on cost and benefits management and include questions about *why* the results are as they are.

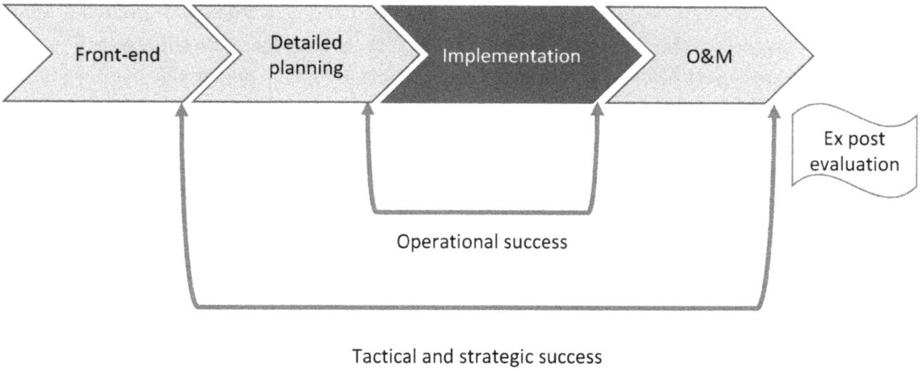

Figure 18.5 Closing the loop between ex-ante and ex-post evaluation through measuring different perspectives of success.

Thus, there is a need to "close the loop" between ex-ante and ex-post evaluation through systematic ex-post evaluation to improve the planning and implementation of future projects and to strengthen the strategies for benefit and cost management (Volden & Welde, 2022) (Figure 18.5). Effective learning requires that projects be followed over time, from the front-end phase through detailed planning and implementation to the operation and maintenance phase. It is insufficient merely to consider cost performance or user effects in the first year after implementation. Evaluations should be based on operational success (often referred to as the achievement of objectives for time, cost, and quality) and tactical/strategic success concerning long-term societal goals and sustainability.

Samset and Volden (2022) argued that evaluation should be based on the project's logic model, that is, the link between project activities/inputs and intended effects and impacts. It should take a broad and multifaceted view of project success. They also argued that project failures could be avoided if project planners and managers learned better from their experiences. Ex-post evaluation should be a mandatory part of a project governance framework to facilitate this.

Conclusion

Project appraisal, planning, and estimation take place against a background of uncertainty. The research literature on project performance has demonstrated that many projects have failed to consider this uncertainty, as costs often turn out to be higher than estimated and benefits lower. This means that error, or deviation between estimates and real outturn values is inevitable as perfect knowledge of the future is impossible. Paired with bias, a natural part of human behavior, this increases the risk of project underperformance and failure. Therefore, we need to account for uncertainty and risk factors in project plans and, as far as possible, debias the project development and decision-making process. The discussion of error or bias has been the subject of much academic debate over the last few years. The purpose of this chapter has not been to support one side in the debate or the other but to draw on lessons from projects that have worked and that have improved cost performance and goal achievement.

In the chapter, we have argued that the front-end of projects is vital for project success, even if other practices during later project stages may be crucial. Projects that fail don't just end badly; they start badly. Therefore, to improve project performance, we must focus on the left side of project development, where the problems are discussed, alternatives considered, and risks investigated.

We contribute to practice by demonstrating how various activities are necessary to reduce risk and avoid cost overruns and benefit shortfalls. We have provided advice regarding the governance, delivery, and operation of projects. Our advice is based mainly on research conducted by the Concept

Research Program in Norway, which researches large government projects. The projects within the programe's research portfolio have all been subjected to a stage-gate project planning and delivery model with mandatory decision points, external quality assurance, and requirements regarding how mature projects must be before they can receive government funding. Most of our advice, based on Norwegian data, overlaps with academic and consultancy reports based on data from other countries, which is reassuring.

We also contribute to theory by demonstrating the need to learn through continuous data collection from completed projects. Much of the academic literature has focused on projects that have gone wrong, such as experiencing cost overruns. However, governments worldwide deliver a welter of projects yearly – most of which are probably completed pretty much as planned. Volden and Welde (2022) suggested that there may be a bad news bias in the academic literature on project performance.) Collecting data from these and disseminating experiences needed to improve future project performance should be at the heart of the practical project literature.

The advice is empirically based in that it is based on a large number of completed projects. A potential weakness is that past projects and experiences do not necessarily provide the best recipe for all future problems. Most Norwegian government projects have traditionally been based on conventional procurement strategies such as design-bid-build contracts. The construction industry, in particular, is increasingly basing project delivery on utilizing the competence and skills of contractors through alliancing and contracts aimed at balancing the incentives of different parties (Walker et al., 2022). Another look at the issues discussed in this chapter in light of potential lessons in a few years may be in order.

Ex-post evaluation is essential for collecting empirical data on project performance to provide lessons from what has worked well and less well, improve future appraisal, and develop more successful projects. Both front-end activities and activities relating to project delivery, operation, and evaluation should be included in a standardized governance framework that ensures quality at entry, supports the selection of projects, and ensures that responsibility for the realization of benefits is allocated throughout the project life cycle.

References

Ahiaga-Dagbui, D. D., and Smith, S. D. (2014). Rethinking construction cost overruns: Cognition, learning and estimation. *Journal of Financial Management of Property and Construction*, *19*, 38–54.

Andersen, B., Samset, K., and Welde, M. (2016). Low estimates – high stakes: Underestimation of costs at the front-end of projects. *International Journal of Managing Projects in Business*, *9*, 171–193.

Bakke, C., Johansen, A., Mahmood, K. M., and Grenland, S. (2019). Feeble project mandate equal higher cost? *Procedia Computer Science*, *164*, 433–440.

Bénabou, R. (2013). Groupthink: Collective delusions in organisations and markets. *Review of Economic Studies*, *80*, 429–462.

Berg, H., Holgeid, K., Jørgensen, M., and Volden, G. H. (2021). Hvordan lykkes med digitalisering? En undersøkelse av nyttestyring i IT-prosjekter i offentlig sektor [How to succeed with digitalisation? A study of benefit management in public IT projects]. Concept-rapport nr. 64. Trondheim: Ex ante akademisk forlag.

Beste, T., and Klakegg, O. J. (2022). Strategic change towards cost-efficient public construction projects. *International Journal of Project Management*, *40*, 372–384.

Cicmil, S., and Braddon, D. (2012). Fading glory? Decision-making around the project – how and why "glory" projects fail (pp. 221–255). In T. Williams and K. Samset (eds.). *Project Governance: Getting Investments Right*. Palgrave Macmillan.

Dysert, L. R. (2006). Is "estimate accuracy" an oxymoron? AACE International Transactions. www.costengineering.eu/images/papers/Is_Estimate_Accuracy_an_Oxymoron.pdf.

Dysert, L. R., and Elliott, B.G. (2020). Early conceptual estimation methodologies. AACE International Transactions. http://ccg-estimating.com/uploads/1/3/2/8/132807526/wp-earlyconceptualestimatingmethodologies.pdf.

Edkins, A., Geraldi, J., Morris, P., and Smith, A. (2013). Exploring the front-end of project management. *Engineering Project Organization Journal*, 3, 71–85.

Ewerhart, C., and Fieseler, K. (2003). Procurement auctions and unit price contracts. *The RAND Journal of Economics*, *34*, 569–581.

Flyvbjerg, B. (2013). Quality control and due diligence in project management: Getting decisions right by taking the outside view. *International Journal of Project Management*, *31*, 760–774.

Flyvbjerg, B. (2021). Top ten behavioral biases in project management: An overview. *Project Management Journal*, *52*, 531–546.

Flyvbjerg, B., and Budzier, A. (2011). Why your IT project may be riskier than you think. *Harvard Business Review*, *89*, 23–25.

Flyvbjerg, B., and Gardner, D. (2023). *How big things get done*. Pan MacMillan.

Flyvbjerg, B., Bruzelius, N., and Rothengatter, W. (2003). *Megaprojects and risk: An anatomy of ambition*. Cambridge University Press.

Flyvbjerg, B., Stewart, A., and Budzier, A. (2016). The Oxford Olympics Study 2016: Cost and cost overrun at the games. WP 2016-20. Oxford, Saïd Business School.

Flyvbjerg, B., Ansar, A., Budzier, A., Buhl, S., Cantarelli, C., Garbuio, M., Glenting, C., Skamris Holm, M., Lovallo, D., Lunn, D., Molin, E., Rønnest, A., Steward, A., and van Wee, B. (2018). Five things you should know about cost overrun. *Transportation Research Part A: Policy and Practice*, *118*, 174–190.

Hofbauer, J., Sanders, G., Ellman, J., and Morrow, D. (2011). *Cost and time overruns for major defense acquisition programs*. Center for Strategic and International Studies.

HM Treasury and Cabinet Office (2011). Major Project Approval and Assurance Guidance.

Hollmann, J. K. (2002). Best owner practices for project control. AACE International Transactions. https://validest.com/library.html.

Hoque, J. M., Erhardt, G. D., Schmitt, D., Chen, M., Chaudhary, A., Wachs, M., and Souleyrette, R. R. (2022). The changing accuracy of traffic forecasts. *Transportation*, *49*, 445–466.

Infrastructure and Projects Authority (2021). Cost Estimating Guidance. www.gov.uk/government/publications/cost-estimating-guidance/cost-estimating-guidance.

Kashiwagi, I. (2018). A global study on ICT project performance. *Journal for the Advancement of Performance Information and Value*, *10*(1), 8–27.

Ika, L., Pinto, J. K., Love, P. E. D., and Pache, G. (2023). Bias versus error: Why projects fall short. *Journal of Business Strategy*, *44*(2), 67–75

Lovallo, D., and Kahneman, D. (2003). Delusions of success: How optimism undermines executives' decisions. *Harvard Business Review*, *81*(7), 56–63.

Love, P. E. D., and Ahiaga-Dagbui, D. (2018). Debunking fake news in a post-truth era: The plausible untruths of cost underestimation in transport infrastructure projects. *Transportation Research Part A: Policy and Practice*, *113*, 357–368.

Love, P. E. D., and Ahiaga-Dagbui, D., Smith, S. D., Sing, M., and Tokede, O. (2018). Cost profiling of water infrastructure projects. *Journal of Infrastructure Systems*, *24*, 04018023.

Love, P. E. D., Sing, M.C.P., Ika L., and Newton, S. (2019). The cost performance of transportation projects: The fallacy of the Planning Fallacy account. *Transportation Research Part A: Policy and Practice*, *122*, 1–20.

Love, P. E. D., Ika, L. A., and Sing, M. C. P. (2022). Does the Planning Fallacy prevail in social infrastructure projects? Empirical evidence and competing explanations. *IEEE Transactions on Engineering Management*, *69*, 2588–2602.

Odeck, J., and Kjerkreit, A. (2019). The accuracy of benefit-cost analyses (BCAs) in transportation: An ex-post evaluation of road projects. *Transportation Research Part A: Policy and Practice*, *120*, 277–294.

Odeck, J., and Welde, M. (2021). Cost overruns of transportation infrastructure projects (pp. 483-489). In R. Vickerman (ed.). *International encyclopedia of transportation*. Elsevier.

Odeck, J., Welde, M., and Volden, G. H. (2015). The impact of external quality assurance of costs wstimates on cost overruns: Empirical evidence from the Norwegian road sector. *European Journal of Transport Infrastructure Research*, *15*, 286–303.

Olsen, O. E., and Lindøe, P. (2004). Trailing research based evaluation; phases and roles. *Evaluation and Program Planning*, *27*, 371–380.

Park, J. E. (2021). Curbing cost overruns in infrastructure investment: Has reference class forecasting delivered its promised success? *European Journal of Transport and Infrastructure Research*, *21*, 120–136.

Pfeifer, S., and Warrel, H. (2021). MoD's poor practices blamed for project cost overruns and delays. www.ft.com/content/9da15fa5-da6c-4b44-ad9a-7b121f80415c.

Project Management Institute (2021). *A guide to the project management body of knowledge: PMBOK® Guide*. 7th ed. Project Management Institute.

Rigsrevisionen (2019). *Budgetteringen av Vejdirektoratets vejprosjekter [The budgeting of the Road Directorate's road projects]*. Rigsrevisionen.

Sager, T. (2016). Why don't cost-benefit results count for more? The case of Norwegian road investment priorities. *Urban, Planning and Transport Research*, *4*, 101–121.

Salci, S., and Jenkins, G. (2016). Incorporating risk and uncertainty in cost-benefit analysis. MPRA Paper No. 74161. https://mpra.ub.uni-muenchen.de/74161/.

Salling, K. B., and Leleur, S. (2011). Transport appraisal and Monte Carlo simulation by use of the CBA-DK model. *Transport Policy*, *18*, 236–245.

Samset, K. (2010). *Early project appraisal: Making the initial choices*. Palgrave Macmillan.

Samset, K., and Volden, G. H. (2016). Front-end definition of projects: Ten paradoxes and some reflections regarding project management and project governance. *International Journal of Project Management*, *34*, 297–313.

Samset, K., and Christensen, T. (2017). Ex-ante project evaluation and the complexity of early decision-making. *Public Organization Review*, *17*(1), 1–17.

Samset, K., and Welde, M. (2019). Mandater for konseptvalgutredninger. En gjennomgang av praksis [The terms of reference document for conceptual appraisal: A review of current practice]. Concept-rapport nr 58. Trondheim: Ex ante akademisk forlag.

Samset, K., and Volden, G. H. (2022). Closing the loop. Ex ante and es post evaluation in order to learn from mistakes and successes (ch. 7). In T. M. Williams, K. Samset, and G. H. Volden (eds.). *The front-end of large public projects. Paradoxes and ways ahead*. Routledge.

Solberg, H. A., and Preuss, H. (2007). Major sports events and long-term tourism impacts. *Journal of Sports Management*, *21*, 213–234.

Terrill, M. (2016). *Cost overruns in transport infrastructure*. Grattan Institute.

Volden, G. H. (2019). Public funding, perverse incentives, and counterproductive outcomes. *International Journal of Managing Projects in Business*, *12*, 466–486.

Volden, G. H., and Samset, K. (2017). Governance of major public investment projects: Principles and practices in six countries. *Project Management Journal*, *48*, 90–108.

Volden, G. H., and Welde, M. (2022). Public project success? Measuring the nuances of success through ex-post evaluation. *International Journal of Project Management*, *40*, 703–714.

Walker, D. H. T., Vaz-Serra, P., and Love, P. E. D. (2022). Improved reliability in planning large-scale infrastructure project delivery through alliancing. *International Journal of Managing Projects in Business*, *15*, 721–741.

Wikipedia (2022). Law of the instrument. https://en.wikipedia.org/wiki/Law_of_the_instrument.

Welde, M., and Odeck, J. (2017). Cost escalations in the front-end of projects – empirical evidence from Norwegian road projects. *Transport Reviews*, *37*, 612–630.

Welde, M., and Dahl, R. E. (2021). Cost escalation in road construction contracts. *Transportation Research Record*, *267*, 1006–1015.

Welde, M., and Klakegg, O. J. (2022). Avoiding cost overrun through stochastic cost estimation and external quality assurance. *IEEE Transactions on Engineering Management*. DOI: 10.1109/TEM.2022.3173175.

Williams, T. M. (2022). Project success (ch. 2). In T. M. Williams, K. Samset, and G. H. Volden, (eds.). *The front-end of large public projects: Paradoxes and ways ahead*. Routledge.

Williams, T. M., Samset, K., and Volden, G. H. (2022). *The front-end of large public projects: Paradoxes and ways ahead*. Routledge.

Worsley, T. (2015). Ex-post assessment of transport investments and policy interventions: Prerequisites for ex-post assessments and methodological challenges. ITF Roundtable Reports, No. 162. Paris: OECD.

Zwikael, O., and Smyrk, J. (2012). A general framework for gauging the performance of initiatives to enhance organizational value. *British Journal of Management*, *23*, 6–22.

Zwikael, O., and Gilchrist, A. (2022). The logic of the project front-end (ch. 3). In M. Williams, K. Samset, and G. H. Volden, (eds.). *The front-end of large public projects: Paradoxes and ways ahead*. Routledge.

Afterword

A Fundamental Problem with Projects or Project Management?

STEWART CLEGG

Introduction

A curious reader of a dictionary that might wish to determine what is a project, will find that it is usually defined in terms of an individual or collaborative enterprise carefully planned to achieve a particular aim. The Project Management Institute (PMI) is a little more specific, defining a project as a sequence of tasks that must be completed to attain a certain outcome in a temporary endeavor with a definite beginning and end. APM's body of knowledge, or other normative guides, such as PRINCE2, are similar. If these authorities are to be believed, by following correct procedures, projects will succeed. Yet, project management has an everyday problem that forms the raison d'être for this book. Project management continues to see the same planning setbacks, over and over again, since error and bias keep creeping into project plans.

Considering the matter of a project with a little more theoretical sophistication, it is worth considering Alfred Schütz's (1967) phenomenological conception of a project. For Schütz, human agency is characterized by projects. These projects have a normative character; they are rule-guided. Our evaluations of states of affairs, as well as of events that disrupt what we take for granted as a state of affairs, and of the meaning of agencies unfolding and remedying these states of affairs, are only meaningful in relation to conceptions of what is normal. Normalization is a process achieved in relation to agency. For any phenomenon there is a range of agential typification of that which is constituted as normal.

Building on Schütz's Temporal Concerns

In considering the notion of human agency projecting forward, temporally, into a future, to achieve a particular aim, as Morujão (2023) suggests, after Schütz (1967), several things need to be considered. Any project has a temporal character. Temporality, as a characteristic of a project, is constituted by the project in a double sense. First, in terms of ebbs and flows in project unfolding rather than the unvarying repetition of routines. Second, in the finitude of the project; at its inception, its temporal ending is already foreseen, already planned, with the hope that it can be achieved according to the plan, a "blueprint," that is, planning-in-practice, as an accomplishment in time and space, will materialize. Between the blueprint and the materiality resides an indeterminacy in which temporality inheres in project consciousness, constituted in communication about what the nature of the project is intended to be. Thus, any project is an expression of problematic intentionality. We can only ever interpret a project's meaning from those signs and symbols that express it. Projects are essentially future-oriented. The unfolding of projects occurs in a future-perfect tense (Pitsis et al., 2003); a plan that is planned in detail in the here-and-now is projected through imagination into a future in which it will have been accomplished. Hence, time is at the center of managing any project. It is what explains the dominance of scheduling as the primary form not only of planning the present but also of committing agencies and resources into the future. Planning involves diverse media of communication between different forms and embodiments of agency, constructed symbolically.

Because the future is always uncertain, any project tackling it typically strives to create and communicate standing conditions for that project. All science occurs in the context of what realist philosophers of science refer to as "standing conditions." These standing conditions provide for the prevalence of the sense that the science makes of the world of object-relations against naturally occurring conditions. A science of objects needs to appear to be context-free; otherwise, it cannot provide a general theory. Standing conditions are definite sets of contextual experimental conditions, such as ensuring a sterile laboratory environment or maintaining a vacuum or a stable temperature. Without these conditions, maintained by the experimentalist, the predicted relations that the research setting seeks to display would not occur. Thus, a context for stable object relations has to be artfully contrived so that the context has no effect other than that sought experimentally.

Any putatively closed system designed in the context of an open future is an act of faith concerning the presence of events that are unforeseen, unknown, or unknowable. Any open future is likely to be marked by the occurrence of events ranging from the known and expected, through the potentially knowable, or those that fall into the category of unknown unknowns. Events are known through temporal units of meaningful communication that strive to make sense of that which has happened (Luhmann, 2012). Networks of recursively linked events of communication construct futures. The contingency of events can engender unexpected evolutions in projects. By definition, events are contingent, as they are neither necessary nor stably apprehended; there is no routine assignment of an event's meaningfulness. Signs and symbols have to be mobilized to make an event meaningful.

Morujão (2023) further suggests that signs and symbols that strive to create closure and order lack *essential* meaning; their meaningfulness inheres in their relational constitution as a communicative sign or symbol. Consider, the totality of the "bill of works," an assemblage of signs and symbols contained in bills of quantities and materials, digital twins, contracts, and other relevant signs and symbols. All of these are communicative devices. To understand them, to appreciate what they mean, takes a combination of trained competencies and implicit understanding of much that is tacit. We might term this combination, inasmuch as it forms a communication system enabling discourse employing a code, situational and contextual theorizing. Our world is composed of fragmented social systems with specific discursive codes and, as Luhmann (1995) shows, such fragmentation makes coordination difficult in a differentiated world of discrete socially situated systems of knowledge and discourse.

Coordination in the world of projects is usually referred to as system integration. In engineering, system integration is usually defined as the process of coordinating component sub-systems into an overall functional system in which each subsystem plays its part. In information systems, doing this entails linking different hardware and software systems to act as a coordinated whole. A system integrator integrates discrete systems. In engineering and information systems what is under consideration is usually machine and software systems. In project management, system integration can never be a wholly material process; it is socio-material.

Sociologically, the codes of system integration require social integration (Lockwood, 1964; Archer, 1996; Clegg, [1989] 2023), a normative universe premised on a world of meaningful communication, according to rules fixing and re-fixing relations of meaning and membership. These rules are not all formal, literal, or concerned with system integration. Those may be termed constitutive rules; these constitutive rules, however, require preferential rules in their mundane enactments. How literally should a specific instruction be interpreted? These questions arise when "the calibration of behaviours is made according to a vague and muddled reference to normative objectives" (Roy, 2024, p. 11). These normative objectives inhabit the world not of systems but social integration. To coordinate the sociomateriality of large complex projects, linking clients, investors, key stakeholders, project organization, and sub-contractor systems, a specific kind of coding is conventional. Conventionally, these codes are known as contracts and in any large complex contract there will be thousands of these codes. What these codes strive to achieve is closure of what is an inherently open system, a system oriented to the production of a specific future that does not yet exist, apart from various imaginaries of what it will become.

Autopoiesis and Coding

For future-oriented projects, the world of project management, it is the organization and management of projects that strives to realize this future-perfect of the project, a future-perfect that reduces the contingency of communication and absorbs uncertainty through planning. The concept of autopoiesis was conceived by Maturana and Varela (1991) as a characteristic of a machine organized as a network of processes of reproduction and transformation of components that interact and transform, continuously regenerating and realizing a network of processes and social relations that produced them, constituting that network in time and space by specifying a self-contained space. These spaces and their temporality are self-contained in the communicative codes that produce them; hence, they are not independent of communication but constituted by it (Luhmann, 2017).

Projects engage a material world of objects, things, and nature. The world is complex and so are major projects, which are characterized by high levels of uncertainty, incomplete control of endogeneity, and a necessary openness to exogeneity in the form of events as unknown unknowns that disrupt project parameters. Hence, projects should be seen as practical experiments whose standing conditions, carefully crafted and planned, cannot always prevail. A project is not a controlled experiment, conducted under strict laboratory conditions. Consequently, any communicatively constitutive system for achieving closure can only ever be a "rough guide" to future prospects. When events occur, as they will, then conditions should encourage creativity and innovation in dealing with them. Again, whether this will ensue cannot be predicted, as it is only ever a retrospective judgment as to whether what elapsed in a project, such that of the Sydney Opera House (Gaim et al., 2022), was a creative triumph or an accounting failure. In fact, it can be constituted as both a creative triumph and as an accounting failure. With sufficient short-termism, the Opera House was an accounting failure, while in the longer-term it was a magnificent aesthetic triumph and a masterpiece of value creation.

The inability to predict accurately does not strike one as surprising although it may be problematic for the agents involved in project delivery, faced with lengthening schedules and escalating costs, as well as changing project parameters. Prediction is possible in closed systems, such as laboratory conditions, but projects are not conducted as closed systems however much agents might try to stabilize closure through the use of binding contracts that are always incomplete. The essences of this lack of completion resides in their indexicality (Clegg, [1975] 2013). No contract can ever stipulate the circumstances of its enactment and interpretation. Incompleteness provides opportunities for human agencies to manage contracts rather than being managed as automatons by contracts as blueprints for action. The combination of openness, indexicality, and the complexity of contractual coding and related devices that strive to limit openness and indexicality, plus the large numbers of stakeholders and interested parties involved in major projects, makes it highly probable that multiple agential interests will be in play in enacting project actions. Consequently, in action designed to deliver materialities, things will change, and these changes will neither preserve past conditions nor those interpretations of these that might once have prevailed. Projects are performances that always include unexpected improvisational enactments (Cunha et al., 2016) rather than just scripted occurrences.

Probable prediction undoubtedly can apply in open systems where nonsymbolic elements are involved, in which, for instance, the effects of interactive variables to cause climate change can be predicted with some accuracy (Steffen et al., 2015). However, it is a chimera in open symbolic systems that are sociomaterially constituted by codes. These codes, taken as just constitutive communication, always run the risk of being treated as explicit in and of themselves – a legally precise set of terms that brook of no implicit meaning, no indexicality in interpretation. These codes strive to be literal and unambiguous, as Wittgenstein (1958) argues when discussing a prototypically coded communication between a foreman and a building laborer. Coding does not handle implicit meanings well; it requires precise terms and assumes a correspondence between words and things. As Roy (2024, p. 101) states, "This is precisely what is required by coding in general. Socialization is secondary and any polysemy, irony or nuance is a source of error." Roy (2024, p. 102) is describing the condition of being on the autism spectrum and in doing so demonstrates that the "need for systematic explanations ... [and] ... indifference to the cultural nature of social codes" is an abnormal form of sociability, one in which everything is a code.

Any project is a communicative constitution of normative expectations about possible futures. As such, this applies both to the practical projects of everyday life and its business, in all its facets, as well as any professional formal theory that reflects on these projects. In Schütz's (1967) view, formal theory, as a recursive social system related to everyday theories, must be able to account for the latter. Specific social systems' communication represents different universes of meaning. Any metatheoretical reflection about the everyday theorizing that is constituting meaning situationally in project design and delivery, creating specific states of affairs, inhabits a double hermeneutic. By this I mean that it is an autopoietic theorization of mundane theorizing that is itself autopoietic in constituting the field to which theoretical practice attends.

Everyday theory comprises common stocks of knowledge, most of which is uncodified, communicated through socialization over the life course. Some is formally pedagogical. The nature of the pedagogy can vary between constitutively state-sanctioned schooling and the preferentially preferred corpuses of knowledge that are legitimated either by the institutions of science or the institution of standards, between which there may well be a difference. Project Management falls into this category of difference, ranging from the PMBOK Guide 2021 to more esoteric theorizing found in collections such as this volume, which, undoubtedly, will become a preferentially constitutive element in the education of future project management scholars.

Project management is a hybrid practice drawing on hybrid knowledge; some is derived from other disciplines such as the various branches of engineering or from accounting and economics as well as other social sciences; some of it draws on the codification of practice that forms the project management body of knowledge. Given that any project is the meeting place of many diverse communication systems interpreting each other's codes in making the future, any complex project is an occasion and meeting ground for many codes in practice and many codes in analysis, as this handbook signifies.

The Impossibility of Closing Open Systems

As noted at the outset, project management has an everyday problem forming the raison d'être for this book. Project management continues to see the same planning setbacks, over and over again, since error and bias keep creeping into project plans. I want to relate this notion of error and bias to the communicative constitution of project management as a codification that seeks to establish standing conditions in and through normative communication oriented to reducing error and bias. Project management as a communicative constitution of an everyday field of action unfolds within a contractual framework and its allied communicative devices that strive to close what is an inherently open system. Creating a closed system in an open field of practice is legislatively impossible because of the role of events.

Whitehead notes that the term "event" is used sometimes in the sense of a nexus of actual entities and sometimes in the sense of a nexus as objectified by universals (See Whitehead, 1985, p. 230). Events have two faces, revealed in the Latin etymology. *Eventum* means the act taking place as seen from inside of the event's unfolding, whereas *eventus* refers to that which has happened when seen from the outside, as a datum whose meaning has been institutionalized. While the former is lodged in the becoming of an event, the latter is elapsed; to be outside of the event means that the event has a significance not evident as it unfolded.

An event cannot be separated from that which it interrupts and there is a constant move between events as process and structure as closure. The structure (as communicative abstraction) is submitted to variations that arise from events. Existing communicative structures unfold and change shape during event occurrences. Formal order is always threatened by the logic of sensemaking that has produced that ordering, as the result of past events, if only because future events, by definition, are unknown. Every form of present ordering will be submitted to a succession of events to come in the future. Closing the system communicatively cannot hold the future and its unfolding events at bay.

An event offers a potential space for action, including inflections of structural rules and design (Linstead & Thanem, 2007). Events can either have been made endogenously meaningful to any putative closed system that is created, or they can exogenously disrupt the normativity on which that closure is premised. In the latter case, their meaningfulness relates to a decentralizing of the structured flow of daily "nonevents" that constitute the routine actions of project organizing. Events generate moments of questioning in which the routine realities of project organizing are rethought and reimagined. It is on these occasions that the moral order of the iron triangle, premised on replication in practice of the communicative sign system as prescribed, as an abstract system of signs and symbols, is potentially disrupted. A moral order requires repetition; it must be enacted again and again to prevail. Any event can potentially deform the structural regularities in which it is embedded. *Thus, the concept of an event relates to both difference and repetition.*

As a putatively closed system in an open field of practice, we should not see failure from the irruption of events as a result of either error in an open system or bias arising from the forms of closure that are attempted but rather see the attribution of either of these as an attempt to maintain the legitimacy of communicative codification as a means of closing inherently open systems. Hence, error and bias as attributes of projects justify further exercises of communicative codification that addresses, theoretically, their communicative codification as an ongoingly flawed project. From this perspective, it matters little which of the "Five Hands" is in play. Each of these five accounts achieves its purpose; it normalizes existential uncertainty about the meaning of things and the meaning of the meaning of abstractions, signs and symbols planning to make a future. They each do so through the application of an ontology that preserves the legitimacy of the overall corpus of theorizing. Each does this through a distinct meta-theorizing about the everyday theorizing of project agents, those implicated in the progressive unfolding of a simulacra of the essentially normative project envisaged in symbolic communicative coding.

Project Practice: The Communicative Constitution of Organization

Contracts as devices are used to control agential behavior and project parameters in an open system. These are inherently uncontrollable because of the limitations of our bounded rationality. While closed systems are easy to control, open systems are not. Confronted by the infinitude of potential openness, project makers strive to design a closed system because of our inability to predict the future and manage its openness. Whatever the plan, expecting deviation should be normal. In project practice, deviation typically means a difference from the coding of contractual commitments. Contractual commitments are a significant part of a communication system that strives to effect closure on the open system of project unfolding. Contracts, as texts, as previously noted, are inherently indexical (Clegg, [1975] 2013) because they cannot provide for their interpretation. Studies that take interpretations as their frame of reference are only ever as ontologically secure as these intersubjective interpretations are stable in situated contexts. In the sphere of projects, all attempts at organized sensemaking rely on the project participants' power to secure this sense. PMBOK, PRINCE2, and other sensemaking devices seek to secure a certain sense. Potentially, any power to do this may be subject to the confounding of the sense being made, defined as a diminished capacity on the part of the actor to maintain the set of standing conditions that, contextually, enabled this power to structure particular episodes in terms of its preferences. Events, as I have argued, can be particularly erosive. Erosion may also derive from the failure of existing imagination on the part of projects as well as from random and arbitrary acts that serve to destabilize the rationality of existing contexts. Rationality is always situational. And because it is always contextually situational it is always implicated with power. No context stands outside power. If that were the case, then it would exist nowhere, outside of understanding, outside of possibility, outside of sense.

Foucault (1977, pp. 27–28) says "power produces knowledge ... power and knowledge directly imply one another ... there is no power relation without the creative constitution of a field of knowledge, nor any knowledge that does not presuppose and constitute at the same time power relations." In such a view, rationalities and powers are fused. Different power actors will operate in and through different rationalities or "institutional logics" (Dille et al., 2021). The different rationalities will have their different rules for producing sense and whose will prevail is most often a matter of power relations. Rather than being law-like phenomena, rules are always constituted locally, in context, by the actors themselves, rather than being the objective instantiation of a general principle or law. Contextualism implies that whatever regularities occur empirically will always be situational rather than the result either of remote laws operating behind the backs of the actors concerned or the result of an idiosyncratic researcher's interpretation of the scene in question. To the extent that the researcher has researched the situational ethics of the context at hand then they will have a sound grasp of the socially and historically conditioned context within which sense is made. With these understandings, researchers can avoid the relativism that they are sometimes charged with. Their understandings will be framed within deeply embedded foundations that the actors find normal and acceptable to use.

Unlike phenomena in an object realm, where the matter at hand has no understanding of itself, actors who possess understanding always populate projects. Their understanding extends both to an appreciation of each other as well as those artifacts that they constitute (which sometimes constitute them – for instance, a machine operator) and with which they interact. Thus, projects are always sociomaterial realms. Projects are somewhat like the cities they change; they are organic, constantly recreating themselves, tearing out the present heart and soul, routing new freeways through the existing geography, creating new aesthetics that overwhelm but never entirely eradicate the old, leaving traces of lost realities, past triumphs, and buried beliefs. Having no static essence, the city can never truly be represented cartographically any more than projects can ever be truly represented statistically. A city exists, with a history embedded in its being there and buried in its constant becoming. All cities have their dramas chronicled by their admirers and detractors, pointing out their triumphs and their errors, the errors most often being attributed to the result of past projects. Attribution of such errors in projects, residing in textual formulation, interpretation, or implementation, cannot be established other than retrospectively, in the wake of some triggering event, which serves as a stimulus for a judgment to be determined through some form of deliberation and decision. Judgment is always a matter of language and communication.

The theoretical approach that comes closest to being able to make sense of project organizing and its errors and successes is that which sees project organizing constituted in and through human communication. Much influenced by Luhmann, a perspective coined as the CCO approach (for Communicative Constitution of Organization, see Cooren et al., 2011) has developed in recent years in organization studies. Communication is the means by which project organizing is accomplished, ongoing and precarious accomplishments realized, experienced, and identified in communication processes that are "tiled" on top of one another and drawn upon in distributed sites in the conduct of coordinated activity through decision-making. Decision-making becomes paradoxical because it is a complexity-reducing mechanism that creates greater complexity for subsequent organizational decision-making and nondecision-making. Increasing complexity occurs as project processes unfold because decisions display contingency with respect to option for choice; thus, decisions resist closure and any final decidability. Project organizing constantly requires decisions to align its communicative constitution with its empirical unfolding in process, especially as events occur. It is only in and from the ongoing processes of interaction and its heuristics that organization emerges. If we really want to understand project organizing, its alleged biases and errors, we must be there, ethnographically, in the Project Management Office (PMO) and elsewhere where these things are constituted as such (Clegg, [1975] 2013), or marshal the historical and narrative skills of a Robert Caro (1974) in charting how the dominance of one person, Robert Moses, the "planning czar" of New York City for much of the twentieth century, could shape the city and the thinking of urban planners elsewhere, as well as their critics (Jacobs, 1961).

The Battlefield of Project Success and Failure

The nature of project success and failure has become a scholarly battlefield. As Kreiner (2020) argues, projects always entail risks, as the uncertainties and difficulties that will unfold in future-making cause people to take more significant risks than they intend. To attribute an initial bias or distortion to project failures in terms of cost, schedule, and benefits is to propose that professionals routinely behave in ways that are unprofessional. We know that sometimes they might; we do not know that nearly always they will. A post-hoc rationalization that if initial plans are not realized, then individuals' cognitive processes must be responsible is hardly illuminating, whether the attribution be to human bias or error. There is frequently little evidence connecting presumed biases to the project processes that ensue. Causal paths can only be constructed retrospectively, when errors can be accounted, such as the implications of changing scope, inflation, and capabilities for dealing with them but bias, as a putative mental state, cannot. Project processes create futures that are always invariably unpredictable in all their features; organizations plan to try to minimize these, but in the face of unique and complex projects unfolding over time and encountering unknown variables, it is hardly surprising if plans have to be altered, improvisations made, costs accrued, and futures altered. To assume that these occur as a result of inbuilt biases on the part of those who plan, practice, and process projects is another matter, one of sometimes dubious attribution, other than through legal process.

The world of major projects is paradoxical in that project failure in terms of cost, schedule, and benefits happens repeatably, not because of a conspiracy of bias making for bad planning or error in delivering otherwise sound plans, but because such projects have innate risks that even the best planning and project management cannot predict. TBMs get stuck and sinkholes open, not necessarily because of error, but because of a lack of human omniscience or its obverse, an abundance of human ignorance. In open systems, with infinite variables, prediction is a chimera and paradox an ever-present possibility. What is important is how paradox is used: is it as something to be suppressed in the light of plans made in partial ignorance of the events defining the present situation or as an opportunity for creativity, ingenuity and paradoxical idea work? We can only know this through close attention to the organizational constitution of communication. One way of gaining this wisdom is through ethnoventionist research (van Marrewijk et al., 2010; van Marrewijk & van den Ende, 2022), "shadowing" (Czarniawska, 2007) a project through its meetings, in its PMO and indeed, wherever the project leads that can be followed. Exercises such as that of Flyvbjerg's (1998) odyssey of planning in Aalborg in Denmark show the worth of such intimate knowing.

Flyvbjerg's book, *Rationality and power: Democracy in practice* (1998), was impressive and interesting, a detailed ethnographic case study of the complex politics of an urban renewal project in Aalborg, Denmark, that used a large variety of data sources over a long period of time. Flyvbjerg's (1998) study of planning in Aalborg was based on many thousands of hours of data, collected over many years of dedicated empirical inquiry in official documents, media reports, unofficial inquiries, surveys, and whatever sources of information could be accessed. A simple plan for a new bus station became a saga that unfolded over a decade of decision-making and nondecision-making, contestation, and struggle between different interests.

Later, Flyvbjerg published *Making social science matter: Why social inquiry fails and how it can succeed again* (Flyvbjerg, 2001). The main argument of the book is an attack on "physics envy" and a promotion of "phronesis," an Aristotelian term, referring to a discipline that is pragmatic, variable, context-dependent, based on practical rationality, and inherently unlaw-like. Phronesis, as practical wisdom, is expounded both theoretically and in relation to projects in Africa with which Flyvbjerg has been engaged. In retrospect, one can see phronesis clearly in the pages of the 1998 book. The urban planning saga associated with the Aalborg bus station redevelopment was a long and complex exercise in decision-making whose rationality was always context dependent because, as Wittgenstein (1972) demonstrated, no rule could ever account for its own interpretation – thus, context cannot be reduced to rules.

Of course, some practices, such as accounting, are entirely rule-bound. The accounting statistics at its completion judged the Opera House the most spectacularly failed megaproject of all time. Sixty years later, the Opera House is inseparable from the city and its conflicts, its power struggles over real estate, its aesthetic imagining of its possibilities, as well as its history, are of no consequence. It is organic, contested, and peopled, a space for human possibilities, impossible dramas, overweening ambitions, and great tragedy. Allowing the case narrative of the Sydney Opera House to "unfold from the diverse, complex and sometimes conflicting stories that people, documents and other evidence tell ... leaves ample scope for readers to make different interpretations and to draw diverse conclusions" (Flyvbjerg, 2001, p. 86). Hence, the possibility of multiple interpretations is admitted and structured into the accounting that one does. As Flyvbjerg (2001, p. 166) stresses, "we must drop the fruitless efforts to emulate natural science's success in producing cumulative and predictive theory; this approach simply does not work in social science."

In a later book with Gardener (Flyvbjerg & Gardener, 2023), Flyvbjerg distills success in terms of projects into a simple rule of combining slow planning and fast action, arguing that this is best attained in modular and scalable projects. On these criteria, as remarked earlier, all but five reference class of projects are predicted to fail, over and over, again. Which version of Flyvbjerg is preferable will become evident subsequently. In making his later argument, Flyvbjerg was explicitly criticizing Hirschman's (1967) view of the "Hiding Hand," a criticism that in some respects triggered the central debate with which this book is concerned. It is to this that we next turn.

The Central Debate

Against the Planning Fallacy advocated by Flyvbjerg and others, there is an opposing view that has become known as the "Hiding Hand," based on Hirschman (1967), a view that has most recently been argued for by Kreiner (2020). In Chapter 1, by Lavagnon Ika, he recounts what he characterizes as the rise and fall of the "Planning Fallacy" or the "Malevolent Hand," a view of the reasons for project success or failure that is opposed to that of the "Hiding Hand." The Planning Fallacy denotes the tendency for forecasts of project schedules, costs, and benefits to be unrealistically close to best-case scenarios. The agents involved in projecting projects engage in "optimism bias," perhaps in order to gain assent for the legitimacy of a project that might not otherwise be acceded to but which, as it unfolds, exceeds its project cost and/or schedule significantly. Bias is an abstraction that depends on a conception of statistical deviation from a norm. Events happen; things change, drifting the project away from its initial symbolic constitution and creating new significance, symbols, and meanings through autopoiesis. Bias can always be assigned to these changes post hoc. Attribution of optimism bias cannot be known other than by retrospection that attributes it to outcomes that do not correspond to those projected, an attribution that cannot be empirically tested because its causal mechanism is defined as agential intentionality. The latter is essentially unknowable other than through agent's accounts, which are hardly likely to be confirmatory and that cannot be trusted as anything other than accounts, irrespective of their content. They certainly do not index intentionality as a prior causal mechanism. It could be argued, as Flyvbjerg and Gardener (2023) do, that planning slowly and using reference class forecasting to do so will shield agents from committing to improbable project optimism as a bias. It might well do so, but it would also institutionalize a conservatism in launching large-scale complex projects because all but five of a substantial number of reference categories have ever been deemed "successful" by these authors. These are solar, wind power, thermal, energy transmission and road construction projects. If all projects have to conform to the reference class of success, future-building looks to be very restricted indeed.

To assume probability in a complex and open system, as Ika et al. (2022) argue, one where unknown unknowns are always likely, is to assume a degree of faith in one's convictions that is likely to blindside one to uncertainties. Against an excessive reliance on a statistical analysis of risks, Ika et al. (2022) suggest that heuristics are better tools. There is one overarching reason why heuristics may be better tools. The reason is that a heuristic is not a statistical device but a communication device, one that is founded on project experience (Wenzel & Stjerne, 2021). And one thing that seasoned project managers share is a considerable degree of project-based experience in which they have been party to much project organizational storytelling. Heuristics thus become a part of a communication system, in which experienced project managers and leaders can draw on their cache of stories to make sense of events. A heuristic taps into everyday theorizing, everyday storytelling, the stuff lived experience. A project may be constituted by a communication system of planning, contracting, and engaging but all this is put in place, usually, long before its doings. These doings will involve complex technical rationalities and sociomaterialities that are brought into being by the project as a communication system of signs and symbols, but their sociomateriality is real and fallible. Cranes topple, Tunnel Boring Machines become stuck, and operatives sicken.

Each of the views of the Five Hands that Ika et al. (2022) advance is flawed in this analysis, although, admittedly, the Fifth Hand is least flawed but also the least theoretically well-constituted. That is, it is correct insofar as what it says, but it lacks a theoretical account of how what it says is possible. The pragmatic consideration of projects as complex, messy processes, as plural and paradoxical, is indeed concordant with the argument that I have made but it lacks theoretic motive power. Projects attempt system closure in a resolutely open field of events. Such events are not errors; to see them as such suggests they are a deviation from what was expected, for which some agency may be held responsible. Events are the irruption of unknown unknowns, whose meaningfulness confounds the immediacy of not knowing they would be manifest. My argument, to restate it, is that any project is a clash between an attempt at system closure in a resolutely open field in which events will disrupt the closed system that the communicative constitution of the project conjures. Conjuring does not always create the appropriate illusion and there may be many contingent events that serve to create disillusion. We should expect that such disillusion is likely to be the case with large complex projects with many stakeholders interpreting the symbols and significations that constitute the project in which many events of the "unknown unknowns" variety are anticipatable as disruptors of the assumptions of the closed system.

The discussion launched by Ika in Chapter 1 is continued in Chapter 2 by Graham Room. A number of critiques made by Flyvbjerg of Hirschman's "Hiding Hand" approach are skillfully and elegantly neutralized. Hirschman was not a "sloppy" researcher; he investigated a small number of projects at first hand; Flybvjerg has a database of many projects, but the data is impersonal in that little or none of it is derived from fieldwork familiarity. Flyvbjerg draws on the legitimacy of major figures in behavioral psychology, associated with the ideas of Daniel Kahneman (2011) while Flyvbjerg and Sunstein (2016) only "engage fleetingly with questions of power." For the author of *Rationality and power: Democracy in practice,* this fleetingness might seem peculiar. In this earlier book, Flyvbjerg is much closer to the strategic approach to power, deriving from Machiavelli, than to that associated with Dahl's (1959) behavioral science approach, as I have drawn these distinctions elsewhere (Clegg, [1989] 2023).

Hirschman seems more allied to the fecund spirits of March's (2008) creative approach to a "technology of foolishness" or the "muddling through" of Lindblom (1959) than to Flyvbjerg and Gardener's (2023) dictum of planning slowly and acting fast. Flyvbjerg's earlier work was acutely aware of politics in planning but in his criticisms of Hirschman he seems to have forgotten their role. Still, Flyvbjerg is confident that the first year of any project is sufficient to predict how it may transpire, however long the elapsed time takes to reach that point where it is considered done. Perhaps Flyvbjerg is not familiar with Gersick's (1988) concept of punctuated equilibrium, that roughly halfway point where a project team regroups to drive to project completion. Perhaps, because it is based on small team research, it is not relevant, although one might think small teams were closer to project practices than the cognitions of individual decision-making. Hirschman seems closer to Gersick's ideas; lots of muddling, lots of strategy, lots of uncertainty. As Room concludes, the notion of responsibility that is essential to vocation a la Weber, differs markedly between the two approaches, especially, one might add, when we ask the key question: Responsible for what to whom? Think of this question as a balancing act between the costs in the here-and-now and the legacy for the future. The latter is a matter of phronesis and should be a concern for policymakers, while the former is primarily a concern for accountants. Room characterizes a dichotomy existing between Flybvjerg's positivism and Hirschman's humanism; however, if the comparison was with Flyvbjerg (2001), with its stress on phronesis, would the comparison have been quite different?

Setting Realistic Project Goals and Heuristics

Zwikael et al. (Chapter 13) are concerned with how to identify realistic major project goals. Project goals, they argue, are unrealistic when underestimated prior to a project's commencement (e.g., project life cycle cost) and/or overestimated beyond the target benefits that expertise evaluates. The latter are frequently and recurrently common due to "ambition, a lack of knowledge, uncertainty, the planning fallacy, cognitive bias, errors, invalid assumptions, political pressure and strategic misrepresentation." Projects can be said to have failed when they do not meet project goals; hence, it is the initial future perfect projection of a goal to be achieved that determines whether a project is successful. Hence, success is not a matter of what occurs in the project but whether what occurs in the project meets the outcomes initially projected.

What can create this disjuncture, leading to project failure? Factors at the individual, project, and environmental level. Individually, cognitive bias may pertain to a lack of success. Cognitive bias is defined as cases where "human cognition reliably produces representations that are systematically distorted compared to some aspect of objective reality" (Haselton et al., 2015, p. 968). How cognitive bias can exist in relation to a projected outcome that is not existentially real, a yet to be completed project, is unclear. Indeed, it seems that what one might think to be the case is not so. Each of the three cognitive biases (*optimism, endowment, and anchoring bias*) that are explored is not concerned with project outcomes but project initiation, seen retrospectively from the perspective of a project already deemed unsuccessful in terms of goal achievement. Some other theory suggests ten biases exist (Flyvbjerg, 2021). In each of the cases, whether the biases are three or ten, the bias is and can only be known and attributed after the event of the project is complete. Thus, the bias is an effect of the project's completion while conceptually it is also assumed to be a cause of it. Readers may find this a strange conception of causality, in which effects are causes; I certainly do. It seems a case of post hoc rationalization rather than an attempt at theorizing failure of goal achievement, on the lines of *the project was a failure, these are common accounts of why projects fail, this account seems to be the likely case.*

As evidence, one might conclude that reasoning that is highly circumstantial is hardly sufficient to elicit conviction. Rather, one might say, there are a number of available accounts that are widely known and shared among scholars premised on accounts that accrue out of practice as well as, in some cases, being embedded in theoretical reflections on practice, drawing on psychology and other behavioral sciences. Thinking sociologically, one cannot see how these accounts, which exist as explanations of what happened in the past, can be taken as anything other than accounts, rather than causes. That these accounts are rated as plausible by expertise in relation to seven major projects, all deemed unsuccessful in achieving project goals, simply attests to the availability of plausible accounts; it does not constitute a causal explanation.

The discussion concludes with a list of ten practices that can contribute to effective goal appraisal; all of these suggestions are sensible but theoretically many of them suffer from the same flaws in reasoning as those already alluded to. Factors such as the unreliability of data, the invalidity of assumptions, risk costs, etc., can only be known after the event of the project's completion. However, the completion of a project is hardly the most significant of the many events that attend any project's unfolding and any of these many events may be those unknown unknowns that will damn the project as less successful than it should have been. Creating a project goal, defining it in terms of factors such as cost, schedule, and value of the completed project, will always be a risky business. Still, when the results are in, it is useful to have plausible accounts available for retrospective sensemaking. However, it should be clear that a retrospective account of things that went wrong has considerable difficulty in being a causal factor; it only explains after the fact and thus is not terribly useful for those deeply involved in the project process who cannot know in the moment what it is that they are doing or not doing that will have what effects in the future. However, experienced project managers and observers may well have a rough and ready calculus of heuristics that are likely to have worked in the past and that may, if events are propitious, work in the present, but they can only ever know in the future.

The autoethnography by Mahalingam (Chapter 16) supports the heuristic view and also suggests that a reconceptualization of error may be in order. He states, "It was the emergence of new information, particularly geotechnical, that led to errors in the original plans, and the consequent reorganization of work that led to the observed outcomes." Considering this statement, what is error? Error is identified as the absence of information at the time that the plans were completed. How can something that was an unknown unknown at the inception stage be an error? An error is a measure of the estimated difference between the observed or calculated value of a quantity and its true value. In this instance, however, the "true value" could not have been known without the geotechnical survey; how could the geotechnical survey, occurring after the plans and in the process of delivering on them, have led to errors in the original plans? The original plans were not in error based on what was known at the time that that they were decided. There might have been error in not having sufficient information at the planning stage but that will never be the case because it is only through the materialization of the project that one can begin to determine what "sufficient" means in this unique context. There is no standard measure of sufficiency that can be used to plot a deviation as error; the deviation from what was planned only becomes evident as the project's materiality unfolds. The plans were not in error, based on what was known, when they were formulated.

The disorganization of the trades' multiple presences on the site toward completion was not an error; it was an event that occurred that had consequences of delay, in part caused by the well-known patterning of temporal activity by tradespeople as one job winds down and another starts up. At the time of planning, the likelihood of the market and opportunities for trades to be tied up in other projects could not be known any more certainly than could the future state of the monsoons, the resources of the well water, or any other events. These are not errors; an error is a technical term for a measure of the estimated difference between the observed or calculated value of a quantity and its true value. Events are not errors because they are fundamentally unknowable until they occur. Only through their becoming can the true value of their being be known. Project hubris might try to plan a perfect closed system in which errors will not occur, but any realist should realize that such hubris will be misplaced. This does not mean that we should not plan; we should plan, but we should not be unduly surprised if reality surprises our plans. It is not surprising; what is surprising is that planners of projects should be surprised by events. Of course, based on experience, as Mahalingam suggests, projects go through phases and there may well be patterning to the various kinds of projects that can inform heuristics. Heuristically, all projects should come with a bold warning that any variation will impose costs; however, many years' familiarity with television programs such as Grand Designs suggests that such a covenant would not change minds that only begin to appreciate what is unfolding as it unfolds and that clients only gain a realistic – that is, actual knowledge – of the costs accruing as they proceed. Once started, a project cannot be reversed; if it is to be completed, once underway, the blank slate is being inscribed and what is written cannot be predicted precisely, if only because precise prediction is only possible in closed systems with stable standing conditions, and most projects do not meet these criteria. Rather, as Vine and colleagues suggest (Chapter 3), they are "voyages of discovery." As the history of megaprojects constantly reminds those who chronicle these things, voters, elected officials, stakeholders, shareholders, and critics enrolled and opposed to these projects will find that a final bill will always fall due, often as an event so momentous that its accounting, in the sociological sense, has to marshal as much practical rationality as talk of error or bias will permit. In the final analysis, all accounts are social constructions.

Voyages of Discovery and Disruptions to Understanding

To regard a major project as a voyage of discovery is a conceit likely to terrify most project management consultancies. Lenfle and Loch (2017) have argued that major projects do their best to avoid uncertainty through stressing stage-gate reviews that match progress against plans and costs against budgets. Deviations are to be deplored despite the fact that is through deviance that learning often occurs. One consequence, as Vine et al. argue, is that innovation is discouraged; innovation introduces uncertainty because it is not part of a planned outcome, by definition. Planning drives out innovation in most cases, a point made at the dawn of the twentieth century by Max Weber, in noting the rigidity and limits of a purely technical rationality.

Against a fixation on project management as an overly rationalized enterprise steered by managerial controls, Vine et al., drawing on project practice in the successful Heathrow T5 project, point to the importance of distributed democratic deliberation in delivering highly complex projects on budget, scope, and time, an insight reinforced by the experience of the construction of a key piece of Sydney 2000 Olympic infrastructure by Pitsis et al. (2003). There, leadership was collective, with rotating responsibilities for key performance indicators, which served as an effective way of both promoting organizational learning and facilitating social integration across functionally divided systems. A cultural design that stressed that alliance project partners should do "whatever's best for project" in the Olympic case (Clegg et al., 2002) and in which there was a risk/reward incentive structure encouraging innovation in meeting all the KPIs was mirrored in many respects in T5. In the latter, plans did not inhibit innovation but served as aids to learning that facilitated it. In terms used elsewhere, a more "socialized leadership" model prevailed (Whyte et al., 2022) rather than the more standard models of leadership derived from conventional leadership studies (Clegg et al., 2025). It should be clear that project delivery is not highly pre-codified in such approaches to innovative projects but is something that unfolds in a dialogue with and around such prefigurative coding as is present. Critical conversations, rather than scripted conformance, become the norm.

Deviance from codes, or as Pinto and Usher (Chapter 17) terms it, their disruption, is an ever-present possibility in major complex projects. Indeed, the more complex the codification, the greater the probability of events disrupting it, creating deviations from plans. Counterfactually, the more complex the codification the more fragile it becomes because there are many more opportunities for potential indexicality in interpretation, many more variables over which control is assumed, and many more occasions for interested parties' interests not to align. As Taleb (2012) argues, more simply coded systems beat more complexly coded systems because the former provide more room for maneuver, learning, innovation, and recovery when events cause deviance and disruption. Pinto and Usher argue that projects as systems have an originally posited value that should be remedially protected as projects play out, creating resilience in terms of returning to normal, or demonstrating their fragility if events destabilize them, while if events provide opportunity to lead in new directions they become "antifragile," creating more value than that originally posited.

The crucial question, however, is value for whom, a question that they do not ask. Projects have many stakeholders and projects that deliver value for some constituencies of stakeholding such as investors, or project owners may have project outcomes that deliver value for users such as the communities that use or are affected by it. A major public private partnership in Sydney has delivered a new motorway system called Westconnex, that will undoubtedly deliver long-term value to stakeholders, such as its monopoly capital owners, Transurban, and its investors, as well as being produced with minimal risk to government finances. However, in prioritizing the flow of tolled traffic and squeezing 10 lanes of non-tolled traffic into four lanes, it has delivered extreme adverse value to about 80,000 motorists a day whose journeys to work have lengthened from about 15 minutes to an hour as a result of changes to the road system.[1] Value for the many was not considered over profit for investors and the relatively few using the new toll system. Value has to be defined in terms of who benefits and the worth of value is not restricted to definition by project sponsors, owners, or investors.

Strategic Alignments, Stakeholders, and Governance

Uncertainty, and coping with it, is one of the strongest tropes of organizational contingency theory and is also frequently encountered in project studies. Martinsuo and Tuominen (Chapter 8) are no exception in their charting of uncertainty's sources and projects coping, which in classical contingency fashion they relate to the organization size. Their focus is on innovation project portfolios facing uncertainty that arises from the environment, parent organization's complexity, and individual projects. Environment is not conceptualized as such but is a list of exogenous factors likely to be troubling for project portfolio management. Organizational complexity is likewise not conceptualized but comprises a list of factors, many of which have substantial literatures dedicated to them in the broader field of organization studies, which do not show up in this context. Individual projects may vary in terms of the parameters of time, cost and quality, as well as the assessment of these and the complexity associated with them.

COVID-19 features in the discussion as an extreme event that had an impact on the project portfolios of five organizations researched. In the organization theory literature, COVID-19 would be known as an environmental jolt, explanatory theoretical frameworks for the study of which have been much cited, but not in this chapter (Meyer, 1982; Meyer et al., 1990). In the terms of Donaldson (1987), such environmental jolts are one of many causes for organizations to perform

[1] Sean Tarek Goodwin, Rozelle interchange traffic chaos warnings were ignored, NSW upper house inquiry told, ABC News. www.abc.net.au/news/2024-04-10/rozelle-interchange-inquiry-traffic-chaos-warnings-ignored/103690990.

a structural adjustment to regain fit, a strategic realignment in terms of the chapter. Had the chapter discussed the range of similar ideas to their own to be found in the neighboring discipline of organization studies what is an interesting but descriptive account of strategic realignment in the world of project portfolios could have drawn on a relevant field of practice. The unfortunate segmentation that seems to separate many contributions in project management from those in management and organization studies, more generally, serves only to weaken the field. There is sophisticated discussion in cognate fields and a little trade would be fruitful.

Davis et al. (Chapter 9) discuss stakeholder theory, defining it as concerned with who has input in decision-making as well as with who benefits from the outcomes of such decisions. As might be implied by some earlier remarks, one might regard this as a far too restricted view. The crucial question is who benefits, with the implication being that where there are beneficiaries there may well also be those adversely effected; are they not stakeholders as well, if the value of their being is diminished? This is not to adopt a zero-sum view of stakeholding because there may well be beneficiaries whose gain is not the cause of some others' loss. The project processes and outcomes create the winners and the losers, with neither gaining nor losing at the others' expense. These stakeholders need not only be humans; they may be other fauna as well as fora. Clearly then, I do not consider stakeholders only in terms of those that Davis et al. define as primary because they are contractually connected to the project. I am considering secondary stakeholders, especially those that act in the name of mute species such as nonhuman animals and ecologies for which projects often have significant potential. Such stakeholders frequently define their participation in projects through their resistance to them. Just as projects may use reference class forecasting to be forewarned about likely troubles for cost and schedule so they might also use it to consider stakeholders that are overlooked but potentially significant. In addition, they might want to conduct strict ecological and civil management surveys of any territory in which they are going to make an impact in order to plan to minimize harm and maximize benefits. Local knowledge and advice can be channelled in ways that are project productive and that lead to less subsequent resistance, an implicit message of new stakeholder theory and one that informs the latter part of the chapter. One aspect of stakeholders that is not addressed in the chapter is the ways in which social media and web-based communication may be a useful tool of project governmentality (Ninan et al., 2020, 2021).

A further discussion of stakeholders by Fran Ackermann (Chapter 5) starts from a paradox perspective, an influential approach in contemporary management and organization studies (Berti et al., 2021; Gaim et al., 2022, 2024). Posing three questions about the uncertain identity of stakeholders, concerning who they are, how to engage them, and when to involve them, she suggests that there are complexities, "relating to process (recognizing the socio-political considerations), complexities relating to content management (dealing with the extensive, interconnected, and often competing issues and values), and dynamic complexity (reflecting the shifts in personnel and norms)." Part of the reason for these complexities might be that these complexities display a potentially paradoxical state of contradiction between these elements that is persistent. Dalcher (2020, p. 3) identifies a key part of the paradox being consideration of doing "business without ethics or ethics without business," in consideration of issues raised by the increasing press of claims for corporate social responsibility and environmental, social, and governance factors.

In addressing who stakeholders might be, various matrix, network, and web analyses are suggested as aids. All the presumed stakeholders are humans. This is not adequate; social scientists increasingly recognize the posthuman condition as appropriate, one in which the human is not considered to be at the center of the conceptual universe. The awareness of anthropocentric climate change has led to a realization that human centeredness is threatening life on Earth in its many forms and that present and future calculations of science need to be post-anthropocentric, which entails adopting a position of posthumanism – hence a convergence of post-humanism and post-anthropocentrism (deVaunjay et al., 2024). An ontology that places the human at the supreme center of being, consigning other forms of life to exclusion, is replaced by an enhanced sense of the connection of social, psychic, ecological, and planetary relations creating a shared living space (Gheradi et al., 2024).

Posthumanism changes the politics of uncertainty that projects confront. Coping with uncertainty underlines most stakeholder analysis, in which coping means eliminating or neutralizing phenomena. In the past, where these phenomena were nonhuman, such as flora and nonhuman fauna, coping with uncertainty about them was accomplished through non-consideration. In a posthuman/post-Anthropocene ontology, lack of consideration in regard to Anthropocene and that which is other-than-human is not optional. Projects in the material world, such as major pieces of infrastructure, have a material impact. Some stakeholders do not have voice. Some are yet to be human, future generations; others lack voice by virtue of being nonhuman or dead. The material past of burial and sacred sites are conduits to our pasts that actors in the present sometimes demand are worthy of respect. Being voiceless does not mean that the future can be ignored or that present nonhuman entities be dismissed from consideration. For one thing, the voiceless find representation in social organization such as Friends of the Earth, or local social groups that organize to save a species or habitat. Considering who are stakeholders and which need to be attended to is something that should be scoped in advance, which might entail bringing new competencies into the portfolio of project management, as Ackermann notes in relation to Juukan Gorge (Wensing, 2021; Clegg & Ninan, 2024). The politics of uncertainty in these circumstances is less about controlling or coping with uncertainty to diminish it and more with enlarging the sphere of uncertainty in order to make concern with it a "big tent," one whose erection is planned before materiality is physically engaged. As Ackermann realizes, this project managing will increase complexity, but it should minimize the range of dissenting "informal" stakeholders, and it will reduce control over decision-making, which, paradoxically, is both a necessary and a good thing, because it socializes project leadership (Whyte et al., 2022; Clegg et al., 2023), placing it in a world of knowledge that is reflexive about being part of the Anthropocene.

These ideas are advanced significantly in the latter part of Maude Brunet's exposition (Chapter 10) of Actor Network Theory in her contribution to this handbook. To cut to the core of the argument, projects as bundles of practices (Schatzki, 1996, 2002) are actants formed through temporary action nets that connect people, processes, materialities, and technologies (Pollack & Clegg, 2023). The project life cycle has its rhythms and what Vaagaasar et al. (2020) term temporal shifts, some of which are punctuated by reactive or proactive turning points, with the latter being seen as a turn with more potential benefit. Some of these turns can be across the range of governance as hierarchical, heterarchical, or network, as Brunet suggests. It can also be seen in a range of governmentalities, as Clegg and Ninan (2024, p. 8) argue. These range through *contract*, where high-trust professionals will enjoy governmentality, as management through their professional freedoms; through *alliancing*, where governmentality is extended to all employees, contractors, and sub-contractors, through a designed culture; through *influence*, where social media enrolls interests to the projects' progress, seeking to translate them to the project interests; by *co-optation*, where resistance to projects is countered by co-opting the resistors into the organization's governance structures; by *incorporation*, where those in the project ecology that might otherwise have suffered from and resisted the project are incorporated in its design from the outset. The latter form of governmentality requires prior planning, in what is known as the project front-end, through the use of participatory planning using agent-based models (Levy et al., 2016) as scenarios and incorporation of those deemed critical to the project in its oversight at the planning stage.

Of course, as with all ideal types, these are not "pure" and one would expect to see hybridity in practice and in process, as shifts occur. From a posthumanist perspective, governmentality by incorporation from the outset affords more opportunities for beneficial outcomes across the board and, to the extent that it will minimize resistance and maximize social license, it should diminish significant realms of possible complexity. The trick is, as Brunet recognizes, to see the project as a material actant mobilizing actors, actants, and resources in a specific context and temporality, in an open system whose standing conditions are constantly shifting.

Chapter 7 by Ralf Müller provides a systematic overview of the topic of governance. Couched in terms quite different from those of Brunet, it focuses on the behavior of actors in and around projects, as well as of the project as itself an actant typified by a system's dynamic and behaviors perspective, in pursuit of the "broadening of levels of analysis" that Geraldi and Söderlund (2018, p. 58) describe. To return to where the afterword started, with the phenomenology of Schütz, one would want to suggest that the notion of behavior, as an objectivist conception, should instead be seen in terms of social action that is made meaningful by the sensemaking that actors both in and around the project render as salient. This is a basic distinction made by Schütz (1979) in his discussion of Weber's (1978) concept of social action. The meaning of a social action may be stipulated by the interested observer but must also take into consideration the accounts that subjects themselves make. These accounts cannot be given any primary legitimacy for they are merely indices of what is plausible and socially, contextually available. Rarely would one expect different observer and observed accounts to align other than in a highly coded institutional context. In multi-institutional contexts, in which many megaprojects unfold, such communicatively common constitution of sensemaking through professional norms is unlikely. Such sensemaking will be oriented to the project as an actant, the actants it encompasses and affects, as well as the actors that comprise and contest it, and interpretation will be launched from many different angles. Governance is always of subjects and objects; the extent to which the subjects are treated as objects varies with the project governmentality.

Critical Subjects, Objects, and Events

The constitution of critical subjects and objects by projects occurs in the project front-end (PFE); where it does not occur there, it is likely to irrupt later, affecting project practices or outcomes at a later date. Harrison et al. (Chapter 15) regard the PFE as the time when the formal rules referring to contractual governance mechanisms and relational normative governance mechanisms establish project coordination and control. In contradistinction to their analysis of macro, meso, and micro levels, one would want to propose that the project, as an actant, exhibits a flat ontology. Moreover, it is one in which the relations of system integration through the contractual codes of relational governance often exist in tension with normative social integration, an insight as old as Fox's (1974) *Beyond Contract: Work, Power and Trust Relations*. Where trust is low, the contractual coding will be high, lessening trust further as the codes of control become denser; where normative social regulation premised on trust is high, the contractual coding can be lower. There is an inverse relationship between contract and its non-contractual normative elements, so it is hardly surprising that "while contractual control is more effective in mitigating opportunism, relational control is more effective in improving relationship performance." The more complex the contractual coding the more opportunities for indexical interpretation to lower trust further between the contracting parties, creating inflexible project options hindering project innovation (Cantarelli & Genovese, 2023). The relations between the two forms of integration, if not inverse, will be paradoxical. Where the inverse relation is highly loaded on the power side of the equation and is low on the normative side, what Harrison and colleagues refer to as project misbehaviors, have a higher probability of occurring.

Van Oorschot et al. (Chapter 6) report on a project in which ostensive control passed from the oversight of the project manager to three sub-projects as the project elapsed and the sub-projects acquired different temporalities and rates of problems, which, given the overall relative lack of visibility that the project manager had of the three sub-projects, led to the assumption that the average progress was satisfactory. The difficulties in maintaining oversight are indicative of the need to socialize project leadership as Whyte and her colleagues suggest – in this case by replacing the hierarchy with a leadership group that encompasses all three sub-projects. Van Oorschot focuses on the *quantity* of problems in the analysis; she might also have suggested focusing on the *quality* of the problems, in the ways that they ranged from being of severe to little concern for project KPIs in terms of project sensemaking.

Sticking with the theme of different project temporalities, Langley and McGivern (Chapter 4), reaffirm the insight of Bansal et al. (2022) that project management necessarily embeds "temporal work" that individually, collectively, or organizationally strives to frame temporal assumptions or structures shaping project action. Their perspective, by focusing on temporal work in a process approach to projects enables the field of project studies to make many fruitful connections with the broader field of organization studies and the flowering of process rather than the more static variance approaches of project management. Temporal work can be variably oriented toward temporal closure or temporal ambiguity. In the former, time is tight and tightly policed as "timelines"; in the latter, the future endpoint for project completion is subject to events taking their toll, whether derived from variables exogenous to the project system or arising from its political practices, processes, and tensions. Timelines function as performative boundary objects for scheduling, synchronizing, and allocating tasks in relation to project temporalities that are constituted as obligatory passage points (Clegg, 2023) – at least until some event or events, or just the passage of time on a slower schedule than anticipated, causes their temporal redefinition, often with implications for other obligatory passage points, such as budgeted costs control or completion date. The process is then one of a dialectic between what is planned and what occurs in practice, where practice is emergent rather than scripted according to project codes. Events disrupt codes, especially the more tightly they are prescribed. Looser prescription, for instance, through heterarchy rather than hierarchy, allows more relative autonomy in interpretation, redundancy, and coupling of codes and practices. As the complexity of projects increases and with it the probability of temporally disruptive events occurring, the dominant authorities in power relations play a dominant role in defining priorities and coding responses to disruptions, creating downward pressure on those that have to manage shifting temporalities in practice, often with toxic results (Clegg et al., 2023).

Projected temporalities and their disruption create polarities between what is planned and what is possible in practice that are better managed through duality than dualism. Rather than reifying the projected temporality as coded, use the opportunity to think creatively and paradoxically about how the event is an opportunity for learning. Those engaged in practices closer to the disrupted temporality will be in a better position to redefine these practices than those at some remove; for the former, the coding will probably be less materially constraining than those at more remove. Paradoxically, project planning and its elaborated coding that made no provision for events that arise may well be restrictive of emergent practices that are more likely to deal with events.

Corruption

When Transparency International still measured corruption according to sectors,[2] the most corrupt sector was construction. Regis Signor and Peter Love (Chapter 12) discuss two of the most famous global cases of corruption, both from Brazil; the first is Operation Car Wash, the scandal that unraveled to implicate Petrobras, that state-owned refinery, its directors and engineers, as well as politicians and construction companies; the second, concerned the construction of stadiums for the FIFA World Cup in Brazil in 2016. The corruption in each was staggering in the amount of bribes and rigging of the bid process in the former and in the unnecessary expenditure on stadiums rather than social welfare needs in the latter. Politically corrupt decisions drove megaproject planning and procurement to generate bribes, aided and abetted by project management and

[2] They stopped publicising the Bribe Payers Index in 2011.

engineering practitioners that colluded in undertaking corrupt practices.

It is suggested that establishing a whistleblowing policy could deter corruption. Insight from researchers specializing in whistleblowing as a practice might temper optimism on this score (Kenny, 2019). More developed institutionally is the idea of an independent body that might advise governments on the viability and benefits of projects as a way of avoiding corrupt and/or infeasible projects, but this would depend on politicians passing a law making it mandatory for all public procurement above a certain base value being impossible to proceed without first having been evaluated by such a body. In the country's most likely to be corrupt, according to Transparency International, this seems an unlikely case on the principle of turkeys not voting for Christmas. The example of the Concept Research Program of the Norwegian Ministry of Finance which rigorously evaluates large government projects, which Morten Welde and Gro Holst Volden discuss in Chapter 18, would be a case in point. Such arrangements seek to ensure public funds are directed toward those delivering the best outcomes for taxpayers.

Wolfgang Seibel and Katharina Eåmeyer (Chapter 11) add to the discussion of malevolence and how not to counter it by considering what happened in a federal system in which law enforcement is a regional state responsibility discharging federal state responsibilities. The German federal state transferred investigative powers from a fragment regional state system and assigned them to a federal agency with little or no experience in criminal investigation of issues of money laundering. Part of the responsibility for this was due to the necessity of enacting legislation to a timetable enacted by EU directives. In short, the project management of the process was highly politicized due to the exogenous contingency of the EU timetable and the turf warfare of the agencies involved in the short time that ensued between drafting and legislation, which ensured that a common logic of action of the constituent political and administrative parts to the new arrangements did not occur. The front-end phase of planning the project was never accomplished appropriately because of both the limited time and the politics of the turf wars that ensued as different interests sought to capture the project.

Welde and Volden are concerned to identify protocols for establishing oversight institutions in the processes of committing to projects and delivering them. A first step would be determining whether the projects proposed should be initiated. Scenarios for alternative solutions to the problem identified that a proposed project would resolve are necessary. Too many projects are "garbage can" (Cohen et al., 1973) solutions attached to convenient problems, in which the consequences of benefits and costs are rarely conserved as a totality. They recommend that a broad, multidisciplinary appraisal of consequences should be presented to decision-makers early. Not only decision-makers, I would suggest, but also potential users and communities that the proposed project might have an impact on should also be party to simulations of the project and its scenarios. In this way, potential stakeholders will be emergent early in the project process. They note that while costs can be assessed post hoc with clarity, benefits are much more difficult to reduce to a cash nexus. During the project process, they recommend stage gates as providing opportunities to terminate, change, or continue a project. Oversight of the project should not only be intra-project but include external quality assurance. Several other basic premises of project management protocols follow, with the suggestion that ex post evaluation, which is rarely done, should be standard and not simply restricted to costs but also include benefits. Dynamic learning from successive projects can ensue.

In Chapter 14, Geraldi et al. return us to the beginning, noting the penchant in certain project management circles to believe in the myths of rationality that populate economic theories and, on the basis of these "rational myths" (Meyer & Rowan, 1977), "lament human deviations" from them and devise ever more rational solutions in the hope of repairing what is, in essence, the fundamental foolishness of the initial gullible assumptions contained in the rational myth, or they might endorse Ika et al's (2022) espousal of simple rules of thumb. As Geraldi and her colleagues note, however, simple rules of thumb are not likely to really cut it in institutionally complex projects in which communicative constitutions of organization will be plural and not necessarily shared. Instead, they decide to do what good empirical social scientists do, to study a crucial decision to either bid or not bid at tender, looking at how factors enter into "saisficing" (Simon, 1955). It would have been good to say that they did this by studying the processes in practice but instead they made do with studying it in accounts of practice, gleaned through interviews with senior decision-makers. According to their account of senior executives' accounts, these decision-makers prioritize eliminating potential project disasters over selecting excellent opportunities. Minimizing risk rather than assessing value is paramount. Second, they do so through a rapid technique that the researchers name as "thresholding." In essence, three decisions were made. First, to accept that the project passed the clearance threshold and should be accepted; second, that it alerted the blocking threshold; third, that factors that might clear a project had to be counterbalanced against those that might block it. What was important was what might go wrong and this most evidently guided decision-making.

Conclusion

Projects can often be costly beyond their estimates of time, cost and benefits and this simple datum has been the fulcrum for the contributions to this book. It has been somewhat less of a fulcrum for this afterword other than in providing the raw material for reflection. The key points in this reflection were the following.

First, that projects are essentially open system interventions that strive to create closure through the extensive coding of standing conditions through contract. Given the openness that they confront in which events will always be possible, this is always going to be problematic. Realism might caution against constantly striving to codify risk in ever more restrictive and prescriptive ways when events can always surprise the calculus used.

Second, projects are autopoietic, as they are systems capable of producing and maintaining the futures that they strive to make by generating their own processes. The import of this for project management is that the nature of its practice is an account of the practices of practitioners in a double hermeneutic, based on the understandings of the project management community, which in turn are often based on prescriptive standards institutionalized by professional and commercial bodies, which in turn, often inform the accounts of these practices' efficacy that academic project management accounts provide. There is ample opportunity for both a degree of circularity and confusion in untangling these practices.

Third, in many cases in the handbook but not all, the theoretical sensemaking that is made is largely contained within the loop of the codes that constitute this recursivity. On occasion, the sensemaking breaks out of the loop to address a broader based social science sensemaking from organization studies, which does make the self-referential quality of project management studies less obvious and does connect it to broader constructs.

Fourth, on account of this recursivity, accounts given by practitioners of their reasons for success or failure are not causally predictive of actual successes or failures that occur but are retrospective accounts drawn from those that are available in a community of practice for making sense of the world in which they work. Such sensemaking is always conditional on plausibility, retrospection, salience, identity, context, enactment, and ongoing events, which cannot necessarily be known in advance.

Fifth, the recursivity is surprisingly humanist given the very sociomaterial nature of many project processes and practices. Such humanism is most evident in discussion of stakeholders; in the vast majority of cases these are regarded as human subjects, more especially as human subjects that have a constitutively coded interest in the project. Sociomaterially, it is not only these forms of stakeholders that are implicated in projects but all those that use the project in its future and all those that either benefit from or are damaged by the project. In the posthuman Anthropocene, this means that the effects of climate impacts resulting from human practices on planet, people, other animals, and fauna must be such that both human and nonhuman subjects should be considered as stakeholders of projects that create material futures.

Sixth, projects are always in a state of becoming (Bjørkeng et al., 2009), they are always in process and their processes and practices are the empirical traces they produce in their autopoiesis. In research terms, this would suggest that these empirical traces that can be observed and recorded in situ provide a more naturally occurring data set for analysis than accounts that proffered in response to interview questions. The reason for this is that sensemaking in practice is observable in the former, while the latter provide second-order accounts of experience. With Silverman (2024), I agree that the latter are not uninteresting as accounts. They should not be taken for granted as indexing anything other than the availability of accounts. As accounts, they bear no causal relation as precedents to what practice; they are mutually constituted in practice. Only through practice-based research in flow will we be able to capture the reality of project processes.

Finally, projects are sites of power relations both within project processes as they unfold and in relation to the materialities and stakeholders that they create. These power relations, conceived as circuits of power, arise in relation to both endogenous sources of change and those that are exogenously unleashed by events that arise as project environment contingencies. Events, as Deroy (2024, p. 101) suggest "introduce contingency into routines while their relations construct a network of intertwined events" – and this is the essential feature of projects as future-oriented sociomaterial forms of temporary organizing autopoietically differentiating their processes and practices and their effects from the codes that constitute them.

The handbook is an organizational constitution of communication oriented toward making accounts of not bringing projects in on time, on budget, to specifications, the persistent failure addressed by this handbook. Why the cost blew out, the specifications were not met, or the outcome not as promised after so much more time than was promised, is a valid concern. In unpicking why these states of affair occur, over and over again, the handbook has engaged directly with the "five hands" that nearly everyone in project management will understand. In addition to discussing the contributions to the handbook, I had two further aims.

First, to connect understanding and interpretation in project management with a wider realm of social science sensemaking constituted by classical debates in sociology such as those concerning the meaning of social action and its distinctiveness from that of behavior. Basically, behavior is describable without attribution of meaning while social action is not. That suggests to me that we should, perhaps, shift from seeking to understand project "behavior" and turn instead to deeper consideration of project "action." Second, that in doing this, I suggest that the institutional constitution of project management as a self-referential activity might be productively broadened by a closer relationship with the worlds of sociology, especially as its vector overlaps with that of organizations as a topic. From a project management perspective, there is much about projects that is unique but there is also much about organization and its sociological understanding that is not, which can be applied to project management. I have sought to balance the many contributions to the handbook by looking at them from a position that is neither wholly inside nor outside of project management as a discipline but that intersects with management and organization studies, albeit with a sociological bent.

References

Archer, M. S. (1996). Social integration and system integration: Developing the distinction. *Sociology*, *30*(4), 679–699.

Archer, M. S. (1982). Morphogenesis versus structuration: On combining structure and action. *The British Journal of Sociology*, *33*(4), 455–483.

Berti, M., Simpson, A., Pina e Cunha, M., and Clegg, S. R. (2021). *Elgar introduction to organizational paradox theory*. Edward Elgar.

Bjørkeng, K., Clegg, S. R., and Pitsis, T. (2009). Becoming a practice. *Management Learning 40*(2), 145–159.

Cantarelli, C., and Genovese, A. (2023). Innovation potential of megaprojects: A systematic literature review. *Production, Planning and Control, 34*(14) 1–21.

Caro, R. A. (2015). *The power broker: Robert Moses and the fall of New York.* Random House.

Clegg, S. R. ([1975] 2013). *Power, rule and domination: A critical and empirical understanding of power in sociological theory and organizational life.* Routledge and Kegan Paul, International Library of Sociology. Republished in Routledge Library Editions: Organization: Theory & Behaviour, vol. 6.

Clegg, S. R. ([1989] 2023). *Frameworks of power*, 2nd ed. Sage.

Clegg, S. R., Pitsis, T, and Mount, M. (2025) *Managing and organizations: An introduction to theory and practice*, 7th ed. Sage.

Clegg, S., and Ninan, J. (2023). Unravelling governmentality in project ecologies. *Project Leadership and Society, 4*, 100099.

Clegg, S., Loosemore, M., Walker, D., van Marrewijk A., and Sankaran, S. (2023). Construction cultures: Sources, signs and solutions of toxicity (pp. 3–16). In S. Addyman and H. Smyth (eds.). *Construction project organising*. Wiley-Blackwell.

Clegg, S., Sarkar, S, Waldman-Brown, A., and Roy, R. (2023). Socialized leadership and improvisational responding to COVID-19 supply voids. *Project Leadership and Society*, 100088.

Clegg, S. R., Pitsis, T., Rura-Polley, T., and Marosszeky, M. (2002). Governmentality matters: Designing an alliance culture of interorganizational collaboration for managing projects. *Organization Studies, 23*(3), 317–337.

Cohen, M. D., March, J. G., and Olsen, J. P. (1972). A garbage can model of organizational choice. *Administrative Science Quarterly, 17*(1), 1–25.

Cooren, F., Kuhn, T., Cornelissen, J. P., and Clark, T. (2011). Communication, organizing and organization: An overview and introduction to the special issue. *Organization Studies, 32*(9), 1149–1170.

Cunha, M. P. e., Neves, P., Clegg, S. R., and Rego, A. (2016). Tales of the unexpected: Discussing improvisational learning, *Management Learning, 46*(5), 511–529.

Czarniawska, B. (2007). *Shadowing: And other techniques for doing fieldwork in modern societies.* Copenhagen Business School Press DK.

Dalcher, D. (2020). In whose interest? Repositioning the stakeholder paradox. Advances in Project Management Series, *PM World Journal, 9*(9), 1–9.

de Vaujany, F. X., Gherardi, S., and Silva, P. (2024). *Organization studies and posthumanism.* Routledge.

Deroy, X. (2024). Posthumanism as a system of codifying events (pp. 101–126). In F. X. de Vaujany, S. Gherardi, and P. Silva (eds.). *Organization studies and posthumanism.* Routledge.

Dille, T., Soderlund, J., and Clegg, S. R. (2018). Temporal conditioning and institutional pluralism: Exploring the nature and dynamics of inter-institutional temporary organizations. *International Journal of Project Management, 36*, 673–686.

Donaldson, L. (1987). Strategy and structural adjustment to regain fit and performance: In defence of contingency theory. *Journal of Management Studies, 24*(1), 1–24.

Flyvbjerg, B. (1998). *Rationality and power: Democracy in practice.* University of Chicago Press.

Flyvbjerg, B., and Sunstein, C. R. (2016). The principle of the Malevolent Hiding Hand; or the Planning Fallacy writ large. *Social Research, 83*(4), 979–1004.

Flyvbjerg, B., and Gardener, D. (2023). *How big things get done.* Macmillan.

Foucault, M. (1977). *Discipline and punish.* Penguin.

Fox, A. (1974). *Beyond contract: Work, power and trust relations.* Faber.

Gaim, M., Clegg, S. R., and Cunha, M. P. e. (2024). *Organizational paradoxes.* Sage.

Gaim, M., Clegg, S. R., Cunha, M. P. e, and Berti., M. (2022). *Organizational paradox.* Cambridge University Press.

Gaim, M., Clegg, S., and Cunha, M. P. E. (2022). In praise of paradox persistence: Evidence from the Sydney Opera House Project. *Project Management Journal, 53*(4), 397–415.

Gersick, C. J. (1988). Time and transition in work teams: Toward a new model of group development. *Academy of Management Journal, 31*(1), 9–41.

Haselton, M. G., Nettle, D., and Murray, D. R. (2015). The evolution of cognitive bias (pp. 1–20). In D. Buss (ed.). *The handbook of evolutionary psychology.* Wiley.

Hirschman, A. O. (1967). *Development projects observed.* Brookings Institution.

Ika, L. A., Love, P. E. D., and Pinto, J. K. (2022). Moving beyond the Planning Fallacy: The emergence of a new principle of project behavior. *IEEE Transactions on Engineering Management, 69*(6), 3310–3325.

Jacobs, J. (1961). *The death and life of great American cities*. Random House.

Kahneman, D. (2011). *Thinking, fast and slow*. Allen Lane.

Kenny, K. (2019). *Whistleblowing: Toward a new theory*. Harvard University Press.

Kreiner, K. (2020). Conflicting notions of a project: The battle between Albert O. Hirschman and Bent Flyvbjerg. *Project Management Journal, 51*, 400–410.

Lenfle, S., and Loch, C. (2017). Has megaproject management lost its way (pp. 21–38). In B. Flyvbjerg (ed.). *The Oxford handbook of megaproject management*. Oxford University Press.

Levy, S., Martens, K., and Van Der Heijden, R. (2016). Agent-based models and self-organisation: Addressing common criticisms and the role of agent-based modelling in urban planning. *Town Planning Review, 87*(3), 321–338.

Linstead, S., and Thanem, T. (2007). Virtuality and 0rganization: The contribution of Gilles Deleuze. *Organization Studies, 28*(10), 1483–1496.

Luhmann, N. (1995). *Social systems*. Stanford University Press.

Luhmann, N. (2012). *Theory of society*, 2nd ed. Stanford University Press.

Luhmann, N. (2017). *Organization and decision*. Cambridge University Press.

March, J. G. (1988). *Decisions and organizations*. Blackwell.

Maturana, H. R., and Varela, F. J. (1991). *Autopoiesis and cognition: The realization of the living*. Springer Science & Business Media.

Meyer, A. D. (1982). Adapting to environmental jolts. *Administrative Science Quarterly*, 515–537.

Meyer, A. D., Brooks, G. R., and Goes, J. B. (1990). Environmental jolts and industry revolutions: Organizational responses to discontinuous change. *Strategic Management Journal*, 93–110.

Meyer, J. W., and Rowan, B. (1977). Institutionalized organizations: Formal structure as myth and ceremony. *American Journal of Sociology, 83*(2), 340–363.

Morujão, C. (2023). Subjective meanings and normative values in Alfred Schutz's philosophy of human action. *Phenomenology and Mind, 24*, 130–139.

Ninan, J., Clegg, S. R., and Mahalingnan, A. (2021). Power in news media: Framing strategies and effects in infrastructure projects. *International Journal of Project Management*. https://doi.org/10.1016/j.ijproman.2021.09.003.

Ninan, J., Mahalingam, A., and Clegg, S. (2020). Power and strategies in the external stakeholder management of megaprojects: A circuitry framework, *Engineering Project Organization Journal*, 9, https://doi.org/10.25219/epoj.2020.00104.

Pitsis, T., Clegg, S. R., Marosszeky, M., and Rura-Polley, T. (2003). Constructing the Olympic dream: Managing innovation through the future perfect. *Organization Science, 14*(5), 574–590.

Roy, O. (2024). *The crisis of culture: Identity politics and the empire of norms*. Hurst.

Lockwood, D. (1964). Social integration and system integration (pp. 244–257). In G. K. Zollschan and W. Hirsch (eds.). *Explorations in social change*. Routledge & Kegan Paul.

Schatzki, T. R. (1996). *Social practices: A Wittgensteinian approach to human activity and the social*. Cambridge University Press.

Schatzki, T. R. (2002). *The site of the social: A philosophical account of the constitution of social life and change*. Pennsylvania State University Press.

Schütz, A. (1967). *The phenomenology of the social world*. Northwestern University Press.

Silverman, D. (2024). *Interpreting qualitative research*. Sage.

Simon, H. A. (1955). A behavioral model of rational choice. *Quarterly Journal of Economics, 69*, 99–118.

Steffen, W., Richardson, K., Rockstrom, J., Cornell, S. E., Fetzer, I., Bennett, E. M., Biggs, R., Carpenter, S. R., de Vries, W., de Wit, C. A., Folke, C., Gerten, D., Heinke, J., Mace, G. M., Persson, L. M., Ramanathan, V., Reyers, B, and Sorlin, S. (2015). Planetary boundaries: Guiding human development on a changing planet. *Science, 347*(6223), 1259855.

Taleb, N. N. (2012). *Antifragile: Things that gain from disorder*. Allen Lane.

Vaagaasar, A. L., Hernes, T., and Dille, T. (2020). The challenges of implementing temporal shifts in temporary organizations: Implications of a situated temporal view. *Project Management Journal, 51*(4), 420–428.

van Marrewijk, A. H., Veenswijk, M., and Clegg, S. R. (2010). Organizing reflexivity in designed change: The ethnoventionist approach. *Journal of Change Management*, *23*(3), 212–229.

van Marrewijk, A., and van den Ende, L. (2022). Shaping interorganizational strategic projects through power relations and strategic practices. *International Journal of Project Management*, *40*(4), 426–438.

Wensing, E. (2020). The destruction of Juukan Gorge: Lessons for *planners* and local governments. *Australian Planner*, *56*(4), 241–248.

Wenzel, M., and Stjerne, I. S. (2021). Heuristics-in-use: Toward a practice theory of organizational heuristics. *Technological Forecasting and Social Change*, 164(7), 120517. DOI:10.1016/j.techfore.2020.120517.

Whitehead, A. N. (1985). *Science and the modern world*. Free Press.

Whyte, J., Naderpajouh, N., Clegg, S., Matous, P., Pollack, J., and Crawford, L. (2022). Project leadership: A research agenda for a changing world. *Project Leadership and Society*, *3*, 100044.

Wittgenstein, L. (1958). *The blue and brown books: Preliminary studies for the "philosophical investigations."* Harper & Row.

Wittgenstein, L. (1972). *Philosophical investigations*. Blackwells.

Index

For EU product safety concerns, contact us at Calle de José Abascal, 56–1°,
28003 Madrid, Spain or eugpsr@cambridge.org.

www.ingramcontent.com/pod-product-compliance
Ingram Content Group UK Ltd.
Pitfield, Milton Keynes, MK11 3LW, UK
UKHW050954290926
15470UKWH00006B/1806
9781009322768